EUROPE AND
THE FRENCH REVOLUTION

Albert Sorel was born in 1842, the son of a rich Norman industrialist. He entered the Ministry of Foreign Affairs in 1866, and was subsequently appointed Professor of Diplomatic History at the École des sciences politiques. In 1885 he published the first volume of *l'Europe et la Révolution française*. He died in 1906, two years after the eighth and final volume appeared. His other books include a study of the Franco-Prussian war and of the Eastern Question in the eighteenth century.

Alfred Cobban was Professor of French History at University College, London, till his death in 1968. He had been Visiting Professor at the Universities of Chicago, Harvard and Johns Hopkins. He was the author of a well-known history of modern France, as well as books on the political ideas of Burke and Rousseau and several studies of French history in the eighteenth century.

J. W. Hunt has been head of the History Department at the City of London School since 1946. He has been a Vice-President of the Historical Association and first Chairman of the History Committee of the Schools Council.

ALBERT SOREL

EUROPE AND
THE FRENCH REVOLUTION

*The Political Traditions
of the Old Régime*

TRANSLATED AND EDITED BY

ALFRED COBBAN

&

J. W. HUNT

ANCHOR BOOKS
DOUBLEDAY & COMPANY, INC.
GARDEN CITY, NEW YORK
1971

L'EUROPE ET LA RÉVOLUTION FRANÇAISE:
*Les Moeurs et Les Traditions
Politiques*
First published in 1885
The first English translation published by
Collins and the Fontana Library
1969
This edition published by arrangement with
William Collins Sons and Co. Ltd.

Anchor Books edition: 1971

Library of Congress Catalog Card Number: 77-113075
English translation copyright © 1969 by
William Collins Sons and Co Ltd

Contents

Contents   vii

The Maps

THE FOOTNOTES

Footnotes repeated or translated from those
of Sorel are indicated by *numbers*; those provided by the Editors are indicated by *symbols*

Editors' Introduction[*]

From any serious list of historians of the first rank the name of Albert Sorel could never be omitted. Yet he had no training as an historian. He was born in 1842, the son of a rich industrialist of Honfleur in Calvados, and never forgot his Norman origins. He went through the ordinary preparation for an official career by attending the law schools of Paris and in 1866 joined the Ministry of Foreign Affairs. During the Franco-Prussian War he was with the Ministry in the delegation of the French government at Tours, and reputedly the author of many of its despatches. His real aspirations were perhaps literary for he wrote poetry and two novels. He was to become an historian almost by accident. One factor in his abandonment of a career in the diplomatic service was his marriage, after the war, to a German Protestant girl whom he had met when he was studying the German language in Saxony in 1866. In 1872, with no historical education and no historical publications to his credit, he was appointed to the chair of diplomatic history at the Ecole des Sciences politiques. He was also, from 1876 to 1902, Secretary General to the Presidency of the Senate, but this must have been a very unarduous post for it seems to have interfered not at all with his teaching and writing. His first publication was a *Histoire diplomatique de la guerre franco-allemande*,

[*] The biographical details in this introduction are derived from Gabriel Monod, 'Albert Sorel', *Review historique*, xcii (1906), pp. 91-9; E. Boutmy, 'Albert Sorel' in *Etudes politiques* (1907); *En l'honneur de Albert Sorel: discours prononcés pour l'inauguration du monument érigé à Honfleur, 2 et 3 septembre 1922* (1922).

in 1875, in which he printed many despatches he had probably written himself. This was followed in 1877 by *La Question d'Orient au XVIIIe siècle* and by a volume of essays on
various diplomatic questions. The first volume of the work
which was to give him lasting fame, *L'Europe et la Révolution française,* appeared in 1885 and the eighth and final
volume in 1904. During the twenty years that were devoted
to this major theme he also wrote short books on *Montesquieu* and *Madame de Staël,* and many articles in periodicals.
He died in 1906 at the age of 64.

This bare outline of his career seemed necessary, but it
tells us little about Sorel as an historian. If we want to penetrate deeper we must begin by noting that he belongs with
the school of Montesquieu, Guizot and Tocqueville, not only
in his basic approach to the course of history but also in the
liberal political outlook—with its limitations as well as its
more generous aspects—which he shared with them. The
story is told of Sorel stopping before an inscription on a gate:
'Propriété nationale; le public n'entre pas'—'Property of the
State; no admittance to the public'. That, he said, is the spirit
behind our national institutions. If Sorel had been concerned
with social and economic questions his characteristically
nineteenth-century suspicion of the activities of the State
might have limited the permanent value of his history. Dealing with international relations it was an advantage, for it
enabled him to see them in a more realistic light and to judge
the noble professions of politicians with a healthy measure
of scepticism. Again to refer to an *obiter dictum,* the principal
maxim in politics, he is reported as saying, is, 'Ote-toi de là
que je m'y mette'—'Get out so that I can take your place'. To
which he added that the inconvenience of such changes was
reduced by the fact that the newcomer nearly always copied
his predecessor, by virtue of a second fundamental maxim,
'Moi, c'est bien différent'—'It's not the same thing when I
do it'.

Sorel's approach to history was thus almost precisely the
opposite to that of his—at the time—more famous contempo-

rary Taine. Where Taine started from a general, abstract principle, and then examined the documents for facts with which to support it, Sorel began from the actual historical evidence. His method was to assemble in parallel columns under the exact date all the facts that seemed of any importance, which safeguarded him from the ever-present danger of the inversion of dates and attribution of false relationships which chronology could disprove. Beginning, in this way, with a full account, he subsequently pared off the inessentials, condensed, summarized in often memorable phrases, and gave elegant literary form to a soundly based historical analysis. He differed from Taine also in seeing the nuances in a situation whereas Taine could only judge in terms of black and white. There was in Taine the spirit of dogmatism of the second-rate scientist, the older sociologists and most philosophers; Sorel brought to his studies a sense of balance, of the interweaving of a multitude of influences that went to make up every historical event. Hence individuals played a part in his history that they could not in the determinist system of Taine, though his brilliant portraits are never mere sketches of individuals for their own sake but are always justified by their contribution to the understanding of the historic situation. Because his aim was simply to bring out what the evidence showed, Sorel was also immune from the temptation to speculate on what might have been. He did not propose to ask what might have happened if Napoleon had lost the battle of Austerlitz, if Metternich had been *modeste* or Danton had lacked courage. 'Ne refaisons pas le passé, je vous en prie', he said—'Do not try to alter what has been, I beg you'.

No historian, of course, can escape the general ways of thought of his own age. History had to be written in the nineteenth century in terms of nations and nationalism. This was not a handicap in so far as it enabled Sorel to appreciate the importance of national traditions, overriding all revolutions and changes of régime. He was also an ardent patriot, and when in the eight volumes of *L'Europe et la Révolution française* he came to the Napoleonic period his balanced judgement for once gave way to his patriotism. In contradiction to what he himself had written earlier of Louis XIV, he saw Napoleon as pushed into continual wars against his will instead of by his own fantastic schemes and bellicose spirit. The latter volumes of Sorel's great work, it must be admitted, are inferior to the earlier ones. After 1795 his treatment becomes slighter, there is less reliance on detailed research and more recourse to rather empty patriotic rhetoric. It is not merely a personal judgement that his first volume, *Les Moeurs politiques et les traditions,* was his masterpiece. The remainder of this introduction must be devoted to a consideration of it.

For some historians their study is the realm of the contingent. Great events are made up of the accumulation of little ones, and for the sake of a nail in a horse's shoe a kingdom is lost. War and foreign policy are apt to seem particularly dependent on the play of circumstance and personality. 'Put a strong ruler on the least powerful throne in Europe and weak ones on all the others', wrote Ségur, 'and he will do what he likes with them.' A contemporary of Frederick the Great might well have thought this. Yet with the coming of the French Revolution the achievements of a Frederick were to seem superficial phenomena, rapidly obliterated by deeper forces moving beneath the surface and carrying irresistibly before them, in a great seismic wave, the day-to-day changes of political life.

A different school of historical interpretation, including such great names as those of Bossuet and Montesquieu, and after the Revolution, Tocqueville, saw history as primarily concerned with these profounder movements. As has already been said, it is to this school that Sorel belongs. On his first page he takes his stand unambiguously with them. His aim, he says, is to discover the *'causes éloignées'* of the momentous events he has to treat of. He wants to show the French Revolution not as a breach with the course of French history but as the natural and necessary sequel to all that had gone be-

fore. But where Bossuet had seen in history the working out
of God's Providence, Montesquieu the operation of natural
laws and Tocqueville of sociological forces, for Sorel the
most powerful determining factor in all countries is the national tradition. His volume is thus, in a sense, both an interpretation of the Revolution and an explanation of the whole
history of France and to a less profound degree of Europe.

Reminding us that the disciplines of geography and history have always been closely linked in French education,
the basic facts in the French national tradition as Sorel sees
them are geographical. The memory of Gaul, kept alive by
classical studies, he believed, followed France down through
the ages. The sea and the mountains formed on all sides except the North-East a framework which the Capetian kings,
century after century, aimed to fill with a homogeneous
nation and a united state. Their greatest successors, the cardinals Richelieu and Mazarin in the seventeenth century,
planned to round off the frontiers on the one exposed side
by extending them to the Rhine: having established strong
frontiers they would then rest content with defending them.
This, according to Sorel, was the classic French foreign policy—'*la modération dans la force*'. The recognition of such a
limit to French expansion was the essential condition, he
pointed out, of the creation of that system of client states in
Germany which was effected by the Treaty of Westphalia
and which guaranteed the strength and security of the
French position in Europe.

There was, however, another tradition, perpetuated in
medieval poetry and legend, which went back to the empire
of Charlemagne. It re-emerged, Sorel believed, in the territorial ambitions of Philippe le Bel, when the first of a long
race of lawyer-diplomats, Pierre du Bois, put forward a claim
to universal monarchy in the name of the kings of France.
When Louis XIV moved from the struggle for frontiers to
the 'wars of magnificence' he was reasserting the claim to
the Carolingian empire. The fatality of this tradition was
that it inevitably united Europe against France and so be-

came self-defeating. In the end Louis XIV was only to be saved by chance from total disaster. Both traditions, at least from the time of Louis XI and division of the Burgundian inheritance, involved a Franco-Austrian struggle, but the conditions in which it was to be waged were bound to be unfavourable if French ambitions brought in the rest of Europe on the side of her enemy.

In the light of these historical considerations Sorel proceeds to subject the diplomacy of eighteenth-century France to a closer examination. Despite the defeats brought about by the excesses of Louis XIV's policy, France's position after 1715 was a favourable one. She had no dangerous opponent in Europe, and a new field of expansion had opened up on the seas and in the colonies, where the enemy was England. On his own principles Sorel might well have suggested that the half-heartedness of the French response to this challenge was perhaps not unconnected with the absence of any national tradition of extra-European expansion, contrasted with the strength of the commitment to continental politics. The real disaster for France, however, lay in the inability to concentrate on either policy. The reign of Louis XV, at least after the decline of Fleury, whose achievement Sorel perhaps hardly appreciated, represented a hiatus in national history, when weak and divided governments, by their lack of policy, sacrificed French tradition and interests alike. This very circumstance enables him to examine the eighteenth century as an age in which international politics can be seen in operation in their present form, unadulterated by considerations of sentiment and unconcealed by any veneer of ideology.

The illusion that Europe before the Revolution constituted in any sense a single Christian commonwealth, as Burke had dreamed, he sweeps away at the outset. The State was all in all; *raison d'état* was its principle, war its means, aggrandisement its end. This was an age of dynastic politics, of wars and of succession and partition treaties. Deceit and treachery were the rule of diplomacy, brutality the essence of war.

The only principle, that of balance of power, was no guarantee of order and justice, though it provided the one check there was on the ambition of states, that of self-interest. Sorel's earlier study of the Eastern Question had revealed to him the ruthlessness of the diplomacy of the age and the blatant hypocrisy of the professions of international good faith and benevolent intentions put forward as a screen for their plans of aggrandisement by the so-called enlightened despots. The *ancien régime* throughout Europe, he believed, was morally bankrupt. The only aim of its rulers was to increase the power of their States. If they ever appeared to undertake reforms, it was with this end in view.

In the last phase of its *ancien régime*, however, France reverted to a wiser policy. Vergennes, last of the great foreign ministers of the French monarchy, successfully checked the distortion of the Franco-Austrian alliance to the detriment of France; in the war of American Independence he inflicted a severe defeat on English power overseas; he successfully joined in the resistance to Joseph II's plans for annexing Bavaria. After this, French interests lay in the preservation of European peace, and Vergennes set about maintaining this by his Commercial Treaty with England of 1786 and his Russian treaty of 1787. 'Ce n'est plus le temps de conquêtes': this opinion, which Sorel quotes, sums up the final foreign policy of Vergennes. The Constituent Assembly of 1789 shared the same pacific views. Nothing in the principles of 1789, Sorel believes, was incompatible with the peace of Europe. The aims of the Revolution of 1789 were reconcilable with the foreign policy of a Henry IV and Richelieu, though not with that of a Louis XIV and Louvois.

But neither France nor Europe was ready for such a policy of peace. This is not to dispute the sincerity with which the Constituants of 1789 held their principles. Nor does Sorel deny the importance of principles. One source of his strength as an historian is his awareness that human behaviour, whether of individuals or nations, is not a mere reaction to external stimuli. Nations can only be led and inspired by the appeal of principles, to which their governments have at least to pay lip service. The revolution of 1789 opened a period, like that of the wars of the sixteenth century, when political struggles within and without nations were to be waged in the name of principles. Like the religious disagreements of the sixteenth century, the ideas of the French Revolution opened a new era in the history of the world, and this was what the rulers of old Europe failed to understand. Revolutions were not new; one government fell and another took its place, the other powers accepted the new government as soon as it had consolidated its position and everything went on much as before. It was natural that the powers of Europe should at first, and indeed for a surprisingly long period, assume that they were confronted with a revolution of the old type and react to it in the old way. They did not realise that it was a new phenomenon and that their previous experience provided them with no clue how to deal with it.

Having brought all this into light brilliantly, however, Sorel does not stop at that. He appreciated something that was to be forgotten in a later age of ideological warfare but that is now becoming of relevance once again. National traditions can temporarily be overlaid by a revolutionary ideology, but if they are to change—and doubtless they do change —it is only by a much slower process and over a much longer period of time than the space of a single revolution can provide. Without professing to underestimate the internal consequences of the Revolution, Sorel believed that in matters of foreign policy the best guide to the way in which a revolutionary nation would behave after the revolution was the way in which it had behaved before it. Even in its internal developments, as de Tocqueville had shown, the Revolution did not break the essential unity of French history. In Sorel's chosen field of foreign affairs the continuity of tradition was even more unmistakable—once it had been pointed out. He had discovered, however, as has been said above, that there were two very different traditions. Mirabeau, Talleyrand, the Constituants of 1789, Barthélemy in 1795, con-

tinued the policy of moderation of which the latest exponent
had been Vergennes. But, despite Vergennes, revolutionary
France was not ready for a peaceful policy, or at least its
rulers were not. Its policy was to be determined not by such
ministers but by descendants of the lawyers of Philippe le
Bel. Their tradition of territorial claims and conquests was
passed on to the generals and the lawyer-diplomats of the
Convention. The Revolution took up the inheritance of Louis
XIV and Europe responded with a renewed Grand Alliance.

In the struggle that ensued, the divine right of monarchs
and the sovereignty of the people were the banners under
which the opposing armies marched to battle, but power
politics was the reality behind the conflict of principles almost from the beginning. There was much in common between the hostile factions, for in being transferred from the
king to the people the nature of sovereignty had not changed,
nor had the habitual ways of practical politicians. Revolutionary France, by adopting the practices of the *ancien
régime*, falsified its own principles. The rights of national
sovereignty, which France had asserted for herself, she subsequently denied to other nations. Humanity, which had
been the ideal of 1789, was identified with France, the spread
of French ideas with that of French power, and liberation
with French conquest. The consequence, as Sorel saw it, was
that the spirit of national independence which had made
the strength of the armies of Revolutionary France was
turned against her, and a revolution which began by appealing to the brotherhood of man ended by substituting for the
cosmopolitan Europe of the eighteenth century the nationalist Europe of the nineteenth.

In France national traditions proved stronger than revolutionary principles, and the same was to be true of her enemies. Sorel's chapters on the characteristic reactions of the
peoples of Europe to French aggression lack the depth and
scope of the analysis he devotes to French history, and may
sometimes seem too schematic and simplified, but they are
none the less penetrating sketches of the historic tendencies

in the different states. If the governments, as Sorel says, followed *raison d'état*, the nations followed their traditions. National policy and international relations, as they emerged from the interaction of these two influences, are the subject of this history.

The influence of Sorel can be seen in practically every history of the eighteenth century that has been written since. What were at first penetrating insights may now seem commonplaces, but they recover their originality in Sorel's own words and their brilliance in the setting which he gave them. Isolated from his broader historical picture, his epigrams and paradoxes also appeared to be over-simplifications. They possessed a clarity rather shocking to those brought up on the minute *pointillisme* of modern historical research, on the accumulation of detail for its own sake and so long as it did not add up to any coherent picture. Clarity came to be suspect and avoidance of interpretation was the test of historical integrity. The better historians, of course, never fell victim to this 'I am a camera' illusion, which is now rapidly fading. Moreover, since history is no longer photography it is possible to admit once again that it is a literary art, as it was in Sorel. Although historians have inevitably, and perhaps sometimes unconsciously at second or third hand, made use of his ideas, the kind of history that is represented by his famous first volume has long been out of fashion. Now that the current of opinion has changed, Sorel's first volume has ceased to be merely a rather old-fashioned classic and has become once again a major contribution to the understanding of modern European history and of the whole course of the history of France.

Note on the Translation

The absence of a translation into English of a major French historical classic such as the famous first volume of Sorel's *L'Europe et la Révolution française*, published some eighty years ago, must seem surprising. Students of history, it may be said, should be able to read such a work in the original. Even in the past this was sometimes the expression of an ideal rather than a fact. In so far as it was a valid argument it represented the situation at a time when it could be assumed that if any foreign language was known by British students it would almost invariably be French. On the other hand one had only to do a little teaching in America to discover that when a foreign language was known there it was just as likely to be Italian or Polish or German or some other European language. In Great Britain, now, though the history schools of universities still give French pride of place, the progress of studies of the history and civilization of other European and extra-European societies is inevitably bringing with it a shift in the balance of linguistic knowledge. As for the great academic developments in Africa and Asia, the more advanced studies there will to a large extent be carried on, unavoidably, in English. If the contributions of French scholars to history are to be known then, in many cases it will have to be through translation. This may be a second best, but it is better than that a great school of history should remain a closed book to the majority of students.

It would also be a mistake to think of this problem purely in academic terms. Great works of history belong to the intellectual heritage of mankind. We would not wish to be excluded from Herodotus and Thucydides because we could not read Greek. The first volume of Sorel may not be quite in this class, but there is no absurdity in mentioning it in the same breath. It is far more than a mere text-book history or a monograph on a single historical theme. Sorel's viewpoint enables him to sweep through the centuries. He envisages the dramatic scenes that opened in 1789 against a many-coloured backcloth of the development of the nations of Europe from the time of Caesar and of Charlemagne, and his work is a contribution to literature as well as to historical understanding.

This presents a problem to the translators. A strictly literal translation of a nineteenth-century work, packed with similes and flashing with epigrams, might seem overdrawn and meretricious, neither of which Sorel is. On the other hand, to tone down the bright colours of the original into a muddy monochrome would be to rob it of its vitality and hopelessly weaken the impact it should make. We can only hope that we have kept as faithful to Sorel's spirit as the different geniuses of the two languages and the different styles of the two ages allowed.

In respect of footnotes the principles on which a selection has been made need to be explained. In the first place, references for quotations, and support for statements in the text by reference to original sources, have normally been kept. They are generally reproduced in the form in which Sorel gave them. Cross-references are also retained. Additional comments and citations by Sorel in the notes have been kept where they seemed of interest. Otherwise they have been omitted, as have references to secondary works which a modern historian would be unlikely to regard as of value.

Finally, editorial comments have been kept down to the minimum. We felt that the reader would not wish to be aware of the editors continually at his elbow, nudging him to point out that this or the other statement by a great historian can no longer be taken as the last word and requires modification in one direction or another. However, some references are explained, and some brief biographical notes inserted; and—more important—where there has been a major change in historical interpretation, especially in respect of French history, which is the prime subject of the book, we have felt obliged to draw attention to it. There are now so many excellent bibliographies that it seemed unnecessary to add one to this volume. On the other hand, Sorel's argument frequently turns on geographical considerations. A good historical atlas is a necessary accompaniment to it, and since this is not always available, and even good atlases do not invariably provide the precise information that Sorel's history calls for in an easily comprehensible form, a number of outline maps have been added to this edition.

A.C.
J.W.H.

Alfred Cobban died on 1st April 1968. He had seen the whole of the material for this book prepared for the press, and he was gratified to be able to complete the task, with so many others, before he was overcome by the illness with which he had contended for so long. It was an invaluable reassurance to me that his guidance was available until the work was done; it was sad that he could not see it in its final form.

J.W.H.

Introduction

The war between Europe and the French Revolution lasted almost a quarter of a century. It began at Valmy and finished only at Waterloo. In the end Europe in coalition triumphed over the French armies; yet it could not be said that France emerged vanquished from the struggle. She had entered on it to defend her independence as a nation, the integrity of her territory, and the reforms she had accomplished in her laws and her political constitution.* The peace cost her only the restitution of the lands she had conquered; she withdrew to her former boundaries; the body of the nation remained intact. The essential results of the Revolution stood: France kept the Civil Code and representative government. These sufficed to render the achievement of 1789 indestructible and to ensure the working out in the future of its full consequences.

* The power of myths in history is illustrated by Sorel's assertion that the Revolutionary War was begun to defend French independence and the reforms of the Revolution against the attacks of the old Europe. In fact, despite the agitation of the émigrés, and the bellicose language of Catherine II, hoping to push Prussia and Austria into a war in the West so that she could swallow up Poland unopposed, the Powers of Europe had no intention of attacking France. This does not mean that the revolutionaries did not fear an attack, instigated by the émigrés and supported by foreign arms; but the declarations of war all came from the Revolutionary Assemblies, as did the initial military aggression. Sorel repeats a few pages below the view that the war was undertaken for the defence of French territory, though the opposite view would not only be more in accord with the facts but would accord better with his own interpretation of the Revolution.

My aim is to bring together the principal features of this epoch, and search in them for what is the very essence of history—the remote causes of 'those great events to which there was so great a reaction'.[1] The ever-surprising developments in this long-drawn-out tragedy, the breadth of its scene of action embracing all Europe, the multitude of actors, the starkly contrasted scenes of heroism and atrocity, the gripping interest of its successive episodes, and the crash of the final catastrophe disturb the soul of the observer and blind him to the sequence of events. Yet, remarkable as they appear as single crises, the episodes of the drama are even more so in their relations one with another and in their interconnection.

The French Revolution, from the outset and solely by reason of its basic principle, undermined and brought down in ruins the whole structure of the old monarchical Europe. It proclaimed the sovereignty of the people, it set forth its doctrines as self-evident and universal truths, it threatened all established authority, it called on all nations to revolt and set themselves free. What is most strange in this is neither the character of the doctrine nor the ardour with which it was preached, but the apathy of the European governments. The signs of the storm escaped their notice; when it burst, they regarded it with egotistical indifference; they became alarmed only when the banks gave way and the flood waters were upon them.

They no more knew how to cope with the danger than they had been able to recognise its signs. They confronted it only with disorganized efforts, contradictory measures, and plans that invariably went awry. Threatened by a people in revolt and by a doctrine of subversion, they had neither a principle of conservation to oppose to the doctrine nor a public force to confront the sedition. In France everything was overturned; in Europe, it seemed, everything remained the same. France had neither government nor funds; hardly

[1] Bossuet, *Discours sur l'histoire universelle*, 3e partie, ch. VIII.

the framework of the army remained. The old monarchies disposed of all the resources of strong governments: their forces were on a war footing; their generals, schooled in the theory and practice of war, led obedient and well-drilled troops. They had training, discipline, numbers, supplies, weapons. It seemed that France must go under. But against all expectation it was anarchy that was organized, and organized force that crumbled. France not only beat the coalition; she did something more astonishing—she divided it. 'These brigands', wrote one of the allied sovereigns, 'desire neither friends nor allies; they require accomplices and victims.'[2] Except for England, which had however on her own account seized the French colonies and meant to keep them, all the allied states defected in turn and became the accomplices of the victorious French in order to share in the spoliation of the victims. The crusade undertaken by the kings against the French Revolution for the defence of established rights ended in the sharing out of the continent between the champions of monarchical right and the powers born of the Revolution. The old Europe was wound up in a cynical bankruptcy.

To treat with the French Revolution, the old Europe abandoned its principles; to treat with the old Europe, the French Revolution betrayed its own. France had solemnly renounced all conquests. She was to bring peace to the world and invite the nations to general concord: tyranny, it was said, had driven them apart, liberty would reunite them. What cause would one have to envy another, when all were equally happy? When war came, it appeared to some that this wonderful Utopia was at hand. What in fact happened was unfortunately much more in conformity with the nature of things and of human passions: victory made the Revolution bellicose. The war, begun for the defence of the land of France, continued with the invasion of neighbouring ter-

[2] Instructions of Catherine II to her ambassador at Berlin, 6 June 1794. Martens, *Traités de la Russie avec l'Allemagne*, t. II, p. 167. Petersburg, 1883.

ritories. Having conquered them in order to set them free, France partitioned them so as to hold on to them.

But at the same time as France profited from the war she submitted to its logic. The French had committed the soul of the Republic to the army and there it remained. Rome brought to life again produced a Caesar. Bonaparte presented himself to France and to Europe as the instrument of the Revolution. France believed him—hence her enthusiasm for him. Europe tried to resist him; he overcame her as much by policy as by force. His genius made him the master in war, and the greed of his adversaries gave him the advantage in the ensuing peace, the pursuit of which, in his hands, became more deadly than war. France and Europe then presented the same spectacle. Those who had made the Revolution and those who had combated it found themselves together in the same bonds. Whilst in France there arose from the ranks of the most ardent democrats a whole regicide nobility, whilst at the Tuileries one could see beside a count who had drafted the law of suspects a prince who had presided over the Committee of Public Safety, there were in Europe sovereigns of the oldest reigning families who accepted royal crowns from the hand which in Paris conferred these strange investitures and, by a stroke of the pen, proscribed entire dynasties. By 1808 the Revolution had on the Continent only victims and allies. Successfully imposed upon the states of Europe, it only now remained for it to conquer the last stronghold to which these princes, defeated or else won over, had retreated—their family pride. It remained only to rob them of the sole superiority of which they had hitherto been able to boast—the blood of which they were so proud, and which made them a race apart from the other races of Europe. In 1810 this happened. The man who to Metternich was 'the Revolution incarnate'[3] married the great-granddaughter of the Empress Maria Theresa. Only seventeen years had passed since Marie Antoinette had per-

[3] *Mémoires*, t. I, p. 51, Paris, 1882.

ished on the scaffold when another Austrian archduchess came to sit in her place on the throne of France, by the side of Napoleon. This, from the point of view of the old Europe, was the most extraordinary event in the whole history of the Revolution.

For France, what followed was even more extraordinary. In 1792 she had declared war on kings and proclaimed peace to the nations. She had triumphed over the kings; it was to the effort of the peoples that she succumbed.* In France the Revolution had ceased to progress and, so to speak, had been congealed into a military despotism; but through the work of this very despotism it continued to propagate itself in Europe. It was spread among the nations by conquest. Though in a degenerate form, it still had sufficient vigour to rouse them, and the language of liberty, distorted as it was in the camp, still profoundly moved men's hearts. War simplified the map of Europe surprisingly. Many frontiers had disappeared; nations formerly cut in pieces were reunited. At the same time as by force of arms France brought men under one government, she taught them through the writings of her thinkers that nothing is finer for nations than independence, that there is no surer way of achieving it than unity, that nations are sovereign, and that the first use they must make of their sovereign power is to gain freedom. The peoples of Europe easily understood this language; they understood too the example France had given them in 1792. What they did not understand was that, using this language and presenting this example, France should seek to enslave

---

* It was a favourite belief of the nationalist historians of the nineteenth century that Napoleon, having conquered the rulers of the old Europe, was himself overthrown by a spontaneous revolt of the nations. There can be no doubt that Revolutionary and Napoleonic Europe witnessed the rise of the modern movement of nationalism, or that national feeling inspired the resistance of, say, Great Britain or Spain to the Napoleonic Empire. Nevertheless Napoleon was beaten not by nations but by the armies of the old Europe and the navy of Great Britain, under their traditional rulers.

and exploit them. Nor did they make any distinction between France and the man who ruled her; they did not seek to understand the phases through which the French Revolution had passed or the manner in which the Republic had been transformed into the Empire. They knew the Revolution only in the form of conquest. It was in this form that it spread its principles among them, and in this form, and in virtue even of these principles, they held it in abomination. They rose up against its dominance.

Reduced to their own strength and their classic system of government, the kings of Europe had been vanquished by a nation which fought with enthusiasm first for independence and then for glory. When the nations joined in the war the rôles were reversed: it was France that found herself reduced to her bare political resources, while Europe turned her own weapons against her. The nations of Europe, as was only to have been expected, were carried away by the passions that had aroused them in the first place. Having armed themselves to secure independence, they remained in arms for vengeance and for conquest. Each brought to the struggle the hatreds, rancours, ambitions which accumulate unseen throughout the centuries, to burst forth in great crises like hidden volcanoes revealed by earthquakes. The shock was such that Europe feels it still. The end of the wars which proceeded directly from the French Revolution marked the beginning of a European revolution whose consequences France has felt only too sharply. It was the advent of the nations. The French Revolution had signalised its beginning; but far from this new era bringing to the old world a principle of order and peace, it was left more divided against itself, a prey to more rivalries, and threatened with greater strife than it had ever been before.

These singular vicissitudes, this surprising process bringing in its train such apparently contradictory events, cannot however be explained by chance causes. If facts remote from one another are arbitrarily brought together, it seems that there can be no relationship between them; but if one considers these facts in their proper order, each is seen to be linked to it predecessor, and item by item the connection can be built up. So one may reach the same conclusion on this great modern revolution as Bossuet on those of ancient times: 'Everything is surprising if one looks only at particular causes; nevertheless, everything proceeds according to a regular order.'[4]

It is this order that I propose to discover in the history of France and Europe during the French Revolution, at least during the essential period of the Revolution, that is up to the end of the Convention. All the causes of the events are then present, all the chief results have been manifested, all the fundamental connections have been determined. To grasp them, one must consider what were at the end of the ancien régime the relations of the states and the dispositions of the peoples of Europe; on what principles the society of states rested; what rules governed their conduct; what views of the general interest—or what calculations of particular interests —determined their policy; what ideas were current among the nations, what sentiments moved men's hearts; and in what condition governments and peoples found themselves when there began that great convulsion of the old world which shook it to its foundations, set all the armies in motion and forced all the people of Europe out of their homelands to join in the *mêlée*.

The principles of the French Revolution were abstract and universal; it was this that made their propagation so easy; but it was this also that produced such widely differing consequences according to the milieu into which they were carried. These beautiful ideas retained their metaphysical purity only in the conscience of the *philosophe* or in the intelligence of the mathematician. The slightest breath of real life deranged and transformed them. Whoever wished to apply them identified himself with them, and in making them his own changed their nature. The dialectic escaped

[4] *Discours*, 3e partie, ch. VIII.

the mass of mankind. They received these ideas not as a law which must guide their thoughts, but as a mould into which they poured in confusion all the instincts, feelings, notions, prejudices and errors that their incomplete education, their muddled experience, the sum of family and national influences had amassed in their minds. The chemist analyses the passing air, reducing it to a formula, but people breathe it; and, according to the germs borne upon it and the organs it enters into, this air can bring them either fever or health.

Pure reason is the concern neither of politicians, who are ruled by raison d'état, nor of peoples, who are ruled by their passions. But both states and peoples have traditions, as old as their history, which spring from the same source as their history and follow a course parallel with it. Their action on men's minds is entirely instinctive, and the less men are conscious of their influence the more imperious they are. In crises which take them unawares men find no other resource; whether they wish it or not, whether they are aware of it or ignore it, lend themselves to it or try to escape it, they undergo the influence of received ideas and of the passions which have found a lodgment in their minds and their environment. It is with this kind of mental equipment that they conceive new ideas and seek to realise them. It was in this way that the French and the other peoples of Europe interpreted the principles of the Revolution and adapted them to the traditions of their past.

I do not claim to have succeeded in explaining these great historic phenomena, but I should consider my work not to have been useless if I had attained this result: to have shown the French Revolution, which appeared to some to be the subversion and to others the regeneration of the old European world, as the natural and necessary consequence of the history of Europe, and to have demonstrated that this Revolution brought no development with it, even the most surprising, that did not flow from this history and is not explicable by the precedents of the ancien régime.

BOOK ONE

*Political Customs
and Reforms*

I. The Ways of Politics

I. EUROPE

There is one prejudice which must be put aside in setting out on this history. It is the representation of Europe under the ancien régime as a regularly constituted community of states, in which each directed its conduct by principles recognised by all, where respect for established law governed international relations and treaties, and good faith marked their implementation, where the sense of monarchical solidarity assured both the maintenance of public order and the permanence of engagements contracted by princes. This 'Christian republic', as some have been pleased to call it, has during modern times been nothing more than an august abstraction. The only period when, in fact, it seemed near realisation was during the Middle Ages; but even this tentative approach failed at the moment when the grand vision of the medieval papacy—the government of the Catholic world by a theocracy—vanished. The Renaissance brought ruin to this conception, as it ruined the feudal system and scholastic philosophy. Nothing of it remained but vague memories to lull the minds of utopians.

A Europe in which the rights of each derived from the duties of all was something so foreign to the thinking of the statesmen of the old régime that it took a quarter of a century of war, the most tremendous that had yet been seen, to force the idea upon them and to demonstrate the necessity of it. The attempt made at the Congress of Vienna and the subsequent Congresses to provide Europe with the elements of an

organization was a step forward, not a return to the past.[1] In
the eighteenth century such progress was only one of the
more attractive hypotheses of the *philosophes*. Towards
1789 it tended to gain a hold, especially in France, on the
minds of some politicians;[2] but they were rated mere dream-
ers, and the great majority of those concerned with government in Europe, confusing the idea with the chimerical project of perpetual peace, continued to regard it as the wildest
of paradoxes.

However, if there was in Europe no Christian republic,
there were nations and states. So long as they existed, and
there were relations between them, there was such a thing as
public law. 'Even the Iroquois have one', said Montesquieu.[3]
What did it mean in the Europe of the ancien régime? I am
not thinking, of course, of the public law put forward by
reformers as an ideal for a future commonwealth. 'They
seem', said Voltaire of these plans, 'to be looked on as a way
of consoling people for the evils caused by government and
the use of force. They give as much idea of justice as portraits do of famous men whom one cannot see in the flesh.'[4]
What we can see are the actual policies of governments; and
we must try to understand the habits they acquired, on which
their relations were based. They did not envisage these habits
in terms of juridical deductions from abstract principles, but
simply as the statement of relationships which derived from
the nature of things. 'Public law is founded on facts', wrote

[1] The results achieved at Vienna, incomplete as they appeared
in conception, and empirical, arbitrary and even unjust as were
some of their applications, nevertheless secured for Europe the
most productive period of peace it had ever enjoyed. There was
perhaps no more than a framework; but at no time have diplomats
built a better ordered structure on more solid foundations, nor
accomplished a task more beneficial to civilisation.

[2] See below. Book II, Chapter II: France, Foreign Policy, § 10:
The Problem of the Frontiers: the views of Vergennes.

[3] *Esprit des lois*, livre. II, ch. III.

[4] *Siècle de Louis XIV*. Personnages célèbres. Article Barbeyrac.

an international lawyer justly recognised as an authority in the chancelleries. 'To understand it, one must understand history; it is the heart of this study, as of politics in general.'[5]

2. STATE AND GOVERNMENT

In the public law of the ancien régime there was one fundamental conception, that of the state; it dominated and governed politics. It was the state on the Roman model—a collective entity, sovereign and absolute. In Rome it had been incarnate in a ruler to whom was attributed the majesty, the omnipotent authority, which belonged to the Republic. With this conception were merged the Christian idea of the prince as God's elect, representing divine authority on earth, and the feudal idea of the monarch as a universal suzerain. In this way was formed the idea of the sovereign as Bossuet and the whole Continent conceived it. 'The entire state is in the person of the prince; in him is the power, in him is the will of the whole people.'[6] It was because the monarch was the state itself that he was thus clothed in majesty; he derived his authority from the state, and it returned to the state when there was no monarch to embody it. The principle of divine right, according to which sovereigns were regarded as holding their rights from God Himself,[7] was applied to the state before it was applied to individuals; it was a simple consequence of the doctrine that all power comes from God. This doctrine made no distinction as to the form of power or its mode of transmission. 'It must reside in the state to which over a long period a people has become accustomed; that is why God takes

[5] Bielfeld, *Institutions politiques*. The Hague, 1760, t. I, ch. II, § 13.

[6] *Politique*, liv. VI, art. 1. prop. 1. Cf. *ibid.*, liv. V, art. 4, prop. 1.

[7] 'They are consecrated by their responsibility as representatives of the divine Majesty, deputed by his Providence to execute his designs.' Bossuet, *Politique*, Livre III, art. 2, prop. 2.

under his protection all legitimate governments, in whatever form they have been established.'[8] 'Through Him all kings hold sway, both those established by right of birth, because He is the Master of Nature, and those who are elected, because He presides over all councils. There is no power on earth that He hath not ordained: "Non est potestas nisi a Deo", saith the oracle of Holy Scripture.'[9]

The Pope, the German Emperor and the King of Poland were elective rulers, but no distinction was made between their rights and those of the King of France. When Napoleon, placing on his own head the crown of Italy, pronounced the sacramental formula, 'God has given it me, woe betide him who shall touch it!' he in no way distorted its meaning and was in no danger of scandalizing the old Europe; he was speaking its own language. 'Charlemagne'—thus the *Mémoires de Louis XIV*—'had risen to his peak of glory not by the process of election, but by his courage and his victories, which were the suffrages of Heaven itself, since it had resolved that all princes should be submitted to one alone.'[10]

This was why the origins of the powers that be must be veiled. The rights of rulers depend entirely on prescription. Nothing could be more obscure than the foundations of these rights. The mystery whereby the naked fact becomes legitimate right is something to be decently hidden from the sight of men. These are regions of fearful mist; it would be temerity to venture there. Above all it is essential that the people shall not force its way into the sanctuary. 'Better,' said Pascal, 'that it should not know of a usurpation which, unjust in origin, has since become just and must be regarded as such. If the usurped power is not to come to a rapid end, it must be thought of as having been just from all time, and its

---

[8] *Id., ibid.*, livre II, art. 1, prop. 12.

[9] *Id. Troisième Sermon pour le dimanche des Rameaux: Sur les devoirs des rois.*

[10] *Mémoires de Louis XIV*, année 1661, éd. Dreyss, Paris, 1866, II, p. 449.

beginnings left obscure.'[11] In this matter the empiricist agrees
with the philosopher. 'The rights of peoples and those of
kings never agree so well as in silence', wrote Retz.[12] The
scepticism of the eighteenth century reached the same conclusion. Without provoking the censure of the chancelleries
or incurring the blame of the courts Voltaire could write:
'Time, occasion, usage, prescription, force, are the making of
all rights.'[13] This was indeed the basis of the thinking of
the men who managed the affairs of Europe at the end of the
eighteenth century.

A sovereign government became legitimate in the eyes of
other states simply by the recognition that they gave to it.
This recognition moreover implied no condition about the
origin of its power. It was even accepted that the relationships between states were independent of the form of their
government and of the revolutions which might modify it.
When M. de Bordeaux, sent by Louis XIV to England, was
received on 21st December 1652 before the Parliament of
the Commonwealth, he declared, 'The accord which ought
to exist between neighbouring states is not affected by the
form of their governments; and so, although it has pleased
God, in His providence, to change what was formerly established in this country, there has not ceased to be a need for
commerce and communication between France and England.
This realm may have changed its complexion, and from a
monarchy become a republic, but geographical conditions
have not changed; our peoples still remain neighbours, with
mutual interests in trade; and the treaties which exist between
nations are binding not so much on princes as on peoples,
since they have as their principal object the common
utility.'[14]

All forms of government existed in Europe, and all were

[11] *Pensées*. Edition Havet. Paris, 1866, Article III, no. 8.
[12] *Mémoires*, 2e partie, ch. III.
[13] *Annales de l'Empire*, livre II.
[14] Guizot, *Cromwell*, livre III. Paris, 1860.

considered equally legitimate.[15] 'To preserve our general
society', wrote an historian of the sixteenth century, 'we have
introduced three kinds of republic—the royal, the seignorial,
the popular. Each legislator considered that his own was the
best.'[16] In the eighteenth century they were called monarchy, aristocracy and democracy. They were discussed in
terms of their common purpose, which was the good of the
state; but no one thought of establishing any kind of priority
among them. People of good society had long thought the
most reasonable and expedient course was 'to deem that government under which a man was born the best of all and to
submit to it'.[17] This was the doctrine of the Church;[18] and
the writer who had most profoundly studied and best defined
the constitutions of states, Montesquieu, followed the same
prudent maxim: 'I am a good citizen,' he said, 'but in whatever country I had been born I should have been the same.
I am a good citizen because I love the government under
which I was born.'[19]

The idea of attributing to one type of constitution an
absolute superiority over the others, the idea that there could
be an ideal constitution applicable to all countries, above all

[15] Theocracy in the States of the Church, autocracy in Russia,
sheer despotism at Constantinople, absolute monarchy in France,
Spain, the states of the House of Austria, Prussia, etc; constitutional monarchy in England; an empire formed from confederated
states in Germany; federal republics in the United Provinces and
Switzerland; a republic with an elective monarchy in Poland;
and in Venice, Genoa, Ragusa and the free cities of Germany all
the varieties of republican government that had survived the
Middle Ages.

[16] Etienne Pasquier, *Lettres*, livre XIX, lettre VII. *Œuvres*,
Amsterdam, 1723.

[17] La Bruyère, *les Caractères*, ch. X.

[18] 'It appears in the antiquity of other forms of government
(than monarchy) about which God has given no precise instruction to the human race, so that each people should follow, as a
divine command, the government established in its country.' Bossuet, *Politique*, Livre II, Conclusion.

[19] *Pensées*.

the idea of making this an object of propaganda, never entered the minds of statesmen. The words republic and democracy were not in any way associated with the idea of revolution. It was reckoned, however, that republics or democracies
were suitable only to small states; they entailed pacific ways
and modest policies.[20] The English republic passed for an
exception, but it had owed its strength only to Cromwell.
The republics of that time were all more or less in decline;
several seemed to be threatened, none appeared threatening.
The Swiss cantons leaned towards neutrality; the United
Provinces were absorbed in commerce; Venice was solemnly
foundering; Poland was dissolving in anarchy. 'Sweden',
wrote Frederick, 'was experiencing the fate of any monarchical state that changes into a republic—it becomes enfeebled.'[21] When towards the end of the century a great
republic was established in North America, it was in this
light that the European monarchies regarded it. 'It takes
time', they said in the chancelleries, 'to shape a conquering
people. It is even more difficult to endow a republic with the
spirit of conquest than the head of a government entrusted
to a single person.'[22] It was according to these axioms that
the politicians of the old Europe judged the French Revolution at the outset. They saw in it an enfeeblement of the
French state, and framed their policy in that light, according

[20] Montesquieu agrees with Rousseau on this point; the great
observer reaches the same conclusion as the great revolutionary:
'It is in the nature of a republic that it should have only a small
territory; otherwise it can hardly survive. . . . The spirit of monarchy is war and aggrandisement, the spirit of a republic is peace
and moderation.' *Esprit des lois*, Livre VII, ch. XVI and Livre
IX, ch. II. 'Monarchy is suitable only to rich nations, aristocracy
to middling states, democracy to small and poor states.' *Contrat
social*, Livre III, chs. IV, VI, VIII.

[21] *Histoire de mon temps*, ch. I.

[22] Examen des motifs et des conditions du traité de paix à faire
avec les insurgents, avec les Anglais et avec nos alliés, 1782. Published by Bancroft, *Histoire de l'indépendance des Etats-Unis*.
Translation by M. de Circourt, Tome III, p. 35, Paris, 1876.

as they thought this advantageous to their interests or otherwise.

3. RAISON D'ETAT

The state is an end in itself. It is sovereign; it recognises no authority beyond its own. The doctrine stated: 'They are gods. Only God can judge their judgements and their persons.'[23] The Catholic sovereigns themselves recognised no superior authority in the Sovereign Pontiff. Except in matters of dogma, he was a prince like the others. 'Who should be judge of these things?' wrote Richelieu. 'Who could consider them disinterestedly and without passion? Not the Pope, who is a temporal prince, and has not so far renounced the splendours of the world that he can be indifferent to them. God alone can be judge. Therefore kings sin only before Him, to Whom alone belongs cognisance of their deeds.'[24] To appeal to God in these terms was to appeal to history, which alone could reveal the designs of Providence. In reality, in dealing with contingencies and even with the ordinary course of affairs, some guidance, some rule of judgement, was required. The state could find none outside itself. It drew from its own omnipotence what it needed. In all things its final argument was raison d'état, that is to say the old doctrine of the public good, as practised and taught to the world by Rome. It had never disappeared from politics. The Renaissance restored it to a place of honour; its development proceeded along with the growth of the great modern states. They borrowed from Rome the spirit of their politics as well as the mould of their institutions.

The name of Machiavelli is justly linked with this doctrine; but Machiavelli is less a theorist than an observer, and the whole force of his work arises from the realistic character he was able to give to it. He describes what he sees and simply

[23] Bossuet, *Politique*, liv. V, art. 1, prop. 2.
[24] *Mémoires*. Année 1626. Ed. Petitot, t. III, p. 24. Paris, 1823.

puts in general terms the actual political behaviour of his contemporaries. So thought Richelieu, who did not fail to draw inspiration from the author of *The Prince,* and deemed 'indispensable' the maxims of 'this solid and veracious writer'. In an *Apologie pour Machiavel* composed by a disciple of the Cardinal* it is stated: 'His maxims are as old as history and as states. He teaches nothing extraordinary and nothing outrageous, but merely recounts what our predecessors have done, and what the men of the present time still practise usefully, innocently and inevitably.'[25]

The most profound thinker and the greatest statesman of the old France are at one on this point, and their agreement is no matter of chance. 'States would perish if one did not often bend laws to necessity. . . . Being unable to fortify justice we have justified force', said Pascal.[26] Richelieu, who had so rigorously applied the doctrine of the public good, pushed it in his *Testament Politique* to its logical conclusion: 'In matters of state he who has might often has right, and he who is weak will find it difficult to avoid being wrong in the eyes of the greater part of mankind.'[27] The reign of Louis XIV did nothing to alter public opinion. 'The supreme law, which is raison d'état', in the words of Saint Simon, continued to govern the behaviour of princes.[28] In the eighteenth century I see only one exception, and that is of the kind that is said to prove the rule; it is Frederick II and his *Anti-Machiavel.* Frederick, when he composed this

---

* Canon Machon began his *Apologie pour Machiavel* in 1641 on the instructions of Richelieu, who died before it was completed. It was only published in the nineteenth century. Whether Richelieu would have approved all the arguments of Machon in defence of Machiavelli is doubtful. *Cf.* A. Cherel, *La pensée de Machiavel en France,* 1935.

[25] See Céleste, *Louis Machon, apologiste de Machiavel. Annales de la Faculté des lettres de Bordeaux,* 1881, p. 446.

[26] *Pensées,* éd. Havet. Art. XI, no. 6, art. VI, no. 7.

[27] *Testament,* ch. IX, section IV. Paris, 1764.

[28] *Mémoires,* Year 1703, with reference to Philip V and the affairs of Spain.

dissertation, was engaged in a mere academic exercise. As soon as he had cast off the leading-strings he threw his school books to the four winds and looked for something very different from the rewards of virtue. Machiavelli had his revenge. The end of the century had still more startling revenges in store for him, as we shall see; but there was nothing new in this, and nothing to surprise men of judgement. 'Everybody condemns this author,' said an associate of Mazarin, 'but everybody follows him and practises his principles— especially those who condemn him.'[28a] In the eighteenth century both ideas and men sank to a lower level. Instead of the elevated irony of a Pascal and the rough frankness of a Richelieu there were the disparaging mockery of Voltaire and the cynicism of Frederick; these could be suitably combined, and they set the tone of the period. Without pushing it too far, the parallel can be continued; deeds ever more outrageous were regarded with increasing complacency. The further it was refined and the more subtly depraved it became, the more despotically did raison d'état hold sway.

It prevailed wherever men felt strong enough to pursue with impunity the designs that it suggested. It inspired the same purposes at Vienna as at Berlin.[29] It was taught to young princes and future ministers. One may read in Bielfeld's *Institutions Politiques*,* 'Whatever the situation in

[28a] Statement by Gabriel Naudé to Gui Patin. *Lettres de Gui Patin*, éd. Réveillé–Parisse, Tome II, lettre 251, to M. Spon. Paris, 1846.

[29] Frederick wrote to Cardinal Fleury, 12 September 1742: 'I am very little worried by anything that can be said against me by a fickle and ill-informed public opinion. Kings are judged by posterity alone.' *Politische Correspondenz*, 1742. Berlin, 1879.

Joseph II wrote to his brother Leopold, Grand Duke of Tuscany, 6 May 1775: 'In my opinion the world must be calmly left to say what it likes, provided that it lets us do what we like.' Arneth, *Joseph II und Leopold II von Toscana*. Vienna, 1872.

* James Frederick, baron de Bielfeld, 1716-1770, was a German publicist and official who represented Prussia at the court of Hanover, and was appointed Inspector of the Prussian universities in 1747. On the outbreak of the Seven Years War he retired and

which a state may be, the fundamental principle of raison
d'état remains always the same. This principle, adopted by all
peoples ancient and modern, is that the public welfare is always the highest law.'[30] An Austrian diplomat wrote in
1791, 'The great powers should conduct themselves conformably with raison d'état. Their interests should prevail
over every kind of sentiment, however just it may be.'[31]

If raison d'état was the rule of policy aggrandisement was
its object. 'Who gains nothing, loses', wrote Catherine II.[32]
The idea of the greatness of the state was closely linked with
that of its extent. These ideas are as old as human commu-
nities. Ever since men have lived in societies they have struggled to conquer and to defend themselves. Pillage and conquest are as old as covetousness, and that was born with
mankind. Princes of all ages have made it a matter of honour.
'The desire to expand and to extend one's frontiers', said
Machiavelli, 'is very natural and common, and when men
do so and are successful they are to be highly praised or at
least not blamed.'[33] The apologist of the seventeenth century
develops this maxim. 'It is based', he says, 'on this principle
and this truth—that princes having nothing other than what
they have usurped, the stronger lay down the law to the
weaker and take whatever suits them. For whatever is useful
they think just, and they consider that states have no other
boundaries than those that are conducive to their own security—though damaging to that of their neighbours.'[34] It

sought asylum in Hamburg, his birthplace. His *Institutions politiques* was published at the Hague in 1760.

[30] Tome II, ch. V: *Des engagements réciproques des souverains*; § 8 and 9: *De la raison d'Etat*.

[31] Memoir of comte Louis de Cobenzl, Austrian ambassador at
St. Petersburg, 1791 (in French). Beer, Die orientalische Politik
Oesterreichs, p. 761. Prague, 1883.

[32] To Grimm, February 1794. Publications de la Société d'histoire de Russie. *Correspondance de Catherine II avec Grimm.*
Petersburg, 1878.

[33] *The Prince*, ch. III.

[34] Machon, Céleste, *op. cit.*

was this that led Montesquieu to conclude in the following century that 'the spirit of monarchy is war and aggrandisement'.[35]

4. RULES OF CONDUCT

The principle and the object of politics thus posited, rules of conduct can be deduced from them. The chief is that one must always be fit and prepared for action and ready to seize any opportunity. 'The negotiator will always find eventually the right moment for attaining his objective.'[36] Success comes to the farsighted and the clever. Certainly it is necessary to reckon with chance; but chance, which is often only the product of muddlers, proves of advantage to superior men. 'Again, if one looks merely at particular episodes chance seems to decide the establishment and the fall of empires, but in a broad view it is a game where the cleverer player carries the day in the end. In fact, in this bloody game in which nations have disputed empire and power, he who has been most far-sighted and diligent, who has endured the longest in great labours, and who has known when to thrust on in an encounter and when to hold back, is the one who at the end has the advantage, having made chance serve his purposes.'[37] The majesty of this language must not deceive us as to the nature of the facts. Never have more generous euphemisms disguised more unscrupulous tricks of policy. Let us leave the galleries where Bossuet paints his vast frescoes, and let us enter the cabinet where the statesman, his courtly dress and ceremonial manners cast off, shows himself as he is. La Bruyère provides a finished portrait of him; whoever understands it has no more to learn of the politics of the time.[38]

[35] *Esprit des lois*, liv. IX, ch. II.
[36] Richelieu, *Testament politique. Des négociations.*
[37] Bossuet, *Discours.* Partie III, ch. II.
[38] *Les Caractères*, ch. X. *Du souverain et de la République.*
Having brought together many documents on the governments of Europe in the eighteenth century, one finds that one has simply

'The minister or the plenipotentiary is a chameleon, a Proteus'; but he only changes his physiognomy deliberately and of set purpose. 'He considers the time, the place, the opportunity, reckons with his power or his lack of it, the genius of the nations with whom he deals, the temperament and character of the persons with whom he negotiates. All his views, all his maxims, all the refinements of his policy are directed to one sole end—never to be deceived, but to deceive others.' One of the surest means of success, moreover, is to speak the truth; this he brings to a fine art. 'He is profound and dissimulating, so as to hide a truth while stating it, for it is important that he should have said it, but that it should not be believed. Or he is frank and candid, so that when he conceals what should not be known, it is nevertheless thought that he has told everything and that one is ignorant of nothing that one would wish to know.' He supports his allies, 'if he finds that this is useful and promotes his aims'; he even upholds the weak and unites them against the strong 'in order to redress the balance', though he may next join with the strong in order to tilt it, and sell his protection and his alliance to the weak at a good price. Moreover, he is a man of the world, *Honnête homme*—the honest man above all—and exquisite in observance of the proprieties. He has a feeling for all the nuances of language, he is thoroughly versed in everything the times require, he excels in finding noble pretexts. 'He speaks only of peace, of alliances, of general tranquillity, of the public interest; in fact he thinks only of his own, that is to say the interest of his master or of his state.' But he is not the dupe of his own phrases; he has no belief in them. 'In his intrigues he keeps always in mind what is solid and essential, always ready to sacrifice to them trifling matters and imaginary points of honour.'

---

compiled notes for an edition of *L'Esprit des lois*. Having ransacked the letters of a host of diplomats of the ancien régime, one finds that one has merely spun out in detail this admirable summary by la Bruyère.

In the eighteenth century the tone changes—but only the tone. The epithets, which are a matter of fashion, the pretexts, which are a matter of opinion, are modified according to the taste of the moment and the prevailing doctrine. High-flown language is in favour, scepticism lords it over all. Politics takes up the fashion for incredulity, even about its own proceedings. 'Everybody', says Voltaire, 'has received from nature the urge to aggrandisement; a chance seems to offer itself, some intriguer seizes upon it; a woman won over by money, or by something which should be more effective, tries to bring the business to nought; another sets it going again. Circumstance, mood, a caprice, a misunderstanding, a trifle decides the outcome.'[39] 'That's the way of the world,' Frederick concludes; 'it's all jobbery.'[40] Really, Frederick believed nothing of the kind, and while sacrificing in public to the good goddess, Her Sacred Majesty Fortune, as he called her, he remained the most reflective and sagacious of politicians and left nothing to chance. We can take note of his table-talk and of his political maxims. The latter are those of Richelieu. 'Make no mistake: fortune, luck, are words which signify nothing.—Seize the opportunity and go forward when it is favourable, but do not strain it by abandoning everything to chance.—Politics requires patience, and the mark of an able man is to do each thing at the right time.—He who has best calculated his course will prevail against those who have acted with less deliberation.'[41] These are his real thoughts, from which he never wavered.

When the wind veers to philosophy, the statesman becomes philosophical. He loves truth, he is 'generous'; he calls himself a 'citizen'; he preaches tolerance; he speaks only of the happiness of the human race; having in the previous century been '*honnête*' he now becomes '*vertueux*' in obedience

[39] To Frederick, 5 August 1738.

[40] To Voltaire, 6 December 1771.

[41] *Considérations sur l'état présent de l'Europe*, 1738. *Histoire de mon temps*, preface, 1775.

to ideas of proper behaviour and knowledge of the world. This was an easy virtue moreover, like the sentiment of honour it replaced. There was nothing extreme about it and it did not require abstinence in any respect. It was enough to be a gentleman, to appear to be free from prejudice, to keep to the accepted forms, to use the expected language and to observe its nuances. Apart from the Trenck scandal* Frederick would have passed as 'humane' if he had 'secularised' himself with less fuss. Talleyrand would have been reckoned to have 'virtue'. The statesman could when need arose exhibit sensibility: he could display enthusiasm, love Nature, shed tears. Diplomacy, which had its encyclopaedists, was to have its *Nouvelle Héloïse*. 'She wept, but she took it all the same', said Frederick of Maria Theresa after the partition of Poland.

In fact, then, the whole world went the same way, and all these refinements led only to the same end, 'which was not to be deceived but to deceive others'. All men knew it, and brought to their dealings an incurable mistrust which was only too well founded. 'A state', wrote a former minister of foreign affairs, 'should be always at the ready, like a gentleman living among swashbucklers and quarrellers. Such are the nations of Europe, to-day more than ever; negotiations are only a continual struggle between men without principles, impudently aggressive and ever greedy.'[42]

5 . GOOD FAITH AND TREATIES

Since raison d'état was the sole guide of policy, the interest of the state was the only guarantee of its undertakings—which means that there was no guarantee. There never had been

---

* Frédéric, baron de Trenck was disgraced and imprisoned by Frederick for communicating with the enemy during the Second Silesian War, in 1745. Trenck in his *Mémoires* (Strasburg and Paris, 1789) proclaimed his innocence.

[42] D'Argenson, *Mémoires*, éd. Rathery, t. II, p. 326, année 1739. Paris, 1859-1867.

any that were worth much. In the sixteenth century Bodin had noted the fact with sorrow: 'For the last two or three hundred years this opinion has gained currency—that there is no treaty, however fair, that cannot be broken; so that the view has almost gained the force of a maxim that a prince constrained to conclude any peace or treaty to his disadvantage may ignore it when the opportunity presents itself.'[43] The seventeenth century, in this respect, was no whit behind the sixteenth; the eighteenth outdid them both. Frederick, at the beginning of his *Mémoires,* treats of 'cases for breaking alliances'. He distinguishes four: the defection of the ally, the need to forestall a defection, *force majeure,* insufficiency of means. He forgets a fifth, which was the most common, and one that he knew from personal experience—raison d'état or political interest, whichever one prefers to call it. Like Machiavelli, Frederick was here doing no more than describe the behaviour of his times. He was not writing a satire, he was setting forth a protocol.[44] 'When one is dealing with fools, rogues, personal enemies and rivals,' said Cardinal Dubois, himself one of the craft, 'prudence dictates that one should undertake no engagement with them except with great precautions.'[45]

There were no precautions that could avail against unbridled greed and the sophistries of raison d'état. This ap-

43 Baudrillart, *Bodin et son temps.* Paris, 1850.

44 I read in a memorandum written in 1741 by a *maître des requêtes,* M. Mandat, entitled *Nouveaux Intérêts des princes de l'Europe:* 'In matters of political interests, neither gratitude nor treaties count for anything; treaties are made through force or interest, and it is through force or interest that they are broken.' *Archives des Affaires étrangères.*

D'Argenson said (*Mémoires,* éd. Rathery, tome IV, p. 245): 'The sentiments of rulers are at the bidding of their interest.' Also, in 1746, à propos of a letter from an Elector of Cologne who did not wish to sign a treaty: 'I should value this letter as much as a treaty, which would be no better kept than a *parole d'honneur.*'

45 Aubertin, *l'Esprit public au dix-huitième siècle,* p. 100. Paris, 1873.

pears in the very middle of the century in an event which portrays the customs of the time to the life—the War of the Austrian Succession. Everything that public law offered in the way of resources and guarantees had been exhausted by the Emperor Charles VI to ensure the succession of his daughter Maria Theresa to his hereditary domains. He established her rights by an organic law, a *Pragmatic Sanction* which he had sanctified by all the diets of the Monarchy. He obtained from the pretenders solemn renunciations. *The Pragmatic Sanction* was then notified to all the powers, who expressly recognised it, and engaged themselves by formal treaties to respect it in perpetuity. Nevertheless, no sooner was Charles VI dead than the princes who had renounced their claims to his heritage and those who had guaranteed it to his daughter tore up their signatures, broke their pledges and leagued themselves together to share out the spoils of Maria Theresa's empire. Never was raison d'état more shamelessly opposed to the most elementary rules of honour and justice. England alone held to her pledges, and it must be said her interests and her inclinations urged her to keep them. These were the customs of the epoch—the customs of all Europe. A French diplomat, the most honourable of men, full of good sense and discretion, wrote at the end of the century, in commenting on the writings of a famous publicist who was a determined adversary of the House of Austria: 'What Favier* has to say of the brittleness of treaties and the bad faith of the Vienna government is very true; but unfortunately history proves that it is equally true of all the governments of Europe.'[46]

This was the public law which they observed in their relations with one another. 'In politics', said the baron de Biel-

---

* Jean-Louis Favier was one of the secret agents and adventurers with whom French diplomacy abounded in the eighteenth century. He is best known as a publicist, for his writings on French foreign policy. See below, II.2.ix.

[46] Comte de Ségur, *Notes sur les Doutes et questions sur le traité de 1756, par Favier. Œuvres*, Paris, 1824-1830.

feld, 'one must disabuse oneself of the speculative ideas held
by ordinary men about justice, equity, moderation, candour,
and the other virtues of nations and their rulers. *In the end
everything depends on power.*'[47] Power carried along with
it, and even gained approval for, all kinds of actions otherwise
barred, as with its successful usurpations of property rights.
Cynics declared quite bluntly that the end justified the
means; scholars were reduced to saying that if it did not
justify them, at any rate it caused them to be forgotten. It is
no good, as a statesman wrote in the last years of the French
monarchy, comforting oneself with the thought that the
King of Prussia is making himself odious by his enterprises.
'In time, the hatred of the means by which a monarchy has
grown great will disappear, but the power it has gained will
remain.'[48] It was in this way that even honour was understood, and this conception is what one must appreciate to
grasp the spirit of the age. Montesquieu, speaking of education under a monarchy, says: 'Under them the actions of men
are not judged as good but as grand; not as just, but as great;
not as reasonable, but as remarkable. As long as honour can
find in them something noble, there will be either a judge to
pronounce them legitimate or a sophist to excuse them.
Deceit is allowed as long as it is associated with grandeur of
conception or with great affairs, as in politics, where guile
does not offend. Adulation is forbidden only when it is separated from the idea of a great success.'[49]

War was the great instrument of rule, the supreme argu-

[47] *Institutions politiques,* t. II, ch. IV. *De la puissance des
Etats,* § 30.
[48] *Recueil des Instructions données aux ambassadeurs et mini-
stres de France de 1648 à 1789,* tome I, Autriche. Paris, 1884.
Instruction du baron de Breteuil, en 1774 par M. de Vergennes.
The statement is the more significant in that, in the same document, Vergennes passes a justly severe judgement on Frederick:
'Any understanding with that power is impossible unless one is
resolved to tread justice and humanity underfoot.'
[49] *Esprit des lois,* liv. IV, ch. II.

ment of raison d'état. The moment it was found necessary it was considered just. It was the means of conquest and of preservation, of defence against attack or its prevention. Coligny, urging Charles IX to take Spain by surprise when her attitude was threatening, concluded 'that it is better to set fire to our neighbour's house than to wait until he sets fire to ours'.[50] 'Great kings', said Henry IV, 'must resolve to be either hammers or anvils, and I would rather strike two blows at my enemies than take one from them.'[51] Descartes, though he had no liking for Machiavellianism, found nothing contrary to philosophy in its argument. 'Justice between sovereigns', he said to a great lady who asked his opinion on the politics of *The Prince*, 'has different limits from those that apply to individuals. . . . Distinction must also be made between subjects, friends or allies, and enemies; for, in respect of these last, almost anything is permissible provided that some advantage is gained for the ruler or his subjects; I do not disapprove in such cases of joining the fox to the lion and adding trickery to force. I go so far as to include in the word enemies all those who are not friends or allies, for there is a right to make war on these when it yields advantage, and when they become doubtful or dangerous, they give cause for mistrust.'[52] The famous passage in *L'Esprit des Lois* on preventive wars merely summarises these ancient maxims.[53]

If a war to forestall danger is held legitimate, it may be thought necessary to hasten its onset so as to surprise the enemy and the better to upset his plans. The brutal aggressions of Frederick are often cited—his attacks and his conquests, more like ambushes or burglaries—yet he only undertook boldly and carried out with success what his con-

[50] Pierre Matthieu, *Histoire de France. Charles IX*, liv. VI, 1631.

[51] Sully, *Economies royales*, éd. Petitot t. VII, ch. VIII, année 1607.

[52] *Œuvres de Descartes*, éd. Cousin, t. IX, p. 387 ff. Letter to Madame Elisabeth, princess palatine, September 1646.

[53] Liv. X, ch. II.

temporaries contemplated but dared not do, or tried to do without success. 'A great power with a grand design', Louis XV's secret counsellor, the comte de Broglie, told him, 'sets about putting it into effect regardless of clamour. Then comes the reckoning with neighbours, but the balance of account will always be on its side.'[54]

In 1755 the English attacked the French on the sea, taking them unawares and without a declaration of war. At Versailles England was thought to be in league with the court of Vienna. 'The military', reports Bernis, 'thought that the English aggression should be regarded as the beginning of a scheme long prepared and agreed with England's allies, and therefore that their plans should be upset by taking possession of the Austrian Netherlands.' The King of Prussia urged this, saying that he had 140,000 men ready and that he would invade Bohemia while the French seized Belgium.[55] He was not listened to, and it was just as well, for at the very time when he was putting forward these specious suggestions to his French ally he was negotiating with England a treaty directed against France. These things happened in the months of July and August 1755. Maria Theresa was warned of them, and at the beginning of September she revealed Frederick's defection to Louis XV; she then proposed to the King of France that they should turn the tables on Frederick and attack Prussia in order 'to set proper limits to his ambition'.[56] Louis XV refused; he was only willing to discuss a defensive alliance. Maria Theresa turned to the Russians, and on 25 March 1756 her ambassador at Petersburg declared that she was ready to attack Frederick with 80,000 men.[57]

[54] De Broglie, *Le Secret du Roi*, t. II, p. 83. Paris, 1879.

[55] Bernis, *Mémoires*, éd. Frédéric Masson, t. I, p. 210 ff. Paris, 1878.

[56] See Bernis, *Mémoires*, ch. XIV, p. 223. *Recueil des Instructions, Autriche*. Instructions of the comte de Stainville, 1757, pp. 362 ff.

[57] Martens, *Traités de l'Autriche et de la Russie*, t. I, p. 190. Petersburg, 1875.

She was in a hurry 'to get the affair launched', Bernis tells us,
and with good reason, for it was not to be thought that Frederick would wait to attack his enemies until they had had
time to form their coalition.[58] 'Have I got the kind of nose
that people can punch?' he asked the English ambassador.
'This lady wants war; she shall have it. All I have to do is to
steal a march on my enemies. My troops are ready; the conspiracy must be split up before it becomes too strong.'[59] He
invaded Saxony and marched on Bohemia. Thus began the
Seven Years War.

I have cited this precedent because it is typical. It became
case law, and we shall see in the sequel that, in 1792, the
advocates of war with Austria did not fail to quote, in justification of the attack they were proposing, the example of
Frederick in 1756.[60]

6. THE BALANCE OF POWER

States recognise no judges other than themselves and no laws
other than their own interests; but the very force that tends
to drive this doctrine to excess serves also to temper it. The
antidote to the paradoxes of raison d'état is common sense;
the curb on the excesses of covetousness is self-interest properly understood. This, the only rule states understand, is
the sole foundation of their justice. Ambition may dictate

[58] See Bernis, *Mémoires*, t. I, pp. 243 and 289.

[59] De Broglie, *Secret du Roi*, t. I, p. 162.

[60] 'In a similar situation, a king whose talents alone could provide an excuse for despotism, Frederick the Great, only withstood
the efforts of the league which the court of Vienna had formed
against him by forestalling its schemes.' Gensonné, 13 January
1792, in the name of the diplomatic committee. 'Examples would
not be lacking to prove the justice of this attack. . . . Remember
the famous Saxon campaign of the renowned Frederick. . . . Four
powers threatened him, and, forestalling them, he turned the
storm against them. And indeed, our cause is more just than his.
. . . Circumstances provide us, like Frederick, with the justification for our attack.' Brissot, 17 January 1792.

the plan, but prudence should govern its execution. Frederick
held to the principle that one must know when to stop. 'If
you overwork your luck you will lose it; if you always want
more you are never happy.'[61] This is an empirical moral—or
rather it is not a moral at all, but a matter of calculation and
policy.

It was said long ago, in reference to Alexander, that death
is meted out to petty thieves but altars are erected to great
ones. It is all a matter of degree and proportion. A man is
hailed as famous for seizing a province but execrated for
taking a hamlet. A skirmish in which a village is burned is
reckoned a massacre; a battle in which hosts of men are
slaughtered is a great achievement. A statesman must try to
allow for people's prejudices. In great enterprises it may be
impossible to avoid offending them, but it is stupid to provoke
them by pinpricks. The sins the public is least ready to forgive its heroes are the venial ones. That is why the conscience
of politicians shows itself so complaisant towards great in-
justices and so scrupulous about small ones. 'It is wrong to
break your word without good cause', said Frederick. 'You
are then reputed inconstant and a trifler.'[62] Richelieu considered that to keep treaties was on the whole the wisest
course. 'It is the greatest strength of sovereigns.'[63] Likewise,
usurpations should only be committed for good reason. 'As
to the Duchy of Warmie,' said the King of Prussia, 'I have
left it alone because the game is not worth the candle. It is
such a meagre morsel that it would not compensate for the
outcry it would raise. Grasping at trifles gets one a reputation
for insatiable greed.'[64] Frederick came straight to this cynical
conclusion and was proud of it. Maria Theresa reached a
similar one after much heart-searching and plenteous tears.

[61] Letter to Podewils, 11 June 1742. *Politische Correspondenz.*
[62] *Exposé des raisons que je puis avoir pour rester dans l'alliance avec la France.* 1742. *Politische Correspondenz.*
[63] *Testament politique,* 2nd part, ch. VI.
[64] To Prince Henry, 24 January 1771. *Œuvres. Correspondance.* Berlin, 1846-1857.

'One must know how to be generous, and not, for a meagre profit, lose one's good name before God and before men', she wrote to her minister, Kaunitz.[65] She was indeed generous, and on a large scale. It came about that the august matron of Vienna and the philosopher of Saint-Souci foregathered, shook hands, and took communion together; the bread was the body of Poland. The Empress wept, the King sneered. But the difference between them was that she demanded of him an extra portion of Poland to assuage her remorse and a bonus of Poles to satisfy her scruples. She got them, and this was the only tribute paid to morality in the whole affair.

Conquest, the starting-point and the goal of these enterprises, is limited only by the conditions necessary for success. The abuse of force frustrates its purpose. To conquer requires strength; to keep what is conquered requires justice and wisdom. Rabelais, who saw in the French monarchy an example of conquests wisely conceived and cleverly effected, expounded the principle in magnificent prose. . . . 'The way to keep and hold a newly conquered country is not, as certain tyrannical men, to their loss and dishonour, have thought, to pillage, bully, harass and vex the people, ruling with a rod of iron. . . . Like a new-born babe, they need to be nourished, lulled, and petted. . . . Like a person convalescing after a long and severe illness, they must be coddled, and nursed back to health. By gently administering philtres, potions and love-charms, what has been gained with difficulty may be kept with safety. Whether he be king, prince or philosopher, the conqueror will not reign more than a brief hour unless valour is seconded by justice. He who behaves otherwise will not only lose what he has gained, but will be the object of scandal and opprobrium, for his prize having died in his hands, he will be judged wicked and wrong in his conquest. . . . And even if he has peace-

[65] 13 January 1772. Arneth, *Geschichte Maria Theresia's*, t. VIII, p. 596, Vienna, 1877.

ful enjoyment of it during his own lifetime, but it then wastes away under his heirs, none the less will odium rest upon him and a curse descend on his memory for his wickedness.'[66]

Rabelais saw far ahead. The experience of three centuries was to confirm his penetrating judgements. Montesquieu, having considered how France had acquired and kept Alsace, Roussillon, Flanders, Franche-Comté, summed up his observations in these maxims: 'The object of war is victory; of victory conquest; of conquest, conservation. A conquest is an acquisition; the idea of acquisition entails the idea of preservation and use, not that of destruction.'[67] There is therefore a natural limit to conquest; it is fixed by the possibility of assimilation. What cannot be held should not be taken; and it can be held only by being assimilated. 'It is for a conqueror to make reparation for some of the evil he has done. Thus I define the right of conquest: a necessary and legitimate, yet unrewarding right, which always leaves an immense debt to be paid to balance the account with mankind.'[68] Only by the settlement of this debt can conquest truly be legitimised and made rightful. 'This law of conquest, which originates in force', said Bossuet, 'passes, so to speak, into common and natural law, by general consent of the people and through peaceable possession.'[69]

Let it be said, moreover, that states cannot grow indefinitely. By growing too large they become weaker. Frontiers stretched too far complicate the task of defence and offer the enemy too many chances of attack. Besides, all greatness is relative. 'One must take care that in increasing actual greatness, relative greatness is not diminished.'[70] It is often better to have on the frontiers states which are weak and disunited than to conquer them and share them with a pow-

[66] *Pantagruel*, liv. III, ch. I.
[67] *Esprit des lois*, liv. I, ch. III; liv. X, ch. III.
[68] *Esprit des lois*, liv. X, ch. IV.
[69] *Politique*, liv. II, art. II, prop. 2.
[70] *Esprit des lois*, liv. IX, ch. IX.

erful neighbour, who may through a temporary combination
have become an ally, but who always remains a rival. Here
another limit to aggrandisement appears—the coincidence of
ambitions. As there were no unclaimed territories in Europe, one country could only enrich itself at the expense of
another. But all the great powers were agreed in refusing to
let any one of them raise itself above the others. Any of
them that wished to play the lion would find the others
leagued against it. Thus the great powers constituted a kind
of joint-stock company, in which all kept what they possessed, made profits according to their holdings, and prevented any of the associates from laying down the law to the
others. This was called the balance of power, or the European equilibrium.

This actually existed after great wars, when all the powers were exhausted and near to ruin. Then for a time they
paused and came to terms, and their opposing aims and
forces produced a kind of balance. But the very causes which
had produced it tended to destroy it. Its continuance implied immobility, which was impossible. It would have required, in fact, a changed world, in which there were no
longer strong and weak, miserly and spendthrift, indolent
and grasping, competent and half-witted. It only needed one
state to decline and another to revive for the balance to disappear.

In the words of a mid-eighteenth-century document, 'It
is a matter of pure opinion, which each interprets according
to his particular views and interests'.[71] It was invoked
against those who aimed at hegemony—by France against
the house of Austria, by England against the house of France.
In the alliances which were formed each followed only its
own interest, and if this often required that the powerful
states which were aggressive should be contained, it seldom
suggested help for the weak states which might be despoiled.

[71] *Recueil des Instructions, Autriche.* Instructions of marquis
d'Hautefort, 1750.

Keeping the powers on an even level required partition and the use of makeweights. These the weaker and the defeated states provided, and the operation inevitably worked to the advantage of the strong, the ambitious and the clever. The rise of Prussia was a logical result of this system; she had served as a makeweight, until she felt strong enough herself to control the balance.

The balance of power, then, was neither a principle of order nor a guarantee of law. Contemporaries understood this so well that the more clearly defined the operation of the idea became, the more thoroughly they armed themselves. 'A new malady is abroad in Europe', wrote Montesquieu; 'it has infected our princes and caused them to maintain an inordinate number of troops. . . . As soon as one state increases the number of troops it calls up, the others immediately increase theirs, so that nothing is gained, but all are ruined. Every monarch keeps on a war footing all the forces he would need if his people were in immediate danger. And this state of mutual stress is called peace.'[72]

To sum up, there was no security but in a sound understanding of self-interest, no principle of order but in the conflict of interests. The rules of conduct could be summed up in these empirical maxims: what is worth taking is worth keeping—a prompting of greed to which all responded. If prudence counselled that nothing is worth taking except what is worth keeping, this was a counsel followed by few. The dictate of ambition is that we must expand; let us make a deal with the strong and share with them if we must— the main thing is that we should ourselves determine the conditions of the bargain. Wisdom replies: it is better to reign among divided inferiors than to dispute control with equals. Finally, experience taught that it is well to undertake only what can be achieved. This calculation was the one and only safeguard of states against the lures of their own ambition and their only security from the excesses of

[72] *Esprit des lois*, liv. XII, ch. XVII.

other states. It is not in this light that the Europe of the ancien régime has generally been seen. But this is what in fact it was like, and it must be envisaged in this way if its reaction to the French Revolution is to be understood. With this we may proceed from a consideration of the prevailing political morality to a survey of the concurrent political behaviour.

7. PARTITIONS

What are the consequences of the political maxims we have discussed? They rebound on the state that practises them. It is a system of public policy that is self-destructive. It has no sanction other than raison d'état, but that is enough, for it is fatal and implacable.

The state being identified with the person of the sovereign, and heredity being in most states the mode by which sovereignty was transmitted, succession quarrels became international conflicts. Every diplomat had to be a jurist. Marriage contracts and wills were most serious matters of policy; and as there was no tribunal to adjudicate the resulting lawsuits, the only trial was by war and the decision was by force. The reign of Louis XIV has been described as one long lawsuit contested with armed might. The names of the wars which occupied the eighteenth century denote their character: the Wars of Spanish Succession, Austrian Succession, Bavarian Succession.

There was in truth no *right* recognised and respected by all, but *rights* which each state was ready always to assert. There was a jumble of feudal customs complicated by all the subtleties of Roman jurisprudence. What Torcy* said of the Emperor Charles VI could be applied to most sovereigns: 'He looks upon states of which he is not the master as so many

---

* Jean-Baptiste Colbert, Marquis de Torcy, 1665-1746, son of Colbert de Croissy; Secretary of State for Foreign Affairs, 1689-1715.

usurpations of his rights.'[73] The ruler's domain being considered inalienable and imprescriptible, the lawsuit was unending. 'Sovereigns', wrote a seventeenth-century French publicist, 'never bring legal claims against one another, because there is no judge before whom they can plead the unjust retention of their property; they wait until force is on their side to recover what belongs to them; and for this proceeding there is no time limit fixed, not even the thousand years laid down by an ancient jurisconsult.'[74] 'Great princes', said Richelieu, 'consider themselves always free to reclaim their rights against usurpers, and to secure them by force.'[75] This is why Mazarin, who was a man of foresight and well versed in this ancient chicanery, wrote on 20th

[73] *Recueil des Instructions, Autriche.* Instruction du comte du Luc, 1715.

Le P. Lelong, in his *Bibliothèque historique de la France*, devotes no less than 360 articles to treatises on the rights of the King in regard to foreign states.

A curious and characteristic specimen of this literature is the treatise on *Intérêts et maximes des princes et Etats souverains*, a revised and expanded edition of the treatise on *l'Intérêt des princes et Etats souverains de la chrétienté* by the duc Henri de Rohan, Cologne 1666. In this are set forth the 'interests' of the Emperor in respect of France, England, Prussia, Poland, Silesia; of the King of France in respect of Navarre, England, Flanders, Genoa, Naples, Luxemburg, Lorraine, Liége, Metz, Toul, Verdun, the county of Burgundy, Tuscany, Avignon, the Venaissin, Orange, Nice, Cambrai, Corsica, Castile and Hainault; of the King of Spain in respect of the duchy of Burgundy, Catalonia, Roussillon, Portugal, Navarre, Milan, Jerusalem, Siena, England, Tuscany, Malta, Genoa, Parma, Savoy; of the King of England in respect of Normandy, Guienne, Poitou, the crown of France; of the house of Austria in respect of Bohemia, Utrecht, Moravia, Switzerland, Friuli, Carniola, Alsace, Breisach, Rheinfeld, Nuremberg, Cleves, Jülich, Berg, Dalmatia, Epirus, Transylvania, Moldavia, the Morea.—See below, Bk. II, Ch. II: the Political Traditions of France, foreign policy.

[74] Memoir on *Le plus sûr moyen de réunir à la France les duchés de Lorraine et de Bar.* D'Haussonville, *Histoire de la réunion de la Lorraine*, t. I, pièces. Paris, 1854.

[75] *Mémoires*, year 1633.

January 1646, when the marriage of Louis XIV and Maria Theresa was as yet a distant project: 'The Infanta being married to His Majesty, we could hope for the succession to the dominions of Spain, whatever renunciation we had had to make.'[76] A century later Frederick, judging that he had a good chance to possess himself of Silesia, recalled that he had ancient rights in regard to this province. His minister, Podewils, timidly remarked that these rights had been cancelled by solemn treaties. 'The question of law is a matter for ministers', replied the philosopher prince. 'That is your business, and it is time to get secretly to work on it, for the troops have been given the order to march.'[77]

Since everyone kept in his archives claims on anything that affected his interests, and believed himself authorised to vindicate them whenever he had the means to do so, there could be neither assured inheritance nor peaceful possession. The established pattern of behaviour thus turned against the dynasties the very principle of dynastic rights. They did not stop at dispossessing heirs; they carved up their inheritance. Rights never became void, but they were divisible. Those who claimed them joined together to make good their claims. Hence formal contracts and partition treaties. The principle of balance prescribed their clauses and established a regular jurisprudence on the subject. While the King of Spain was still living, Louis XIV divided his succession, in 1668, with the Emperor Leopold; in 1698 he provided for its division by a tribunal of arbitration on which were seated England and Holland. These transactions set the tone for the diplomacy of the century that followed. In reality, it was raison d'état alone that gave guidance to these combinations; as the eighteenth century wore on, nobody concealed this fact. Legal pretexts were relegated to the background. Partition was a method of destruction, and was so avowed by all concerned. The War of the Austrian Succession was only the re-

[76] Mignet, *Succession d'Espagne*, t. I, p. 33.
[77] *Politische Correspondenz*, t. I, p. 90.

sounding climax to a policy customarily determined by expediency. 'The death of the Emperor Charles VI, last prince of the house of Austria, is a sign that the moment for the annihilation of this dynasty has come', wrote the Duc de Choiseul in an official document. 'The jealousy and the alarms inspired in the whole of Europe by the huge amalgamation of states which the late Emperor had tried to unite in the hands of his eldest daughter; the attitudes of various rulers of some substance who put forward claims to the succession; the loss by this family, through the death of the last Habsburg prince to possess it, of the imperial crown which had been the link between so many scattered states, all seemed to favour the plan of destroying this power by sharing it out. It was in pursuance of this idea that France adopted the project of partitioning the states of the Austrian inheritance, conformably to the rights of the claimants, so skilfully adjusting the shares that the new owners would be continually occupied in resisting each other's attempts at aggrandisement, thus preventing the erection of a new power as redoubtable and as menacing to France as the former house of Austria had been. In this way the future tranquillity of Europe could be made secure and durable.'[78]

From this it was only a logical development to regard the dismemberment of a state no longer as a transaction to settle rival claims and a forced sequel to succession wars, but as a normal resource of diplomacy, and a means of preventing wars by satisfying in advance the ambitions about to be unleashed. This consequence of the principle of balance, paradoxical as it at first appears, in fact presents itself as soon as a definition of the principle is attempted. Sully's 'Grand Design' implied a general overturning of territorial rights in Europe. The whole system of the Westphalia treaties rested

[78] *Recueil des Instructions, Autriche.* Instruction du comte de Choiseul-Praslin, 1759. The project, however, was not new. A first rough sketch of it had been made with Charles XII in 1718, and with Sardinia in 1733. See D'Argenson, *Mémoires*, tome I, p. 29; tome IV, pp. 218, 273, 275.

on the expropriation, for the sake of expediency, of the ecclesiastical territories. These secularisations, as they were called, provided a precedent. The Revolution found it in the records and put it to good use.

There were two states whose geographical position and internal condition destined them to be objects of transactions of this kind—Turkey and Poland. Their possessions were so great that they might satisfy everybody. The idea of their dismemberment was therefore far from new. It had wide currency in the eighteenth century. In 1782 Russia and Austria agreed to divide the Ottoman Empire between them; in 1772, because they could not at that time agree on the partition of the Turkish Empire, they had, in concert with Frederick II, shared out part of Poland. It was the King of Prussia who set the operation going and guided it to its conclusion; but the same idea had occurred to them all. Poland was up for auction, and the bidders had no scruples about speculating to promote their interests. In less than a year, between December 1768 and August 1769, Kaunitz, her Chancellor, proposed to Maria Theresa that they should buy the Prussian King with Polish Prussia. The King of Prussia demanded of Russia two Polish provinces as the price of his alliance; Russia agreed. The French minister suggested a partition of Poland to Vienna in order to detach Austria from Prussia, and at the same time made the same suggestion to Berlin to detach Prussia from Austria. And finally the Turks, who had gone to war to protect Poland's independence, were ready to deliver up their ally to Austria to get her support against Russia.

The partitioning governments of 1772 invoked ancient rights. But in the perpetration of this iniquitous deed these were a mere matter of form. The rulers in reality attached no value to them and did not expect anyone to be convinced by them. 'I have a poor opinion of our claims', Maria Theresa admitted. 'The Austrians are taking two starosties', said Catherine, 'Why should not everyone else take something too?'

Frederick agreed, and opened the bidding; but, he added, 'When one's claims are not very sound, it is better not to go into them in detail.'[79] The declaration of 1772 subordinated these pretended claims to the principle of expediency, the only one that could be invoked: 'Whatever may be the extent and boundaries of the respective claims, the resulting gains should be exactly equal.'

'This', wrote Frederick, 'is the first example history shows of a partition planned and concluded peacefully among three powers.'[80] It was not to be the last. Having resorted to partition first to settle differences, and then to prevent them, the powers would next proceed to divide up a state simply to maintain good relations. The dismemberment of monarchies became both the end and the means of policy. Weak states viewed with alarm the growth of this practice, which threatened them all. It busied the minds and filled the files of all the governments in the last days of the ancien régime. It was a self-contained system; it figured in the normal pattern of conduct of the governments of Europe, and replaced the simple doctrine of balance, which it both refined and completed. It had a name, the *co-sharing system*, which passed into the language of the chancelleries and became an item of the diplomatic repertoire. It had a principle —with a false air of legality: 'Acquisitions should be perfectly equal.'[81] It had its casuistry, which confused the equity of the deed with the equality of the shares, the justice of the operation with the niceness of the balance, and disregarded the difference usually considered to exist between judges and thieves.[82] It had its case law, which, 'to maintain

79 *Le Question d'Orient au dix-huitième siècle*, pp. 142, 147, 265.

80 *Mémoires*, éd. Boutaric, t. II, p. 359. Paris, 1866.

81 Declarations of 19 February 1772 for Austria, of 28 February for Prussia, of 5 March for Russia. *Question d'Orient*, p. 224. 'This proposition, which was *just*, was accepted without difficulty', says Frederick in his *Mémoires*, *id.*, p. 216.

82 'I was always opposed to this iniquitous partition—it was so

this just balance', came to calculate portions according to the fertility of the soil, the population, the political value, which must be taken to mean, according to one commentator, not merely the actual quota of the population, but its kind and quality.[83] It had its procedure and its formulas, which were those of chicanery: the contracting of the mortgage to guarantee the fulfilment of the deal. It had its jargon, which was that of second-hand dealers: 'swaps' to compensate for differences in value, 'extras to make good the loss on the swap'.[84]

I have thought it necessary to set forth these customs and to define their meaning because the French Revolution found them in full vigour in the old Europe. This was the public law which would have been applied to France, and which, in default of her submission, was applied afresh to Poland. France did not introduce it into Europe in 1792; she was threatened with subjection to it, and if later she practised it herself this was not innovation but imitation. Far from having imposed this system on Europe to undermine the rights of others, she was led to adopt it in order to come to terms with the old-established states. It was on these conditions that she treated with them and obtained her citizen-status in Europe. By so doing she betrayed, corrupted and destroyed her own principles and the new system of right which she wanted to make prevail, but she did not betray, corrupt, or destroy the ancient law of Europe; its foundations had been undermined by the old Europe itself. The Revolution did not dig the bed of the torrent, it only swelled its waters. The habits of the ancien régime had indeed brought results of most grave and extraordinary import.

---

unequal', wrote Maria Theresa to Mercy, 1 February 1773. Cf. *Question d'Orient*, pp. 274 and 219.

[83] *Question d'Orient*, p. 241.

[84] All these terms are taken from the correspondence. The reader will come across them again later in these studies. See in Vivenot, *Quellen*, Vienna, 1873, the report of Ph. Cobenzl of 8 August 1792, tome II, p. 164.

8. DETHRONEMENT AND REGICIDE

Few scruples were entertained about dividing up states and
dispossessing sovereigns and there were just as few about ex-
changing kingdoms and displacing dynasties. There could be
nothing more unstable than rights of possession in Europe
at the end of the seventeenth and still more in the eighteenth
century. The name of Alberoni* characterises this state of
political chaos, as the name of Machiavelli characterises the
system of raison d'état. Alberoni agreed that the place of
policy had been taken by 'the caprice of certain individuals
who, without rhyme or reason except, perhaps, reasons of
their own, cut up and gnaw away states and kingdoms as
though they were Dutch cheeses'.[85]

The treaties made by Louis XIV to settle the Spanish succession involved a complete revolution in the map of Europe,
an odd transference of dynasties, an astonishing migration of
sovereigns and governments. In 1698 a Bavarian was to rule
over Spain, the Indies, Belgium, and Sardinia, a Bourbon
over Naples, Sicily, the Presidios, and Guipuzcoa,* while
an Austrian would have Milan. The arrangement collapsed;
Louis made another, from which the Bavarian disappeared:
the Austrian would take Spain and the Indies; the Bourbon
would have Milan, which he would exchange for Lorraine;
he would moreover take Naples, Sicily and the Presidios,
which he would exchange for Savoy, Nice and Piedmont.
The Belgians, meanwhile, were to set up a republic and ally
themselves with Holland in order that they should avoid
being partitioned to provide a makeweight in the bargain.

---

* Cardinal Giulio Alberoni, in charge of Spanish policy from
1716 to 1719, pursued an adventurous foreign policy in the interests of the family ambition of the Queen, Elizabeth Farnese.
[85] Letter cited by Sismondi, *Histoire de France*, t. XXVII,
p. 324.
* The Presidios were Spanish strongholds on the coast of North
Africa; Guipuzcoa was a small province in northern Spain.

A treaty, conceived virtually on these lines, was signed in 1699. The process having been thus started, the eighteenth century suffered the results. From 1731 to 1748 Parma, where the dynasty was extinct, passed first to Spain, then to Austria, then to a cadet branch of the Spanish family. Sardinia, allotted at first to Spain, was given to Austria in 1714 and to Savoy in 1720. A king of Poland obtained a life interest in Lorraine; the Dukes of Lorraine were transferred to Tuscany. Naples and Sicily, separated and reunited by turns, suffered the most peculiar vicissitudes and received the most unexpected rulers. The Treaties of Utrecht gave Naples to Austria and Sicily to Savoy, which in 1720 exchanged it for Sardinia; Austria reunited them for a time; fifteen years later they passed to the Spanish Bourbons.

At that time Italy provided the great market for kingdoms; soon it was to be Poland, and later Germany. But it was the same process continuing and spreading; the French Revolution merely accelerated it, and Bonaparte drove it to its final conclusion. Europe had, so to speak, already been kneaded into dough for the conqueror's fist.

These migrations of rulers had become familiar; so had the sight of homeless dethroned monarchs. 'Who would have believed', said Pascal, 'that the King of England, the King of Poland and the Queen of Sweden would be unable to find a retreat, an asylum, anywhere in the world?'[86]* The seventeenth century saw two Kings of England turned off their thrones. The eighteenth could show a whole series of princes who contested each other's titles, dispossessed, expelled, and sought to destroy one another. There is no more mordant satire on the morals of the time than the chapter of

[86] *Pensées*, éd. Havet, art. VL, no. 35. The allusion is to Charles I, Christina of Sweden and John Casimir, dethroned by Charles X Gustavus.

* Charles II, not Charles I, was in exile from 1651 to 1660; Christina had voluntarily resigned her throne in 1654; John Casimir was only briefly in exile in Silesia in 1655 before recovering his kingdom.

Candide in which Voltaire describes the strange supper his
hero had in Venice in the company of foreign kings: Achmet
III, who had dethroned his brother and been dethroned by
his nephew; Ivan, dethroned while still in the cradle;
Charles Edward of England; Augustus of Saxony and Stan-
islas Leczinski, both Kings of Poland; and finally Theodore,
King of Corsica—put in as an ironic finishing touch. 'As they
rose from the table, there arrived in the same hostelry four
Most Serene Highnesses who had also lost their states by the
hazards of war, and who came to spend the rest of the carnival season at Venice; but Candide hardly noticed these newcomers.' This novel was read in all the courts of Europe and
the whole fashionable world found diversion in this macabre
carnival.

One is amazed by the frivolous indifference of contemporaries; what can be said of that of their descendants? Voltaire
was jesting, and exaggerated for the sake of mockery. But
some years later the farce became sinister reality. In 1808 at
Erfurt, Napoleon, an Emperor born of the Revolution, was
surrounded by a retinue of kings, and there took place, not
indeed the comic supper-party of Voltaire's imagination, but
a real and most august supper-party which brought round
the same table a legion of dethroned sovereigns—the Bourbons of France, of Spain and of Naples, the Prince of Bra-
ganza, to say nothing of bishops, grand dukes, abbots, counts
and most serene highnesses.

But exile was not all. There were worse extremities. 'I
have said you are gods', cried Bossuet. 'Nevertheless, O gods
of dust and ashes, you will die as men die. You will fall as
the great fall.'[87] Fall they did, but their fate hardly stirred
the feelings of the survivors. One is surprised by the absence
of shock in Europe at the deaths of Louis XVI and Marie
Antoinette—the tepid indignation, the shabby mourning,
the speed with which they were forgotten, the easy under-

---

[87] *Politique*, liv. V, art. IV prop. I. Cf. *id.*, *Troisième Sermon
pour le dimanche des Rameaux*, Sur les devoirs des rois.

standing established with the Revolution as soon as it took on habits of order, agreed to compromise, and substituted a policy of partition for one of propaganda. By 1798 there was a regicide ambassador in Berlin, a second in Naples, and three others successively accredited to the Holy Roman Empire at the Congress of Rastadt.[88] The niece of Marie Antoinette* found several of the most famous regicides grouped around her throne. This flexibility of morals and this condescension on the part of sovereigns was nothing new; and if the precedents of the ancien régime in this delicate matter are borne in mind there will be infinitely less cause for astonishment.

I say nothing here of political assassination openly taught and practised in the sixteenth century; I speak only of sentences passed on sovereigns by the state, for state crimes, in virtue of raison d'état. In modern Europe the earliest precedent is that of Mary Stuart; in it are subsumed all the others. Mary Stuart was a queen. She was prosecuted for acts of sovereignty by another sovereign.† When on this ground she contested the competence of the commission which was charged to condemn her, the president of the tribunal answered: 'Wherefore lay aside the bootless privilege of royal dignity, which now can be of no use unto you; appear in judgement and show your innocency.' Elizabeth was not content with the findings of the commission; she had it ratified by the English Parliament; and sixty-two years later this Parliament applied the same law to the grandson of Mary Stuart, whom the accidents of fortune had placed on the throne where Elizabeth had sat. The question at issue be-

[88] Sieyès at Berlin, Lacombe Saint-Michel at Naples, Treilhard, Jean Debry, Bonnier at Rastadt.

* Marie Louise, wife of Napoleon, was actually a great-niece of Marie Antoinette.

† This is quite inaccurate. Mary was found guilty on the charge of participation in plots against the life of Elizabeth while she was living in constraint in England, whither she had fled as a refugee from Scotland.

tween two sovereigns in conflict over their sovereign rights
was now debated between the English nation, which had
declared itself sovereign, and the King of England, who
claimed the immunity of a sovereign. 'I would know', said
Charles I, 'by what power I am called hither . . . England
has been for nearly a thousand years a hereditary kingdom.'
'Sir,' replied the President of the High Court, 'we do not
sit here to reply to your questions. Answer to the charge—
guilty or not guilty.'[89] In these two phrases is summed up
the whole trial of Louis XVI.

What was the attitude of rulers in face of these attacks
on the majesty of monarchs? Henry III tried to intervene on
behalf of Mary Stuart—she had been Queen of France.* He
made it known in London that he would consider her condemnation 'as an act against the common interest of all
kings.' Elizabeth took no notice, and Henry did not press
the matter. The King of Spain, an enemy of England, tried
to avenge the Queen of Scots, but Elizabeth defeated him.
Some years later, when allied to the French King Henry IV,
and respected or feared by all monarchs, she left her crown
to her victim's son, who by that time was her obedient servant. It could be said, of course, that this was only a monarchs' quarrel, and that royal rights were not in dispute. But
in the case of Charles I the issue was between a legitimate
sovereign and a people in revolt; the outcome was the same.
Europe was indeed moved by the death of Charles I, but
each government displayed its emotion in proportion to the
extent of its interests. The most indignant were Holland,
which was a republic, and Russia, which was a barbarous
despotism; Holland was in deadly rivalry with England, the
Tsar of Muscovy had no relations with her and so had no
cause for fear. Spain and France, on the other hand, having
made a mild protest against the trial and execution of the
King, vied with each other in their haste to recognise the

[89] Guizot, *Charles Ier*, t. II, liv. VIII. Paris, 1862.
* During the brief reign of her husband, Francis II.

Commonwealth. Useless to argue that Charles I ruled by the same title as Louis XIV, that his Queen was a daughter of France, that the revolution that overthrew the English throne threatened all thrones; nothing availed against the fact that the Commonwealth was strong, and that it was in France's interest to have a good understanding with it. The implacable reasoning of raison d'état prevailed over all motives springing from honour, religion and established right. 'It would seem', wrote Mazarin to the Regent, Anne of Austria, 'that if we were guided by the laws of honour and justice, we should not recognise this republic, for the King could do nothing more prejudicial to his reputation than to desert the cause of the legitimate king, his near relation, neighbour and ally, and nothing more unjust than to recognise usurpers who have dipped their hands in the blood of their sovereign. But as the laws of honour and justice should never lead us to do what is contrary to the dictates of prudence, we must consider . . . that a prolonged refusal to recognise the Commonwealth would do nothing to augment or to confirm the rights of the king . . . Besides, there is reason to fear that if the Spaniards are once closely linked with the English, they may prevent them from entering into good relations with us, and may get them, if not to make open war on us, at least to give Spain powerful assistance against us. There remains therefore no doubt that we should without delay enter into negotiations with the English republic, and give it such title as it may desire.'[90] Louis XIV recognised the Commonwealth, and all Europe followed his example.

'O tempora! O mores!' exclaimed La Bruyère,[91] 'O wretched times! O age full of wickedness!—when a man[92] could say: "I crossed the sea, I robbed my father of his patrimony, I drove him, with his wife and his heir, from his

[90] Guizot, *Cromwell*, liv. III, p. 234.
[91] *Des jugements*.
[92] The Prince of Orange, who became King of England as William III after having overthrown James II.

territories and his domains"; and he had indeed done as he
said. He should have had to fear the resentment of many
kings against this outrage upon a monarch's person; but they
took his side. They virtually said to him, "Cross the sea,
despoil your father, show the whole world that one may
drive a sovereign from his kingdom like a petty seigneur from
his château or a farmer from his holding! . . . Royal dignity
no longer has privileges—kings themselves have renounced
them!"' But these are the words of a jaundiced observer,
not those of a politician. Only to philosophers and theologians was regicide a sacrilege, and royal dignity a sacred
thing; politics was a matter of security and the pursuit of
interests. The passions of men knew no lèsemajesté. At
Speyer, in 1689, the soldiers of Louis XIV sacked the cathedral, in which eight emperors were buried. Their ashes were
thrown to the winds—Louvois meant to terrorise the Germans and overwhelm them with contempt. There was no
fear even of unleashing popular frenzy and the blind fanaticism of crowds. In 1691 the rumour spread in Paris that
William III had just died. 'Each man', wrote Louvois, 'awoke
his neighbour, and without any orders given, they lit bon-
fires in celebration, and drank a great deal of wine.' The
police, somewhat bewildered, tried to still the ebullience,
but the people surrounded them, embraced them, and drew
them into the riot. The movement reached the provinces.
Everywhere the nation, mad and raging, celebrated the death
of its enemy. It was an anticipation of the *carmagnole*, but it
was a *carmagnole* instigated by royalty. Reading this contemporary account we might think that we were in the next
century, in the full tide of sansculottism: 'Throughout several
days and nights one could see the effigies of the prince and
princess hanged, drawn, flayed by the butchers, dragged
through the streets, mounted on asses with outrageous in-
scriptions, torn to pieces by pupils of the Jesuit schools
dressed up as demons. The galleries of the cemetery of the
Holy Innocent are still full of prints of these two personages
in all kinds of scandalous postures. There was plenteous

drinking—on credit—to the confusion of the defunct ruler; the heavens were split with cries against the usurper. . . .'[93] This was the way the Paris populace, in the reign of a prince who was described as 'invincible defender or prompt avenger of outraged majesty',[94] interpreted, with the tolerance of the police, the maxims of raison d'état. They learned that kings can commit crimes, that they can be tried, that a traitor king or an enemy king is no longer a king. Pursue the argument, remove the idea of sovereignty, and the people will soon turn against the king the precedents set by royalty; the king himself becomes the usurper, the traitor, the enemy par excellence. It is a short straight road to 1793.

The eighteenth century took this road with cynical frivolity. Raison d'état no longer had the peremptory and grim conciseness of the previous century; it was expounded by way of discussion and dissertation, with elegant sophism and pride of style. In 1718 the Tsar Peter had his son decapitated for crimes against the state. Some moralists thought they should protest. Voltaire reminded them of order, of history, of the maxims of Roman law and the canons of classical tragedy—which the thinkers of those days so readily confused. 'Peter was a king before he was a father, and sacrificed his own son to the interests of a founder and legislator. . . . If Alexis had reigned, all Peter's work would have been destroyed. . . . When this catastrophe is considered, men of feeling tremble but the stern approve.'[95] If necessary, however, raison d'état could be presented agreeably and with fair words. In 1742, Elizabeth, Peter's daughter, called out the Russian soldiery, and marching at their head broke into the palace and put the Queen-Regent in prison. The Tsar was an infant aged two, named Ivan. She pitied him, took him in her arms and embraced him. Then, this concession made to 'men of feeling', she sought counsel of 'the stern'.

[93] See Camille Rousset, *Louvois*, IV, ch. XIII, p. 425.
[94] Bossuet, *Oraison funèbre de la reine d'Angleterre*.
[95] *Histoire de la Russie*, ch. X.

She consulted the French ambassador, the marquis de la Chétardie; he was young, tender, passionate, and in this gross court he represented the refined manners of the West. Elizabeth had taken him as a lover, and he had powerfully aided her in getting possession of the throne. 'I could not', he wrote, 'oppose any means by which all trace of Ivan VI could be removed. It is in fact only by this expedient that Russia can be secured, now and in the future, against the misfortunes which chance might bring about, and which the example of the false Dmitri must still cause one to fear in this country.'[96] The matter was expressed in very gallant terms; the hypocrisy of the manner only makes plainer the cruelty of the advice. Louis XVII died more quickly—he was less robust; but he suffered under the same law, and despite the circumstances which made this atrocious incarceration of a child a historic event, his imprisonment and death hardly produced more effect than the case of the unhappy Ivan, victim of the same raison d'état.

The world became more and more used to it. Russia greatly enriched the store of precedents. But what is astonishing is not to find barbarous customs in a state still barbarian; it is the indifference with which the governments of the old Europe beheld the spectacle. In 1762 a German princess, married to the Tsar Peter III, plotted to remove him from the throne.* The Tsar was arrested, deposed and assassinated in prison. Diplomats reported the fact as the most natural thing in the world. They were neither scandalised nor moved by it; there were even some who sent congratulations—those who reckoned that the change would benefit their courts. Of this number was the comte de Mercy, ambassador of Maria Theresa, the same who resided so long and

[96] Albert Vandal, *Louis XV et Elisabeth de Russie*, ch. II. Paris, 1882. See the letter, no less cruel, of Frederick, of 20 April 1743, *Politische Correspondenz*. He advises sending Ivan to Siberia—an oubliette where he would disappear.

* Princess Sophia Augusta of Anhalt-Zerbst, who became the Empress Catherine II.

played so big a rôle in Paris. He relates the adventure and concludes: 'Such has been the course of one of the greatest and most fortunate events that have ever come to pass. . . . This nation was exasperated against Peter III and the only difficulty was to know how to put an end to his insensate rule.' The Frenchman M. Béranger, who was a mere Chargé d'Affaires, was the only one to indulge in certain considerations of morals and philosophy: 'What a picture! On the one hand, the grandson of Peter the Great dethroned and put to death; on the other, the grandson of the Tsar Ivan V languishing in irons, while a Princess of Anhalt usurps the crown of their ancestors, attaining the throne by regicide.'

The agents set forth the facts, governments judged them according to their interests. For Frederick, whom the friendship of Peter III had barely saved from catastrophe, it was 'a thunderbolt'; for Maria Theresa, whom Peter III had deserted, it was a stroke of luck. 'I bow before divine Providence, who has watched over Austria, Russia and Christendom,' she wrote to Mercy. 'Never has news rejoiced me as much as this happy accession to the throne.' The English 'cordially congratulated' the new Tsarina. As for Louis XV, who expected to have the same reasons for rejoicing as Maria Theresa, he did not stint his expressions of admiration, and he sent to his ambassador, the baron de Breteuil, as follows: 'The dissimulation of the Empress-Regnant, and her courage in the moment of the execution of her project, mark her out as a princess capable of conceiving and carrying out great enterprises. I am convinced of the urgency with which not only courtiers, but even foreigners and all the envoys who dwell in the presence of this princess, will pay their respects, and even take pains to make them specially marked, in order to attach Russia more intimately to the interests of their masters. It is this respect towards crowned heads which should be the basis of your conduct towards and your discourse with the Empress.'[97] As to discrowned heads, it seems

[97] De Broglie, *Le Secret du Roi*, t. II, p. 19.

that respect for them was nobody's concern. The story of
Catherine's accession was promptly known. Rulhière told it
in a report which appeared in 1773; he hid nothing—the
Tsarina's plotting, her intrigues, her amours. The book was
talked of by everyone; Catherine wanted to read it, and asked
Diderot, who was then with her, for a copy. The philosopher, who rather prided himself on his effrontery on occasion, nevertheless thought it wise to take oratorical precautions. 'As to what concerns you, Madame,' he said, 'if
you put a high value on propriety and virtue, trifles which
your sex sometimes affects, this work is a satire against you;
but if you are more interested in grand conceptions, mascu-
line and patriotic ideas, the author presents you as a great
princess, and, altogether, does you more honour than harm.'
'You make me wish all the more to read this book', replied
the Tsarina.[98]

In relations between sovereigns everything could finally
be put on the basis of their interests: savoir-vivre was the
standard of behaviour. The observance of the code was a
delicate matter, and required a singular degree of vigilance.
Thus in 1781 the Grand Duke Paul of Russia, the heir, if
not the true son, of Peter III, paid a visit to Vienna, where
he was given a magnificent reception. Gala performances
were arranged—at the Opera, *Orestes*, with a ballet, while
at the Comedy they were producing *Hamlet*. Though it was
accompanied by music and dancing, *Orestes* lent itself all
too readily to pointed allusions. But *Hamlet* passed all
bounds. It was the comedian Schroeder who saw the point,
and so relieved was everyone at avoiding, thanks to him, so
great a blunder, that he was given a present of fifty ducats
in recognition of his tact.[99] The precaution was the more
valuable because the Grand Duke was much troubled in the
mind, and the phantoms of the Prince of Denmark con-

[98] Rapport de M. Durand, 9 November 1773. *Publications de
la Société d'histoire de Russie*, t. XVII, p. 288.

[99] Wolf, *Œsterreich und Preussen, 1780-1790*, p. 70. Vienna,
1880.

stantly haunted him. 'This prince', a French agent wrote some years later, 'follows in the footsteps of his unfortunate father in every respect; and unless the heart of the Grand Duchess is the temple of all the virtues he will suffer the same fate as Peter III. He expects it—he told her so himself.'[100] The event of his death in 1801 and the way in which it was welcomed in Europe showed, in fact, that neither in the Russian court nor in the older courts had traditions changed in this respect.

9. REVOLUTIONS IN THE SEVENTEENTH CENTURY

The way in which sovereigns regarded outrages upon other sovereigns explains the attitude of governments towards revolutions, which were also assaults upon sovereignty. Many had occurred in Europe, and no one thought of considering revolutions in the abstract or apart from the particular circumstances in which they took place. Revolution in itself, regarded as a normal and continuous process in society, was an idea as foreign to the statesmen of the ancien régime as was the idea of dynastic legitimacy as an unchanging and absolute basis of sovereignty. Both of these highly abstract conceptions took shape in men's minds at the same time, in the course of the French Revolution, and were dictated by the same philosophical systems. The French Revolution was 'an event unique in history', wrote Joseph de Maistre in 1796.[101] That was why the men of the ancien régime were so completely mistaken about its character. They judged it simply in the light of precedents, and behaved accordingly.

The men of this period knew from history, and had indeed seen for themselves, risings resulting from the perpetual wretchedness of the people, from the harassments inflicted upon them from crude greed, from the instigation of fac-

[100] Report of Genet, 16 September 1791. *Affaires étrangères.*
[101] *Considérations sur la France,* ch. IV.

tions, the conspiracy of intriguers; or even from the anarchy that spontaneously develops when government is hopelessly bad or authority is weakened. They had observed 'those outbursts to which nations are naturally prone'.[102] They had traced their course in the Italian republics; they knew the violence of factions and the means they employed—exile, confiscation, death, sedition, civil war. They had seen the same happenings with the same sequels in France and England. They knew too that man, lacking restraint, reverts to the fierce, stupid and bewildered savage that nature made him. All this they knew, and the conclusion seemed clear enough: these were the chronic maladies of states, the ordinary sequences of their decline and death. The origin of the evil was to be found within states themselves, in the wearing out of their organs through age or through excess; it was not caused by wounds or by contagion brought in from outside. One of our early historians—and one of the most judicious— writes: 'Bodies politic are founded on certain principles whereby their beginnings, the course of their existence and their end are predetermined. There is nothing more natural than that they should decay when the principle by which they have grown has itself decayed.'[103] Bossuet unhesitatingly fastens the responsibility upon the rulers. 'However far we may seek in history for instances of great reversals of fortune, we find that they have always been caused by the weakness or the violence of princes. When rulers neglect to acquaint themselves with the business of government or with the state of their armies . . . to watch over the laws and to observe moderation, when they cause their subjects to lose their respect, and govern them in such a way that the evils they are suffering seem to them worse than those they might fear from change, then their patience will be exhausted and the extremes of violence will menace the ruling dynasty.'[104]

102 Pascal, *Provinciales*, letter XIV.
103 Etienne Pasquier, *Lettres*, liv. XII, letters VII and VIII, to M. de Sainte-Marthe.
104 *Oraison funèbre de la reine d'Angleterre*.

In the light of these ideas, governments envisaged a revolution in a foreign state only as an isolated episode; they judged it from the standpoint of their own interests; they exacerbated or calmed it according as it suited their purpose to strengthen or to enfeeble the state concerned. This was one of the favourite fields of political manœuvre and one of the classic resources of diplomacy.

The finest opportunities of this kind that history could show were provided by the great upheaval which had taken place in central Europe in the sixteenth century and plunged it into war until the middle of the seventeenth. It has been called an age of iron; it was therefore pre-eminently an age of war and diplomacy. The political riches of those times were a matter of pride, just as men vaunted the wealth of the mines of Peru, in which whole generations were sacrificed to load the galleons of Spain with gold. Governments were so impressed by the results of the upheaval that its true nature escaped their notice. It was just the same two hundred years later with the French Revolution. Like the social and political revolution of the eighteenth century, the religious revolution of the sixteenth was abstract in principle and cosmopolitan in action; it arose from universal ideas, and so could appeal to all peoples. It brought together nations which had been divided, divided those which had been united. It stirred governments into mutual hostility or linked them in alliances; it aroused sedition and involved states in civil strife. It gave birth to apostles, proselytes, martyrs, fanatics. It overturned the whole of Europe, and threw back into the melting-pot the elements of which it had been constituted. But the chaos was, after all, only a matter of appearance, and when the crisis was over, these elements were seen to have arranged themselves according to their natural affinities.

The Reformation appealed to all nations, but each interpreted it in the light of its own tendencies, particular traditions and inherited ideas. Thus in Germany it caused the antagonism of north and south to erupt in violence; in England it was associated with the establishment of free govern-

ment; in France, according to the region, it might serve as
pretext either for the claims of the great nobles against the
monarchy, or for the claims of the people against the great
nobles. Nations adapted the Reformation to their traditions,
governments fitted it into their systems. Because Spain and
France were bitter rivals, Spain took advantage of the wars
of religion to stir up rebellion in France, and became the
paymaster of fanatics and the patron of demagogues. The
French sought in Germany a diversion of the power of the
Habsburgs. The house of Austria fought against the Reformation because it wanted to centralise the government of the
Empire; the princes of North Germany upheld it because
they wanted division. Austria aimed at universal empire, and
could only secure it through religious unity and the support
of the Roman Church; Charles V and Philip II of Spain
were uncompromising Catholics. The King of France, to oppose the hegemony of the Austrians, egged on the Protestants
and became the champion of German liberties, which were
closely linked with the success of the Reformation. The German princes who accepted it were aiming at independence
from the Emperor and the Empire. The King of France,
while giving them all the help he could, repressed the Reformation in his own Estates, since he wished to keep them
under control, for his nobles were trying to use them against
him as the princes of the Empire used the Diet against the
house of Austria. The great crisis in religion was thus transformed into a political crisis; conflicts of power took precedence over conflicts of principle, and the struggle appropriately ended in a readjustment of frontiers.

The essentially secular and political character of the
Treaties of Westphalia bears ample testimony to the spirit in
which the governments of Europe had reacted to the Reformation. Certainly these treaties contributed to the establishment of freedom of conscience, but they did so indirectly,
and by force of circumstances rather than of set purpose.
What prevailed in the famous maxim 'Cujus regio, ejus reli-
gio' was the religion of the state; it was raison d'état applied

to questions of conscience—a state of affairs far closer to intolerance than to liberty. The whole transaction between the participating states was based on the principle of confirming each one in its independence, and of the great profiting at the expense of the small. For the sake of peace the Catholic states, which represented the old order, compromised with the new order, and consented to the secularisation of church property. The fundamental law of the Middle Ages was betrayed in principle and in fact; on the one hand unity of faith and the supremacy of the court of Rome disappeared; on the other hand the small feudal properties were absorbed by the larger states. If the treaties of 1648 are compared with those of 1801 and 1803, it can hardly be questioned that the public law of Europe was as seriously assailed by the former as by the latter. The settlements of the Napoleonic era were no more than a sequel and an imitation of those of the seventeenth century. Faced with the French Revolution, in its political consequences so analogous with the Reformation, the governments of the end of the eighteenth century behaved in the same way as had those of the sixteenth. From this famous precedent derived all the international law of the ancien régime in respect of revolutions.

It found its earliest and most fruitful application in the form of intervention in civil wars. These followed on the private wars of the feudal period, and preserved their characteristics. The feudal system, substituting the lordship for the fatherland, parcelling out the state and proliferating entangled suzerainties, involved the utmost elasticity in the matter of alliances. Nobles, in their struggles against one another or against their sovereign, did not scruple to call to their aid other nobles and even other sovereigns. Where feudalism survived, as it did in Germany, these habits persisted, and the Treaties of Westphalia sanctioned them. In France, where the royal authority had overthrown feudal power, the same pattern of behaviour had outlasted the circumstances which had given rise to it. The traditional conduct followed in waging feudal struggles was now adopted in revolts against the sovereign state. Factions called upon foreigners for help, each considering itself to be in the right, for each claimed that it was itself the state and should prevail over its opponents. Regarding itself as the state, each regarded itself also as the fatherland—the two conceptions were confused in men's minds. At La Rochelle Richelieu fought the Huguenots and the English together; Mazarin had to contend with the Frondeurs in league with the Spaniards. The moral lapses of the two great heroes of the century are only too well known. Those who had done most for France against the foreign enemy, Turenne and Condé, in turn allied with the foreigner against their country. Yet in spite of this the conceptions of the sovereign, the state, and the fatherland were becoming more distinct and precise. 'Never is there just cause', wrote Bodin in the sixteenth century, 'for taking up arms against king and country.' High treason came to be more strictly defined and more systematically punished. Nevertheless, the practices of the sixteenth-century wars and of the Fronde were far from having disappeared by the time of the French Revolution. In similar situations these practices automatically reasserted themselves. From them derived the behaviour of the émigrés, taking up arms in alliance with the hostile Coalition—a final manifestation of feudal politics coinciding with the extinction in France of the last traces of feudalism. It was at this moment, and actually as a result of the resort to force by the émigrés, that the separation of the idea of 'la patrie' from the idea of the ruler occurred. This separation, which was one of the main features of the French Revolution, had indeed been prepared earlier by the monarchy itself, but it was not, however, complete in the minds of all, particularly of those who were to be defeated by it— those who appealed to the feudal past. This was what made possible the armed émigrés, organizing a state against the state, concluding alliances with foreign powers and invading France side by side with foreign armies, and all in the belief that they were acting within their rights, for the émigrés claimed to have on their side both state and country, and to be fighting only against usurpers.

This attitude was general in Europe, and governments made use of it in their struggles with one another. Not content with encouraging factions, they instigated them; from supporting civil strife they went on to provoke it; to exploit revolutions was not enough—they fomented them. 'Is it a counsel of prudence and justice', Richelieu had asked, 'to wait for others to be devoured only to suffer the same fate after them?'[105] In an apology for the policy of Louis XIV written by a contemporary we read: 'If it is shameful in a prince to foment a rebellion of subjects against their legitimate ruler, this is a policy in which Austria has for a long time led the way. If it is indeed the established practice of sovereigns to harm each other as much as possible, why should it be a fault in us to do what is common the world over?'[106] Everyone in fact boasted, according to Saint Simon, of brewing up revolutions in other countries. The English did not fail to do so against Louis XIII and Louis XIV— who repaid them with interest. Le Grand Monarque believed in stirring up sedition in every enemy state. 'I kept up correspondence with groups in Hungary,' he wrote in his *Mémoires*, 'so that I could start trouble for the Emperor as soon as he tried to meddle in my affairs.'[107] But the most striking example, and the most typical precedent, was found in the relations of the French court with England during the revolutions of the seventeenth century. These demonstrate in advance the shifts of policy which marked the behaviour of the great powers, especially Austria, towards France during the Revolution.

Charles I fought to uphold the royal prerogative. The French monarchy was engaged, at the same time, in a similar struggle. If the revolutionary party triumphed in England, the factions in France would naturally be encouraged.

[105] *Lettres et papiers d'Etat*, t. VIII, p. 214, year 1635.
[106] See Camille Rousset, *Louvois*, t. III, ch. IV.
[107] Year 1666.

But the government showed not the least concern. 'The situation', wrote Louis XIII's ambassador in London in 1637, 'seems most favourable for embarrassing the King of England.' Richelieu did not miss the opportunity. Whilst he incited the malcontents, on the other hand he secretly stirred up the court. The Queen wanted to take refuge in France. He dissuaded her. 'In a situation like this, to give up is to lose everything', he instructed her.[108] His aim was to promote disorder in the state and the consequent enfeeblement of England. Mazarin's policy was the same. The agents he sent —d'Harcourt in 1644, Bellièvre in 1647—had instructions to cause the utmost possible confusion. Parliament declared itself sovereign; in Mazarin's opinion 'this was not the time to dispute about formalities', and he recognised the sovereignty of Parliament.[109] Queen Henrietta, sister of the French king, felt herself abandoned, betrayed; she wept, complaining bitterly of this perfidious policy. At a later stage, however, the English revolution began to seem menacing, even on the Continent. That sectarian spirit of which Bossuet spoke, 'which would abolish all monarchies and level all men—the dream of seditious characters, the impious and sacrilegious chimaera of the Independents', seemed to be abroad. France herself was in the throes of civil war. The Frondeurs cited the example and asked the help of the English Commonwealth. This republic was now threatening to spread into other realms the ardour by which it was itself being consumed. It was thought to be planning union with Holland, which had the same kind of government and religion. *'Faciamus eos unam gentem'*, wrote an envoy of the Parliament from Holland. They were becoming arrogant too. 'I will make the name of the English', said Cromwell, 'as great as that of the Romans.' He was considering a league of all the Protestant states, directed by himself. It was an-

108 Guizot, *Charles Ier*. Pièces, no. 6.
109 *Flassan, Histoire de la diplomatie*, livre VI. In 1791, after Varennes, Austria was to recognise the constitution of the Republic in the same way.

nounced that he would invade France at the head of his army. He was reported to have said that 'if he were ten years younger, there would not be a king in Europe who would not have cause to tremble; and, having a better motive than the late King of Sweden, he felt capable of doing more for the good of the people than the Swede had ever done through his ambition.'

Thus warned and threatened, Mazarin, it might be thought, should have hastened to form a counter-alliance. He did nothing of the kind. Seeing Cromwell and his republic firmly established, he thought it better to have them as friends than as enemies. He came to terms with them; and as this suited their interests also, they were quite ready for his approach. So the Most Christian King was allied with a Protestant and regicide republic; while this republic made war on the only state on the Continent that shared the same religion and the same form of government—Holland. 'I shall not speak', exclaimed Bossuet, 'of the all too fortunate sequel of Cromwell's enterprises, nor of his famous victories, by which virtue was outraged, nor of the long period of stability which so astonished the world.' Astonishment was quite out of place; if in some quarters Cromwell's successes seemed inexplicable it was certainly not at Louis XIV's court. The most regal of kings did not hesitate to address Cromwell as *prince,* assuring him that he considered him 'one of the greatest and most fortunate rulers in Europe'.[110] Cromwell's prestige in Europe was immense. An account of his life is like an anticipatory summary of Bonaparte's. He was feared, admired, sought after. He received ambassadors from Sweden, Germany, Italy, and even Poland. The prince de Condé wrote to him in 1653: 'I consider the people of the three kingdoms to have attained the height of fortune in that their goods and their lives are entrusted to the guidance of so great a man. For my own part, I beg your Highness to believe that I should be most happy to be of any service to

[110] Guizot, *Cromwell,* t. II, p. 369.

you.' The admiration inspired by Cromwell survived his power. After he was dead and the republic overthrown, this phrase appears in the *Mémoires* of Louis XIV* for 1662: 'Cromwell, in whom genius, opportunity, and the misfortune of his country had inspired ideas far above his birth.'

While ambassadors flocked to the Protector's presence in London, the legitimate heir to the English throne, Charles II, wandered from city to city on the Continent, begging secret audiences for his envoys, pensions for his servants, an asylum for himself and his relatives. Everyone found him a nuisance and showed him the door; he got nothing but private condolences and public insults. It reads like an earlier version of the history of the Bourbons during the French Revolution and up to 1814. Charles recovered his throne, and Bossuet gave Louis XIV the glory of it: 'The shame of kings has been avenged.' But Louis XIV did not allow himself to be dazzled to the point of forgetting traditional politics. His *Mémoires* for the year 1666 announce, 'I was supporting pensioners in Ireland to rouse the Catholics there against the English, and I opened negotiations with certain refugees from England to whom I promised considerable sums to revive the remnants of the Cromwellian faction.'

If this was how he behaved towards Charles II, a legitimate sovereign, recently his protégé and his paid client, he behaved still worse towards William III, a usurper and the bitterest of his enemies. This note of 1666 precisely conveys the style to which the eighteenth century conformed.

10. REVOLUTIONS IN THE EIGHTEENTH CENTURY

Many revolutions occurred during this century. They were quite unrelated, and there was no connection between types

---

* The nature and authenticity of Louis XIV's *Mémoires* have been much discussed. See *Les Mémoires de Louis XIV, édités par Jean Longron*, E. Esmonin, *Etudes sur la France des XVIIᵉ et XVIIIᵉ siècles*, pp. 449-54, 1964.

of government and their attitudes towards other states in these periods of crisis. Since each pursued its own immediate interests and nothing else, policies continually changed as circumstances altered. England seemed to the French, and to continental statesmen in general, to be a country torn by factions. 'The government of this island is more stormy than the seas that surround it', said Voltaire.[111] 'What in other countries would be merely a murmur of sedition in England becomes a revolution.' Diplomats were always describing it as on the verge of an upheaval.[112] The politicians of Versailles rejoiced. 'We are in no hurry', wrote M. de Choiseul, 'to see a stable ministry installed in England. Indeed I hope that anarchy will prevail for some time. I wish it would last a century.'[113] In 1762 the rumour spread that the Russian boyars had some desire to imitate the Polish magnates and set up a sort of royal republic. Louis XV, being at that time in a bad humour with Russia, wrote to his ambassador, 'Anything that may plunge the country into chaos and thrust it back into darkness is advantageous to my interests.'[114]

Thus it was that Poland's neighbours so jealously protected the liberties which kept that republic in a state of anarchy and laid it open to intervention and partition. With its anachronistic constitution, Poland re-enacted in eighteenth-century Europe the confused and gloomy chronicle of mediaeval private wars. Every faction sought foreign help, and every foreign state sustained a faction. It was a principle at Vienna, St. Petersburg and Berlin to oppose at all costs any reform which might tend to strengthen the Polish state. Its very constitution provided the conditions for its neighbours to stir up trouble, and the subsequent disorders supplied them with excuses for intervention in the affairs of the republic and the completion of its ruin. In this way

111 *Lettres philosophiques*. Letter VIII.
112 Montesquieu, *Notes sur l'Angleterre*.
113 To M. Durand, 4 August 1767. Cornélis de Witt, *Jefferson. Pièces.* Paris, 1861.
114 Vandal, *Louis XV et Elisabeth de Russie*, p. 424.

they fomented civil war in 1768, and in 1771 claimed that Poland's dismemberment was justifiable and necessary to put an end to the endemic anarchy which threatened the interests of neighbouring states.

The Swedish constitution resembled in some respects that of Poland. Though it did not offer Sweden's neighbours such inviting opportunities, it seemed to them highly advantageous and they set great store by it. The enemies of Sweden spoke of Swedish liberties in a tone worthy of the Roman Senate. The instructions given to the Danish minister in Stockholm in 1767 read: 'Every power, every person who upholds in Sweden liberty and the laws may claim the friendship of our King, his concurrence and his support; every power that attacks them is his enemy, and every man who contends against or betrays them incurs his displeasure.'[115] When the precious liberties of Sweden seemed to be threatened, Frederick of Prussia displayed a *'générosité'* which would have surprised Lafayette, and Catherine a *'vertu'* by which Mme. Roland would have been abashed. In 1764 and in 1769 these two despots undertook by formal treaty to oppose 'the re-establishment of sovereignty' in Sweden. Gustavus III attempted to revive royal authority, and France, needing an ally in the north, helped him. He brought off a coup d'état which beyond doubt saved the Swedes from the fate just suffered by the Poles. He received encouragement from Versailles, but threats from St. Petersburg and Berlin. This ruler, engaged in restoring royal power, was obliged to excuse himself to the neighbouring sovereigns. The terms of his apology are well worth study; they show how weak was the cause of monarchy when a king was reduced to defending himself in this way against other kings. Writing to his uncle, Prince Henry of Prussia, Frederick's brother, Gustavus III said: 'Tell me, in God's name, what I have done to bring upon myself the storm which you say inevitably threatens me. Have I not demonstrated my peaceful intentions in

[115] *Correspondance ministérielle du comte de Bernstorff.* Copenhagen, 1882.

the plainest manner? If it is a question of the change in the form of government of my realm, you are too just not to appreciate that this is not a matter to be discussed with foreign powers. It has been done and ratified by the Swedish nation, which understands what is to its advantage. What right can foreign powers possibly have to seek a quarrel with me for having sought the welfare of my subjects? If that is to be a cause for war, there is no more justice in the world. . . . What shall I gain by treaties and guarantees with powers which know no law but their own desires, and rely on arms alone to enforce them? I cannot believe that I am to be attacked in disregard of every principle of right and justice. Such an act would undermine the rights of all sovereigns and of all independent nations.'[116]

A liberated nation could have justified its independence by precisely the same arguments. The object of the revolution, whether the freedom of the people or the power of the sovereign, mattered little. A democratic revolution and a royal coup d'état were treated in the same way. At the moment when in Sweden she was taking the side of the king, in the American colonies France was supporting the people in their rebellion against England. While this struggle was still in progress, the same king and the same minister—Louis XVI and the comte de Vergennes—intervened in Geneva against the democratic party. Thus in the space of a few years, having upheld the monarchy against the aristocracy in Sweden and Poland, and having tried to uphold the aristocracy against the monarchy in Russia, France was attacking in Geneva the democracy that she defended in America. She would have been hard put to it to establish any relationship of principle between these opposite policies. There was in truth no principle but the interest of the state, and that was considered enough. 'The insurgents I am expelling from Geneva are British agents,' wrote Vergennes, 'whilst the American rebels will be our lasting friends. I have treated

[116] January 1773. Geffroy, *op. cit.* The *coup d'état* was on 19 August 1772.

both, not in the light of their political systems, but in the light of their attitudes towards France. That is my "raison d'état".'117*

This was in fact the basis of all policy, and a new example was soon forthcoming. It was the last provided by the ancien régime, and the most significant. In 1787 revolts of a revolutionary character broke out in the Austrian Netherlands and in the Dutch republic, in Belgium and in Holland. In Belgium, the aristocracy, with the support of the Catholic clergy, demanded the retention of the ancient liberties, which had been swept aside or threatened by the centralising government of Joseph II. In Holland, democrats and patriots took up arms against the Stadtholder, who was scheming to set up a kind of dictatorship and overthrow the republic.† In both countries the peoples were defending their national liberties, and princes were aiming at absolute power. Nothing better demonstrates the complete lack of principle or of consistent policy than the behaviour of the European powers in these circumstances. France supported, secretly in Belgium and openly in Holland, the party of freedom—the party she had opposed in Sweden. England, who had just been fighting her rebellious subjects in America, was partial to the Belgians in their revolt against Austria, but energetically supported the Stadtholder against the Dutch patriots. Thus in Holland the absolute monarchy which reigned at Versailles championed the rights of peoples; the limited monarchy of England gave its help to a ruler who was trying to destroy ancient liberties. Joseph II and Kaunitz, who looked so fa-

---

117 Soulavie, *Mémoires*, t. V, p. 275. Paris, 1801.

* The *Mémoires* of the abbé Jean-Louis Soulavie on the eighteenth century and the Revolution are indigestible compilations of mingled truth and falsehood.

† Sorel puts the situation the wrong way round. Rather than aiming at dictatorship, the Stadtholder was trying to defend the relics of his constitutional authority against the attacks of the Patriots, who had practically taken control of the country, supported by the French, during the War of American Independence. See A. Cobban, *Ambassadors and Secret Agents* (1954).

vourably on anarchy in Poland, sought to deprive the Belgians of the liberties they thought so precious to the Poles. And the Prussians, who incited and subsidised the revolution in Belgium, intervened with an army to crush that in Holland, and to set up there a government of the kind they would not tolerate in Stockholm or Warsaw or Brussels.*

Among all the instances of intervention in the eighteenth century I find only one league formed between crowned heads, and it was directed against royal power—the league of the northern powers against Poland and Sweden. As to the powers of western and southern Europe, I find only one case in which they combined in furtherance of a common object, and that was the suppression of the Jesuit order. It was a characteristic episode: it showed up, as in a kind of bas-relief, some of the salient features of the politics of the time. All the Bourbons and the Braganzas—France, Spain, Naples, Parma and Portugal—had, for purely political reasons, proscribed the Jesuits. They acted in the fullness of their sovereignty, for in none of these states was there a constitution or fundamental law to limit, in this connection, their absolute power. But expulsion of the Jesuits would not be enough if the order could rally itself elsewhere. Every possible refuge must be closed to them and their very existence suppressed. Their survival in fact depended on the weakest rulers of the Continent, for the stronger promptly combined to subject the Society of Jesus to their will. What they required of the Pope was an act stemming from his spiritual power; therefore, if they had had any respect for the rights of the Church, they should have proceeded only by way of persuasion. Their representations should have been restrained and deferential, as would befit personages honoured with such titles as Most Faithful, Catholic, Most Christian King. To look for such respect and tact would be

* Sorel's picture of the contradictory attitudes of the various Powers towards the Dutch and Belgian revolts is justified, but he is mistaken in suggesting that the British government favoured the revolt of the Austrian Netherlands.

to mistake the manners of the time. Their demands were urgent, haughty, arrogant; they were accompanied by threats and supported by force. Pope he might be, but Clement XIII was to them only a ruler—and the worst armed of all rulers; he was treated accordingly. As the Pope was invested with a double sovereignty, it was a double usurpation. In his capacity of temporal sovereign, he was required to close his frontier to the proscribed order; in his spiritual capacity he was required to suppress it. Both sovereignties were thus infringed. Moreover, it did not stop there. The two powers being confused, the one was attacked through the other; the temporal being the more easily got at, it was through this that siege was laid to the spiritual power and its capitulation enforced. The Church being also a state, it was subject to the law of states—which meant that it ceased to be inviolable. The powers allied against the Jesuits treated the Holy See just as Louis XIV, after the Revocation of the Edict of Nantes, would have treated the Dutch Republic if the proscribed Protestants had had no other refuge, and if the Dutch had had neither armies nor allies to defend them.

Clement XIII tried to resist. One of the confederates, the weakest though not the least enterprising, the Infant Duke of Parma, was within the Pope's power. This duke had reformed ecclesiastical jurisdiction in his states and disputed the suzerainty claimed there by the Holy See. By virtue of this suzerainty the Pope, in a brief of 30th January 1768, declared the decrees of the Infant null and void, and called upon him to retract them under pain of excommunication. To this usurpation of the rights of a prince of their House the Bourbon of France retorted by occupying Avignon and the Comtat (Venaissin), the Bourbon of Naples by the occupation of Benevento and Ponte-Corvo—over which moreover he claimed sovereignty. Then, in identical notes handed to the Holy See in January 1769, France, Naples and Spain called upon the Pope to suppress the Jesuits. Some days later Clement XIII died. The allies were soon busy finding a suitable successor. 'If the Pope follows the principles of Clement

XIII,' wrote Choiseul, 'the monarchies will exact by force
what they previously asked of the Holy Father as an act of
goodwill.'[118] Ganganelli promised to suppress the Jesuits,
and became Pope with the name of Clement XIV. Then
he played for time. He struggled for more than four years;
but the allies held on, and would yield on no item of the
pledge. 'The King', wrote d'Aiguillon on 11th January
1773, 'possessed himself of this territory—Avignon—only because the House of Bourbon was dissatisfied with the conduct
of the late Pope towards the Infant, and has kept it only because the King of Spain has asked him to defer its restitution until the Pope should give him satisfaction over the affair
of the Jesuits. As soon as he obtains it the King will give back
Avignon.' And Louis XV's ambassador at Rome, Cardinal de
Bernis, reported on February 17th: 'It is most advisable that
France should always have at her disposal a sure means of
bringing back the Roman Curia to a suitable disposition if it
should depart from it. We can seize Avignon whenever we
wish, and this possibility will always enforce respect from
the Papacy.' Naples followed suit, and the restitution of
Benevento in fact was conditional, like that of Avignon, on
the suppression of the Jesuits. The Pope capitulated, the
Jesuits were suppressed, and the Holy See recovered its territories.

For a full appreciation, however, of the scepticism of the
old Europe and the anarchy of 'the Christian commonwealth', this strange business of the Society of Jesus must be
pursued to its conclusion. While the Catholic governments
proscribed the Jesuits and in this way usurped the authority
of the Pope, the heretics and schismatics welcomed the
banned order and prided themselves on being more papist
than the Holy See. Frederick needed teachers for his subjects of the Roman faith; here was a good opportunity to
obtain them cheaply, and he took it. 'Since my brothers, the

[118] To Bernis, ambassador of France at Rome, 9 May 1769.
Masson, p. 119.

Catholic, Most Christian, Most Faithful and Apostolic Kings have driven them out,' he said to the Prince de Ligne, 'I, heretic though I am, gather in as many as I can.'[119] He had nothing to fear; scattered among a Protestant population and closely regulated by Prussian officials, the Jesuits had to obey. 'I know very well', he wrote to Voltaire, 'that they have been plotters and have always been mixed up in politics; but that is the fault of government for allowing it.' He laid down his conditions, which were harsh, and the Jesuits submitted to them. The great Catherine followed her neighbour's example, and like him did well out of it. The Fathers, so unaccommodating towards Catholic governments, showed themselves most tractable and obliging towards these two despots, who were not so much dissidents as freethinkers. In particular, the Jesuits preached to the Poles the duty of obedience to the Orthodox tsarina and the Lutheran king who had annexed them.

Considering all these things, I conclude that if anything appeared at the end of the ancien régime to be improbable, and indeed contradictory of all established practice, it was a condition founded upon international law for the defence of that law. 'A pope', said Frederick, 'who now wished to preach a crusade would hardly muster twenty rascals.' A Holy Alliance before 1789 would have been a veritable historical paradox. The old Europe was incapable of it, and it took the French Revolution to make the conception possible.

II. THE DIPLOMATIC SCENE

Diplomacy is the expression of political customs. The diplomats of the ancien régime, living in the most brilliant society in Europe, formed a particularly refined and exquisite circle. But their intellect, manners and language are not our concern; it is the fundamentals that we must seek to know.

[119] Prince de Ligne, *Mémoires*, on Frederick II, p. 39.

It is their opinions and their actions that we must consider if we are to understand how this diplomacy was so easily adapted to a revolutionary situation, and how the men of the Revolution learnt its ways so easily.

The negotiations of this period wear the appearance of intrigue conducted on a higher political level and for more substantial gains. That was the essence of the subtle art of diplomacy. States were guided only by self-interest; but there were ways of thwarting or falsifying its calculations. Raison d'état was the reigning principle, but passions really held sway and determined men's actions. These were the real stuff of international politics, and so it was often degraded, sometimes utterly base. The old Europe was not troubled by scruples, and did not pride itself on a false delicacy. The eighteenth century could show nothing more scandalous than the spectacle of Louis XIV's court in the seventeenth, when 'the most powerful ministers and all those formerly great'— the King of England, the Queen, the ambassadors—trembled before the 'puny widow of the famous cripple, Scarron, governess of the royal bastards'.[120] In Louis XV's time, Maria Theresa did not scruple to make use of Madame de Pompadour, 'who was', according to an official document, 'the vehicle of that sovereign's most secret overtures to the King'.[121] The Empress had opened her heart to the mistress of Louis XV to obtain a French alliance;* when some years later she wished to obtain recognition of the partition of Poland—concluded despite that alliance and to her disadvantage—she went even further. It was a dirty business, only to be carried through at the price of pretty thorough humiliation. Maria Theresa had a daughter of seventeen who was about to marry

---

[120] Saint-Simon, *Parallèle*, p. 79. Cf. *id.* 24, 277.

[121] *Recueil des Instructions, Autriche*. Instructions of comte de Choiseul, 1759. See *Mémoires de Bernis*.

* Though Mme de Pompadour played a minor rôle as an intermediary, the view that the king's former mistress exercised a leading influence in the famous Reversal of Alliances of 1756 is no longer accepted.

the Dauphin of France. She instructed her to wheedle the du Barry.* 'I do not require anything degrading,' she wrote to her ambassador, 'still less intimacies, but the attentions due to her grandfather and sovereign, in consideration of the good that may result to us and both our courts; the alliance may depend on it. I look to you to make every effort and to my daughter to employ all her charm, setting aside such prejudices as might suggest a different course for her. Nothing could be more valuable than the good that she could do.'[122]

When the most worthy of sovereigns, herself most devout and entirely virtuous, was reduced to such humiliation, it is understandable that the complete sceptics, who handled their affairs rather differently, comported themselves with perfect ease on so congenial a field for their manœuvres. As well as mistresses at Versailles there were favourites at St. Petersburg to be won over by the same base methods. The same game was played everywhere, and sometimes it was carried, at least in intention, far beyond the limits of gallantry. To someone who was hoping in 1723 for the death of the King of Poland, an agent wrote: 'This event cannot now be far off. All that is needed is for the King of Poland to have a new mistress, witty and charming, and it might occur quite soon.'[123] To provide a mistress for a king, a lover for a queen or an empress, or indeed for a princess royal, wife of the heir presumptive, was one of the favourite devices of diplomacy. Persons of this type played a part of great importance, and held the stage for long periods in the great theatre of world affairs. Their careful briefing and secret instructions are summed up in the well-known lines:

---

* All the Empress was asking was that Marie Antoinette should exhibit a few minor politenesses to the king's *maîtresse en titre*, instead of completely ignoring her.

[122] To comte de Mercy, 2 July 1772, Arneth et Geffroy, *Correspondance de Mercy-Argenteau*, Paris, 1874.

[123] Vandal, *Louis XV et Elisabeth*, p. 62.

'What are my orders, sir? How shall I act?—
You have to please this lady, and make love.'[124]

Corruption was the chief instrument in all these manœuvres. Venality was rife almost everywhere. The marquis
d'Argenson pointed out, with justifiable pride, a notable exception to this general degradation. 'Corruption has not
found its way into the Ministry of Foreign Affairs. This is to
be welcomed almost as a miracle and one highly creditable
to the French nation,' he said, 'especially in view of the sal-
aries it pays its clerks and their small hope of promotion.'[125]
D'Argenson claimed that the practice 'of relying on money
to achieve diplomatic success' had originated in England. It
was indeed used there a great deal, but so it was also on the
Continent. The most ancient treatises on the art of diplomacy put faith in it; La Bruyère lists among the qualities of
the diplomat the art of knowing when to offer bribes, and
certainly of seeming willing to receive them. 'He knows how
to win the interest of those with whom he deals; he does not
wish to be thought impregnable on this point, but allows
some concern for his own fortunes to appear. In this way he
encourages proposals which betray the most secret ideas of
others, their deepest schemes and even their ultimate aim, for
his own advantage.'

Most diplomats of the eighteenth century made use of
bribery to the limit, and did not content themselves with
hints. They were quite crude about it. In 1716 Dubois was
treating with Stanhope. 'I risked an approach,' he wrote to
the Regent, 'and I have never been more joyful than when
he allowed me to speak out—even to name the sum, which I

[124] See in the *Secret du Roi*, by the duc de Broglie, the story
of the mission of the baron de Breteuil, tome I, p. 368. It concerned the future Catherine II, then Grand Duchess; a helpful
precedent could be found in the relationship of the marquis de
la Chétardie with the Empress-regnant Elizabeth. See Vandal,
op. cit.

[125] *Mémoires*, éd. Rathery, t. IV, p. 150 ff.

fixed straight away at 600,000 livres, a proposal which he graciously received without being at all put out.'[126]* At the time of the outbreak of the French Revolution, Thugut, who had been Internuncio at Constantinople, and who was to be called to direct Austrian policy in this great crisis, had been in receipt of a pension from the King of France since 1768. Apart from this kind of everyday business there were the great markets that were open periodically—the Swedish and Polish diets. In 1763 that of Sweden cost France 1,400,000 and in 1766 1,830,000 livres. In 1773 the Russian minister Panin proposed to his associates in Vienna and Berlin that they should 'guarantee a fund for buying votes', and set up an office for concerted operations. The market par excellence, however, was the Diet of the Holy Roman Empire. There everyone was ready to give or to receive. In 1741, when a Bavarian was to be made Emperor, Belle-Isle pushed up the bidding, but being prudent, was careful to pay only after the vote had been cast. This was no empty precaution, for the Elector of Cologne, who had received 100,000 florins from Austria, got his confessor's permission to go back on his word without repaying the money. The same procedure was applied even in papal conclaves. 'The King', wrote a minister of Louis XIV, 'should not neglect any means at his disposal; he should use tact, insinuation, and even money, which is the quickest and surest means of all, and one long in use at the court of Rome, in order to obtain a Pope wiser and less partial than the last.'[127] The item for secret funds and pen-

126 Aubertin, *l'Esprit public au dix-huitième siècle.*

* By order of the Regent Dubois at one point offered Stanhope £3,000, and renewed the offer several times, finally on the day of his own departure from Hanover. There would have been nothing unusual in acceptance of such a gift on the conclusion of a treaty, but Stanhope refused, and Dubois reported to the Regent that it was the only point in the negotiation in which he had '*totalement échoué*'—totally failed.

See Basil Williams, *Stanhope*, Oxford, 1932, p. 223.

127 The reference is to Innocent XI. See Camille Rousset, *Louvois*, tome IV, ch. X.

sions had a pre-eminent place in the budgets of the chancelleries.

As though the cabals of official diplomacy were not enough, and there were not enough matter for repugnance in this school of intrigue, corruption and deceit, it was reduplicated in a secret diplomacy which was so entangled and confused by its own plots that the history of the negotiations of this century becomes an impenetrable labyrinth. There had at all times been secret agents pursuing shady pacts or initiating risky negotiations, but never had this been carried to the extremes we see in the eighteenth century. Rulers, sated with absolute power, seem to have developed a taste for romance, conspiracy, adventure. Their scepticism was so radical and their mistrust so profound, they carried their stratagems to such an extreme, that they came to distrust everybody, their own confidants above all. To reassure them they had to negotiate through nameless individuals who approached them mysteriously with passwords or other prearranged signs of recognition. There was established a kind of diplomatic freemasonry, with its initiates and its go-betweens. What began as an expedient developed into an institution. With Louis XV this passion became a positive mania, yet he did no more than refine upon the general practice. Europe was swarming with secret agents. This rôle gave such a feeling of self-importance that everyone hankered after it. Financiers, who had correspondents everywhere, and men of letters, to whom all doors were open, were tickled in their vanity by such employment, and found a new stimulus to their amour-propre in thus playing—if only in the antechamber—the part of negotiator and statesman. Voltaire was contemptible in this rôle, Diderot insignificant; Grimm, who was a German and had a smattering of the craft, rendered some service to his masters—he was even admitted to the ranks of the regulars. Men of ambition tried to climb by way of these backstairs. It was by this means that Dumouriez launched himself on the world. The records of secret diplomacy are thick with illustrious names. There were none more famous than those two to whom the imminent death of Frederick gave the opportunity in 1786 to make a start, up-stage and as confidants; the day was not far distant when they would fill the premier rôles in the great tragedy of the century. At Talleyrand's suggestion Mirabeau was sent as an observer to Berlin. It was a kind of improvised rehearsal in which both practised their parts: Mirabeau took the part of an ambassador, and the future negotiator of the Treaties of Vienna that of minister *in partibus*.

The recesses of the theatre, the wings and corridors, teemed with adventurers. They crowded the hostelries, listening at every keyhole, insinuating themselves by every passage, trafficking in secrets, bargaining for news, veritable political panders ready to sell anything that was for purchase, and to buy anything that was for sale. Like Beaumarchais' hero—a faithful portrait—'welcomed in one city, imprisoned in another', the adventurer was, however, more often asked in than shown the door. He was the intermediary par excellence in this contraband trade, the bill-broker of this smugglers' exchange, the commercial traveller of this clandestine commerce. A cynic like Casanova, a charlatan like Cagliostro, penetrated even into courts; a double-faced adventurer, a sort of androgynous Figaro, the Chevalier d'Eon, achieved rank in the diplomatic corps. The marquis de Poterat, conspirator and gambler on the stock exchange, on the run from the police and the bailiff's men, card-sharper, hired spy, literary assassin, rejected by all circles and general ne'er-do-well, was able to present himself at Vienna, where he was received and listened to, as plenipotentiary of the government of the Directory. A comte d'Antraigues, worth as little and described as 'the prince of clowns' by one of those who employed him, became 'the soul of the emigration'.[128] Another who lived on his wits, Roques de Montgaillard, was also briefly a leader of it. The Revolution did not create the bands of intriguers

[128] D'Avaray. See Forneron, *Histoire des émigrés*, t. II, p. 78. Paris, 1884.

who prowled about the byways of Europe. They were already there lurking in the depths; the Revolution merely brought them to the surface and cast them up on the shore amid the flotsam and jetsam. They set to work, for the time was propitious for creatures from the underworld. They were suited to their task, since they had been used for it before, and indeed most of them were already known—though not to their credit. They now found ample employment, and disproportionate importance, not only on the side of the Revolution, but on that of the émigrés and even in the service of the old courts of Europe.

Tricking information out of foreign agents, corrupting or debauching them, were rather risky and expensive methods. There was a simpler and less costly way of discovering the secrets of diplomats, and that was by the interception of their correspondence. 'This kind of perfidy, which common practice seems to sanction,' said the author of *Institutions Politiques*, 'is so well known, so commonplace, that means of defeating it have been adopted nearly everywhere by using an indecipherable code.'[129] But the key could be bought, and in those times at any rate there was no code that did not yield up its secret sooner or later. The *cabinet noir* was a state institution; the *interceptes*, as they were called, were a constant source of intelligence. There were experts in the arts of unsealing, deciphering and re-sealing letters. Those of Paris were reckoned extremely clever;[130] those of Vienna were no

[129] Tome II, ch. III, § 13; Correspondence, spies, relations with the post office; ch. X, § 18, on the art of cipher, deciphering, opening and re-sealing letters. Bielfeld writes as an expert.

[130] In March 1794 an employee of the former *cabinet noir* submitted to the Committee of Public Safety a memorandum intended to demonstrate the usefulness of that institution. He paints a picture of it which, despite the florid style and the garish colours, does not lack interest: 'Before the Revolution there existed in France (and similarly in England and the principal states of Europe) an institution for official supervision. This institution when well managed has the property of serving as guide or compass to those who hold the reins of government; and the advantages, more

whit inferior. The latter had not only the cypher of the French ambassador, but also that of Louis XV's secret correspondence. It was through this very devious channel that the Minister of Foreign Affairs, d'Aiguillon, knew about *le secret du Roi*, which for a long time had been no secret to the court of Vienna. The Cardinal de Rohan, then ambassador to that court, had bought one of the agents of the 'cabinet noir', and among other precious documents thus revealed to him were the letters sent by the Comte de Broglie to one of the embassy secretaries, without the knowledge of the ambassador or of the Minister of Foreign Affairs.

There was only one way of avoiding 'interceptions', and that was to entrust despatches to reliable, brave and conscientious couriers, but even this was a rather precarious method. 'Do not fail to put your despatches carefully into cypher,' wrote Montmorin in 1788 to a French agent in Italy,

---

or less extensive, which it secures are related to the geographical situation of the different states where it is practised and the aptitude of the persons employed in it. In the first respect, France is the country most favourably situated, because through her territory pass the most important despatches in Europe. And as to the second the theory of decoding ciphers has been developed to a point which other powers do not as yet believe possible. The establishment in question is known by the name of the *Secret des postes*, thus concealing from the public its true purpose. This was thought to be simply a police supervision over individuals, whilst in fact matters of state were its main concern; . . . there was a mechanical process for opening (letters) and closing them again with such speed, without altering the imprint of the seal, that when they reached their destination it was impossible to tell if they had been examined.' The ciphers, badly devised, gave themselves away by their very complexity. Frederick was very proud of his, but they had decoded it in Paris. 'Initiation into the *Secret des postes* was roughly in these terms: You find yourself admitted to business of the highest confidence; you have and always will have adequate emoluments; but remember that you do not leave this office at your own wish, and that if, through chance or otherwise, you should come to leave it before age or infirmity compel you to withdraw, your place of retirement will be the Bastille.'—*Affaires étrangères.*

'even those you entrust to Spanish couriers. Not to mention other accidents, Spanish couriers can be kidnapped, as several instances have shown.'[131] There were indeed classic examples. In the month of June 1685, Louvois, informed that a courier of the Emperor would pass through Alsace on his way from Spain, wrote to M. de Montclar, the commander at Strasbourg, 'His Majesty considers it a matter of importance, in the present situation, to rob this courier and get his despatches. So you are ordered to position, in a village close to the post-route between Saverne and Strasbourg, three or four reliable men who will rob the courier and seize his despatches, which must be most carefully sought out, on his person as well as in his saddle, on pretext of searching for money.'[132] If the courier defended himself, he might lose his life. His life might be taken in any case in order to put up a better show of a hold-up by professional bandits. 'For this rough work', wrote the wise Bielfeld, 'only stout fellows of tried fidelity must be chosen.'[133]

Couriers were small fry; they disappeared without trace; everybody knew that the roads were infested with brigands, and all governments confessed that their police were unable to suppress them. To waylay and rob ambassadors themselves was more audacious and more difficult. It happened nevertheless, despite the well-known safeguards of international law. The kidnapping of Maret and de Sémonville in 1793* was no more than a repetition of an outrage perpetrated at the same place and in similar circumstances in the sixteenth century. Then the French envoys who were passing through the Duchy of Milan to present themselves at the court of

131 Montmorin to Cacault, chargé d'affaires at Naples, 23 September 1788.

132 Camille Rousset, *Louvois*, t. III, p. 270.

133 *Institutions*, t. II, ch. II, § 25.

* Maret and Sémonville, appointed in 1793 as its representatives respectively to Naples and Constantinople by the Committee of Public Safety, were captured *en route* by the Austrians, in defiance of the principles of international law, and flung into prison.

Suleiman were assassinated by order of the imperial governor, who wished to gain possession of their papers. The Rastadt outrage of 1799* also had its precedents, less ancient, certainly, but of equally high authority. During the Congress of Cologne, in 1674, Louvois wrote to the comte d'Estrades: 'It looks very much as though M. de Lisola (plenipotentiary of the Emperor) will soon leave Liége to return to Cologne. It would be a great advantage if on his return he could be seized, and indeed far from inconvenient for him to be killed if he or those with him should defend themselves, for he is a man of highly impertinent speech who works most industriously and relentlessly against the interests of France; you would not believe how much you would advance yourself in his Majesty's favour if you could carry out this project.'[134] Lisola managed to avoid the trap, but this way of conducting foreign affairs was so much a matter of custom that one month later the Emperor's soldiers seized the Prince of Fürstenburg, plenipotentiary of the Elector of Cologne and client of Louis XIV, and carried him off to Vienna, where he remained a prisoner until peace was signed.

The eighteenth century only continued the same tradition and developed already customary abuses. Frederick carried to its logical conclusion the practice of investigation by

* By the terms of the Treaty of Campo Formio the Emperor agreed to the meeting of a Congress at Rastadt to deal with the affairs of Germany. It opened in December 1797 and negotiations dragged on until, in March 1799, Austria openly joined the Second Coalition by declaring war on France and declared the Congress at an end. The French envoys, Bonnier, de Bry and Roberjot, were ordered to leave by Austria but instructed to remain at their post by the French Directory. Under Austrian pressure they took carriage for Strasbourg on the night of 28 April. They had barely started their journey when, in the outskirts of the town, they were stopped by Austrian hussars, their papers and possessions pillaged and Bonnier and Roberjot assassinated on the spot. The only explanation for the outrage ever offered by the Austrian government was that it was 'an unfortunate misunderstanding'.

[134] Camille Rousset, *Louvois*, t. II, p. 2.

means of 'interceptes'. Suspecting in 1756 that a plot was being hatched against him and that the proof of it would be found at Dresden, he occupied that city without a declaration of war, and laid hands on the state archives. The point of the lesson was not missed, and more than one application of it will be met with in the course of these studies. The seizure of the duc d'Enghien on neutral territory, his summary condemnation and clandestine execution were merely a case of kidnapping followed by assassination; the invasion of Rome, the arrest of the Pope, the seizure of the Vatican archives were simply the ultimate term in the series.

12. WAR

While peace pursued by means of perfidy rested on a precarious foundation, war was characterised by extreme atrocity. Yet, unrestrained and barbarous though it was, war was in a sense less discreditable than peace, being at any rate more honest, in so far as it was more appropriate to its end, which was the triumph of force. It retained a certain nobility derived from the customs of chivalry. If the standard which it upheld, the right of the stronger, was crude and base, the means employed, strangely enough, did much to raise its moral level. War called for the highest virtues of which man was capable. Honour was its guiding principle; among all those who bore the sword there was a kind of brotherhood of arms which engendered a mutual esteem, even when they fought each other with the utmost ferocity. It was in war that the old European society, the French in particular, showed at its best. Besides, fighting was a career—the noblest of careers—governed by the same rules in all European countries. Wars were not then national conflicts; though violent, they were not marked by the bitterness of international struggles. It was quite common for officers to pass from the service of one state to that of another, remaining completely loyal, and incurring not the slightest blame, still less suspicion. So between army staffs, before and after battle, there were rela-

tions of high courtesy which tempered to a certain degree the
ferocity of war. The mitigation indeed was small. War strips
man of his veneer of civilisation, exposes his faults of character, gives rein to his vices, unbridles all his passions. To
preserve self-control in war requires a deep-seated discipline
and the latent resources of a long-established civilisation.
But the men of the eighteenth century, beneath an exterior
of polished refinement, were still brutish and violent. While
most of them could discourse elegantly of 'humanity' very
few were humane. 'Sensibility' was a mere matter of fashion;
they powdered and preened themselves, but at bottom they
retained all the crudity of the previous century. Had it been
otherwise, we could not explain the heroism or the violence
of the Revolutionary wars. This violence was not peculiar to
the improvised armies thrown into battle by the Republic;
it can be seen just as plainly in the army of the émigrés,
which was composed of gentlemen, and in the regular
forces of the Coalition. It must not be forgotten that the
struggle opened with the Brunswick Manifesto, which was
simply taken from the military code of the ancien régime.

The history of seventeenth-century wars is nothing more
than a sinister commentary on the engravings of Callot and
Romain de Hooge. The soldiers appear brutal, the armies
an undisciplined rabble. By implacable custom war must
nourish war. Everything was subject to requisition; all coffers
were emptied, even those of the churches. The invader took
all that the population could pay. This was the means not
only of sustaining the army, but of building up a treasure to
provide for future wars, the profits of war being in those
days one of the most dependable resources of financiers. Add
to this pillage, rape, arson. The occupied country bore the
brunt of war, and it was a crushing burden. Inhabitants
reputed dangerous, or even suspect, were proscribed. Others
took fright, and to escape the peril which threatened not
only their property but their persons and the honour of
their wives and daughters, fled the country. Then a tax was
put on absent persons, and those who did not pay had their

houses demolished. The classical method of stimulating payment was arson. 'As regular as a bout of fever,' wrote Luxembourg in 1672, 'every other day we burn down the houses of those who are fools enough to drive us to it.' The Elector Palatine protested not against the deed but against its abuse. 'I thought', he wrote to Turenne, 'that strictly one should only set fire to places where contributions have been refused.' Again, houses were burned down and inhabitants hanged in any village where the people had fired on the troops. 'The inhabitants of cities, towns and villages', said the Manifesto of 1792, 'who should dare to defend themselves against the troops of their Imperial and Royal Majesties and fire upon them, whether in open country or from the windows, doors or apertures of their houses, will be punished on the spot according to the full rigour of martial law, and their houses demolished or burned down.'[135]

Louvois was an implacable perpetrator of bloody deeds, but nothing he did was new—he only regularised to some extent the established usages and applied with method the procedures which his contemporaries employed haphazardly. He believed that systematic terror would more quickly force people to submit. In the case of the Palatinate he wrote, 'It is absolutely necessary to bring these people to reason, either by hanging them or by burning their villages.' The Germans put up a stubborn resistance; the troops vied with one another in brutality; the cruelty of the reprisals inflamed passions still further. 'Inhumanity against the Germans must be stepped up', cried Louvois, 'if they are not prepared to wage war honourably.' The Germans regarded the French as 'cannibals'; the French said the Germans had 'nothing but the faces and shapes of men'. Louis XIV had fifty German houses burned down for one French house destroyed; for every house burned by the French, the Germans shot two prisoners.[136] If a place held out for an unreasonable time, the garrison was

---

[135] C. Rousset, *Louvois*, t. I, p. 393; t. II, p. 79.

[136] C. Rousset, *Louvois*, t. IV, pp. 394, 183, 239; t. III, pp. 238, 380.

threatened with being sent to the galleys. If émigrés or rebels were found in it, they were imprisoned and then, if few they were hanged, if many decimated, the survivors being sent to 'row for His Majesty'.[137] 'I must tell you', wrote the Prince de Condé to Louvois in 1673, 'that I find the spirit of these people quite different from last year. They are given over to despair.'[138] From 1793 onwards this was to be the lugubrious and monotonous refrain of all generals with a shred of humanity, of all commissioners not blinded by fanaticism. The same laments can be found in the correspondence of foreign soldiers and diplomats. The military code of Louvois was to be enforced on France by her enemies, and the revolutionaries were to treat foreign countries in the same way.

This is how war was understood and how it was waged by the men of the eighteenth century. D'Argenson received many complaints during his ministry, and was moved by them. But he was told that 'war and pity do not go together'.[139] Indeed they did not. The wars of this period were notorious for the indiscipline of the armies, the exactions of the conquerors, and the scandalous fortunes made by many of the commanders. The armies were accompanied by 'a crowd of parasites hanging on to their flanks' and living on their pillage, peripatetic *faubourgs* where officers and soldiers came to buy and sell and dispose of their loot. Lumbering across the countryside, these rapacious caravans infested and ruined the land; they were a drag on the army's movement, an encumbrance which disbanded when there was a victory and broke up under defeat. A contemporary wrote in 1741, after Frederick's passage through Moravia: 'Never since the Goths has war been waged in such a fashion as this.'[140] In 1744 the Austrians advanced to the frontiers of Lorraine and called on the inhabitants to submit; those

137 Louvois to Créqui, September 1670. C. Rousset, *Louvois*, t. I, p. 300.
138 C. Rousset, *Louvois*, t. I, p. 448.
139 *Mémoires*, t. IV, p. 403.
140 De Broglie, *Frédéric II et Marie-Thérèse*, t. II, p. 210.

who resisted, they proclaimed, would be hanged, 'after being forced to cut off their own noses and ears'.[141] The Seven Years War surpassed all previous wars in atrocity. The Count of Saint Germain wrote in 1757: 'The countryside for thirty leagues around is sacked and ruined as though a fire had raged through it.' 'We are surrounded by hanging corpses,' wrote another witness, 'and the soldiers do not hesitate to massacre women and children as well if they resist the ransacking of their houses.'[142] Frederick sometimes enrolled prisoners in his own army, and if this was their lot they were lucky—for at other times, as at Crefeld, all who laid down their arms were massacred. The ferocity of Russians and Prussians towards each other was terrible. The Russians occupied Memel in 1757, enrolled all the garrison and deported the townspeople. 'Nothing like it has been seen since the invasion of the Huns. Inhabitants were hanged after their noses and ears had been cut off, their legs torn off, their hearts and entrails cut out.'[143] In the following year at Küstrin the Prussians took their revenge. 'The Russians', Frederick relates, 'lost two thousand prisoners and at least fifteen thousand men they had left there, for the soldiers gave no quarter.' In 1788 Prince Potemkin laid siege to the Turkish town of Otchakof for six months. He was a courtier and a man of the highest refinement. He prided himself on his literary taste and feeling. 'The cruelties of the Spaniards in the New World and of the English in the Indies', wrote a Russian, 'are nothing in comparison with our military philosopher, who is busy translating Rousseau's *Héloïse* and in putting to death all those who have valuables to tempt his greed.'[144] On December 16th the assault was launched. Of 20,000 Turks who defended the place 10,000 were killed. The town was

141 Voltaire, *Siècle de Louis XV*, ch. XI.

142 Grimm. See Sainte-Beuve, *Causeries du lundi*, t. VII, article *Grimm*.

143 Hermann, *Geschichte des russischen Staates*. Gotha, 1832-1866, t. V, p. 142.

144 Rostopchine, *Correspondance*. Moscow, 1876.

put to the sack, the pillage went on for three days and more than six thousand inhabitants were slaughtered. 'The fury of the Russian soldiers was such', says Ségur, 'that two days after the assault, when they found Turkish children hidden in forts and underground refuges, they seized them, threw them in the air, caught them on the points of their bayonets and cried, 'These anyhow will never do harm to Christians!''[145]

Hostages were taken to ensure not only security on the march, but also the safety of detachments left in the rear. When he abandoned Prague in 1742 Belle-Isle carried off sixteen notables, four each from the nobility, clergy, magistracy and burghers; they were to answer for the garrison which stayed in the city. More than this, territories were seized and even whole countries occupied by the same title. The Duc de Choiseul wrote from Vienna in 1757: 'I have urged Count Kaunitz to tell the Hanoverian minister firmly that if the 15,000 English who are supposed to be about to land in France carry out the smallest exaction contrary to the rules observed among civilized nations, the Electorate of Hanover will be made answerable for the damage, and that every French village burnt by the English will irrevocably entail the burning down of a Hanoverian town.'[146] Bernis, then Minister of Foreign Affairs, thoroughly approved of this step: 'Those who think us capable of sparing an enemy at bay have too low an opinion of us. . . . The territories of the King of England must be regarded in some sort as a hostage in our hands.'

If the standards of the time, and particularly those of the states which formed the coalition against France, are to be fully appreciated, they must be seen in operation, not in a hostile and invaded country, but in an occupied country which those governments wished to keep—as in the Polish provinces which the powers had just shared out and taken

---

[145] Ségur, *Mémoires*, t. III, p. 442.
[146] Filon, *L'Ambassade de Choiseul à Vienne*. Paris, 1872. Hanover was of course the patrimony of the King of England.

into their possession as pledges for their claims. The Russian soldiers, 'more highwaymen than soldiers' in the words of Rostopchin, vied with the Poles they fought against in violence, and often outdid them. Everywhere they killed, robbed, burned, raped, and held to ransom—in the name of religion. Muskets and whips were the means mutually employed for conversion. Saldern, the Russian commander, was described by a witness as 'a madman who had been given a sabre'. Frederick exploited the usurped territories for military purposes, setting up magazines, revictualling troops, levying contributions, filling up the ranks of his army, and requisitioning Polish girls like flocks of animals to people Pomerania, where, he said, they were short of women. 'This rigour', wrote the Saxon Resident, 'has driven the people to despair.' The Austrians, more civilised, prided themselves on keeping to the law. They delimited the frontiers, inspected title-deeds, claimed their rights, and then applied to the 'reincorporated' populations the same harsh government as in their hereditary states. Really, beneath these plausible appearances and formal procedures, their rule was as bad as that of the Russians and Prussians. 'In the name of the benevolent Maria Theresa', reports a French historian, 'two men—Pergen, in charge of administration, and Hadik, commander of the armed forces, took what we should call revolutionary measures against these unhappy lands, and applied there a code which anticipated that of our Revolution.'[147] Emigration was considered a crime, the inhabitants being forbidden to leave the territory; those who remained were mulcted to the limit, while those who tried to find refuge from an odious occupation in flight were punished with confiscation; Branicki, whom the King of Poland had sent on a mission to Versailles, was held to be an émigré and his property was confiscated. Polish judges had to take an oath of allegiance to Austria and in its name to condemn their compatriots. Most people were

[147] Ferrand, *Histoire des trois démembrements de la Pologne*, liv. V, Paris. 1820.

cowed by fear and obeyed. At the court of Vienna, however, these two proconsuls were thought to be too moderate and to have shown too much lenience. 'Count Pergen is reproached here', said Joseph II, 'with being too inactive, and the truth is he has so far done nothing.' Hadik was no better. 'He is too old for this job, too slow and too much inhibited by his Hungarian prejudices, which are out of place here.'[148]

Such were the customs of war at the end of the ancien régime. The terrorists found them easy to accept and adapted them without difficulty; yet they added to them not only the ferocity of fanatics but also a new and particularly revolting depravity—the hypocrisy of humanitarianism. To resist this general impulse, whether in the form of tyrannical military orders or the contagion of spreading reprisals, a singular strength of mind was required. Where it appeared, it was the finest glory of the heroes of our national wars.* Philosophical veterans like Dugommier, enthusiastic young warriors like Marceau or Desaix, they knew how to add to the military virtues of the old armies their own generous ardour.

13. THE DOWNFALL OF EUROPE

What conclusions are to be drawn from all this? The political traditions of Europe on the eve of the French Revolution are epitomised in two episodes—the War of the Austrian Succession and the Partition of Poland. The first shows how the undertakings of governments were regarded, the second how much respect was paid to established sovereignties. These iniquitous deeds were the testament of the old Europe, which having signed it had only to die, bequeathing to those who set out to reform her ways, but who, to their confusion and the public misfortune, could only imitate them, the pernicious tradition of the abuses through which she perished. These abuses were the product of custom, but custom had

---

[148] Arneth, *Maria Theresia*, t. VIII, p. 418.

* Sorel does not resist the temptation to idealise 'national wars'.

never hitherto been interpreted with the cynicism of utter logic or pushed to such scandalous extremes. Here was its *summum jus*, but here also lay its supreme injustice, its sophism and negation. The ancien régime had reached those dubious confines where law, twisted from its purpose, degenerated into abuse. The example of past ages, and their own precedents, which had all led states into these deeds, also led them insensibly to these exaggerations of their own principle. They did not see that excess meant self-destruction. Their law was nothing but prescription, and rested on the mere facts of possession, which were justified simply by their existence, and were supported only by their own weight. *Mole sua stat.* The veil which hid the sanctuary of states they tore violently aside, and exposed the mystery of sovereignty to the masses. They showed the nations that two things took precedence over the rights of states—the power of the state and the convenience of its sovereign. They opened the gates to a revolution which, to overthrow their thrones and destroy their empires, had only to turn their own methods against them and follow the example they had provided. It was thus that by strictly following established ways the rulers who most fully represented the ancien régime prepared its downfall, unwittingly justifying the profound saying of Pascal: 'Custom is the basis of right for the simple reason that it is accepted, this is the mystical source of its authority. To try to go back to its original principle is to destroy it.'[149]

All that remained of international law was raison d'état as its principle and supreme end, intrigue as its means and force as its only law. Politicians cynically avowed as much. 'Force is the supreme law', said an Austrian diplomat, 'and one has to acquire more of it even though one has plenty already.'[150] It was a terrifying state of affairs, and from all those contemporaries who viewed the scene with detachment and re-

[149] *Pensées*, éd. Havet, art. III, no. 8.

[150] An observation made at the Congress of Teschen, 1779, and reported by a French official. *Affaires étrangères. Frédéric II et Marie-Thérèse*, t. II, p. 198.

flected upon it one gets this impression of fear. No one saw more deeply or spoke in more arresting terms than Mallet du Pan,* who, in the crisis which he so clearly foresaw, was to be the adviser of the old Europe, always far-sighted and always misunderstood. In 1792 he wrote: 'Never perhaps anywhere in the world have there been such likely prospects for the success of the engineers of social upheaval. Divided among a number of diverse governments, Europe offers little basis for a common resistance, and the first great continental nation that changes the face of society will be confronted only by disunited members. Because of the character of European politics during the last century, and the nature of the conventions on which it has been founded, it has become difficult to set in action for a common interest thirty rulers who all fear each other. For a hundred years their ministers have been accustomed to base their own security on indifference to the danger of any state they suspect of being able some day to harm them.'[151]

While the European commonwealth was dissolving in anarchy, and the bonds, always frail and artificial, that united governments seemed everywhere to be broken, the same principles of ruin and dissolution threatened the established order within states. Everything was crumbling and decaying at once; the same crisis that ruptured relations between states

---

* Jacques Mallet du Pan, 1749-1800, was a Swiss publicist. At an early age he was introduced to Voltaire, who helped him to obtain a post as Professor of Literature and History in Hesse-Cassel. Later he was appointed editor of the *Mercure*, a journal which provided a reasoned analysis of the debates in the Constituent Assembly from 1789 to 1791. On the outbreak of war he was sent by Louis XVI on a confidential mission to the rulers of Austria and Prussia. This failed, and thereafter he lived in exile, finally in England. His writings include *Considérations sur la nature de la révolution française*, London, 1793; *Correspondance politique pour servir à l'histoire du républicanisme français*, Hamburg, 1796; *Mémoires et correspondance de Mallet du Pan*, Paris, 1851.

[151] *Mercure*, number for January. *Mémoires et correspondance*, I, p. 251.

upset the relations of governments and citizens. In both its manifestations the crisis arose from the same excess and proceeded from the same causes. In foreign and internal affairs alike the ancien régime perished by the abuse of its own principle. The same revolution threatened all states; they were no more capable of perceiving their peril than they were of combining against it. The study of European politics explains how this revolution was able to develop in Europe with impunity and to triumph over the alliances formed to repress it. A rapid survey of governments and nations will enable us to give an account of the particular character it assumed and the means whereby it was propagated.

II. Governments and Reforms

1. GOVERNMENTS IN CRISIS

'At present every power is in a state of crisis', wrote Catherine the Great in 1780.[1] The writings of contemporaries were full of sinister predictions. There was a general complaint of decadence; revolutions were expected and catastrophes foretold on every side.[2] In France breakdown seemed imminent; the machinery was too old and complicated; it had lost its power, and the controlling hand had lost its skill; the whole state was out of gear. While France was sinking into decrepitude Prussia on the other hand was exhausted by pre-

[1] *Publications de la Société d'histoire de Russie*, t. II.
[2] Grimm wrote in 1757: 'I am very far from thinking that we are entering upon an age of reason; indeed it would not take much to convince me that Europe is threatened by some catastrophic revolution.' Linguet wrote in 1779: 'The peoples are suffering, the governments are dissatisfied; on all sides appear the disturbance and restlessness that precede great crises of whatever kind.'

mature growth. She was 'an artificial power', presenting to
Europe a flimsy and shaky façade, behind which there was a
tottering erection recklessly built upon sand, lacking foundations; only through the genius of the architect did it stand
erect. 'If ever', wrote Mirabeau, 'an unintelligent ruler should
ascend the throne, we should see this formidable giant suddenly crumble; Prussia would collapse like Sweden.'[3] Maria Theresa lamented the threatened downfall of her monarchy: 'No civil or political bond is holding firm; everywhere
people and provinces seem increasingly wretched and deca-
dent; and things will get worse if we go on as we are.'[4] Mallet
du Pan portrayed England as 'overburdened with taxes, torn
by party rivalry, corrupted by greed for money, and threatened by all the political prophets, as Venice was, with inevitable ruin'.[5] And what of Spain? The causes of her decline were already a commonplace for the *philosophes* and a
text-book exercise for students of politics. As for Poland, the
doctors had given her up and she was reduced to a choice
between the formulas of alchemists and the panaceas of
quacks.[6] 'I see all the states of Europe rushing to their ruin',
wrote Rousseau in 1772, 'monarchies, republics, all these
polities so grandly established, all these fine governments so
wisely elaborated, all are fallen into decrepitude and threatened with an early demise. All the great nations are groaning,
crushed by their own weight.'

The causes of this breakdown of the ancien régime were
everywhere the same—excessive expenditure on courts and
on war, sumptuous building, prodigal or avaricious mistresses,
greedy favourites, and, above all, the incessantly growing demands of armaments, now swollen out of all proportion.*

[3] *Monarchie prussienne*, Paris, 1788, liv. VII.

[4] To Joseph II, 2 January 1778. Arneth, *Maria Theresia und
Joseph II*. Vienna, 1867.

[5] *Annales politiques*, t. III, 1782.

[6] See Rousseau, *Gouvernement de la Pologne*. Mably, *Du gouvernement et des lois de Prologne*, etc.

* This version of the causes of the fall of the ancien régime is
supported in the original by a footnote reference to Taine, who

'The ruin of Europe has gone so far', wrote Montesquieu, 'that if individuals were in the situation that faces the three wealthiest states of this part of the world, you would say they had nothing to live on.'[7] States were hopelessly encumbered, unable to get credit, crushed under a weight of debt; the lesser more exhausted than the greater, for though their resources were smaller, their extravagance was as great. There was only one state that had sound finances, and that was England, despite the formidable size of her debt; this was due to the good management of Pitt's government. Prussia possessed a reserve of precious metals, and could show a balance, thanks to Frederick's implacable parsimony. But in fact she had neither a regular budget nor sound accounts. A few years of squandering by Frederick's successor reduced Prussia from this relative prosperity to the same state of bankruptcy as the rest. The French Court was preparing in 1791 to leave Paris, form a government in the provinces and rally the army on the frontiers—but it needed money. Marie Antoinette begged help from her brother. The ambassador, Mercy, replied: 'The Emperor was hoping to obtain a loan from Holland; he gave up the idea, because the city of Amsterdam was raising twelve millions to save its own bank from collapse. Russia has raised eight to ten millions; Sweden has borrowed six by pledging her iron mines; Poland has tried to raise four to six millions, but could not get them. All the money is in England. It is known with certainty that

---

was still an oracle when Sorel wrote. So far as France is concerned its source can be found in the anti-monarchical propaganda of noblesse and parlements which preceded the Revolution and was taken up by the Third Estate. In fact, the whole expenses of the Maison du roi amounted to about one-ninth of the annual expenditure. The burden which ruined French finances was the debt, and this came above all from the cost of French wars, especially the intervention in the War of American Independence financed by Necker at the price of borrowing at exorbitant rates of interest.

[7] *Esprit des lois*, liv. VIII, ch. XVII.

the Landgrave of Hesse-Cassel[8] has a treasure of fifteen to twenty million florins and that he would like to lend some of it; but he has so little confidence in borrowers that he cannot reach a decision—he has refused two great sovereigns.'

While all governments were reduced to borrowing, the service of their debts swallowed up much of the revenue, and they were perpetually in deficit. It was the fundamental vice of the régime, and the rest of Europe, if not worse than France in this respect, was certainly no better. The same consequences were everywhere apparent. Mirabeau wrote in 1788, 'Taxes are raised in an abominable manner everywhere in Europe.' Everywhere on the Continent, as in France, the richer the taxpayer the less he paid. As taxes went up, the privilege of exemption from them was extended. It was the system of progressive taxation in reverse. Nobles escaped payment, bourgeois obtained exemption; the crushing weight fell on the people of the countryside. In addition to the dues the sovereign laid upon them as subjects they bore those which the lord exacted from them as vassals. Feudal rights were the same everywhere, and were in fact least onerous, if not least vexatious, in France.

Of Russia I do not speak; serfdom was established there in the sixteenth century, just at the time when it was disappearing or being relaxed in the rest of Europe. In Poland it was kept up without any of the mitigations brought about by the relative softening of manners, the enlightened self-interest of lords, and above all in Russia by the intervention of the state. In Germany it persisted almost everywhere. The peasant could neither quit the manor, nor marry, nor change his occupation without the permission of his master. He worked during childhood as a servant in the lord's manor house; later he was liable for dues and for labour service

---

[8] William IX, son of the notorious trafficker in men who carried on a trade in soldiers, and grew rich through the armaments which brought ruin to his fellow-rulers. Mercy was writing on 21 April 1791. Arneth, *Marie-Antoinette, Joseph II und Leopold II.* Vienna, 1866.

which might be required on as many as three days a week.
Only with difficulty could he become a proprietor; in any
case his property was not his to do what he liked with and
did not pass intact to his children. This system gave rise in
Germany to general complaints. There were, however, very
considerable differences in its application. In the territory
of Zweibrücken the customs were particularly outrageous.
The estate of a Mecklenburg noble was likened by Pertz
to the den of a ferocious beast ravaging and silently devour-
ing everything around. The Lusatian peasant was a slave.
The Landgrave of Hesse sold his subjects to the English at
a hundred crowns a head. The Bavarian ruler reduced his
to the level of beasts. 'It is an earthly paradise', said Frederick, 'peopled by brutes.'[9] 'In the states of the house of
Austria', reports a contemporary, 'the common people are
poor, the businessman and the middle class in general comfortably off, the great nobles and the gentry rich, yet the
ruler is almost always at his wits' end to find the necessary
funds to keep the state going.'[10] The government did its
best to improve the lot of the peasant—and thereby the yield
of the taxes. The Empress, benevolent and intelligent, describes her subjects as 'downtrodden and overburdened' even
in time of peace.[11] A report on Bohemia addressed to the
Council of State in 1769 affirms: 'One sees with astonishment, with real shock and deep emotion, the extreme
wretchedness of the peasant, languishing under the loads
his lord piles upon him.' 'It is worse than in Hungary', wrote
another agent—and he could not think of a more dreadful
comparison. Joseph II toured the country, and returned in
consternation at what he saw.

In Prussia the peasant was rather less wretched. Frederick

[9] Pertz, *Leben des Ministers Freiherrn von Stein.* Berlin, 1849-
1855.
[10] Bielfeld. *Institutions,* t. I, ch. X, § 12.
[11] Arneth, *Maria Theresia,* t. IX, ch. XII and XIV: *l'Administration et les finances;* t. X: *les Provinces.* Vienna, 1879.

squeezed his subjects hard, but with discretion. He insisted that the noble should live on his estate and look after his peasants. Any one of them could address himself to the King, who read every petition. Government officials watched over the management of the land; the state gave assistance to agriculture and protected the vassal against excessive demands by the lord. Nevertheless the peasant's lot was very hard; he still paid seven times as much as the lord in direct taxes, while indirect taxes, thanks to Frederick's excessively protectionist system, bore heavily on his clothes, his victuals, and even the tools of his trade. Innumerable dues, more complicated and confused even than in France, encumbered rural property. It was reckoned that in Brandenburg, on thirty acres of land yielding nine and three-quarter écus the peasant paid the state just over eight écus, without counting what he owed to the lord and the clergy. In Pomerania, where the soil was less barren, he paid a little over sixteen écus on an income of seventeen and a half écus. In the most wretched dominion of the King of Prussia, the country of Cleves, the peasants despaired of making a living and the land lay waste.

The life of the Danish peasant was no different from that of the German. North and central Italy, on the other hand, was one of the regions of Europe where the countryman suffered least. He led a placid existence under the benevolent eye of his lord, who, especially in Piedmont, softened the rigours of the system. The existence of the peasant was easier in this countryside of small-scale farming with a resident nobility. All the same, conditions were harsh, and strange abuses not unknown. Goethe, travelling through Verona in 1786, questioned an inhabitant: 'I asked whether there were not also some rich peasants.—Yes, certainly there are.—And what do they do with their money?—They have lords who take it from them.'[12]

In France, the lesser nobles lived on their estates, but did not manage them, except in the west, where the old customs

[12] *Voyage en Italie*, trans. Porchat. Paris, 1862.

were retained—which explains the armies of the Vendée.*
The greater nobles neither resided on nor administered their
estates. Nowhere was this state of affairs so notorious or so
widespread as in France. There remained elsewhere more
or less marked traces of the feudal system, but, except in
England where they controlled local government, and Prussia where they partly held on to it, nobles almost everywhere
tended to live in the French style—they dissipated their fortunes, neglected their duties, inflated what should have been
the countervailing rights, and so completely lost their raison
d'être. In Prussia, where the king kept the nobles in check
and employed them in governmental duties, the nobility,
though arrogant and harsh, was respected by the peasantry
and was the chief strength of the nation. It was the same in
Piedmont. In Hungary, on the contrary, in Bohemia, and
in the hereditary dominions of the House of Austria, the
government was powerless to restrain the nobility, and the
peasant appealed in vain to his sovereign against the lord.

This right of appeal was the peasants' one recourse; but
there was none in the states of the Empire, Suabia and Franconia, which belonged to the *noblesse immédiate*. They were
called this because they held their power only from the Emperor—which means that in fact they held it from no one.
Nothing that in the greater states lessened the abuses of the
system—neither government, superior courts of justice, safeguards, protection, nor police—could be found in these territories. Apart from certain families of intellectual culture and
elevated principles—the glory and the pride of Germany,
where the father administered his estates as a patriarch, and
the sons travelled and sought careers at the great courts of
Europe (the Gagerns and the Steins for example)—all these
counts and barons of the Empire prided themselves on their
isolation, their moral bankruptcy and their political crudity;

---

* Simple explanations, such as this, for the revolt of the Vendée,
which was the result of the interaction of many different factors,
are no longer possible. See, for example, Charles Tilly, *The
Vendée* (1964).

these were the bar sinister of their bastard sovereignty, and they gloried in them. Veritable village tyrants, stupid parodists of the Prussian despotism which they emulated only in its violence, they formed in the heart of Germany a sort of archipelago of islets, more cut off from Europe by the closed frontiers of their domains than they could ever have been by the waves of the ocean. 'In many a place', said a German publicist—attached though he was to old customs—'you have only to note the appearance of a village to be sure that it belongs to a noble of the Empire. This nobility had once had its raison d'être, and amidst the disorders of the Middle Ages had rendered great service to the people; since then it has done nothing but harm. In former times it protected the peasant against the abuse of force; now instead it abused force by turning it against him. Privileges seemed more burdensome and more insupportable there than elsewhere.' There was nothing more unpopular in the whole Empire.[13]

The nobles of Sweden thought of nothing but diversion, while those of Denmark left their vassals to the exactions of government officials. In Spain, they dissipated in the expensive boredom of the court the money they painfully extracted from their estates. Their lands, badly managed, yielded little, and the people remained obedient only through indolence. The system seems to have been less harsh—as throughout Europe—on the estates of the clergy; ancient customs were there rather better kept; but the lenience in exploitation, only relative in any case, was accompanied by much neglect. Besides, the exemption from taxes enjoyed by the lands of the Church involved additional taxes upon the peasantry. Hence arose discontent and restiveness which, even in Spain, broke out in public disturbance.

Thus in all the countries of the Continent the same evils were produced by the same causes of disorder. Governments were aware of the effects, and tried to overcome them. Thinkers studied the ills of the time and suggested remedies.

13 See Hæusser, t. I, livre I, ch. V.

And so as decline proceeded there could be seen developing throughout Europe a movement for reform. The way in which reform was conceived must now be considered.

2. IDEAS OF REFORM

The source of these ideas was to be found in France. From France they radiated throughout Europe; but as they travelled they became differentiated, and the differences were important. Among the thinkers who had most influence, the earliest and the most readily listened to were those who, aiming only to remove abuses, sought to reform the state but by no means to destroy it. Montesquieu seemed the most profound, most stable and wisest of these; he had studied the facts, he respected the evidence, he subordinated pure reason to the observation of things as they were. He showed that each polity bears within itself, along with its raison d'être, its causes of duration and downfall. He showed how each can adapt to its own particular constitution the elements of civilisation which are the honour and the interest of all alike. He warned states of the common danger that threatened them—the abuse of their own principle. But his ideas were too far ahead of those of the politicians of his time to be within their grasp. In Europe generally he was more often admired than read, more often read than understood. His influence was exercised remotely and indirectly: only the details of his work received attention; from the great laws which he discovered his contemporaries culled no more than a few isolated formulas. The politicians of the day, cultured though they were, remained frivolous in their thinking, hasty, inconstant and worldly. What they wanted was not a powerful lens which would concentrate the beams of enlightenment but a crystal whose facets would scatter the light in a dazzling cascade. Voltaire was the perfect genius for the old Europe. He understood it, he saw beneath its surface, he had taken its measure. He taught it to laugh at

itself, and while he diverted it he was teaching it. He reigned
by virtue of his defects as much as by his qualities; the enthusiasm he imparted to the man of the world was never
likely to make him overstep the mark. His gusts of gener-
osity refreshed the atmosphere of the courts without disturbing it. The depth of scepticism his readers found in him
was precisely what kept him in constant sympathy with them.
They were enchanted by the marvellous limpidity of his
prose, and reassured by the limitations of his mind. In him
they thought they recognised themselves—and they admired
what they saw. Men of his kind, rare at all times, have always been the world's great charmers. Voltaire was accommodating, amiable and encouraging. He never, like Montesquieu, took on the desperate air of the hippocratic healer,
who finds the deeper causes of all ills and believes that only
by their removal can a cure be wrought. The state was perishing of excess; Montesquieu advised moderation in conduct
and a wide division of powers. In this way, by a wise disposition of forces flexibility and harmony might be renewed
in the State, so that the blood which had flooded to the centre and stifled it might flow back to the extremities. Voltaire, on the other hand, did not ask his patients to change
their habits or tame their passions; his only medicine was a
well-savoured and appetising diet of ideas which relieved and
revived them, but only for the moment. He believed the state
could do everything and it was his constant aim to strengthen
it. 'Liberty and property are the English watchwords; they
are the command of Nature!' But he meant liberty regulated by a master and property guaranteed by strong government. His political ideal was despotism tempered by tolerance and enlightenment.* While Montesquieu called for
intermediate bodies and a whole clutter of complicated ma-

---

* Though some justification can be seen in Voltaire's letters and
works for interpreting him as an adherent of enlightened despotism, his political views cannot adequately be summarised in this
way. See, for example, Peter Gay, *The Party of Humanity*
(1964).

chinery, Voltaire was content with much less. If we look again at the article in the *Dictionnaire philosophique* entitled 'Civil and Ecclesiastical Laws' (it was later printed under the title of '*Cahiers de Voltaire aux Etats Generaux*') we shall see that it is the complete programme for 'enlightened' government—in two words, it is enlightened despotism. 'It is not a question', wrote Voltaire to d'Argental in 1769, 'of making a revolution like that of Luther and Calvin, but of bringing about a revolution in the minds of those called to govern.'

This was the first current of ideas. There was another, pursuing a quite different course, which advanced further every day, and threatened the old world with a total cataclysm. It could only fertilise the land after having first submerged it; it could only enrich with its silt a countryside first devastated by the torrent of its waters. These new doctrines mingled the most just and opportune proposals for reform with the most chimerical of revolutionary hypotheses. They were supported by the most persuasive texts; the whole arsenal of the sciences was placed at the service of all the subtleties of dialectic. Men's minds were conquered through their passions, which were erected into principles; they were enraptured, intoxicated with the spirit of self-glorification. The new ideas were the more attractive because they proposed the most appealing remedies for acknowledged evils.

In this respect what happened in France was repeated on the Continent wherever books were read or ideas talked of. In Germany particularly can be found the same mixture of restlessness and enthusiasm, the same impatience, the same anxieties followed by the same outbursts of hope. Jean Paul* wrote in 1803 that the revolution, more intellectual, more vast than that of Paris, but just as murderous, which was surging up in the minds of men, was not so much an effect of the French Revolution as the result of movements prior to it and analogous to those from which it had arisen. In 1765,

---

* Jean Paul Richter (1763-1825), novelist and satirist, was a fervent democrat and enemy of aristocracy and monarchy.

Nicolaï and his friends attempted through their *Universal German Library** to do what the *philosophes* had accomplished in France—to destroy in men's minds all respect for the past. By 1789 they had almost achieved their end: traditions were no longer respected, everyone was convinced of the wrongness of the old ways, of the absurdity and decrepitude of established institutions. 'Things cannot remain as they are', said Forster† in 1799; 'all the signs show this clearly.' He prayed for the salutary crisis by which the world should be renewed. The price—even a price in blood—mattered little to him. He wrote in 1782, 'Europe seems to me to be on the eve of a terrible revolution. The body is so corrupted that a blood-letting may well be necessary.' Another German thinker, Jacobi,‡ declared at the same time: 'I would wish for some kind of inundation, even were it of barbarians, to sweep away this infected bog and uncover the virgin earth.' 'The masses', wrote Stramberg,§ 'were not precisely demanding change, but they suffered under their ever-present troubles. A vague yearning for unknown changes pierced even to the heart of the family. Even the housewives had seen enough of their old furniture. The birth pangs of the new age were soon to be experienced.'

With these aspirations there developed in men's minds the idea that reason should govern the world, that it would be sufficient by itself, for being able to comprehend everything it could accomplish everything. To the law defined by Mon-

* Nicolaï's 'Allgemeine Deutsche Bibliothek', through which he and his friends propagated the ideas of the Enlightenment, was founded in 1765.

† See below, p. 409.

‡ Jacobi had accepted the ideas of the Enlightenment and welcomed the beginning of the reforming movement in France, but rapidly turned against the Revolution.

§ Probably Christian von Stramberg, whose *Denkwürdiger und nützlicher Rheinischer Antiquarius, welcher die wichtigsten . . . geographischen, historischen und politischen Merkwürdigkeiten des ganzen Rheinstroms . . . darstellt* was published at Coblenz between 1851 and 1860 in 22 volumes.

tesquieu and founded on facts it opposed natural law
founded on reason; and the latter, more simple, more logical,
more easily grasped, prevailed everywhere, but especially in
Germany, over the former. Pufendorf* was well read in it;
Wolf† was an almost despotic authority on it. He taught,
by a process of deduction and in a geometrical form, that
there are rights inherent in human nature, that every man
should enjoy them equally, and that all are entitled to resist
anyone who tries to hinder their exercise. From his doctrine
logically follow the sovereignty of the people and the right
of insurrection. Frederick II saw this clearly, and he held the
author in small esteem. He said at the beginning of his
Mémoires, 'I make no mention of Wolf, who chewed over
Leibnitz's system and drivelled tediously over what Leibnitz
had written in letters of fire.' But this was not the opinion of
Germans in general. Bielfeld, who was proud of having read
l'Esprit des Lois, and had in fact drawn from it the basis of
his *Institutions Politiques*, nevertheless admired Wolf and
his ponderous dissertations. 'In his book', he wrote, 'can be
found the reason for everything, the origin and foundations
of all the world's laws, at least of all that are wise. It is a
complete system. . . . The immortal author has also epitomised this colossal work in a modest octavo volume called
Institutions du droit de la nature, which is of the greatest
use.'[14]

In its abstruse form, however, this doctrine was only
within the reach of thinkers schooled in the algebra of metaphysics. Rousseau, with his strange genius, breathed life into
it, and threw it, palpitating, into the minds of the people.
The cold, faint light of dialectics did not touch their emotions. With Rousseau its beams stirred the senses and dis-

---

* Samuel von Pufendorf (1632-94) published his *De Jure Na-*
turae et Gentium in 1672. He was one of the most influential of
the theorists of Natural Law.

† Christian, Freiherr von Wolf (1679-1754) was a disciple and
populariser of Pufendorf and Leibniz.

[14] *Institutions*, t. I, ch. II, § 9.

turbed the heart. In France he was the prophet par excellence of the Revolution;* in Germany his influence was at least as great, if not even more exclusive and decisive. A German historian compares it to that of the scholastic philosophy in the Middle Ages. The education of the Germans prepared them to understand it; their sentiments urged them to admire it. Germany was going through the epoch of bizarre agitation and passionate involvement which is known as the period of *Sturm und Drang.* Inexhaustible springs of tears only awaited the impulse to flow; floods of enthusiasm were ready to burst forth; men's souls were full of passions avid for transformation into virtues and seeking purification in the act of expression. Nowhere else was Rousseau to find so fertile a soil. His effect was such that the great succumbed to it as completely as the mediocre; at the same time as he spawned a generation of muddled sophists, turgid speechifiers and tearful libertines, he inspired the poets and instructed the philosophers: from him issued Schiller and Kant. He invaded Italy and conquered it as he had done Germany. He was perhaps less dominant there, but the foremost Italians came under his influence, even if for reasons of prudence they avoided acknowledging it: this was true of Beccaria,† and above all of Filangieri.‡

---

* Sorel repeats below (e.g. p. 137) and in even stronger language the belief that Rousseau gave the impetus to the revolutionary movement and that the *Contrat social* provided the programme for the revolutionaries. This view, which could only be made at all plausible by transferring the general literary cult of Rousseau into political terms, was first given wide publicity by Burke in his *Reflections.* In fact it has been shown that the influence of the *Contrat social* before the Revolution was negligible, and that in the opening phases of the Revolution his authority was appealed to more by counter-revolutionaries than by revolutionaries. See Joan Macdonald, *Rousseau and the French Revolution* (1965).

† Cesare, Marchese Beccaria (1738-94), a Milanese, author, in 1764, of the famous *Treatise of Crimes and Punishments.* In the original Italian and in translation it went through many editions and played an important part in stimulating the reform of the

In response to this impulse, there arose in Italy and Germany, with the same generous illusions and the same enthusiasm as in France, the religion of humanity, the faith in reason, the urge to strive for the welfare of the human race, and the belief that the time was near when, thought being emancipated, man would awake regenerated for ever. Humanity having no fatherland, the believers in this faith knew no frontiers; they were cosmopolitan. 'Everyone', Goethe wrote, 'desired absolutely to be one with mankind; people were no longer concerned with news and gazettes; our business was to learn to know Man; as to men in general, we willingly left them to do as they pleased.' Schiller said in 1784: 'I write as a citizen of the world. It is a good time to have lost my country if I have exchanged it for the whole world. Germans!' he cried, 'Do not seek to be a nation, content yourselves with being men.' Lessing declared emphatically that he had no idea what love of country could be.

All nations, it was held, must think of each other as friends; the cosmopolitans were thus led to celebrate all revolutions, and, as a peculiar consequence, to applaud in others the patriotic virtues which they affected to have discarded themselves. Paoli was for a moment the hero of Europe.* The American Revolution set the Continent aflame. Instead of soldiers (these were sent by the French) the Germans dedicated volumes of poetry to the Americans. 'I vividly recall', wrote a Norwegian, 'what took place at Elsinore and in the roadstead, the day when the peace was concluded that

---

penal law. Its basic ideas derive from the school of Locke, but the ground had also been prepared for its moral and emotional appeal by the influence of Rousseau.

‡ Gaetano Filangieri (1752-88), a member of the Neapolitan aristocracy, published his *Science of Legislation* in 1780.

* In 1768 the Republic of Genoa sold its rebellious possession, the island of Corsica, to France. For a year the Corsican insurgents, under the leadership of Pasquale Paoli, held out against French forces before the occupation was completed and Paoli had to take refuge in flight.

assured the triumph of liberty. The roadstead was full of
vessels of all nations. . . . All ships were dressed with flags.
. . . Their crews shouted with joy. . . . My father wanted
us to be imbued with the sentiment of political liberty. He
brought us to the table and made us drink with him and
his guests to the health of the new republic.'[15]

The same admiration was felt for the reforms of Louis
XVI and the ministry of Turgot. 'A thousand vows', said
Goethe, 'had been sworn on behalf of the Americans; the
names of Franklin and Washington were resplendent on the
horizon. When a new King of France, desiring to do good,
showed every intention of limiting his own authority, and
sought by abolishing a host of abuses to achieve the most
admirable results and to reign through order and justice
alone, smiling hope spread throughout the wide world, and
confident youth felt able to promise itself—to promise the
whole world—a splendid and magnificent future.' This enthusiasm, this intoxication of thought, as Mme. de Staël
called it, found in Schiller the most eloquent of interpreters.
Don Carlos, which he published in 1787, is only the poetic
representation of this ideal of humanity, which was the
dream of the age. The marquis de Posa represents the statesman, reformer of the world, whom all hearts acknowledge
and all souls await. 'Man is greater than you think; he will
break the yoke of his long sleep. . . . Be generous like the
strong! Let happiness spill freely from your hands. Be for us
the example of whatever is eternal and true. See around you
Nature in her splendour—she is founded on liberty; and
how rich she is in her liberty! Consecrate to the happiness
of the people the power which for so long has redounded
only to the grandeur of the throne. Give back to humanity
the nobility it has lost!'

These adjurations were by no means pure rhetoric. Schiller proclaimed only what he believed to be possible; the age
believed with him, rulers and statesmen along with all con-

[15] *Mémoires de Steffens*, cited by Tocqueville, *Mélanges*, p. 70.

temporaries. It was not merely through frivolity, indifference, or presumption on their strength that they let these doctrines develop around them; it was not simply the seduction of language that hid the danger from their eyes; it was not even that the air was saturated with these thoughts and that everyone breathed them in with his life. It was that fundamentally the propositions of the philosophers answered to the secret preoccupation of the politicians; both were agreed on the starting-point and on the objective—reform achieved through the state and in the interest of the state. This idea is central to the understanding of the affairs of this period.

In the eyes of the politicians, the state was omnipotent, raison d'état was sovereign. The whole policy of the *philosophes* amounted to putting the state's omnipotence at the service of the infallibility of reason, making pure reason, so to speak, a new raison d'état. On this principle all kinds of opinion were agreed. Voltaire extended a hand to the encyclopaedists; the physiocrats,* dissidents in all else, were orthodox in this. 'The state', said Mercier de la Rivière, 'must govern according to the rules of social order, and when it does so, it must be all-powerful.' 'The King', wrote the marquis de Mirabeau, 'in fact rules over goods and over life, and not less over opinion.' This conception of the state bred the most profound scorn for the English constitution. 'Here', said Letrosne, 'reforms which change the whole state of the country can be accomplished in a moment, while with the English such reforms can always be held up by the parties.' This was a bond of union between the physiocrats and Rousseau. 'The idea of representation is modern;† it comes to us from feudal government, that iniquitous and absurd system which

---

* The physiocrats maintained that land was the source of all wealth and that by immutable natural law the interests of the ruler as supreme landowner must be identified with the interests of his subjects. They came nearer than any other group of French thinkers to the idea of enlightened despotism. Among them were the elder Mirabeau, Letrosne and Mercier de la Rivière.

† i.e. as opposed to ancient, the normal usage of Rousseau's time.

degrades the human race.'[16] He jeered at 'the stupidity of
the English nation', and held it up to the scorn of his contemporaries. His conception of revolution was to move the
seat of sovereignty, to bring it back to its classical origins,
which meant to restore it to the people, conceived as the
people had been in the republics of antiquity. The embodi-
ment of sovereignty, however, remained the same—it was the
state. The object of the revolution would be not to abolish
it, but to take possession of it. It was not a question of reducing its omnipotence to the gain of individual liberty, but
of using this omnipotence to constrain the citizens to receive
the baptism of the new religion. Let the *philosophes* hold
power for a few hours, and by an operation of the grace of
the state, by virtue of which the miracles they so readily
mocked at would seem entirely natural, not only the face
of the world but the very soul of man himself would be
changed. They thought it quite possible for government, and
quite easy for those who wielded its power, to regenerate
even Poland, to re-establish the finances even of Spain, even
to organize perpetual peace. 'Bring into being the European
republic for a single day,' said Rousseau, 'and this is enough
to make it last for ever; . . . if we could have a Henry IV
and a Sully perpetual peace would become a reasonable project.'[17] 'March at the head of the kings of Europe', cried
Schiller. 'A stroke of the pen you hold in your hand, and
the earth is created anew! . . . You will have made your
kingdom, Sire, the happiest of all; next it will be your duty
to subjugate the world.'[18]

This way of conceiving of the state and its reforms led
the reformers and revolutionaries to the same conclusions
as those to which the doctrine of raison d'état had brought
the politicians. The main one, from the point of view of this
study, was the justification of the coup d'état—it became legit-

[16] *Contrat social*, livre III, ch. XV. Cf. *Gouvernement de
Pologne*, ch. VII.
[17] *Jugement sur la paix perpétuelle.*
[18] *Don Carlos*, act III, scene X.

imate when its object was to make doctrine prevail. If the author of it made a boast of his philosophy, the philosophers would applaud the deed. Their very language, in general so elegant and precise, veered into sophism, and their integrity, so justly praised, was compromised when they lowered themselves to their surprising concessions to raison d'état. They were always ready to interpret virtue as love of philosophy, liberty as the rule of the enlightened, the rule of the enlightened as that of the *philosophes*. It is less surprising to find such famous disciples hailing 18 Brumaire as the coming of liberty when one remembers that the masters themselves had celebrated as the finest achievements of philosophy the coups d'état of Catherine the Great and Gustavus III.

Frederick had no need to indoctrinate the *philosophes*; the admiration they professed for him was perfectly reasonable. They expected everything from 'enlightened' rulers;* never did a ruler show himself so 'enlightened' as Frederick. Never had a sovereign held a higher opinion of his rights or greater respect for his duties towards the state; he was at the same time the absolute master and the most zealous servant. Contemporaries approved his doctrine and admired his conduct. Hence the enormous prestige he enjoyed in Europe. He was the king who personified the spirit of the age. In that time the most generous aspirations of that spirit were joined with the most shocking licence of thought; enthusiasm rubbed shoulders with cynicism. That of Frederick, which we find so repellent, degraded him no more than *La Pucelle* de-

* Voltaire's connection with Frederick and Diderot's with Catherine have led to exaggerated ideas of the extent to which the *philosophes* were committed to the support of enlightened despotism. Their political ideas, though in most cases not very clearly formulated or detailed, were liberal in the broadest sense of the term and almost without exception they condemned despotism. One source of the misunderstanding has been a confusion between the *philosophes* and the small sect of the physiocrats. See Alfred Cobban, *In Search of Humanity* (1960), and note above p. 94 (n.).

graded Voltaire in the eyes of people of good society, no more than *Le Rêve de d'Alembert* degraded Diderot in the view of those with morals,* no more than the depravities of the *Confessions* degraded Rousseau in the opinion of men of feeling. If Frederick cheapened himself, he did so in company with the finest and greatest minds of his time, and his intellectual debauchery only added to the celebrity of his name. 'All his acts are governed by passion and hatred', wrote Maria Theresa, only too conscious of what he had inflicted on herself. 'Yet the multitude is on his side, which is incomprehensible. It shows what the prejudices of the public are worth. His agents, great and small, are everywhere, and he keeps them contented with trifles; everybody is taken in.' The spirit of the age was the only agent he needed. On it Frederick was borne aloft; it was thus that he had so many flatterers, and had them so cheaply. In the end, all his other qualities were eclipsed by the heroic. The Seven Years War left him without an equal. His steadfastness in the unequal struggle and the strength of character he showed in defeat compelled the admiration of contemporaries. For friends and enemies alike he became Frederick the Great. A few protested against the partition of Poland; the great majority pardoned it, because the deed seemed a masterpiece of cleverness, and the result a triumph for enlightenment and tolerance. Only one voice, at least among those that have reached our times, was raised in opposition to this concert of opinion:† it was that of a poet, an Italian—Alfieri.‡ But

* Voltaire's *La Pucelle* is a satiric history in verse of Joan of Arc, larded with a good deal of obscenity. Diderot's *Rêve de d'Alembert*, though not without its 'shocking' passages, is essentially a serious and brilliantly written exploration of scientific speculations far in advance of his time.

† There were two other notable voices raised in protest against the first Polish Partition, those of Edmund Burke (anonymously but almost certainly) in the *Annual Register* for 1772 (p.2) and of Rousseau in his *Gouvernement de Pologne*.

‡ Count Alfieri (1749-1803), Italian poet. He at first welcomed, then turned violently against, the Revolution. *Misogallo*, 1790-

Alfieri was not a philosopher, and he was to exhibit the same
hatred for the French Revolution as for the King of Prussia.
His diatribes against Frederick and his *Misogallo* arose from
the same source.

The most famous men of the age prostrated themselves
before the Solomon and the Semiramis of the North. Leading the procession and dancing before the ark, Voltaire was
the Coryphaeus of the age. Raynal,* his words ampified by
Diderot, poured out adulation in high-flown prose: 'We are
in turn struck dumb with astonishment and proclaim our
admiration to the world. O Frederick, Frederick! Thou wert
looked upon as a model of the warrior king. There is a title
yet more glorious, that of citizen king. Make Prussia happy.
Dare more—give peace to the earth.'[19] All that the King of
Prussia lacked, Diderot thought, was a little more willingness to learn. Catherine, in his opinion, lacked nothing at
all: 'Oh! my friends, what a sovereign! You must all agree
that there is the heart of Brutus with the face of Cleopatra!'[20]† Rousseau himself was quite ready to bow down;
he only asked a small sacrifice to his particular gods. 'Take
from before me this wounding sword. Look into your heart,
O Frederick! Could you reconcile yourself to death before
you have become the greatest of men? Let me see Frederick,
redoubtable and just, fill his lands with happy people whose
father he should be, and Jean-Jacques Rousseau, enemy of

1798, comprised satirical sonnets, interspersed with prose, against
the French.

* The abbé Raynal (1713-96) was one of the most effective
popularisers of the ideas of the *philosophes*. The colossal reputation of his *Histoire philosophique et politique des établissements
et du commerce dans les deux Indes* is now difficult to understand.

[19] Raynal, *Histoire philosophique*, liv. V, ch. X.

[20] *Lettres à mademoiselle Voland.*

† Though he was not wholly proof against the flattery, or the
financial aid, of Catherine, in the *Mémoires* Diderot drew up for
her he maintained his liberal political principles and condemned
even enlightened despotism. See M. Tourneux, *Diderot et Catherine II* (1899), p. 143.

kings, would come to die with joy on the steps of his throne.'[21] Mirabeau, who penetrated the defects of the Prussian establishment with such remarkable perspicacity, also intoned the canticle, and acclaimed 'the transcendent enlightenment' of Frederick, 'for ever illustrious among the children of men.' He lauded 'the boldness of his thought, the sagacity of his mind, the force of his prudence, the firmness of his character, his profundity of judgement, his greatness of soul'. He praised him for having made of his state 'for the science of despotism, what Egypt was for the ancients who sought instruction'; and he concluded, 'If Prussia were to perish, the art of government would return to its infancy.'[22]

The reformers called upon the princes; their doctrines committed them to do so; moreover, it was only from the princes that they could expect the implementation of their reforms. Wherever in the eighteenth century there were assemblies, estates, deliberative bodies, they showed themselves enemies of innovation and jealous guardians of their privileges. Everything that was done to improve the lot of the people or to perfect the system of government was done by the rulers and in spite of the assemblies. The diets and assemblies of nobles in Sweden, Germany, Poland, Hungary, Bohemia, were always in opposition, just as the parlements in France fought against the projects of Turgot. 'Wherever provincial assemblies had kept their ancient constitution', said Tocqueville, 'they held up the progress of civilisation more than they helped it. They were strangers to the new spirit of the times and unaffected by it. Thus the feelings of the people were turned away from them and towards the princes.'[23] The *philosophes* showed the kings that nothing was easier for them than to become well loved while becoming strong. They showed them ways of promoting the happiness of mankind while increasing their own power.

[21] Letter to Frederick, 30 October 1762.
[22] *Monarchie prussienne*, livre VIII.
[23] *L'Ancien Régime*, livre I, ch. IV.

The alliance between them was quite natural. The kings needed the support of public opinion—the *philosophes* commanded it. The *philosophes* needed the support of the secular arm—the rulers lent it them. Each worked in his own interest, the ruler for the triumph of absolutism, the *philosophe* for the rule of enlightenment; but they set forth together and made common cause in their campaign against the past.

This was why the princes looked so calmly upon the audacities of philosophy, and proved so indulgent to the unruliness of the *philosophes*. They thought they could keep them on a tight rein, and lead them into their own paths. They looked on them as a body of auxiliaries or scouts, the condottieri of their army; in a word, they made use of them without qualms. Philosophy was for rulers both an instrument of government and an entertainment. Frederick and Catherine appreciated the French *philosophes* in the same way as Francis I did the Italian artists or Louis XIV the poets of Paris. Perhaps also there was a touch of a Louis XI's or a Medici's fancy for alchemists and astrologers. The great practitioners of politics have always liked to play with the prophets. There was also a large element of calculation in their taste for literature. What official gazettes could compare with the correspondence of Voltaire, Diderot, or d'Alembert? Carried by these marvellous messengers, the 'winged words' of princes flew around Europe. This 'official press' worked also for posterity. The enlightened rulers could be sure that they would be talked of as long as French was spoken and wherever there were people of intelligence. The great fraud of the age would be perpetuated to posterity. But if the age was duped, the rulers were not. They never lost their sense of responsibility, or their sang-froid; philosophic incense never turned their heads. They believed in the influence of the stars only when the stars led them where they wished to go. In this they were superior to their illustrious courtiers. If one of these went so far as to try to play the counsellor of state, Catherine quickly called him to or-

der in haughty and caustic tones, like the German she was.
Diderot, who was scarcely a diplomat, once expressed his
surprise that his discourse, to which the Tsarina listened with
such enthusiasm, produced so little effect. 'With your fine
principles', she told him, 'you can make beautiful books, but
they don't work out in practice. You forget the difference
in our positions. You only work on paper, which will put up
with anything; while I, a poor empress, have to work on
men's skins, which are ticklish and easily irritated.'[24] She
did not believe in the innate goodness of man, nor in the
infinite perfectibility of the human race. 'The moralists', she
said, 'strive to correct abuses; but is it really certain that humanity is capable of perfection? They have refined everything—learning, the arts, Nature herself, but man has always
stayed the same.'[25] *Sensibilité* made her laugh; *Le Contrat
Social* made her sick. 'Rousseau', she concluded, 'had put
men down on four paws.'[26] Frederick was not displeased
to see his *philosophes* in the same position. He felt a deep
scorn for them, and made it crudely apparent. Perchance
after supper, when the effect of the wine had worn off and
the intimate gathering had broken up, it might occur to them
to take his sarcasms literally, and to remind the King of Prussia of the divagations of the philosopher of Sans Souci. He
would then bring them back to cold reason, to the tolerance
which in his view they interpreted so stupidly, and to the
necessities of government, of which they understood nothing.
The transcendent height of scepticism from which he judged
them was beyond their reach.

The *philosophes* took their revenge on weak rulers and in
petty courts. There they reigned despotically, as in the salons
of Paris. There they were courted, admired and blindly followed. These courts took their tone from Frederick and Catherine; they modelled themselves on France, which set the

[24] Ségur, *Mémoires*, t. III.
[25] *Lettres au comte Czernichef*, 1780. *Publications de la Société d'histoire de Russie.*
[26] Letter to Grimm, 29 April 1791.

fashion. Reforms were in the wind, reformers were in vogue; in calling Turgot to his councils and trusting him with the government of the state, Louis XVI was only following the example of the kings of his house and with them all the rulers of the Continent.

3 · ENLIGHTENED GOVERNMENT

This was the age of enlightenment; it saw the reign of enlightened sovereigns, the government of philosophical ministers. The shining stars were St. Petersburg and Berlin. Let us look at the satellites. In the north there was a prince in whose features everyone saw the lineaments of a great man. This was Duke Ferdinand of Brunswick. The tragic deceptions of fate only made him more famous. Mirabeau, who compared him with Alcibiades, thought him alone capable of continuing Frederick's work in Prussia. In 1792 the chief leaders of the Revolution thought that he alone could take up in France the work of Henry IV. 'He lacks only a crown', wrote a revolutionary journalist, 'to be, I will not say the greatest of kings, but the restorer of liberty in Europe.' Even in 1799 there were to be politicians in France, some of the most judicious, Talleyrand for example, and some of the most thoughtful, like Sieyès, who were to think of entrusting him with the task that was to be Bonaparte's. Behind the Duke of Brunswick marched the whole procession of German princes, all of them protectors of the arts and friends of mankind—Charles Augustus of Weimar, who had Goethe as his minister; Charles Frederick of Baden, who went to study politics in France, at the school of the Marquis de Mirabeau; Joseph Emmerich, Archbishop-Elector of Mainz, who prided himself on his love of philosophy; Clement de Saxe, Elector of Trier, who prided himself on his love of belles-lettres; Gustavus III in Sweden, Charles III in Naples and Spain, Leopold of Austria in Tuscany, completed the company. Joseph II, on the imperial throne, was at the very centre of the movement.

While in France there were a Choiseul, a Malesherbes, a Turgot, a Necker, whom philosophy could call her own by various titles,* she was honoured to have rulers throughout Europe for her friends or disciples. In Prussia there were Henry, Frederick's brother, a great giver of counsel and maker of plans; Möllendorf, who commanded armies; Carmer, who drafted the code; Struensee, who administered the finances; Zedlitz and Hertzberg, certified pupils of the great king; Dohm, who was his negotiator in Germany; Goltz, his representative in Paris. Montgelas planned to regenerate Bavaria; Fürstenburg devoted himself to similar work at Munster, Stadion at Mainz, Abel at Stuttgart. Struensee had attempted it in Denmark, and Bernstorff took up his work.† More timid, cautious and restrained, but inspired by the same ideas and moved by the same impulse, van Swieten, Sonnenfels, Martini and Riegger served Maria Theresa. Tanucci, a fervent *philosophe*, governed in Naples, where one of the most kindly and convinced of reformers was called to power. Villamarina, Sambucca, Caracciolo were trying to civilise Sicily. Du Tillot was all-powerful in Parma, where Condillac‡ was tutor to the heirs to the throne. Verri§ and Beccaria were consulted in Lombardy; Neri, Tavanti, Manfredini collaborated in the government of Tuscany. Philosophy could number also among its followers Pombal¶ in Portugal,

---

* While Malesherbes and Turgot had affiliations with the *philosophes*, to bring Choiseul and Necker into the same category is to extend it considerably.

† Struensee was a German physician at the court of Christian VII of Denmark. He made the queen his mistress and gained absolute power in the state in 1770, only to be overthrown by a palace intrigue in 1772 and executed. Bernstorff introduced the reforms of the Enlightenment in Denmark subsequently by more moderate and gradual measures.

‡ See note below, p. 153.

§ See note p. 375.

¶ The marquis of Pombal was the all-powerful minister of Joseph I of Portugal from 1750 to 1777. There was more absolutism than enlightenment in his policies.

Aranda, Grimaldi, Florida-Blanca and Campomanès in Spain, and in Sweden Creutz and baron de Staël.

With such encouragement everywhere, but especially in Germany and Italy, intellect was fostered: schools were opened, universities expanded. Religious tolerance reigned in Prussia; Gustavus III introduced it in Sweden. Even the ecclesiastical princes recognised its advantages. In 1783 the Bishop-Elector of Trier issued an edict in favour of heretics: 'On the one hand,' he declared, 'by putting aside all appearance of persecution our holy faith will become more worthy of respect; on the other hand, thanks to the establishment of rich businessmen and manufacturers, the country's trade will develop, the poor unemployed will have work, and the wealth of foreigners will flow into the land.' Serfdom tended to disappear; it diminished in Prussia under Frederick, in Bohemia, Moravia, Galicia and Hungary under Joseph II. It was suppressed in Baden in 1783, in Denmark in 1788. Efforts were made everywhere to reduce the corvées and to improve the dreadful lot of the peasant.

Penal laws were amended: torture was abolished in Tuscany and Sweden, and its actual use declined in Baden, Denmark, and Austria. The reform of civil law was more complicated, for it involved a reform of the fundamental laws of the state, as was seen in France in 1789. Nevertheless, it was under discussion everywhere, and always with the same inspiration.

The great commission summoned by Catherine from 1766 to 1768 to elaborate a code of laws for Russia was very much a phantasmagoria, but the homage paid by the legislators of Moscow to the ideas of the age was none the less noteworthy. 'The nation', they said, 'is not made for the ruler, but the ruler for the nation. Equality for the citizens means subjection only to the law; liberty is the right to do anything not forbidden by the law. It is better to spare ten guilty men than to condemn one innocent. Torture is an excellent method of ruining an innocent man in weak health and saving a guilty one who is robust.'[27] The committees of the Convention would have found no fault with these maxims; nor would Catherine's proconsuls in Poland have disavowed the commissioners of the Convention. Both had learned their theories in the same college and practised them in the same school.

The Prussian legislators seemed infinitely more in earnest than the Russians. The code which Frederick had had drawn up by the most experienced statesmen and jurists of the realms was only promulgated in 1794 in the reign of his successor; but it belonged, in its origins and principles, to the period of 'enlightened government', indeed it was in a way its most significant manifestation and product. The word 'state' alone was used to designate the sovereign power. Thus the person of the ruler was absorbed into the state and merged with it. The sovereign represents the state, and the state represents society. The good of the state and its subjects is the aim of society and the boundary of the law. Each member of society must work for the common good, that is to say the good of the state. The rights of individuals must give way to general utility, except that the state must indemnify individuals for any property it takes from them. The laws and ordinances of the state can only limit the natural liberty and rights of citizens in the interest of general utility. The common rights of men are based on the natural liberty of each to seek his own good, provided that he does not encroach on the rights of others. It is the mission of the head of the state to promote the general good; he is authorised to direct to this end all the actions of individuals. He makes the laws, does justice, and protects the citizens. He must provide them with the means of developing their aptitudes and resources so that each may turn them to the greatest advantage of himself and the state.

This was a veritable 'Declaration of the rights of the state and the ruler'. This type of government was in fact very like

[27] Rambaud, *Histoire de Russie*, ch. XXXI.

that which obtained in France in the year VIII. When one
of the most famous of revolutionary prophets, Sieyès, had to
accommodate the doctrines of the *Contrat social* and the
forms of popular sovereignty to the requirements of despotism, infinitely less innovation was involved than was usually thought—or than he himself was pleased to think.* In
1781 a Tuscan, the senator Gianni, planned an ideal constitution for his country; it was to be submitted to the people,
who, in voting for it, would at that moment recover their
full natural liberty. The Grand Duke Leopold, to whom this
project was submitted, though he does not seem to have
thought of putting it into effect, admired the arrangements
and approved the principle. From this arose a very curious
document which he addressed to his sister Marie-Christine in
1790, and which could be regarded as the *Profession of
Faith of an Enlightened Sovereign*:

'I believe that the sovereign, even when hereditary, is only
the delegate and servant of the people, for whom he is created. In every country there should be a fundamental law or
contract between the people and the sovereign to limit the
latter's power; if the sovereign does not keep it, he forfeits his
position—which is given to him only on this condition—and
no one is any longer obliged to obey him. The executive
power rests with the sovereign, but the legislative with the
people and their representatives, and they, at each change
of sovereign, may add new conditions to his exercise of
authority. The sovereign owes the people an exact and

---

* Sieyès' pamphlet, *Qu'est-ce que le Tiers Etat*, in which he
maintained that the Third Estate alone represented the nation,
established him as the leading prophet of the sovereignty of the
people. But he always denied that he had learnt anything from
Rousseau, and his political principles differed in fundamental respects from the *Contrat social*, especially in his distrust of direct
democracy. This appears in the Constitution of 1791, in the drafting of which he took a large part, and also in the Constitution of
the Year VIII, drawn up after the *coup d'état* of Brumaire, which
Bonaparte was easily able to convert into a cover for autocratic
rule.

annual account of the expenditure of the public revenue; he has no right to impose taxes arbitrarily. He must render account and get approval for all changes of system, new laws, etc. Finally, I believe that the sovereign should rule only through the law, and that his constituents are the people, who can never renounce, or be deprived, by any prescription or tacit and forced consent, of the imprescriptible right, which is that of nature, by which they have consented to have a sovereign, that is to say to accord him pre-eminence so that he may promote their welfare and happiness, not as he wishes, but as they wish and understand it. For the single end of societies and governments is the welfare of individuals.'[28]

I have frequently quoted Bielfeld's *Institutions Politiques*. It contains not only a description of governments but the wishes and, so to speak, the *cahiers** of the governed.[29] Composed for the education of a Prussian prince, this work was placed in her library by Catherine beside that of Montesquieu. The reforms accomplished were nothing compared to those proposed. Because everybody believed in the omnipotence of decrees, everybody became persuaded of the virtue of formulas and the efficacy of axioms. Political theory consisted simply in deducing their consequences, and political practice in applying them. The art of government was thus reduced to the elements of political geometry. 'Their ideal constitution', wrote Möser, a German publicist who contested these doctrines, 'must have the uniform beauty of a French tragedy, and could be set forth, at least in plan and outline, on a small sheet of paper, so that any official would

[28] Wolf, *Marie-Christine und Leopold II*. Vienna, 1867.

* Sorel is drawing a parallel with the *cahiers* or statements of grievances drawn up on the occasion of the elections of States General for representatives of the three Orders to present to the king.

[29] See particularly Vol. II, the chapter which deals with the Council and the ministers.

need only a scale to measure its dimensions and could then implement it.'[30]

In this respect, the ruler who best embodied the spirit of the age was not Frederick, but Joseph II. Frederick was born the master, Joseph the disciple, and it is by their disciples that teachers are judged. The King of Prussia embanked the waters and harnessed them to his use; the Emperor threw himself into the stream and let himself be carried away. In Frederick the statesman was always uppermost, always proposing and deciding in the last resort; the *philosophe* had a subordinate function—for the results accomplished by policy he provided the abstract raison d'être and theoretical justification. With Joseph II the rational concept preceded the political calculation and determined it. He had a wideranging intelligence, but it was superficial; his mind overflowed with ideas. He wanted to be magnanimous, and had a passion for greatness; but in him there was nothing profound but ambition, and that was ambition on the rebound—reflected ambition. He wanted to surpass Frederick; his whole behaviour was only an awkward, imprudent, ill-advised imitation of this prince whom he had made his hero, but whom history made his rival, and whom he copied while detesting him. The political genius of Frederick was made up of good sense and moderation; in Joseph moderation was completely lacking. He was a man of theory; his greatness was only in his impulse. His education was a poor one, limited by the method of the Jesuits. Into this narrow mould he poured a medley of notions hastily borrowed from the French *philosophes*, especially the physiocrats. Thus he aspired to political ideals of the vaguest sort, and had a quite unrealistic idea of his ability to realise them. 'Since I ascended the throne and assumed the premier crown of the world', he wrote in 1781, 'I have made philosophy the legislator of my Empire. Its logical application will transform Austria.'

He set about reforms everywhere at once. For him history

[30] Hæusser, liv. I, ch. V.

had never happened, and neither traditions nor established facts were of any account. Such things as race, time, circumstance, did not exist; there was only the state, and the state could do anything. He wrote to the Bishop of Strasburg in 1782: 'In a realm governed according to my principles prejudices, fanaticism, and the slavery of the mind must disappear, and each of my subjects must be reinstated in possession of his natural rights.' He needed a united realm and, as a prime condition, a *tabula rasa*. Yet fate had decided that his work must be done in the most heterogeneous, incoherent, disunited and discontinuous state in Europe. His subjects had nothing in common, neither language, traditions, nor interests. Therein, he thought, lay the great defect of the monarchy. 'The German tongue is the universal language of my empire. I am the Emperor of Germany, and the states in my possession are provinces which form a single body with the state of which I am the head. If the Kingdom of Hungary were the most important of my possessions, I should not hesitate to impose its language on the other countries.' He therefore imposed the German language on Hungarians, Croats, Czechs, Poles—on all the Slavs. He suppressed the ancient territorial divisions, which recalled the successive agglomerations, the irregular accretions which had built up the monarchy. He established thirteen governments and divided them into circles. The diets disappeared; government was handed over to intendants, after the French formula. In the towns the burgomaster, chosen by the state, became an official. The already very restricted share in government which nobles had kept in certain parts they now lost. He taxed them; he taxed churchmen; he wanted to establish a tax proportional to income, payable by all classes alike. He protected the peasants, lightened serf obligations, reduced the corvées, built hospitals and, even more, schools, in which the state would mould pupils into obedience. His ideal would be the equality of his subjects under the uniform rule of his government. He codified the laws; he instituted courts of appeal with a supreme court for the whole

Empire. He regulated industry, and subjected commerce to a rigorous protective system. Finally, he treated the Church with a high hand and established toleration. 'Grant liberty of conscience,' he declared in 1777, 'and there will be only one religion, which will be that of directing all the state's inhabitants to its good.' This immense revolution was accomplished by means of decrees in less than five years. If we compare the state of cohesion to which the Bourbon government had brought France by 1789 with the disunity of the Austrian monarchy at the death of Maria Theresa in 1780, it will be seen that the revolution achieved by the Constituent Assembly was nothing to that which was attempted by Joseph II.

Thus in the last years of the ancien régime we see a state of crisis developing in the governments of the Continent, and a reform movement analogous to that in France. The reforms which the *philosophes* demanded, and which they expected of the established authorities, were made in the interests of the state. Their aim was to make men happier under a stronger and more beneficent master; they never aimed at making them more independent under a more moderate government. Everywhere on the Continent could be seen preparations for a programme of social and civil reform operated by the state and for the profit of the state, but by no means the preliminaries of a political reform destined to limit the power of the state. Everywhere could be seen the elements of enlightened despotism, everywhere the progress of religious toleration and civil liberty—but nowhere the elements of political liberty. Those which yet remained as a heritage from the Middle Ages tended to disappear with the vestiges of the feudal system.

4 · THE COLLAPSE OF THE OLD INSTITUTIONS

In the Middle Ages feudal institutions had prevailed everywhere in Europe. Now, where not already destroyed, they were under attack or collapsing in ruins. The Roman conception of the state, propagated by the teaching of Roman law and inculcated by the jurists, was spreading throughout the Continent from France, where it already dominated. All rulers were dazzled by the great success of the royal house of France, by the power and majesty of her monarchical establishment; she was envied—and imitated. Roman institutions and the all-powerful authority of Roman law combined to promote the interests of the state. They were made 'not for the liberty, but for the obedience of men',[31] and gave admirable support to the claims of rulers. The jurists who interpreted this law became their most influential counsellors, justifying their lust for power and the acts of their ministers, each zealous to put his own ambitions at the service of his sovereign's. In the state as organized by the Romans and conceived by the jurists can be seen the framework of the structure which, behind composite façades and modern décor, the enlightened ministers, disciples of the *philosophes,* were building, or dreamt of building. 'In Rome they no more recognized bounds to the actual power of the ruler than to the theoretical sovereignty of the people.'[32] The ruler commanded armies, made peace and war, levied taxes, fixed their incidence, regulated expenditure. He had the power of confiscation; he conferred noble rank; he made laws; he was judge; he was sovereign pontiff—'he holds all religion in his hand and exercises a right of supervision over all priests'. He was the administration, law, religion; he was master of all things, protector of all men. The senate which assisted him was no more than a council of state, a consultative commission. Precisely on these principles were built the governments of Louis XIV, of Frederick, of Joseph II.

Whatever crises they might undergo, governments always found the same remedy—to strain every resource in order to extend their power to the utmost, to annihilate every obstacle, every curb or restraint. The state required for its pur-

[31] Fustel de Coulanges, *Histoire des Institutions,* t. I, p. 66.
[32] *Id.,* t. I, p. 73.

poses disciplined, silent and servile agents. The treasury was the provider and at the same time the 'control'; it was the motor of the machine; the other parts of the government served only as its driving belts. This machine impinged on everyone; it penetrated everywhere and turned the whole country to its own use. The same system was set up by Peter I in Russia, it operated in Prussia, Joseph II introduced it in Austria. Everywhere the ground was cleared, inaccessible fastnesses opened up, the walls of ancient fortifications sapped by this same implement; everywhere the same plough passed across the same ruins, the same harrow levelled the soil. Montesquieu found this alarming: he saw in it the collapse of all the barriers which mark off monarchy from arbitrary power; he saw monarchy undermining its own foundations and reeling under its own weight. He gave a warning in those admirable chapters of *L'Esprit des lois* where he deals with the corruption of the principles of government;[33] but the statesmen of his time gave no heed, and those who came after only improved upon earlier precedents.

In Germany the Austrian emperor aimed at absorbing the Estates of the Empire, in the same way as in France the Capetian king had absorbed the great feudatories and vassals. He strove to extend his prerogatives as the kings of France had extended their jurisdiction and supremacy. He contested the constitution of the Empire and tried to abrogate it in detail, to atrophy it by disuse, to whittle it away by successive encroachments upon the treaties of 1648 which guaranteed it. In an instruction prepared in 1774 for a French agent bound for Vienna appeared this: 'The imperial publicists treat this fundamental and sacred law, the very palladium of German liberty, as a decayed relic, ruined by decrepitude and by the changes of time and circumstance. They would like to take as their model of government the laws made by the Roman emperors, whose imitators the German emperors have always been. The traditions of the Empire are preserved

[33] Liv. VIII. Ch. VI, VII, VIII.

only as empty honours and formulas, kept alive by pedantry
and ignorance, which may be turned into the formal titles
of an absolute authority.'[34] In Bohemia Maria Theresa summoned the Diet only to ratify her decrees or to vote fresh
subsidies; all its administrative functions were transferred to
the Council of State sitting in Vienna. The Diet of Hungary,
which should have met every year, assembled only three
times in the Empress's reign, that is to say in forty years. It
was the same with the other diets. Maria Theresa deprived
them of their rights; Joseph II ceased to summon them at all.
'In Germany', wrote Mirabeau in 1788, 'only princes of the
second rank are still limited by their estates in respect of
taxes. The King of Prussia is free from all restraint in this
matter.' The princes of the second rank were similarly impatient to free themselves, after the example of the King of
Prussia and in emulation of the Emperor. 'Men are con-
scribed and taxed at the pleasure of the ruler', wrote Möser,
a saddened defender of the old institutions. 'Assemblies and
subjects are permitted to complain, as long as they pay. But
if they show themselves recalcitrant, the best justified and
most humble remonstrances are treated as disobedience,
crime and rebellion.' Some assemblies were permitted to survive as an act of grace on the part of a tolerant ruler. Attempts at resistance in Wurtemberg and Mecklenburg only
angered the authorities and drove them to excess. In the imperial cities municipal life was extinct; of their former republican institutions there remained only an empty show and
meaningless formulas.

The Cortes survived in Spain, but their function was
merely to recognise the sovereign and to confer on him powers which he then used to abolish their prerogatives. 'The
law', as royal edicts declared, 'is to be valid as if it had been
voted and promulgated by the Cortes'. This was all that remained of the liberties of Spain. Since 1713 the Cortes had
not been consulted on any serious matter. 'However pressing

[34] *Recueil des Instructions, Autriche.* Baron de Breteuil, 1774.

the needs of the state,' said Florida-Blanca, one of the enlightened ministers of the time, 'beware of calling on the
Cortes for help; they would soon become your rulers and
judges.'[35] Pombal, also an enlightened minister, one of the
most esteemed of the age, had the same view. 'In governing,'
said a contemporary, 'he had no other aim than to concentrate authority in himself, humiliate the nobility, and keep
the nation in the most servile obedience.'[36]

In Denmark absolute government, set up in 1660, was
merely more firmly established. It triumphed in Sweden
through the coups d'état of Gustavus III in 1772 and 1789.
The Prince of Orange vanquished the patriot party, thanks
to the support given by Prussian arms in 1787, and transformed the ancient republic of the United Provinces into a
disguised monarchy. In Russia there were no independent
political institutions, and Peter I, by his famous *tchine*,* had
established a hierarchy of nobles which was midway between
the Chinese mandarins and the democratic nobility set up by
Napoleon. Only in Poland were the ancient institutions preserved; they were considered by all good citizens the worst of
evils; only the enemies of the republic wanted to maintain
them, and all its friends strove to restrict the ancient liberties
for the benefit of the state.

In the endeavour to exalt their power the Catholic states
met with only one redoubtable adversary—the Church. It
had occupied the dominant positions since the Middle Ages
and intended to keep them. In the development of its political principles and its institutions it had followed the same
evolution as the state. The Council was reduced in power
and finally effaced itself, like other great assemblies of the
Middle Ages. The papacy took precedence over it and tended
to absorb it, aiming at absolutism and infallibility. The papal

[35] Baumgarten, liv. I, ch. II.

[36] Malouet, *Mémoires*, t. I, p. 10. Paris, 1874.

* The name given to the table of ranks which regulated the
status of Russian nobles, drawn up in 1722 and arranged in three
parallel hierarchies—army, civil service and court.

theologians, pupils of the same school as the royal jurists, adopted the same plan. The Church as they conceived it was the Roman state in the religious domain. Antagonism was thus inevitable between two powers which were in constant contact, interlocking everywhere, and both claiming supremacy. Moreover, while the state was burdened with debt the Church was rich; its property escaped taxation and presented the government with a constant object of irritation and envy. There were few politicians who in this situation did not see the advantages of schism, or even find sufficient reasons for engaging in heresy. 'The Catholic princes', wrote Voltaire to a Russian friend in 1768; 'are not bold enough to declare that the Church must be subject solely to the laws of the sovereign. Only your illustrious ruler follows the right course: she pays the priests, she opens and shuts their mouths; they are under her orders, and everything remains undisturbed.'[37] Princes who had enslaved the nobility and subjected or dissolved the assemblies were not likely to accept the existence in their realms of a numerous, rich, powerful and disciplined body, subject to the authority of a sovereign who claimed to be arbiter over all others, who governed the consciences and disposed of the souls of their subjects, and who, to exercise this redoubtable authority, enclosed himself in a sanctuary inaccessible to their forces. Louis XIV tried, if not to force an entry, at any rate to invest the approaches and control its communications. He never ceased to hammer at the Church's frontiers, and more than once he invaded its domain. He had not driven the Huguenots from his kingdom in order to hand it over to the ultramontanists. He wanted neither parties nor dissidents in the state—least of all masters; the Revocation of the Edict of Nantes and the declaration of the French clergy on the Gallican liberties are two chapters of the same book. And it was in this school that the Bourbons of Spain learnt to regulate the relations of Church and state.

[37] To comte Schouvalof, 3 December 1768.

From the beginning of Philip V's reign to the end of Charles III's, that is to say for more than eighty years, the rulers of Spain never ceased to strive for the supremacy of the king over the Church. They limited its jurisdiction, suppressed its right of sanctuary, cut down its revenues, restricted its right to acquire property, and consigned the Inquisition, through enforced slumber, to oblivion.[38] The names of Aranda, Florida-Blanca and Campomanès are associated with this struggle; they endeavoured to deprive the Church of its educational function as well as taking away its powers of censorship. Pombal followed their example in Portugal. Charles III began on the throne of Naples the work he continued in Madrid. Tanucci, *philosophe* minister of this enlightened prince, excluded clergy from tribunals and from schools, made marriage a civil contract, and forbade the publication of papal bulls without royal authority—all this, in the words of an edict of 1767, 'by the supreme independent authority which the King holds directly from God, inseparably united to sovereignty because of his omnipotence'. Ferdinand IV, who succeeded Charles in 1759, closed convents and forced bishops to institute each other. In Parma, du Tillot, minister of Duke Ferdinand, rivalled Tanucci: he refused payment of the firstfruits owed to the Holy See, intercepted bulls, presented to benefices, prevented establishments in mortmain from acquiring real estate, and forbade monks to receive bequests. Leopold reserved to himself in Tuscany the censorship of papal bulls, abolished the tribunal of the papal nuncio, suppressed convents, regulated and reduced public devotions. The movement even spread to the Republic of Venice, which set about copying the monarchies.

The Prince-Bishops of Germany took the same line as the lay rulers of Italy. In their relations with Rome they often forgot that they were bishops, never that they were princes. The Elector of Cologne, younger brother of Joseph and Leo-

[38] From 1746 to 1759 it burned only six persons; four from 1759 to 1788.

pold, made excellent use in his electorate of the maxims of his elder brothers. In 1785 the Bishops of Trier, Mainz, Cologne and Strasburg notified the Roman Curia of the prerogatives they intended to maintain; one of the chief was the censorship of bulls. Failing this concession, they threatened to summon a national church council. Maria Theresa was pious, even devout, but before all else she was empress. She forbade papal nuncios to travel in her lands, bishops to correspond directly with Rome, priests to take part in the drafting of wills. A report addressed to her in 1769 by Kaunitz, her Chancellor, showed how the power which of all in Europe most respected the rights of the Church intended to conduct relations with it.[39] After recalling that 'during several centuries of ignorance and superstition', the popes, having escaped from dependence on the Emperors, had tried to fasten their yoke upon them, the Chancellor added: 'Suppose we attempt to maintain and enforce the existing laws on the subject of acquisition in mortmain, which is so contrary to the balance of property necessary for the preservation of the social order; or suppose we want to tax the temporal possessions of the clergy, in respect of which they should be, in justice and reason, on a par with all the other subjects and citizens of the state; suppose we wish to restrict the influence which the clergy have acquired over censorship, over the marriage contract, over laws of inheritance, or to diminish the number of religious festivals, to abolish the dreadful tribunal of the Inquisition, to cut down the excessive wealth of the clergy or merely check its growth in order to prevent the total ruin of civil society—at every point we find the Pope and the clergy blocking the way. . . . If we do not put an end—and that promptly—to these pretended doubts and uncertainties about the limits of the sovereign power, the result will be that schisms will appear, and perhaps we may shortly see entire kingdoms and nations breaking completely

[39] Arneth, *Maria Theresia*, t. IX, ch. I, VI and VIII.

away from the See of Rome, to the utmost detriment to Catholicism.'

Maria Theresa restrained her sons and her Chancellor. But when they obtained control they set to work on the grand scale. Leopold dreamed of reconstituting the Austrian Church on the plan of the Gallican Church, adopting Bossuet's famous declaration as its charter. Joseph thought this would leave it too much independence; besides, the bishops would have none of it. He acted without them, claiming however to touch 'neither dogma, nor rite, nor internal discipline'. His work, which was in all respects the prelude to the *Constitution civile du clergé*, was vitiated by the same basic contradiction: Joseph II, like the Constituants who subsequently imitated him, tried to remain a Roman Catholic while by his own authority, and without the agreement of the bishops or the acquiescence of the Holy See, he completely overturned the ecclesiastical constitution of his states. It goes without saying that he reserved to himself the censorship of bulls; he totally prohibited the teaching of those that defined the prerogatives of the Holy See;[40] he increased the number of country curés, reduced the powers of the bishops, instituted civil marriage and divorce, decreed toleration of dissenters and waged relentless war on the monastic orders. He forbade them to recognise any head residing in Rome or to have any relations outside the bounds of the monarchy. In 1781 he closed 600 monasteries at one fell swoop—all those of the contemplative orders; the number of religious fell from 63,000 to about 8,000. Soon it was the turn of the mendicant orders. I pass over in silence the petty details, the pinpricks, the stupid formalities; but it will not do to forget the question of money, which was the essence of the matter and brought it to a conclusion. Maria Theresa had forbidden the religious to send funds abroad, especially to Rome; Joseph forbade this also to bishops, and with the property confiscated from the monasteries he established a treasure for political

[40] The bulls *In cœna Domini* and *Unigenitus*.

and military expenses which was called 'the religious fund'. The operation was not very profitable, for the convents were usually in debt; when the debts were paid off there was little left—beyond the deed and the principle, which were what mattered.

Catherine the Great had no account to render to Rome, and so had fewer difficulties to face. Not content with dispersing monks, closing convents and taxing church property, she secularised it, in her own way also anticipating the work of the French Revolution. The Russian clergy owned almost a million serfs; the Tsarina confiscated them and handed over the administration of Church property to a commission; the monasteries, now pensioners of the Crown, received allocations from the state.

The Church put up a determined resistance to these violent assaults. The suppression of the Jesuits was only one episode in the struggle. 'They are an advanced outpost of the court of Rome', said Frederick to d'Alembert. This famous society had made a unique contribution to the establishment of absolute power in the Catholic monarchies. But having helped the state to suppress all dissidents, it aspired to independence for itself. The state could not allow this one obstacle to remain when all others had been removed. The struggle which was begun against the Jesuits, however, continued against Rome, and when the advance guard had been dispersed an attack was launched on the main body of the ecclesiastical army. Rarely had the Church seemed in greater difficulties than at the end of the ancien régime. The *philosophes* attacked its doctrine, the princes its discipline; the popes had to defend their spiritual authority against the former and their temporal prerogatives against the latter. The spiritual and the temporal were everywhere mixed and entangled; the princes enrolled the *philosophes* as their auxiliaries, and the *philosophes* boasted the patronage of the princes; the Pope invoked the secular arm against his adversaries when he could, and was not averse to creating political diversions in their states; ministers on their side did not

scruple to seize his property to force him to abandon his principles, to take material guarantees from him as head of a state
in order to overcome his moral resistance as Pontiff; they
found in Benevento, in Avignon, in the Comtat, the means
of applying to a recalcitrant Holy See a kind of *question
ordinaire et extraordinaire*. And so the Church, threatened
with constitutional schism and with invasion of its territories,
found its empire over men's souls and its political influence
simultaneously shaken.

Yet after all, it was with France that the Papacy got on
best. After violent conflicts a friendly understanding was re-
established. Louis XV made peace and restored Avignon;
Louis XVI sincerely respected religion and dealt gently with
the clergy. But outside France the crisis was general. Three
of the most powerful monarchies, England, Russia and Prussia, and in addition to Prussia half of Germany, were outside
the Church. With the Catholic courts—Austria, Parma, Tuscany, Portugal—the Church was in a state of either open
strife or latent conflict. Its relations with Spain were indifferent, with Naples impossibly bad. 'The Pope', wrote Leopold of Tuscany to Joseph II, 'will not nominate to any of
the forty-two vacant bishoprics; he tries surreptitiously to stir
up the people, above all the great nobles through Galeppi,[41*]
and the provincial populace through the mendicants.'[42] Not
only the course of events but the tone was significant. 'The
obstinacy and stubbornness of the Pope are inconceivable',
wrote Leopold;[43] 'he would do well to remember that in the
early centuries of the Church the bishops were nominated
by the people and the representatives of dioceses, and given
their office by the sovereign; that the metropolitans consecrated them, and that thereafter they simply sent a letter of
recognition to the Bishop of Rome, and later to the popes,
who were never more than the first among them, never their

[41] The comte Galeppi, auditor of the nunciature.
* Auditor of the papal nunciature (embassy) in Tuscany.
[42] Leopold to Joseph II, 17 December 1787.
[43] To Joseph II, 6 March 1787.

masters and absolute spiritual sovereigns, as is now claimed in Rome, especially in the improper and absurd oath administered to bishops at their consecration.' From 1768 Joseph considered that the court of Rome had made itself 'almost despicable'.[44] When he came to reign alone, he made a point of treating it with scorn, not sparing threats,[45] still less mockery and impertinence. Pius V came to Vienna in 1782. 'I went as far as Neustadt to meet him,' wrote Joseph, 'and to avoid all ceremonial or compliment of any kind, I met him on the high road, in the presence only of postillions; I immediately made him descend from his carriage, took him into mine, which seated two, and brought him straight to Vienna.'

The rulers who emerged from the French Revolution, from beginning to end of their struggle with the Church, under the Constituent Assembly and under Bonaparte, were to take no different view of their relations with Rome, nor use any different language in regard to the Holy See. For they were to adopt the same maxims on the omnipotence of the state as the governments of the eighteenth century, and they were to be actuated by the same passions—those which the *philosophes* had everywhere aroused against the Church.

5. UNREST AND SEDITION

This campaign of governments against the forces of the past provoked resistance; at the same time their tendency to take everything on themselves and the corresponding tendency of public opinion to expect everything from them were productive of trouble.

In bringing down the nobles and attacking the Church, the state believed it would conciliate public opinion and be strengthened by its support; in fact, while humouring popular passions, at the same time it excited them—and aroused

---

[44] Arneth, *Maria Theresia,* t. IX, p. 551.

[45] 'As for the Pope and the priests and monks . . . their turn will come.' To Leopold, 19 July 1787.

them against itself. As everything was thought to be possible
for government, there was much more irritation at what it
failed to do than satisfaction with what it did. Incomplete,
doubtful and partial reforms aroused hopes more than they
fulfilled desires. The reforms gave credence to the idea that
the old world was in decay and needed rejuvenation, and
accustomed people to sudden changes; they created the taste,
the appetite, and the need for them. The idea of a necessary
order in the life of nations disappeared everywhere, and instability was thought to mean progress. A muffled discontent, a deep disquiet spread through the nations.

Germany was particularly disturbed, and in Germany it
was the best organized state in which this tendency declared
itself. It was developed by the very achievements of enlightened rule. Frederick showed up best from a distance. The
theorists whose formulas he made use of admired him infinitely more than the people on whom they were tried out.
The brilliance of the King of Prussia was least dazzling in
Berlin. There enthusiasm was less noticeable than impatience
with the yoke. 'The cords are stretched so tight', wrote Mirabeau in 1786, 'that they must surely be relaxed. The people
have been so oppressed, harassed, persecuted that they must
have some relief.'[46] Frederick was too much feared, and his
people did not weep for his passing. The great vacuum left
by his death seemed a deliverance. It was in Berlin as it had
been in France upon the death of Richelieu. 'Everyone is in
mourning, but no one is sad', Mirabeau reported. 'Everyone
is affected by it, but no one feels afflicted. Not one regret,
not one sigh, not one word of praise . . . Two-thirds of Berlin are now falling over themselves to prove that Frederick
was an ordinary man, and perhaps even a lesser man than
many . . . !' This then was the outcome of the great reign—
everyone longed for it to end! 'People are tired, worn out and
have had too much to put up with', wrote the Austrian min-

[46] *Histoire secrète de la cour de Berlin.* Paris, 1789. Cf. the
originals and the version examined by Talleyrand in *Affaires
étrangères.*

ister.[47] However, Frederick had engendered in Prussia such
an idea of the power of the state that the people had the
highest hopes of his successor, and similarly this prince
thought himself equal to fulfilling their wishes.

In Austria, on the other hand, there was general discour-
agement both in ruling circles and among the governed. The
benevolent and relatively moderate rule of Maria Theresa left
behind as much apathy as the extreme methods of Frederick.
This great Empress was very sad in her later life. Her letters
are one continual complaint. 'I have sacrificed thirty-five
years to the people', she wrote in 1775; 'I am so disheartened,
so upset by the thought that I do more harm than good.'[48]
When she died, the people, according to one witness, burst
out in almost indecent rejoicing at her funeral.[49] By 1782
Joseph was as discouraged about his reforms and disillusioned
with his reign as his mother had been at the end of her life.[50]
'You have to row in that galley', he wrote to his minister
Kaunitz in 1786. 'You have to row until the finish. Perhaps
if you batter away at the same spot something will come of it
in the end.' All that did result was chaos in the state and disturbance among the people. All classes and all the countries
of the monarchy in 1789 felt that the world was upside
down, and security was no more.

There was sedition everywhere. Maria Theresa had tried
to improve the lot of the peasants in Bohemia, and in 1773
she issued an edict on the corvée. The peasants imagined
that the Queen wished to free them from all dues, that the
nobles were opposing this, and that the officials of the government were misinterpreting the sovereign's orders. They rose
in revolt. The ancient Hussite fanaticism—the only surviving
form of Czech patriotism—was reawakened in their hearts.
The destitute joined with the fanatics. Roving bands terrified

[47] Wolf, *Œsterreich und Preussen*, p. 50.
[48] See her *Correspondance* with Mercy, and Arneth, t. IX, ch.
XII.
[49] Wolf, *id.*, p. 21.
[50] See Beer, *Joseph II, Leopold II und Kaunitz*. Vienna, 1873.

the countryside. 'They commit frightful excesses,' wrote an official in 1775, 'pillaging the chateaux, carrying off and wrecking everything that falls into their hands, leaving the fields unsown and even forcing others to do likewise. . . . They have already sacked several churches, broken down the altars and images of saints, carried off the vessels and thrown down the Host.' They marched on Prague, where, they said, traitors had hidden the charter of enfranchisement. The troops had great difficulty in dispersing them and saving the city from the threatened pillage.[51] The disturbances spread to Moravia, and then to other regions. 'I fear widespread disorder', wrote the Empress in 1778; 'already in Styria they want neither to pay dues nor to work.' In Hungary it was the same. 'These people perpetrate horrible excesses.'[52] Joseph attributed the evil to vacillation in the exercise of power—'so many promises not kept, so many threats not carried out.'[53] When he reigned it was worse.

If the timid and cautious reforms of Maria Theresa had stirred up such grave disorders, those of Joseph II, radical and arbitrary, violently expressed but feebly applied, aroused general revolts, almost revolutions. The clergy demanded their immunities, the nobles their privileges, the people their enfranchisement. The nobles and the clergy, vexed by the government, deserted it. The people thought anything was permitted. State officials, bewildered and harassed by the contradictory instructions of the ruler, dazed by the changes they were imposing—which they themselves had undergone without understanding them—obeyed with a bad grace and ceased to command obedience. Violent and unexpected repression, followed by inexplicable lenience, caused irritation instead of appeasement. Under the yoke of German centralisation that was being imposed on them the peoples recalled their origins and sought in their national traditions their titles to independence. In Bohemia they began to speak

[51] Arneth, t. X, ch. XII.
[52] Arneth, *Maria Theresia und Joseph II.*
[53] Letter to Leopold, 9 August 1775.

Czech once more, and demanded the summoning of the Estates. In Hungary they demanded a meeting of the Diet. The nobles of Galicia were restive. In 1789 there was a state of extreme ferment in all the provinces of the monarchy. Revolution threatened in Bohemia, Hungary and Galicia, and actually broke out in the Netherlands.

So one of the most enlightened rulers of the eighteenth century met the same fate as the most fanatical of the despots of the sixteenth. The 'philosophic' reforms of Joseph II produced the same effects as the Catholic tyranny of Philip. For both, the Spaniard and the German, though pursuing very different objectives, proceeded with the same lack of understanding of the interests of the people and the same scorn for their traditions. The Belgians had not changed: obsessed by their national independence, strongly attached to their customs, inspired by their religion, they still combined a devotion bordering on superstition with the ancient spirit of revolt which had so long stirred in the Flemish communes. Each province had its own administration, its estates, its charter. Each voted the taxes, and if it did not actually make the law, the sovereign could only change it with the consent of the estates. When he came to power he swore to maintain 'the rights, privileges and constitutions' of the provinces. The most famous of these Belgian charters was that of Brabant, which was called the *Joyeuse Entrée*. 'It is true', wrote one of the governors of Belgium, 'that these countries are very much attached to their privileges, and I would even venture to say that they carry them to the point of folly; but they are all brought up in this prejudice, and it is a sore subject best left alone, since all sovereigns have not only confirmed them but sworn to observe them; so they look upon their privileges as fundamental laws of the state. I would say that these provinces are very easy to govern, for with gentleness and the least favour that Your Majesty deigns to show them, you may be assured that you may do what you like with them.'[54]

[54] Prince Charles of Lorraine in 1763 to Marie-Thérèse.

Ruling them was all the easier because their social condition was comparatively good. The nobles lived on their estates; the clergy, who had vast properties, administered them well and were popular; in short, the classes were less divided and the feudal régime less onerous than elsewhere in Europe. Maria Theresa thought well of the Belgians and understood them. She was their idol, said de Pradt. But even under her rule Belgium was for the house of Austria only a 'continental colony', a lucrative farm appreciated mainly for the revenues it yielded. Joseph II regarded it solely from this fiscal point of view. He was always ready to 'swap' it for Bavaria, which would suit him better. Not being able to 'swap' it he took it into his head to reform it—so as to exploit it more effectively. He did not know the country; he paid a short visit in 1781, and then, after this hasty glimpse and a few weeks of improvisation, he broached his scheme of reform. It bore mainly on religion. Edict succeeded edict from 1781 to 1786, putting the Church completely into the hands of the state. That done, he set about the lay institutions, and by an edict of 1st January 1787 he took away the administration of justice from the provincial estates, divided the country into circles, in which he established intendants, courts of first instance and courts of appeal. This was a flagrant violation of sworn charters. If the religious reforms had exasperated the country, the administrative reforms provoked it to revolt. Joseph II was in open conflict with the Church; and he united against himself all those in Belgium who prized national rights and ancient institutions.

There appeared at the head of the opposition a man whose name will recur more than once in this book—Henry van der Noot. He was an advocate of the council of Brabant. He displayed neither elevated ideas, firmness of character, nor sureness of judgement. But he possessed the essential qualities for the task he undertook—energy and fervent patriotism. He was of the stuff of which agitators are made, but he was found to be incapable of ruling. The other provinces followed suit, the monks and priests summoning the people to defend themselves and preaching resistance. Militias arose all over Belgium. Some men thought of forming a confederation and gaining independence like the United States of America, and asked France for support. The news gave Joseph pause. But instead of seeing in the troubles an effect of his imprudent reforms, he attributed the resistance to the intrigues of those powers that were interested in stirring up trouble. He would only see in it the hand of France, the work of 'priestcraft' and the court of Rome, which made use of the priests and above all the Capuchins to move the lower classes to revolt, fomenting sedition 'through the confessional'.[55] Whatever the real cause of the danger may have been, he took due account of it, and in the summer of 1787 revoked his edicts. But soon reassured by the internal difficulties of the French government he restored at the end of 1787 the arrangements concerning the Church, and enjoined General d'Alton, who commanded in Brussels, to employ, in case of opposition, 'the dire method of cannon and bayonets'. Under this threat the council of Brabant, which filled much the same rôle as the Parlement of Paris in France, registered the edicts. The seminaries of Malines and Antwerp were occupied by troops, the bishops put under arrest. It was announced that unlawful assemblies would be dispersed by firearms. Troops were posted as in a conquered country. The terror produced silence, and in September 1788 d'Alton was able to write: 'Calm still reigns'.

The submission was only apparent. This revolution was not of the kind that peters out in a scuffle; it steadily gathered force. The Belgian troops refused to march against their compatriots; the estates of Brabant and Hainault refused to vote subsidies.[56] Joseph declared that by this refusal they had violated the charters and released him from his oath. He restored the estates of Brabant, which gave way, and decreed

[55] See his correspondence with Leopold, July 1787.
[56] *Id.*, November 1788.

the dissolution of those of Hainault, which resisted. Then, hoping with this bait to win over the multitude, and to disconcert the nobles and clergy and the bourgeois oligarchy by a democratic diversion, he modified the charter of Brabant, 'deciding', he said, 'in justice to restore to the small towns and municipal franchises, which pay so considerable a part of the public charges, the exercise of their public and constitutional rights'.[57] He reckoned on reducing the great communes through the small ones, but the council of Brabant and the estates of the province, though they deliberated in the midst of armed men, refused to register the new edicts. The Emperor decreed the abrogation of the charter itself, and revoked the *Joyeuse Entrée*. Implacable orders were given to d'Alton. On 7th June 1789 Joseph wrote to him: 'Whatever the cost in blood of such an operation, it is not to be reckoned when it is a question of saving everything and finishing with these perpetual outbreaks once and for all.'

The risings began. This revolution, developing parallel with that in France, had quite different causes; the rôles were completely reversed. Here it was the sovereign who was the revolutionary and the people who defended the ancien régime; but at bottom the public liberties and national independence were at stake. To defend them the Belgians employed the same means and the same language as the French. A deputy of the nobility exclaimed in the estates of Brabant in 1787, 'This magnificent country is conveyed like a piece of real estate for sale or barter, for trafficking in the cabinets of princes or in public documents, so much against one province and so much against another.' The estates of Brabant claimed 'natural law' in support of ancient custom and their old liberties. When the deputies resisted they were acclaimed; they were declared 'fathers of their country', national cockades were handed out, and the populace, stirred up by the monks, pillaged the houses of those they supposed to be on the side of the government. A revolution made to

[57] *Id.*, 29 April 1789.

maintain the ancien régime proceeded just like the one in France which aimed to overthrow it.

Meanwhile, in addition to the party favourable to the ancient customs, which was in the majority, there appeared another, composed of lawyers, doctors and former priests, who demanded a share in government, extension of electoral rights and the suppression of privileges. Joseph's reforms only displeased them because they issued from him, and because in order to impose them he abolished the national liberties—which they on the other hand wanted to extend. This party, directed by a lawyer called de Vonck, desired a democratic revolution; the party of van der Noot demanded the re-establishment of the aristocracy. These two parties were destined to dispute between them the government of Belgium, but for the moment they united to reconquer it. Both were equally ardent patriots and they were filled with the same hatred of Austria. Joseph II had thus united all the Belgians in opposition to him, just when a revolution was beginning in France which would soon bring all the peoples into alliance against their oppressors. Later we shall see the grave consequences which resulted from the diversity, not to say the antagonism, of the feelings which animated these two revolutions. At the moment it is sufficient to note that they broke out at the same time.

Others seemed imminent. The Dutch patriots, subjugated by Prussian arms, were still active, organizing in secret, burning to take revenge on the Stadtholder and to recover—if possible extend—their national rights. In Sweden, Gustavus III had upset everybody—the nobles, because he had cut down their privileges, and the people, because he had done nothing to help them. Lastly, Geneva burst into revolt, and this revolution deserves particular attention. 'I am studying the quarrels of Geneva,' said Vergennes, 'for it is to be feared that their writings, having nourished discord among themselves, may spread the fanaticism that possesses them beyond their frontier, and their neighbours may proceed from curi-

osity to imitation.'[58] This was unusual language for a statesman of the old régime; the presentiment resulted from an
accurate and penetrating political insight. In fact what was
being prepared in Geneva in 1782 was the French Revolution. It was being rehearsed in miniature, so to speak, on
this minor stage.

It was Rousseau who gave the impulse. The *Contrat social*
was the programme, the *Lettres de la Montagne* the war-cry,
of the revolutionaries. The struggle was less between two
parties disputing power than between two classes that hated
and aimed to dominate, exclude and proscribe one another.
On one side was the reigning oligarchy, the patriciate, which
filled all offices; on the other side the bourgeoisie, sovereign
in principle but in fact shut out of government and eager to
govern in its turn. Their leaders were Duroveray, Dumont,
Clavière, Reybaz. Against their violent propaganda the aristo-
crats tried to invoke the intervention of the powers which
had guaranteed the constitution. The revolutionaries denounced this appeal to the foreigner as treason, and anticipated it by a coup d'état. They imprisoned the more formidable of their adversaries, and invited the more timorous to
surrender. 'The remains of the Senate have met,' reported
Mallet du Pan, 'to be informed of the proscription of the
senators and to confirm it. They have been ordered to submit.' The victors formed a 'commission of safety' and organized a 'Roman dictatorship'. Terror reigned in Geneva,
and for the vanquished it became a prison. Not content with
spoliation and imprisonment, the revolutionaries indoctri-
nated their captives. To subdue them was not enough—they
must be converted. This was a new feature; starting in Geneva, it spread far. 'These people boast of virtue while indulging guilty passions; they exercise despotism over opinion
while demanding approbation for monstrous deeds in the
name of reason and equity; they congratulate themselves as
if they had fulfilled sacred duties; they invoke humanity

[58] Soulavie, *Mémoires*, t. V, p. 227.

with bloodstained hands, write panegyrics on the fatherland while tearing it asunder, and invoke the rights of peoples while outraging the liberties of individuals.' The rule of these sinister babblers was soon wrecked by their furious jealousies. While they quarrelled, the French, Sardinians and Swiss, guarantors of the constitution, intervened to restore it.* The security commission decided on defence to the last, and decreed that the Genevans should follow the example of the Saguntines. Barrels of gunpowder were piled up in the churches; the destruction of the city was prepared. But while they awaited the enemy there were disputes, proscription, massacre. Then the enemy occupied the city, and the revolution was ended by a military coup d'état. The revolutionaries, hunted in their turn, fled to England to beg asylum until France should be opened to them. They became the professors and brokers of cosmopolitan revolution, instructing the disciples of the *philosophes* in the practice of popular revolt. From Dumont, friend of Talleyrand and collaborator of Mirabeau, to Clavière, who became a minister, they would all be found soon in Paris.

6. THE ANCIEN REGIME IN FRANCE

Thus a state of crisis was general in Europe; at the moment when the French Revolution was in train the ground seemed to be thoroughly prepared for social and political revolution all over Europe. If the revolution which seemed everywhere imminent broke out in France it was not because abuses were worse there than elsewhere, that the feudal system weighed more heavily on the people, that government was more unintelligent, more haphazard or more despotic, that wretchedness was more intolerable or men's hearts more sickened by a

* The aristocratic constitution of Geneva was guaranteed by France, Zurich and Berne, but the powers which intervened to restore it in 1782 were France and Berne, Zurich abstaining. Its place was taken by Sardinia.

more odious yoke. The motives which produced the revolt were the contrary of these.[59] A revolution made to destroy the institutions of the Middle Ages began in the country where these institutions were in course of disappearing and were crumbling of their own accord. The truth was that their yoke seemed the more intolerable as it became less burdensome; it exasperated those whom it no longer crushed. Vestiges of serfdom remained only in some corners of the eastern provinces. The peasant had not only ceased to be a serf, he had become a proprietor. The land was so split up that agronomists complained. Localised centres of power, which are always vexatious, were subordinated to royal authority; the Frenchman had a hundred ways of evading them. Unity was secured through the laws. Even feudal rights, attacked by the jurists and restricted by royal authority, were relatively less burdensome; the most objectionable and vexatious, those which affected a man's person, dignity or honour, were falling into disuse. In short, as a contemporary said, 'oppression was less severe in France than in Spain, Portugal, Austria, Prussia or Turkey; these countries however remained quite tranquil, while France had a revolution.'[60] This was precisely why she did so.

The peasant proprietor was directly affected in his work and in his property by corvées and feudal dues; he suffered from them much more than if he had worked for someone else. He no longer accepted so easily the sacrifice of his time and labour when he could devote them to his own profit, and when the results of his work could be inherited by his children. The noble who exploited him gave nothing in return for what he took; the peasant no longer received from him any of the services which had formerly justified his demands. The Frenchman, being served and protected by the state alone, no longer recognised any obligation except to-

[59] This has been expounded in the clearest manner possible by de Tocqueville.

[60] Adrien Lezay, *Des causes de la Révolution*, 1797.

wards the state; and since the noble received more from the state than himself, he expected him to pay more in proportion. 'One part of the institutions of the Middle Ages having been destroyed,' wrote de Tocqueville, 'what remained became a hundred times more odious.' As it was the state that had accomplished the first part of the task, it was expected to do the rest, and this was demanded all the more impatiently since the task seemed more simple and already far advanced. So true is this that the parts of France where the storm of Revolution burst most impetuously and raged most violently were those where progress had been most noticeable. The only districts which showed some degree of attachment to the ancien régime were those where the régime survived most completely—Brittany, the Vendée, Poitou. Here the qualifications were preserved along with the abuses; noble privileges were accompanied by noble duties. Nobles lived on their estates, and shared the lives of the peasants. The classes understood each other, they remained united and made common cause. Everywhere else the noble seemed a usurper to be driven out.

The prosperity enjoyed in France during the first part of Louis XVI's reign precipitated the movement, for it made men more conscious of the vexations that remained and more determined to get rid of them.* And, finally, France was the country where ideas of reform were most widely spread, where minds were the most cultivated, where men were most alike, the government most centralised, the nobility most reduced in status, intermediate bodies most subjected to the state, the nation most homogeneous, the state most closely knit. Thus the need for a revolution seemed most evident

---

* Sorel's argument is justified in principle though not exactly correct in fact. After its early years the eighteenth century was one of economic progress in France, but the reign of Louis XVI was marked by an economic regression culminating in the disastrous harvests which preceded the Revolution of 1789. See C.-E. Labrousse, *La Crise de l'économie française à la fin de l'Ancien Régime et au début de la Révolution* (1944).

just when the means of accomplishing it seemed most ready to hand.

These were characteristics peculiar to France. They explain why France had a revolution before the other nations of Europe. It remains to show how the French Revolution gave the impulse to all the others, and so became not only French but European.

III. *The Influence of France*

1. THOUGHT AND THE LANGUAGE

There is a European climate of opinion which prevails everywhere, though being French in origin it naturally finds its fullest expression in France. The ideas that shape both government and thought descended from Greece to Rome and from Rome to France. This is commonly called *l'esprit classique*. The principle of this classical spirit was abstract thought, its method pure logic.[1][*] It has been diffused in the

[1] See Taine, *l'Ancien Régime*, liv. III, ch. II, *l'Esprit classique*.

[*] Taine, with his dazzling style and clear-cut ideas, was probably the most influential writer of his time in France. Sorel followed his interpretation of the thought of the eighteenth century and its effect on the Revolution without question. Only those historians who are committed to seeing the Revolution as the consequence of the Enlightenment, or the Enlightenment as the seedbed of democratic tyranny and totalitarianism, can still accept Taine's work as sound history. In fact he himself was a conspicuous example of the French tendency, which he criticised, to classify everything in abstract, logical categories. The Enlightenment was not immune from this tendency, but in it scientific empiricism went further towards outweighing Cartesian rationalism than perhaps in any other intellectual movement in French history. Taine altogether failed to see this.

modern world through three great channels—the teaching of
religion, the teaching of law and the teaching of letters.

The Church was shaped in the mould of ancient thought,
which it preserved and bequeathed to the modern world. It
did more: it proclaimed that ideas should rule the world. It
nourished in men's minds the conception of an absolute truth
and a universal law, and along with these the notion of a
superior virtue, residing in unbounded faith in a principle
which allows of no qualification. It set before the minds of
men the aspiration for an ideal city, made up of nations
united by a common principle and governing themselves according to it. By its example it preserved the tradition of a
cosmopolitan and profoundly democratic society, in which
all are called and in which the lowest and the humblest may
be raised to the government of mankind. In the domain of
the state it taught that God is the fountain-head of sovereignty
and the people its channel; that sovereignty comes from God
by way of the people and that kings are not irresponsible
before men; that though power comes from God, the same is
not necessarily true in respect of the man who wields it or
the purposes he chooses; that the people are not made for
kings but kings for the people;[2] and finally that the law, as
St. Thomas says, is 'a rational order constructed for the common good'.[3]

Here the Church was at one with the jurists, so often
armed and leagued against it, whose doctrines, however, derived in part from the same source, fundamentally followed
the same course, and were propagated through the same channels. For them Roman law was the formulation of reason.
The supreme authority of the Digest derived from the fact
that it was seen as a sort of repertory of natural law. This is
how it was envisaged by the great French jurist Domat, the
contemporary and friend of Pascal. Boileau described him

[2] Saint Thomas, *De regimine principis*, III, c.xi.
[3] *Somme théologique*, 2nd part, quest. 90. See Janet, *Science
politique*, liv. II, ch. III.

as 'the restorer of reason in jurisprudence'. D'Aguesseau said that his works formed 'the best-ordered general plan of civil society that has ever appeared'.[4] The spirit of Domat was essentially classic. In 1694 he composed a treatise entitled *Les Lois civiles dans leur ordre naturel*, in which he presented Roman Law as the foundation of public law, itself the repository of natural law and *raison écrite*. 'All men are equal by their nature', he wrote;[5] but a government is needed to maintain order in society; and in this government it is proper to distinguish two kinds of laws, those which are the commands of power and which are called 'arbitrary laws', and those which are derived from natural law and which, being the necessary consequence of the principles of justice and equity, are immutable, and the same everywhere and always.[6]

These were only theories; the study of classical literature gave them substance. The rules of logical thought and the laws of political society were learnt from the ancient world; the illustrations which gave reality to the theories and the literature by which they were disseminated came from the same source. The same spirit prevailed in Church and state, religion and politics, philosophy and letters, laws and taste: which is why literature was such a powerful vehicle of that spirit. This spirit was pre-eminently French, just as it was French literature that above all gave it expression. Both developed in France concomitantly with the emergence of the language, the growth of national consciousness, the definition of the state and the clarification of its political traditions.

If we examine the turmoil of Renaissance France, we find in it the whole spirit and language of the French Revolution, along with all its passions. Brutus provides a precedent for the legal treatment of tyrants and the Catholic League invokes against a Huguenot king the ancient maxim of the

[4] Viollet, *Précis de l'histoire du Droit français*, p. 190.
[5] *Le Droit public*, tit. I, sect. I.
[6] *Avertissement* and *Préface* of *Traité du droit public*.

sovereignty of the people. These same influences were so
strong on all sides that the Protestants, who claimed that they
went back to the springs of Christian thought and repudiated
the influence of Rome, dogmatised, abstracted, and deduced
as imperturbably as their opponents and according to the
same logical methods. We find the same spirit, fiery and subtle, rational yet full of passion, beneath the magnificent dra-
peries of Corneille. It bursts out in full flame in the memoirs
of Retz. 'The people', he writes, 'were in an uproar. Some
voices were even heard calling for a Republic!'[7] In 1648, at
Saint-Louis des Jésuites, a prelate preaching before the court
adduced, as a decisive argument, 'Natural law which is above
all other laws'.[8] This was Gondi,* and here are his thoughts
when he was on the point of flinging himself into the revolution: 'I recalled to my mind all the most striking ideas and
especially all those most suited to mighty projects that my
imagination had ever conceived; I let my pride be flattered
with the title of head of a party, which I always admired in
the Lives of Plutarch, . . . and I abandoned my destiny to
the impulse of glory.'[9]

This type of mind reached maturity with the poetry of
Corneille, the politics of Richelieu and the philosophy of
Descartes. It subsequently became concentrated and engrossed
in itself and reached its quintessence with Louis XIV, but at
the same time it disintegrated. The absolute monarchy, the
Politique tirée de l'écriture sainte of Bossuet and the tragedies of Racine are fruits grown from the same seed and borne
on the same tree. They all fell together in the following
century, withered, dried up and decomposed. The state disintegrated, ideas became over-subtle; but being more diffuse

[7] 2nd part, ch. XIII, 1649. Ed. Champollion, Paris, 1873.

[8] 2nd part, ch. I, p. 153, note.

* Paul de Gondi, later Cardinal de Retz, was Coadjutor to his
uncle, the Archbishop of Paris. He was one of the leaders of the
first Fronde in 1648 and played a prominent part in the subsequent struggles, from which he emerged with a cardinal's hat.
His Mémoires were published in 1717.

[9] 2nd part, ch. IV, 1648.

they were propagated the more easily, as they rose higher above mundane affairs and were universalised. In this respect also and in this shape, although degenerate, they remained very French. The national character and language lent themselves marvellously to this development.

'Two particular characteristics distinguish you from all the other peoples of the world', said Joseph de Maistre of the French: 'the spirit of association and that of proselytising. Ideas with you are always national and always ardent. It seems to me that a prophet, with a single stroke of his proud brush, portrayed you to the life two thousand five hundred years ago, when he said: Every word of this people is an incantation. . . . The slightest idea that you launch on Europe is a battering-ram with thirty million men behind it. Always greedy for success and influence, it might be said that you only live to satisfy this desire; and as a nation cannot have been given an objective without the means of accomplishing it, you have been given this means in your language, by which your influence has been established much more than by your arms, even though these have shaken the world. Your literary empire has not been confined to the present state of the language: it is as old as the language itself. Already in the thirteenth century an Italian wrote the history of his native land in French, *because the French tongue is understood throughout the world and is more delectable to read and listen to than any other*'.[10]—'A dangerous book written in French', declared Bonald, 'is a declaration of war against all Europe.'

The reason was that all Europe spoke and understood the French language. 'Most German scholars have been hacks', declared Frederick, 'the French are artists.[11] This is why French works are universally known and why the French language has taken the place of Latin. To-day, anyone who knows French can travel through Europe.' The French lan-

[10] *Soirées de Saint-Pétersbourg*, 6me entretien.
[11] *Histoire de mon temps*, ch. I.

guage was suited to the genius of the eighteenth century, as
Latin was to that of the Middle Ages. It is a language which
simplifies and generalises; it can be borrowed and used anywhere, like the barest mathematical formula. The expansion
of the French language and spirit was a *fait accompli* by
1750. The previous century prepared the way for it; the excesses and errors of Louis XIV contributed as much to it as
did the glory of his reign. Those who were proscribed after
the Revocation of the Edict of Nantes were scattered through
Europe and carried the seeds of French genius with them.
They laboured for the honour of their country at the very
moment when it had cast them out; and they opened, un-
knowingly, new paths for the spread of its influence at the
very time when many of them were passionately taking up
arms to fight it. They established, notably in Prussia, colonies
which became, at the time of the great struggles of the Revolution, nuclei of a French party, often even hot-beds of propaganda and in any case centres of French influence and pro-
French sentiments. When the governments that emerged
from the Revolution tried to revive the traditions of Richelieu,
while adapting them to their own principles and passions,
they found in Germany a remarkable predisposition to share
their views. This is not surprising if one remembers that the
statemen with whom they had to deal had learnt their history
from the same sources as themselves, and imbibed from their
refugee teachers along with the language the political traditions of France.

In 1783 the Berlin Academy set as the subject of its competition the question, 'What has made the French language
universal?' The answer of Rivarol was: 'It is because of all
languages it is the only one which combines clarity with
brilliance. Reliable, apt for conversation, rational, it is no
longer merely the tongue of France, it is the language of the
human race.' The admirable talent of the author was as good
as proof of his thesis. Rivarol obtained the prize. The Berlin
Academy thus gave formal recognition to the primacy which
the French mind had long possessed in European civilisation.

French was the language of thinkers; it provided an international form of expression for universal ideas. Anyone who wanted to launch an idea on the world did it in French. Thus Formey,* the disciple of Wolf, published the *Belle Wolfienne* and the *Abrégé* of the works of his master, while Bielfeld composed his *Institutions politiques* in French for the instruction of the princes and statesmen of Germany. Gibbon wrote his first book in French. Vattel, who was in the service of Saxony and addressed himself particularly to the Germans, presented them with his famous treatise on the *Droit de la nature et des gens* in French. A substantial and interesting book has been written on French literature outside France in the eighteenth century.[12]

French was the language of rulers. Despatching an ambassador to Berlin in 1770, the Austrian Chancellor Kaunitz said that he gave him his instructions in French, 'because it is customary to use this language in addressing the King of Prussia'. It was similarly the custom in the courts of Poland and Sweden, nearly everywhere in Germany and even in the court of Vienna. Frederick, Catherine II, Maria Theresa, Joseph II, Leopold, though all German by birth, wrote in French. Mercy did the same in the confidential reports which he sent to the Empress on the conduct of Marie Antoinette in France. French was the language of elegant and polished society. Diplomats employed it in their conferences: it was the language of conversation, and in diplomacy all business is done by conversing. Manifestoes, diplomatic notes, treaties, were drawn up in French: French was the tongue for addressing all Europe and rival claims vanished before its acknowledged superiority. In addition it was essential, in these important matters, to be clear and to be understood—at least, if one was not it had to be by intent. Moreover the habit of

* Jean-Henri-Samuel Formey (1711-97) was perpetual secretary of the Academy of Berlin. His popularisation of the philosophy of Wolf under the title *La belle Wolfienne*, in 6 volumes, 1741-1753, obtained a great success.
[12] Savous, *Le dix-huitième siècle à l'étranger.*

using French was not the result of a mere tacit convention: it arose out of the nature of things. There was no lack of occasional protests, of assertion of the rights and privileges of other languages, of declarations with each new precedent that it was not to count as such. This was the case, for example, with the treaty of alliance of 1757 between France and Austria: a secret article was added for the express purpose of establishing that if the treaty was drawn up in French this was because the Germans wished it to be so. The custom was none the less established, and the reason for it was expressed very clearly in a despatch sent to the French minister to the German Diet. The Germans had complained that they were not addressed in Latin, which was the official language of the Holy Roman Empire. 'It would be wrong to suppose', said the French government in this connection, 'that by keeping to the custom which we have followed up to the present we are asserting the preeminence of the French language and attempting to compel other powers to recognise this: they are all entirely free to employ their own tongues as we have used ours. If the latter has been generally employed in recent times this is solely because it is known throughout Europe, because it is very precise, and because Latin . . . is no longer the customary language, especially of diplomacy, and is, so to speak, relegated to colleges and universities.'[13] The author of the *Institutions politiques* says the same thing and concludes that it is now no longer permitted for a statesman to murder the French language.

However, this was hardly correct. In passing thus from mouth to mouth the language was distorted; in such varied climates its nature changed; by being diffused it became turbid, the stream was swollen by unforeseen tributaries, it lost its primitive limpidity and its natural savour. In this cosmopolitan society everyone bent the foreign tool he had learnt to use in the direction prescribed by his own character and the idiosyncrasy of his nation. The French language suffered

[13] 18 February 1792. *Affaires étrangères.*

the fate of Latin, whose place it had taken. There had formerly been a 'refugee' style, now there was a European style, which was to the French of Voltaire and Jean-Jacques what the jargon of the Middle Ages was to the language of Cicero.

But we are not concerned here with vocabulary and grammar; what matters is that every word that came from France found its way into men's hearts. This was a fact with notable consequences even in politics. 'Enlightened' Europe did not confine itself to conceiving universal ideas or studying cosmopolitan science in French: it learnt its own history in French. The *Essai sur les moeurs* and the *Siècle de Louis XIV* were the brilliant manuals from which men of the world, rulers and statesmen drew their common fund of historical knowledge. Despite all the wear and tear of life, the imprint always remained on them. The unpleasant traits and the lack of patriotism in Voltaire's character have been rightly pointed out; he was better as an historian than as a man. But his leading ideas, above all in the *Siècle de Louis XIV*, remained essentially French; and it was from this point of view that educated Europe envisaged its history. The consequence was curiously advantageous for France. When France aimed to extend her rule in the train of her ideas, she found Europe as well informed of her political designs as of her social ideas, and as ready, so to speak, to receive her system of government as her revolution.

Books alone could not have achieved this: the spoken word, the propaganda of actual individuals, was also necessary; and these were legion. They spread throughout Europe. Voltaire gave the signal; Diderot traversed Holland and travelled as far as Russia; d'Alembert carried his brilliant mind, Raynal his 'providence', Condillac his system and all his precision tools of thought, through Europe. As for the nomadic lesser gods, the list is too long to enumerate. This astonishing generation had a sort of passion for travelling and spreading its ideas. Bernardin de Saint-Pierre* set off for

* Bernardin de Saint-Pierre, 1737-1814, trained as an engineer, wandered through Europe with a plan for social regeneration and

Russia to act there the rôle of legislator, strayed from his
path in Poland and hoped to discover in these harsh countries the genius which he was only to find in the Ile de
France. Dumouriez* could be found at every cross-road and
in every inn, leaving for Italy knapsack on back and stick in
hand, trying his skill at intrigue in Spain, at civil war in
Corsica and at revolution in Poland, and waiting for the
moment when chance would put the honour and the fate of
his fatherland into his hands. In addition to personalities
who were invited or fêted, and nobodies who roamed about
and knocked on any door, there were the mere travellers,
who journeyed just to see the world, for experience and
education. To these may be added the cosmopolitan body of
diplomats, military men, scholars, philosophers, publicists,
ranging from Maurice of Saxony,† for example, to Milord
Maréchal Keith‡ and Grimm,§ who constituted a sort of

---

travelled as far as the Ile de France (Mauritius). His first book
decribed this latter journey. He subsequently wrote other books,
the best known being *Paul et Virginie*, which made him a leading
figure among the pre-romantics. He was a friend of Rousseau's
last years and a precursor of Chateaubriand.

* Dumouriez, adventurer and secret agent before 1789, was to
be the victorious general of the revolutionary armies at Valmy and
Jemappes.

† Maurice de Saxe, 1696-1750, Marshal of France, illegitimate
son of Augustus II, Elector of Saxony and King of Poland, made
France his adopted country and distinguished himself as a soldier
in her service; he associated with many of the famous men of the
time and was honoured by Frederick the Great.

‡ Milord Maréchal Keith, 1685-1776, hereditary Marshal of
Scotland, fought under Marlborough, but supported the Old Pre-
tender in 1715. Took service in Spain and later went to Prussia,
where he was entrusted by Frederick the Great with important
missions. In Neuchâtel he met Rousseau and became his friend
and protector.

§ Grimm was a German baron from Ratisbon who entered
French literary society with the aid of Rousseau and Diderot. He
is best known for the long series of newsletters, mainly about the
French literary world, which he circulated in manuscript to noble
and royal subscribers in Germany from 1753 to 1773. From 1774
to 1796 he corresponded with Catherine II.

artificial *patrie* for Frenchmen of the dispersion. France drew as many of them as she could to herself. At one moment there was a proposal to entice Goethe, then a student, to the German chancellery of Versailles. To cut a long story short, this chaotic and noisy swarm of rumour-mongers, news-mongers, speculators, secret agents, jacks-of-all-trades, gamblers in every currency, although it worked on the lower levels, none the less deepened in its own fashion the bed in which greater rivers were to run.

'The time has come', a contemporary wrote, 'when we can speak of "*le monde français*".'[14] Like all conquerors, the French were admired and feared at the same time. They were fawned on and envied. Their domination was accepted with concealed resentment and a secret impatience to escape from it. They astonished, inspired respect, periodically aroused enthusiasms and more often provided entertainment. I cannot say that they were loved, still less that their country was. Only the extreme inconsistency and chronic weakness of the government of Versailles reassured Europe as to the political consequences of this prodigious expansion of French genius. Europe profited by it and took pleasure in supposing that in this way the French were being weakened. It was a short-sighted view. The intellectual expansion of France in the eighteenth century was not a deviation from its history but a natural development of it. France continued to exercise a dominant influence in the way most appropriate to the age. It was her peculiar good fortune that the great periods of her history were also the great periods of modern society. She offered Europe the picture of a superior civilisation both in the nation and in the state: the nation took up and completed the task of the state. 'In the seventeenth century,' said Guizot, 'it was the French government which influenced Europe; in the eighteenth it was French society.'[15]

14 Rivarol, *Discours sur l'universalité de la langue française.*
15 *Civilisation en Europe*, lesson XIV.

The century was not to end without the state gathering in the fruits from the seeds sown by the nation.

2. EDUCATION

The intellectual 'magistracy' exercised by France[16] required minds that had been prepared for it. This sovereignty called for subjects ready to accept it, and these had been produced by a system of education that was everywhere the same. Never had educated men been shaped so completely in a single mould as at this time. Rousseau deplored it. 'To-day', he wrote in 1772, 'there are no longer Frenchmen, Germans, Spaniards, even English, there are only Europeans. All have the same tastes, the same passions, the same manners, because none of them have derived a national character from their own institutions.'[17] They were trained in the same schools, in which a wholly abstract method was applied, and their teachers belonged to a cosmopolitan order. Up to 1762 the Jesuits were the great educators of Europe. Proscribed in the Catholic states, they continued to teach in the others, and even where they were expelled their methods continued to be imitated. By the nature of their Order they were a master-piece of the classic spirit. None contributed more towards propagating that spirit and preparing the way for its dominant influence, and since it was the spirit of the age their most ardent opponents were also their most servile imitators. The philosophers turned their own intellectual weapons against them; the Jacobins imitated their skilful organization and implacable discipline and employed all their methods of propaganda in the service of revolutionary proselytising.

The children of ordinary gentlemen and bourgeois went to colleges for their education; sons of great lords and princes had tutors, who were philosophical priests or *philosophes*,

16 This is the term of Joseph de Maistre, *Considérations sur la France*, ch. II.
17 *Gouvernement de la Pologne*, ch. III and IV.

themselves educated for the most part in clerical schools. Condillac* drew up for the duke of Parma his *Cours d'études*. In his *Traité de l'art d'écrire* he offered as examples of style to his noble pupil phrases such as: 'An enlightened prince believes that all men are equal'.[18] 'Peter III', said Rulhière,† was brought up in the love of equality.' His grandson Alexander was taught by the Swiss La Harpe, friend of enlightenment and humanity. In Sweden, under Gustavus III, the whole of fashionable society went into raptures over *Emile*, which provided the programme of enlightened education.

After college, those who were not destined for the army went on to study law at the universities. The University of Strasburg was celebrated throughout central Europe; Schoepflin and Koch taught there. Young Frenchmen—such as Talleyrand, Narbonne, Ségur, Tracy, Rayneval, Bignon—went there to find a window on Europe. They met young Germans who had come to study France. Besides the greatest, such as Goethe and Herder, there were many budding diplomats, like Metternich, who was there in 1788, and Cobenzl. It was through this door, above all, that French ideas penetrated into Germany; and so was built up that whole school of professors and jurists which was the kernel of the French party at Mainz and was to provide the connections which facilitated the conquest of the left bank of the Rhine.

Education as a 'man of the world' completed the work of college and university: it was again wholly French. 'I have several times said, and I really believe it,' wrote Lord Chesterfield, 'that a Frenchman who combines a moral basis, edu-

---

* The abbé de Condillac (1715-80) was the chief exponent in France of the sensational psychology derived from Locke; his *Cours d'études du prince de Parme* is dated from 1769 to 1773.

[18] Livre I, ch. II.

† Claude de Rulhière was secretary of the French embassy to Russia in 1762 when Peter III was overthrown and murdered and Catherine II proclaimed Empress. He wrote a history of these events.

cation and common sense, with the customs and etiquette
of his country has reached the perfection of human nature.'
European society copied, with varying degrees of crudity or
finesse, French society. Even at Weimar, where in the last
third of the century the prevailing spirit was German, one
could find, though doubtless in a more serious and sedate
fashion, all the marks of the cultured society of Paris. There
the Germans exhibited the same interest in science, the same
craze for novelties, the same joyous irresponsibility, the same
intoxication with illusions, often combined with the same
mocking and disparaging scepticism. They grew sentimental
with Rousseau one day and jeered with Voltaire the next.
Sensibility was universal and incredulity widespread. The
Bishop-Elector of Cologne founded in 1786 an Academy
inspired by the *philosophes*. In Catholic Germany indifference proceeded from the weakness of religious education and
the looseness of morals.[19] The shallowness of the French
saved them from the excesses of their own ideas, which exercised a more arbitrary influence elsewhere in Europe than
in France.

The same jargon had spread throughout Europe, so that
polished society, before the Revolution, not only anticipated
the spirit but used the actual vocabulary of the Revolution.
It had been learnt from French writers, who themselves took
it from Latin. The younger Racine laid down the maxim,
'Under a citizen king every citizen is king.'[20] Bossuet declared in the chapter of his *Politique* on 'Love of the Fatherland':[21] 'Duty calls on the citizen to sacrifice at need
everything he holds most precious.' The tragedies of Voltaire
propagated similar principles. The books of Rousseau give
them new life. Virtue was fashionable in the smart society of
Europe before it appeared on the agenda of the Revolutionary
assemblies. Men were citizens and patriots or they were noth-

19 See below, Book III, the chapters on Germany and Prussia.
20 *Au Roi rentrant à Paris, à son retour de Metz,* 1744.
21 Livre I, article 6, prop. I.

ing.[22] Rulers boasted of the same titles. 'The cause of the Empress', wrote an official of the house of Lorraine in 1742, 'has become that of every prince of the Empire who is a true patriot.'[23] The same description can be found in the most unexpected places. A letter addressed by the Russian government to the Austrian minister at St. Petersburg, to inform him of the revolution which had dethroned Peter III, reads, 'Her Majesty the Empress, having to-day, in response to the unanimous desire of all loyal subjects and good patriots of that empire ascended the imperial throne of all the Russias, has given instructions for all foreign ministers residing at her court to be informed of this event.'[24] Reading the correspondence of sovereigns, their manifestoes and above all the lampoons they drew up, or caused to be drawn up, against their enemies, one would believe oneself in Paris at the height of the revolutionary tragedy.

Hearing the pathetic appeal, 'Can His Majesty present me at the same time with his royal heart and a dagger?' we might think we were listening to a patriot minister betrayed by the court; in fact it is the child Emperor, the Bavarian Charles VII, addressing to Fleury his complaint at being abandoned. 'What infamous rogues are we dealing with,' we find in another place, 'and how, surrounded by cowardly and venal riff-raff, can we uphold the Constitution . . . and resist the frantic brigandage of the cursed Viennese tyrant?' This is not Brissot denouncing the Austrian Committee in the Assembly, it is the King of Prussia writing to one of his ministers.[25] Here is an orator with the elevated tones of some open-hearted Girondin addressing the Poles: 'For centuries all Eu-

[22] 'Vauban, as good a patriot as he was a great conductor of sieges.' Saint-Simon. *Parallèle*, p. 277. Cf. Littré, article *Patriote*. In 1764 a vessel named *le Citoyen* was launched at Brest. *Archives de la Marine*.

[23] Marquis de Stainville to Fleury, cited by de Broglie, *Frédéric II et Louis XV*, t. I, p. 43.

[24] *Archives des Affaires étrangères*.

[25] Ranke, *Die deutschen Machte*, t. II, p. 242, pièces (in French).

rope has witnessed your struggle to resist oppression, to defend and save the Fatherland from unjust usurpation, and fight for liberty. It is the duty of the human race to come to the aid of those who exhibit such great and noble and also natural sentiments, counting itself fortunate to be able to assist those who have shown the virtues of true citizens and great souls!' Alas, this has no reference to Poland, it is Catherine the Great congratulating Paoli.[26] Finally, a pamphlet of Frederick's in 1760 already reads like Camille Desmoulins, in his *Révolutions de France et de Brabant,* denouncing the conspiracy of kings against France: 'Is there any difference between a gang of petty brigands murdering and robbing private individuals, and an alliance, dignified by the most august names, the aim of which is to despoil by force another ruler (here we may translate 'people') with nothing to rely on but his own strength? To obtain associates in their crimes, your ministers engage in corruption and intrigue in all the courts of Europe. They guarantee success and promise a share in the loot; and so by appealing to the ambitions and self-interest of other states, they conjure up a plot that will be fatal to the peace of Europe.'[27]

The arts of republican eloquence spread from French to foreign literature. Alfieri composed against the French, whom he hated, works modelled on their own. His dramatic writing was wholly classical; its characters were abstractions; his aim in his tragedies was to make men 'free, strong and generous', to intoxicate them 'with virtue and love of the fatherland', to teach them to know their rights. In 1789 he composed a treatise against tyranny. German poets styled Frederick 'Father of his country'. Others, less obsequious, for example, Stolberg,* rhymed the advent of liberty and portrayed it

---

[26] See Rambaud, *Etudes sur Catherine II (Revue des Deux Mondes).*

[27] *Lettres d'un Suisse. Œuvres,* t. XV.

* Friedrich Stolberg wrote a 'Song of liberty of the Twentieth Century' in 1775 and later an 'Ode to Liberty'. He welcomed the Revolution but gradually turned against it, called the French 'The Huns of the West' in 1793 and became an extreme opponent.

bursting on the world like a torrent red with the blood of tyrants.

The works of Schiller at this period are one passionate ode to humanity, a sincere and rapturous song of liberty. The brilliance of his style and the originality of his images should not conceal from us his essential thought: it is wholly republican, and as he said himself somewhere, entirely Roman and classic.[28] Although he broke away from the superannuated mould of tragedy and rejuvenated and invigorated a decayed dramatic art, he none the less started under French influence. His verses are animated with the same inspiration as the orators of the Constituent Assembly. *Die Räuber* is the drama of blind and frantic revolution.[29] *Kabale und liebe* is a stirring satire on the abuse of power, the corruption of the great, the depravity of the little German princelings pillaging their own states and trafficking in their own subjects. 'In the depth of the heart of Posa is to be found a republican virtue', wrote Schiller in *Don Carlos*. He advocated this virtue in *Fiesko* and did not draw back from tyrannicide. He attributed the failure of his play to the apathy and lumpishness of the Germans. 'Republican liberty is but an empty word here,' he said; 'there is no Roman blood in the veins of the people of this country.'

The English prided themselves on having less Latin ancestry than any other people; yet the spirit of the century moved also in them. The philosophy of 'simple ideas', that of

[28] *Lettres sur Don Carlos*, letter II.
[29] 'The law never made a great man,' says Carl Moor. 'It is liberty that giveth birth to Titans. Oh! if the spirit of Hermann could rise again from his ashes! Put me at the head of a troop of men like myself, and I will make Germany a republic beside which Rome and Sparta would seem like convents of nuns.' *Die Räuber*, Act 1, Scene II, 1782. The playbill appeared with a frontispiece showing a raging lion and the caption, 'In Tirannos'. In Germany there arose a Euloge Schneider to take this programme literally, as in France there was a Hébert to translate into massacre Diderot's *Eleuthéromanes*.

Locke, a clear and inspired liquor which Voltaire distilled and poured out over all Europe, originated in their island. The troubled waters flowed through every channel there also, and stirred up 'the fever of destruction and rebuilding' which was agitating the whole continent, with 'deism, atheism, materialism, scepticism, ideology, back to nature, the rights of man, the recklessness of Bolingbroke, Tindal, Mandeville, the daring ideas of Hartley and Bentham, and all the revolutionary doctrines'.[30] In addition, oratory was there the art of government. No people gave way so easily to the abuse of hollow rhetoric and abstract logic. This was the milieu most suited to the dominance of the classical spirit, as the English discovered. In this government, said Macaulay,[31] 'the power of speaking is the most highly prized of all the qualities which a politician can possess; and that power may exist, in the highest degree, without judgement, without fortitude, without skill in reading the characters of men or the signs of the times, without knowledge of the principles of legislation or of political economy, and without any skill in diplomacy or the administration of war. . . . From the Book of Dignities a curious list might be made out of Chancellors ignorant of the principles of equity, and First Lords of the Admiralty ignorant of the principles of navigation, of Colonial ministers . . . [who could not repeat the names of the colonies,] . . . of Lords of the Treasury who did not know the difference between funded and unfunded debt, and of Secretaries of the India Board who did not know whether the Mahrattas were Mahometans or Hindoos.'*

[30] Taine, *Histoire de la littérature anglaise*, livre IV, ch. I. Paris, 1863.

[31] For what follows, see Macaulay, *Lord Chatham, William Pitt*, trans. Guizot. Paris, 1862.

* Essay on William Pitt (the Younger) written in January 1859. The clause in parentheses is omitted from the French.

Unfortunately Sorel relied for many of his references to English history on Macaulay's *Essays*, which, apart from the brilliance of their style, reveal the English historian's weaknesses rather than

What was required was not knowledge of affairs of state
but the ability to talk about them in a way that satisfied the
majority of the representative assembly. This was what the
Parliamentary leaders excelled in. Fox was by nature a great
orator, but his education was limited to political history; he
knew nothing of the natural sciences or of finance and commerce. He had a generous heart, a seductive eloquence, brilliance, charm, and above all a familiar acquaintance with
the models of antiquity. This was also, along with an unusual command of argumentation and invective, the essence
of Burke's talents. Composing dissertations rather than
speeches, he opposed monarchical abstractions to revolutionary ones. This is the explanation of the profound impression
he made on his contemporaries, even the French. Sheridan
and Erskine used the pathetic appeal and could move their
audience by the grand gestures of the tragic stage. The debates in the English Parliament have become famous, as they
deserve to be; but they were oratory in the classical style,
which is here the significant point. A young Frenchman who
visited England in 1754 went to Parliament and heard Lord
Egmont attacking a bill to enlarge the army, denouncing it
as a menace to liberty. He spoke 'with the pride of a republican', wrote our young traveller, who had just left college.[32]

If we turn from the orators of the opposition to the men in
power and the best-known statesmen, it is the same story.
They had an identical upbringing, and it bore the same fruits,
only they were more solid ones supported on a stronger
branch. Lord Chatham knew nothing thoroughly. He had
not devoted himself consistently to any study. Law was as
foreign to him as finance. He was even ignorant of the rules
of the House of Commons. But he was a wonderful orator,
with every quality required to fascinate an assembly. He possessed 'the strange power of inspiring affection and confidence

his strength. Contrary to what is said here, the government of
the Younger Pitt was marked by important administrative reforms,
as Sorel himself points out later (p. 387).
[32] C. Rousset, *le Comte de Gisors*, p. 58.

in great bodies of men; an eloquence which charmed the ears, stirred the blood in the veins and filled the eyes with tears'. He argued poorly and was prodigal of contradictory images. He launched into violent apostrophes. His theatrical behaviour was so inveterate that he could not check it even in committee. His death in open Parliament, in the crisis of the war and in the midst of a solemn debate, was his final *coup de théâtre*. Ancient tragedy had never presented to its audience so grandiose a catastrophe as that day struck dumb the House of Lords.

Chatham was compared to Demosthenes. He brought up his son on the speeches of the Athenian orators. William Pitt's education was exclusively in the classical writers together with some elements of mathematics. His father collected for him selected pieces of eloquence, made him read sermons, trained him in commonplace and in extempore speech, in gesture and stance. At Cambridge Pitt only studied the art of oratory. He attended lectures on Quintilian, analysed the speeches in Thucydides, Sallust and Livy and filled note-books with their finest phrases. Between whiles he composed a tragedy and to strengthen his mind read Locke's *Essay on the Human Understanding*. This was his total intellectual baggage when he entered Parliament at the age of twenty-three and threw himself into the struggle. After that he had no more time for studies and learnt no more except in scraps, from day to day, through conversation, according to the needs of the occasion and the demands of politics. His secretaries analysed dossiers and books for him and he gathered from their notes, to form the basis of his speeches, the arguments which would carry weight. His eloquence did the rest. 'Legislation and administration', said Macaulay, 'were with him secondary matters. To the work of framing statutes, negotiating treaties, of organizing fleets and armies, of sending forth expeditions, he gave only the leavings of his time and the dregs of his fine intellect. The strength and sap of his mind were all drawn in a different direction. It was when the House of Commons was to be convinced and persuaded that he put forth all his powers. He accordingly became the greatest master of the whole art of parliamentary government that has ever existed. . . .'* With this we come to France and its revolution.

3. THE EUROPEAN COMMUNITY

A common education and intellectual development established a surprising affinity between contemporaries. 'I see with pleasure', wrote Voltaire to a Russian in 1767, 'that a great republic of cultivated minds is being formed in Europe.' The French *philosophes* and their disciples were the first citizens of this republic; they were recognised as such everywhere and for polished society to admit them the appearance of respectability was all that was needed. The path had been opened which would be followed when the Revolution had given their pupils the reins of government. As soon as the Revolution had produced a regular government, the old Europe was ready to enter into relations with its members; in fact all it had to do was to renew with former acquaintances a relationship that had been interrupted. However violent it became, the crisis could not break bonds established by the whole civilisation of the century. This aspect must be discussed, because by examining it more closely we can understand some of what were at first sight among the most surprising developments in the history of the Revolution.

The bourgeois origin of the French republicans did not frighten Europe. It was long since used to parvenus. I do not mean only those of wealth, who have always been courted, nor those who had worked their way up by intrigue, who have always been recognised. I mean those who had risen by their political or military talent, their genius or their courage. The state had been taught by the Church to choose its servants from all ranks; from the moment that it took them into

* *William Pitt* (the Younger). The final sentence is quoted from an earlier passage of the essay than the rest.

its service it counted them as nobles. The great statesmen of the time of the Renaissance—Ximenes, Wolsey, L'Hôpital—were roturiers. Pope Sixtus V came from a peasant family. In the seventeenth century the affairs of Europe were managed for ten years by an English country gentleman and an Italian adventurer. They dealt on equal terms with kings. Cromwell married his daughters to lords, one of whom, Fauconberg, became an ambassador to the court of France. All Europe knew that Mazarin had secretly married Anne of Austria.

Even the most famous ministers, for example Richelieu, were not great nobles; most came from the *noblesse de robe* or were roturiers, such as Louvois, Lionne, Colbert and all the retinue of 'vile bourgeoisie' with which Louis XIV was surrounded.* There is no need to recapitulate the well-known names of those who, from the President Jeannin to Barthélemy,† formed an unbroken chain of bourgeois diplomats. Dubois was a very odd individual. None the less the Pope made him a cardinal and the Regent made him his first minister. Struttman, Chancellor of the Holy Roman Empire under Leopold I, was a mere lawyer of the little state of Jülich. The Neapolitan, Stella, whom Charles VI made his counsellor, had been a mule-driver, then a brigand, and subsequently a soldier. We find him in 1715 at the Court of Vienna with the title of count. There he met in the Council

* Sorel does well to put the phrase 'vile bourgeoisie' in inverted commas. As he says, the ministers of Louis XIV were mostly *noblesse de robe*. Their families often came from the ranks of the lesser nobility, even though they had acquired financial office under the crown. Saint-Simon's denunciation of them as mere bourgeois should not be taken at its face value.

† Pierre Jeannin (1540-1623), a président in the Parlement, wrote in *Négociations* an account of diplomatic relations, in which he took part, between France and the Netherlands in the latter part of the sixteenth century. François Barthélemy began his career in the bureaux of the Ministry of Foreign Affairs and was subsequently secretary in various embassies. He played a leading part in diplomatic affairs after 1789.

a marquis of Perlas, who began as the notary of a village near
Barcelona. Bartenstein, who cut a figure at Vienna and died
a baron in 1767, was the son of a teacher at Strasburg. Spielmann, who held an important post at the time of the Revolution, was the son of a shoemaker, and Thugut, who was in
control of foreign affairs in this great crisis, was the son of a
petty clerk and brought up by charity. I am referring to the
court of Vienna because it was regarded, and not unjustly, as
the most exclusive. That of Prussia professed in this respect
to be entirely open-minded; nearly all its officials were of
humble origins, recently ennobled or given titles. In Spain,
Alberoni was the son of a gardener. Monino, the minister of
Charles III, was the son of a notary; he was made Count of
Florida-Blanca as the result of a treaty which gave this colony
to Spain. Pombal, who was all-powerful at Lisbon, was a
gentleman of modest birth; he was made count and marquis.
A Danish doctor, Struensee, became in 1770 the lover of the
Queen, who made him her chief minister in 1771. I need
hardly mention Godoy; there will be only too much to say
subsequently of his scandalous elevation in the world; nor
of the Russian favourites and accomplices of Catherine, conspirators and even assassins risen from still lower, whom she
made barons, counts and princes.

'To allow prejudice against low birth to affect appointment
to ministerial posts', a German writer[33] declared, 'is not
worthy of a *philosophe.*' The welfare of the state should
override such imaginary influences. The control of public
affairs was to be allocated on the basis of talent, not of the
dubious merit of birth. Parvenus were ennobled. Peter the
Great, in his *tchine,* only systematised for a new and half-
barbarous society what was practised in the old societies of
the continent. The old aristocracy accepted these upstart in-
truders ironically; they had to wait before they were recognised by select society. But such exclusion from fashionable
society and limited cliques had no effect abroad, where in

[33] Bielfeld, t. II, ch. II, § 25.

political and diplomatic relations such distinctions were less appreciated. The antiquity of a title or the number of quarters possessed by its owner were not looked at. Rank took the place of birth and the office determined the rank.

Doubtless to rise from humble origins to high position was exceptional; but such cases were frequent enough and sufficiently hallowed for no one to exhibit surprise when France made a rule of it. Moreover, the statesmen whom the Revolution elevated, who laid down its principles at the beginning and reorganized it after the years of anarchy, came precisely from those bourgeois and *parlementaire* families from which the ancien régime had for long recruited its officials, intendants, councillors and even ministers.* They possessed the education which had become everywhere the mark of the world of society and which had reduced its members, not only in France but throughout Europe, to a single pattern. They all belonged to the same political world. They would have been admitted to it even before the Revolution imposed them on it. Was there any government in Europe which equalled in extent of knowledge and ability that which included such men as Portalis, Mollien, Roederer, Treilhard, Merlin, Lebrun, Siméon, Tronchet, Bigot, Reinhard?† When Napoleon

* These are generalisations of the kind that a contemporary historian would not venture on without a detailed study of the personnel involved. The phrase 'ce monde parlementaire', which Sorel employs, is ambiguous. If he meant by it the great families of *conseillers* and *présidents* of the Parlements, very few members of these became leaders of revolutionary France, though some came to office under Napoleon and more during the Restoration. The same can be said of intendants and ministers. On the other hand, the secretaries and clerks and lesser officials of the Parlements, venal courts, intendancies and ministries rose to much higher office after 1789.

† Portalis was Minister for Religion under Napoleon; Mollien had charge of the Treasury; Roederer held a series of major offices in France and the Empire, including that of Education; Treilhard had been a member of the Directory and played an important part in drawing up the Napoleonic Codes; Merlin, also a Director, after a distinguished career during the Revolution was for

conferred titles of baron or count on them he merely copied the traditional procedure of the old governments. This is why the latter showed no surprise and so easily recognised the new nobility. Europe, indeed, would have been in the wrong if it had made difficulties. Such scruples had been abandoned long since. A prejudice which could be overcome by mere wealth could hardly hold out against talent. As a prince Cambacérès was better value than a Potemkin;* and taking regicide with regicide, a French count who had condemned Louis XVI to death was at least on a par with a Russian count who had executed Peter III. Courts which admitted one could hardly exclude the other; they were accepted all the more easily because of their intelligence and personal worth.

With soldiers the noblesse came back to its origins. They were not lacking in glory and were not grudged admiration. Europe had never worried about the ancestry of its heroes. Finding them in the republican armies it gave them its admiration. The funeral ceremony of Marceau recalled the finest features of the age of chivalry.† The same virtues received the same recognition later, when a bellicose republic, by being transformed into a military monarchy, had made

---

thirteen years under Napoleon public prosecutor at the Court of Appeal; Lebrun, Third Consul in 1799, Prince and Arch-Treasurer of the Empire, was governor-general for Napoleon in Genoa and subsequently Holland; Siméon presided over the legislative committee during the discussion of the Code Napoléon; Tronchet was president of the Appeal Court and one of the compilers of the Code Napoléon; Bigot de Préameneu also contributed to the Code and was later Minister of Religion; Reinhard's career was mostly in diplomacy.

* Cambacérès, a member of the Convention but not a regicide, became Duke of Parma, Prince and Arch-Chancellor of the Empire. Potemkin played a minor role in the overthrow and murder of the Czar Peter III. He subsequently became one of the lovers of Catherine II and was loaded with favours and power.

† Marceau was killed in battle against the Austrians in 1796 and given an honourable burial with a salute of guns in the Austrian camp at Coblentz.

the greatest of its soldiers into an emperor. What ruler would not have envied the General Staff with which he was surrounded! What military leader, in former times, had ever possessed a military council such as assembled on the morning of Austerlitz—Murat, Lannes, Bernadotte, Soult, Davoust![34] 'If I were to live as long as the world lasts,' wrote a witness, 'the impression of such a sight could never be effaced from my memory.'[35] These were all to be ancestors of ducal families. Two were to become kings, and one of these, Bernadotte, not by the chance of war or the will of his master but by the choice of the Swedish nation and with the agreement of the old Europe, which even thought, at one moment, of putting him on the throne of the Bourbons. Many of these soldiers, of very humble origin, had not even had an elementary education. They learnt the ways of war, politics and society in the camp. So had a famous general of the old armies, Albert of Saxe-Teschen,* and no one had been astonished at it. When we add the ever-present spirit of the age and the great freemasonry of arms which enemies shared, we can understand how even during the most violent struggles, honour and mutual respect for bravery preserved traditions of military courtesy. They mitigated the cruelty of war and even played a part, later, in preparing the way for peace.

This is the point at which the strength and extent of the bonds which the eighteenth century had created between France and Europe can be assessed. As soon as the Revolution ceased to rely on mere force, men's hearts turned again to France and reconciliation seemed possible. Even at the height of the struggle some had not despaired of this; they had been prepared to facilitate it and in the end to accomplish it.

[34] Murat, Lannes, Soult, volunteers of the Revolution; Bernadotte, private and sergeant-major before 1789; Davoust, officer before 1789, volunteer in 1791.

[35] Philippe de Ségur, *Histoire et Mémoires*, t. II, p. 463. Paris, 1873.

* Albert of Saxe-Teschen, 1738-1822, a second son of Augustus III, King of Poland, commanded an army in the Austrian Netherlands in 1792, the first year of the war against France.

Without such tendencies the negotiations between the Republic and its enemies would be inexplicable. That the French had been able to defend themselves and to conquer was much; to make themselves heard and be understood was more. It was possible because at bottom they and their enemies spoke the same language.

Such were the paths that the old France opened for the new. In a Europe thus prepared by the intellectual developments of a whole century we can see the French armies, zealous for their cause and carried forward by victory, embark on the conquest of the old world, which they believed it was their task to rejuvenate. They proclaimed generous principles; they abolished abuses that would be thought unbearable if the peoples had not borne them for so long. They proclaimed reforms which responded to the aspirations of thinkers and the claims of the lowly. The soldiers in their armies and the propagandists of their revolution were inspired with a burning national ardour; yet they were convinced that Frenchmen alone were rational beings. Their patriotism, which to them was a religion, confused the welfare of the Republic with that of civilisation: they believed all the gains of France to be conquests for humanity. Their impetus was prodigious and Europe could not withstand it.

4. RELIGIOUS REVIVAL AND SUPERSTITION

However, the Revolution did not limit itself to the diffusion of 'lumières' by invasion, the establishment of enlightenment by conquest, and the propagation of liberty by war. This was only the political consecration of the influence France had exercised during the eighteenth century; the state had completed, for its own gain and glory, the work begun by the nation. From the beginning of the Revolution there was, side by side with the broad and clear current flowing, so to speak, out of the whole history of France, a different one, disturbed, violent, tumultuous, swollen by all the storms, which overflowed into the other and drove it from its bed, mixed their waters together, swamped the fields and covered them with a common flood. A wild proselytising took the place of patriotic fervour, enthusiasm degenerated into fanaticism. The Revolution ceased to be an event in history, a series of contingent and actual facts: it became a doctrine, a religion, a god. The *philosophes*, who had prepared the way for it,* repudiated this 'mania for conquest', 'this fanatical, dark and cruel madness'.[36] They were proud of being antichristian; several plumed themselves on their atheism. Yet their disciples behaved after the fashion of the most narrowly fanatical sects. Their bloodthirsty missions, their savage inquisitions, their frightful *autos-da-fé* are no longer to be compared to the crusade against the Albigenses. We must go back to Islam and its conversions by force of arms to find in history a parallel for such terrific invasions and such tremendous apostolates. 'In one hand they bore the sword and in the other the rights of man', cried a contemporary.[37] They had their armed missionaries, their neophytes and their martyrs. Their doctrine, like the dogmas of religion, was universal, exclusive and despotic. There was only one truth and they were its prophets. The world was corrupt; theirs was the duty of regenerating it. They were virtue incarnate; their mission was to establish the reign of virtue. Fanaticism, like absolutism, is always the same. The human spirit has only one shape for this obsession: the fanaticism of reason took perforce the mould of the fanaticism of faith.

* The attribution of the French Revolution to the influence of the *philosophes* is to be found as early as Burke's *Reflections* of 1790. It was almost an article of faith in the nineteenth century and is still ardently upheld by some historians. It is generally realised now that the relationship of ideas to political and social developments is a much more complex one than used to be supposed, and that in any case the ideas of the *philosophes* have more bearing on the reforms of the second half of the eighteenth century than on the political revolution.

[36] Voltaire, *Dictionnaire philosophique*. Article *Fanatisme*, sections I and II.

[37] Mallet du Pan, t. II, p. 135.

However, an abstract and universal character is common to all doctrines, even those which remain purely speculative. It is not sufficient by itself to explain the nature of the revolutionary propaganda. If the doctrines of the eighteenth century gave birth to this kind of proselytism it was because a particular predisposing condition was present. Revolutionary principles were combined with mystical aspirations. A yeast of sensual and sentimental religiosity was fermenting in men's minds. The same hand wrote the *Profession de foi du vicaire savoyard* and the terrible clause of the *Contrat social* which banished atheists from the republic and punished blasphemers with death. Fiery patriots, who did not shrink from coups d'état or shut their eyes to massacres, saw in the success of the great revolutionary *journées* the hand of Providence. Even during the worst excesses of the Revolution and at the height of the reign of terror this trait appeared in the cult of reason, in the religion of nature and in the base hierophants even at the level of the foolish gnosticism of Catherine Théot,* in the fête of the Supreme Being and the priesthood of Robespierre.

In the time of Louis XIV, beneath the pulpit of Bossuet and the oratory of Port-Royal, there flowed an underground but 'direct and uninterrupted' current of libertinage which led to 'the great heresy of these latter days, scepticism', as Nicole called it, and prepared the way for Voltaire.[38]* Simi-

* The letters of Catherine Théot, who suffered from religious mania, to Robespierre fell into the hands of his enemies on the Committees of General Security and Public Safety, who used them to cast ridicule on him. His Rousseauist deism and his promotion of a great public fête in honour of the religion of the Supreme Being had already exposed him to the attacks of the more violent anti-clericals and atheists in the Convention. One of the charges brought against him on the ninth of Thermidor was of aspiring to be a high priest of the Revolution.

[38] Saint-Beuve, *Port-Royal*, livre III, ch. XVI; livre V, ch. VII. Paris, 1867.

* Pierre Nicole was one of the Jansenist theologians and educationalists who gathered in the middle years of the seventeenth century at the convent of Port-Royal.

larly in the eighteenth century, in the midst of the war against religion preached by the *philosophes* and waged by the rulers, the minds of men were affected by a sort of disquiet, and vague disturbances appeared here and there which announced a wind of change. The bizarre mysticism and the sectarian fanaticisms of the Revolution were signs of the times, symptoms of the crisis set in motion by the Revolution. The violent and absolute doctrines by which the Revolution became a religion in reverse were suddenly succeeded by no less absolute and violent doctrines which made religion into a revolution turned inside out. In 1793 there was the religion of reason, in 1794 that of the Supreme Being. The first composition of Bonald dates from 1796, and Joseph de Maistre published his first book in the same year.[39] At the same time, almost in opposition and unbeknown to them, the inspiration of the *Génie du Christianisme** was being foreshadowed. Men's minds were moving of their own accord in that direction. Saint-Martin,† 'official defender of Providence' as he described himself later, was living in the expectation of a new age. 'I need God', he said, and sought him in himself and in nature; he deified everything around him.[40] Ballanche‡ dreamed of revelation and palingenesis. The letters of Ampère§ cast a delightful light on a sensitive and mystical little society in the neighbourhood of Lyon, with which we come close to Geneva and Protestantism.[41] The ideas of Rous-

[39] Bonald, born in 1754, published in 1796 his *Théorie du Pouvoir*; J. de Maistre, also born in 1754, published in 1796 his *Considérations sur la France*.

* Written by Chateaubriand and published in 1802.

† Louis Claude de Saint-Martin (1743-1803) was an *illuminé* and mystic.

[40] Sainte-Beuve, *Causeries du lundi*, t. X, article *Saint-Martin*.

‡ Pierre-Simon Ballanche (1776-1847), Christian mystic.

§ André-Marie Ampère (1775-1836), physicist anf precursor of electrodynamics, also wrote on the philosophy of science. His *Journal et correspondance* was published posthumously.

[41] *Journal et correspondance d'André-Marie Ampère*. Paris, 1872.

seau disturbed his mind. He envisaged a 'religion of man without temples, altars, rites, confined to the internal worship of almighty God, the pure and simple religion of the Gospel'. This was a long-prepared reaction, for the religious thought of a whole century preceded it. It led straight to the rationalist and sentimental Christianity of Schleiermacher.*
In 1788 Necker drew upon himself the mockery of Rivarol and all smart society by his book on *L'importance des opinions religieuses*. This was the background of Mme. de Staël, whose *Religion de l'enthusiasme* was maturing in her mind at the same time as it was being spread in Germany. She only understood it so well and bore such eloquent witness to it because she had long before been initiated and spontaneously converted to it.

The religious revival in Germany preceded the French Revolution. In Germany, moreover, incredulity had only spread among the aristocracy. The Prussian people remained religious and rejected the strange doctrines of clerical Voltaires that emerged from the fantastic consistories of Frederick. The death of the philosopher king in 1786 was followed by a savage reaction against philosophy, by which the new reign courted popularity. Official orthodoxy took over the state university, and a government of *dévôts* replaced that of atheists. Throughout Germany, even in the places where piety had disappeared, there had remained a substratum of emotional religiosity, in which Rousseau and all those who were influenced by him found something to build on, as well as the Catholic revivalists such as Stolberg and others, who undertook a task in Germany similar to that of Chateaubriand in France. But it was in England, where the philosophy of irreligion had first appeared, that the reaction had its greatest effect. The established religion was desiccated, Catholicism banned, and scepticism prevailed among the enlightened classes. The movement for religious revival and

* Friedrich Schleiermacher (1768-1834), German theologian and philosopher.

reform emerged from the people. The Methodists, Wesley and Whitfield, travelled the country preaching the Gospel and calling for the reform of the Church. Their faith was infectious and deep. England was covered with their missionaries and everywhere crowds surged around them and seemed to hang on their words. The established Church itself was affected by their influence and reanimated by it. The older dissenting sects—Presbyterians, Independents, Baptists —were aroused by their example and joined with the newcomers in the struggle to satisfy the newly awakened need for religion.

Without this remarkable spiritual development in Europe, events in France would have remained merely bizarre, grandiose or sinister episodes in an extraordinary drama; they would not have reverberated beyond their own setting and would have found no echo in men's minds. All the enthusiasm and all the passionate proselytising would not explain the effect of this propaganda if there had not been hidden tendencies which predisposed men in its favour. Without these there would have been only revulsion and opposition, increased by the attempt at conversion by force. What is most surprising, said de Tocqueville, 'is not that the French Revolution employed the methods that it did, or conceived the ideas that it manifested: the great novelty was that so many nations should have reached the stage at which such methods could be effectively employed and such principles easily accepted'.[42]

The fact is that not only were men prepared for its principles, they were also schooled in its methods. The French revolutionaries borrowed their system of propaganda from the religious sects. They took their organisation from the most powerful of the associations ever established within the Church. And even in this they were not innovators. Before the Revolution Europe was covered with secret societies, formed on the same pattern and animated with the same

[42] *Mélanges: De la Constituante au 18 brumaire*, p. 187.

spirit. 'Most', says the historian who has examined this subject in the broadest scope, 'had been purely philosophical
or religious; but subsequently they all turned towards politics and became absorbed in it. Their methods differed, but
the end was to regenerate society and reform its government.'[43] The most important of these were the Freemasons.
Their main centre was in England, but they had spread elsewhere, to France, Italy, Sweden, even Russia, and above
all Germany. Princes and nobles were proud to preside over
its lodges and accept the title of Grand Master. In Prussia,
after the Seven Years War, a Society of *Amis de la Patrie*
was set up and Frederick II hastened to join it.

Out of one of the students' associations which swarmed
in Germany grew the famous sect of the *Illuminés*. Weishaupt, who founded it, was a Bavarian professor of canon
law. The aspirations of Freemasonry seemed to him too
vague and its lodges too independent. He proposed a more
simple and coherent doctrine, but one which was frankly
revolutionary in its principles; it was founded on the natural and imprescriptible rights of liberty and equality. Since
society interfered with the exercise of these rights it was an
obstacle to human perfectibility; individual property was arbitrary and abusive; civil and religious laws were so many
attacks on the primitive rights of man. These rights must be
restored to him, and the means to achieve this was the total
destruction and reconstruction of the social fabric. Such were
the principles, and they were immutable; but the *Illuminés*
did not propose the use of violence or haste in their application. They believed that methods of infiltration were preferable to an attempt to storm the citadel by force. Not being
able to destroy the social fabric, they thought it expedient to
instal themselves within it. They canvassed for places and
exhibited remarkable skill in obtaining them. These regenera-
tors of the world were also very skilful politicians; in their

[43] Tocqueville, *Mélanges*, unpublished chapters of *L'Ancien
Régime et la Révolution*, ch. I.

cénacles they were past masters of intrigue. They were to be found everywhere, pushing themselves into jobs, outwitting princes and enlightened ministers. They moderated their language, introduced mental reservations into their teaching, and spoke less of tyrants and more of democratic rulers. The Elector of Bavaria was surrounded by them. Most of the statesmen and diplomats of the lesser courts were affiliated to the sect. They even included Catholic priests like the canons of Mainz, the Coadjutor of Dalberg, the Curator of Benzel and a host of others, who replaced devotional images with the symbolic pictures of philosophy. However, it was not possible to provide all the faithful with official prebends, and some were impatient. After 1759 these broke with Weishaupt and founded dissident lodges in which they organized for battle against nobles, priests and kings. French propaganda found sympathisers in the former and associates in the latter. They were numerous in the Rhine states; they had supporters in Italy; and it was among them that the conspiracy which led to the regicide of 1792 in Sweden was framed.

However, towards the end of the century and under the influence of the reaction which was secretly troubling men's minds, many of those who had formerly been influenced by the Freemasons and the *Illuminés* began to become alarmed at both the doctrines and their consequences. They seemed to be leading to anarchy. The doctrines seemed desiccated. Their practical effects were alarming and their theories unsatisfying. Since pure reason revolted their heated imaginations, science was too slow for their impatient spirits, and they were not yet ready to return to religion, they flung themselves into mysticism and superstition. The Freemasons, especially those of the strict observance, had already propagated a whole system of solemn but puerile rites which they pretended to be derived from the East, and in which, by the operation of a masonic grace, the disciples of Voltaire were able to participate without dissolving into laughter. André

Chénier, who before denouncing the crimes had unmasked with such a lively zest the folly of his contemporaries, shows us the *Illuminés* 'adapting a whole accumulation of ancient superstitions to the ideas of their sect, preaching liberty and equality like the Eleusinian or Ephesian mysteries, translating natural law into an occult doctrine and a mythological jargon'.[44]

The superstition which always lurks in the depth of the soul now came to the surface. Man was dazzled by his own enlightenment and intoxicated with pride. He supposed that the world only existed by his thought and must obey his will, that reason which could conceive all could also accomplish all. But though reason accepted the pattern of his thought, the world obeyed its own laws and nature eluded the commands of his mind. He became impatient and angry; his teachers had spoiled him. As they did not enable him to achieve his impossible desires, he revolted against their teaching, broke the alembics which had proved too crude to distil the essence of things, smashed the scales which were too clumsy to weigh atoms, discarded the books which only gave the tentative results of incomplete experiments, and turned to the alchemists. Over-simple formulas had produced disillusionment. The clear, thin light of reason, concentrated on one object, left whatever surrounded the luminous point in too profound a darkness, which involuntarily attracted attention. Mystery, which had been driven out of the human mind, took its revenge. The eternal aberrations of the mind and the old errors, which had been thought forgotten for ever, reappeared, decked out in philosophical trimmings and disguised as science. A Cagliostro* could cut a figure in society; Mesmer's bucket aroused more enthusiasm than the

[44] *De l'esprit de parti*, 1791.

* Italian adventurer and worker of wonders. He claimed to be a count and won the patronage of members of the highest society. Among these was the Cardinal de Rohan, through whom he was involved in the affair of the diamond necklace.

discoveries of Lavoisier.* The most subtle minds, that of a
Lavater† for example, inclined in the direction of the cabal
of mystics. Goethe himself strayed into these dubious paths
and had his Walpurgis night; it took all his strength of mind
and genius to resist temptation and keep his balance.

It was at this time that a barely known sect, the Rosicrucians, founded in Germany in the previous century, emerged
from obscurity. By chance it seemed to provide an answer
to the confused aspirations of humanity and it took advantage
of this fact. As both magicians and *philosophes*, the Rosicrucians offered a doctrine and a bond of union to unquiet
spirits whom rationalism did not satisfy and Christianity satisfied still less, and who combined a vague desire for marvels
with the humanitarian sentiments at work throughout Europe. They were respectful of established authority, declared
enemies of the reformers and of the revolutionary sects of the
Illuminés in particular. Their object was to evict them from
the governments and courts. They preached good news to
princes and called on them to work for the happiness of
mankind by strengthening their own authority. They reconciled despotism with virtue and flattered simultaneously
the imagination and the ambition of the despots. They
claimed the secret of making gold, a precious one at a time
when all treasuries were empty, and that of reforming governments without weakening the authority of princes, no less
useful a secret at a time when discontent, if not revolt, was
seen to be smouldering everywhere. They claimed that they
could command the forces of nature. Science meant very little to them. They rejected its methods, just as in politics
they had rejected tradition and experience. They communed

* Mesmer was an Austrian doctor who propounded the theory
of animal magnetism as a healing force and held séances at which
the participants joined hands round a tub of water. His arrival in
Paris in 1778 began a fashionable craze for mesmerism. Lavoisier
was one of the greatest of French scientists and the founder of
the modern science of chemistry.

† A Swiss pastor who believed that character could be scientifically deduced from facial appearance.

directly with nature and put it at the service of their adepts. They did more, they put them in touch with the great minds of past ages, who became thus their mystical advisers and secret collaborators. Theosophists and charlatans, humanitarian Tartuffes, sentimental hypocrites accommodating to the weakness of the great, courtiers and intriguers, they were ready to use any methods to achieve success. They made a career out of their crude mysticism. The Landgrave of Cassel paid a high price for the apparitions presented to him by clever rogues. Gustavus III was an ardent and convinced follower of the sect. He had a sorceress whom he consulted, he took part in cabalistic rites and had a vision of Charles XI. But nowhere was the influence of the Rosicrucians, or the rôle of conjurers, greater than in the court of Prussia after the death of Frederick II. These crude and cunning mystifiers set up their weird apparatus in the rooms of Potsdam where formerly the philosopher king had amused himself with Voltaire in tracing to the bottom the follies of mankind. The Rosicrucians had worked themselves into the confidence of Frederick William, heir to the Prussian throne. As soon as he succeeded they usurped his authority, governed in his name and dominated Prussia. In 1789 they were all-powerful, and it will be seen that they exercised at one moment a decisive influence over the greatest affairs of Europe.

Thus, at the same time as the germs of revolution were fermenting everywhere in Europe, and everything seemed to favour revolutionary propaganda, elements of reaction and resistance were appearing. All these were, in two very opposed forms, the result of the same tendencies of the human mind, and they were not confined to the French. The same causes of disturbance were shaking the foundations of all states and analogous crises seemed imminent in all nations.

5. NATIONS AND IDEAS

The Revolution broke out in France and spread from thence; some peoples accepted its principles straight away, others re-

pudiated them. Some governments fell because they opposed
it, some survived by struggling against it, and others found a
way, while resisting its conquests, to identify themselves with
its spirit and regain strength by imitating its example. If the
French Revolution became propagandist, and if its propaganda produced such different results in different places, we
must not look for the explanation of this in the prevailing
doctrines, because they were everywhere the same. The cause
is to be found wholly in the varying characters of the different nations. Doctrines and ideas could only spread in the way
they did because they were abstract and universal: every
nation was susceptible to their influence because each could
interpret them in the light of its own temperament, its feelings and its established ideas. It followed that the same formulas served for the expression of very different sentiments
and the same phrases enshrined very different ideas. It was
precisely over the meaning of generally accepted propositions that there was a conflict. As soon as mutual exploration
was attempted, differences of opinion began. This was of
major significance for subsequent history and it is important
to make it clear.

The nations, by interpreting the doctrines they were taught
in their own way and each picturing abstract man in its own
image, were only bringing the doctrine back to its initial point
and abstract man back to his origins. They each returned to
reality through the route by which they had left it. These
famous systems—and I refer above all to political ones—were
universal only in form. They assumed the formal pattern presented by the age. The world was misled into taking what
was only, most of the time, the classical method of exposition
for the basic principles. A careful analysis and examination
of the beginnings of the best-known of these theories shows
more or less clearly that they derive from specific facts, which
were then isolated, abstracted, generalised and turned into
maxims. This was the case with Hobbes in his *Leviathan*
and Locke in his *Civil Government*. Each concerned himself
with England and its government alone; the former was

driven towards absolutism by the sight of revolution and the latter towards liberty by the experience of absolutism. Bossuet described the monarchy of Louis XIV, idealising it to bring it closer to the precepts of Scripture. The abbé de Saint-Pierre looked to the Holy Roman Empire, and his perpetual peace is only a reformed and developed version of its constitution. Kant had only Germany in view.

All these examples, however, vanish before that of Rousseau. The *Contrat social* was written solely for Geneva; it expresses the wishes of a Genevan democrat for his country.* This is the key to its comprehension, and it shows that the reforms proposed by Rousseau, though radical, had nothing utopian about them. Geneva was a city-state of the classic type; its tradition was republican; even with an extensive citizenship all citizens could take part in the actual government. Direct government by the people, at a pinch, need be neither a fiction nor a fraud. Rousseau idealised all his passions; he saw the world in himself and humanity in his fatherland. In reality all he had studied and knew was Geneva. 'What will you think, Monsieur,' he wrote to a Genevan, 'in reading this short and accurate analysis of my book? I can guess your answer, you will say to yourself: here is the history of the government of Geneva! . . . I have taken your constitution, which seems to me a good one, as the model for political institutions, and in putting you forward as an example to Europe, far from seeking to destroy you I have set forth the means of your preservation.'[45] Does it follow that he believed the same system good for all states and an infallible prescription? This idea was far from him. Educated as

* Most commentators on Rousseau would now regard this as an exaggerated verdict, but the influence of Geneva on Rousseau's political ideas is still a subject for debate. More recent discussions than those cited by Sorel are G. Vallette, *Jean-Jacques Rousseau genevois* (1911), J. S. Spink, *Jean-Jacques et Genève* (1934), A. Cobban, *Rousseau and the Modern State* (revised edition, 1964).

[45] *Lettres de la Montagne*, letter VI.

he was on Plutarch, he knew that Sparta had disappeared from the face of the earth and that a copy of it was no longer to be found even at Geneva.[46] He judged that a republic was only appropriate to small and poor states.[47] The only hope he saw for great states was in the federative system.[48] In respect of constitutions, he declared that 'each is the best in some cases and the worst in others'.[49] The essential thing was that nations should remain true to themselves. On these grounds he flattered himself that he was the least cosmopolitan of men. 'If you arrange it so that a Pole can never become a Russian, I guarantee that Russia will never subdue Poland. National institutions shape the genius, the character, the preferences and the customs of a people. They make it what it is. They inspire it with an ardent love of the fatherland, founded on customs which cannot be uprooted. They make it perish of boredom amid other peoples and in the bosom of pleasures it lacks in its own country. . . . *Ubi patria, ibi bene.*'[50]

Divested of the artifice and illusion of style, here is the true basis of Rousseau's thought. This is why, outside Geneva, only the formula and the abstract features were grasped. When it was put into practice the doctrine was falsified, in different ways according to the different nations. In France, for example, the idea of the direct government of the people led to power being given up to armed crowds and the clubs of Paris. The principle of the sovereignty of the people, interpreted under the influence of the traditions of Rome and applied in a centralised state, resulted in the despotism of a handful of sectaries. The past of France and the imperatives of its history made federalism seem a crime. Consequently there was no longer any element of moderation,

[46] *Lettres de la Montagne*, letter IX.
[47] *Contrat social*, liv. III, ch. VIII.
[48] *Contrat social*, liv. III, ch. XV.
[49] *Contrat social*, liv. III, ch. III.
[50] *Gouvernement de la Pologne*, ch. III; cf. *id.*, ch. IV: *Education*.

any corrective in the system; there remained only the paradox of tyranny. In Germany, on the contrary, where federal institutions prevailed, where there was a host of petty principalities and where the essential vice of the state was the dispersion of power and the division of the nation, the doctrine of the contract promoted the strengthening of the state and the concentration of the nation; it fell in quite naturally with the stream of history. The disciples of Rousseau, who were revolutionaries in France, became reformers in Germany.

Thus a study of the nations leads us to the same result as the study of states, and we draw from an examination of ideas the same consequence as from the examination of political institutions. In the revolution which was coming governments only followed raison d'état, that is to say their interests envisaged in the light of their experience. Nations only followed their hereditary genius, that is to say the character, emotions, instincts they had evolved in the course of centuries. The peoples, beginning with the French, interpreted the Revolution according to their national traditions, and the governments dealt with it according to their political habits. Therefore we must go back to these traditions and habits to understand the relations of France and Europe during the Revolution: they provide the key to this whole history.

BOOK TWO

Political Traditions:
France

I. The Nation and the Government

I. TRADITIONAL MONARCHY

Whether France under the ancien régime possessed a constitution is a much debated question. We might rummage through the most secret archives of the kingdom without finding one; our kings never believed in one and their lawyers denied its existence.[1] True, whenever the state got into difficulties and authority was weakened, there was always an

[1] Louis XVI declared to the Parlement of Paris, on 19 November 1787: 'The principles to which I wish to recall you are of the essence of the monarchy and I will not allow them to be disowned or tampered with.'—The Keeper of the Seals, Lamoignon, set them out in these terms: 'These principles, universally accepted by the nation, bear witness that *the sovereign power in the kingdom belongs to the king alone*; that he is accountable only to God for the exercise of his supreme power . . . that the king is sovereign head of the nation and is one with it; finally that the legislative power resides in the person of the sovereign, independent and indivisible. It follows from these ancient maxims of the nation, witnessed on every page of our history, that to the king alone belongs the right of convoking the *Etats généraux*, that he alone can judge whether the convocation is useful or necessary; that he has need of no extraordinary powers for the government of his realm; that *for a king of France the representatives of the three orders of the State are only an extended royal council, composed of members chosen from a family of which he is the head, and that he will always be the supreme arbiter of their representative capacity and their grievances*'—speech of the king to the Parlement; speech of M. de Lamoignon, Keeper of the Seals, at the royal session of the Parlement, 19 November 1787, *Archives parlementaires*, Madival et Laurent (1868), i. 264 ff.

appeal to the fundamental laws—which however were nowhere to be found. Everyone called them to witness, but none could specify them. The keenest minds could scarcely discern 'the almost obliterated traces of the wise middle way that our fathers discovered between the despotism of kings and the anarchy of the people'.[2] We must take care not to follow up these will o' the wisps. They lead to quicksands, and anyone who ventures in them is swallowed up. 'As though waking from sleep the people groped about for the laws', wrote Retz of the troubles of 1647, 'but they found none.'[3] 'It's a game at which one is bound to lose', declared Pascal; 'the people, having lent a ready ear to speeches telling it of the yoke it endures, then proceeds to revolt. Better that it should not know of usurpation, which, unjust in origin, has since become just and must be regarded as such. If the usurped power is not to come to a rapid end, it must be thought of as having been just from all time, and its beginnings left obscure.'[4] The foundations of government should remain a mystery. If there is any fundamental law it is this maxim, which takes the place of all others: 'the rights of the peoples and those of kings never harmonise so well as in silence'.[5]

However, a monarchy as powerful as the French does not prevail for eight successive centuries over so many enemies without and so many revolts within, it does not increase continually in strength and glory, without having its own justifications and its principles arising therefrom. By the accumulation of precedents, customs may develop, and from customs may be produced the principles of a constitution. But this is only theory. The whole authority of the French state depended on the history of the past, its whole sanction on the history of the future. No theory could bind the present and politicians took account of none. Montesquieu drew up, on

[2] Retz, *Mémoires*, 2nd part, ch. II, 1646.
[3] *Id.*, 2nd part, ch. III.
[4] *Pensées*, éd. Havet, article III, no. 8.
[5] Retz, *id.*, 2nd part, ch. III.

the basis of this theory, several chapters of his admirable work; but all his genius could not put the *Esprit des lois* in place of *Habeas corpus* for a Frenchman or safeguard him from a *lettre de cachet,* an order of confiscation or the arbitrary exaction of a tax. The attempt to reduce the customs of the ancien régime to their basic elements brings us to the formula which sums up the whole spirit of its politics, just as the theory sums up the spirit of its constitution: 'a prudent monarch served by intelligent ministers'. 'The frivolity and inconstancy of the French', said Richelieu, 'can only be overcome by the presence of a master. They are equal to anything, provided that their rulers show them clearly what they should do. I make bold to tell your Majesty that if you find leaders worthy to command, you will not lack subjects ready to obey. Unquestionably, the general opinion in the world that the French are incapable of order and discipline reflects only the unfitness of leaders who do not know how to adjust their means to their ends.'[6] This sums up the whole monarchical constitution and reveals the essential cause of the greatness and the decline of the French monarchy.

Great kings with good ministers, or at least cautious kings with great ministers, were needed. Henry IV and Sully, Louis XIII and Richelieu, are the perfect models of the old government, in which individuals were everything and institutions nothing. In the absence of men of superior talent there was only a void, for there were no laws which would enable the state to do without them or even to mark time till they appeared. Thus brilliant and prosperous reigns were succeeded by long periods of sterile disorder.

This was not caused by the whims of a despot or the chance appearance of an ambitious man. It was a result of the general conditions of development of the nation and state, of the very nature of things. By the fourteenth century, one historian says, it had already been settled, to the sorrow of

[6] *Testament,* ch. VI.

the kingdom and the people, that the monarchy should be absolute and that France should be a stranger to liberty.[7] The causes go back to the origins of the monarchy and derive in a way from its very raison d'être. In France, the nation and the state were formed and developed together. Feudalism split both into fragments; but the nation naturally tended to reunite and the crown provided it with a rallying point. The first condition of success was the destruction of the feudal system. The crown could not increase its power, or the nation take shape, except at the expense of the feudal barons. To the king they were rivals and rebels; to the bourgeois and the peasant, oppressors. The people turned to the king for aid, and their hatred of feudal rule strengthened the king's hand in his struggle with the barons. This is the essence of the nation's history, which gives it consistency from the Middle Ages to the Revolution. The parallel impulses which drove the monarchy towards centralisation and the nation towards the king operated through the same agents —the lawyers, who came from the bourgeoisie, became ministers of the king, and established the principle of royal supremacy.

In this respect no histories are more contradictory than those of France and England. The great contrast between them is evident from the start. In France the whole development was against the feudal system; the essential nucleus of the nation was the third estate, which allied with the king against the nobles. In England the national struggle was directed against the crown; the nation crystallised round the gentry, who allied with the bourgeoisie against the king. Everything in France tended towards centralisation, everything in England towards a division of powers. The national expression of the old England was a powerful Parliament, that of the old France a great king. The English, moreover, did not have to reckon with foreign invasion; in their struggles

---

[7] Lavisse, *Du pouvoir royal en France sous Charles V.* (*Revue politique*, 1880, and *Revue historique*, 1884).

against royal supremacy and in the civil wars which followed, they had no fear of foreign intervention. On the contrary, this anxiety was the dominant preoccupation of the French in their internal troubles. The threat of conquest always hung over them, and they were not free for long at a time to pursue their internal quarrels without being exposed to pressure from abroad. It was in periods of disorder and anarchy that the great demands of the English on the crown were put forward. The French in such times had neither liberty to act nor a free choice of their course of action. If they took advantage of the struggle to fetter their king, the foreigner would take advantage of it in advance to fetter them. They attended first to what was most pressing, and the sentiment of national independence took precedence over the desire for political liberty.

All these national characteristics became fixed in the course of the great crisis of the sixteenth century. The two monarchies emerged from it fully grown, at their full stature and with their definitive cast of countenance. The reason why France had no Great Charter or House of Commons is also the reason why the Reformation failed there. It appealed to argument against Catholic dogmatism; it appealed above all to conscience and grace. It called for liberty and did much to hasten its arrival, though liberty was not its prime and immediate object. The Reformation was essentially a Christian reaction against the unbelief and the free-thought of the Renaissance,* the revival of a faith which had been strained almost to dissolution by the soothing scepticism of Rome, a protest against the serene pagan joys of Italy, a return to the conscience, to spiritual unease and agony, a retreat across the Middle Ages to St. Augustine and St. Paul. In the field of religion it shattered the unity of the Church; in the field of politics it led by way of the self-government of the parish to that of the commune, and so

* Sorel's summary over-simplifies the relation between the Reformation and the Renaissance.

tended to break up the unity of the state. Since the idea of toleration had not entered into men's minds, a dissident church could only survive with the support of an armed faction. Religious divisions implied political ones. But it was not in the nature of the state to tolerate schism; either it had to accept the Reformation, or the adherents of the Reformed Church had to form a sort of state within a state. These were the decisive considerations.

France was too deeply imbued with classical culture, too naturally drawn towards rationalism, too enamoured of pure logic, to be able to accept a compromise between reason and faith. Among its rulers, the moderates, the *politiques* as they were called, were indifferent in religious matters, while the devout were fanatics. The Reformation seemed unprofitable to the former and criminal to the latter. Moreover both were, politically, firmly on the side of unity, and on this ground they joined in condemning the Reformation. If it was favoured by nobles, this was only because it gave them the opportunity to resume their struggle against the crown. To these feudal aims were added, in certain towns, vague ideas of republicanism. If the great nobles and the republicans, momentarily united, had won, their success would have led, in all probability, not to the strengthening of public liberties by setting up a parliament like the English one, but to the breaking up of the state and its dissolution into a confederacy. France would have moved not in the direction of England and the Revolution of 1688, but of Germany and the Treaty of Westphalia.

Moreover other Powers were mobilised and waiting their chance: when it came they seized on it. Called in by the French factions, Spain and Germany in turn urged them on and stirred up the flames of civil war. All they wanted was the spoils. The king did not intend to share his power with the leaders of the Reforming party or his kingdom with the allies of the League. By defending the unity of the state against the former and the integrity of French territory against the latter, he responded to the deepest sentiments of the nation. It did not want either the rule of the nobles or the intervention of foreign Powers: it preferred dictatorship. That was its instinct, which we find still alive and impassioned in the Revolution. The sixteenth-century dictator was the king. As against the Huguenots, suspect of federalism, and the *Ligueurs*, committed to Spain, he alone represented the national tradition. The idea of the Reformation was contrary to the main trend of French thought, and its practical consequences to that of French polity. Hence it did not prevail. I do not say that this result was good for France and that we have to congratulate ourselves on it. But to imagine France with Magna Carta and the Reformation would be to turn it into England and to reverse all the conditions of its history. Our regret should not be so much for the 'great refusal' of France as for the deep-rooted causes which made it inevitable. It was the same causes which were in the end to bring the monarchy to disaster and leave the French no way out of the impasse in which they found themselves, no other recourse than revolution.

Such is the secret power of great historic forces. In France, where the Reformation threatened national unity and the absolute monarchy, it strengthened them; in England, where it was directed against public liberties, it confirmed them. The English Reformation was initiated by a despotic king, Henry VIII, under the influence of his passions—impatience with the yoke of Rome, desire for the lands of the Church, and ambition for absolute power. He believed that by making himself head of the Church he would control the minds of the English. But their spirit was too independent, the Reformation was for them a liberation of conscience, and all the devices of the crown could not prevent them from seeing it as a religious Magna Carta. Far from subjugating them to the authority of the king, the Reformation, on the contrary, inspired them in their struggle for public liberties with a new conviction and feeling of pride. Like the constitution, it became identified with the nation; and it made the constitution somehow more intimate and dearer to the English by linking it with their religion. Political liberty provided a natural basis for the Reformation, and the monarchy was to find in the sects to which it gave birth more formidable and desperate opponents than the political factions had ever been.

The result of the religious revolution settled the fate of those revolutions which followed. In England, as in France, national traditions were the decisive factor. In England they went back to the institutions of the Middle Ages and the struggle against the royal attempt to gain absolute power. In France, on the other hand, they were derived from a violent aversion for the same institutions and from the struggle against the feudal aristocracy which was attempting to revive them for its own advantage. The English revolutions of the seventeenth century prepared the way for the final triumph of free government; in France the chaotic and rash disturbances of the Fronde ensured the triumph of the absolute monarchy.

However, the monarchy, to be able to maintain its great rôle, constantly needed to reconquer its ground and gain new strength from its original source. It could not afford to be under a misapprehension about either its raison d'être or the conditions of its success. It was in duty bound to exercise its power with all the more moderation because there was no check on it. The nation had abdicated its rights but not its judgement. Since it had abandoned everything to the crown, it expected something substantial in return. It had given itself into the hands of the king in order to be governed well, with foresight, order and moderation. Henry IV understood this. He accepted Catholicism for the sake of the unity of the state; but he conceded to the Huguenots all the liberty of conscience that the conditions of the time allowed. The Edict of Nantes was complementary to his conversion; they cannot be separated. His conversion gave him the crown, and the Edict assured him of the submission of the kingdom. He introduced into the laws a toleration that was still unclear and uncertain in men's minds. He set up the government which will always be the most popular in France, that of intelli-

gence and common sense. He did more: he believed that by
securing supreme power, and making himself the head and
the representative of the nation, he had taken on himself the
obligation of leading the nation towards those ends which
it vaguely desired without being able to achieve them. He
was a reforming king, and in that respect also, and even
more deeply, he entered into the traditions of the monarchy.

To assume that the nation was indifferent to affairs of
state and capable only of obedience would be to misunder-
stand its character. France had not lost the taste for liberty
in subordinating it to the public weal. There is a long tradition of independence in its history; from time to time the
nation's rights were asserted; and the French never let despotism establish itself for long without opposition. The spirit
of democratic liberty never appeared in a more striking form
than in the communes of the Middle Ages. The *cahiers* of
the States General, from the fourteenth to the seventeenth
century, anticipate essentially all the demands of 1789. If
the Estates failed in their attempts to take over the government, it was because they were only summoned in time of
trouble, in face of disaster and in the midst of disorder. Lacking the experience and the powers needed for government,
they could merely formulate their desires. It was for the
monarchy to put them into practice, to extract from the
cahiers the elements of practical reform, and to carry out in
orderly fashion those things that the Estates had confusedly
put forward. By securing for the people the chief advantages
that they hoped for from liberty, the monarchy led them for
a time to forget the principle itself. 'The actual text of the
cahiers was in front of those who drew up the ordinances
of Charles V and Louis XII.'[8] Again, after the troubles of
the sixteenth century the reforms of L'Hôpital* appeared,

---

[8] Picot, *op. cit.*, t. IV, p. 296. Cf. t. I, pp. 208 and 537; and, for
Henry IV, t. III, p. 274; *Résultats de l'Assemblée des notables.*

* Sorel's disposition to find repetitive patterns in history has led
him astray here. Michel de l'Hôpital, appointed Chancellor in
1560, was dismissed from effective power in 1568. His great re-

and the reforms of Sully, which marked the reign of Henry IV, came from the inspiration of the Assembly of Notables.

Similarly, after the disturbances early in the seventeenth century and the meeting of the Estates in 1614, there was the great constructive work of Richelieu; and after the Fronde, the years of pacification and fruitful reorganization associated with the name of Colbert. A great historian has compared these times to the Consulate, a comparison which explains both the rise and the success of Bonaparte.[9]

With Louis XIV the monarchy reached its apogee. The apotheosis of the king was decreed, statues were raised to him; he was a Roman emperor, one of those placed among the gods. 'It was', declared Michelet, 'the most complete triumph of monarchy, the most perfect harmony of people and king that had ever been seen.'[10] Towards the middle of the reign, and in the later years of the century, the tide which had carried the monarchy along with it gradually slackened, and the waters piled up as they flowed back on themselves. The promulgation of the Edict of Nantes by Henry IV had signalised the maturity of the monarchy; the Revocation of the Edict by his grandson marked its decline. Up to that point it had possessed coherence without being systematised: it was now to make a system for itself and out of the system to create a dogma. It had lived by compromises, it now became uncompromising. Moderation had given it strength; by using this strength immoderately it was to ruin itself. The monarchy no longer ruled in the interests of the nation; it no longer ruled for the state; it ruled for itself and for itself alone. It became an end in itself, and a god to itself. It was absorbed in its own cult and was overwhelmed. It had grown like a great oak which gathers in its sap all the goodness of the

forming edicts came at the very beginning of the civil wars of the sixteenth century, not after the troubles, and they remained merely paper enactments, since their practical application was frustrated by the opposition of the Parlements and the Guise faction.

[9] Guizot, *Civilisation en Europe*, lecture XIV.
[10] *Précis de l'histoire moderne*.

earth round it and gives back in return the coolness of its shade and the wholesomeness of the atmosphere it creates. Yet at the very time when the tree seemed most majestic, in the brilliance of its finest summer, the sap stopped flowing in its branches and they fell one by one. The trunk dried up and wasted inwardly. The roots were rotten and no longer held to the soil, its branches were bared to the wind, the rains wore it down from above and parasites attacked it from below. Formerly it had been a shelter against the storms, henceforth it could no longer weather them; it would be shattered and uprooted by the first tempest that broke upon it.

For the monarchy to survive and renew itself it had to persevere in reform and continue in the task of national emancipation; it had to combine glory with moderation; the state had to be prosperous and the people content; extremes had to be avoided and abuses removed. Having abolished the political power of the noblesse, the monarchy should have suppressed the accompanying economic advantages, which now lacked justification; it should have freed the land and completed the enfranchisement of the people. In the sixteenth century there had been a need for a 'tolerant' monarchy, in the seventeenth century for a powerful and in the eighteenth for an enlightened one. If it declined or evaded the task, the nation had acquired sufficient awareness of itself and its rights to insist on the fulfilment of its hopes; and the king was to find leading the campaign against him the very lawyers who during five centuries had fought for him against the nobles.* Having aided him to gain power, they claimed to exercise it with him, or if he resisted, against him.

The monarchy had disarmed itself, dismantled its strongholds and handed over the gates to its enemies; resistance

* Sorel rightly saw in the struggle of the eighteenth-century Parlements against the ministers one of the chief sources of the Revolution, but he was mistaken in regarding the Parlements as the advocates of enlightened reforms. It was the reforming activities of the royal administration that aroused their opposition, in which they allied with the privileged orders against the crown.

was excluded, since any resistance would be against the nation. 'Tout est devenu peuple devant lui', said Saint-Simon of Louis XIV.* The state towered like a colossus over an undifferentiated mass: there was nothing to protect it from attack. Louis XI subjected the appanages to the monarchy; Henry IV overcame the religious factions, Richelieu the political ones. As for the noblesse, for four centuries the monarchy had struggled to deprive it of all its influence, organization and political functions. The structure of the State was ambitious and glorious beyond compare; but it resembled one of those Gothic cathedrals in which the height of the vault and the opening of the arches were carried to the point of paradox, narrowing and making gaps in the walls in proportion as they rose higher. That done, to clarify and open up the outline of the building, the aisles and the buttresses which held up its walls were demolished. The result was that the edifice visibly tottered on its foundations; at the least blow against the walls it would crumple up under the pressure of its vaults and the crushing weight of its towers.

Louis XIV pushed the monarchical principle to extremes; he abused it excessively and in every way. He left the nation crushed by war, maimed by proscriptions, and chafing under a yoke which now seemed ruinous. His ministers were worn out, the treasury empty; all the springs of the state, strained beyond endurance, were broken, and in its huge frame there remained no other recourse than the chance appearance of genius. Things had reached the point where only a great king could forestall a great revolution.

2. THE CRISIS OF THE MONARCHY

The revolution was incubating throughout the eighteenth century. Its symptoms appeared one after another: muffled

* Saint-Simon means that Louis XIV had reduced the higher orders in the state to the level of the populace. This is, of course, a great exaggeration.

sounds were heard, fissures appeared in the ground, and along the walls the cracks which foretell the earthquake. The situation that developed was the most unbearable of all —chaotic despotism, irresolute omnipotence, centralised anarchy. Everyone looked after his own interests. All the forces of society were in conflict. Bishops and Parlements quarrelled; the government struggled with the clergy and the magistrature. Lampoons proliferated and authority was relaxed. Divisions among the leaders stimulated disorder among the people, who became accustomed to despise them by witnessing their mutual enmities. Only during the ministry of Fleury was there some respite; but his uneventful term of office was of greater duration than consequence. Louis XV, when he took charge, showed himself jealous of his authority, uneasy, apathetic and apprehensive. He was incapable of ruling personally, but he would not let his ministers govern in his name; and as he dared not contradict them he conspired against them and impeded them in secret. For their part, they intrigued against one another and quarrelled violently. 'The councils of the ministers in the time of the Marshal de Noailles', wrote d'Argenson, 'were the most frightful things in the world; celestial thunder could not have been heard in them.'* The honourable gentlemen took counsel like an assembly of demagogues. 'The Marshal went all out against anyone who argued with him; he stamped with his feet, threw his hat about the room, and changed his principles at every meeting. M. de Maurepas yapped, joked and produced epigrams that he thought to be unquestionable maxims of State. The Cardinal de Tencin resorted to Moréri† at every commonplace that he did not know, which was frequently the case.' The meetings of the Council were fol-

* Marshal de Noailles (1678-1766), Minister of State 1743-1756.

† Author of *Le Grand Dictionnaire historique, ou le Mélange curieux de l'histoire sainte et profane*, 1674. It acquired great authority and went through many subsequent editions and enlargements.

lowed by those held in the King's presence, which were no
better. 'The King', wrote one of his ministers, 'is more detested and despised by the members of his Council than he
could be by the most fanatical republicans.'[11] He paid them
back in kind by changing them at his whim or at the arbitrary
will of his mistresses.* The instability and disorder of the
French government were proverbial among foreign observers.
Towards the end of the reign, a clever adventurer, who had
plotted with the King against his own government, and who
had inadvertently been consigned to the Bastille, could reply
to an ill-advised judge who interrogated him: 'I have learnt
from the King himself to distinguish between his sacred person and that of his ministers, for in the seventeen years that
I have been in his service, his Majesty has disgraced or dismissed twenty-six ministers.'[12]

Royal finances only survived by periodic bankruptcies. The
army was in dissolution. It remained brave, capable of brilliant deeds in the face of the enemy and even of fine examples of steadfastness, as in the retreat from Prague.† But,
as a whole, it was a broken-down machine, jerked about er-
ratically under the impulsion of strings pulled from Versailles. The generals felt themselves constantly under threat
of recall, disgrace, trial, exile, or the Bastille. Their aim was
to please rather than to conquer, to negotiate rather than to
fight, to intrigue at Court rather than to harass the enemy.
Politics invaded the camps, their factions hated one another
and discipline vanished in a network of intrigue. The type
of soldier remained good, but with the example he was given

[11] D'Argenson, *Journal et Mémoires*, t. IV, pp. 139-146.

* As an absolute monarch and the heir of Louis XIV, Louis XV
was a complete failure; but the picture of him drawn by a dismissed minister such as d'Argenson must not be taken as the
exact truth. Louis disliked being parted from those he was used
to, and the instability of his ministers, after Fleury, is not to be
attributed merely to his whims. Also, the political influence of
his mistresses has been greatly exaggerated.

[12] Dumouriez, *Mémoires*, liv. II, ch. I.

† Conducted by Belle-Isle in 1742.

he became an impudent pillager and plunderer. It was a story of decay. 'The principal cause', writes a Marshal, 'is the total ignorance, from ensigns to general officers, of the duties of their position. . . . The lieutenants and the captains do not know how to manage or command their companies, and colonels, brigadiers, *maréchaux de camp*, in turn, know no better how to lead their regiments, brigades, divisions. . . . Our officers all have, individually, as much courage, talent and intelligence as those of the enemy, but they fail in one essential point: there are few among them, even in the lower ranks, who have not their own plan of campaign and find fault with the general's; and there is practically none who does not think his rank beneath what he deserves.'[13]

This was the essential vice, and it is the prime cause of all revolutions—the exaggeration, ruin and bankruptcy of authority. The spirit of sedition is always latent in men's minds and only requires the dykes to break for anarchy to overflow. Paris was full of tribunes ready to harangue the crowds, and of poor wretches, scoundrels and hotheads ready to enlist in their train. The legend of demagoguery survived underground and was a living tradition. The revolutions in Paris during the Hundred Years War were the prototype of all that followed. The leaders of the gilds formed themselves into a Commune and seized power. They had their *journées*, invaded the Palace, identified the armed bands which followed them with the will of the people, massacred ministers under the eyes of the king, set up a dictatorship and governed by terror. Etienne Marcel* reminds us of Danton, Caboche† foretells Maillard.‡ In the sixteenth century the

[13] Report of the Maréchal de Broglie in 1759. *Le Secret du Roi*, t. I, p. 343.

* Leader of the popular party in Paris, 1355-58, during the captivity of Jean II in England.

† Caboche put himself at the head of the butchers of Paris in the early fifteenth century and became the leader of a faction which attached itself to the Burgundian party and for a time terrorised Paris.

‡ Son of a minor officer of the law courts; he played a part in

Ligue added religious fanaticism to the spirit of anarchy. It already foreshadowed the formidable organization of the Jacobins, and was denounced and feared as that famous Society was to be later. Saint-Simon spoke of the henchmen of Guise as Joseph de Maistre was to speak of the zealots of Robespierre—'these raging preachers, that scum of fanatics who produce so much confusion in the uneducated minds and weak consciences of the people. . . . That hydra-head of the League which devoured Europe, but was frustrated in its plans and hounded to its death.'[14]

Rioting has its precedents and its classic form. In 1648, Retz relates, 'The unrest was like a sudden and violent conflagration spreading from the Pont-neuf through the whole town. Everyone took up arms. Children of five or six carried daggers, sometimes provided by their mothers. More than twelve hundred barricades appeared in Paris in less than two hours, with flags flying and defended by the arms left behind by the League.' A century later a minister of Louis XV wrote, 'With inflammable materials everywhere, a riot may turn into a revolt, and a revolt into a full revolution, which will set up tribunes of the people, revolutionary committees, communes.'[15] Again, 'The Parisians are in turmoil. . . . A magistrate told me that if the Court of the Châtelet is suppressed he is sure there will be barricades and in that way the revolution will begin.'[16]

Towards the middle of the century political agitation was appearing everywhere. In 1749 a pamphlet apostrophized the king: 'Louis, if you were fomerly the object of our affection, it was because we did not yet know how corrupt you were: if Frenchmen still live in this kingdom, depopulated by your crimes and delivered like a prey to the mountebanks who reign with you, it is to curse you.' In the same year

the attack on the Bastille, the October Days and the September massacres.

14 *Parallèle*, pp. 47 and 121.
15 D'Argenson, *Journal*, 1751.
16 D'Argenson, *Journal*, 1753.

another lampoon began, 'Awake, shades of Ravaillac!'[17]* As early as 1720 handbills had been scattered through the town with the words, 'Kill the tyrant and never mind the consequences.' Friendly, gay, pleasing as the French, and Parisians in particular, may seem, they are always capable of turning again to savagery, and going over, as Voltaire said, 'from the Opera to Saint-Bartholomew.'[18] The fact is, poverty was frightful, years of dearth followed one another, revolts broke out here and there in the provinces, the roads were infested with bandits, and the focus of all these smouldering discontents was Paris. The agitators and the firebrands, to use Roederer's description, had only to appeal to hunger to excite acts of cruelty. Nobody doubted it. In 1754 d'Argenson believed that it would begin with 'tearing priests to pieces in the streets, even the Archbishop of Paris'. In 1750 there was a rumour that children were being kidnapped to populate the colonies. The *faubourgs* rose, and some of the police archers were killed. The mob gathered in front of the house of the Lieutenant of Police, saying that it would massacre him and *eat his heart* and then burn Versailles. The Lieutenant, 'ghastly as a drowned man', only saved himself by handing over to the rioters an officer of the watch, who was at once dragged into the gutter and beaten to death. To conclude, we may cite two ministers of Louis XV: 'Everything is falling to pieces.' 'All is in decay: if we prop up the building on one side, it crumbles on the other. . . . We are approaching the ultimate period of decadence.'[19]

All these facts existed, their causes were in operation and consequences manifest before the Seven Years War and while the influence of the *philosophes* had hardly made itself felt. The *Esprit des lois* appeared in 1748, the first vol-

[17] Rocquain, *l'Esprit révolutionnaire*, liv. IV.
* Who assassinated Henry IV.
[18] Letter of 1776. *Lettres inédites*, published in 1856 by M. de Cayrol. Sainte-Beuve, *Causeries*, t. XIII, article *Voltaire*.
[19] D'Argenson, 1752, VII, p. 295. Bernis, 1758, II, pp. 221, 238.

ume of the *Encyclopédie* in 1751; Voltaire was in Prussia
working on the *Siècle de Louis XIV*; Raynal was almost unknown, Rousseau known only for the two *Discours* written
in 1750 and 1754 for the Academy of Dijon, and Mably by
his compilations on public law. But the spirit of enquiry and
criticism was in the air, along with a general restlessness and
discontent. When the parlements acted as though they were
a Roman Senate, when one could read in the opinions of
lawyers, as early as 1726, that 'The laws are effective conventions between those who govern and those who are governed';[20] when, in its Remonstrances, a Sovereign Court
could declare, 'If subjects owe obedience to kings, for their
part kings owe obedience to the laws', and that 'The nation
is above the king as the Church is above the Pope',[21] the
times were already ripe for revolutionary doctrines. The
propaganda came at the right moment to arouse public feeling. Public opinion was ready for it. In various ways the
state had opened the gates to its enemies and the disasters
of the Seven Years War provided the impulse. The revolutionary situation was a result of the faults of the government,
but the *philosophes* gave it leaders, cadres, a doctrine, direction, the temptation of illusions and the irresistible mo-
mentum of hope. They did not create the causes of the revolution, but they made them manifest, actuated them, gave
them emotive force, multiplied them and quickened their
pace. The writings of the *philosophes* were not responsible
for the disintegration of the ancien régime: it was because
it was disintegrating of its own accord that their influence
promoted the Revolution.

If the Revolution did not break out during the reign of
Louis XV, this was because France remained profoundly
monarchical, and because it had, in the words of a contemporary, the expectation of a new reign. In this crisis, as in all
previous ones, the nation, when it lost its bearings, looked
to the king. It expected everything of him, because it be-

[20] Rocquain, pp. 56-57.
[21] *Remonstrances* of 1753, 23 May.

lieved that to him everything was possible. Doubtless many talked of political liberty, but most had only a vague idea of what it meant and none had any practical knowledge of it. They desired it above all for the sake of the results it was expected to bring, and these results were reforms which the state itself could in fact have carried out.

The first and the most essential of these was civil liberty: liberty of person and property, the basic liberty which is the necessary condition of all others. It consisted simply in the destruction of the last vestiges of the feudal régime. The second was the fair distribution of taxation between all citizens. Both were in the interest of the state: the first would give it more loyal subjects and the second a more ample revenue. They were only prejudicial to the privileged classes, the nobles and the clergy, that is to say to the classes which for five centuries the state had been striving to reduce to full obedience. The state would thus increase at the same time its wealth and its popularity, and so crown its achievement. That is why these reforms were constantly in the minds of its ministers and lawyers. Their portfolios were full of plans for reforms: the committees of the revolutionary assemblies, and the Councillors of State of the year VIII, had only to pull them out by the handful.

The idea of codifying the laws was an old one. D'Aguesseau* had invited all the parlements of the kingdom to join in the great work: 'The perfection of the Laws', he said, 'is to be as simple and as general as possible. The Law must be the expression of a principle.' Pothier† undertook part of the task; his writings were to be the daily bread of those who drafted the Civil Code. Machault‡ planned the reform

* H.-F. d'Aguesseau, 1668-1751, Procurator-General of the Parlement of Paris 1700-1717, Chancellor of France 1717; ceased to be Garde des Sceaux with effective authority in 1722, but remained Chancellor till his death.

† R.-J. Pothier, 1699-1722, famous French jurisconsult and author of several learned works on French law.

‡ Machault d'Arnouville, Controller-General from 1745 to

of taxation; Mollien, who carried it into effect later, had already investigated the problem as a member of the ministerial bureaux. As early as 1769 Lebrun, who became a duke at the time when Mollien was made a count, had prepared for Maupeou, whose secretary he was, a whole plan of reorganisation of the judiciary. It was nearly enough the one which was carried into effect at the beginning of the nineteenth century. La Chalotais,* Guyton de Morveau† and Roland‡ had the idea of putting education into the hands of the state; the University of France, with its *Conseil supérieur*, its inspectors, its *écoles normales*, appears in germ in their writings.

Some of the men of the ancien régime went further and worked out plans for reforming its whole institutional framework. They did this with the interests of the people in mind; but the clearest advantage would have been to the interests of the state. I am not thinking of utopists but, for example, of an intendant, one who had passed his years in the administration and who became a minister: it was Turgot who told the king, 'So long as your Majesty does not depart from justice, you can regard yourself as absolute in making the law and count on the good will of the nation to execute your orders.'[22] The aim Turgot put before himself was to concentrate the power of the nation in the hands of the king so

---

1754, introduced the *vingtième* in 1749, but his attempted reform was frustrated by the parlements and the clergy.

* La Chalotais, Procurator-General in the Parlement of Brittany, took a prominent part in bringing about the suppression of the Jesuit order in France. He drew up a plan, published as *Essai d'Education nationale*, for a national system of education, which was highly regarded by Voltaire and others.

† Guyton de Morveau, 1737-1816, distinguished scientist, who played also a political rôle during the Revolution. He published, in 1762, a *Mémoire sur l'éducation publique*.

‡ J.-M. Roland, 1734-1793, politician, Minister of the Interior 1792-93, published a *Mémoire sur l'éducation des troupeaux*, Paris, 1779.

[22] Turgot, *Œuvres*, t. VII, p. 389.

that he could use it effectively.[23] Education was to give the people discipline and to shape their minds. 'Your Majesty will find everywhere talent, virtue, disinterestedness, honour and enthusiasm. Honesty will even become customary. No superhuman effort will be needed to unleash the strength of a united realm.'[24] To support the king in his task Turgot conceived of a hierarchy of municipal councils leading up to a 'grand national municipality' which would meet for six weeks every year in the presence of the king. It would administer but not rule, express its wishes but not pass laws, limiting itself to the discussion of principles without laying down rules. 'The royal authority will be enlightened without being hindered, and public opinion will be propitiated without danger.'[25] Lebrun proposed the summoning of Estates to form a king's council, adding, 'With the help of their votes the king's government would no longer need to be restricted or balanced by any other power.'[26]

This was the spirit of enlightened rule, the spirit of the century, and that of the French monarchy in its most fruitful years. It was by taking up, similarly, the ideas of their times that Charles V, Louis XII, Henry IV and Louis XIV had become great rulers and founded such a strong dynasty. There was nothing in the task which exceeded the strength of the monarchy or contradicted its traditions. 'If there had been on the throne a ruler of the stature and temperament of Frederick the Great,' wrote Tocqueville, 'I do not doubt that he would have carried out several of the great changes in society and government that the Revolution introduced, not only without the loss of his crown, but even to the increase of his authority.'[27]

This is what was discerned by the only great political figure to be brought forth by that time of troubles. Mirabeau

[23] *Id.*, t. II, p. 506.
[24] *Id.*, t. VII, p. 682.
[25] *Mémoire de 1775.*
[26] *La Voix du citoyen*, 1789.
[27] *L'Ancien Régime*, liv. III, ch. III.

wrote in 1790: 'A hereditary monarchy in the Bourbon dynasty; a permanent legislative body, periodically elected and restricted to making the law; an undivided executive, with wide scope and supremacy in all matters relating to the administration of the kingdom, the execution of the laws and the control of the police; a legislative body with exclusive authority over taxation; a new division of the kingdom; free justice; liberty of the press; ministerial responsibility; the sale of royal domain and the lands of the Church; the establishment of a Civil List; the abolition of distinctive orders, of privileges and of financial exemptions; the end of feudalism and of the parlements; an end to corporate bodies of noblesse and clergy and to provincial estates and provinces: this is what I mean by the bases of the constitution. It limits royal authority only to make it stronger; these principles are perfectly reconcilable with monarchical government.'[28]

What was wanted in 1774, when Louis XV died, was infinitely more modest. There was confidence in the king, and public opinion would not have haggled with him over the extent of his authority if he had employed it for popular reforms. Henry IV had never been so much hoped for, or Richelieu so praised. People dreamed of a king who would be a legislator, and by a curious piece of atavism the *philosophes* were pleased to represent the sovereign of the future under the lineaments of the legendary heroes of the Middle Ages. The lawyers of the first Capetians, at the beginning of the dynasty, invoked before these weak rulers the great name of Charlemagne. They pictured him as the imperial founder and sought the titles of the monarchy in vague memories of his reign. Eight centuries later, the *philosophes* again put forward his example to show Louis XVI how a state should be reformed. 'Mably', said a contemporary, 'reveals Charlemagne as the *philosophe*, the patriot, the legislator. He shows him renouncing an arbitrary power which is always fatal to

28 Bacourt, *Correspondance entre Mirabeau et le comte de la Marck*, Thirtieth note. Paris, 1851.

princes and recognising those imprescriptible rights of man which had fallen into oblivion.'[29] The great figure which had towered over the dawn of the monarchy reappeared in its twilight. Philip Augustus had been inspired by his example; Bonaparte was obsessed by his memory. Louis XVI was more modest in his aspirations.

3. LOUIS XVI

He had a difficult task. To curb such uneasy spirits, channel the turbulent current of opinion and yet make use of it, keep the nation under control and at the same time emancipate it, was a daunting programme. Again, to overcome the opposition of the privileged classes and keep them obedient while despoiling them of their privileges, to shore up the foundations of the building and give it new buttresses at the very moment when what remained of the old ones was being destroyed—such a task called for boldness, vision and flexibility. What was needed was a Henry IV, subtle and strong, a bold, ingenious and enterprising statesman. Though endowed with the qualities to make a dynasty popular in a prosperous age, Louis XVI had none of those necessary to establish one in time of trouble or re-establish it in the midst of disorder. He was a ruler fashioned from the illusions of his time, a prince out of an idyll or a moral tale, in no respect the heroic figure called on to play a part in the tragic story that the century was unfolding. He was not uninformed, but his mind was sluggish and inconstant; he had intelligence without will-power, common sense without strength of character. The impression he produced was that of an unassuming, rather dull, submissive individual. 'The weakness and indecision of the king', said his brother, the count of Provence, 'are beyond description. Imagine balls of oiled ivory that you try in vain to hold together.'[30] Through indifference, optimism, or dis-

[29] *Eloge de Mably*, by abbé Brizard, 1787. See Mably, *Observations sur l'histoire de France*, liv. II, ch. II.

[30] Bacourt, *Mirabeau et La Marck*, t. I, p. 125.

trust of himself and others, he let those he should have commanded do whatever they wished; he made no effort to control events. Always toying, touchingly, with good ideas, while incapable of carrying any into effect, always liable to sudden changes through goodness of heart, apathy or scruples of conscience, he spent his time trying to reconcile contradictions which could only be resolved by being reduced to nullity.

In the absence of a great king France needed a great minister. But, lacking that capacity for daring which was the genius of Henry IV, Louis XVI equally lacked the gift of discernment and the ability to be a king that took the place of genius in Louis XIII. Indifferent to other men because he did not understand them, fearing above all determined characters, alarmed and disconcerted by the resolution in others which he was vaguely uneasy not to find in himself, he could not have discovered, still less have supported, a Richelieu. A minister of the English kind would have seemed humiliating to him. He could never have endured the tutelage of a Pitt; yet the personal exercise of authority frightened him. Energetic policies were repugnant to him. He loved his people and liked to believe himself beloved by them; the idea of severity was horrible to him. When he fell from the idyll to the tragedy, he turned away his eyes, full of anguish, and drew back from bloodshed. The only things at all steady or determined about him were his personal feelings and his religious beliefs; in default of political virtues, of which he was devoid, he possessed all the private ones— a tender heart, loyalty in his affections, modesty to the point of self-abnegation, gentleness and self-sacrifice. Attacked in the ultimate fortress of his personality, he suddenly roused himself; what remained in him of the blood of St. Louis revived and greatness appeared. 'The king is a nullity', wrote a foreign ambassador.[31] He was mistaken. Louis XVI was

[31] M. de Staël, 22 October 1789. _Correspondance_, published by Léouzon-Leduc, Paris, 1881.

a good man and a Christian; but he was not a king. He could love and forgive and suffer and die; he could not rule.

He was not built to control the Revolution but to endure it. The weakness of his government precipitated the crisis, but the contradictions in which he involved himself appeared at the very beginning of his reign. He tried to govern with the support of public opinion, by recalling the parlements and entrusting the government to reformers. Having formerly been struck down because they refused to obey, the parlements were emboldened by their restoration. They resisted the reforms that were proposed all the more stubbornly because they felt their authority had been confirmed.

Turgot, who had won over Louis XVI to his ideas, represented what was most noble and elevated in the aspirations of contemporary statesmen. No one was more suited to become the 'enlightened minister' of a 'virtuous prince'. He continued in the particular fashion of his time the work of centralisation begun in previous centuries. All his plans were directed towards uniting nation and government. He began with social and economic reforms. Louis XVI decreed free trade in corn and the abolition of the corvée, the jurandes* and the corporations. This was a revolution in commerce, industry and agriculture, and consequently one that involved the whole social fabric. To make it effective Turgot counted on two auxiliaries, which failed him simultaneously: public opinion, which demanded reform but was in no way prepared to accept its practical consequences; and the monarchy, which no longer had the prestige needed either to give a lead to opinion, or if necessary to resist it. Turgot himself, although an expert administrator, was too much a visionary and not sufficiently aware of practical difficulties. He argued abstractly, worked as though on a *tabula rasa* and disdained history, and so was led to disregard the real nature of things.

Turgot wanted the king to have absolute legislative power.

* Gilds; these and the corporations had rules restrictive of trade.

This was the opposite of what the parlements wanted and they refused to register the edicts. Public opinion, which favoured the edicts, had no focus and no organ: it was everything and it was nothing. The opposition of one of the great bodies of the state, representing only a handful of men, was therefore all-powerful. Among the opponents, most felt the need of reforms; they called for reform in general, but resisted any that affected them in particular. The plan was popular as a whole; but every step that was taken to put it into effect produced a combination against its execution. However, these combinations could have been overcome. Assessing the situation from above, it would have been possible to paralyse them by using the mutual opposition of the very elements which composed them. In fact, if society remained divided into separate groups, individuals had come closer to one another; they could have been managed by appealing to the ideas they had in common, instead of alienating them by attacks on their different interests. Though everyone defended his own privileges, each was ready to abandon the privileges of the others; and they were all unanimous in condemning the very notion of privilege. This is why partial reforms met with so many obstacles, and a total revolution with none. The privileged classes themselves gave up to the people, in a single night, the fortress which they had defended so tenaciously against the king's first approaches.

The essential thing was that the king should break down the opposition. Louis XVI did not have the courage; instead he sacrificed his minister. Turgot, who had come into power in 1774 with the highest hopes, resigned two years later utterly discouraged. Under his ministry the numbers of the discontented had increased. He had brought out in a dazzling light two truths equally fatal to the monarchy: the necessity for a great reformation and the powerlessness of the monarchy to achieve it. With him all hope of recasting the government in its ancient mould vanished. All that remained was to try to carry it on. Unable to attack the source of the disease, subsequent ministers attempted to dissipate the symptoms. Necker tried to deal with the problem of finance, but only two remedies were open to him—to restore them to order and to introduce economy. In applying these he came directly into collision with the abuses, and indirectly with the privileged classes. He failed, like Turgot, and for the same reasons, and withdrew in 1781. The monarchy fell back on routine, on expedients, on rule-of-thumb methods. After the aged Maurepas it had recourse to underlings, such as Joly de Fleury and d'Ormesson. Then, giving up in despair, in 1783 it handed itself over to a sort of political quack, Calonne, a spendthrift of ideas and money, who flattered the caprices of the courtiers, dazzled high society with his boasts, stunned it by his self-confidence, squandered the last resources of the treasury, lost the last stakes in the political game and irresponsibly pushed the monarchy on towards catastrophe.

The attempt that had been made to gain the support of the people having failed through the resistance of the privileged orders, it was the support of the latter that the government then attempted to obtain. Because they had defeated the government it was assumed that they represented a stable force. After having fought them, the monarchy tried to rally them to its cause. There was a kind of reaction in favour of the noblesse, which was particularly noticeable in the army. An ordinance of 1781 which exacted titles of noblesse for the higher ranks provoked the roturiers deeply. Those who were affected by the measure saw no hope of promotion except through a revolution. Moreover the spirit of the army was factious and the noble officers intrigued as much as any others. Changes in discipline irritated the officers and strained the loyalty of the soldiers; discontent fostered insubordination. In 1788, at the training camp of the prince de Condé, says a contemporary, 'The policies of the Brienne government were the subject of all conversation, the resistance of the parlements was openly applauded, the behaviour of the court mercilessly criticised and its muddles exposed

and exaggerated.' The rights of the people were discussed,
English officers were admired and envied as 'freemen and
not the puppet soldiers of a despot'.[32] In short, the army
was in chaos. From this there followed that defection which,
as Rivarol put it, was not one of the causes of the Revolution
but the Revolution itself.

The parlements were in open revolt. Far from thinking
of strengthening the state they were trying to weaken it.
They believed that the government was too strong. The solution of the crisis, according to them, was to diminish its
power. This was why they were so ardent in defending privilege and in asserting those claims which they thought would
help in their unacknowledged struggle to rival the power of
the Parliament of Great Britain. For this purpose, they called
on those famous fundamental laws which could not be
evoked without undermining the whole fabric of the monarchy. They could not give the people leadership, but they
could arouse it by their agitation. They initiated the demand
for the States General, which soon became the cry of the
whole nation. It was an appeal to hope which found an
echo in every heart.

It was generally felt that existing conditions could not last,
that the government was no longer equal to its task, that a
crisis was inevitable. Sectional interests all hampered and
diverted one another. However, it was believed that the general will could not err: if men were brought together they
would speak with a united voice, which the nation would
recognise as that of reason and justice. The monarchy having
abandoned its task, the idea arose that it could be undertaken
without the monarchy. Power proved to be limited and government difficult, but the thought that liberty was being
achieved was an easy consolation. Given liberty, it was believed, everything would immediately be possible and easy to
achieve. Liberty became the object of a sudden wild enthu-

[32] Miot de Mélito, *Mémoires*, t. I, pp. 3 ff. Paris, 1873. Miot
was at that time *commissaire des guerres*.

siasm; there was a blind belief that its advent would avenge all disappointments. The voice of the people seemed truly to be the voice of God, which would level the mountains, calm the oceans and transform men's minds.

For a time French governments still hesitated to appeal to the unknown, which remained, in spite of everything, frightful to them. They feared to approach that mysterious shore towards which they felt themselves being driven by an irresistible current. They tried to coast alongside. Provincial assemblies were summoned, in which the Third Estate was dominant and soon well-organized. The government, which itself had been unable to introduce reforms, 'conferred the power of enacting them upon those who had been most angered by its refusal to grant them'.[33] The Provincial Assemblies completed the ruin of the ancien régime. They made the convocation of the States General more urgent by showing both that it was increasingly necessary and that it could easily be accomplished. The ministry fell back upon a final palliative by calling, in 1787, an Assembly of Notables, from which the same conclusions emerged in a still more urgent form. No other alternative remained.

So many hesitations and vicissitudes had ended by exhausting the machinery of state. From top to bottom and from the centre to the extremities, the whole hierarchy was paralysed. The government faced total defeat, public authority was weakened and its agents were disheartened. In the army discipline was breaking down; there was neither ability to command nor readiness to obey. The repression of civil disorder was therefore impossible. Such was the balance-sheet of the ancien régime at the moment when it presented its accounts. It had exhausted all its great servants and all possible expedients. Having no longer any resources in itself, it sought for them elsewhere and called on the nation to provide them. Thus the States General were convoked in 1789.

[33] D'Arbois de Jubainville, *L'Administration des intendants.* Paris, 1880.

4 . THE NOBLESSE AND
THE THIRD ESTATE

Having appealed in vain to the king, the French appealed to liberty. This was a new kind of language, but they adopted it with passion, without, for the most part, knowing exactly what it meant. They employed it as one does a dead language, into which one cannot without distorting the meaning translate ideas that are foreign to it. France continued to think in terms of absolute rule. A few men, more enlightened or more penetrating than the rest, and who were in advance of their times, favoured, like Montesquieu, a constitution similar to that of England. They were only a kind of academic élite; the general trend of opinion flowed in quite a different direction. The English constitution, resulting from century-old compromises, was the least rational of conceptions. In this respect it seemed to most Frenchmen a third-rate piece of work. They saw in it nothing but the bizarre relics of some shapeless edifice of the Middle Ages, and they were as incapable of understanding the detail or grasping it as a whole as they were of appreciating the beauty of a Gothic cathedral. They thought that with a single effort they could produce something much better. Moreover, the English constitution was aristocratic; that alone was enough to make it unpopular. Actually, it was quite inapplicable to France, because the elements of which it had been constructed in England had almost entirely disappeared there, and the precise object of the French Revolution was to destroy their last traces.

The Revolution was directed against the noblesse. Despite the forward-looking liberalism of a few nobles, it was not to be expected that the noblesse would ally with the Revolution, or that the revolutionaries would entrust the leadership to it. The representatives of the noblesse in the States General were those who were most fiery in opposing the constitutional monarchy; English constitutional ideas had no more violent critics. They were opposed to the idea of an upper house because there would not be places for them all in it, and because by raising some nobles above the others the corporate spirit of the noblesse, according to them, would be destroyed. Moreover, they possessed neither leadership nor influence. They had long since ceased to be an aristocracy. The old noblesse had paid with its blood for the dazzling rôle it had played in the military glories of France. If nobles could still be courageous at the head of their troops, in politics, lacking both sanction from the past and effective support in the present, they could only provide the weakest and most unstable of opposition parties. They could appeal for support neither to historic traditions nor to new doctrines. They united against themselves all the precedents of the monarchy and all the passions of the people. It was, said the most penetrating and impartial of those who have passed judgement on the ancien régime, a remarkable phenomenon to see a whole noblesse, 'established for a thousand years, find itself suddenly rootless, without any means of maintaining its position, a whole upper class unable to find any other section of the nation with which it could unite. It was like a corps of officers exposed to the fire of its own troops. That is its condemnation and in this particular case its excuse.'[34] It is also the conclusion of Tocqueville's history. From the very beginning of the Revolution the chief members of the noblesse in the Assembly gave up the game. They saw no remedy but in recourse to force, and not being able to find this force in the nation or in themselves, they sought it in foreign alliances, which completed their ruin.

The logic of facts dictated the preponderance of the Third Estate. Constituting a numerical majority of the three orders, it assumed the leadership and promptly took over the other two, thus rounding off its history by acceding to power, as the nobles had rounded off theirs by their downfall. The ideas of the Third Estate were basically democratic. Liberty as they conceived it was above all civil liberty: political liberty

[34] Tocqueville, *Mélanges*: notes et pensées.

was in their eyes only the means to this and its guarantee. They wanted it less for its own sake than for what it might achieve, which was the overthrow of the feudal régime and the establishment of equality. The Third Estate was not only a class demanding its rights; it was composed of individuals who were claiming posts under the state. Personal ambition added emotional force to all their principles. 'For men who felt themselves called on to achieve great things,' declared one of the most clear-sighted observers of that generation, 'for young men urgent to put into effect their great superabundance of vigour, who thought it an inalienable right and a duty to utilise fully the gifts of nature, equality of rights seemed essential. In this way careers might be opened for the ambitions of all those with personal and political ability to the greatest offices and dignities, both civil and military, and to all the distinctions that society could offer to talent, virtue and service of the highest order. . . . But, when all this has been said, the Revolution meant less an increase in affluence or in personal security than the triumph of national pride. The French clung to it not so much because it was to their interest as because it made them respected.'[35]

A share in the exercise of power was not sufficient for the French; they had to have a monopoly of it. 'The Third Estate is a nation in itself and the whole nation', declared Sieyès. 'Conquest upsets all social relations and the noblesse has crossed to the side of the conquerors. Well, we must send it back to the other side; the Third Estate will become noble when it conquers in its turn.' Rabaut-Saint-Etienne wrote at the same time, 'The Third Estate is a whole society; what remains is a useless redundancy. Not only should the nobles not be the masters, they scarcely have the right to be citizens.'[36] These democrats did not understand liberty in the way of an English subject, who consented to the limitation of his own rights as a means of limiting those of others. They

[35] Roederer, *L'Esprit de la Révolution*, ch. I. *Œuvres*, t. III.
[36] *Considérations sur les intérêts du tiers*, 1788. See Tocqueville, *Mélanges*, unpublished chapters, ch. V.

understood it in the way of the French king, who recognised no other right than his own and did not admit the existence of any authority superior to his own. Liberty was to them a synonym for sovereignty.

It was what was called Roman liberty, and this conception, restored by Rousseau and the Genevan school, adapted itself wonderfully to the classical formulas long accredited in France by the monarchy. It belonged to the habits and traditions of the French. The study of classical literature had propagated this spirit. It had survived throughout the civil wars and the struggles of the Parlement. Moreover, 'curtailed and distorted' as it was, this liberty was still productive. 'This', said Tocqueville, 'was what, at the very time when the effects of centralisation were more and more levelling, weakening and reducing all individuals to a passive role, preserved in many of them their native originality, their distinctive colouring and contrasts. It kept their self-respect alive in their hearts and often ensured the predominance of the thirst for glory over their other passions. It created the vigorous, proud and audacious spirits we shall meet, who made the French Revolution at once an object of admiration and terror to the generations which followed.'[37]

In some, this Roman pride was allied to strength of character and constancy of spirit. They fought for their principles, died with stoicism or retired with dignity after the defeat of their party. Others, the greater number, exhibited above all a political kind of pride. They were jealous and suspicious of rivals, merciless towards the defeated and arrogant towards foreigners; but when they met a stronger, they easily reconciled themselves to submission to any master, whether it was a crowd, a faction, a dictator or a general, whether it was called the people or the Committee, Robespierre or Bonaparte. They possessed the primordial virtue of democracy, which is to identify love of the *patrie* with the love of equality; but they lacked the virtue necessary for republics, which,

[37] *L'Ancien Régime*, liv. II, ch. XI.

according to the *Esprit des lois*, lies in self-abnegation.[38] When he wrote his famous pamphlet on the Third Estate, the abbé Sieyès certainly never guessed that a seigneurial estate and the title of Count would be the outcome for him; yet the whole system of the noblesse of the Empire was there in germ from the beginning. The mixture of noble sentiments and generous ideals with personal passions and ruthless ambitions produced a violent and confused agitation which was one of the chief elements of strength in the Revolution. This is why we see in it so much heroism side by side with so much baseness, such high achievements and such complacency in the face of degrading atrocities.

The spirit of the Third Estate was above all that of the lawyers. They predominated among the deputies of the bourgeoisie and consequently in the Assemblies. This fact was decisive for the doctrines of the Revolution. The *philosophes* provided the ideas and laid down the principles; the lawyers translated them into legislative acts. They prepared, and often carried out in their practical aspects, all the positive achievements of the Revolution, what was worst and what was best in it, from the Law of the Suspects to the Civil Code. The nation elected them in such numbers because the work which was in hand was in the beginning one above all of legislation, and because in every small town or city they were the best known and thought to be the most capable members of their order. By electing them when it inaugurated its sovereignty, the people were appropriating and continuing the traditions of the crown. It chose its representatives from the same courts out of which the monarchy had so often drawn its own councillors and ministers.

[38] Montesquieu, *Esprit des lois*, Avertissement: 'To understand the first four books of this work it must be remembered that what I call virtue in the republic is love of the fatherland, that is the love of equality.' This definition is as necessary to understand the Revolution as to understand the *Esprit des lois*—'Love of the republic is in a democracy that of democracy; love of democracy is that of equality.' Livre V, ch. iii.

Chosen in this way, they continued in the Revolution the work that their predecessors had undertaken for the monarchy: they poured it into the classic Roman mould. Faithful to the maxims of the powerful school from which they emerged, and wholly permeated with its doctrines, they applied to the new sovereign all the traditions of the old one. Indeed it seemed as if, in these matters of state, only the terms were changed. Sovereignty passed from the king to the people; but in altering its principle it did not change its nature. At bottom things returned to the point from which they had started. For the Romans, the Republic or the state was 'a sort of absolute monarch before whom all did obeisance'.[39] The Emperor assumed the whole authority of the Republic. 'If the Emperor is all-powerful,' said the jurists, 'it is because the people of Rome has conferred on him its omnipotence.' In Rome the Empire had been set up by transferring to the prince the rights of the people; in France the Republic was set up by transferring to the people the rights of the king.[40] For the lawyers, the king was the Emperor of the *Digest*; the state was embodied in his person. The monarch was suppressed in 1792, but the state remained what it had been— 'the absolute ruler before whom all must bow', which explains how an Empire on the Roman model could emerge so promptly from the Republic.

By restoring sovereignty to the people it became a kind of abstract and impersonal despot and was treated as such. Scarcely was it recognised and installed in its omnipotence than it found courtiers, flatterers and flunkeys. The vices of the declining monarchy thus corrupted the new-born democracy. 'Know that you are kings and more than kings. Can you

[39] Fustel de Coulanges, *Histoire des institutions*, t. I, l. II, ch. I.
[40] A *Mémoire sur les Etats généraux* published in 1788 declares, 'The Third Estate is the people; the people is the State itself; the totality of national power resides in the people; through it the whole State exists.' These are the formulas of Bossuet reshaped by a disciple of Rousseau. The author, d'Antraigues, was then a violent democrat; he subsequently became a violent royalist. Chérest, ii. 267.

not feel the blood of sovereignty circulating in your veins?'
cried a demagogue.[41] Those who expressed themselves thus
were not addressing the people in general; they were speaking
to a group of individuals, each of whom attributed and applied to himself literally the homage of the crude flatterer.
The first comer who was greeted thus did not interpret his
sovereignty in the way of the *Contrat social*, which he had
not read, nor in that of Roman law, which he did not understand. He interpreted it simply by way of his impressions and
his instincts. He felt himself a sovereign like the royal child
to whom but lately had been said, as he was shown the palace, fields, soldiers and the assembled multitude: 'Sire, all
that you see is yours!' And he used it accordingly. Hence
those petty tyrants who set themselves up wherever they
found power to be used, whether the Republic conferred it
on them or they usurped it from the Republic.

They were assured successively that they were Englishmen,
Americans, Romans, Spartans. They remained on the morrow
what they had been on the eve, eighteenth-century Frenchmen, and the spirit of the old government reappeared in the
very institutions destined to destroy it.

5. THE REVOLUTION AND
ITS PRECEDENTS

The same theory, or rather the influence of the same pattern
of behaviour, led the National Assembly promptly to concentrate all power in itself. It declared itself sovereign and understood the term as Louis XIV had done—that is to say, it invested itself with the entire authority of the state and was
prepared to exercise it. The king remained no more than a
clerk directing from a subordinate position lesser clerks, the
ministers and their copyists. But the Assembly was itself a
mob, too numerous to exercise direct rule. Like the people,
it had to govern by choosing delegates. The idea of a col-

[41] See Taine, *La Révolution*, t. II, l. IV. ch. I, § 4.

lective authority was familiar to France: an experiment in it had been made at the beginning of the century, and more recently the Provincial Assemblies had brought it back into fashion. Rousseau set it up as a principle for great states ruled by sovereign assemblies. He recommended the Diet of Poland to entrust the executive power to councils of varying composition, whose members, constantly renewed, would exercise their authority only under the inspection and control of the Legislature.[42] The Constituent Assembly ruled through its committees, which gave orders to the ministers. In effect, it confused the legislature with the executive, and so proceeded to the ultimate excess of centralisation at the very moment when it was claiming to decentralise.[43]

Nobody contributed more than the lawyers to these strange developments. Such vicissitudes did not surprise them, for they believed that they had remained consistent throughout. The fact is that they were only concerned with the state, by whatever name it was described. They served the state alone, and conceived it always in the same way and served it in the same fashion. They passed quite naturally from 'those steps of the throne where a ruthless and formidable Richelieu hurled thunderbolts at mankind rather than governed it'[44] to the seats of the Convention, where the people, by its votes, took over this dreadful power and governed men by destroying them.

Events brought them suddenly into power. Even if they had had a taste for liberty, they would not have had time to serve their apprenticeship to it. At the beginning of the Revolution there was an onrush towards the ideal: everything was to be destroyed, everything renewed. France was, men thought, to be recreated after having been annihilated. But these absolute formulae bore no relation to what actually occurred. France continued to act, as it had always acted, in the way its character dictated. When the sap could no longer run

[42] *Gouvernement de Pologne*, ch. VII.
[43] Cf. Tocqueville, *L'Ancien Régime*, l. III, ch. VII.
[44] *Mémoires de Retz*, t. I, p. 94.

as it was wont, it proved intractable. It gathered, burst through the bark into misshapen excrescences, and all went awry. There was disorder, anarchy, civil war. Foreign war was added. The Republic was in danger, France was invaded. The republicans had to defend at one and the same time the independence of the nation, the territory of the fatherland, the principles of the Revolution, the supremacy of their party and their own lives. This was no easy task.

War has urgent and imperative commands; it does not admit of utopias, of gambles which may turn into disaster. It requires a government that can muster men, arm them, feed them, lead them into battle. But government was just what France lacked. It was left to visionaries to seek out what would be the ideal government; but when they thought they had discovered the great specific remedy for the evils of the state, it was only to learn that the time was not ripe for it to be applied in this world. In the meantime government had to be carried on as well as it could and as necessity dictated. As it was necessary to act quickly, the simplest form of government and that most ready to hand was chosen. Thus by the force of circumstances the traditional forms of behaviour and ideas prevailed. Pure reason having failed them, men fell back on a rough empiricism. They returned instinctively to habit, routine, precedent; none of these was on the side of liberty, but there were innumerable precedents for despotism. Thus in the guise of expedients all the procedures of the ancien régime stole silently back into the Revolution. Once back, they remained unchallenged. All that was left for the theorists to do was to disguise and conceal them.

The Assembly had been set up to represent the people, but it was found that it lacked unity. So power was concentrated first in a committee of twelve, then in a Directory of five, in a Consulate of three, and finally in an Emperor. Under the ancien régime the heart of the state, the central motive force, was the king's council. It was the court of justice, it drew up and issued the laws, settled taxation, maintained public order and dealt with all important state business. The intendant, who was its delegate, combined a plurality of powers. He was 'the unique agent in the provinces of all the decisions of the government'.[45] Hence the title of *commissaire départi*, which he held from the beginning. When it was realised, in 1793, that the government was being shackled by the network of departmental, district and communal councils, there was a return to executive agents. The revolutionaries thought they were copying the Roman Senate when they were merely copying Cardinal Richelieu. The Committees of Public Safety and General Security took the place of the King's Council, the *commissaires* that of the intendants. This was only a beginning. A few years later the Conseil d'Etat of the year VIII, councillors on mission and the whole hierarchy of the prefectures appeared. It was an evolution that happened almost without anyone being aware of it. Those who established these posts and filled them were just the same kind of men as those to whom similar posts had been entrusted under the ancien régime. The only difference was that instead of receiving them as inferiors, they took them as masters. As for the troop of officials, it was sufficient to open the lists and they reappeared of their own volition.

In practice, especially in the finance of the state, which was the open wound of the ancien régime, arbitrary expedients had always been the rule, extending, if necessary, as far as confiscation. The property of the Church was always in danger. In time of dearth there was recourse to the *maximum* on prices. In time of war armies lived off the enemy country. War supported war and sometimes also the state. It was controlled from Paris or Versailles, and it was not the generals who finally decided the fate of the armies. Richelieu, observed the historian of the princes de Condé, took his generals from wherever he could. 'He found them in the Church, in his family, among the obscure; he shifted them about, changed them, tried to uphold, sometimes for a long time, those who were his own creation, but broke them when

---

[45] Tocqueville, *L'Ancien Régime*, l. II, ch. II.

he recognised his error; sending some to execution and some
to the Bastille, burying others in sinecures.'[46] Under Louis
XIV the great war minister was a lawyer. Louvois and his
clerks kept the 'court generals' well under control. They
were not allowed to win battles without the approval of the
bureaux. The same tradition reappeared in the committees
of the Convention.

In crises the government operated by coups d'état, by
journées, for the term is an old one, even in its sinister meaning. The government had accustomed people to sudden
changes effected by force. We need not go back to the time of
the Estates, to the history of the duc de Guise and of the
maréchal d'Ancre;* at the height of the eighteenth century
and on the very eve of the Revolution magistrates who dared
to oppose the orders of the king were treated in the same way.
They were arrested, exiled and their offices confiscated.
Armed men were sent into their meeting-hall to hunt them
from their seats. In May 1788 the Parisians saw, once again,
troops lighting their camp-fires round the Palais de Justice.
As has been appropriately said, the longest established government in Europe had taught them 'to defy the majesty of
the oldest institutions, to violate the rights of one of the more
revered of their ancient authorities in its own precincts'.[47]

The Revolution seems bolder and more original in its treatment of the Church. In reality it was no more an innovator
in this field. Faced with its greatest problem, it could only,
once more, imitate the ancien régime; but the precedents, up
to this point very amenable to the new pressures and very
adaptable to the new theories, this time recoiled against the
revolutionaries. The gun which they intended to discharge

[46] Duc d'Aumale, *La Première Campagne de Condé, Revue
des Deux Mondes*, 1883.

* The Duke of Guise and his brother the Cardinal of Guise
were murdered by order of Henry III at his Chateau of Blois in
1588. Concini, maréchal d'Ancre, favourite of Marie de Medici,
suffered the same fate by the order of Louis XIII in 1617.

[47] Tocqueville, *Mélanges*, p. 92.

burst in their own hands. The reason was that its mechanism was such that they could not use it without misusing it. In their other policies everything had been straightforward and the ancien régime had so to speak prepared the ground for future excesses; but in respect of religion and the Church, it had been compelled to observe a moderation which it had abandoned in other matters; here the smallest practical error could destroy the whole theoretical justification.

Undoubtedly the king believed, as his lawyers maintained, that the Church in France was under royal authority in temporal matters, and that its property, granted by the crown, could be taken back if it judged proper. When the clergy opposed the state, its temporal revenues had been seized. When the Holy See showed itself recalcitrant, the king occupied Avignon, and if need be threatened Rome itself with armed force. He could employ a more serious threat, the opposition of the French clergy, which might involve a breach of relations and a schism. Such were the facts, but to isolate them in this way is to distort them. To draw from them political maxims for use at the same time against the French clergy and against Rome was to fall into the most dangerous of misapprehensions.

In practice, the state had always compromised. It asserted, in principle, its overlordship of Church property, but it contented itself, in fact, with the *don gratuit* that the Church granted it. The Church reserved its rights, but nevertheless paid, because it was dependent on the state, which ruled but also protected it. The king was its secular arm, what was described as kind of 'external bishop'. He left the control of education and the cure of souls to the Church; in return, it taught his subjects the duty of obedience. Moreover, as a proprietor it was attached to the soil, it was national; and if it upheld its privileges against the king, it upheld them equally against the Pope. The whole strength of the state in its conflicts with the Holy See proceeded from the support of the French clergy. Their disputes were often extremely lively, but at bottom they were quarrels over the boundaries of power: on both sides principles were excluded from the dispute. The king did not challenge the spiritual supremacy of the Pope in the Church, or the Pope the temporal supremacy of the king in his realm. Like two neighbours holding property by identical titles, they did not challenge one another's right. Their lawsuits dealt only with the claims which they had on each other's respective fields of jurisdiction, or with the possession of some disputed enclaves. However extreme his political claims might sometimes be, it was a matter of honour for the king to remain in all religious matters most Christian and the eldest son of the Church.

This is what the lawyers of the Revolution never understood. They kept the letter but falsified the spirit of the policy, when, despoiling the French clergy of its property and its moral supremacy, they demanded its support, in spite of itself, against Rome, and when, deprived of this necessary alliance, they tried to employ against the Holy See methods that had only been efficacious formerly because of the support of the French clergy. Everything, in fact, in this complex and composite pattern was mutually dependent and reciprocally upheld: a religion of the state, a national clergy, a 'Very Christian' king. The Gallican Church was necessarily a landowning and privileged church. When it no longer had lands or privileges, it had to look for a basis of support outside France, in Rome, and it became ultramontane.

The attempt to adapt a jurisprudence which rested entirely on the principle of a state religion to a régime based on the religious neutrality of the state, but in which actually an irreligious philosophy prevailed, was paradoxical. One of the most serious crises of the Revolution resulted from this mistake. The opposition of the clergy and the faithful discomfited all the revolutionaries and exasperated the militants, who cared little for the subtle compromises of the ancien régime. They claimed the right of reducing the Church to obedience and they quite simply applied to the clergy and the recalcitrant Catholics the measures which the monarchy had taken against heretics. These were unhappily the logical result of a theory that was only too accessible to unsophisticated minds and the application of them came only too naturally and familiarly to zealots.

Since the time of Richelieu there had no longer been a state within the state. The government had achieved political unity. This was not enough for Louis XIV: he wanted the unanimous support of men's minds. Obedience in action was not sufficient for him: he also needed to control men's consciences. 'To try to distinguish between the obligations of conscience and the obedience which is due to kings', wrote one of his intendants, 'is an illusion which can only be the result of blind prejudice.'[48] The theory of the ancien régime could be summed up in the maxim: *Une foi, une loi, un roi.* The law, in the ideas of the Jacobins, absorbed into itself the king and the faith; it no more tolerated opponents than the Church tolerated heretics or the monarchy tolerated pretenders. For the Jacobins the opponent was worse than a heretic: he was an unnatural monstrosity, someone to be put outside the law. To prosecute him and bring him into subjection all the frightful methods of inquisition and repression amassed by the monarchy were employed. From that store the Committees helped themselves liberally.

All the precedents for the revolutionary legislation against the priests and the nobles are to be found in the edicts of Louis XIV against the Protestants. The only means of safety for members of the Reformed Church had been flight, and this was made a crime. Their property was confiscated. They were persecuted through their children. If they resisted they were massacred. The war in the Cevennes exhibits all the characteristics of the war of the Vendée. The Terror was sketched out in this sanguinary preface. There was even a foretaste of the sickening mawkishness of Barère. 'It is by winning the hearts of the heretics', the king wrote to a bishop,

[48] *Mémoires de Foucault,* published by Baudry, p. 139. Paris, 1862.

'that you will tame their obdurate spirits. . . . They will perhaps never be brought back to the bosom of the Church by any other way than by the *road strewn with flowers* that you have offered them.'[49] It was not only heresy that the ancien régime perseuted, it was dissidence of any kind. The Jansenists were treated like the Huguenots, and laws of confiscation, dispersal and exile became so much part of the general pattern that in the eighteenth century Catholic governments applied them to the Jesuits. The revolutionaries learnt at the feet of the ancien régime how to be implacable in order to become irresistible. 'Punishments', said Richelieu, 'are a more certain means of keeping men to their duty; they are the less forgotten because of the impression they make on our feelings.'[50] To provide these terrible examples there were special tribunals whose verdicts were based on raison d'état. The system of *lettres de cachet* kept the tradition alive and passed it on to the revolutionary Committees.

In putting forward these facts and trying to explain them, I am in no way excusing them. I am not at all suggesting as an attenuating circumstance the fact that, having overthrown the ancien régime, the revolutionaries copied its worst abuses. What I want to demonstrate is the permanence of the same pressures, the propensity of accumulated habits, the strength of tradition. The older excesses and those of the Terror cannot be set off against one another; it cannot even be said that the former produced the latter. They all derive from the same source, which is a very different matter. The terrorists had no idea at all of avenging the victims of Louis XIV; the perpetrators of the massacres of September were not having their revenge for St. Bartholomew; the *noyades* of Carrier were not reprisals for the *dragonnades*. Whether in the sixteenth, the seventeenth or the eighteenth century, the same fanaticism produced the same results. Considered in this way,

---

[49] Puaux, *Les Précurseurs français de la tolérance au dix-septième siècle*, p. 19. Paris, 1881.
[50] *Testament*, ch. IV.

the Terror is deprived of the sophistical prestige with which its retrospective apologists have tried to surround it. The only great thing about it was the extent of its plagiarism.

What would have been truly extraordinary in the Revolution would have been the triumph of liberty. The ancien régime had no pretensions to this. It did not admit, in principle, liberty of conscience, political liberty, or even civil liberty; though it allowed in part, with more or less indulgence according to its whim or its enlightenment, the exercise of one or the other. The severity of its theory was often attenuated in practice. In spite of the rigour of the laws, which decreed the punishment of death for the authors of writings tending to attack religion and the authority of the king, none of the *philosophes* died on the scaffold. Diderot did not suffer the fate of André Chénier.* Under the terrorists it was precisely the opposite: the theory was humanitarian and sentimental, the practice barbarous. All the liberties that had been granted in general were taken back in detail. It was not an Edict of Nantes, an act of toleration and guarantee promulgated in favour of part of the nation that was revoked in 1793, it was the *Declaration of the Rights of Man*, the very raison d'être of the Revolution and the common right of all Frenchmen. Although we may explain to ourselves the lamentable contradiction between the acts and doctrines of the revolutionaries in terms of precedents in the customs and education of the ancien régime, we should not pass the same judgement on governments which, although they coincided in certain excesses, nevertheless were founded on absolutely opposite principles. If the ancien régime was self-consistent in its despotism, in copying it the Revolution was not. It saddens one to see Bossuet proscribing the Huguenots, but one recognises that it was in the logic of his theory. It is not possible without indignation to conceive of Descartes proscribing Pascal. Yet that was what the world now saw.

* Guillotined in 1794.

6. THE REPUBLIC OF LETTERS

The *philosophes* and men of letters were the inspiration of
the Revolution.* It owes to them its most liberal ideas and
its most fatal innovations, the humanity of its beginnings and
the ferocity of its mid-career, its enthusiasm and its fanaticism. Anyone who neglects the history of the literary and
philosophical struggles of the eighteenth century must
totally fail to understand the corruption of such high principles, the bitter hatreds of men whom everything should
have bound together, their frightful struggles to usurp from
one another the gains won by a common effort, and those
fine-spun differences of opinion which were translated into
bloody proscriptions. On the other hand, if it is appreciated
that it was the rivalries and dissensions that had earlier ravaged the republic of letters which were carried by the writers
in all their violence into the political assemblies, the problem
disappears.

Schools of thought became sects and coteries turned into
factions. 'These factions', said Saint-Just, himself one of their
most fanatical members, on one occasion, 'born before the
Revolution, have followed it through its career, like reptiles
following the course of a stream.'[51] Even while they were
only struggling to influence opinion, they already manifested
a spirit of intrigue and bitter jealousy. The members of rival
factions spied on, denounced, accused, excommunicated one
another. Not only opinions came under fire, but also the
men who held them. No line of attack was barred. Lacking
any better court of appeal they played to the gallery, stirred
up public indignation or ridicule regardless of the truth of

* For a comment on the defects of Sorel's assumptions about the
relationship between the ideas of the *philosophes* and the Revolution see note, p. 168. It is difficult, on the other hand, to refuse to
allow some perceptiveness in his reference to 'the corruption of
such high principles'.

[51] Sainte-Beuve, *Causeries du lundi*, t. V, article *Saint-Just*.

their allegations, and took pleasure in their own foul language. Hence those charges of corruption, theft, poisoning, assassination, perversion with which their polemics are filled; and that vocabulary of lurid invective, full of 'treason' and 'scoundrelly deeds' which appeared to be composed for the sycophants of the clubs or the revolutionary tribunal. Proof of a charge was unnecessary: the suspicion was enough by itself. Anyone who contradicted it was a rogue, every rival was dishonest, every opponent an 'enemy of virtue'. 'On both sides', observes a contemporary, 'I have seen intense hatred and all the consequences of the spirit of faction.'[52] These were the worst of all, for they exhibited a failure of reason more wretched and more frightening than the weaknesses induced by passion, combining as they did an inflated egoism and its sophistries with the distortions resulting from vanity, from the fanaticism of a coterie and from doctrinal infatuation.

The sentiments and the style of writing of the eighteenth century exhibit in advance all the passions of the Revolution. 'This century', declared the most eloquent, embittered and fervent of the tribunes of the factious republic of letters, 'is above all spiteful and malignant.'[53] When Fréron* died it was asked who would write his epitaph, and the answer—'The first to spit on his tomb.' 'The arrogance of modern philosophy', it was said, 'has pushed egoism and conceit to their highest point. The inclination of all members of the younger generation towards such a comfortable doctrine has caused it to be taken up with passion and taught with the same fiery intolerance. They have accustomed themselves to bring into social relationships the same air of mastery with which they deliver the oracles of their sect, and to treat with open contempt, which is only a more insolent kind of spite, anyone

[52] Soulavie, *Mémoires*, t. VI, ch. XIV: *La République des lettres*.

[53] J. J. Rousseau, *Deuxième Dialogue*, 1775-1776.

* Elie Fréron (1718-76) was a persistent critic of Voltaire and the *philosophes*, who retorted with immoderate abuse.

who dares to hesitate to accept their verdicts. . . . Enslaving themselves in order to enslave others, they conclude by interpreting any opposition as total rebellion. A tyrannical generation cannot be either very gentle or very peaceable. Hence the hateful dispositions which distinguish this generation. Moderation is no longer in men's minds nor honesty in their affections. They do not so much love themselves as hate everything that they cannot identify with themselves. . . . They have forgotten how to do anything but hate; they are not bound to their own parties by affection, still less by esteem, but simply by hatred of the opposing party. The hearts of the disciples are soaked in the same rancour as is poured out in the writings of their masters.'

It was these disciples who, a quarter of a century later, having obtained control of France, quarrelled over its government with even greater violence, for it was no longer just a matter of personal reputation and glory but of sovereignty and of life itself. There was only one further step: when passions had been sufficiently aroused they passed from literary polemics and ostracism to political proscription and extermination. 'National cruelty', said La Rochefoucauld, 'produces fewer crimes than vanity.' Under the ancien régime the law confined writers to a battle of words; when they obtained power the first use they made of it was to put their metaphors into practice and one another to death.

The line of descent is so clear that the order in which the disciples expelled and succeeded to one another was almost the same as that in which their masters had taken the leadership in the republic of letters. Montesquieu and the supporters of limited monarchy in the English style came first—a small group of high intellectual value but wielding little influence and quickly pushed on one side. Voltaire came next with the constitutionalists, and the early Rousseau of the *Nouvelle Héloïse* and *Emile* with some of the Gironde; the *Encyclopédie* with Condorcet; Diderot with Danton; and the later Rousseau, of the *Contrat social* and

the *Dialogues,* with Robespierre.* And just as on the fringes
of literary circles swarmed the crowd of 'obscure followers',
to quote Taine, of those who had lost their way, of fanatical
zealots, the missionaries and inquisitors of atheism, anarchy,
communism and massacre, so round the clubs and even in
the Assemblies, stirring up the people and terrorising its representatives, swarmed the troops of fanatics and madmen
from Hébert to Marat. These plumbed even lower depths.
The eighteenth century broke out like a plague spot in the
monstrous degeneracy of the marquis de Sade, whose dreadful logic pushed its doctrines to the ultimate point. It was
almost as though he was trying to demonstrate through sheer
disgust the absurdity of d'Holbach's *Système de la nature.*
The subtle poison of sensuality, which seeped in everywhere,
was in the air. It was the especial evil of the age: Diderot
was affected by it, Rousseau contaminated, Mirabeau blighted
in his finest hour. Some, like Laclos,† added to it a calculated
depravity, a taste for refined cruelty, and de Sade a wickedness and madness which extended to criminality. They were
the fanatics of vice. The link between books and men,
thought and action, finds a savage and hideous corollary in
the deeds of Carrier.‡

7. NATIONAL CHARACTER

Thus, everything was ready for revolution. The ancien régime was in decay, government was discredited and bankrupt, men's minds were dazzled with illusions and agitated
by passions, and a wild frenzy was brewing among the
masses. And when the revolution came it was to be a far-
reaching one, which would give rise to anarchy, degenerate
into fanaticism and finally spawn atrocities. All the same,

* This attempt to schematise the Revolution in terms of the
literary schools of eighteenth-century France reflects the influence
of Taine and should not be taken seriously.
† Author of *Les Liaisons Dangereuses* (1782).
‡ Notorious for his terriorist activities at Nantes.

France survived. The political and social reforms which were the raison d'être of the Revolution became irrevocable the moment they were decreed. France emerged from anarchy stronger and more confident and burning to achieve greater things, and her power reached greater proportions than ever before. And when she lost her political supremacy it was only to recapture, with a lustre which recalled that of her finest years, the generous leadership in literature, in the arts and sciences, which she had formerly exercised, and to attain to greater heights in peace than she had reached in war. France was to consolidate her new destinies by establishing representative government, of which the Revolution had only been able to lay the foundation and corner stone.

The fact is that the Revolution did not, as has too often been said, break the chain of French history. It was only one episode in it—the most astonishing perhaps, but still only an episode. The geographical consequences resulting from the situation of France in Europe had not been altered, nor had the temperament or the character of the French nation changed in the course of this great crisis. In its long history it had undergone more than one test of the same kind, and it was in consequence of these vicissitudes that it became the most closely knit, the most traditional country in Europe, and the one in which nation and state were most nearly identical. By an alternation of ebb and flow, or growth and stagnation, France slowly took shape. It had had its parched summers and passing storms, its winters of disaster and tempest; but the soil was a good one, and as soon as the sky cleared there was always a revival of life and a new outburst of fruitfulness.

The French, experiencing turn by turn either a fanatical admiration or a blind hatred for their rulers, greedy for liberty to the point of licence, and for peace to the point of slavery, preserved violent passions under a veneer of refinement. They were 'capable of sensibility to the point of enthusiasm and of all extremes in their affection as in their

discontent'.[54] They kept in their hearts a foundation of instinctive 'Atticism', an imperative need of order, method and
sense of proportion. Wit and common sense were the only
things they desired insatiably. No nation is more capable of
being intoxicated by sophisms and paradoxes or afterwards
more impetuous in revolt against them. None has been truer
to itself under an appearance of inconstancy and none more
practical under an appearance of folly. France revolts to
achieve the impossible and is purified as soon as there appears a certainty of obtaining what is practicable. Violence
is employed to gain the most moderate ends. No nation has
envisaged vaster designs and none has more often been satisfied with modest achievements.

Its traditional resilience saved France in the Revolution
of 1789 as in previous ones. Because the crown failed to
achieve reform, the nation revolted and overthrew the monarch; but it remained what the monarchy had made it. The
omnipotence of the state had brought about the ruin of the
government; but for the same reason—the absorption of the
patrie in the state—the nation felt that by dissolving the state
it would destroy itself, and so it became reunited. The passion for unity constantly fostered by the ancien régime saved
the Revolution from its own excesses. All that was needed
was for the French to see the threat of evils without remedy
for them to regain their self-control and recover their senses.
They still possessed what is the soul of a nation and the true
principle of the public weal—love of the fatherland. Patriotism was reborn in the excitement of a revolution which
was also a liberation. The two ideas were fused into one,
and Frenchmen defended at the same time their national
independence and the liberty they had won.

They wasted no time in doing this. To avoid foreign rule
or the re-establishment of the ancien régime they put up with
everything, even the degrading tyranny of the Terror. They
concentrated their gaze on the enemy. But when they had

[54] Voltaire, *Siècle de Louis XIV*, ch. XII.

conjured away the external danger, they experienced as much horror of the domestic anarchy as they had felt for the invasion. They looked on the yoke of the terrorists with the same aversion as that of the foreigner. They rejected with disgust the remnants of the bloodthirsty factions which had torn the nation in pieces under the pretext of defending it. The same impulse which had made them destroy the ancien régime, reform the constitution of society and the state, and defend the country against foreign invasion, led them successively to overthrow governments which proved unable to safeguard the end which they had steadfastly pursued—civil liberty, combined with order and peace. Having given up everything to the state in order to save the Revolution, they expected from it orderly government in return.

The actual crisis that France had passed through had created the men who were capable of bringing it to an end. Those among the revolutionaries who had a capacity for statesmanship emerged out of the turmoil. Months of these terrible struggles counted for years of peaceful manœuvring. 'We must change our ways,' wrote a minister of Louis XV in desperation, 'and this task, which would require centuries in another country, might be accomplished in a year in this, if there were men capable of it.'[55] Such men had been born when he wrote, and the youngest were of age by 1789. With the Revolution they could become members of the nation's assemblies. When the revolutionary storm had subsided, they found many others, trained in public business by the ancien régime, who were attracted to the new régime by their ideas and who could help and direct them in their task.[56] This mighty generation constituted the nucleus of the government which organized the Consulate. Under the Restoration it became the inspiration of representative government.

[55] Bernis, letter to Choiseul, 31 March 1768, II, p. 196.
[56] Portalis, Siméon, Mollien, Lebrun, Beugnot, Malouet, etc. See the descriptions of Mignet and Sainte-Beuve.

After this long detour, and after so many aberrations and such an arduous apprenticeship, the men of 1789 returned to the fundamental idea, which had somehow gone astray in the course of the Revolution: the idea that political liberty is the only guarantee of the other liberties. They had been satisfied with decreeing democracy. They thought that they had taken adequate precautions for its survival by taking over the government. When they found that liberty was in danger, they realised that the only effective recourse for its defence was liberty itself, and they became its most ardent champions. The teaching of experience and the influence of the new spirit of the times were such that the monarchy, in order to re-establish itself, had to have recourse to the same means that democracy had used to sustain itself. Those who wanted to stop the Revolution, and those who wanted to continue it, the partisans of limited monarchy and those of absolutism, the constitutionalists, republicans, Caesarean democrats, Bonapartists and royalists, had the same interest and demanded the same guarantees for their various rights and claims. The generous emotions of 1789 still survived and reappeared, matured and strengthened by experience; and the generation which had begun the Revolution could conceive the hope of terminating it. The France of tradition thus carried within itself, as well as the seeds of dissolution, the elements of regeneration and recovery.

At the same time, in this crisis as in the similar ones of the fourteenth, fifteenth and sixteenth centuries, France had not to take account simply of her own problems, but had also to reckon with Europe. The Revolution of 1789 was followed by a war which lasted until 1815, for in fact there was no peace between the wars but only a truce and a few months of armistice. The Revolution became essentially bellicose: this was its greatness and its ruin. The armies overflowed into the nation and war absorbed the state. It exercised the decisive influence, not over the reconstitution of the government —it would have been reconstituted in any case—but over the form which the reconstitution took, the character it assumed.

It was in war that revolutionary France found its most amazing achievements, though their causes and explanations are to be sought in the past history of the nation. External as well as internal affairs had their permanent historic determinations. The French have shown, in their relations with Europe as well as in their internal history, besides the spirit of moderation and compromise under which the country has had great policies and prosperous ages, gusts of romantic ambition, a sort of intoxication with conquest, and a fickle bias towards glory and adventure. Along with that *'modération dans la force'* which is the very essence of the French genius there exists a craving for the impossible which diverts it into aberrations. The Revolution brought each of these opposed instincts into operation in turn. 'It is contended', wrote d'Argenson, 'that in France a republic would be no wiser than the kind of monarchy which has ruled us for fourteen centuries: the national character would remain the same.' 'In the spirit of the nation', he adds, 'lies the whole strength of the monarchy.'[57] I shall try to define this spirit.

II.   Foreign Policy

1. THE ORIGIN OF TRADITIONS

The policy of the Capetians, considered historically and in respect of its traditions, had two principal objects: internally to create a nation which should be homogeneous and a state which should be coherent, and externally to ensure, by securing good frontiers, the independence of the nation and the strength of the state. The monarchy, which had responded to national aspirations by setting up the authority

[57] *Mémoires*, éd. Rathery, t. IV, p. 216.

of the state, did so equally by extending its power in Europe. The external and internal ends coincided: the one was the consequence and the complement of the other. The Capetians found France confined and divided. Despite the separatist tendencies of the feudal régime, the common traditions and aspirations of the people enabled its kings to unite the nation, to centralise authority and create a state. In this early period the history of the nation was identical with the history of the royal domain. It took shape in proportion as that domain was extended; it was unified to the extent to which royal supremacy prevailed. After the kingdom was set up, the kings endeavoured to enlarge its limits just as they had enlarged their domain. The process which had been begun within the narrow limits of the monarchy was extended beyond them, wherever there were populations connected in origins and traditions with those which the monarchy already ruled. These were the peoples of ancient Gaul, who had been reunited under Charlemagne. They drew their civilisation from the same sources, had been shaped in the same mould and preserved the same memories. Hence, despite frontier struggles, local enmities and quarrels over leadership, there was a common foundation on which royal policy could build with confidence.

This policy derived, in both objects and methods, from the nature of things. Bounded by the Atlantic Ocean, the Pyrenees, the Mediterranean and the Alps, the French monarchy could only expand to the east and the north, in Flanders and the areas which constituted, at the accession of the Capetians, the kingdoms of Lorraine and Burgundy. It was led in that direction by nature and by necessity. As soon as the French monarchy had been set up, an inevitable conflict with Germany followed for the possession of these intervening territories, which both states claimed. From the fifteenth century, the history of Europe is full of brutal wars to conquer them and desperate ones for their preservation. The struggle assumed different forms according to the changing spirit of the times. Varied pretexts were put forward to

support the different claims, and the theories invoked
changes within the system of international law; but if the
means were different, the end remained the same. The consistent pursuit of the same end, while ideas and facts underwent so many revolutionary changes, can only be explained
by the peculiar conjunction of circumstances which created
and perpetuated the great traditions of these nations and
states. There are mysterious principles established at the birth
of nations from which the laws of their historical development subsequently emerge. They can be seen in France from
the earliest times.

The policy of the French state was determined by geography; the nation was instinctively aware of it before the lesson was taught by raison d'état. It was based on a fact—the
empire of Charlemagne. The starting-point for the great lawsuit which fills the history of France is the insoluble dispute
over the inheritance of the Emperor. That provided the motive for the ambitions of its kings, therein its lawyers found
the origin of the rights they asserted; and there was the source
of the popular tradition which led the kings to put forward
their claims and the lawyers to find justifications for them.
The monarchy had no sooner emerged from the mists than
historians and poets recalled to its kings the lost greatness
of their predecessors. At the beginning of the eleventh century, Adalbéron,* in a poem addressed to Robert, proclaimed
the power of the kings of France, 'first in the rank of kings'.
'From the time of our fathers the kingdom of the French
has subjugated the kings of other states.'[1] All other crowns,
he held, were subordinate to that of France.

According to a chronicler of the same period, Glaber,†

---

* Adalbéron Ascelin, bishop of Laon, born mid-tenth century in
Lorraine, died 1030, author of 'Poëme satirique' in 430 hexameter
verses, dedicated to King Robert.

[1] Guizot, *Collection des mémoires relatifs à l'histoire de France*,
t. VI.

† Raoul Glaber was an eleventh century chronicler, born in
Burgundy. His chief work, a chronicle of the years 900 to 1046,
was printed in the *Historiae Francorum* of Pithou in 1546.

supremacy and empire belonged to France. 'The kings of France, the strongest and most powerful in Christendom, were distinguished for their justice . . . and the Empire over which they ruled for so long was the symbol of their triumph.'[2] As time went on the image of the great Emperor grew to colossal proportions. From Philip Augustus to Napoleon it towers over the history of France. The chronicles of Charlemagne provide the primal origin of that political tradition which, by a strange reversion to the past, was to bring about the realisation in the nineteenth century, before the eyes of an astonished Europe, of a great Western Empire, which the poets of the Middle Ages had presented to the popular imagination as a marvellous myth.

> *Quand Dex eslut nonante et dix royaumes,*
> *Tot le meillor torna en doce France.*
> *Li miudre reis ot à nom Charlemaine:*
> *Cil aleva volentiers doce France.*
> *Dex ne fist terre qui envers lui n'apende:*
> *Il ala prendre Baviere et Alemaigne,*
> *Et Normandie et Anjou et Bretaigne,*
> *Et Lombardie et Navarre et Tosquane. . . .*
> *Rois qui de France porte corone d'or*
> *Preudons doit estre et vaillant de son cors;*
> *Et s'il est hom qui li face nul tort,*
> *Ne doit garir ne a plain ne à bos*
> *Deci qu'il l'ait ou recreant ou mort;*
> *S'ainsi nel fet, dont pert France son los:*
> *Ce dist l'estoire, coronez est à tort.**

---

[2] *Chronique de Raoul Glaber,* liv. I, ch. I. Guizot, *id.*

* 'When God divided the world into a hundred kingdoms he placed the best one on the sweet soil of France. The name of the best of the kings was Charlemagne, who much desired the greatness of France. Every land God had made was subject to him. He took Bavaria and Germany, Normandy, Anjou, Brittany and Lombardy, Navarre and Tuscany. . . . The king who bears the crown

At the time when the *chansons de geste* celebrated these past glories, France was in sad decay. The English occupied part of the kingdom and the first need was to drive them out.* This was the plan which the Norman Wace, author of the *Roman de Rou*, accused the French of forming.

> *Se li Franceis poeient lur pensez achever,*
> *Ja li reis d'Engleterre n'avreit rien deça mer:*
> *A hunte l'en fereient, s'il poeient, passer.*†

This prime necessity did not prevent Philip Augustus from cherishing more extensive ambitions. When he was barely twenty, one of his barons, seeing him preoccupied, asking him of what he was thinking. 'I am thinking of one thing', he replied, 'it is to know whether God will grant to me or to one of my heirs the grace of raising France to the height it reached in the time of Charlemagne.'[3]

What was only a dream and an intense desire in Philip Augustus became, a century later, a set plan in Philippe le Bel. The aggrandisement of his kingdom was the constant preoccupation of this ruler. Historians depict him as 'always obsessed by the memory of Charlemagne, whose heir he claimed to be, always watching for a chance of extending the influence of France in Germany, of winning over the towns

---

of France must be wise and valiant. Any man who offends him must not escape his vengeance by forest or by plain; and the king must not stop until that man is dead or cries for mercy. If this is not done France's honour is sacrificed and in the judgement of history he is wrongfully crowned king.'

* The struggle between the Plantagenet dynasty of Henry II and his sons, deriving from Anjou, and the Capetian Philip Augustus, based on the Ile-de-France, can only anachronistically be represented as a struggle between English and French.

† 'If the French could realise their intentions, the king of England would soon have nothing on this side of the sea; had they the power to do so they would drive him back across it with ignominy.'

[3] Guizot, *Histoire de France*, t. I, p. 459.

and turning the Rhine princes into his pensioners.'[4] His reign was a major one in the history of France, abroad as well as at home. At this time French policy emerged from its tentative beginnings. It appeared in its stark reality and in the form it was constantly to assume under ambitious kings. Its object was conquest, its method process of law, its agents the royal lawyers. At the same time as the great plan of the monarchy took shape, there appeared the race of men who, along with the churchmen and even more than they, were the teachers of those who were to negotiate, chicane, plan and provide pretexts. They emerged, ready and armed for the struggle, from their provincial law-courts and appeared suddenly on a wider political scene. They put forward proposals for negotiation. They knew Europe and its rulers even better than they knew France and their master. They were living witnesses to the tradition which had been established in the nation, for without this tradition they would be inexplicable.

Such was Pierre du Bois, the chief and the first of them in date. Born in Normandy, he studied law at Paris and in the year 1300 was *avocat des causes royales* at Coutances. From there he addressed his *Traité de l'abrégement des guerres et des procès* to the king, Philippe le Bel. 'This work', says his learned biographer, 'exhibits an extensive knowledge of European politics and of the secret plans of the French dynasty.'[5] Du Bois was familiar with the *Digest*, which he cites constantly, but he was above all 'nourished on the popular poetry of the Carolingian *chansons de geste*, which he took for genuine history'. He adduced Charlemagne, who reigned, it was said, one hundred and twenty-five years and 'who had no equal',[6] as the finest model for the kings of France. The Carolingian legend and the *Digest* are the two sources of his ideas: the former suggested to him projects

---

[4] *Histoire littéraire de la France*, t. XXVI. *Pierre du Bois, légiste*, by Renan.

[5] Renan, *Histoire littéraire de la France*, t. XXVI.

[6] *De recuperatione Terrae Sanctae*. (*Histoire litt., id.*).

which were often immoderate and chimerical, while the *Digest* furnished him with pretexts which were often specious and involved, but always crafty and practical. His dominating idea was to extend the royal authority. He worked passionately to increase French power in Europe. When it was reported that the king had just gained 'the sovereign territory of Arles, the lands situated on this side of the Rhine (*citra rivum coloniensem*) and of Lombardy, from the Southern sea to the Northern', Du Bois offered his congratulations;[7] but this did not satisfy his ambitions. His dream for his master was the imperial crown, which 'had been transferred from the Greeks to the Germans in the person of Charlemagne'. Philip, he held, should make it hereditary in his line. The Electors of the Empire were to receive, in exchange for the high dignity which they would lose, lands and money taken from the German churches.[8] The system of secularisations, which the negotiators of the Treaties of Westphalia found so useful and the lawyer-diplomats of the Revolution had so much at heart, was clearly not a modern invention; this method of providing compensation for acquisitions of territory in Germany is almost as old as the idea itself of the acquisitions.

Du Bois did not stop here. Along with the crown of Charlemagne, it was dominion of the world, universal monarchy, that he wished to see bestowed on the kings of France. Philip was to establish everywhere, as far as Constantinople, his sons, brothers, nephews, cousins. He would be the general suzerain of the old territories and the new. He would take over the patrimony of the Church, and make the Pope his dependent, to decide all doubtful cases in his favour and excommunicate recalcitrant princes. In return the king would endow the Papacy richly and free the Holy Land from the yoke of the infidel. However, in order to accomplish this great enterprise the king would need the co-operation of Eu-

[7] *Traité de l'abrégement*, text cited by de Wailly.
[8] *Pro facto Terrae Sanctae* (*Histoire litt., id.*).

rope. This could only be obtained if the princes were assured that they would not be recalled from the east by the attacks of their neighbours. It was essential therefore that perpetual peace should reign among Christian rulers. The only way of ensuring this was for the Pope to command peace and the king of France to enforce the command. Perpetual peace and a crusade were pretexts to lend colour to this vast plan of domination. If he succeeded in executing it, the king was to content himself with putting one of his brothers on the throne of Germany and keeping for himself 'all the lands on this side of the Rhine, with direct rule and suzerainty over the counties of Provence and Savoy'.[9]

There was much that was chimerical in these plans; but even in that respect the legist was doing no more than providing a specious form for ideas which were stirring in men's minds. Such ideas were widespread, and the very incoherence of the statements in which they occur demonstrates their prevalence.

In 1291 the people of Valenciennes called on the protection of the king. They claimed that they were French, invoked their titles, produced charters and reminded Philip that several of his predecessors had been emperors. Nothing is more characteristic than the history of the alleged treaty of Vaucouleurs, which Philip was supposed to have signed in 1299 with Albert of Austria. 'It was said to have been agreed', relates Guillaume de Nangis, 'with the consent of King Albert and the barons and prelates of the kingdom of Germany, that the kingdom of France, which on this side only reached up to the Meuse, should extend its boundaries as far as the Rhine.'[10] Other chroniclers also report the fact and give the king credit for it. In fact, there is every reason to believe that the treaty is apocryphal: nevertheless it was one of the titles to fame of Philippe le Bel. Two hundred

[9] *De recuperatione Terrae Sanctae*. (*Histoire litt.*, id., and t. XVII, p. 737, notes).
[10] *Chroniques*, year 1299.

years later an advocate cited it in a speech in the Parlement.[11]
The treaty was enshrined in a popular work, and the reputation which redounded to Philip enhanced the high regard
that his subjects had for his authority. An *Eloge de Paris*
written in 1323 says, 'The monarchy of the whole universe
belongs to the most illustrious and sovereign house of France,
simply by right of a native impulse towards that which is
best' (*ex nativae pronitatis ad melius jure*).[12]

This right was worthy in its principle; in practice it was
open to all sorts of interpretations. There was no claim which
could not be buttressed by it. We should not fail to recognise,
however, the generous and naïve qualities in the patriotic
enthusiasm of these Frenchmen of olden times. For them
the happiness of the world was bound up with the greatness
of France. It seemed for them beyond question, and to their
minds nobody could doubt it. All the same, the more the end
seemed to them just, the more they were indifferent to the
means. They thought all methods legitimate to achieve such
a great object, and all arguments good in support of such a
cause. They cited all the texts that were furnished by the
confused erudition of the time, all the measures which the
brutal habits of the century suggested. They put uncritical
learning at the service of unscrupulous policy. They identified the king with the state; and in the service of the king,
and in the interests of the state, any ruse was allowable and
all violence lawful. Contradictions never worried them. 'In
the eyes of Du Bois, the Pope could do nothing if he was
Italian and an enemy of France; when he became French
and a creature of the king, he could do anything.'[13] Thus
they employed against foreigners, as arguments which could
not be refuted, the papal bulls which they refused to acknowledge when their own interests were affected. It was

[11] Boutaric, *loc. cit.*
[12] *Tractatus de laudibus Parisiis*, by Jean de Jandun. *Histoire
générale de Paris. Paris et ses historiens au quatorzième et au
quinzième siècle*, by Leroux de Lincy, Paris, 1867, p. 61.
[13] *Histoire litt., loc. cit.*

the same with the principles of the Roman law. *Si veut le Roi, si veut la loi*: this maxim summed up their jurisprudence, their politics and their philosophy. Skilful subordinates but dangerous counsellors, they were fascinated by royal authority and sought to dazzle their masters with it. This is how Pierre du Bois addresses Philippe le Bel: 'You possess an inexhaustible treasury of men, which will suffice for all wars that may come about. If Your Majesty knew the might of his people, he would unhesitatingly undertake the great enterprises which I have just described . . . provided, of course, that he is inspired by the right motives, that is to say by a desire for the general weal.'[14]

Such was the political system and such its original and primitive character. All that remains is to trace its development and the ways in which it was pursued by those who came after. The councillors of Philippe le Bel were the first of the line. They founded a dynasty, and throughout history we shall find affinities between the members of this strange and powerful race—men of chicanery and of war, who well deserve the odd description given them of *chevaliers ès lois*. Louvois is only the most famous representative of a dynasty which includes du Bois and Nogaret among its ancestors. We must remember one Pierre Flotte, who fought and died 'comme un chevalier' at the battle of Courtrai, if we wish to understand the strange inheritance of the lawyers Danton and Merlin de Thionville, who, in 1793, infused emotion into a war of conquest.

The jurists of Philippe le Bel were in advance of their time. His weak successors, who had to assert their right to the throne of France and reconquer their own kingdom from the English, were not in a position to put forward claims to foreign territory. This struggle occupied five reigns and a whole century. The nation and the monarchy emerged from it more united and more sure of one another. National feeling was freed from its trammels. All classes in the kingdom

[14] *Traité de l'abrégement*, de Wailly, loc. cit.

shared in the deliverance, which was, in its decisive phase, essentially the achievement of the people. The Maid, whose inspiration was the salvation of France, sprang from their loins. At last France existed, vital and loved, so that the humblest of its children gave herself as a sacrifice for the liberation of her country. Patriotism had been growing slowly in men's hearts: its full revelation came with Jeanne d'Arc.

2. ORDINARY WARS AND WARS FOR GLORY

As soon as the war of independence was concluded, the war of frontiers began again. The tradition had not been forgotten, the poets kept it alive. One of those who, at the beginning of the Hundred Years War, stirred up Philip of Valois against the English addressed him thus:

> *Fais leur tantost apercevoir*
> *Que Gascoingne est de toy tenue*
> *Et te fais seigneur droit clamer*
> *De tout ce qui est deça mer;*
> *Soit la mer borne et dessevrance*
> *De l'Engleterre et de la France.* . . .
> *Flandre aussi deça soit vostre.*[15]*

The kingdom was hardly delivered from the English, France had hardly begun to breathe freely again, when ambitious advisers urged the king to plunge anew into foreign adventures. He was reminded that the territories of Burgundy and Lorraine to the east, which seemed to offer themselves for his conquest, had formerly belonged to the crown and that there was a legitimate claim to them which it would

[15] Jubinal, *Nouveau Recueil de contes*, t. I, p. 73.
* 'Make them realise forthwith that Gascony is yours and have yourself straightaway proclaimed lord of all that is on this side of the sea; let the sea be the bound and dividing line between England and France. . . . Let Flanders also on this side be yours.'

be just to enforce. In 1434 Guillebert of Metz, proclaiming the excellent merit of the kingdom of France, wrote, 'I do not tell you, indeed, of all the kings of France, or of their kin, who were kings of Austrasia, whose principal seat was at Mes in Lorraine, which ancient chronicles called France.' Recalling the great deeds of Charlemagne, and summing up his conquests, he outlined a programme for his successors— 'Liége, Flanders, Hainault, Brabant, Guelders, Jülich, upper and lower Burgundy, Provence, Savoy, Lorraine, Luxemburg, Metz, Toul, Verdun, Trèves, Cologne, Mayence, Strasburg.'[16]

From the same period, and on the same theme, there is a more striking piece of evidence. It is the *Débat des hérauts d'armes de France et d'Angleterre*.[17] When the French herald wishes to demonstrate the superiority of French valour over English, the model he proposes to French warriors is Charlemagne—'Charlemagne son of Pepin, who was such a great king and did such great deeds of valour, above all against the Saracens, and who brought all Spain to the Catholic faith and conquered so many lordships in Germany and in Lombardy. . . . And thus the said Charlemagne became Emperor and even you of England acknowledged his rule.' Marvellous adventures, epic endeavours, the conquest of empires— such wars were great and noble, they were *guerres de magnificence*. As for wars over frontiers, *guerres communes*, these, according to the herald of arms, hardly deserved to be mentioned.

All the same, kings and their advisers thought them worth undertaking. They left ambitious dreams and the legendary deeds of Charlemagne to the poets and the writers of the romances of chivalry, and held on to the part of the tradition that was practical. As soon as their hands were free they

[16] *La Description de la ville de Paris et de l'excellence du royaume de France. Paris et ses historiens*, pp. 144, 146.
[17] Written between 1453 and 1461. Published by Pannier and Paul Meyer in the volumes of the *Société des anciens textes de France*, Paris, 1877.

reached out for it. The king mobilised his troops and his lawyers their texts; diplomatic negotiations and military operations began simultaneously.

Germany, or rather the Germanies as they were called then, provided both the opportunity and the pretext for aggression. The Holy Roman Empire was profoundly divided: the princes were struggling against the Emperor, and the cities against the princes. The alliance of Charles VII was sought at the same time by the Emperor against the Swiss and by the Duke of Lorraine against the imperial towns. Charles VII promised assistance to both. In the marches of Lorraine the frontiers of the Empire were changing and ill-defined in the extreme. The imperial cities were suspended, in a sense, between Germany and France. In this area there was hardly any prince or local lord who was not at the same time a vassal of both the French monarchy and the Emperor. There was no need to search out historical precedents, to make involved changes in procedure, to take pledges. It was urged in the court, reported Aeneas Sylvius, that the French should take advantage of the situation to assert the ancient rights of the French crown over all the territories on its side of the Rhine.[18] This was what they did. In 1444 the Dauphin, later Louis XI, led his troops into Switzerland to make war on the Swiss leagues. He then concluded peace with them, withdrew to Alsace and proclaimed that he had come there 'to assert the rights of the kingdom of the Gauls, which extends up to the Rhine'.[19] Meanwhile the king, Charles VII, at the head of another army, had penetrated into Lorraine and summoned the towns between the Meuse and the Vosges to recognise his authority. 'Let it be known', he declared on 11 September 1444, 'to all present and to come that, as we did not long ago, we have entered into the marches of Bar and Lorraine and towards the Germanies for

18 Henri Martin, t. VI, p. 413.

19 *Jacobi Wimpfelingii Germania ad rempublicam Argentinensem.—Thomae Murneri ad rempublicam Argentinam Germania nova.* Strasburg, 1874.

great matters touching us and our lordship, and especially to provide a remedy for various usurpations and attacks on the rights of our kingdom and the crown of France in the several provinces, seignories, cities and towns being on this side of the Rhine, which from olden times used to belong to our predecessors, the kings of France.'[20]

Toul and Verdun recognised him as their protector. Metz resisted and pleaded its privileges. The royal lawyers were ready to challenge them. 'The said king of France and those of his council', reports a chronicler, 'for their part intended to make war on legal grounds, saying that from long past and in ancient times town and city had been and duly were held under the sovereignty of the crown of France'.[21] The president of the Parlement, Jean Raboteau, informed the inhabitants of Metz that he was in a position to prove this, 'as well by charters as by chronicles and histories'. Invoking in turn the support of the King against the Emperor and of the Emperor against the King, the towns of the intermediary zone tried, in fact, to make themselves independent of both, like the Swiss leagues and cantons. 'The King', said Jean Raboteau, 'was well aware that they were accustomed to invent or discover such wiles and excuses, and as when the Emperor of Germany came . . . in full power and with the intent to constrain them to obey him, for their defence they at that time alleged themselves to be subjects of the King of France and tenants of the French crown; similarly when former kings, predecessors of the King of France, had come to enforce their obedience, they then declared themselves to belong to the Empire and to be subjects of the Emperor.'[22] The people of Metz did not let themselves be persuaded; the Germans protested, and the king withdrew; but the initial pleadings had been made and the case remained henceforth in the courts and ready for decision.

During the following reign the problem of the Burgundian

[20] *Ordonnances des rois*, t. XIII, p. 408.
[21] Mathieu de Coussy, ch. III.
[22] *Id.*

inheritance was posed in all its amplitude. The king could not abandon the French provinces which were part of the inheritance without betraying the interests of France; and he was led naturally to wish to add to them the former Burgundian territories which had escaped French allegiance. As soon as he heard the news of the death of Philip the Bold, Duke of Burgundy, Louis XI gathered his troops, called the bâtard de Bourbon and Philippe de Commines to his side, and 'entrusted them with the necessary powers to summon to obedience all who were willing to accept his rule'. He also gave them sufficient forces to constrain those who were not willing. He launched a general attack, alleging in each place a different justification. At Abbeville he had it proclaimed that this territory, leased by Charles VII in 1435, 'should return in default of heirs male'; at Arras, that 'the king claimed the town by "reason of forfeiture"' and the territory should go with the town. In Burgundy he invoked the right of 'garde noble'.[23] He occupied Hainault and the imperial territories on the grounds of *nantissement préalable* and subject to giving them up if necessary after judgement. In Flanders he appealed to national feeling, and introduced into his claims an argument which was destined to have a great future. 'If my cousin were well advised,' he told the inhabitants, 'she would marry the Dauphin. You Walloons, who speak French, need a French ruler, not a German.'[24]

Instead, the heiress of Burgundy married Maximilian of Austria. The inevitable consequence was the rivalry of the houses of France and Austria. The conflict was dictated by the interests of France and the instinct of the nation. There is nothing surprising in the fact that the policy was a popular one for the monarchy; it emerged, so to speak, from the deepest traditions of France. The marriage, said an historian at the end of the seventeenth century, 'gave birth to a war of more than two hundred years, which looks like lasting much longer. Occasionally interrupted by the exhaustion of the

23 Commines, liv. V, ch. X and XI.
24 Guizot, *Histoire de France*, t. II, p. 432.

combatants, it was only to return like an intermittent fever as soon as the infected matter had gathered again. In its course rivers of blood have been poured out and an infinity of burning, ravaging and human misery perpetrated. . . . France and the house of Austria have involved in this quarrel most of the princes of Christendom. So long as there remains one inch of land to be won it will be an irritant and an un-failing source of new wars.'[25] The pretext, if not the cause, of the war which broke out in 1792 and inaugurated the mighty struggle of the French Revolution with Europe was the disputed sovereignty over the middle lands. It was one more episode in the long trial by battle between Austria and France which had been waged since the fifteenth century. This struggle was an essential condition of the existence of the French state. The Archduke Philip, son of Maximilian and of Mary of Burgundy, married, in 1496, Joanna the Mad, heiress of the crown of Spain. Their son Charles, when he succeeded to the throne, ruled over Spain, Naples, Sicily, the Low Countries, Franche-Comté and the Indies, to which he added the Imperial Crown. Henceforth France, encircled by the Spaniards and the Austrians, met them on whatever road she took.

The French method was first to establish her claims for-mally and then to enforce them with armed might. The King's councillors drew up the titles on which his claims were based. A long process of investigation and legal proce-dure laid the foundation for the greater annexations. Prin-ciples were laid down and precedents established. In the same way as legal cases had been used to expand the royal domain and royal power within France, so precedents were invented for use outside France. The tangled network of sovereignties and feudal suzerainties furnished an unlimited supply of pretexts for political claims. Roman law, which was being studied more closely and was now better known, provided an inexhaustible arsenal of arguments and maxims.

[25] Bayle, *Dictionnaire historique*, art. *Louis XI*, note.

Local customary law was added to them. Royal supremacy
was fortified by the traditions of Roman rule. The domain
was declared inalienable, indivisible and imprescriptible. It
was laid down that the king could alienate none of his rights,
and these rights were discovered wherever there were any
claims to pursue.

The interests of the crown found a powerful prop in the
revival of classical learning. Knowledge of authors whose
writings not only provided a model but were also a source of
authority was spread through the invention of printing. It
was no longer sufficient to invoke the memory of Charlemagne and rely on a legend. History and policy provided a
deeper and more substantial foundation. The rights of succession to the great emperor were sought for in the very beginnings of his empire. The search was pushed back to ancient
Gaul. Caesar, who described its boundaries as lying on the
Pyrenees, the Cevennes and the Rhine, was quoted as a witness to the origins of the nation. The fact being incontestable,
from it was deduced an imprescriptible right. His *Commentaries*, which won the admiration of literary men, became
the breviary of statesmen. The kings and their lawyers took
the idea of the frontiers of Gaul from the Romans, as they
had taken their principles of international relations. Classical
authors provided the mould of the monarchy and the frame
within which it was to grow and be delimited. They fastened
on to the idea with all the more determination because it was
at once spacious and uncomplicated, because nature and history both seemed to support it, and because it opened up for
national ambition the finest field that could have been imagined. The writings of Strabo* were translated into Latin,[26]
and every enlightened Frenchman could read the passages
from which were drawn successively and according to the
times historical precedents, maxims of state, and a system of

---

* Stoic and traveller, c.64 B.C.-A.D.19, wrote *Geographica* in
Greek, describing the physical geography of the chief countries
of the Roman world.
[26] Venice, 1516; Basle, 1571; Geneva, 1587.

political philosophy. Gaul, it said, was bounded by the Pyrenees, the Alps and the Rhine; these are 'the natural frontiers' and geography knows no others.* As for 'the frontiers drawn by rulers at different periods and from different political motives, these are as changing as the motives that inspire them.' In Gaul the pattern of rivers and mountains seemed to have something providential about it. 'What should above all be observed in this country', it was said, 'is the perfect relationship which prevails between the different parts, through the rivers that water them and the two seas into which they flow. . . . Such a happy disposition of territories, by the very fact that it seems to be the work of an intelligent being rather than the result of chance, is sufficient to prove the existence of Providence.'[27]

Thus the titles of France seemed to have been inscribed by God himself in the nature of things, just as they had been by history in treaties and charters. But if these latter were numerous, they were obscure. The political lawsuits in which they were adduced gave rise to continual and unexpected

---

* The memory of the frontiers of Roman Gaul certainly exercised an influence over French history. It was sometimes suggested that France should extend to the Rhine: a poem by Jean le Bon, in 1568, includes the somewhat cryptic couplet:

Quand Paris boira le Rhin
Toute la Gaule aura sa fin.

The Foreign Minister, Lionne, in 1662, referred to the Pyrenees as the natural boundary between France and Spain. But the idea of nations being delimited by 'natural' frontiers does not have the long tradition in French history that Sorel supposes. It belongs to the intellectual climate of the revolutionary period, when, for example, it could be said that the closing of the Scheldt was 'against nature'. It was Danton who, in January 1793, after the victories of Dumouriez and Custine in the Austrian Netherlands, proclaimed the doctrine of natural frontiers and so staked out a claim to the Rhine frontier for France. See C.-G. Picabet, *La diplomatie française au temps de Louis XIV* (1930); P. Rain, *La diplomatie française d'Henri IV à Vergennes* (1945); G. Zeller, 'La Monarchie d'Ancien Régime et les frontières naturelles', *Revue d'Histoire Moderne*, viii (1933).

[27] Strabo, trans. Letronne, liv. IV.

difficulties and disconcerting objections. A superior law was needed to interpret doubtful precedents, to apply the precepts of Roman law to feudal cases and to trip up the enemy's jurists. Such a rule already prevailed in the relation of states: it was raison d'état. It guided the conscience of kings, controlled the policy of diplomats and inspired the jurisprudence of the lawyers. It was the first step in the legal confrontation and the last one in the decision. All schemes were based on it and all enterprises justified by it. It was the ultimate law and there was no appeal from it: *salus populi, suprema lex esto*.

The lawyers and publicists of Germany fought their cases and upheld their claims with the same mad logic and the same uncontrolled erudition. They invoked the same texts and relied on the same authorities. It was a war of citations and syllogisms, in which the subtleties of the *Digest* were combined with the cavils of scholasticism. Geography and astrology, history and myth, the *Commentaries* of Caesar and the deeds of Charlemagne, the Theodosian Code and the laws of the barbarians, the precedents of the Roman Empire and the charters of the Middle Ages—any source which provided an argument was worth citing, even the worst at least adding to their number. Rabelais has left us incomparable parodies of these barbarous polemics. But at bottom the issues were not such as could be settled by texts or abridged by maxims. The very uncertainty, the confusion and triviality of the pretexts invoked on one side or the other, are sufficient proof that the real issues did not lie in the field of law and jurisprudence.

These heavy-handed legal debates represent only the formal aspects of the conflict. In reality it was one of those struggles which are the essential basis of all history. The problem of frontiers was not one that could be settled by appeals to Roman or to feudal law. Frontiers are the dividing lines which mark the boundaries of nations, that is to say of populations with similar traditions, identical aspirations and a common civilisation. The great question which was being posed and was developing beneath the complications and the obscurities of political discussion was precisely to know towards which of the two empires and the two peoples who were contesting the intervening territories the populations in dispute would feel themselves sufficiently drawn to form with it a single nation and state.

Whilst such ideas looked to the future, royal policy deviated from them and strayed into mistaken paths. Charles VIII allowed himself to be tempted by the legend; he turned away from the Holy Roman Empire to follow in the steps of the Emperor in Italy. 'With my help you will become greater than ever was Charlemagne', Ludovico il Moro told him;[28] and Charles set out on the conquest of Naples and Constantinople. This was one of the most dangerous aberrations of French policy, and it is for this very reason that it must be mentioned here. Moreover this adventure of knight-errantry was to have a curious repetition in the wars of the eighteenth century, when a democratic republic, at the height of its struggle with Europe, was to find its efforts against Austria diverted, just as those of the Valois had been, to Italy. Bonaparte revived, with the idea of carrying to its conclusion, the grand design of Charles VIII; a Pope fled distracted before the Conqueror; Naples fell into the hands of the French; the exploits of Championnet* recalled those of the son of Louis XI; and the victory turned rapidly against the victors, through the fickleness which made the French tire of their conquest even more rapidly perhaps than the Italians became tired of their rule.

These Italian expeditions were 'wars of magnificence' if ever there were any, but they were disastrous wars. Some of the king's advisers were fully aware of this. 'The greatness and the peace of the kingdom depend on the possession of

---

[28] Commines, liv. VII, ch. VI.

* Jean-Etienne Championnet led the French army which captured Naples and briefly set up the Parthenopaean Republic in 1799.

the Low Countries', Crèvecoeur told Charles VIII.[29] It was
towards the north and the east that French power should
have been directed. 'The French would have done better to
seek gains on that side rather than on the side of Italy', wrote
the author of the *Mémoires de Gaspard de Saulx** a century
later. These would have been 'ordinary wars', it is true, but
they would have been in the real interest of the monarchy.
Experience was to prove it only too well, and the actual deviation in policy only strengthened the national tradition. It
reappeared under Henry II more strongly than ever; he returned to it, and for long after there was no straying from
its path.

3. RIVALRY WITH
THE HOUSE OF AUSTRIA

The house of Austria already ruled a large part of Europe,
but Charles V aspired to universal monarchy. Not only did
he check the advance of France, he hemmed her in on all
sides and aimed to overthrow her. France, looking in all
quarters for allies against him, found them in the Turks,
then in their heyday and at the height of their success against
Christian Europe. They invaded Hungary, besieged Vienna
in 1529 and threatened it again in 1532. France looked also
to the German princes who had gone over to the Reformation and who needed French assistance in their fight for religious and political independence from Charles V. These
were effective allies for France, but only on very specific conditions, about which no mistake must be made. French intervention in Germany had to be for the purpose of guaranteeing the liberties of the princes of the Empire; on this
condition the princes would support France against the house
of Austria. But France could not simultaneously protect and

[29] Guizot, *Histoire de France*, t. II, p. 475.
* The Memoirs of Gaspard de Saulx de Tavannes (1509-73),
maréchal de France, were written by his son Jean de Saulx,
vicomte de Tavannes.

subjugate Germany. It was essential that she should abstain
from conquests at the expense of her allies. It followed that
she could only expect from them 'compensation,' or 'satisfaction' in the intervening territories, chiefly those belonging
to the house of Austria. If France claimed more, and became too threatening, her German allies would turn against
her and join themselves, if need be, with Austria to expel her
from Germany. Such reversals of policy, which often took
the form of defection from the alliance, can be seen in the
relations of France and the German princes from the very
beginning.

In 1552 several of the princes, 'badly treated under the
yoke of the Emperor, ran for aid', in the words of a contemporary.[30] They warned Henry II that Charles V intended to occupy Metz, Toul, Verdun, Strasburg and other
of the Rhine towns. This would be, they said, 'the total ruin
of the Empire',[31] and they called on Henry to exorcise the
danger. The king's Council met. 'The way', said the Marshal
de Vieilleville, 'is quietly to occupy, as opportunity offers, the
aforesaid towns; this would mean a gain of about forty
leagues of territory without the loss of a man, of an impregnable bulwark for Champagne and Picardy, and moreover
the opening of an easy route by which to break into the
Duchy of Luxemburg and the territory beyond as far as
Brussels. In addition, you will make yourself the master in
the long run of many fine and great towns which have been
torn from your crown, and at the same time regain the sovereignty of Flanders, of which you were deprived by fraud
and which had belonged to the kings of France for more than
a thousand years from immemorial antiquity.' Some time
after this, Vieilleville opposed a measure which would have
been personally advantageous to him, but which seemed to
him contrary to the grand plan. He refused a brilliant post
because he preferred, he said, 'to die rather than let myself or

[30] Brantôme, *le Grand Roy Henri II.*
[31] Vincent Carloix, *Mémoires sur la vie du maréchal de Vieilleville*, liv. IV, ch. VIII.

my posterity suffer the reproach that for the sake of the government of a province I deprived the crown of France of a frontier of such a kind and extent that it extended right into the kingdom of Austrasia, which was the first crown of our former kings'.[32]

It was in this way that conquests necessary for the security of the state were turned into an assertion of the rights of the state. French military leaders had their minds full of classical memories. They found in antiquity both examples to follow and titles to produce. Rabutin called his account of the expedition, *Commentaires des dernières guerres en la Gaule Belgique*. He dedicated his book to the Prince of Cleves. Remember, he told him, referring to their campaign, 'how greatly you praised Julius Caesar'. The war was popular. Rabutin celebrated 'the intense zeal of the French for their king'. Vincent Carloix pictures the urban youth stealing away from father and mother to enlist, the workshops shut for lack of craftsmen, 'so great was the ardour in all classes to join in the adventure and to see the river Rhine'. But all these descriptions fade before that which Rabelais has left in the prologue to the third book of *Pantagruel*: 'Considering on all sides this most noble kingdom of France, . . . everyone to-day is earnestly at work using his strength, some for the fortification and defence of the *patrie*; some to repulse the enemy and to hurt them; the whole regulated so well and ordered so finely, and to such evident advantage for the future (for henceforth France will have magnificent frontiers and the French will be assured of their peace), that little prevents me from entering into the opinion of the good Heraclitus, and affirming war to be the father of all good things, and to believe that war is in Latin called *belle*, not by antiphrasis . . . but absolutely and plainly because in war everything appears that is fine and good. . . .'

The king occupied Metz, Toul and Verdun. It was a great step forward, but it was not enough for the ambitions of

[32] Vincent Carloix, *id.*, ch. XIV.

some. Jean de Saulx-Tavannes, in the memoirs which he wrote of the life of his father fifty years later, reproached the king with not having annexed Alsace and Lorraine. 'This would have been', he said, 'the re-establishment of the kingdom of Austrasia, joined to that of France. The king was not sufficiently skilful, and the Constable, who favoured it, would have been opposed by the Duc de Guise, who was beginning to equal him in influence.'[33] Moreover the Germans did not give Henry II the time for this conquest. When they saw the French in Strasburg they became reconciled with the Emperor, and France had to make peace before they all joined in a hostile alliance.[34]

What the father had failed to achieve, Coligny never ceased from pressing the son to accomplish. The conquest of Flanders was his dominant idea and the basis of his anti-Austrian policy. 'Whoever prevents war against Spain', he said, 'is no good Frenchman and has the red cross at heart.'[*] He assured Charles IX that the local population would surrender without a struggle out of hatred for the Spaniards, so that, he added, 'without great cost they would make him ruler of all the Low Countries, the greater part of which had been filched from the French crown, usurped unjustly from the king's predecessors, and could rightly be recovered by force of arms since by force of arms they had been lost'.[35] Brantôme reports that a few days before his death, reverting to the affair of Flanders, of which he unceasingly thought, Coligny said, 'God be praised, all goes well. Before long we shall have chased the Spaniard out of the Low Countries and made the king master of them, or we shall all die there, myself the first, and I shall not regret the loss of my life if I lose it in such a good cause.' Fanaticism intervened. The massacre of Saint Bartholomew occurred instead of the Flan-

---

[33] *Mémoires de Gaspard de Saulx*, year 1552.
[34] *Id.*
[*] A red cross was the emblem of Spain.
[35] Pierre Matthieu, *Histoire de France*, t. I, p. 338. Paris, 1631.

ders expedition and the Admiral was assassinated.* 'An unhappy death for all France,' concludes Brantôme, for 'he
was about to conquer a country as large as a kingdom and
add it to France.'[36]

The line of advance was henceforth clearly marked out.
With Henry IV the monarchy came to full possession of its
strength and its motivation. The national tradition was consolidated, defined, simplified, disengaged from the legend and
the dream. The *politiques* had taken over. The rôle of the
jurists expanded as they rid themselves of the confusion and
crudity of earlier times. Their learning became less obscure,
their ideas were clarified. They added to a still lively sense
of their country's greatness a deeper respect for its dignity, a
juster appreciation of its obligations, and in consequence a
stronger and more positive conviction of its rights. They gave
France the first of her great historians and one of the greatest
of her negotiators, in Etienne Pasquier and the President
Jeannin. I do not mean that they were unaware of the legend
or insensible to the enticements of tradition. Pasquier recalled
them in his *Recherches de la France*. Bongars, who was employed by Henry IV in so many great matters, was familiar
with the writings of Pierre du Bois and celebrated the great
deeds of the kings in his *Gesta Dei per Francos*. But all
acknowledged to themselves that there was a necessary limit
to ambition, which was prescribed by interest properly understood. What could not be kept should not be conquered.
Exaggerated conquests exhausted the strength of the state
and stimulated rivalry. There was henceforth a level of
power which could not be passed without provoking the formation of a dangerous hostile coalition. France must not

* It is true that the Admiral Coligny had devised a plan, to
which he had secured the adherence of the young king Charles
IX, for a French invasion of the Netherlands. This meant the outbreak of war with Spain, which, given the domestic situation of
France, racked by the internecine struggles of noble factions and
religious parties, would have been the occasion not of a triumph
but of a major national disaster.

[36] Brantôme, *M. l'amiral de Chastillon.*

arouse against herself the resentment which she made use of against Austria.

Sully was full of such fears; they reappear at every point in his letters and his conversation with Henry IV. This was the basis of the policy of his *Œconomies royales.* 'Every king of France, whoever he may be,' said Sully, 'must rather meditate how to acquire sure friends, allies and confederates, held to him by bonds of common interest, which are the best of all, than by venturing to the edge of schemes exceeding his true strength draw on himself the irreconcilable hatred and the armed forces of one enemy after another.'[37] Etienne Pasquier, who praised Henry II lavishly for his conquests in Lorraine, nevertheless held that it was important above all to tailor one's plans to the actual strength and interests of the state. He makes the philosopher in the *Pourparler du prince* say, 'I understand you when you tell me that you are extending your boundaries; but alas, unhappy man, you fail to see that to give your kingdom good boundaries you must first put bounds to your own ambitions and desires.'[38]

Where were such boundaries? Sully did not fail to recall that France under Charlemagne had re-established the Western empire—'la monarchie occidentale'—and that subsequently the kings of the third race* saw 'their dominion reduced by half to the narrow limits in which it is at present restricted'.[39] He noted that nature had laid down certain frontiers, that of the Pyrenees for example.[40] He admitted that 'the sole and only means to restore France to her ancient glory and to make her greater than all the rest of Christendom'[41] would be to regain the neighbouring territories which 'formerly belonged to her and seem to be properly within

[37] Tome IX, éd. Petitot, p. 33.
[38] *Lettres*, liv. I, letter XI.
* The Capetians, in succession to the Merovingians and Carolingians.
[39] *Œconomies*, t. VIII, chap. XI, p. 183.
[40] *Id.*, t. IX, p. 471.
[41] *Id.*, t. VII, ch. X.

her limits, namely Savoy, Franche-Comté, Lorraine, Artois, Hainault and the provinces of the Low Countries, including Cleves and Jülich'.[42] But would it be possible to keep these without provoking bitter rivalries and ruinous wars, above all without arousing in the royal house ambitions which would be more dangerous to France than all the hatred of her enemies? 'Consider', he wrote to the king, 'what might be the thoughts of princes less wise, moderate and unambitious than you are, as your successors may chance to be . . . and whether they would be able to content themselves with these limits, without such extensive frontiers giving rise to ambitious desires and insatiable greed for the further growth of French dominions and the title to the empire of the West.'[43] One might think that, in writing these lines, he was prophesying Louis XIV and Napoleon.

Sully feared excess in the use of power. According to him France was self-sufficient: she was strong enough to have nothing to fear from other states and to be feared by all. But if he tried to moderate the desire for gain, he was far from losing the taste for domination. He was too smitten with the greatness of his country, too devoted to the glory of his king, too imbued with the old national traditions, to wish to restrict the rôle of France in the world. On the contrary he aspired to extend it and raise her to a height from which she could dominate all Christendom and the civilised world. This was the origin of the strange and vast plan which has wrongly been called the *Grand Dessein* of Henry IV and which could more justly be called the grand design of Sully. To overthrow the house of Austria and reduce it to the possession of the Iberian peninsula, split up Europe into a number of spheres of influence which would mutually limit one another, combine them into a republic of Christian states with the Pope presiding and France ruling over it, weaken the rivals of France and strengthen her client states, surround her with a belt of neutrals, her protégés in principle, her

[42] *Id.*, t. VIII, ch. XII, p. 258, and t. IX, ch. II, p. 28.
[43] *Id.*, t. IX, ch. II, p. 28.

vassals in fact, a bulwark for her defence and an advance guard of French influence; and finally, with peace established among the Christian states, to expel the Tartar and the Turk from Europe and restore the empire of Constantinople —such was in its main lines the famous plan of Sully. What it essentially did was to make France the constitutional ruler of Europe; and for all that it was dressed up in a learned and involved constitutionalism, it none the less would have amounted to the establishment of a universal monarchy.

It was in this form and without any beating about the bush that d'Aubigné presented the final schemes of Henry IV. He said that Henry was getting ready for nothing less than 'putting the imperial crown on his head with a single effort. Other governments', he said, 'would judge the merit of the plan by the merit of the planner' and would resolve to share in victories that they could not stop. 'The consent of the people, which is often the voice of God, seemed to offer its blessing. The nations, having abandoned their enmities, would be willing to pull up their boundary-stones for love of Henry. Germans would adopt the weapons of the French in order to fight like them. . . . The Marquis of Brandenburg would demand the utmost service from the nobility of Pomerania, and the Swiss would call to life their motionless rocks. And all this to set up a Christian Emperor whose power would keep the Turks at bay, reshape Italy, tame Spain, reconquer Europe and make the universe tremble.'[44]

This project of a Christian Empire had already been adumbrated in the fourteenth century by Pierre du Bois in his treatise *De recuperatione Terrae Sanctae*, though only in the rough and ill-defined terms of the political thinking of his day. Sully revived the idea, freed it from the crude acquisitiveness which was concealed beneath the fantastic imagination of the medieval jurist, and gave it the mystical appeal of a utopia. We meet it again, nearly three centuries later, disguised in the austere academic robes of an ideology, as the

[44] *Appendix ou Corollaire des Histoires.*

grand design of Sieyès. He envisaged a France surrounded by dependent republics, dominating Europe by her alliances, providing political leadership, imposing peace and propagating the doctrines of the Revolution among the nations.

After the sixteenth century, the spiritual family whose history I am trying to sketch splits into several branches. Some exalted and some moderated the ambitions of the kings; some advisers stirred them up to widespread conquest and others diverted them from it. Aggression was to have its apologists, and justice and prudence their defenders. Some were to pursue great and chimerical projects, and some to dissimulate their ambition under the pretence of utopian pacifism. The inherited traits appeared in all: the skill in finding new excuses for century-old claims and in justifying by established law and the fashionable philosophy the execution of an unchanging plan. Some pursued it with blind passion, some with blatant greed, and yet others with the wise patience of true statesmanship.

Those who laid the basis for modern French diplomacy, who perpetuated and clarified the traditions of the past and laid down the policy for the future, belong to this last class. Henry IV, Richelieu and Mazarin were the architects of the great European achievement of the old France, which was the Treaties of Westphalia.

Henry IV was the least chimerical of men, but he loved subtle argumentation and reasoning. It amused him to listen to the speculations of Sully; but in the plans of the minister there were two assumptions which the king could not accept: peace, which he did not believe possible, and disinterestedness, which was not to his taste. 'Indeed,' he told Sully, 'would you have me expend sixty millions to conquer territories for someone else without keeping any for myself? That is not my idea.'[45] We do not know where he would have stopped if he had succeeded in the great plan he was maturing at the moment when he was snatched away from France.

[45] Sully, t. VIII, ch. VIII, p. 124.

A ruler of such wisdom would certainly have found it best only to conquer what he judged he could keep; but it may be surmised that his ambitions extended at least to Flanders and the whole of Lorraine. Sandraz de Courtilz, in a work published in 1688, even claimed that 'Henry IV wanted to give back to France its ancient boundaries and to extend its frontiers on the east as far as the bank of the Rhine, in the south to the Alps and the Pyrenees, and in the west to the ocean'.[46] Two *Lettres savoisiennes*, which appeared in 1600 and 1630, attempted to justify the annexation of Savoy. According to the author, France owed it to herself to take the Alps for her frontier on the Italian side and the Pyrenees on the Spanish.[47] Pierre Matthieu attributes a significant observation to Henry IV. In 1601 the king, who had annexed Bresse and the Pays de Gex, received the representatives of his new subjects. 'Among other things that the king said to them,' the historian reports, 'the following were remembered: "It is reasonable, since you naturally speak French, that you should be subjects of the king of France. I am quite willing for all who speak Spanish to belong to the king of Spain, for those who speak German to join the Germans, but all whose language is French should owe allegiance to me."' And Matthieu adds, 'This might have come about through his military achievements, which were so great that without French treacheries he would have made one part of the world French, as Probus had made one part Roman.'[48]

4. RICHELIEU

Such was the tradition of Henry IV. Richelieu was bred in it. At the beginning of his memoirs, in the year 1610, referring to the plans of the great king, he added, 'Perhaps the appetite might have grown with what it fed on. In addition

[46] Cited by Charles de la Combe, *Henri IV et sa politique*, p. 394. Paris, 1877.

[47] Lelong, *Bibliothèque historique*, no. 29088.

[48] *Histoire de Henri IV*. Paris, 1631.

to the plan which he had made for Italy, he was resolved to attack Flanders, whither his thoughts sometimes turned, as well as to put the frontier of France on the Rhine. . . .' Not only Richelieu was imbued with this tradition, but also a large body of opinion which was at the same time national and monarchical. This was the party of the *politiques*. It was because Richelieu relied on this party, and defined its aims so clearly and vigorously, that he rose so quickly into power and established his authority so effectively. In the year 1612 he wrote to a friend, 'As for external ills, I would call them by another name if they gave us the opportunity to extend our frontiers and cover ourselves with glory at the expense of the enemies of France.'[49] Contemporaries say that he liked to read the *Argenis* of Barclay,[50] and that he saw the principles of his policy in that confused allegory. In fact, in the concluding chapter, entitled *Prédiction de felicitez*, Poliarque, 'the greatest king of the Gauls', marries Argenis and a seer announces to him that, among other successes, 'you will extend the limits of your empire: the Rhine will see you victorious on one side and the ocean on the other'.[51] In 1627 Malherbe wrote of Richelieu to Racan, 'I assure you, there is something superhuman in that man. . . . The space between the Rhine and the Pyrenees did not seem to him a large enough field for the fleur-de-lys. He wished them to flower on both sides of the Mediterranean and their scent to be wafted to the farthest countries of the East. The extent of his schemes was the measure of his courage.'

Richelieu was a master architect and builder par excellence. His plans were positive; his views clear, simple and penetrating. His great superiority lay in his capacity for seizing his opportunities and taking advantage of them; of only proposing what was opportune, only undertaking the possible, only carrying out policies that would endure. By 1633

[49] Gabriel Hanotaux, *Histoire du cardinal de Richelieu*, t. I and II.
[50] Paris, 1621.
[51] French translation, Paris, 1624.

the kingdom was pacified and the Huguenots subjected, and there was reason to believe that if he supported the cause of the Protestant German princes against the house of Austria, these princes would transfer 'all that they held on this side of the Rhine' to the king. He showed, in a memoir addressed to Louis XIII, 'that the advantages to the king of such a policy would be great and the risk slight. . . . It would enable him to extend his kingdom to the Rhine without striking a blow.' But it was first necessary to clear the way, that is to say to seize Lorraine, whose Duke had taken the side of the Emperor. 'With that done,' added Richelieu some months later, 'we could imperceptibly extend the limits of France to the Rhine and be in a position soon after to intervene in Flanders, if by a general uprising or obvious collapse of Spanish interests an opportunity appeared in the spring to do so.'[52]

Such was the policy. It remained to settle the rights of the matter, that is to say, to find justifications, pretexts, and a mode of procedure. For this purpose Richelieu had one of his councillors compose a memoir entitled *'Quel est le plus sûr moyen pour réunir à la France les duchés de Lorraine et de Bar?'* This declared, 'The Emperor has no rights in the lands on this side of the Rhine except by usurpation, and all the less because the river was the boundary of France . . . for five hundred years. And when the county of Champagne was united to the crown by the marriage of the heiress of Champagne with Philippe le Bel, he concluded a treaty at Vaucouleurs with the Emperor Albert and the bishops and barons of the Empire, in which it was laid down that the frontiers of France should extend to the bank of the Rhine as they had done formerly.' The jurists provided the legal arguments and the method and mode of prosecuting them, and then delivered judgement. The King referred his grievances against the Duke of Lorraine to his Parlement. While the case was being heard he occupied the territory as a pledge, in order that, when judgement had been given, if the Duke

[52] *Mémoires*, year 1633.

refused to recognise the suzerainty of France, the King would be able to 'reunite' the Duchy legally and according to feudal law. This would close the door to any complaint in law, and to the prayers and intercessions of foreign princes whom the Duke of Lorraine might call in, all the more effectively because it would be the King's own Parlement which had given the verdict.

Richelieu was not satisfied to pursue his claims only by diplomacy and war. He aimed at a national policy which would be backed by public opinion. Hence the series of writings which he inspired, and which appeared both under his own government and in the first days of his successor. The object was to instruct the French as to the raison d'être and the consequences of the vast system of war and diplomacy which was to lead up to the treaties of 1648. Their arguments were all ready-made; they only had to be gathered from the national traditions and adapted to the spirit of the age. The publicists of the seventeenth century, who were the direct and legitimate descendants of those of the fourteenth, saw to this. It will be the less surprising to see the lawyers of the Convention, such as Merlin, Cambacérès, Reubell, Treilhard, as soon as they obtained power, take up the old tradition of royal conquests and adapt them so easily to the new pattern of public law, when we consider that those who founded it in the fourteenth century and those who developed it in the seventeenth had the same origins, had received the same education, were all inspired with the same spirit, emerged from the same law-courts and bureaux, and were steeped in the same records and archives.

The first of the line of Richelieu's royal publicists was Chantereau-Lefèvre, who began his career as an official of the Gabelle and was subsequently intendant of the Duchies of Lorraine and Bar. He produced, in 1642, the *Considérations historiques sur la généalogie de la maison de Lorraine*, with a 'map of the ancient kingdom of Austrasia, the true and original inheritance of the crown of France'. He dedicated his book to France: 'I am one of the least of its children. Nevertheless I venture to claim that I have had the good fortune to bring out of obscurity a truth which is important for the peace of France.' This truth was the fact that the Franks had conquered all Gaul, that is to say, 'the great extent of territory situated between the ocean and the Mediterranean Sea, which is bounded by the river Rhine, the Pyrenees, the Alps and the Apennines, and which has always been known under the name of Belgic, Celtic and Aquitainian Gaul'.[52a]

Chantereau-Lefèvre felt himself upheld by the thought that in proclaiming its rights he was serving his country, and that the happiness of the whole world was bound up with the prosperity of France. Here, once again, was a belief which the publicists of the seventeenth century held in common with their predecessors of the fourteenth and those who were to emulate them at the time of the Revolution. Pierre du Bois had proposed in a treatise on the *Abrégement des guerres* that the king of France should have supremacy in Europe; and the legislators of the year III similarly believed that to increase the power of France in Europe was to work for the peace of the world. Chantereau-Lefèvre did not doubt that once the question of frontiers had been settled, peace would reign for ever between French and Germans. 'The reestablishment of these frontiers', he concluded, 'will restore an honourable and sure peace, not only to France, but to the whole of Christendom. It has continually been disturbed, since the year 720 A.D., by those who, after they had overrun many fine and great possessions of the Franco-Gaulish crown, struggled to ravish what remained and to reduce all Christian princes to bondage under the ostentatious title of a fifth monarchy, which they held destined to engulf all the West.'

Chantereau-Lefèvre was ambitious, but he was also a practical politician: his ideas were precise and limited. Denis Godefroy, the historian of France and a son and grandson

[52a] Liv. I, p. 64.

of jurists, upheld the same thesis in his *Mémoires et Instructions pour servir dans les négociations et affaires concernant les droits du Roy*.

By the time of the Treaties of Westphalia it was an accepted fact that in annexing Alsace and Lorraine France was only reconquering lost territory which was rightfully hers. A book published in 1648 under the title *Les affaires qui sont aujourd'hui entre les maisons de France et d'Autriche* characteristically says of the rulers of Europe, 'Among these is the king of France, whose state includes Narbonnensian, Aquitainian, Celtic and Belgic Gaul. Nevertheless he does not in fact possess all these.' What he did not possess, he was justified in laying claim to whenever the opportunity offered of doing so with advantage. However, rights and pretensions were not confined to lands which had formerly been French possessions. Once started on this slope, imagination and rhetoric were uncontrollable. The jurists discovered claims wherever they saw interests, and rights wherever they saw claims.

A royal lawyer at the court of Béziers, Jacques de Cassan, produced in 1643 a work entitled *La recherche des droits du Roy et de la couronne de France sur les royaumes, duchés, comtés, villes et pays occupés par les princes étrangers*. He expanded French claims to cover almost the whole of Europe. There was no country which could safeguard itself from them, not Spain, nor Portugal, Sicily, Naples, the Milanese, Sardinia. This author's scholarship was a tissue of absurdities. What mattered, however, was the general plan and the practical aim, in which the fantasist found himself at one with the statesmen.

There was a pre-judicial action to be settled before the case under dispute was begun: it involved one initial and essential point. The Franks had inherited Gaul and all its dependent territories: therefore France had to 'reunite' Savoy and Nice, and to recover Lorraine, since it was one of those territories on this side of the Rhine 'which had been usurped from France'. This was the kingdom of Austrasia. 'By whatever name it is called', adds our jurist, whose patriotic ardour at this point suddenly elevates and clarifies his normally flat and heavy style, 'it was always a rich jewel in the crown of France, like a precious stone found in the same rock, the same mine, or gold dug from the same earth. . . .' To it must be added Flanders and the Low Countries, he held, because Julius Caesar had included them in the Gallic provinces. Also Roussillon; and here the reason given should be noted. It represented a transition to a set of ideas that the Convention was much later to borrow from the ruling philosophy, without guessing perhaps that it was reviving the ideas of Strabo and of a lawyer of Louis XIII from the court of Béziers: 'As the ancient ramparts of Gaul to the east were the Alps, so have the Pyrenees, which border this country, always been on the west. These were the limits which nature seemed to have drawn with her own hand and which the former kings, to whom the establishment of their monarchy was due, gave to their State.'

Finally, there is a piece of evidence which shows better than all the others the extent to which this political programme was accepted by the government of Richelieu. In the Latin Testament of Richelieu there is the famous sentence: 'The aim of my ministry has been to give back to Gaul the frontiers destined by nature, to give the Gauls a Gallic king, to identify France with Gaul, and to re-establish new Gaul wherever the old one had been.' The authenticity of his *Testamentum politicum* has been challenged, and not without reason;* but from the point of view of national tradition

---

* Richelieu's *Testament politique* is the subject of a still unfinished academic debate, begun by Voltaire, who was convinced of its lack of authenticity. It has also suffered from the absence until recently of a scholarly text and from being confused with quite different writings. It was not a testament but a statement of views on the government of France possibly compiled under the influence of Richelieu in the early 1630s. See the *Testament politique du Cardinal de Richelieu. Édition critique publiée avec une introduction et des notes* by Louis André, Paris 1947. Rémy Pithou in 'A propos du Testament Politique de Richelieu' (*Revue suisse d'Histoire*, lvi, fasc. 2, 1956) concludes from a careful ex-

the essential thing is that its compiler, whoever he was, interpreted the thought of the Cardinal in this way, and wishing to honour his memory found nothing better to put forward for the admiration of the French. 'When, two hundreds years hence,' wrote Voltaire, 'those who come after us . . . learn that in the time of his ministry the English were beaten and driven away, Pignerol captured, Casale relieved, the whole of Lorraine joined to the crown, the greater part of Alsace brought under our rule . . . and when they see that so long as he presided over our affairs France had no neighbour from whom she had not gained territory and whom she had not defeated in battle, if they have a drop of French blood in their veins and any desire for the glory of their country, will they be able to read such things without conceiving admiration for him?'[53]

Such was the memory that was left of Richelieu. This was why he was to become, through his example and his maxims, for governors as well as governed, the highest model of the French statesman of former times. His ideas were spread so widely that a century and a half later we rediscover them in the men who were called in 1794 by the chance of revolution to rule France, without their having been prepared for it in any other way than by the education of any enlightened Frenchman of their time. They did not have his knowledge of public affairs, his tact in dealing with men, his vigorous common sense, his firmness of character, the extraordinary penetration of his views, nor above all the remarkable balance of his genius. They were rash imitators and immoderate disciples. They preserved only his general maxims, which they distorted into a set of abstract sophistries. But they justified

---

amination of one passage on Levantine trade that it could not have been written by Richelieu or that his part in it is negligible, and that in any case further research is required before a firm conclusion can be reached. The phrase quoted by Sorel is not from Richelieu's *Testamentum* but from the *Testamentum Christianum, testamentum politicum* of the Jesuit Père Labbé.

[53] 24 December 1636, letter LXXIV.

themselves by his example; they claimed the honour of descent from him; and for all that their spirit was more bitter and more violent, they were none the less at bottom his heirs.

Mazarin continued and completed his work. Thanks to him France garnered the inheritance of Richelieu. The tradition was so strong that it was on his foreign policy that Mazarin relied for the support of his domestic government. The doctrine had been so deeply rooted that it passed from polemics into State papers. Article 4 of the Treaty of 1659 declared, 'The Pyrenean mountains, which in ancient times separated Gaul from Spain, shall henceforth be the dividing line between the two kingdoms.' Mazarin effected important 'reunions' of territory with France and planned even more extensive ones. In 1646 he attempted to have Nice and Savoy ceded to France by treaty. Of all his schemes the annexation of Belgium was perhaps the one he had most at heart. 'We would have extended our frontiers up to Holland,' he wrote to d'Avaux, 'and on the German side, which is the greatest source of alarm, up to the Rhine, by the retention of Lorraine and Alsace and by the possession of Luxemburg and the County of Burgundy (Franche-Comté). . . . This would be to emerge from the present war with so much gain and prestige that the most malicious would be hard put to take exception to it. The most critical could not but hold so much blood well shed, and wealth well spent, if they saw the whole of the ancient kingdom of Austrasia annexed to the crown. . . .'[54]

The peace concluded in 1659 was far removed from these magnificent hopes. Critics found in it much to complain of and material for stinging sarcasm. They reproached Mazarin with his prudence and timidity. That masterpiece of irony, the letter of Saint-Evremond to the marquis de Créqui on the Treaty of the Pyrenees, is well known: 'What a difference, Monsieur, between such profound wisdom and the mental disorder of the Cardinal de Richelieu!' There seems

[54] 20 January 1646, *id.*, p. 270.

to be nothing to add to this cruel dart. In praise as in blame, when an unchallengeable comparison was wanted by which to elevate or to lower the reputation of one's contemporaries, nothing more effective than this one could be found. Posterity, less prejudiced, has linked the two cardinals together in a common admiration; and has found their achievement the more admirable as, with the progress of time, its right proportions and soundness have come to be better appreciated.

5 . THE CLASSIC SYSTEM

The house of Austria had been weakened and humbled, France had separated its two branches, German and Spanish. There had been no great changes in territorial sovereignty but all the relations of states had been altered. Formerly the house of Austria surrounded France; henceforth it was itself divided by France. Spain offered hostages in the Netherlands and Franche-Comté and was only formidable by her alliances. Through the involvement of the German branch in the Empire the Spanish branch had been deprived of its strongest support. The league of the Rhine barred to the Austrians the road to France and the Netherlands. The Germanies saw their rights guaranteed by the French, so that France found more clients than enemies in Germany. Thus constituted, instead of a threat the Empire became peaceful, and instead of being the chief obstacle to French greatness in Europe became an instrument of her power. French power had increased much more than her territory; apart from the house of Austria it aroused no jealousy, for it seemed destined to protect the rights of the other states. By means of her alliances France had interested Europe in the maintenance of her power. Foreign policy was thus brought back to the principle which had been, internally, the source of the success of the monarchy: *la modération dans la force*.

This is what must be understood when we study what is called the 'classic system' of French diplomacy. Its moderation was its essential principle; whenever it was extended, by however little, the result would be to distort it. The network of alliances, so carefully woven, was only formidable because of the kind of mutual bond that linked all the parties together. Within this system, Germany, Sweden, Holland, Savoy, Poland, even the Turks, were protected by one another against a common adversary. But let France threaten them herself and they would turn against her and all the ties would be loosened. A German ruler who had not hesitated to combine with France and to share with her a fragment of Germany would turn against her for the purpose of regaining favour with other German states. By defending what remained of the Empire, he would obtain authorisation to keep what he himself had taken, and would compensate in a sense for his own illegitimate seizures by helping to despoil France of hers.

The Treaties of Westphalia had increased the territories of a number of princes. These remained sufficiently dependent upon France and at odds with one another to present no danger of defection or hostile alliances; but only on condition of a cautious moderation in French policy. To push this policy to extremes, to suppress too many principalities, bishoprics, abbeys or counties in Germany, to concentrate power there in a few hands, above all—to use language the meaning of which was to become very plain in the following century—to create, under the pretext of restraining Austria, a power which would try to overthrow her and take her place, would be utterly to misinterpret, and in fact betray, the policy of Richelieu.

Richelieu looked on Italy as he did on Germany. If he thought of creating a confederation there it was for the purpose of ensuring 'its public liberties against perpetual disturbance and invasion by the Spaniard',[55] not to substitute for the formidable, but indirect and unwillingly tolerated,

[55] *Lettres et papiers d'Etat*, ed. Avenel, t. IV, p. 668. Cf. Chéruel, *Minorité de Louis XIV*, t. I, p. 51.

influence of Spain the supremacy of an Italian house which would be infinitely more dangerous to France.

This policy depended throughout on compromises. The only unchanging thing in it was its essential basis, which was French interests. This provided its only unity, but it was a more valuable foundation of policy than any other. Henry IV, Richelieu, Mazarin were not theologians or politicians. The idea of subjecting the policy of the state to a dogma or an abstract principle would have repelled them. Richelieu defended the German Protestants for the same reason as he opposed the French ones: they formed a state within the state. It suited the cardinal that there should be such a state on the other side of the Rhine to weaken the house of Austria; it did not suit him to have one on this side against the house of France. In short, these great statesmen were systematic without being hidebound. The plans they formed were of the kind which, to use the expression of Bossuet, were upheld by their own consequences.

These plans were appropriate to the spirit of the nation. In French foreign policy, as in internal affairs, there was always a crusading leaven which fermented, though never for long at a time and never deeply. The French loved war and glory, but soon tired of them; and if ever war carried them far afield, they immediately became impatient to return. At the time of Austerlitz, at the apogee of the military power of France, Napoleon, commanding soldiers carried away by his genius, was forced to admit it. 'If you were to listen to the single voice of the army', he told one of his officers, 'you would hear it call for a return to France.'[56] In these conditions defeat easily became a rout, and to be themselves again the French had to be back in France. They never tired of defending their country; they quickly tired of aggression. In a word, they were little suited to great conquests. 'The French nation', said an English writer of the seventeenth century, 'on its home ground is supremely brave

[56] *Mémoires du général de Ségur*, t. II, p. 459.

and invincible; when it overflows its frontiers it is no longer the same. This is why it has never been able to maintain its rule over foreign nations, and why when it has great power this turns against itself.' Richelieu was well aware of this lack of endurance. 'If their valour had been accompanied by that quality', he said, 'the universe itself would not have been large enough for their conquests.'[57]

In their foreign undertakings there was a certain limit which it was necessary not to go beyond, excess which Europe would not tolerate and which the French themselves were not capable of supporting. That was the basic principle of the classic system: *Louis XIV le dénatura*—he turned it wholly against its own nature.

6. LOUIS XIV AND EXCESSES

His aim at first was to continue the policy of Richelieu but to surpass him. His first wars were wars over frontiers. He treated all rights as equally plausible and invoked one or another as it suited his convenience; but in his claims right was always subordinate to raison d'état. On Lorraine the *Mémoires* of Louis XIV for 1662 say, 'This is the route our armies invading Germany by way of Alsace have to take; it was formerly a gateway through which the foreigner could invade France and a strong frontier lordship which always joined in the internal quarrels in France. Essentially it is part of the ancestral patrimony of the kings of France, which it was our duty to reunite with the body of the monarchy, from which it had long been separated.' The territories in the Low Countries which Louis XIV gained in 1668 were similarly 'provinces which had always belonged to the kings of France'. It was the same with Franche-Comté, which he 'reunited' in 1678—'a large, fertile and important province, which should be part of the kingdom by reason of its language and by legal

[57] Barclay, in his *Icon animorum*, ch. III. Cited by Joseph de Maistre, *Considérations*, ch. VII.

rights as just as they are ancient. Through it I can open an invasion route into Germany and at the same time close one into France to my enemies.'[58] His claims on Luxemburg were more doubtful, but here raison d'état was all-powerful and seemed to contemporaries to be adequate to prove the case by itself. 'It is the finest and most glorious conquest that the king has made in his life, and the one which best gives him security on all sides', Vauban wrote to Louvois; and Louvois replied, 'This conquest seems to me inestimable for the glory of the king and the advantage of his subjects.'[59]

They were not satisfied with asserting the interests of the nation; they strengthened their case by arguing that they were carrying out its wishes. Though they paid little heed to these in domestic affairs, they never tired of appealing to them as a weapon against foreigners. Thus in 1644 the Regent, refusing to restore Lorraine to Charles IV, declared that 'in the interest of her reputation and for fear of giving the French grounds to criticise her, she could not do it'.[60] Similarly in 1685 the king, sending the comte de Vauguyon to Vienna, instructed him to tell the court, 'There was no one in France who did not regard Lorraine as so inseparably united and bound up with the body of the kingdom that the smallest loosening of its bonds could not be proposed henceforth without arousing the indignation of every good Frenchman.'[61]

The foreign policy of Louis XIV found a very active auxiliary in the parlements. His pretexts and his methods of negotiation were wholly juridical. To establish his right to one part of the Low Countries he invoked a local custom. He diverted it from its application in civil law, says Mignet, into the political field, and applied it to the transfer of crowns, or at least of provinces. He used his judges to settle frontier disputes and to establish the exclusive sovereignty of

---

58 *Mémoires de Louis XIV*, passim.
59 C. Rousset, *Louvois*, t. III, ch. IV.
60 d'Haussonville, *Réunion de la Lorraine*, t. II, p. 212.
61 *Recueil des instructions*, *Autriche*, p. 109.

France in the disputed territories.[62] 'Jurisdiction is the sign of royalty, and Louis XIV was determined that other powers should recognise the decisions of his *parlements*.'[63] The *parlements* delivered the verdicts and Louvois carried them out. The *chambres de réunion* had the last word in royal cases. This was Louvois' idea. 'I have given orders to the intendant', he wrote to the king in 1679, 'about all that has to be done to carry the dominions of His Majesty to their proper extent according to the correct interpretation of the Treaty of Münster.' The jurists set to work; they ransacked the dossiers, the *parlements* issued their decrees, and the interested parties had to choose between submission and confiscation.[63a]

In this trial at arms each stage in the procedure was marked by a battle. Wars were necessary to force the Empire and Europe to recognise the decisions of the king's lawyers, and each new treaty in which they were registered became the pretext for a new war. The fundamental one, the Treaty of Münster, the terms of which are still disputed, left the sovereign rights of France over those ceded territories which did not belong to the house of Austria, and which before the cession had been held directly of the Empire, in some doubt. The result was to provide Austria, wishing to recover the lost province, with a means of challenging the rights of the king of France, of weakening his authority, and drawing the Empire into the struggle in support of the claims of German princes with lands in Alsace who were trying to withdraw them from French sovereignty. The king used the same documents to assert his legal rights and to a considerable extent succeeded.[64] Nevertheless the legal argument continued throughout the eighteenth century. The protests of the German princes against the suppression of their feudal rights in

[62] *Introduction à l'histoire de la succession d'Espagne.* Camille Rousset, *Histoire de Louvois,* t. I, ch. II.

[63] Michelet, *Précis de l'histoire moderne,* ch. XIX.

[63a] C. Rousset, *Louvois,* t. III, ch. I.

[64] 'Considérations touchant l'intervention des garants de la paix de Westphalie'. 1792. *Affaires étrangères.*

1789 were only the last episode in it. On this occasion, once
again, it was war which decided the issue.

Louis XIV unhappily was not content with the satisfactory
and practical 'common wars' of his predecessors. He also had
his 'grand design' and 'war of magnificence'. Indeed, this was
his dominant idea. 'The Spanish succession', says the historian of these great diplomatic negotiations, 'was the pivot on
which practically the whole reign of Louis XIV turned. It
was the main concern of his foreign policy and his armed
forces for more than fifty years. It was responsible for the
greatness of his first years and the troubles of his last.'[65] It
all but ruined the work of Richelieu. Louis XIV misused his
inheritance externally as he did within France, and because
of the allurements of the same inordinate ambition and desire for absolute rule. His allies slipped away and were soon
fighting against him. The only remaining leagues in Germany
were those which opposed him. The Revocation of the Edict
of Nantes had alienated the Protestant princes; the ravaging
of the Palatinate joined them in a common indignation with
the Catholics. The Empire united with the Emperor to
make war on France, which was the ruin of the work of
1648. The bitterness of the Dutch paralleled that of the
Germans. Deprived of his natural allies, Louis XIV was faced
by a coalition of England and Austria with the rest of Europe. Having been brought to this pass through oppression of
the weak, he found no way left of satisfying his ambition
except by sharing it with the strong. This was what he tried,
both with Austria and with England. In the end, by aiming
to get everything he risked losing it all.

The part of his reign in which Louvois was dominant
seems to anticipate the wars of the Directory, and the period
of the Spanish Succession the days of the Empire. There was
then a similar coalition, inspired by England, with armies
furnished by Germany. France, thrust back on herself and
invaded, was threatened, after so many conquests, with dis-

[65] Mignet, *Histoire des négociations relatives à la succession
d'Espagne*. Introduction.

memberment. The enemy guns thundered in the night as far as Marly; and this was the unhappy consequence in each case of the same excess of pride and the paradox of greatness. 'If ever any motto has been justified in all respects,' wrote Louvois, 'it is that which was created for Your Majesty: *Seul contre tous!*'[66] This is characteristic of the spirit of exaggeration, derived from the classics, which concealed ambition and greed behind the mask of patriotic virtue. 'Rome', Bossuet told the *grand Dauphin*, 'had neither an army nor leaders; yet in this unhappy condition, with everything to fear, the Senators unhesitatingly decreed that they would perish rather than yield to enemy arms, and offered to grant the enemy fair terms after he had withdrawn his forces. The Senate remained true to its principles, and its decree that it would yield nothing to force became a fundamental law of the Roman state. . . . It was always more malleable in victory than in defeat. . . .'[67] The same spirit appeared in the eloquence of the Convention in its heroic days. Its speeches, from beginning to end, exhibit all the exaggeration of the later days of the Empire. He continues, 'The universal belief that nothing could resist them made their enemies lay down their arms and gave their allies invincible aid. The results of a similar opinion of French armies can be seen in Europe. The whole world, astonished by the deeds of the king, confesses that he alone can put limits to his conquests.'

What saved Louis XIV was not only his own constancy, the steadfastness of his councillors, the loyalty of the people and the glorious resistance which retrieved French fortunes at the end of his reign; it was also the accident of the death of the Emperor Joseph I. Europe suddenly saw itself faced with the reconstitution of the monarchical colossus of Charles V. The threat seemed the more alarming in that France having been defeated, there would no longer be any force on the Continent to counterbalance the power of Austria. There-

[66] *Testament politique*, cited by Mignet, *Introduction à l'histoire de la succession d'Espagne.*
[67] *Discours sur l'Histoire universelle.* 3rd part, ch. VI.

fore peace was possible, and Louis XIV had the wisdom to conclude it. The Spanish Bourbons were permanently excluded from the French throne, and the two crowns were to remain totally separate; but France, and this was the essential thing, kept the frontiers which Louis XIV had conquered in his first years of glory.

7. LOUIS XV AND FAILURE

Louis XIV made France odious to her neighbours and suspect to all Europe. Those who succeeded him needed much prudence and wisdom to mitigate the feelings of fear and jealousy which his long reign of conquest and war had aroused. They were lucky in that the moderation which was forced on them was also the best and wisest policy for France. She kept Alsace, Franche-Comté, Flanders and Roussillon, and because of her expanded frontiers was no longer in danger from her former enemies. The Treaties of Utrecht had changed the whole balance of power.

In future the house of Austria was confined to Germany. It is too often forgotten, when this dynasty and its rivalry with France are mentioned, that the centre of hostility was Spain. It was in Spain that the violent hatreds were born which were attributed, by an error of terminology as much as of interpretation, to Austria alone. But Spain was now no longer dangerous; she was weakened and dependent. A younger son of France, a Bourbon, reigned in Madrid, and dynastically the situation had been reversed. Austria had undoubtedly extended her territories, she had gained the former Spanish Netherlands, the Milanese and Naples, to which Sicily was soon to be added; but her strength was being dispersed. By extending her outposts she offered her enemies new openings for attack. The Netherlands were vulnerable to France; Savoy threatened the Milanese; and in Germany the growing power of Prussia was rallying the opponents of the Empire. France was to complete her task by the annexation of Lorraine. The house of Lorraine was moved to Tuscany, and by the same treaty, that of Vienna of 1738, Naples and Sicily passed to the Spanish throne.

It seemed as though henceforth French policy had only to aim at the maintenance of the *status quo* on the Continent. France was the most compact of the powers. Her chief enemy had been greatly weakened. She was surrounded by lesser states which courted and feared her. She could resume the rôle of moderator of Europe and guardian of the peace which Richelieu had prepared for her, and carry into another hemisphere the superabundance of power and the excess of vigour which is a condition of health for great nations.

Her future greatness lay henceforth in the colonies, where she would come up against England. In this new theatre of war their rivalry flared up more ardently than in the Hundred Years War. To support this struggle, which covered the whole world, France had need of all her resources. While she was fighting in both Canada and India, she should not have launched her armies across the Rhine. Peace on the Continent was the necessary condition of the great future which awaited her in America and Asia. To achieve this it was necessary to renounce continental ambitions. This was possible: France's defensive strength was considerable. None of her neighbours would dare to fire a shot against her. But France unfortunately was far from being capable of such a wise policy. As a result of attempting at the same time to found colonies and to reshape the frontiers of Europe, she compromised her power in both worlds.

England profited from the inability of France to abstain from simultaneous pursuit of European aggression and colonial conquests. Austria became the natural ally of England against France, and the strength of the diversion she could effect tied France down to a war on land. However, with the support of Prussia, Savoy, Poland, and Turkey if need be, the French could still have kept Austria in check by diplomatic methods, if French statesmen had been willing to be content with diplomacy. Unfortunately, hatred of the house of Austria had outlived its justification: the Habsburgs still seemed to them the menace they had been in the days of Balzac.[68] It was not enough to have restricted their power: France could not rest until it had been annihilated. 'It has always been a fundamental rule of our statesmen', said d'Argenson, 'that Habsburg power must be reduced to the point at which the lands of the Emperor are no greater than those of the wealthiest Elector.'[69] When Charles VI died in 1740, leaving only a daughter, it seemed too good an opportunity to miss. Sounding the view-halloo, the French commenced the chase in the spirit of the ballads of ancient days. They were all set to 'make an emperor and conquer kingdoms',[70] but the Bavarian Elector whom they crowned was only a stage emperor; and as for the conquests, they were only too happy when Maurice of Saxony saved those that Louis XIV had won. The only result of the war was the aggrandisement of Prussia.

However, France, beaten at sea, was saved by the genius of Dupleix, who with a handful of men founded an empire in India. But having risked the loss of Canada in order to conquer Silesia for the king of Prussia, France was to lose it finally in the next war for the pleasure of attempting to restore that province to the Queen of Hungary. France, having played the game of Prussia in the War of the Austrian Succession, was to play that of Austria in the Seven Years War.

Frederick was the most untrustworthy of allies. In 1755 he cynically abandoned the alliance and passed over to the English, who had just renewed the war against France. England having gained the alliance of Prussia, to maintain the balance it was necessary that France should join Austria. Maria Theresa offered an alliance and France accepted it. Thus was concluded the famous treaty of I May 1756. Its object was entirely defensive, but France did not understand

[68] *Le Prince*, ch. XIX.

[69] *Mémoires*, t. IV, p. 218.

[70] *Mémoire de Belle-Isle*. De Broglie, *Marie-Thérèse et Frédéric II*, t. II, 8. Cf. above pp. 18, 20, 31.

this. She changed partners but remained the dupe. When he became the ally of Austria, Louis XV's policy was still as blind as when he had been her enemy. The continental war, which should have been subsidiary for France, became her major effort. Instead of controlling the alliance France fell into the secondary rank. She did not even achieve the irrelevant result for which she had sacrificed her most precious interests. Frederick kept Silesia, while France lost Canada and gave up Louisiana; and the Indian empire passed to the English. Under Louis XV a policy whose only raison d'être was the defeat of England had been managed in such a way as to ensure her triumph.

'Above all', wrote Bernis to Choiseul, then ambassador at Vienna, 'make sure that the king does not remain in slavish dependence on his allies. That would be the worst condition of all.'[71] It was in fact the condition of France during the last years of the reign of Louis XV. The alliance of 1756, which had been in the beginning and in its first form a skilful expedient, solidified into the most disastrous of all political systems. France gained no territory but lost prestige. Formerly she had grouped round her all those who were alarmed at Austrian power; now, compelled to choose between them and Austria, she gave Austria a free hand. As a crowning humiliation, on the morrow of a war in which France had sacrificed everything to serve Maria Theresa's hatred of Frederick, she saw the apparently irreconcilable German powers draw together unbeknown to her and make an agreement at her expense to partition, in concert with Russia, the spoils of one of France's oldest dependents—Poland.

Spain, the only ally remaining to France, had been linked with her in 1762 by the Family Compact, the only beneficial achievement of those years of disaster. The alliance proved stable because France and Spain had the same enemy, England. Victorious, but always suspicious and always on the

[71] 29 October 1758. *Mémoires de Bernis*, published by Frédéric Masson, t. II, p. 321.

watch, England was the hereditary enemy and the implacable rival of France. Peace treaties with her were only truces; enmity brooded always. A centuries-old hatred, kept alive by continual injuries to the *amour-propre* of the French, fed their desire for revenge. Contemporaries likened the relations of France and England to those of Rome and Carthage. 'England', said a well-known publicist, 'has adopted the same principle of not letting us regain strength, of keeping unceasing vigil on our ports, on our dockyards and our arsenals, of watching over our plans, our preparations, our slightest motions, and calling halt to them with a lordly air or a threatening show of force.'[72]

France had suffered a terrible decline. The disconnected efforts of Louis XV to remedy by his secret diplomacy the misfortunes resulting from his official policy merely showed the purposeless anxieties of a spirit weary of itself. Its restlessness revealed its weakness. The gallant man who was sacrificed in this thankless equivocal task, the comte de Broglie, exhausted all the resources of a mind capable of conceiving great things, and under another ruler, perhaps, of achieving them. 'The other nations', wrote one of the most enlightened and worthy Secretaries of Foreign Affairs, Gérard de Rayneval, 'concluded that France no longer possessed strength or resources. The envy which had hitherto inspired the policies of other courts towards France degenerated into contempt. The government at Versailles lost its prestige and its influence over other governments. Instead of being, as formerly, the hub of European policy, it became a passive spectator, whose approval or disapproval counted for nothing.'[73]

The nation was conscious of its degradation. It was the more angry in that the new course of foreign policy defied all its traditions. For a century it had been taught to hate

[72] Favier, *Conjectures raisonnées*, ch. X. De l'Angleterre. See the edition by Boutaric: *Correspondance secrète de Louis XV.*

[73] *Situation politique de la France à l'avénement du Roi au trône, 1774. Affaires étrangères.*

the house of Austria. The need to humble this house, and the way to achieve this by alliance with the Protestant states, and in particular with Prussia, had become maxims of state in the public mind. They were learned at college and taken for truths as self-evident as the philosophy of the Enlightenment or the rules of classical tragedy. The name of Richelieu had never been held in greater honour, or the Treaties of Westphalia more admired. The War of the Austrian Succession, in which France was engaged in war simultaneously against her two principal rivals, revived these great memories. The battle of Fontenoy, Napoleon said, gave the monarchy forty years more of life.[74] At the beginning of the Seven Years War, public opinion, faced with the defection of Frederick II, grasped the need for a change of course to restrain Prussian ambitions. It believed it understood the reason for the Austrian alliance and approved it, supposing that by this change of alliance France, freed from Prussian pressure, could concentrate all her efforts against England. But when the country found that its military effort was being directed towards Germany, and that French forces were fighting not in the interests of France but in those of Austria, that Canada was being sacrificed to Silesia, and that, under the pretext of revenging the wrongs of Maria Theresa, the coasts of France were being exposed to the attacks of the English, the policy no longer seemed comprehensible and France felt betrayed.

The king of Prussia, who was popular in France, was not blamed for this. His genius, his government, even his conquests were admired. They found favour in the eyes of the *philosophes*. The constancy with which Frederick waged the struggle won back the good opinion of those who had been angered by his desertion. The hatred which Austria drew upon herself outweighed the resentment which Prussia had earned. 'The nation is more bitterly opposed to the war than ever', wrote Bernis in April 1758. 'The king of Prussia is

[74] *Mémoires de madame de Rémusat*, t. III, p. 288. Paris, 1882.

madly admired, because those who conduct their affairs successfully are always admired. The court of Vienna is detested because it is regarded as a leech on France.' It was a correct and not exaggerated judgement. 'Our policy has been absurd and shameful',[75] concluded this minister of Louis XV, and all France agreed with him. Indignation overflowed when the partition of Poland was known and when it was seen to what a point of 'servile dependence' on the house of Austria the king had reduced France.[76]

The fear of being one day despoiled by such a greedy and unscrupulous ally intensified French anger and resentment at being exploited during the war and duped during peace. 'I predict', wrote Mably several years later, 'that the Emperor will call on us to restore Lorraine, Alsace and anything else he pleases.'[77] 'If France gets involved in an unsuccessful war,' said one of the ministers of Louis XVI, 'who can guarantee that the Emperor will not claim Alsace and even other provinces?'[78] Thus the misuse of the alliance by the Austrians revived all French traditions of enmity with Austria. Add that Maria Theresa was *dévote*, that she was known to be a friend to the Jesuits and an enemy of the *philosophes*, and that in the French court the favourites were reckoned to be won over to Austria, and everything contributed to increase public hatred of an alliance which in any case seemed unnatural. At a time when the partisans of new ideas were beginning to be known as *Patriotes*, all the opponents of these ideas were identified with the 'Austrian Party'.

Great as was the hostility to the Austrian alliance among the disciples of the *philosophes* and the educated public, it

[75] Bernis, *Mémoires*, II, pp. 17, 202.
[76] Bernis to Choiseul, 29 October 1758. *Mémoires*, II, p. 322.
[77] *Notre gloire et nos rêves*, 1778.
[78] See the *Mémoires* read at the King's Council in 1784 and 1785, published after the originals in the National Archives by M. Tratchevsky, *La France et l'Allemagne sous Louis XVI*, Paris, 1880. The passage cited is taken from the *Mémoire* of M. d'Ossun, 11 November 1784. Cf. *Mémoires* of the comte de Ségur, 11 November 1784, and of M. de Castries, 2 January 1785.

was even stronger at court and within the royal family. The Dauphin, father of Louis XVI, although very religious, was committed to the traditional policy. He made no secret of his hostility to the Choiseuls, 'Lorrainers at heart and by origin', and to the alliance of 1756, 'which prevents us from being French'. He wrote that he would search in the history of his ancestors for 'the means by which they detached Spain, Naples, Lorraine, part of the Low Countries, Alsace, Franche-Comté and Roussillon from the house of Habsburg'; and added, 'I must not forget that if I do not preserve the same watchful policy, Austria will recover from me what she took from my ancestors, and not so long ago, for we remember what France was in the days of Charlemagne.'[79] The daughters of Louis XV had the same views; the comte de Provence was imbued with them. It was the watchword of all who prided themselves on their understanding of the international scene and their knowledge of French traditions. On this subject there was only one opinion among the ministers of Louis XVI. It was 'the national war-cry', said one of them; and it was the verdict of that famous bureau of foreign affairs in which tradition was preserved, as a contemporary said, 'like the sacred fire of the Vestal Virgins'.[80]

These feelings were so general at the time of the Revolution that in this respect the émigrés shared the sentiments of the republicans. The 'Austrian Committee' was as suspect and as violently denounced at Coblenz as at the Convention. An émigré officer, analysing in a memoir destined for Catherine II the causes of the collapse of the monarchy, attributed it to 'the disastrous alliance of 1756'.[81] In 1795, the 'Austrian faction' was spoken of with as much bitterness at Verona and at the court of the comte de Provence as in the Committee of Public Safety. Instead of the marriage of Marie Antoinette with the Dauphin sealing for ever the al-

[79] Soulavie, *Mémoires*, t. I, p. 111, Paris, 1801.

[80] *Id.*, t. I, ch. I.

[81] *Mémoires sur les affaires présentes*, by the comte de Langeron, 1792. *Archives des Affaires étrangères*.

liance of 1756, the unhappy princess accumulated on her head the hatreds and prejudices of three centuries of rivalry, stimulated by the still smarting impression of recent wrongs. The very reason for her arrival in France made her suspect to the French. Her association with the alliance, which was in fact the raison d'être of her marriage, was in their eyes her crime. The violence of the passions aroused against her mother and her country must be appreciated if we wish to understand the monstrous unpopularity which pursued her in France. It was summed up, well before the Revolution, in the term which was for Marie Antoinette a verdict of deposition and death—*l'Autrichienne*.

8. LOUIS XVI

When Louis XVI ascended the throne the monarchy was even more humbled in Europe than it was in France; external affairs seemed even more compromised than internal. Louis XVI tried to restore both in the same way, by a return to the traditions of the monarchy while making every effort to adapt them to the needs of a new age. Vergennes, who was entrusted with foreign affairs, was given a task analogous to that of Turgot. Although he lacked the genius of Turgot, he possessed in a high degree common sense, practical experience, and a staunch, wise and far-sighted patriotism. His judgement was sound, his mind enlightened, and he had a feeling for moral principles. He has been charged with lack of a definite policy; but who could have followed one in the confused state of Europe and with such contradictory commitments and interests? He has been accused of inconstancy and even duplicity, and more than one contradiction has been found between the principles he professed and the instructions he gave to his agents. It has been forgotten that he was operating in a world of rogues and sceptics, that his duty was to try to win them over to his views and that to do this he had to use language they understood. His role was by no means a straightforward one. Censor and courtier, moralist and diplomat, he found himself in a self-contradictory and awkward situation. Moreover he was solemn and had a taste for holding forth in the literary style of the century. Yet for all his slight veneer of pedantry he was a man of honour, the wisest minister France had had for many years and the most upright statesman in Europe.

Vergennes' whole career had been in diplomacy. He had belonged to the royal counter-diplomacy controlled by the comte de Broglie. He was a member of 'the king's secret', which in his person now came to office. He did not plan to overthrow the alliance of 1756, but he proposed to bring it back to its original purpose, and to make what had become through the weakness of Louis XV and the incapacity of his ministers an Austrian system once again into a French one. This was exactly what Louis XVI wanted. If Vergennes succeeded in his plans, while Turgot failed in his, this must not merely be attributed to the difference in their tasks, the extreme complication of the internal situation and the comparative simplicity of external affairs; it must be attributed above all to the support which Vergennes had from public opinion and to the king's confidence in him. Opinion was divided over the reforms of Turgot. Private interests, allied against him, were able to paralyse his action. On the other hand, public opinion unanimously desired the restoration of French prestige abroad and as soon as it saw the minister engaged in this task supported him. Moreover, to uphold Turgot and defend him, if necessary despite himself, a strong king would have been necessary; to appreciate the work of Vergennes and accept his policy, all that was needed was an honest intention and a knowledge of the permanent interests of France in Europe, both of which Louis XVI had.

The king understood the affairs of Europe infinitely better than those of France, because he had received instruction in the former, while the latter had been neglected. In any case, by whom could he have been taught? If such a tutor had existed, he would have been the great minister of whom

France had need. The complexity of the domestic government of France repelled the languid and indecisive spirit of Louis XVI. Besides, for the King and from the point of view of the court, these were minor matters, the concern of '*petites gens*', which could be left to the intendants. Foreign affairs were the proper affair of kings; they were the life-work of his caste, his family; they were his personal business. Naturally hard-working, the king applied himself to them conscientiously. He was familiar with the history of his own house and with that of the other dynasties of Europe; he had not learnt it by dry and pedantic lessons but by reading and conversation in the ordinary course of his life as a sovereign prince. His ideas about Europe could be reduced to a few basic propositions, in which he profoundly believed. He added to them a high opinion of the dignity of his crown. Thus prepared, he could accept good counsels and give wise advice.

This was what he did. In these matters his very timidity and distrustful nature were an advantage. He feared the influence of the Queen, and while he often gave way to it in internal questions, where he was not on his guard, he knew how to nullify it in foreign affairs. From the time of his accession he showed that his foreign policy was going to be very different from that of his grandfather.

'Deign to remember, Sire,' Vergennes wrote to him in 1782, 'the situation of France relative to the other powers of Europe when Your Majesty took over the reins and did me the honour of entrusting me with the department of foreign affairs. The lamentable peace of 1763, the partition of Poland, and many other equally unfortunate developments had delivered severe blows to the prestige of your crown. France, formerly a source of fear and jealousy to other powers, then only aroused the contrary feelings. The premier state in Europe was hardly granted a place among the second-rate powers.'[82] To restore France to her rightful place it was neces-

82 Vergennes to Louis XVI, 1782. *Affaires étrangères.*

sary to free her from the dominance of England and shake
off the Austrian yoke. An opportunity had appeared of doing
both at the same time.

When the English colonies of North America revolted,
France aided them. When Joseph II tried to annex Bavaria,
France resisted him. In vain did Joseph invite Louis XVI to
join in the project and offer him as his share of the profits
territorial acquisitions in the Low Countries. Whatever the
gain might be, it would not compensate, in the eyes of the
King, for the harm that would be done to the French monarchy by the introduction of Austrian power into the heart
of Germany. It would put the Empire at the mercy of Austrian ambitions, repudiate the guarantees of the Treaties of
Westphalia, and finally, by the same manœuvre, open the
road into Italy to the Imperial armies. The compensation
offered would indicate to Europe all the more clearly the
reduction of France to a secondary rôle.[83] The Treaty of
Teschen, concluded through Louis XVI's mediation in 1779,
restored her clientèle of minor states to France, who had
shown herself firm and disinterested. Europe, which had
come to discount her power, learned to respect it again. The
defeat which was inflicted at the same time on the English,
the alliance which France concluded with Spain and Holland against them, and the ultimate success of the War of
American Independence, completed the revival of French
prestige.

Henceforth, French policy was directed towards maintaining peace on the Continent. It was not an easy task. Doubtless Frederick, in his old age, had become conservative. He
abandoned an active foreign policy and aimed only at enjoy-
ing his gains. But Catherine the Great, a bold and restless

[83] 'The King felt the necessity of finally putting an end to the
intolerable misuse that the cabinet of Vienna made of his complaisance, his attachment to the alliance, his friendship for Their
Majesties, and of re-establishing equality between the two courts
once again.' *Situation politique à l'avénement du Roi*, by Gérard
de Rayneval, *Affaires étrangères*.

pupil, and the Emperor Joseph, a rash competitor, saw in the American war an opportunity to undertake the partition of the Ottoman Empire. The peace concluded between France and England in 1783 came just in time to halt these conquests. Russia managed to keep the Crimea, as an anticipatory share of the Turkish inheritance; but the court of Vienna took warning that France would not abandon the Ottoman Empire to its ambitions. Whatever price the king attached to the alliance with Austria, wrote Vergennes, he would not hesitate to renounce it 'if it involved abandoning the hope of restoring it to its true principles, and if he became convinced that his ally was determined to take no notice of his appeals and to launch out on schemes which His Majesty could not connive at without sacrificing the prestige gained by the wise policy of the last ten years and without injuring irreparably the essential interests of the kingdom'. As it seemed only too likely that Joseph II would not give up his plans of conquest, Vergennes concluded that 'nothing was more shaky than the alliance', and that it was 'threatened with a not very distant reversal'.[84]

The reversal was not long in coming. Frustrated temporarily in his designs against Turkey, Joseph II turned against the Dutch and denounced the treaties closing the Scheldt. These were one of the foundation stones of the commercial prosperity of the Republic, and it appealed to its allies. France took its side, and the Treaty of Fontainebleau, signed in 1785, ensured the preservation of its rights. This rebuff, by which Joseph II was greatly provoked, confirmed him in his plan to disencumber himself of the Low Countries. His idea was to transfer the Austrian Netherlands to the Bavarian house, which would cede to Austria in return its South German territories. The Austrian Netherlands, combined with the territories of the Palatinate on the left bank of the Rhine, were to constitute a new kingdom of Burgundy or Austrasia.

[84] Instructions of the marquis de Noailles, 1783. *Recueil*, t. I, p. 523 ff.

To obtain French support for the plan, Joseph offered her Luxemburg; but in fact neither the projected manœuvre, nor the name of the new state, was likely to appeal to Louis XVI. He did not confine himself to refusing his co-operation; he encouraged the formation of the German League, or *Fürstenbund*, by Frederick, to resist the aggression of the house of Austria.

The French ministry could justly congratulate itself on having revived the prestige and influence in Germany which France had formerly possessed through the Treaties of Westphalia. Louis XVI was on the way to make himself the arbiter of the peace of Europe. Vergennes crowned his achievements by completing, in 1786, the Commercial Treaty with England, which was designed to consolidate peaceful relations between the two countries. A similar treaty signed in 1787 with Russia sealed an entente between Paris and St. Petersburg which seemed to suit the interests of both. This wise policy, said a contemporary, 'restored to us the prestige which had been lost by the weak reign of Louis XV. Through it Louis XVI enjoyed a reputation appropriate to his virtuous character, that of a moderate, strong and peaceloving monarch.'[85] It was an age of generous illusions and great hopes. 'The kingdom', declared the comte de Ségur, 'appeared so flourishing that without being endowed with a Cassandra-like gift of prophecy it was impossible to have any inkling of the abyss towards which a swift current was bearing us. We thought we were progressing towards perfection, unchecked by any hindrances and fearing none. We were proud to be French, and even more to be Frenchmen of the eighteenth century, which seemed to us an age of gold renewed on earth by the new philosophy. . . . Truly, when I look back on that age of delusive dreams and learned folly, I compare the state in which we found ourselves to that of someone on top of a high tower, whose vertigo, produced by

[85] Ségur, *Mémoires*, t. II, p. 7.

the spectacle of an immense horizon, precedes by only a few moments his dreadful fall.'[86]

The downfall was indeed imminent. So deep-seated were the ills that had eaten into the ancien régime that its latest triumph only hastened its collapse. Vergennes was a good diplomat, but he was not a statesman. He had no mastery of domestic policy, and in the extreme disorder of its internal affairs France needed both a Richelieu and a Colbert. Admittedly, his efforts to restore French prestige in Europe had been successful; but money was needed to wage war and supply the armaments necessary to support his diplomacy. He successively opposed Turgot, whose plans ran counter to his own, and Necker, who preached economy. He contributed, without knowing it, to the involvement of the state in the dubious expedients which led it towards bankruptcy. His ministry was, and could only be, a brilliant interlude in a story of decadence, a momentary diversion which only distracted French attention from domestic affairs for their seriousness to become all the more evident a moment later. What made a reform of the government essential was the disorder of French finances; and to divert public attention from this the debt had been increased. Reform was so urgent that it was necessary, if the government was to devote its efforts entirely to this, to sacrifice altogether the kind of predominance that had been regained in Europe. Vergennes died on 13 February 1787 and so escaped the wretchedness of seeing his work destroyed by the very effects of its success.

9. POLITICAL SYSTEMS

Nothing remained of the 'Austrian system', and even the alliance hardly existed any longer except in name. No one in Europe failed to appreciate this fact, especially at the court of Vienna, but it suited the enemies of the system in France to pretend otherwise. They were not content with

[86] *Mémoires*, t. II, p. 28.

being freed from the Austrian yoke, they wanted the alliance
to be broken. They were not content with the restoration of
the treaty to its initial object, they wanted it to be denounced.
They promoted a patchwork of odds and ends as an alternative French policy. The moment the policy of the government began to falter they attacked it violently. They attributed the sudden eclipse of France in Europe not to the
financial collapse which was its real cause, but to the mistaken policy of the government, which they condemned as
criminal. This was the source of the accusations of treason
directed later against the King, the Queen and the ministers.
Since the ideas of the opposition, which were put into effect
when it came to power, prepared the way for the whole
foreign policy of France during the Revolution, we must
examine carefully both the school and the doctrine that were
destined to exercise so great an influence.

The founders of this school were two men whose reputations are now very different, but in their own time were
similar. These were Duclos and Favier, both well situated
for understanding French foreign policy. Duclos was histo-
riographer royal and Favier one of the chief agents of the
secret diplomacy. More a *littérateur* than a statesman, Duclos
did not have any pretensions to theory; but in his *Mémoires
secrets* he revealed the history of the Seven Years War to the
whole educated public. His *Mémoires* provoked indignation
against the 'shameful peace of 1763'. They spread hatred of
Austria and its alliance as the source of all the ills of France,
and admiration for the King of Prussia, whose friendship,
it was alleged, would have remedied them all. The misuse
of the French alliance by Maria Theresa was condemned
with a severity that was only equalled by the indulgence of
the author for the betrayals of Frederick. This history, in
which the very mistakes gratified their passions, taught contemporaries what judgement they should pass on the policy
of Louis XV. For a long time the *Mémoires secrets* circulated
in manuscript. When they were printed, in 1790, they were
already famous, and were lapped up by a public which was

prepared to admire them blindly. Duclos thus took the first steps to prepare public opinion for the new policy, but it was Favier who was its effective instigator.

Favier was a *déclassé*. Born at the beginning of the century, he started on a diplomatic career, in which he exhibited undeniable ability. He was quietly got rid of because of the licentiousness of his life, the cynicism of his language, a too marked taste for intrigue and an undue willingness to employ police methods and corruption. Dismissed from honourable employment, he was reduced to subaltern and equivocal posts, in which he vegetated miserably. He had travelled widely, seen much and learnt much. Along with a fund of exact and very extensive knowledge, he had a remarkable talent for exposition. The dogmatism with which he put forward his ideas suited the intellectual habits of his readers; and the technical details of the evidence with which he supported his theories carried conviction. When he was expounding them, a lively sense of French greatness and a patriotism made more ardent by resentment at his personal wrongs elevated his style, while he added the spice of impudence made fashionable by Diderot. In the end his diplomatic lessons bordered on the kind of aesthetics that *Le neveu de Rameau* had taught.*

It was from him that Dumouriez, at the beginning of a life of adventure, learnt politics and foreign affairs. They struck up a friendship, and later Favier drew him into the secret diplomacy, which brought them both to the Bastille. There was a moment when one was the inventor and the other the agent of one of those strange plots that Louis XV

---

* *Rameau's Nephew* is a short masterpiece by Diderot, describing a conversation between the writer, upholding the average eighteenth-century belief in moral purpose and the goodness of man, and the nephew, expressing pessimism, cynicism and a determinist view of life. Part of its fascination is that it really does not teach anything, and at the end we do not know which side Diderot is on. Although it includes an aesthetic argument, its ethical content is more relevant to Sorel's comparison.

hatched against his own government. Back-room planners as well as secret agents, they contrived vast schemes in imagination, only to be reduced to the pettiest devices in practice. Their knowledge of affairs of state had all been won in the corridors and they only operated on the backstairs. They combined a weakness for abstract arguments on great theoretical systems with a passion for intrigue and a mania for mystification. Utopians and conspirators at the same time, they were the recruiting agents and instructors of that horde of unofficial diplomats who, in the early days of the Revolution, suddenly appeared in the clubs and the editorial rooms of journals, pending the time when, through a maze of byways and side-roads, they were to overrun Europe.

The teaching of Favier can be summed up in one fundamental proposition: the total destruction of England. England, he held, being the sole obstacle to the expansion of France in the colonies, on the seas and on the Continent itself, she must be blockaded in her island and excluded from intervention in Europe. Since, however, Austria was the only dangerous land power, it was necessary to begin by overthrowing her. The Austrian alliance had distorted the whole of French policy and caused all the ills of France: the only remedy for these was an alliance with Prussia. This doctrine was the crux of the whole argument; it was also its fatal defect. In fact the new system merely turned the old one upside down. It suffered from identical drawbacks—the same application of abstract arguments to affairs of state, and the same failure to understand the requirements of politics and the nature of men. Favier's grievance against the Austrian alliance was that it had abandoned French tradition in the north and the east, and had sacrificed the old allies and clients of France to the ambitions of the house of Austria. He was right, but he abandoned himself to the strangest infatuation when he thought of persuading Prussia to break with Russia, ally with Sweden, support the Turks, defend the Poles, and along with a makeweight of little states, uphold the French protectorate in Germany. It was equivalent to expecting Prussia, as Louis XV had expected Austria, to cease to be herself. It substituted a wild paradox for a fallacy.

However, the paradox was suited to the spirit of the age and the trend of opinion. It had the unusual luck to be backed by tradition and at the same time appeal to the passions of the day. Brandenburg had been one of Richelieu's tools. The king of Prussia was a *philosophe*. Each of his victories appeared a triumph of enlightenment; the 'enlightened' Prussians professed such an intense hatred of Austria that no one in Paris doubted their affection for France. 'Men', declared Rivarol, 'always take the enemies of their enemies to be their own friends.' Prussia seemed the natural ally; to strengthen her was to add to one's own strength. In addition there was the rare satisfaction of working for the happiness of mankind and reconciling political calculation with the principles of philosophy.[87]

Favier's principal book, the *Conjectures raisonnées*,[88] in

---

[87] We should not despise unduly these aberrations of another age. Our own country has witnessed equal or worse ones and the source of them has not dried up. All that Favier and his disciples said of Prussia and humanity we have read about nationality, of the house of Savoy and the Italians, of Prussia and the Germans, of Russia and the Slavs. When shall we at last begin to understand this truth of common sense which a man of intelligence and a good Frenchman put, as a commentary, at the foot of one of the pages of Favier? 'A statesman in Paris should not make himself Spanish, or English, Austrian, Prussian, Russian or Turkish: he should be French and calculate the interests of his country and the alliances which are proper for it according to the times, the respective strength of foreign powers, and *above all according to the quality of those who are in control of them.*' Note by the comte de Ségur in his edition of Favier: *Politique de tous les cabinets de l'Europe*, 1801.

[88] Favier published in 1756 a brochure entitled, *Doutes et questions sur le traité de 1756*. The *Conjectures raisonnées sur la situation actuelle de la France sous le système politique de l'Europe* was composed in 1773 at the request of the comte de Broglie (see the *Secret du Roi*, t. ii, ch. viii). Many copies were in circulation in Paris. The work was published in 1793 under the title; *Politique de tous les cabinets de l'Europe*. The comte de Ségur

which he put the essence of his teaching, was written for Louis XV. He was addressing a ruler whose willingness to oblige the house of Austria was only too well known, and he was not afraid of seeming too dogmatic or too systematic in what he said. He shouted because he knew that the king was deaf. Composed to be read without attention and perhaps with dislike by a declared partisan of the Austrian alliance, the work was devoured by a public which was violently hostile to everything that its author was attacking. What was intended to arouse the patriotism of Louis XV merely excited the passions of the opponents of his policy. Favier became their idol. 'The predictions of this great man are so many prophecies that have all come true', wrote a former consul, Peyssonnel,[89] in 1789. 'I was brought up from my childhood on the papers of Favier', said Sémonville in 1793, when he was on the point of leaving for his mission to Constantinople. Mably was profoundly impressed with them, and though he was less prejudiced in favour of Frederick and less obsessed with the Prussian alliance, he concluded, like the author of the *Conjectures raisonnées*, that Austria was the natural enemy and Prussia the inevitable ally of France. Soulavie scattered the same ideas through the *Mémoires du maréchal de Richelieu*, a 'history of the decadence of the French monarchy' which appeared in 1796.

But the chief propagator of the new policy, the true prophet of the diplomatic revolution, was Raynal. He translated the aphorisms of Favier into passionate rhetoric. It was by means of the gloss in the *Histoire philosophique et politique des deux Indes* that the doctrines of the *Conjectures raisonnées* were transmitted to the men of the Revolution.

---

produced in 1801 an edition accompanied by a commentary. Here we have Favier criticised by a disciple of Vergennes. M. Doutaric has reproduced the text of the *Conjectures raisonnées*, with most of these notes, in the *Correspondance secrète de Louis XV*. Paris, 1866.

[89] *Situation politique de la France, et ses rapports actuels avec toutes les puissances.* 1789.

Due allowance being made for differences, diplomacy, which had had its Montesquieu, now found its Rousseau. The *politiques* of the Revolution derived from Favier, the rhetoricians, the visionaries and the sectaries from Raynal. Favier had disciples and Raynal proselytes. In him, said a writer in 1783, who was in spite of this an enemy of sophism and hostile to exaggeration, the powers of Europe are in turn called before the tribunal of humanity to shudder at the barbarities committed in America, to the tribunal of philosophy to blush for the prejudices which the nations still cherish despite its teaching, and to the tribunal of politics to learn that their true interests are founded on the happiness of the people.[90]

We can already detect that curious mixture of invocations to peace with bellicose exhortations, humanitarian effusions and the zest for conquest, patriotic ardour and cosmopolitan enthusiasm, which was to be found in the speeches of the Convention. In the odd dithyrambs on Richelieu which break out suddenly between two pages of ranting against tyrants, there is a presentiment of the spirit of the authoritarian democrats of the Convention. 'Monarchies need peace and security, republics need alarms and a dangerous rival. Rome needed Carthage.' Yet Carthage had to yield or perish. 'Englishmen,' cried Raynal, 'you have abused your victory. This is the moment for justice or for vengeance. Europe is weary of tyrants; at last it claims its rights—Thus would Richelieu have spoken. All true citizens should condemn him as a man of blood and a murderer, who for the sake of despotic power handed his enemies over to the executioner's axe. Yet the nation and the state must also honour him as the minister who first aroused France to her true rôle and gave her the leadership in Europe which was proper to her strength.' Raynal even added, and it will be seen that the Jacobins did not give him the lie, 'It is thus that Louis XIV, who for forty years knew how to maintain the respect of his

90 Rivarol, *De l'universalité de la langue française*.

contemporaries, would have spoken, for even in his mistakes he remained great, and even when he was humbled by misfortune he never degraded himself or his people.'[91]

However, alliances, whatever they may be, are only the means of policy. The end is frontiers. Let us consider what this meant at that time, and see how this centuries-old problem presented itself to contemporaries.

10. THE PROBLEM OF FRONTIERS

In 1789 the constant end of Capetian policy seemed close to attainment. Doubtless the northern frontier was wholly artificial; but experience had shown that Vauban's girdle of iron was worth more than rivers and mountains. Moreover, what mattered was less the frontier in itself than the kind of nation which it bounded. In this respect the position of France in Europe had never been so favourable. Internally, on French soil, there was the most homogeneous nation, the most strongly centralised state on the Continent. Externally, there were weak and divided neighbours. The Austrian Netherlands, Belgium and Luxemburg were in a sense wide open to attack: France could occupy them before an army sent to their aid from Vienna would have left the hereditary states of the house of Austria. Towards the east there were the electoral bishoprics, the Bavarian Palatinate, the Duke of Deux-Ponts, pacific and feeble princes involved in debts, or mercenary, natural clients of France, who could count on their neutrality so long as she did not threaten to dismember their possessions. Behind them, and behind the Rhine, there was the Holy Roman Empire, divided against itself, a huge body without character or life, which only desired to vegetate peacefully under the guarantee of its neighbours. Prussia and Austria mutually restricted one another, and France, supported by the small states, could lay down the law there, on the sole condition of not invading the Empire. Switzer-

[91] Liv. XVIII, ch. XLVIII.

land was a friendly neutral. Piedmont was ruled by greed and fear: it coveted the Milanese and feared to lose Savoy. Farther away, in Italy, divided between rival dynasties, the Bourbons of Parma and Naples might one day, under able leadership, counterbalance Austrian power. Finally, Spain was joined to France by the closest treaty ever concluded between the two monarchies.

In these conditions statesmen asked themselves if it was wise to contemplate continual aggrandisement as a policy for the future. It was evident, henceforth, that no power in Europe was strong enough to conquer without allies. Poland had provided a peremptory demonstration of this. But such allies were only to be found among ambitious states, which, being strengthened, then became rivals; the only means of aggrandisement was by sacrificing the weak to the strong. But to do this would be to destroy the whole system of the Treaties of Westphalia, which based the supremacy of France on a clientèle of smaller states. Was it not better to remain the most powerful monarchy in a divided Europe than to share with equals, in permanent rivalry, the control of a Europe reduced to a few great powers? Did not a frontier disputed at various points but with neighbours of this kind protect the state better than one which might be more scientifically drawn, but on the other side of which would be strongly organized monarchies always ready to take up arms against France? Those who were wise recalled the maxim of Etienne Pasquier, 'To give your kingdom proper limits, you must first set proper limits to your own hopes and desires.'

This problem, the most serious for the future of France that could be posed, was not a new one. Already, under Louis XIV, Turenne and Vauban had advised the king not to take in war what he could not keep in peace. 'If we wish to hold out for long against so many enemies,' wrote Vauban in 1676, 'we must think of closing our lines.'[92] In 1694 he

[92] C. Rousset, *Louvois*, t. II, ch. IX.

proposed the restitution of everything that had been conquered beyond the Rhine and in Italy. He laid down the
principle that 'if everything on this side of the Rhine properly belongs with France, nothing beyond the Rhine does'.[93]
He did not express an opinion on the extent of the conquests
to be made on the left bank. This was a question of politics
to be settled by time and circumstances. But while he indicated clearly what would be imprudent conquests and inten-
tionally left the possible conquests vague, he vehemently
specified the necessary ones. Among these were Strasburg,
Luxemburg, Mons and the line from Ypres to Courtrai. To
restore these places would be 'to offer our enemies the knife
to cut our throat'. 'Strasburg should no more be given back
than the faubourg Saint-Germain.'[94]

Vauban was interested only in the strength and defences
of the kingdom. According to him this was true policy and
the true object of ambition. In the following century ambitions became even more restricted, because the pattern of
Europe made annexations more difficult and the internal
condition of France did not allow of serious risks or dangerous enterprises. This was the regretful conclusion which
d'Argenson reached. Before entering the ministry he had
kept the hope of fulfilling 'our finest plan, to have only the
Rhine as our frontier in the north and the north-east'. After
two years' practical experience, he wrote, 'The time for conquests is over. France . . . has enough to satisfy her greatness
and to round off her territory. It is time, at last, to begin
governing, having devoted so much effort to winning land to
govern.'[95] Montesquieu came to the same conclusion, but,
judging from a higher level, he did not regret it. He held
that there was a necessary relation between the size of states
and their constitutions; that nature had set their limits not
by rivers and mountains but by the character of their in-

[93] 'Places dont le Roi pourrait se défaire'. *Oisivetés de M. de
Vauban.* Paris, 1843.
[94] *Id.*
[95] *Mémoires,* I, pp. 29, 371.

habitants and their natural economy. France, he believed, had the good fortune that its extent was proportionate to its power and to the moderate spirit of the nation; a great empire was always difficult to defend and could only be upheld by a despotism: 'Just as monarchs must know how to increase their power, they must know how to limit it. In bringing to an end the inconveniences of a small size, they must always bear in mind those of a greater extent.'[96]

This was the basic idea of Vergennes, and he had the opportunity to put it into practice when Joseph II, in order to persuade France to let him annex Bavaria, hinted that he would reward her for her complaisance by the cession of part of the Low Countries. 'I venture to suggest to Your Majesty', said Vergennes, 'that there is no equivalent at all which could compensate for the injury which would result from the aggrandisement of the house of Austria. Even if the whole of the Low Countries were ceded to Your Majesty and Austria acquired a lesser territory, the loss would be none the less real, to say nothing of the damage to public opinion, which would be the most regrettable result of all.'[97] That was the essential point. Was the partition of Poland the misuse of an old right or the application of a new one? Should it be condemned, or instead taken advantage of? Did they want to admire Frederick, absolve him, imitate him, join in the partnership and claim a share? If they declared, as Versailles had done, 'that all association with that power is impossible unless one is resolved to trample justice and humanity under foot',[98] they could not take Prussia as a model. The states on the Rhine were very tempting; they lent themselves marvellously to rounding off French territory.[99] But the consequences of annexing them needed to

[96] *Esprit des lois*, liv. IX, ch. VIII.
[97] Mémoire to Louis XVI, 12 April 1777. Flassan, t. VI, p. 126.
[98] Instructions of the baron de Breteuil, 1774. *Recueil*, t. I, p. 495.
[99] 'If the misfortune of circumstances should compel Your Majesty to agree to a partition, his views should turn most naturally

be considered: the disadvantages would far exceed the advantages. France would be left without a policy and Europe would be given over to anarchy. Every state would excuse its behaviour by the example of other states; there would be no principle other than convention and no law but force. 'What would happen to Europe', cried Vergennes, 'if this monstrous system ever gained acceptance, as please God it never will? All political bonds would be dissolved and Europe would rapidly present only a scene of trouble and confusion.' It was the task of France to keep order on the Continent.

The new system was derived from the very conditions which French policy demanded, and the state found the bases of its new power in the very reasons which prohibited annexations. Or rather, it continued to follow its traditional policy, while adapting it to the needs of the time. Renouncing conquests henceforth, it would make other states renounce them also. Its disinterestedness would be the foundation of its greatness. Grouping round it the lesser states which it protected, it would be guaranteed their alliance by their self-interest; and it could be at the head of a defensive coalition strong enough to repel any aggression. Thus surrounded, France would remain in the first rank and Europe would help to maintain her there. She would be the arbiter of peace and it would be her rôle to preserve a balance between the powers, which could only be overthrown, however much she might gain, to her detriment.

Wisdom counselled this plan; it was a just one and dictated by self-interest rightly understood. In working for general peace, France was working for her own good and ensuring her supremacy. 'France, constituted as she is,' concluded Vergennes, 'must fear aggrandisement much more than desire it. A greater territory would give weight to the periphery

towards the upper Rhine. The political inconvenience would be infinitely less and the advantages more real; but when one reflects on the flagrant injustice it would be necessary to commit, an honest man cannot agree to this plan.' Mémoire de Vergennes. Flassan, *loc. cit.*

and weaken the centre; she has within herself everything that constitutes real power—a fertile soil, precious commodities which other countries cannot do without, zealous and obedient subjects, devoted to their master and their *patrie*. . . . Placed in the centre of Europe, it is the right of France to exercise an influence in all important matters. Her king, like a supreme judge, can consider his throne a tribunal instituted by Providence to ensure respect for the rights and possessions of other sovereigns. If at the same time Your Majesty were to devote all efforts to putting the internal affairs of France in order and so conduct his policy as to establish the conviction that neither a thirst for aggression nor the slightest ambitious project would be entertained and that the only aim was order and justice, this example would achieve more than the force of arms. Justice and peace would reign universally and all Europe would gratefully applaud and acknowledge the blessings which it would owe to the wisdom, the virtue and the magnanimity of Your Majesty.'[100]

The language of diplomacy had never been more elevated. Never had a worthier proposal been put before a just ruler. It represented an entirely new line of thought. It marked the transition from the old international order, which was breaking down through the abuse of its own principles, to the new one which was beginning to emerge from the speculation of thinkers and pass from theory into practice. To appreciate the full scope of the change which was under way, it is necessary to compare the motives of Vergennes with those which had recently influenced the northern courts in their negotiations over Poland. They must above all be compared with those invoked by the French government in 1740 to justify the dismemberment of the Austrian empire.[101] We no longer

[100] Mémoire cité, 1777. Cf. the Mémoire de M. de Castries of 5 January 1785: 'The King, possessing the finest kingdom in the world, cannot have the ambition to extend his territory on the continent.'

[101] See above, p. 32.

have the cynicism of a Frederick or a Catherine, the harshness of a Louvois or the ruthless calculation of a Richelieu. The general interest was now seen as the way of achieving each separate interest: the domination of raison d'état was weakened and considerations of a purely moral order were invoked to check the brutal realism of the traditional policy. Something of the *Esprit des lois* had penetrated diplomacy.

'A king aiming at conquests', Vergennes wrote at the beginning of the reign of Louis XVI, 'would certainly have reason to regret the present position; but a citizen king would congratulate himself on finding himself in a situation so favourable to his pacific and benevolent intentions.'[102] The spirit of 1789 had already entered foreign policy: the Constituent Assembly was to express views no different from these.

Mirabeau and Talleyrand were brought up in the same school and when they entered the Assembly were imbued with these principles. To carry through great reforms external peace was essential. For Mirabeau the resources of France were inexhaustible; to re-establish her greatness all that was needed was time to restore her strength. 'Domestic strength is the most essential element in foreign policy', he wrote in 1787; 'I have long held that French affairs will be conducted badly so long as the Minister for Foreign Affairs is the chief minister.'[103] He condemned the partitions as iniquitous, discreditable and harmful. He judged Prussia to be so strong that it would be dangerous to increase its power; and believed that Germany should be preserved as the principal element in a balance of power on which the preponderance of France depended. As an ally he inclined, despite all prejudices, towards England; having acquired similar institutions, the two nations would have a common motive for de-

[102] Vergennes. Instructions to Breteuil, 1774. *Recueil*, t. I, p. 487.
[103] *Lettres à un de ses amis en Allemagne* (Mauvillon), Brunswick, 1792. Letter of 17 January 1787.

fending them. With their interests united by the Commercial
Treaty, competition would, he believed, increase their
strength tenfold. The enfranchisement of the English colonies would bring about that of the Spanish. This would give
immense markets and they both could share their exploitation
and control of them.

Talleyrand had similar ideas. The partition of Poland had
aroused his indignation, but it also taught him a lesson.
France, according to him, should henceforth renounce its old
ideas of 'primacy and preponderance'. 'True wealth consists
not in invading the territories of others but in making the
best use of one's own.' He believed that what France possessed was enough for her greatness and that it could not be
increased without danger to herself and to the peace of Europe. These sound propositions were the foundation of the
policy of the sensible and tactful minister who was, in 1795,
the real Minister for Foreign Affairs of the Republic, the
lucky and able negotiator of the Peace of Basle, Barthélemy.

France was able then, at the moment of its Revolution, to
base the peace it needed on a respect for the rights it proclaimed. Its permanent interests in Europe could be reconciled with its new political principles. By a rare chance the
teaching of theory coincided with that of experience. The
policy which abstract reason recommended to the idealistic
legislation of the Revolution was that which properly understood self-interest, prudence and reflection had suggested to
the most far-seeing statesmen of the ancien régime. One basic
principle of the Revolution was the sovereignty of the people:
its corollary was the right of all nations to decide their own
fate. 'Bargains between states', Mirabeau had written in
his book on the *Monarchie prussienne*, 'are no less wicked
than annexations to round off one's territory. To effect territorial exchanges without consulting the inhabitants is an act
of violence and tyranny.'[104] The whole international law of
1789 is summed up in that sentence. Honestly applied this

[104] t. VI, liv. VIII, Conclusion.

principle would have prevented all the abuses of conquest; but its basic object was to prevent conquest itself, for national politics might change and practical good sense and empirical conclusions were not an absolute guarantee. The policy of a great state, declared the Preamble to the Constitution of 1791, requires 'simple and incontestable principles,'[105] peremptory maxims, inviolable engagements. The legislators of 1789 were therefore led to translate the propositions of Vergennes into solemn decrees and to make the renunciation of conquests a fundamental law of the state.[106]

This was the last word and the almost paradoxical conclusion of the policy of moderation. Neither France nor Europe was ready for such a radical reform of political habits. The spirit of proselytism soon came to dominate the Revolution; ideas of conquest continued to prevail in Europe and a desperate war followed. The independence of the French was preserved by their patriotic spirit; the divisions of Europe opened the way to the conquests of the republicans and their enthusiasm ensured their victory. When peace became possible in 1795, the Constituents of 1789 had long disappeared from the scene and nothing remained of their outlook. The men who now ruled were powerful legists, armed and armoured, direct descendants of the *chevaliers ès lois* of Philippe le Bel, exaggerated rivals of Richelieu, immoderate successors to Louvois. They transferred to the people all the ideas that their predecessors had applied to the majesty of the king. They aroused in the people a lust for glory, urged them into war, and founded on their passions the power they exercised in their name. They sought for the commentary on the rights of the nation in the collections of *Droits du Roy*, and in this way a policy of conquest replaced the policy of peace and moderation.

[105] Preamble of the 1791 Constitution.

[106] 'The French nation renounces all wars of conquest and will never employ its forces against the liberty of any people.' Decree of 22 May 1790, art. 4—Constitution of 1791, titre VI.

II. NATURAL FRONTIERS

History is the mother of national tradition. Considerations which restrain statesmen do not restrict scholars. Statesmen have to compromise with facts, while the learned have the task of preserving ancient rights and giving a content to prescription. When, in 1738, Dom Martin Bouquet published the first volume of his *Recueil des historiens des Gaules et de la France*, he recalled in his preface that 'Our Gaul, which is the real Gaul . . . was bounded by the Ocean, the Mediterranean and the Alps, and stretched from the Pyrenees to the banks of the Rhine.' A work which was destined to be the breviary of the historians of France and the archive of its diplomats, the *Bibliothèque historique* of Père Lelong, gathered together rights and claims, traditions and treaties, all the evidence and all the procedural documentation.[107] The author revealed to statesmen and political jurists the arsenal of the counsellors of the former kings. The article devoted to the rights of the crown of France over neighbouring states mentioned no less than 360 works, printed or in manuscript. Treating, in Book IV, of the 'Civil history of France', he included in it 'the provinces which belonged to it formerly, according to the bounds of Old Gaul'. They may, he goes on, be divided into three classes: 'The first group includes the twelve governments general. . . . Other provinces, which were formerly part of France but had been separated from it, have been brought back by later kings; finally there are those which do not at present form part of the kingdom.' Between 1727 and 1751 Père Bougeant recounted the negotiations of the seventeenth century. His history of the *Traité de Westphalie* reveals the full extent of the plans of the two cardinals for the greatness of France. In 1764 Forcemagne edited the *Testament politique* of Richelieu, of which there

[107] Lelong, *Bibliothèque historique de la France*, 1 vol. Paris, 1719. 2nd edition by Fevret de Fontette, 1768, 5 vols.

had formerly been only doubtful and incomplete fragments. The maxims of the great minister were given wide publicity and passionately discussed. Finally, Voltaire, in his *Essai sur les moeurs* and his *Siècle de Louis XIV*, shone a dazzling and witty light over this whole history of claims and conquests.

The tradition had never been blotted out in the mind of the people. In this connection there was a characteristic observation. In 1748 a lampoon appeared in which France was criticised for not having annexed Belgium. 'It would have been impossible', wrote d'Argenson, 'to keep such a fine conquest in the face of the whole of Europe, already only too jealous of the house of France: such are the irresponsible ambitions conceived by the populace.'[108]

The government gave up the ambition unwillingly. It had added Lorraine to France and still had its eyes on the Low Countries. Belgium, which should have been the compensation for France after Louis XV helped Prussia to annex Silesia, was to be her reward when, changing his policy, Louis XV planned the return of Silesia to Austria. This was the principal object of Bernis in the treaties of 1756 and 1757;[109] it was also the aim of those who criticised the Austrian alliance and extolled the opposite combination. The occupation and annexation of Belgium and Luxemburg were the common end of all diplomatic plans.

The tradition was kept alive by classical studies, revived by historians, propagated by writers, taught in the military academies and preserved in the archives of the parlements. It was thus transmitted to the two classes of men who exercised a dominant influence over the foreign policy of the Revolution, the lawyers and the soldiers. It descended to them in a remarkably clear and untrammelled form under the influence of the analytical spirit of the age. The data were very simple, unmixed with any element of speculation.

[108] Edgar Zévort, *Le Marquis d'Argenson*, p. 409. Paris, 1880.
[109] See Bernis, *Mémoires*, t. I, p. 211.

Between the system of Vauban and of Montesquieu, and
the dazzling plans of conquest which had been a national
dream for centuries, there no longer remained any differences but those of degree and opportunity. Both groups
were concerned only with positive gains and invoked only
practical considerations. For the soldiers the only elements
in the discussion were the requirements of attack and defence, for the statesmen the needs of domestic government,
for diplomats the needs of European peace. There was agreement on the ultimate frontiers: Savoy and Nice on one side,
the Meuse and the Rhine on the other. The acquisition of
the left bank of the Rhine was put forward as a direct and
definite objective by no one; it was the ideal aim, a plan for
the future, the final term of the series. If this end continued
to be posited, it was because everything needs a limit and
this one seemed to be indicated by geography, history and
policy. Yet the simplest reflection showed that it was perhaps
dangerous to go as far as this, and in going beyond, France
would certainly exceed the strength which the balance of
power in Europe allowed. She would overstep the limits of
what she could rule, defend and keep.

This frontier having been attained, it was held that France
would halt and stand on the defensive. Satisfied with such
great acquisitions, she would not allow any more to take
place. In a memoir composed for the king by a *maître de
requêtes* of the Conseil d'Etat in 1744 can be read: 'France
should remain effectively limited by the Rhine and never
dream of making any conquests in Germany. If she makes it
a rule not to go beyond this barrier and the others which
nature has prescribed on the west and in the south—the
Ocean, the Pyrenees, the Mediterranean, the Alps, the Meuse
and the Rhine—she will become the arbiter of Europe and
will be in a situation to uphold peace instead of disturbing
it.'[110]

[110] *Nouveaux Intérêts des princes de l'Europe*, by Mandat.
Archives des Affaires étrangères.

But to achieve these great plans and impose them on Europe, it was necessary either to conquer it wholly, which seemed impossible, or to divide it, that is to say to gain within it friends and associates. The spoils of the vanquished would serve to balance the accounts. There was an enemy to conquer and divide—Austria. There was an ally at hand eager for gain, ready to listen to suggestions of conquest and favourable to partitions—Prussia. The ecclesiastical principalities of Germany had already served to complete the weight and restore the balance in a similar case. In the last resort there was Poland, now bereft of frontiers, a sort of empty state. Prussia could be given a free hand there and a blind eye could be turned on what she did.

Such were the conditions of a policy of conquest. The generals of the Republic and the lawyers of the Convention brought this tradition to their corps and committees. But the generation to which they belonged was a generation of *philosophes*, which condemned war and rejected conquest; it aspired to build national constitutions and international relations on unshakeable principles. It no longer wanted transactions which were as precarious as the intrigues by which they were concluded, the interests by which they were influenced, or the convenience which decided them. It needed agreements based on absolute, primordial, self-evident right. The peace which the well-being of humanity required must be sealed for ever. The perfect simplicity of the calculations of a Richelieu was no longer within reach of those involved minds. They had the pretension of being wholly free from Machiavellianism. It was no longer enough for them to plead the facts, they had to appeal to right; and as historical rights were not enough, they appealed to natural right. Their doctrine required convenience to be reconciled with justice and raison d'état with abstract reason.

There was only one honest solution to the problem, however. All the *philosophes* saw it and the French Revolution erected it into one of its noblest principles. It was to consult

the people and only add to the state those who came in willingly. The principle was a simple one but its application
difficult. Some populations might be recalcitrant. It was possible, and indeed very probable, that foreign rulers involved
in a territorial deal or partition might refuse, for their part,
to agree to a principle which they judged subversive of their
own authority. Those who provided the doctrine, happily,
had thought of this contingency, and absolute and universal
as was the principle of the sovereignty of the nation, there
was another one even more universal and absolute, so to
speak, which could overrule all others. It was proclaimed by
Raynal: 'To have sold or given away your citizens to a foreign power', he cried, 'will always be a crime before the
tribunal of morality. By what right, indeed, does a prince
dispose of a people which has not consented to change its
master? Should nations be everything or nothing? Have kings
no debt to their nations? Has international law no meaning?
Is it only the rights of princes?' All the same, in practice the
law of nations was not always clear: led astray by treacherous
counsels or degraded by a long despotic rule, they themselves might sometimes fail to recognise it. To those in charge
of their destinies Raynal therefore indicated an infallible
rule: 'The welfare and the safety of the people are the supreme law on which all other laws depend and which recognises no higher law than itself.'[111]

This law, whatever its title to supremacy, was a far from
clear one. Who had the right to interpret it? Who was to
arbitrate in the dangerous matter of conquests and settle the
limits beyond which they could not go? The problem was
to fix bounds to the public interest which would satisfy
France and Europe at the same time. The peace of the world
depended on this, because the bounds would be immutable.
To determine them some principle was needed which would
be superior to the arbitrary combinations of politicians, the

[111] *Histoire philosophique*, liv. XVI, ch. VII.

selfish passions of conquerors and the very blindness of populations unaware of their own rights. This principle was defined by the author of the *Contrat social*. He found it, like all his other essential principles, in the source of all wisdom and all virtue—nature. 'The situation of the mountains, seas and rivers of Europe, which serve as frontiers to the nations which inhabit it, seem to have determined the number and size of those nations. It might be said that the political order of this part of the world is, in some respects, the work of nature. . . . This is not to say that the Alps, the Rhine, the sea, the Pyrenees, are insurmountable obstacles to ambition, but these obstacles are supported by others which strengthen them or bring back the nations to the same limits when temporary struggles have overridden them.'[112]

These maxims should not be forgotten; they embody, in respect of international law, the whole spirit of the Convention. The speeches of Danton and the reports of the Committee of the year III are only their amplification. Thus the *conventionnels*, at the very moment when they were decreeing the Constitution of the Republic, settled, by another decree, its definitive frontiers. Since the rights of the nation come from nature, the exercise of these rights could only stop at the point where nature itself had drawn a line. The same doctrine which derived the laws of republican France from the precepts of the law of nature based international law on the principle of natural frontiers.

These frontiers, traced by nature, were precisely those indicated by legend and delineated by history for centuries. What the study of the past suggested to statesmen, abstract reason suggested to the *philosophes*; the empiricism of the former led to the same conclusions as the rationalism of the latter, and these conclusions were those which, since the fourteenth century, had been successively deduced from feudal law, from Roman law, and from treaties.

[112] *Extrait du projet de paix perpétuelle de l'abbé de Saint-Pierre*, 1760.

12. THE TRADITION OF CONQUEST

Far-reaching as these designs were, however, they were still only plans for a *'guerre commune'*. There is still the tradition of the *'guerre de magnificence'* to be described, because in its turn this was to prevail. As always, before 1789 ambitious schemes assumed two shapes: the utopian and the paradoxical, perpetual peace and universal empire. These were both wonderfully adapted to the new spirit of the age. A great political theorizer, his inspiration peopled with wild chimeras, a Sieyès for instance, could dream of underpinning the constitution of Europe by only allowing republics to survive in it, all organized in the same way; they would be associated in a federation and harmony established between them by complicated and ingenious institutional devices. He did not realise that nations so different in origin and character, even if they were put into the same mould, could only be reduced to symmetry by force. Sieyès believed he was transferring the United States of America to Europe; in fact he was restoring the Roman Empire. The peace which he was planning was the Roman peace, the Augustan peace as it was called, which the peoples of the ancient world achieved not through mutual respect for one another's independence, but by common subjection to the same master. Since this revolution could only be brought about by conquest, the luckiest or the ablest conqueror would occupy the throne, the way to which had been so ingeniously opened to him.

Many minds were already haunted by the fatal project of reshaping the German constitution. The idea was to simplify the map and group its peoples together. The aim was no longer, as it had only recently been, to set up emperors and kings, but nations and republics on the ancient soil of Germany. The confused mosaic of the Holy Roman Empire outraged these logical minds. The quasi-sovereign noblesse and all the feudal paraphernalia shocked their legal spirits. Followers of the *philosophes* could not endure the sight of ecclesiastical principalities any longer. 'The Germans', said Raynal, 'complain that though they share the same name, speak the same language, form a single nation under one head, their Empire enjoys neither the strength nor the consideration that it ought to have.'[113] Why should the Germans not constitute a nation and a state like France? Why should not the great sovereign houses achieve there, in the interests of the German people, what the Capetians achieved in France? There were Frenchmen who took pleasure in this idea. We shall see, wrote one of them, Prussia and Austria, 'fortunate powers', swallow up all the lesser, parasitic states. 'The electorates, archbishoprics, abbeys, baronies of Germany will suffer the fate that the duchies, counties, marquisates had in France. Instead of being oppressed in peace and devastated in war in the name of two thousand phantom sovereignties, this great country will henceforth be dominated only by two powers, both interested in maintaining peace.'[114]

Since Italy suffered in the same way, the same remedy was to be applied there; but first it was necessary to turn out the foreigner and deliver Italy from the German yoke. This had been the plan of Charles VIII. It was one of the articles of the 'Grand Design' which Sully attributed to Henry IV: his proposal was to cut out a kingdom for the house of Savoy in Lombardy, Parma and Montferrat, and to group a confederation of Italian powers round the Papacy. In his book on *The Prince*, Balzac says it reflects great credit on Louis XIII to have tried to free the Italians from their 'tyrants'. Vauban believed that by a neat political manœuvre Savoy could be annexed without difficulty. Chauvelin took up these plans in 1733. It was the leading idea in the ministry of d'Argenson. 'The most important project that had been under way in Europe for many years', he said in his *Mémoires*, 'was that of forming a republic or permanent association of Italian states like the German, the Batavian, and the Helvetic.'[115]

[113] *Histoire philosophique*, liv. XIX, ch. II.
[114] Linguet, *Annales politiques, 1777-1792*, t. IV.
[115] Tome IV, pp. 266 ff., 464 ff.

He proposed that there should be a Diet and that the king of Sardinia should be at the head of the league. This would be a second Germany at the gates of France. The plan was thus all ready to be adopted by the republicans: only the names needed changing for the former projects of the French monarchy to be developed into the idea of freeing the Italian nation and making it into a federal republic.

But what was the use of regenerating Italy and making it an ally if not to open the road to the East for France and the way to greater conquests? This was the thought at the back of the minds of all the visionaries and all the planners. Leibnitz, who as a good German judged it proper to divert the French from the Rhine, made an effort to lead Louis XV into temptation by suggesting to him the idea of fighting the Turks: Egypt was to be the reward of the French. D'Argenson, reflecting in 1738 on the decadence of the Ottoman Empire, proposed the substitution of a number of Christian states for the heathen power: 'Thus ancient Greece and the beautiful land of the Nile would flourish anew.' Kings of Greece, Macedonia, Palestine, Syria, Egypt, even of Barbary and Morocco, would be set up, with an Emperor at Constantinople. Finally, 'a canal from the Levant to the Red Sea' would be dug, which would be owned 'in common by the whole world'.[116] When Catherine the Great began her crusade in 1768, she took advantage of the favour with which these attractive ideas were viewed. Voltaire urged the cause of the Greeks. André Chénier made it the cause of all poets.

Statesmen, however, were concerned with material gains and it was Egypt which continued to seduce them. We are told that Choiseul thought of it and that the occupation of Corsica was for him one stage on the route to the East. When Joseph and Catherine drew up, in 1782, their great plan for the partition of Turkey, they hoped to gain French support by the offer of Egypt. 'I believe,' wrote the Emperor, 'though without being sure of it, that there will be a way of commit-

[116] *Mémoires*, t. I, p. 361 ff.

ting France by offering her facilities in the actual territories of the Porte, and especially in Egypt.'[117] Six years later, in 1788, a work of Volney acquainted the public with these plans. He revealed that the king's council had deliberated on them, that it had been considered whether, being unable to prevent the dismemberment of the Ottoman Empire, it would not be better to join in it; that some had thought of taking the Morea and Crete, some Cyprus and others Egypt. 'Only one gain', he said, 'could adequately compensate France and be worthy of her ambition, and that is Egypt. . . . By way of Egypt we could approach India, re-establish the ancient trade-route across Suez and cause the route by the Cape of Good Hope to be abandoned.'[118]

When Bonaparte entered Italy his spirit was stirred by these grand visions. Beyond mountains and seas he felt the pull of the East. 'Only twenty-four hours' journey away', he wrote when he reached Ancona, 'lies Macedonia.' A little later, revealing his innermost thought, he added, 'Truly to overthrow England we must occupy Egypt.'[119] He did so, and pushing his ideas from that point to their logical conclusion, he conceived the plan of marching on Constantinople. 'There I will destroy the Ottoman Empire and leave a name to posterity; and perhaps then overthrow the house of Austria and return by way of Vienna to Paris.'[120]

What he achieved exceeded in 'magnificence' the wildest dreams since the time of Charlemagne. The legendary deeds of Charlemagne came true and were surpassed. If anyone, in 1790, had told some liberty-loving member of the Constituent Assembly, some cautious and moderate disciple of Vergennes such as Talleyrand, that his work would contribute to the re-creation of the Empire of the Caesars, that

---

[117] To Catherine II, 13 November 1782. Arneth, *Joseph II und Catharina von Russland.*
[118] *Considérations sur la guerre des Turcs.* Paris, 1788.
[119] Letters to the Directory, 10 February and 16 August 1797.
[120] Philippe de Ségur, *Histoire et Mémoires,* t. I, p. 440.

he would be the chief minister of a conquering state, and that this monstrous power would emerge from a revolution of which the first principle had been the renunciation of all conquests, he would have protested that the teaching of history, the system of balance of power, and the opposition of Europe, made such a development impossible, and that the prophecy was absurd. However, paradox proved truer than common sense; yet it was not a miracle, and what that witty Voltairian, too contemptuous of those who had gone before, would have repudiated in theory, a mere scholar, doubtless dull and even a little suspect of the taint of 'superstition', but fed on history and soaked in tradition, a Père Lelong for example, would have taken care not to dispute.

The internal stresses which made the Revolution degenerate into bloody anarchy and only regain order in the shape of despotism already existed before it broke out. The tendencies which led the despotism into conquests covering all Europe emerged at the same time. Swollen by storms, the river became a torrent, a cataract, a flood; yet it still had the same source and flowed in its century-old bed. The contours determined its course and its flooding was but the excess of its natural flow. When the storm was over the river would subside into its former channel and once more flow quietly between its old banks. Then those who had been prudent and circumspect and had taken refuge in the hills or allowed themselves peacefully to be shut in their ark had their revenge on those who had recklessly imagined themselves masters of the storm while they were swept along by it. The belief that such a colossal power could not be supported for long and that sooner or later it would crumble under its own weight was not likely to be mistaken. This was the calculation on which those who resisted the revolutionary conquests relied; they never gave up hope of confining France again within its former limits. And this leads us to ask what other nations thought of France at the end of the ancien régime.

13. FRANCE AND EUROPE IN 1789

If they seemed at first to congratulate themselves on the Revolution it was because they believed that it would for a long time paralyse France, force her to withdraw into herself and break with the traditions of her foreign policy. The satisfaction with which they viewed the commencement of the crisis and the fears which its development soon produced in them had the same origin—their conception of the resources of France and of the peculiar flexibility of the national temperament. The author of the *Institutions politiques* wrote in 1761, 'No statesman should ever let himself fall into the common habit of saying, in time of war, that France or England is beaten. . . . These two powers are inexhaustible.'[121]

Judged thus, and knowing the proud and adventurous spirit of its people, France was feared. Its eclipse in the latter part of the reign of Louis XV only reassured its enemies temporarily. The sudden success at the beginning of the reign of Louis XVI showed them that it was a mistake to suppose that France was in decline. Their conclusion was quite the opposite, and the very exaggeration of their views was a sort of indirect testimony to the power of France, the character of the French and their steadfastness in pursuit of their plans. At bottom, and while hoping that France by a speedy collapse would quickly prove them mistaken, other nations saw her in the colours in which she had been painted by the opponents of Louis XIV. They observed her carefully and noted with eagerness every sign of weakness, every symptom of disorder that appeared. But as soon as they saw renewed signs of strength and health, they did not doubt but that she would resume the natural pattern of behaviour of her great days. This is how they pictured it, in the language of the classical age: 'Their maxims of government are as follows: first, to conduct war always beyond their own fron-

[121] Tome I, ch. X: *De l'opulence de l'Etat en général,* § 13.

tiers. . . . The genius of this nation will never allow the
rest of the world to remain for long in peace and quiet. It
has a fire which needs fuel, and if it does not find this externally it will gather the materials for it within France. The
smoke of conquest is incense to them. They always need
pretexts to remain armed and so have the power to maintain
a royal authority which has so remarkably exceeded the limits of their fundamental laws. Their second maxim is to meddle in everything and make themselves arbiter by force or
cunning. Their third maxim is to have only one rule of
conduct, the interest of the state, and otherwise to be hindered by no loyalty to treaties, no devotion to religion, and
no ties of blood or friendship. . . . Their fourth maxim is,
so far as they can, to keep other states occupied and divided
in their domestic affairs or engaged in foreign wars. . . .
All these maxims are those of an aggressive state and are the
evidence of a great, extensive and long-cherished plan.'[122]

In the eighteenth century Frederick the Great held the
same views, and the pleasure he took later in being able to
hold the government of Louis XV in contempt is evidence
of the very different opinion he had formed of France when
he was young. 'The parallel you draw between France and a
rich and careful man surrounded by prodigal and unfortunate neighbours', he wrote to Voltaire in 1738, 'is as happy
as could be. It brings out well the strength of France and the
weakness of the neighbouring powers. It explains the reasons
for this and enables the imagination to penetrate future centuries and envisage the continued growth of the French monarchy, resulting from a single uniform principle, as that of a
power united under a despotic head, which according to all
appearances will one day swallow up all its neighbours.'

The plan attributed to France was the traditional one. It
was so patent that even foreign states recognised it as a maxim
of French policy if only to oppose it. A memoir drawn up
by Frederick the Great in 1738 reads, 'On the East, France

[122] *Bouclier d'Etat*, 1667. See Rousset, *Louvois*, t. I, p. 22.

is only held back by her own sense of moderation and justice. Alsace and Lorraine, torn from the Empire, have extended the limits of her dominion. It is to be hoped that the Rhine will in future mark the borders of the monarchy. . . . To achieve this there is only the little Duchy of Luxemburg to invade, the small Electorate of Trèves to acquire by some treaty, and a Duchy of Liége to seize because it would be proper to do so. The Barrier fortresses, Flanders and some similar trifles would necessarily have to be included in the reunion; and all that France needs for this is the government of a moderate and mild statesman, whose character would give countenance to the policy of his court, and who under cover of respectable appearances could push his plans to a successful conclusion.'[123] The passage is evidently ironic; nevertheless Frederick did not doubt that it could and should represent the policy of any true French statesman, and he reserved the right of Prussia to oppose it or to profit by it according to circumstances.

In 1760 Bielfeld, writing about the state system of Europe, claimed that 'if the political system of France were confined to obtaining the seas, the Alps, the Pyrenees and the Rhine for frontiers, this would undoubtedly be the dictate of wisdom.'[124]

But this was the extreme limit, and even if Europe allowed France to attain it, which was doubtful, it was to be feared that the very causes which enabled her to attain such great conquests would compromise their preservation and bring about their loss. 'By following the guidance of common sense,' the author of the *Institutions* says again, 'we should expect France to try to maintain herself as the greatest and most powerful kingdom in Europe, but not the only one. Her object must be to extend her conquests to the banks of the Rhine and make this river her frontier as it was for ancient Gaul. But if she achieves this her power will be too

[123] *Considérations sur l'état présent du corps politique de l'Europe.*
[124] *Institutions*, t. II, ch. IV. § 20.

formidable for the rest of Europe and will arouse the hostility of all other nations. Conquests beyond the Rhine would be too difficult to keep, and the slightest reversal of fortune, such as the greatest empires have experienced, would bring about her downfall.'[125]

The issue which was posed in 1792, and which formed the essence of the great debate between France and Europe during the Revolution and the Empire, was precisely to know whether, to reach and maintain this level of power, France would not be obliged to falsify her own genius, transform the state into an armed camp and hand over the Republic to the generals. Would Europe, conquered or won over, resign herself to seeing a peace concluded in such conditions as anything but a truce? Would England, strong behind the sea, cease from forming coalitions to regain by force what had been lost by force? To frustrate the plans of England and win over or defeat her allies, would not France have to form counter-leagues, engage in partitions, undertake new wars and push her advanced posts out ever farther? Would not the inevitable opposition of the English make the destruction of England an absolute necessity for France? In a word, would not a Continental System be the fatal consequence of the complete conquest of the left bank of the Rhine?

A system which involved such extremes would be self-destructive. Even admitting that it could be pushed to its logical conclusion, that is to say to domination over the Continent, the moment of its success would be that of its ruin. This was understood by the one great opponent whom the French Revolution and Napoleon encountered—William Pitt. It was also the one ray of light that shone in the subtle and tortuous mind of Metternich. In the struggle which the former began and the latter prided himself on completing there was no other guiding light. The consolation for Frenchmen like ourselves, who are led by our native temperament

[125] Bielfeld, *Institutions*, t. III, ch. III: *de la France*, § 40.

to nourish such dreams, is the memory of the wisdom of those statesmen who foresaw the catastrophe. The illusions that led us astray were precisely those of which these far-sighted advisers tried to cure us. So well were their views adapted to political realities that when France, after twenty-two years of unrelenting struggle, had been overcome by the enemies leagued against her, driven from the territories she had conquered, and attacked on her own soil, and when, resigning herself to the peace imposed upon her, she wished to sign it honourably and to be reconciled with Europe without forfeiting her historic place among the nations, there was one course open to her. This was to revive the policies prescribed for her by the wisest of her ministers on the eve of the Revolution. No more was needed for her to win back confidence, respect and consideration, and in due course even her former prestige and influence.

The inspiration of the admirable despatches of Vergennes can be detected behind the instructions which were drawn up in 1814, in the name of Louis XVIII and under the influence of Talleyrand, for the French plenipotentiaries at the Congress of Vienna. 'France', it was said, 'is so powerful a State that other nations can only be reassured if they believe her policy is a moderate one, which they will do all the more readily if they see that it is also a just one. She is in the happy position of not needing to distinguish between justice and her interests, or of having to seek her interest elsewhere than in the justice which is the interest of all.'

This was the true French tradition. We shall see in what follows how she deviated from it, what passions led her astray, and what responsibility, in these temptations, should be attributed to the influence of example and of opportunity, to the resistance she met and the collusion she was offered, to the illusions with which she was fed and the miscalculations that were made. Europe played its part in all these developments, and here the history of France cannot be separated from that of Europe. The whole struggle, indeed, is a series of actions and reactions. Europe, in this period, under-

BOOK THREE

Political Traditions:
Europe

I. England

I. INTERESTS AND POLICY

England is a commercial island, and her whole policy follows from that fact. The English can only expand through their colonies, and since they produce more than they consume, they must have outlets. Their navy is the instrument of their wealth, and they aim to rule the seas. The mercantile character of their interests and the envy which it produces; their national character, which is haughty and self-opinionated; the nature of their power—that insular isolation which allows them, as Montesquieu said, 'to scatter affronts everywhere' with impunity[1]—all these combine to infuse their policy with that spirit of arrogance and rivalry which makes them feared throughout Europe. They bring to the pursuit of their commercial interests the same harshness and pride as Louis XIV to the prosecution of his dynastic interests. Their political economy is their raison d'état. And so while maintaining a monopoly of her own colonial trade, as indeed was the general custom, England claimed the right to trade in other people's colonies, and strove by every means to organize a contraband commerce with them which in her own territories she repressed with the utmost energy. As it was impossible for her to come to terms with other nations over this matter, she contemptuously crushed the weak and relentlessly opposed the strong.

She was not in the least willing to share the control of

[1] *Esprit des lois*, liv. XIX, ch. XXVII.

the seas, colonial empire or world trade with France; hence her implacable opposition to any combination which, by extending France's coasts in Europe, would open for her new outlets to the ocean. The supplying of Germany she meant to keep to herself, and above all, she would not allow the French to establish themselves in Antwerp—hence her systematic determination not to tolerate the acquisition by France of Belgium or the left bank of the Rhine. A French agent wrote from London in 1677: 'The lower House has voted unanimously that the English will sell their shirts (these were the terms they used) to make war on France for the preservation of the Low Countries.'[2]

These sentiments were still equally strong and passionate in 1789. The revenge the French had just taken in America was not calculated to soften them. It was a political maxim, a raison d'état with which the least of City burgesses was as thoroughly imbued as the most experienced counsellor of the Crown. To contain, abase, humiliate France if they could, and in any case to mew her up within the Continent, this was the permanent foundation of their plans. As they could not achieve this directly or by themselves, for want of an army, they worked through alliances and sustained their allies with subsidies. Such had long been the motive of their alliance with Austria: the court of Vienna was paid by England to combat France, her rival, and to defend her interests in the Low Countries.

From the accession of George I in 1714, however, England had a footing on the Continent. The King was Elector of Hanover, and he had a strong feeling for the electorate, which was his patrimony. Although the union was merely a personal one, and England was not involved in it, the King's attachment to Hanover became nevertheless a shackle on English policy. It was a pledge which France could seize in the event of war. In this way she found a means of using her armies to balance the superiority of the British fleet. 'We

[2] Camille Rousset, *Louvois*, t. II, p. 309.

can obtain nothing from England except by way of Hanover', wrote d'Argenson in 1745. It was also the principal bond between France and Prussia, who coveted this country. After 1756 the game was reversed; the partners changed sides, but the contest really remained the same. Prussia had reassured the King of England in respect of Hanover, and they became allies. France and Austria made common cause against Prussia, but England still had an army on the Continent to fight the French. These transitory combinations did not alter the effect of national interests. At the outset of the Revolution, France was to detach herself from Austria and threaten the Low Countries, the court of Vienna was to resume its understanding with London, and Prussia, balanced between the two, would again feel the stimulus of her old greed for Hanover.

Towards 1789 England, leaning momentarily towards Prussia, was protecting Holland while controlling her policy. At sea they were rivals; but if their trade interests were opposed on the high seas, their interests in Europe were in harmony. The Dutch no more wished to see the Scheldt a French river than the English, or even to see it free for the ships of all nations. Portugal was a sort of continental colony for the English from which they threatened the Spaniards. Italy concerned them only through the trade arrangements they imposed on her feeble governments. In the Mediterranean the English balanced the influence of France and disputed with her the commerce of the Levant. They tried in the Baltic to exclude her from that of northern Europe. Denmark and Sweden were courted and threatened in turn.

As for Russia, her independent attitude during the American War had considerably cooled her friendship with the English. After considering for a long time that their interests were the same, the English now began to recognise their divergence. The establishment of the English in the Indies, and the progress of the Russians on the shores of the Black Sea, tended to alter all relations between these two powers, despite their former alliance. By becoming an Asiatic power England inevitably became a rival of Russia; she could not contemplate without alarm a Russian threat to the Ottoman Empire; she could not allow a new state of the first rank to open up a direct passage to the Mediterranean. As for Poland, since there was no lucrative business to be had there, the English did not concern themselves with her.

Thus all their alliances were directed towards the double purpose of extending their maritime empire, and restricting, and if possible destroying that of France. This was their constant endeavour. But the very character of this policy meant that it could only be pursued intermittently.

The English made war only for the sake of trade; but because war interrupts trade and makes it difficult, they only took the decision to fight when their interests seemed absolutely threatened. But then, throwing themselves into a struggle which they deemed to be forced on them, they fought with intense and concentrated passion, and an animosity the more stubborn since its motive was egotistical. Their history is full of these alternations between an indifference that seemed to stem from decadence and a fury that disconcerted their enemies. We see them at one time abandoning Europe, at another dominating it, neglecting the greatest affairs of the Continent yet trying to decide the smallest, turning from peace at any price to war to the death.

These reversals of policy arose from their desire to repair their fortunes, if beaten in war, or if victorious, to profit from the victory; in either case, they aimed to settle their accounts. Their wealth allowed them to contract enormous debts, but precisely because they were rich they felt the burden of debt and found financial disorder insupportable. In addition there was the overriding concern with their public liberties, which were always jeopardised in time of war. So it was that after their great success in the Seven Years War and after their reverse in the American War they withdrew into themselves and became absorbed in their internal affairs.

It was at this time that England experienced a formidable domestic crisis. The English paid dearly for their arduous apprenticeship to liberty. They won it, but their political habits were not yet settled nor the exercise of liberty yet disciplined. When they ceased fighting with foreigners they resumed struggling among themselves; the eighteenth century was full of such struggles.

During the Seven Years War, even during the American War, these struggles reached a degree of violence that had not been seen since the dreadful years of the Civil War.* 'The nation', said Macaulay, 'was in a state of angry and sullen despondency, almost unparalleled in history';† Parliament was discredited, the King was hated, politicians found their hold on power precarious, and were faced with all the instruments of anarchy. Power was sought through corruption. Political agitation extended even into family life. 'Women, children, servants called themselves Whigs and Tories. Sermons, like comedies and masquerades, had a political colour.' As if the press did not fan the flames enough, political societies were founded, clubs were organized, and the country was enmeshed in a political net the threads of which were all caught up in London. This propaganda was 'encouraged by an active correspondence, by associations and movements concerted throughout England. The various counties nominated committees of correspondence and association which maintained the agitation, and delegates were sent to London to co-ordinate it.' Language moreover was gross and brutality rife. Men accused each other of lying, impudence, dirty trickery. This was the vocabulary current in Parliament. Members were out for blood and greedy for confiscations. During the Seven Years War they proposed

* Sorel takes Macaulay's highly coloured description of the political struggle in Great Britain at its face value.
† Essay on *William Pitt, Earl of Chatham*, 1834. The further quotations in this paragraph are not from this essay; they have been rendered into English by the translators.

to treat the directors of the South Sea Company as parricides were treated in Rome, and throw them into the Thames.[3]*

The Commons usurped government, decreed arrests, threatened the ministry with impeachment. The populace was naturally disposed to transports of fury and frightful disorders; agitators stirred them up and flung them into the assault. In 1780 the rioters were on the point of invading the Houses of Parliament; at one moment the members were reduced to clearing a pathway sword in hand. In 1782 the mob surrounded the chambers, jostled the peers, harried the bishops, insulted ambassadors, opened the prisons, burned down mansions. For several days London seemed like a captured city. The riots were terrifying.† 'It is in the character of the English to hanker after bloody tragedies', wrote Frederick. They must have victims. Byng had been thrown to them in 1757. The trial of Warren Hastings in 1786 showed that customs had not changed.

Religious fanaticism was added to political passion. In 1778 the populace of Edinburgh, stirred up against the Catholics, destroyed their chapels. In Glasgow their homes were pillaged. They trembled for their goods and for their lives. The Irish, encouraged by the example of the Americans, plotted and took to arms. The eternal demand for independence was complicated by religious dissensions and agrarian grievances. Insurrection was always smouldering in that unhappy island.

'A nation convulsed by faction, a throne assailed by the fiercest invective, a House of Commons hated and despised by the nation, England set against Scotland'—it is in these terms that Macaulay sums up his picture of England in these

[3] Macaulay, *William Pitt, Earl of Chatham*.

* Sorel has made a mistake here. The passage in Macaulay to which he is referring describes the state of public opinion in 1720, when the South Sea Bubble burst.

† Sorel seems to be distributing the Gordon Riots of 1780 over the two years 1780 and 1782.

troubled times.* The English had decapitated Charles I, detested Charles II, driven out James, subordinated William, despised the first two Georges. The third, who ascended the throne in 1760, had reigned for twenty-three years before his subjects began to feel any attachment to him. Ministries collapsed one after the other. The Cabinet of 1771 was the seventh in ten years. Since the accession of George III the only statesman in England, the great political leader and organizer of victory in the Seven Years War, Lord Chatham, was merely a survivor of his days of greatness. His effacement only showed up more clearly the mediocrity of his successors.

George III possessed some royal qualities. He had dignity, consistency, not to say obstinacy, and a lively sense of British honour. He had a jealous love of power, but was little capable of exercising it; at times his mind was clouded. In 1765 he had a first onset of dementia, and after that he was always irritable and temperamental. Impatient of the tutelage of political parties but powerless to form one of his own, he ruled for a long period through favourites, and his favourites ruled through corruption, the chronic sore of English government. In the previous reign Walpole had made it into a system of administration. Lord Bute erected it into a political institution —he called it 'the management of the House of Commons'.†

With public morals at such a low level, private morals did nothing to sustain them. They followed the same profligate

* *William Pitt, Earl of Chatham,* 1834; from the concluding paragraph of the essay.

† What the Victorians called corruption, later generations of historians have learnt, under the teaching of Namier, to interpret as the natural operation of the parliamentary system in the eighteenth century. Great Britain had a parliamentary government with a constitutional monarch. The king had the right of choosing the head of the ministry and the duty of providing royal influence to assist him to maintain a majority in the House of Commons. Charges of favouritism and corruption, though sometimes not without basis, were the small change of political controversy.

course as in Paris, but licence was attended by more cynicism, debauchery by more stupidity and particularly more drunkenness; there was less refinement, less taste—less disguise. George III maintained a relative decency. His son, the Prince of Wales, whose debts exceeded those of many a small continental state, led a life of open scandal. In 1789 there was a question of Sheridan's entering into office. In reporting this the French ambassador wrote: 'Although in this country matters of form count for little, it would be indeed extraordinary if a man of the worst reputation, formerly an actor, and son of an actor, married to an actress, and to crown all a bankrupt, should find himself a minister in Great Britain. However, if the Prince of Wales controlled his party instead of being controlled by it, Mr. Sheridan would be at the head of the administration.'[4]* This letter conveys the tone of the correspondence of foreign diplomats and indicates the kind of opinions of England that were current on the Continent.

2. EUROPEAN OPINIONS

The truth is that Europe did not understand England at all. It only considered her affairs from outside, with eyes blinkered by envy or fear, and with a secret wish to discern the symptoms of some malady which might be as fatal to the English as it would be reassuring to their rivals. The statesmen of the Continent could and should have seen that the crisis taking place in England was not the first. History could have taught them that although she had suffered violent

[4] 6 January 1789. *Archives des Affaires étrangères.*
* The despatch which Sorel quotes also illustrates the capacity of French diplomats for misunderstanding the politics of a parliamentary country. If the Prince of Wales had become Regent in 1789, the prime minister he would have chosen might have been Fox, but certainly not Sheridan; and even with the influence of the crown cast on his side, it is not certain that Fox could have secured a parliamentary majority.

bouts of fever, followed by long periods of somnolence, England had nevertheless continued to cut a great figure in the world. But history, like all long-term experience, was held in slight esteem in the chancelleries; ranged against it were pride and indolence, two vices which unfortunately agree very well with a worldly outlook and political dexterity. It was said in the courts of Europe that having accepted the partition of Poland, the conquest of the Crimea and the independence of the United States, England had clearly abdicated her position, and that the time was approaching when, having finally relegated her to her own island, responsible and stable governments would no longer have to bother with her.

Her people seemed to them turbulent by nature, and her constitution subversive of all authority. Since there was no consistency in men or in affairs, there could be neither a workable policy nor reliable alliances. 'Nothing', wrote Vergennes in 1783, 'could be so inconstant as the policy of the Cabinet of St. James's, nor more subject to the momentary influence of the minister, whose almost daily changes of policy prevent the Council of St. James's from having any fixed principles in European affairs.'[5] With 'so peculiar a government', said Kaunitz, 'one cannot really count on anything.' In the eyes of these statesmen England seemed ready to become a kind of insular Poland, a Poland rich, serious-minded, absorbed in itself, but only preserving an apparent consistency through the lucky chance of having no neighbours. A French agent wrote from London in 1766, having pointed out all the signs of weakness: 'This is what escapes foreigners who see only England's immense fleets and vast magazines. They are imposed on by outward appearances, and few people realise that a mere nothing, a false rumour, or just the audacity of an enemy, will embarrass credit, throw the complicated machinery into disorder, and reveal a fee-

[5] Instructions of the marquis de Noailles. *Recueil*, t. I. *Autriche*, p. 166.

bleness which is only understood by those who are directly involved.'[6]

Catherine the Great found the English lacking in spirit. She laid upon them the banal reproach which is always used by poor and despotic states to cover up their jealousy of those which contrive to be at the same time free and prosperous—'They are too rich!'[7] Frederick thought likewise and spoke of them with scorn. 'These riches, this ridiculous expenditure which goes beyond all reason, the luxury, the spirit of venality, all these things have contributed to the corruption of a government formerly so deserving of respect.'[8] Joseph declared them to be quite simply in a state of decadence. He had said so to Frederick in their conversations at Neisse in 1769, and he repeated it to his brother Leopold in 1783: 'This great power which once held France in check is now fallen utterly and for ever, all influence and force lost, and relegated by a voluntary sacrifice to the rank of a second-class power, comparable with Sweden or Denmark, and probably soon to be, like them, under the orders of Russia.'[9]

This verdict of the greatest princes merely supported the predictions of the most famous students of politics. Mably had noted 'the complete decadence' of the English.[10] Rousseau wrote in 1760: 'It is easy to foresee that in twenty years from now England will have fallen and moreover will have lost her liberty.'[11] And Favier, who in his own time thought the English so formidable, complacently analysed the ferment of dissolution which threatened the breakdown of their power: 'The disproportion and disjunction of the parts of

[6] Durand to Choiseul, August 1766, published by Cornélis de Witt, *Jefferson*.

[7] Letter to Voltaire, 13 December 1770.

[8] Letter to the Duke of Brunswick, August 1782. Ranke, *Die deutschen Mächte*, t. II. Pièces.

[9] Arneth, *Joseph II und Leopold II.*

[10] *Notre gloire et nos rêves*, 1778.

[11] *Extrait du Projet de paix perpétuelle*, note.

which the structure is composed, and their natural tendency to crumble; the convulsive movements of Ireland, tired of the yoke; the approaching and inevitable danger of a breach between the colonies and the mother country; the vast size of the national debt; the continual outflow of precious metals to meet the cost of foreign trade; the imminent peril of bankruptcy, and at the same time the necessity to increase the debt because of the impossibility of creating new taxes . . .'[12]

The war in America appeared to be a peremptory demonstration of the accuracy of these conjectures. It was said, especially in Paris, that the power of England was artificial, and that it was disintegrating; that the success of England in the Seven Years War was due less to her superiority than to the political and military incompetence of the government of Louis XV; that this success itself had ruined her, and that she was more shaken by her victory than France by her defeat. To destroy her it was only necessary to leave her to herself, to her corruption and her discords—apart from nourishing the corruption, and fomenting the discords as necessary. A cabal suitably engendered in Parliament, riots in London, an insurrection in Ireland, a diversion in the Indies, and England would be ruined. Finally, by shutting her up in her island, and turning against her the isolation of which she was so proud, her trade would be cut off and her ruin completed. The idea of annihilating England was widely current at the end of the ancien régime, particularly in France; it seemed simple and natural, and was seriously discussed. The archives are full of projects for a descent on England, and a number of political adventurers proffered their services, hoping for a chance to hatch out their pet schemes. By a bizarre contradiction, but one that frequently arises from the superficial and irrational opinions which nations entertain of one another, England was the object of exaggerated dread in the present, but was to be suppressed with incredible ease in the future.

[12] *Conjectures raisonnées*, 1778.

These views on the English, in all their complexity, were to be those of the men of the Revolution. The idea behind the war of 1793 and later behind the continental blockade, which was already adumbrated by the Committee of Public Safety, proceeded logically from these erroneous notions. The gigantic aberration of Napoleon in 1812 merely pushed them to extremes: England was only a pretended empire, a phantom state; touch it and it would vanish! Napoleon would have pushed his attack as far as India. The snows of Russia stopped him, and the whole prodigious apparatus of war which the French had assembled against England since 1793 was swallowed up there along with his army.

Nevertheless Montesquieu had warned his contemporaries. He had shown them that they should 'seek the friendship of England and fear her hatred all the more because the inconstancy of her government and her internal troubles seemed to suggest that it was not to be feared, for in that country the fate of the executive power seemed to be always to be harassed at home and respected abroad', and that 'if any foreign power threatened the state and endangered its fortune or its glory, the lesser interests would give way to the greater, and all would unite to support the government'.[13] This was in fact what happened when Europe tried to battle against a France aroused by the most terrible revolution and led by the greatest soldier of modern times. In the old monarchies we saw great interests everywhere give way to petty ones. Court intrigues and the rivalries of army staffs paralysed the exercise of power. The traditional governments found their organization, in appearance so simple, inextricably confused. After having for a long time hampered one another, in turn they betrayed the common cause. England, dragged out of her momentary indifference, was alone capable of uniting and directing them. They no longer reproached her with her wealth, for they all had to ask her for subsidies. She displayed more discipline than Prussia, more consistency

[13] *Esprit des lois,* liv. XIX, ch. XXVII.

than Russia, more constancy than Austria. She deployed a natural strength that exceeded anything that these three states had ever aspired to; and the courts of Vienna, St. Petersburg and Berlin in coalition were not capable of developing an executive power to compare in energy, intelligence or tenacity with the government of Pitt the Younger.

3. THE MINISTRY OF PITT

Willam Pitt came to power in December 1783. He was twenty-four years old. In a few months he showed what he was made of, and it was plain that England had found in him the greatest minister she had yet had. In 1789 his ministry was still in being, and it was with him that Europe and France had to reckon during the Revolution. The rôle which he assumed in 1793 and played until his retirement in 1801 astonished the statesmen of the Continent. The greatness of his earlier days had escaped their notice. Remarkably enough, no statesman was every more exclusively English or showed less liking for European affairs. Cautious, and frugal in financial matters, he had none of that passion for the gigantic which had drawn his father into such hazardous undertakings. He knew little of Europe and scorned to learn more of it, and like Walpole he let it be seen very clearly that diplomacy bored him. 'What the English do not know', said Kaunitz, 'is prodigious.' Pitt knew England, and that was enough; this was where he was so far superior to statesmen of the school of Kaunitz, who knew all the world's affairs except those of the nation they had to govern.

Contrary to these statesmen who directed their country from without, and made their conduct of internal affairs dependent on their foreign policy, Pitt governed Europe by way of England, and it was for this reason that he acted with such force and consistency. His base was unshakeable: his power abroad was in a way only an extension of that which he exercised at home. That was where he was so original among his contemporaries. 'Neither for his country nor for himself', says Guizot, 'did he look abroad for great enterprises, for occasions of rivalry or contention; when they presented themselves and were imposed on him by necessity he accepted them without hesitation; but he did not go beyond such necessities, and he did not provoke them by ambitious designs or premeditated plans. The enlargement of England's external power by diplomacy and war was not his dominating desire. The internal affairs of the country, its prosperity, the perfecting of its institutions, progress towards justice for all and the general welfare—these were the first and constant preoccupation of Pitt. Above all he had good government at home and peace abroad at heart, being convinced that good government at home would, when need arose, ensure the greatness and force of his country abroad.' His genius was to be found in his constancy, and his constancy rested on an imperturbable faith in the triumph of common sense.

When he took over the direction of affairs a humiliating peace had just been concluded and the country was in a state of grave crisis. He had to cope with an enormous debt, finances in disarray, quarrelsome factions, a divided nation, an unreliable Parliament, and an opposition led by parliamentary orators and tacticians of the first order—Burke, Fox and Sheridan. To all appearances the situation was analogous to that in France when Louis XVI had ascended the throne nine years earlier. But while in France the troubles were a prelude to the dissolution of the state and the collapse of the monarchy, in England they were only a crisis, certainly violent, yet normal and healthy, in the growth of the nation and the formation of the state. England had institutions which were capable of development and in which all the national passions could be and were to be dealt with in course of time. These conflicts were but the consequence and complement of older struggles, in which her character had been formed and from which she drew her strength. They were moreover conflicts of parties, not of classes; each party wanted to govern the state, not take it over, still less destroy it. And, finally, there appeared in England what was lacking in France—a statesman.

King George was reputed to be jealous of his ministers, fickle, even perfidious, and complacent about the cabals formed by his friends against the Cabinet. Pitt was not a courtier; he was stiff and imperious. The King did not like him; but he liked power, and Pitt was able to control him because he raised the prestige of the Crown. The parties had been proved in turn unfit to rule. Pitt, a Whig in origin and outlook, governed with the support of the Tories, and governed so well that at the end of a few months he obtained from the country a ministerial majority unparalleled in the history of Parliament.* He brought before the House of Commons a rational budget, calmed the fears aroused by the state of the finances, put the accounts in order, and gave a stimulus to trade by restoring confidence and credit. England having lost the American possessions, he organized those of India, and drew up edicts of toleration for Ireland. These reforms, entirely practical, sensible, and in the national interest, became popular and redounded to the profit of the state. Pitt thus wielded, said Macaulay, legally and solely through free institutions, a power equal to that of a Ximenes or a Richelieu. 'He was the most powerful citizen then to be found in Europe. He was now the greatest subject that England had seen during many generations. He domineered absolutely over the Cabinet, and was the favourite at once of the sovereign, of the Parliament, and of the nation. His father had never been so powerful, nor Walpole, nor Marlborough.'†

* This nineteenth-century version of the politics of the reign of George III has not survived modern historical research. In particular, the interpretation in terms of a party struggle between Whigs and Tories has suffered extensive revision. The suggestion that the king was personally hostile to the younger Pitt is mistaken.

† *William Pitt* (the Younger), January, 1859; the first sen-

Rancour against France continued to be intense; it was manifest in the discussion which followed the commercial treaty of 1786. From the English point of view, however, this was an excellent arrangement—its result was that France indirectly reimbursed England for a part of the expenses of the American War. But this pacific reparation did not satisfy the English patriots. Fox, who was later to advocate so brilliantly the policy of entente with France, was at this time all for rivalry. 'France', he wrote, 'is naturally the political opponent of Great Britain. I do not of course go so far as to say that she is and must remain an irreconcilable enemy of England, and that she could not feel a secret wish to live on friendly terms with this realm. It is possible, but it is hardly probable.' Pitt replied, 'My mind rejects this assertion as something monstrous and impossible. It is feeble and childish to suppose that one nation can be the eternal enemy of another.' The two adversaries seemed, in this chapter of their epic struggle, far removed from the rôles they were to play during the wars of the French Revolution. At bottom, however, though they might change their language they did not change their character. Fox remained an orator, Pitt a statesman. The majority thought him right, but he was overwhelmed with insults, and of the kind that could wound. He was described as a degenerate son of the great Chatham, and denounced as a time-server to France.

Pitt had gained power but he still lacked prestige, and this he could obtain only by satisfying English pride with revenge on France. The revolution in Holland in 1787 provided the opportunity. When France supported the patriots, he restrained the Stadtholder and forced France to withdraw. The Treaty of the Triple Alliance which he concluded in 1788 with Prussia and Holland completed his work not only by providing England with a redoubtable defensive system, but

tence, though included by Sorel in the quotation, is not to be found in Macaulay's essay.

by assuring her a means of decisive arbitration in the affairs of the Continent whenever she found it appropriate.

These successes enabled Pitt to pass through the most serious ordeal by which his government could have been tried in home affairs—the King went mad.* The Whigs and the friends of the Prince of Wales now expected to take office. Pitt made a determined stand against them, and got Parliament to restrict the rights of the Regent. The King recovered at the beginning of 1789, and the general joy that burst forth on this occasion showed what progress the monarchy had made in the feelings of the nation. The dynasty seemed definitely established. As for Pitt, he was more popular than ever. England could now show Europe a powerful statesman at the head of a strong government. It was because this government was free and its strength truly national that it was so resilient and formidable.

England was thus revived and regenerated at the very time when France seemed to be in a state of total dissolution. While in France there now appeared to be no remedy for the ills of the state but total revolution, England recovered herself by the normal development and regular progress of her institutions.

4. THE PARTIES
AND THE REVOLUTION

This contrast was the manifestation of a divergence which was as old as the history of the two countries and had become in a sense an historical law.

The English possessed a political sense absolutely lacking in the French, and they possessed a constitution and traditions of liberty. The ancien régime, which in France had established only a caste of nobles, in England established

* It is now held that George III suffered from a physical ailment which temporarily affected his brain but that he cannot be described as mad.

an aristocracy. This aristocracy only kept those privileges which it still justified by its services to the state; these services were valued and considered an honour, and in order to render them, to fulfil its rôle in the nation and take its share of power, the nobility was ready to sacrifice even its immunities. The nobles paid their share of the taxes in order to rule. Moreover, struggles jointly sustained in defence of the same political rights brought them closer to the people. In France, individual differences were much less sharp, but differences in rights remained, and these seemed the more insupportable to the unprivileged in that they considered themselves in principle the equals of the nobles. In England common political rights made men forget the difference in status. Feeling themselves to be free, men were less preoccupied with appearing equal. The aristocracy was, moreover, to a large degree an open one.

The old institutions of local government, the basis of all others, survived in full vigour, constantly renewed and refreshed by use. Political liberty was not an abstract formula inscribed by philosophers at the head of an ideal constitution, developed as a kind of political algebra and artificially applied to all the laws of a people lacking in any experience of it or positive idea of its meaning. Political liberty was a product, so to speak, of the national soil. Instead of being handed down arbitrarily from the state to the local community it was born and bred in the local community, rising thence to the centre by a natural progress, and being distilled in the constitution. Its introduction in France would have required a revolution in the state and in the habits and instincts of the nation—precisely as in England a revolution would have been necessary for its destruction.

As long as the Revolution only aimed at the establishment of political liberty in France and the destruction of the ancien régime, the English remained indifferent to it—it was irrelevant to them. But when it aimed at reforming society and suppressing religion, it seemed to them subversive of their institutions and beliefs, and they reprobated it. Finally, when it degenerated into armed propaganda, and then into conquest, they judged it fatal to their interests, and they fought it. They waged the struggle the more fiercely because the interests at stake were not simply, as in previous wars, wealth and power. To these were added the most exalted motives that could inspire a nation in arms. The age-old rivalry of the two peoples came out even in their different conceptions of right and liberty. It was for these ideas, as much as for world mastery, that they undertook this twenty-three years war.

If appearances only were considered—the costume, outlook, language of fashionable circles—this antagonism between France and England at the end of the eighteenth century would seem inexplicable. But the likenesses were only on the surface, at bottom all was different. The same current of philosophical ideas had passed over both countries. In England it had only touched the heights, but in France it had reached ground level, and whilst in the one country it had left only a few dazzling foam-flakes on the tops of the tallest trees, in the other it had deposited a thick layer which covered and impregnated all the land.*

In England irreligion was only a matter of good form and fashion, a passing spree, an aristocratic refinement or affectation. In France it was a dominating and general passion; it affected all the Third Estate and in many ways it had reached the multitude. In England the gentry, the bourgeois, the peasants, the working classes and the military men remained religious, clinging to their beliefs and always ready to turn faith into fanaticism. Catherine the Great said of England, 'Fanaticism has raised her up, fanaticism sustains her,

* This contrast between the influence of the Enlightenment in France and in Great Britain is greatly exaggerated. It can only be supported to any extent by identifying the Enlightenment with anti-clericalism, which was only one aspect of it and naturally did not develop beyond a moderate degree in a country which being Protestant only experienced a limited measure of clericalism.

fanaticism will cast her down.'[14] But far from destroying her, it in fact preserved her. Fanaticism was with the English a sectarian, not an irreligious force. The most furious levellers of the seventeenth century had based themselves on the Scriptures. There were inexhaustible sources of heresy in England but no deep current of atheism. Every aberration from the faith could recruit a loyal band of followers, but no neophytes were attracted to the cult of reason. In fact there were infinitely more dissenters than revolutionaries. Those who desired change looked to the Bible, not the *Contrat social,* for inspiration.

While in France the war against the Church led to the absorption of the Church by the state, and then to the total suppression of the Church and to official irreligion, in England it produced as a reaction a sect of believers, the Methodists, and also brought a revival of faith in the established Church. In 1779 dissenters had been authorised to preach and teach on the sole condition of declaring themselves Christians. In 1789, at the moment when the Revolution started, a motion was under discussion in London to repeal the Corporation Act and Test Act, and give Catholics the right of admission to public office. The dissenters and Catholics did not seek the overthrow of the constitution, but only asked for liberty. To grant it to them, Parliament had only to conform to the spirit of English institutions. All the sects, moreover, made common cause against unbelief, and in this respect the French Revolution found them all equally hostile. So the spirit of sectarianism and fanaticism which became revolutionary in France became conservative in England, and the chief source of popular agitation turned against the French Revolution. As to the avowed unbelievers, French experience gave them pause; in face of the consequences of these doctrines they began to have serious doubts about their principles. They were moreover men of the world and

[14] Letter to Czernichef, 1770. *Publication de la Société d'histoire de Russie,* t. II.

sceptics before everything else, and in due course unbelief
went out of fashion, and scepticism turned against irreligion.

There was a similar development in politics. Latterly there
had been a great parade of principles in England, a flurry
of speeches and meetings, and a restless group of democrats
had appeared. But really, in the eyes of the English, it was
nothing more than 'a negligible faction, without arms,
money, organization or leaders'.[15] The ties which these
democrats claimed to have established with the French revolutionaries made them odious to the people, who took them
for traitors and accomplices with the enemy. The English in
their patriotism, as jealous and suspicious as that of the
French, hunted down these associates of the Jacobins with
the same fury as did the Jacobins in France the 'accomplices
and mercenaries' of Pitt. The English democrats made no
converts in England, but they made many dupes in France.
They did much to precipitate war between the two peoples
by the hope they gave to the one and the fear they inspired
in the other of an English revolution parallel to that in
France.*

So far did this go that the Whigs, who saluted the Revolution as a new era of peace for humanity, lost their popularity through this declaration of sympathy and admiration.
Some of them, though deserted by their friends and supporters, persisted in their convictions, Fox being the most
noble and illustrious example. Most of them followed Burke,
and with him hurled against the French the major excommunication. These, however, were men of absolute principles
and high thinking. But, contrary to the French, who started
from *a priori* principles and then tried to bend the facts to the
doctrine, the English 'employed their faculties to the utmost

---

[15] Macaulay, *op. cit.*

* This paragraph underestimates the strength of the democratic
movement in Great Britain, though it is true that the French
revolutionary governments grossly overestimated it. The reaction
to events in France did however weaken it and repression drove
it temporarily underground.

to build in all things theory on practice, and to find a philosophy conformable to the facts'.[16] And so it came about that the same education and the same doctrines produced on one side of the water ardent destroyers and on the other determined conservators of the existing order.

The English nation declared itself passionately on the side of the conservatives. Restless, clamorous and turbulent as they were, the English prized their institutions, and for all the fuss they made amended them only by the most modest reforms. While the Frenchman despised his government, detested his clergy, hated his nobility and rebelled against the laws, the Englishman was proud of his religion, his constitution, his King, his aristocracy, his House of Lords. These were so many towers of the formidable fortress into which he withdrew, under the British flag, to sit in judgement on Europe and wither it with his scorn. Inside the fortress the command could be disputed, but no foreigner might come near it. Things English were no business of his, and the feeling of the people was completely against him.

Just as in the political struggles of the Middle Ages the barons were found joining with the people to combat the royal prerogative, so now the commons joined the aristocracy to defend chartered rights and the monarchy against the spirit of revolution. In fighting against the Revolution, England followed the unchanging traditions of her history; the war of resistance was a national war. England was the one redoubtable adversary of the French Revolution because she alone could oppose to it similar forces—national principles and popular passions. If the English played such a great part in this crisis while Europe cut such a wretched figure, it was because they justified the verdict which Montesquieu had formerly passed upon them: 'This is the people of all the world which has best understood how to avail itself of these three great forces—religion, commerce and liberty.'[17]

[16] Rémusat, *L'Angleterre au dix-huitième siècle*, t. II, p. 449.
[17] *Esprit des lois*, liv. XX, ch. VII.

II. Holland

I. CONSTITUTION AND POLICY

'Holland follows England like a longboat which follows in the wake of the warship to which it is tied. The Dutch, as citizens, detest the stadtholderate, which they regard as the road to tyranny; and as merchants, they have no policy but their profit.'[1] In these lines Frederick admirably summed up the opinion of contemporaries, which must be taken into account if the part played by the United Provinces in the first crisis of the French Revolution is to be understood. The Republic comprised seven provinces: Guelderland, Holland, Zealand, Utrecht, Friesland, Overyssel, Groningen. Each was an oligarchy in which the nobility counted for very little while the rich bourgeoisie was all-important; each had its estates and ruled itself in its own way. For affairs common to all the provinces the estates nominated delegates who met at the Hague; they represented the Republic in foreign affairs and decided questions of peace and war. *Leurs hautes puissances les états généraux*, as they were called, were faced by a rival power, that of the Stadtholder, who was also Admiral of the Union and Captain-General of the five provinces of Zealand, Holland, Utrecht, Guelderland and Overyssel. The Prince of Orange, who was invested with this high dignity, had none of the prerogatives in respect of the States General that a sovereign has in respect of a parliament, though he aimed at these, for he was ambitious to add political to military power. Hence resulted a constant conflict between the Stadtholder and the States General.

France had contributed greatly to the establishment of this republic in the time of Henry IV and Louis XIII, and there

---

[1] Frederick II, *Mémoires*. Introduction.

was a very active and influential French party in Holland
from the end of the sixteenth century. But a germ of hostility
was to be found in the very principle of alliance between
France and the Republic. The Dutch were above all an independent and commercial nation. They sought the protection of France to ensure their national independence against
the house of Austria and their freedom of trade against the
English. France gave her protection to Holland to hold off
the house of Austria from the mouths of the Scheldt and the
Rhine, to weaken English influence there and to open for
herself the road through the Low Countries. What the
Dutch feared above everything else was that if France established herself in Flanders and opened Antwerp to her
fleets, their political independence and freedom of trade
would be more directly threatened than they could be by
England or the house of Austria. And so after invoking the
help of France they then resisted her, and France having
freed the Dutch then attempted to subject them to herself.
Hence there was hatred on the one side and anger on the
other instead of gratitude and friendship. The Dutch had not
thrown off the Spanish yoke to submit to the French; all
pretensions opposed to their own interests they ascribed to
tyranny, and when they resisted these pretensions the French
reproached them with ingratitude. Perhaps France could
have reconciled the Dutch to her plans by giving them some
part in them and reassuring them as to the results. But such
guarantees would have required a condescension that was
not to the taste of Louis XIV, and a moderation of which
his policy did not allow.

To understand the course of Dutch relations with the government that emerged from the French Revolution we must
always keep in mind the relations of the Dutch Republic
with Louis XIV. These are two episodes in the same story.
When Louis XIV launched the first of his enterprises against
the Low Countries, the War of Devolution, the Dutch,
alarmed by French progress, joined with the English and
Swedes to check it, and the Peace of Aix-la-Chapelle was

concluded in 1668 by their joint mediation. Glorious and profitable to him as this treaty was, Louis did not pardon the Dutch their intervention, and he invaded the Republic in 1672. His armies were led by Turenne and Condé. The Dutch did not feel equal to the encounter and offered to agree to humiliating terms of peace. They were prepared to accept the union of Belgium with France, to cede Maastricht, 'sHertogenbosch, Breda, Berg-op-Zoom, Dutch Brabant and their part of Flanders, and pay an indemnity of ten million livres. Louvois thought this was still not enough. As long as the Republic retained any substance, he believed that it would be a centre of resistance to France, a stronghold always open to France's enemies. 'The best way of achieving the conquest of the Low Countries', he wrote in 1671, 'is to humble the Dutch and if possible to destroy them.' He demanded Nymegen, Guelders, certain trade advantages, twenty-four million livres, freedom for Catholic worship, and finally the vassalage to France of the seven provinces. This was subjection, if not conquest.

At this the Dutch rose as one man. The moderates, whom they accused of pusillanimity, were thrown out of office, the pro-French elements were exterminated, and the stadtholderate was restored with all the powers of a revolutionary dictatorship. Then they cut the dikes—if Louis XIV was trying to destroy their country, they would submerge it.* This heroism prepared the way for their salvation; the leader they now chose accomplished it. William of Orange was the centre and the leader of the grand alliance of Europe against Louis XIV. The struggle finished only with the Treaties of Utrecht, which, giving the Netherlands to Austria, entrusted her with the protection of Holland, and guaranteed the Dutch what they appreciated even more—the closing of the mouths of the Scheldt to the trade of the Belgian provinces.

* In fact it was only a strip of the country, important for defence, that was flooded, but this served to hold up the French advance.

These great efforts appeared to have exhausted their energy. Having fought so steadily to save their freedom, they thought it was assured for ever, and were concerned only to remove the traces of this long war. They had had the courage to sacrifice their trade for their independence; now they thought of nothing but trade, and bit by bit they sacrificed their independence for it. The accession of William to the throne of England made them first the allies, later the satellites, and then the underlings of this allied power which remained their rival for trade and empire. During the eighteenth century, while they prospered greatly in speculation and trade, they fell away sadly in power and dignity. Diderot, who visited Holland in 1773, could still admire the solemnity of the assembled States General: 'There one can find business men and bankers adopting the imposing accents and majestic air of kings.' But he was forced also to record that 'the ambition of the Republic is wealth, not greatness'.[2] Favier, who had studied Holland closer at hand, was no more deceived by these solemn appearances. 'She fears everything,' he wrote, 'complains of everything, and takes precautions against nothing.'[3]

Believing herself assured of the trade of her colonies, Holland pursued purely financial interests in Europe, placing her capital, lending at high interest to governments in difficulties, and limiting her ambitions to becoming the main centre for managing the public debt of the Continent. But though she detached herself from politics they were bound to catch up with her sooner or later, and even in the effort to shake free of them, she involved herself in European politics despite her wishes, through all the investments she had at stake; in place of treaties, her credits involved her with the European powers. These dealt with her somewhat as needy noblemen treat their bankers—being as arrogant after the contract as they were obsequious beforehand. While still

[2] *Voyage de Hollande. Œuvres*, Paris, 1875-7.
[3] *Conjectures raisonnées*, sect. II, art. IX: *de la Hollande*.

wanting the money of the Dutch they set little store by their government; and from despising a state to violating its rights was but a short step. 'This Republic,' Favier concluded, 'formerly a centre of war and diplomacy, now fearfully awaits her fate at the hands of Europe; her security and her very existence depend on the outcome of great power conflicts, in which she herself has ceased to count.' 'Batavians!' cried Raynal, 'the destiny of every commercial nation is to become rich, craven, corrupt and conquered!' Thus were the Dutch judged by the French Revolution, and they were treated accordingly.

2. THE PARTIES AND FRANCE

However, this revolution, which was to entail the defeat, subjection and finally the total annihilation of Holland, at first found among the Dutch enthusiastic disciples, convinced imitators and innumerable admirers. In the second half of the eighteenth century the remnants of the old republican party formed a party which was pleased to call itself 'patriotic and pro-French' in opposition to the aristocratic party, which looked to England and supported the Stadtholder. The patriciate of rich bourgeois who composed this 'patriotic' party was however anything but democratic. 'While thoroughly republican in face of the Stadtholder they were arrogant towards the other classes.' In the lower ranks of the bourgeoisie, among those who were excluded from government by the oligarchy, a new group was being formed which was not content with claiming ancient rights, but openly announced its intention of modifying the institutions of the Republic in a democratic direction. Imbued with the philosophical ideas which held sway in France, this group showed itself equally hostile to the bourgeois oligarchy and the Stadtholder's despotism.

The French ministry at Louis XVI's accession, which was reviving the traditional policy everywhere, supported the patriciate; it gave no encouragement to the democrats, but it did not disavow them, and this party, which, in fact, served French policy by its opposition to the stadtholderate and the English alliance, expected some real help from France. Its hopes were strengthened by the establishment of the republic of the United States. All the patriots, whether patricians or democrats, were inspired by this example, and as the Stadtholder was all the time attempting further usurpations, the two opposition parties, divided as they were fundamentally, combined against him. The agitation which began to show itself in 1784 developed by 1787 into a veritable revolution.

France, its government paralysed by internal difficulties, was in no condition to give support to the patriots. England threatened them, and Prussia, whose new king was brother-in-law to the Prince of Orange, sent an army under the Duke of Brunswick to his help. The patriots did not put up any serious resistance. The bourgeois oligarchs were unwarlike, and the extreme feebleness of the democrats was apparent as soon as they came up against regular troops. Besides, national independence was not at stake; no one in Holland thought that either Prussia or England was threatening to conquer the country. The conflict was at bottom no more than a question of prerogatives in internal government. The revolutionary aims of the democrats alarmed the more timid spirits, and the business men, who formed the greater number of the rebels, were ready to submit. The Stadtholder became a sort of sovereign after the English manner; Holland took the road to monarchy. From this time the United Provinces found its policy tied to that of Prussia and England.

The weakness of France had cost her the alliance of Holland. But the arrogance of the English and the obvious design of the Prince of Orange to overthrow the Republic in some sort restored the French to favour. They were not feared, and belief in their power began to revive when they were seen setting about a complete reform of the state with so much enthusiasm. The patriots and democrats who had been proscribed in large numbers after the events of 1787 had found refuge in France. They made common cause with the party of the Revolution. The thoroughly cosmopolitan character of the new French principles raised the hopes of the exiles; in wishing success to the Revolution in France they sincerely believed they were hastening the hour of the emancipation of their own country.

Thus the French Revolution found in Holland a hostile government but a sympathetic nation, a power disposed to combat it but a party disposed to assist it. The success of this party would ensure the friendship of the Republic for France. The old alliance of the French monarchy with the Dutch oligarchy could be renewed between the two nations, both freed from the old régime and transformed by similar revolutions into two democracies. But revolutions, even the most profound, do not change the characters of peoples or their world interests. As constitutions become more democratic, national character and policy come out more plainly and the dictates of interest become more insistent. When the two democracies, one at the Hague and one at Paris, had to deal with each other, France and Holland resumed the same relations as in the days of Louis XIV, on the eve of the War of Devolution. The advance of the frontiers of France to the Meuse and the Rhine aroused as much distrust in Dutch democrats as in Dutch patricians. The opening of the Scheldt seemed to them no less ruinous to their trade when decreed by French republicans than if it had been ordered by a King of France. They were above all patriots jealous of the independence of their country; what the foreign conquerors were called mattered little to them the moment they threatened to enslave Holland. As in former times, France could only win them over by moderation or subdue them by force of arms. The Dutch had every interest in remaining allies of a government which would protect them against their enemies without threatening their trade or their independence; they could not, without bringing destruction on themselves, agree to become the vassals of a conquering despotism which would reduce them to the rôle of its paymasters and admirals. Harsh and onerous as the supremacy of England was, it seemed preferable to this: at least the English assured them of peace and prosperity.

'People are convinced', said Saint-Evremond, 'that the Dutch love liberty, and only hate oppression.'[4] They called on Pitt to save them from Napoleon as they had asked William III to save them from Louis XIV. In spite of the many vicissitudes, in spite of the forced submission of the Dutch and the unprecedented triumph of the French, the crisis worked out just the same for the Dutch as it had done a hundred years earlier, but with even more honour and more signal advantages. In 1713 the protection of Belgium had been entrusted to them; in 1814 they were given its government. Their hatred of France on both occasions seemed so strong and their interests so evident that the victorious European coalition could not do better than trust its outposts to the Dutch and make them the advance guard against France. So, at a distance of a century and in very different conditions the same force of circumstances which had brought France and Holland together and then opposed them to each other caused the French, by a necessary chain of consequences, first to set the Dutch free, then to conquer, dismember and ruin them, and finally eliminate them from the roll of European nations. They made them enemies because they did not know how to make them allies.

III. Spana

I. ALLIANCES

Holland veered, under the pressure of conflicting interests, between France and England. Spain, at the end of the ancien régime, seemed to be indissolubly linked with France. The

[4] *Discours sur les historiens français.*

two dynasties, the two governments and the two nations were held together by the strongest bond ever formed between two states: this was the Family Compact, a general treaty of alliance, guarantee and commerce signed on August 15th 1761 at the most disastrous moment of the Seven Years War. It was due to Spain's intervention that France had not suffered a still more abject defeat. The faithful fulfilment of their obligations by the Spaniards did not go unrecognised by the French. While there was widespread and lively criticism in France of the Austrian alliance, the Family Compact, at least in principle, was universally approved. The two states seemed in the nature of things to be drawn together in the same way that ties of blood united the two dynasties. Objections raised against the Family Compact were only in matters of detail; they arose from the ideas, which were in fact fair enough, that the French had conceived about Spain and the Spanish nation.

In spite of the efforts of Charles III and his ministers to revive the power of their country, bring her back into the main stream of European history, and, as people said, to rouse her from her lethargy, Spain was in a state of decadence. For lack of men and money the army had only in appearance returned to its former strength. Everything was sacrificed to the navy. In 1778 it numbered 67 ships of the line and 32 frigates. This fleet was necessary to the Spaniards: drawing all their resources from the colonies, they had to defend their coasts against the enemy in time of war, and during peace to protect their trade from the encroachments of English and Dutch smugglers. Also it had to escort the famous galleons which carried to Europe the gold from the American mines. But the navy which thus ensured the state's revenue itself absorbed the greater part of it. Spain, it could be said, no longer had a merchant marine. She produced nothing; she imported ingots of gold and exported fewer and fewer commodities and manufactured goods. It was because of this that smuggling was so serious. Even in the Mediterranean Spanish goods were carried under foreign flags, so that freight, commission and the purchase of foreign currency devoured all the profits. 'The peoples of Europe', said Montesquieu, 'carried on all the trade of their empire under their very noses.'[1]

Internal trade was meagre for lack of canals and roads. Corn could not be fetched from the regions where it grew, so the coastal areas were forced to import foreign corn, while the farmers were ruined. Moreover, internal customs duties survived because of the independent spirit of the various provinces and the relative autonomy they enjoyed. The Spaniards were blamed for not tilling the land; having few needs and despising labour, they neglected many of their natural riches. The extent of these, however, must not be exaggerated. 'A third of this country is cultivated,' wrote a publicist in 1773; 'another third could be, at great expense of time, trouble and money; the rest is and always will be untillable.'[2] The same factors that caused agriculture to languish prevented the development of industry. As a result of the spirit of the times and the general loss of vigour, of the abuse of entail and the excessive growth of the monastic orders, the population was declining. Favier described the Spaniards as a 'romantic and improvident' nation, hating foreigners, governed by monks, indolent and arrogant, 'two hundred years behind other civilised nations'. An 'incorrigible' administration multiplied the taxes, and as levies increased, so the officials and therefore the vexations suffered by the people multiplied too, producing much more evil than profit. In 1788 the population rose to eleven millions and the total revenue to 200 million francs. 'The King of Spain', said Montesquieu, 'is only a very rich individual in a very poor country.'[3] The chief resource was the treasure in the form of American bullion, which was accumulated in case of war—a precarious resource, for it was unproductive, and maritime war, by cutting off the colonies, could prevent its replenishment.

[1] *Esprit des lois*, liv. XIX, ch. X.
[2] Favier, *Conjectures raisonnées*, art. XII: *De l'Espagne*.
[3] Liv. XXI, ch. XXII.

Besides, income from America diminished as the colonies increasingly felt the effects of the detestable system of exploitation to which they were submitted, and the consequences of the enfeeblement of the mother country. Grievously torn by race conflict, stirred by the winds of revolt blowing from the United States, oppressed and exhausted, trading neither among themselves nor with foreigners, they were affected by all the causes of decadence in Spain and did not find within themselves the forces of passive resistance which Spain drew from her past and her traditions. England was preparing there a striking revenge for the help which Spain had given with such temerity to the revolt of the Americans of the North. Even before 1789 there had been a first attempt at a rising in Peru; the great revolution which was to break out twenty-five years later was already being hatched in secret. The most diverse causes contributed to it. In these countries moral and religious discipline was exclusively enforced by the Jesuits; they alone taught and preached submission to metropolitan Spain. In suppressing them, Spain abolished the chief instrument of her domination, and the dispersal of this order contributed as much to the independence of South America as the example of the United States, the propaganda of the French Revolution, and the encouragement of England. Thus did Spain, who lived on her colonies, ruin them and herself by exploiting them.

The publicists who studied Franco-Spanish relations at the end of the ancien régime thought that a revolt of Spanish America was probable; they did not however consider it impossible to prevent it by modifying the Spanish colonial system. They consciously exaggerated Spain's resources and the possibilities they afforded to a skilful government of restoring trade, agriculture, industry and finance. They judged the alliance to be useful to the French and indispensable to the Spaniards, but they thought France should control the common policy of the two kingdoms.[4] Favier, who should always

[4] 'There are', Favier wrote in 1773, 'natural, necessary and indissoluble connections, based on the common and unchanging

be studied if the diplomacy of the Revolution is to be understood, said, 'Spain's influence on France should be a thing of the past; her need and her actual inferiority in power should put her in the place appropriate to the younger branch of the family. It is for France to guide by her example and so resume, in a manner of speaking, her rights as the elder.'

There was one very sensitive and painful spot in the relations of France and Spain. This was Louisiana, which Louis XV felt obliged to give up to Spain as compensation in 1763. 'We had not only to cede New Orleans, but to use force to hand it over', wrote a contemporary. 'These loyal French passed under the Spanish yoke; let us draw the curtain on this tragedy; the new masters have in their usual fashion gained one more desert.'[5]

France wanted to recover Louisiana; Spain desired with a still more ardent passion to recover Gibraltar. She dreamed also of reconquering Jamaica, lost in 1655, and secretly nursed the ambition to gain possession of Portugal. This was a permanent aim and secret of Spanish policy. 'I endeavour as far as I can to make friends with Portugal', wrote Charles III in 1787. 'This is the policy to adopt so long as it is not possible to reunite this crown with that of Spain.'[6] These ambitions bound Spain to France; they were the classic devices by which French diplomacy drew Spain into her plans against England. And so, in spite of the dangerous example and the obvious peril to his own colonies, Charles III let himself be involved in helping the North Americans in their revolt against England.

---

interests of the two powers, on which their external and maritime security, or the security of their commerce, mutually depend.' Peyssonnel, a former French consul and a disciple of Favier, declared in 1789 that the *Pacte de Famille* would always be regarded 'as the sacred instrument of public welfare'. *Situation politique de la France: vues et développements des avantages que le Pacte de famille peut donner à la France*, 1789.

[5] Favier. Boutaric, *Correspondance secrète de Louis XV*, t. II, p. 218.

[6] Baumgarten, liv. I, ch. I.

2. THE COURT AND THE GOVERNMENT

Charles III had just died[7] when the French Revolution began. He was the best ruler Spain had had for a long time. He left good ministers—Aranda, Campomanès, Florida-Blanca —but it was not given to them to finish his work. A reign of recovery was followed by a reign in which everything went to pieces. Revived for a time by an intelligent ruler, Spain passed in a few years into the hands of an imbecile prince, and foundered in a base intrigue. This disaster threatened from the earliest days of the new king. Charles IV was forty, corpulent, feeble-minded, good-natured, incapable of believing evil of others because incapable of conceiving it himself; loving, chaste, devout, and so even more a slave to his wife than to his own temperament, the first years of his marriage put him in blinkers for the rest of his life. Scrupulous to the point of separating himself from his queen when he no longer hoped to have children by her, he took refuge in the chase, in manual tasks and violent exercise. He enjoyed nothing but the table, music and bullfights, and was exhausted after half-an-hour spent on state business.

Marie-Louise of Parma, petite, dark of complexion, by no means beautiful, but possessed of grace, elegance, and particularly poise, was superstitious, passionate, ignorant and restless. She was fundamentally frivolous, and in her character were found obstinacy without firmness, deceit without intelligence, intrigue without consistency; her greed exceeded her ambition. Her heart was even more empty than her head. Her husband seemed to her brutal and gross and she despised him. She detested her eldest son and took little interest in her other children. When she ascended the throne and it was Godoy's good fortune to cross her path she was thirty-four, with a disordered imagination and turbulent desires, which

[7] 14 December 1788.

were curbed by neither religion nor virtue. Godoy came from the petty provincial gentry. For lack of anything better he had enlisted in the royal bodyguard at the age of seventeen. He was now twenty-one. He was very handsome, with a solemn beauty frequently found in the men of southern Europe, giving them in youth an air of restrained and imperious passion, and in their maturity an impenetrable and imposing exterior well fitted to conceal mediocrity of mind, hardness of heart, domineering egoism, and all the tricks of a corruption the more insidious that it seems to be unconscious. The Queen fell desperately in love with him and gave herself up completely to him; he shamelessly exploited her infatuation. Not content with making Godoy her lover, she wanted to make him a great man, a minister, who should share her power. She brought him to court and made him an intimate of the royal family, where Charles IV docilely went crazy over him too.

At first Marie-Louise showed some circumspection in the successive honours which she heaped upon her favourite and which—assisted by a series of scandals—marked the progress of her passion. But before long her infatuation was complete. Godoy gained an ascendancy over her as great as her own over Charles IV. Since she was jealous and passionate, while he was presumptuous and impassive, and it flattered his vanity as an upstart adventurer to boast of his infidelities, he was soon positively maltreating her, subjecting her to a humiliation as great as that which she inflicted on the King. And so on the eve of the French Revolution these three personages, so strangely linked, began to play in their court costume and in the austere setting of Philip II's palace the comedy—as old as vice and stupidity—of the accommodating husband duped by his wife and the aging mistress exploited by her lover. The piece began, about 1787, like a chapter of *Gil Blas*; it ended twenty years later in a dénouement which might have come from Shakespeare. Having been the laughing-stock of European courts and then the target of their scorn, these wretched people went on their way, through every degradation, to the fatal catastrophe of Bayonne.*

In the early days of the reign Charles IV on principle, the Queen through hypocrisy, and Godoy from policy professed devotion. The Queen wanted power for Godoy, and Godoy wanted power for lucre: for this reason the old councillors of Charles III had to be removed. As they were *philosophes*, while the nation remained Catholic, Marie-Louise and Godoy called the old Spanish fanaticism to their aid. The ministers soon lost all influence, and having for a time consigned them to comparative unimportance, Marie-Louise disgraced them completely as soon as the French Revolution gave her a pretext.

Reaction in Spain was complete. The Church recovered its sway, and the Inquisition was re-established. It thus seemed that the Revolution was bound to find Spain hostile; a Bourbon king and a *dévot* government could not but detest it. But the King was a husband before he was a Bourbon, and Marie-Louise had become a *dévote* only to mask her intrigues. Her passions led her at one time to desire war to make her lover famous, at another to desire peace to make him popular. This feeble and corrupt court seemed a ready prey to every suggestion prompted by fear and to every temptation offered by greed. Those governments that had to deal with Spain did not fail to profit by this weakness to dominate her policy. The court was to be successively tied to England and then to France, in turn to negotiate with the Revolution, to condemn it violently and to oppose it feebly, to seek alliance with the Directory, and finally to give itself up to Napoleon, who destroyed it.

France found Madrid only too amenable to her designs, and the illusions which resulted from this proved more disastrous to her than did the incapacity and turpitude of her

* At a conference at Bayonne in 1808 between Napoleon and the Spanish royal family both Charles IV and his heir Ferdinand gave up their rights and Joseph Bonaparte was put on the Spanish throne.

rulers to Spain herself. The French were led by the habits and traditions of the ancien régime to treat the Spaniards as an inferior nation, destined for the rôle of an auxiliary. Looking on the Spanish court as cowardly and venal, the politicians of Paris forgot to reckon with the Spanish people. They thought it could be divided and governed at will. It was not that they despised it or aimed of set purpose at its subjugation. But they thought the Spaniards had been enervated and enfeebled by the later Austrian rulers, and raised from decadence only by the Bourbons, a dynasty which in its turn had become degenerate. Only another foreign government, more intelligent, more enlightened, more resolute, could take up the work of recovery and bring it to success by means of rigorous treatment and appropriate remedies. What Louis XIV had undertaken solely in the interests of despotism, France, now herself regenerated by the Revolution, had the right and the power to accomplish for the greater good of Spain and of humanity in general.

These calculations, in which the essential factor—the character of the Spaniards—had been suppressed, deceived the Convention, led the Directory astray and ended in involving Napoleon in the most fatal of his enterprises. It was in fact by this roundabout route that he was led to copy the designs of Louis XIV and put one of his brothers on the throne of Philip V. Napoleon, in this matter as in many others, only carried to excess and expanded out of all proportion the political plans which the Revolution had inherited from the ancien régime.

In 1778 Florida-Blanca said to the comte de Montmorin, Louis XVI's ambassador, 'It seems that you look on the King of Spain as a sort of viceroy or provincial governor.' While there were rulers in Spain who were resigned to this rôle, things went well for France, and as long as Charles IV was on the throne the calculations of the politicians of Paris proved correct—they gave the orders and Spain, more or less willingly, obeyed. But when, deceived by this submission, Napoleon thought he could seize the throne on which the

Bourbons submissively reigned, he found himself face to face with the Spanish nation, and all his calculations were upset.

3. THE NATION

The new wind of the eighteenth century had merely passed over Spain; the people had not breathed it in. In a country where the Inquisition became a part of the state machine at a time when the Parlement was becoming established in France, the power of the Church had increased, just when it was diminishing everywhere else. The wholesale reforms of Charles III always remained alien and even hateful to the Spaniards. They did not arise from their laws, and they were repugnant to the country's customs. Charles III and his 'enlightened' ministers never gathered round them more than a small group of men, no doubt very estimable and distinguished, but quite without influence outside the cabinet and the Council of State. They had no hold on the people; as soon as the government lost its grip, the people were no longer with them. The suppression of the Jesuits had been profoundly unpopular. Deprived of their guidance, which after all had made for moderation, the Spaniards put themselves in the hands of the monks and became more fanatical than ever. The only serious opposition in Spain was to the reforms. The reaction which followed the accession of Charles IV was hailed as promoting the public good. When the Cortes met in 1789 to acclaim the king and modify the law of succession, it prostrated itself before Charles IV, who came before the Cortes only to dissolve it.

Strongly attached to the dynasty, indifferent to political liberty in the general affairs of the State, sworn enemies of innovation, the Spaniards could be roused only for the defence of their religion and their provincial liberties. Their superficial obedience to established power concealed an undying spirit of independence. They were really 'less submissive to the government than to their own customs'. As long as authority was content to change nothing, it could do as it liked; as soon as it attempted change it struck at the heart and they revolted. 'It is true that they are ignorant, poor, lazy,' a contemporary reported, 'but they are sober, serious, proud, loyal and tenacious; their instincts are strong, noble and generous, and their devotion is unshakeable. This people, insular in character and withdrawn, almost isolated, by its position, has remained estranged from and indifferent to the progress of European civilisation. Actually repelled by any outside contact, they take pleasure in their isolation, which is intensified by an absolute and superstitious faith and by their submission to the clergy.'[8]

Under foreign conquerors and in face of a revolution which overthrew their dynasty, menaced their religion, upset their customs and outraged their morals, these Spaniards, who had come to count as nothing more than a problem for discussion in Europe by *philosophes* and a living example of national decadence, were suddenly aroused to a fanatical fury and feverish patriotism that disconcerted all the statesmen of Europe. Their heroism derived, however, from the same causes as their collapse. Spain had remained unchanged in a Europe undergoing transformation. 'There is no doubt', wrote Richelieu, 'that the Spaniards surpass us in constancy and determination, in zeal and fidelity to their kings and their country.' Napoleon found them just as they had been ever since the expulsion of the Moors. If the Spanish nation was not, contrary to the opinion of the sages, tired of being badly governed ever since the days of Charles V, it was because the governments it had suffered with such unvarying docility had flattered by turns its passion for romantic heroism and its incurable indolence of spirit. Above all they had been careful to respect its customs.

The Spaniards rose against the invading French from the same motives that had led them to submit to the power of their kings. The defects which had so enfeebled them were

[8] *Mémoires du général de Ségur*, t. III, p. 745 ff.

now a source of strength and turned to virtues. They had seemed 'serious, austere, strange, inhospitable'.[9] Their scorn for foreigners degenerated into fierce hatred. They always nourished in their hearts a deep hostility to the French. 'My father would rise from his tomb', said a Spanish peasant before the Revolution, 'if he could see a chance of a war with the French.' Their poverty made them insensible to the sufferings of war; their religious fanaticism exalted them beyond the power of persecution. The love of adventure and passion for independence which filled the countryside with vagabonds, smugglers and brigands brought together at the first summons those guerillas who became invincible because it was impossible to lay hands on them. Their priests, violent and sectarian, lived amongst them; they incited them to battle and they led them into it. These peasants, fired with enthusiasm, fought like the Turks, dispersing before regular troops in the plains, but meeting the assaults of the enemy, from behind their crenellated walls or mountain entrenchments, with the most ferocious and determined resistance.

The crusading instinct which survived in them together with the fierce ways of the Middle Ages, ferocity co-existing with the refinements of honour, bitter vengeance combined with the spirit of sacrifice, all these made them, as soldiers facing the invader, both heroic and cruel. Everything that had rendered them impervious to modern civilisation during the eighteenth century, everything that maintained them in their lethargy and, so to speak, closed the avenues of Europe to them, conspired to make them invincible in their mountains when the pride that detached them from the world was insulted, when the prejudices that had isolated them were attacked, when their national independence—the only benefit of which they were aware—was threatened.

The Revolution, even in its most beneficent and pacific aspect, was in any case bound to offend them. When it took the form of an invading army and foreign conquest, it

[9] De Ségur, *op. cit.*

exasperated them. If there was one thing they execrated more than invasion and foreign government, it was *The Rights of Man*. This was why, having accepted Philip V, a Frenchman but a Catholic, they drove out Joseph, who became king through the Revolution. Spain thus formed the barrier at which the propaganda of the Revolution stopped, and in trying to force a way through it Napoleon's weapons were shattered. The Napoleonic conquest came up against the same obstacle as revolutionary proselytism—national passions. It took a long time for the revolutionary spirit to penetrate into Spain. When it did, it was caught up in the current on which the hearts of Spaniards were borne along—it became in its turn entirely national, and the spirit of liberty only added to the ferment of hatred of the French. This spirit worked in Spain wholly to the detriment of France. The condition for the success of the French Revolution in that country was that the French should cease to be the masters there.

IV. *Italy*

I. THE ITALIANS

Every factor that estranged the Spaniards from the French seemed to bring together the French and the Italians, or at least those of the north and centre. There the Revolution met with an enthusiastic response, and the conquest also proved easy. Italy was used to the domination of foreigners of old, and social conditions closely resembled those of France. A French victory could bring nothing but benefit to the Italians. They truly constituted a nation with its own traditions, the memory of which they cherished and wanted to revive.* Italy was torn in shreds, but they were shreds of the same material, and even the rents which laid bare the weft bore witness to its ancient texture.

The end of the eighteenth century in Italy reminds one of those times at the dawn of the Renaissance when Italians reawoke to literature, art, science, and finally politics; when, invoking the memory of Caesar, they dreamed of rebuilding their country, and the name of Italy was heard again throughout the world. To their honour be it said, that however much they had been oppressed, they had never let their rights be forgotten. Failing political spokesmen to acclaim them, there had always been poets. There was no such thing in Italy in the eighteenth century as a national policy, but there were a national language, and national poets and historians. 'The day will come', cried Alfieri, 'when Italians will be reborn and will boldly take the field.' He sounded the call in his poems and his tragedies, which breathed the spirit of ancient Roman patriotism. Muratori and Denina reminded the Italians of their origins,† and strove to revive in them a consciousness of nationhood through knowledge of their history. Thus was Italy reborn, as she appeared to Vico in the spacious vision of the future which he revealed to mankind.

Pietro Verri published a review modelled on the English *Spectator* and entitled *Il caffè*.‡ In it he told a story of a man who appeared one day in Milan in company where he was unknown. 'Are you a foreigner?' they asked. 'No, sir.' 'A Milanese?' 'No, sir.' When the perplexed questioner insisted that he must be one or the other, the unknown man replied,

* Sorel is writing under the influence of the nationalist presuppositions of the nineteenth century. Italy was far more fundamentally disunited, in all respects, than this paragraph suggests.

† Ludovic Antonio Muratori (1672-1750), a great scholar and historian from whom Gibbon learned much. His *Annali d'Italia* (1744-49) go down to the year 1500. Denina was the author of *Delle Revoluzioni d'Italia*.

‡ Pietro Verri (1728-97), friend and collaborator of Beccaria, was an economist and administrator.

'I am an Italian, and an Italian can no more be a foreigner in Italy than a Frenchman in France, an Englishman in England or a Dutchman in Holland.' He then followed up and developed this idea; he showed how the division of Italy made intellectual activity impossible. The company were impressed, and thought he spoke like a man of culture and sense and a patriot, and they all lamented the unhappiness of a time when, instead of all Italians 'in the land traversed by the Appennines and bordered by the sea and the Alps being fellow-citizens', the chance of being born in this place or that made one man different from others. The stranger again took up his theme; he showed that the Italians not only had the same origins, but the same character and the same civil laws; they had them when they shared in the honour of Rome; they still had them in the time of Charlemagne, and they had proved in their republics at the time of the Renaissance that they had not forgotten them. He compared Italy to a system of planets, each in its own orbit but each subject to the same attractive force and keeping its place in a general system. 'Let us', he concluded, 'frame our policy on this model. Though divided among several powers and subject to different rulers, let us further the progress of the sciences and arts by forming one system. Let patriotism—that is, love of the general good of our nation—be the sun which lights our way! Let us all be Italians once more, if we would still be men!'

His message was well understood in Europe. Through their literature and art the Italians remained united in spirit despite the political patchwork of their country, and preserved, wherever there were lively minds or lovers of beauty, the memory of a great past and an instinctive hope for the future. Everything, even the wonderful soil and climate, helped to associate with the luminous name of Italy the idea of fatherland. Italy's titles of nobility were the very title-deeds of European civilisation. They were known to everybody. 'Italy waits in hope', wrote Catherine the Great in

1780. The author of *Corinne** expressed an idea very widely held at the end of the eighteenth century when, speaking of 'the mystery of Italy', she added: 'The Italians are more remarkable for what they have been and for what they could be than for what they are at present.'[1]

The Italians cared for their country, but except for the subjects of the King of Sardinia they professed complete indifference to the governments among which they were divided. Apart from Piedmont their rulers were either elective heads, as in Rome and the republics, or nomadic dynasties like those in Parma, Tuscany, and Naples. The rulers were really nothing more than crowned life-tenants of the state; their peoples looked on them as such and judged them simply on the merits of their administration. These tendencies in the Italians made them particularly ready to feel the influence of a revolution which, while overthrowing the institutions and dynasties to which they were indifferent, exalted the sentiments they all felt. The French Revolution both proffered reforms which were ardently desired by the great majority of the people, and proclaimed the principle of national independence; it promised to emancipate and unite them, to reconcile men through the laws and lead them to solidarity through patriotism. The Italians were sure to acclaim a revolution based upon these principles, and their governments, except that of Piedmont, the only one with a national character, had no means of defence against it.

2. THE GOVERNMENTS

By the Treaty of Vienna (1738) the Two Sicilies had been allotted to a cadet branch of the Spanish Bourbons.[2] Don

* Madame de Staël.
[1] *Corinne*, liv. I, ch. V.
[2] Don Carlos, son of Philip V and Elizabeth Farnese, born in 1716, gained from Austria, at the time of the War of the Polish Succession, the Kingdom of Naples. He was recognised as King of the Two Sicilies by the Treaty of Vienna in 1738. He reigned,

Carlos, the first king of this dynasty, was an enlightened
ruler. He tried to cure 'the negligence of a government which
from time immemorial has failed to govern or to civilise its
subjects'.[3] But he could only change things on the surface,
and the condition of the people remained wretched. In the
interior brigandage was rife and on the coast, in Calabria, the
Barbary pirates still decimated the villages. The nation submitted apathetically to beneficial reforms but without understanding their purport. The people were quite familiar, however, with violent revolution. Under the impact of a sudden
shock this somnolent populace could suddenly go frantic.
The country was fit for nothing but anarchy or tyranny;
the French Revolution merely precipitated the transition
from one to the other.

In 1759 Don Carlos was called to the throne of Spain
through the death of Ferdinand VI, his elder brother. He
left the Two Sicilies to his third son, Ferdinand IV, who
was only eight years of age. Charles's ministers formed a
council of regency, and the government remained relatively
intelligent and benevolent. Ferdinand was declared of age in
1767, and the following year married Maria Carolina of
Austria, daughter of Maria Theresa and sister of the Queen
of France. The King was seventeen, the Queen sixteen. It
took them some years to shake off the tutelage of the Council
of Regency, but the retirement in 1776 of Tanucci, its leading spirit, indicated that the royal couple now considered
themselves able to rule alone. Their government was of a
most lamentable description.

Ferdinand was ignorant, coarse and idle. He never wrote
anything—it was said that the only inkwell in the palace was
in the council chamber. He was partial to low pleasures,
petty debauchery, and cheap popularity. He was at bottom
a vulgar despot, always liable to turn savage through fear or

---

under the title of Charles IV, until 1759. At that time the death
of his brother, Ferdinand VI, called him to the throne of Spain,
which he occupied as Charles III until 1788.

[3] *Mémoires du général de Ségur*, t. II, p. 528.

anger. However, limited as he was, and incapable of noble thoughts, he retained a certain royal instinct, and some obscure notion of his duty. A woman of character would soon have discovered how to manage this big spoilt baby, flabby and conceited as he was; she would have given him advisers if not advice. But Maria Carolina was a passionate Austrian, arrogant and vindictive. She wanted to be the focus of all eyes in Europe; she was obsessed by the renown of Catherine, which was a constant spur to her ambition. She had attainments, intelligence, a strong liking for intrigue, and charm. She had no difficulty in dominating her husband. 'My wife knows everything', he would say admiringly, and he let her interfere in all the affairs of government. Despite his lack of interest in state business and his continual quest for pleasure, Ferdinand was jealous of his authority and anxious to preserve the appearance and illusion of it. The Queen could only lead him where she wanted by constantly deluding and distracting him. She thus contrived his degradation, while in securing for herself the direction of the government she did nothing to raise the prestige of the crown. She lacked purpose and consistency. She enjoyed power but used it only to gratify her whims and readily entrusted it to favourites. Moreover she was frivolous, rash, and careless of scandal. Of this she provided plenty during the epoch of the Revolution by her intimacy with her chief minister, Acton. She soon gave still more cause for it by bestowing such ostentatious favour on an English adventuress of great beauty and charm, but dubious reputation, who through life's strange chances had become the wife of the British minister in Naples—Lady Hamilton.

The imperious Maria Carolina did not put up with Spanish tutelage for long. She dismissed the former advisers of Charles III one after another. Relations between Ferdinand and his father during the latter's last years were extremely strained. Permanently at odds with Spain, Naples also remained on bad terms with France. No hope remained of drawing her into the Family Compact. It was said at Naples

that Spain had merely been a dupe, and as France seemed to
be weakening that it was not the time to be drawn into her
wake. The Bourbons were losing influence, but Austria, who
had seized it from them, was not managing to keep it. In
this situation the calculations of Maria Theresa in marrying
her daughter to Ferdinand were upset. In the last years of
the ancien régime Naples was firmly attached to England.
Impatience with family ties, the desire for an independent
policy, and above all the ignorance in which she was kept by
her favoured minister delivered over Maria Carolina to the
English alliance.

Acton, though Irish in origin, was passionately English
in outlook; he did not like Austria and he detested France.
A mediocre politician, conceited, inflexible without consistency and obstinate rather than vigorous, he nevertheless had
some notion of government. Intriguer though he was, he
proved a good navy and war minister. Thanks to his efforts
Naples could put into the field twenty-five thousand men
and maintain forty ships at sea. But they were only forces
for show, since those who controlled them held them in low
esteem and used them only with the greatest caution.

Naples had no quarrels otherwise, except with the Holy
See. This lawsuit was traditional, for its origins went back
to the foundation of the Neapolitan state. Naples was an
ancient fief of the Church, and Rome, which had conferred
the fief, required homage for it. This was now represented
by an annual tribute of 8,000 ounces of gold—about 40,000
francs—and the triennial gift of a white palfrey. Though
this was no more than a symbol, Rome attached as much importance to keeping up the practice as Naples did to letting
it fall into disuse. The court wished to be sovereign in law as
well as in fact. It also coveted the Duchy of Benevento,
which was within its grasp and on which it had claims. The
conflict with the Church which Charles had started for reasons of philosophy Ferdinand continued for reasons of politics. In 1789 the enmity of the two neighbours was glaring;

we shall see to what use it was put by the governments that emerged from the French Revolution.

Rome had completely fallen from its former state. In spirit it was no doubt the same; it was still the Rome of which Saint-Simon spoke, 'where they are willing to attempt anything that may succeed, and jeer at those who put up with it'.[4] But the days were past when Rome could score off compliant victims. Instead of attacking other states she suffered their attacks herself. Clement XIV had been forced to accept the humiliation of the Papacy at the hands of the Catholic monarchs. In 'the department of the faith'—the only one left to the Church, said Frederick—Pius VI[5] had been constantly obliged to defend his frontiers, and his defence was feeble. Bit by bit, through force of circumstances, the prince became more important than the pontiff; the government of the Church was always entangled with that of the Patrimony of St. Peter. The formidable spiritual power was lost in the decrepit body of the temporal state, which shared all its infirmities, and so the paralysis which afflicted the Papal States crept over the government of the Church. 'The court of Rome', wrote Joseph II in 1768, 'has become almost an object of scorn. Internally, its people exist in the deepest misery, wholly depressed, while the finances are in complete disorder and discredit.'[6] 'The internal affairs of the pontifical state are in the greatest disarray', reported the Venetian ambassador Zulian in 1783; 'it is a progressive decline and the government daily loses force and authority.'

Pius VI was a man of pure morals, limited intellect, and proud spirit.[7] Handsome and majestic in person, he loved festivals and ceremonies, the performance of sacred ritual, sumptuous buildings—anything calculated to impress. He was an autocrat and theocrat, 'without other law than his

[4] *Parallèle des trois premiers rois Bourbons.*
[5] Clement XIV, 1769-1775; Pius VI, 1775-1800.
[6] Arneth, *Maria-Theresia*, t. IX, notes.
[7] Masson, *Le Cardinal de Bernis*, ch. XI and XIV, and in particular p. 319.

own good pleasure, without other concern than the advancement of his family, without other counsel than his own vanity'. His government was weak and ruinous at home and absolutely nugatory abroad.

Since he drew the best part of his revenues from the Catholic states, he had to keep on good terms with them, even in religious affairs. Naples had a hold on him through Benevento, and France through Avignon. He had a continual dispute with Venice over the Legations. If these three states should agree to uphold their respective claims by concerted action, the pontifical domain would in large part be lost. We have seen that the Pope was at odds with almost all the Catholic governments, even on church affairs.[8] In the last years of the ancien régime only France could be said to be on good terms with him. So the rôle of the ambassador of the Most Christian King was of considerable importance. Bernis wrote on 5 August 1789, 'I am definitely the second person in Rome.' The Revolution changed this state of things entirely. The hostility of France to the Holy See gained it the sympathies of Europe, and the misfortunes of the Church aroused the concern of governments. By directly attacking religion at the same time as it overthrew the States of the Church, the Revolution restored to the papal government the strength and influence it had lost. In bringing down the sovereign it raised up the Pope.

Tuscany had perhaps the best government in Europe.[9] She managed without a foreign policy, but she had need of neutrality and knew how to preserve it. Leopold, who reigned in Florence, was too profoundly Austrian to love France, but his interest in defending the trade of Leghorn against English attempts on it formed between the two governments a link whose strength was proved by the events of the Revolution. The ruling class was 'enlightened' and sympathetic

[8] See above Book I, ch. I, p. 62 ff.; ch. II, p. 121 ff.

[9] Attached, in 1738, to the house of Lorraine, it was ruled by Francis, husband of Maria Theresa and Holy Roman Emperor. His second son, Leopold, succeeded him in 1765.

to French ideas; these it prepared the populace to accept. The dynasty had not had time to sink roots in the country, and benevolent though it was Leopold's authority proved interfering and tiresome. The people saw him go without regret, and when the house of Lorraine was overthrown by war Tuscany asked of her new masters only that they should govern with moderation and intelligence.

Genoa stood in fear of Austria, which would have liked to overrun the small republic, and sought the protection of France. Her whole policy was a matter of getting her neighbours to leave her alone. 'The Senate of Genoa', wrote a contemporary, 'may not henceforth proceed with any discussion until at each assembly the Doge has proclaimed in a loud voice, "Do not forget, Senators, that the safety of the Republic depends on her neutrality!" '[10] The Revolution landed the Genoese in trouble with both England and France. They struggled feebly under this double pressure. England only claimed to control them, France conquered them.

Venice suffered a similar fate. This republic came to grief through its very excess of prosperity. Its conquests had exhausted the benefits gained by trade, and to maintain the artificial power it had built up it had to have a despotic government and oppressive laws. But this government broke the people's spirit and exhausted the state's resources by misuse. As the Republic's territory grew its revenues diminished, and in the eighteenth century it was generally enfeebled. Yet though the people of Venice had cause to tremble, their diversions were unmatched anywhere in Europe. Under a system of tyranny tempered by carnival, the power of the state's inquisitors threatened no one but flibbertigibbets, scamps and scandalmongers—others were not bothered by it. Its sole function was to paralyse the internal life of the state.

Having for so long battled against the Turks, Venice was now reduced to seeking their protection against Austria. This

[10] Bielfeld, t. III, ch. VII: *De l'Italie.*

was the fate of Poland, and Venice was threatened by the same dangers. 'An ill-governed state invites government by foreigners', said the Doge Renier, who had been ambassador in Vienna at the time of the Partition. 'If ever there was a state which needed peace it is ours, for we possess neither army, navy nor allies, and it is only through luck and by accident that we survive—and thanks to the reputation of Venice for prudence. That is all the strength we have.' This prudence was really nothing more than weakness, and it produced an uncertainty which was in fact the worst kind of imprudence. The Venetians trembled before Austria, which coveted their country, while against her they had only one support, and that was France. The rivalry of the two states enabled Venice to survive, but when war broke out between them the Republic had to declare itself. Yet it was capable of nothing but vacillation, and so provided pretexts for both the combatants on its frontier. When they were tired of fighting each other, they made peace at the expense of Venice.

Of Lucca, Parma and Modena I shall not speak—they were territories, not states. They were so regarded by the Revolution, which continued to deal with them as the ancien régime had done—they were treated as job lots, to be disposed of as convenient.

There was only one state in Italy which kept to a line of policy and took pride in her traditions—Sardinia. Her policy was aggrandisement, and her tradition was to balance herself between France and Austria, serving the first in order to make gains, the second in order to preserve them. It seemed that these two masses, as they drew together, must crush Piedmont, but instead she thrust herself between them like a wedge, expanding her territory as she edged them aside. These instructions were given to a Sardinian representative in 1794: 'It has been by allying themselves first with the one and then with the other, according to what seemed advantageous at the moment, that the princes of the House of Savoy have greatly extended the bounds of their territories in Italy; this has always been the method of their plans of expansion.' The position in which Sardinia found herself thus made opportunism a rule of conduct. It was said that in a certain minor capital the diplomats were accustomed in time of war to ask the Sardinian minister: 'Which side is your master on today?' The ambitions of the House of Savoy were directed primarily towards the Duchy of Milan. 'It is an artichoke', said Charles Emmanuel, 'to be eaten leaf by leaf.'[11] Second to the Milanese it was Genoa that Piedmont coveted most avidly. In 1777 she proposed to Austria a partition of that republic, but Austria would have nothing to do with it. Having wasted her efforts at Vienna, Sardinia tried the same game at Berlin.

For a long time a secret affinity had drawn her in that direction. The two states shared the same destiny. They had risen in concert and had received royal crowns almost at the same time, as the reward for their common dexterity in defection. The parallel between the two monarchies was a classic topic for literary exposition. 'The King of Sardinia is to the house of Austria in Italy what Prussia is in Germany —he can advance only at its expense', said d'Argenson at the time of the War of the Austrian Succession. 'Half of the Milanese remains in the hands of Charles Emmanuel, as Silesia does in those of the King of Prussia', wrote Favier after that war '—something that cannot be forgiven.' Austria did not forgive, and it was this that brought her two enemies together. 'The Prussian alliance is for the house of Savoy the alliance of the future', wrote Count Perrone, then minister for foreign affairs, in 1777.[12]

Sardinia's relations with France were excellent as 1789 approached. The double marriage of the brothers of Louis XVI with the daughters of Victor Amadeus strengthened family ties, and the wise policy of Vergennes bound the two

[11] Bielfeld, t. III, p. 181. Frederick, *Mémoires*, I, p. 52.
[12] D'Argenson, *Mémoires*, IV, p. 278. Favier, éd. Boutaric, *Corr. secrète*, II, p. 329. Bianchi, *Storia della monarchia Piemontese*, t. I, pp. 564-570.

states in closer alliance. When Russia and Austria threatened
the Ottoman Empire the Sardinians, with that political flair
which seldom deserted them, saw that if they wished to cut
a figure in the world they must concern themselves with this
eastern crisis, and that it was in their interests to join with
France and England to check the ambitions of the imperial
courts.

Thus the Revolution found Sardinia perfectly united with
France. The entente had been sealed by necessities which
seemed independent of the form of their governments. The
diplomats of the Revolution thought that the compliance of
Sardinia could be assured by giving her an interest in the
Republic's conquests. But they reckoned too much on the
cupidity of the court of Turin and not enough on its judgement. The Revolution, while proposing an expansion of Sardinia's territory, began by destroying the principle on which
her government was based. For Piedmont to subscribe to this
meant abdicating her power altogether. She was too close to
France, too nearly within her grasp, and too exposed to the
contagion of her ideas to attempt, like Prussia, to associate
herself with the enterprises of the Revolution while defending herself against its propaganda. So the Revolution changed
the whole relationship between France and Sardinia. The
attempt to follow the tradition of the French monarchy in
diametrically opposite circumstances caused a complete breakdown of policy.

The grand design of the House of Savoy was to group the
Italian states around itself. In 1780 Count Napione proposed
to Victor Amadeus the formation of an Italian Confederation
which 'should animate the patriotic spirit in Italy and reunite the countries of common origin'.[13] This was also an
old project of French policy.[14] Expounding it in his
Mémoires d'Argenson laid down the necessary condition.
'The object of this plan', he said, 'is to concentrate the Italian

[13] Bianchi, t. I, ch. VIII, § 4.
[14] See above Bk. II, pp. 257-8.

powers, to drive out the foreigners and to show by example that we have no ambitions for ourselves.'[15] This Italian Confederation should in fact work out like the German one: France could find in it an instrument of influence, but she could not use it as an instrument of conquest without compensating the great states at the expense of the small; she could not make it an instrument of domination without provoking the formation of hostile leagues and so frustrating the whole object of her policy.

These projects were familiar to the publicists and politicians of the Revolution, who naturally adapted them for use in their own propaganda. Thus they proposed that the peoples of Italy should themselves accomplish what in the time of the monarchy had been proposed to their governments. But in these new conditions it was more than ever necessary to remember the wise words of d'Argenson. In freeing Italy, France must not aim to make gains for herself. The attempt to transplant the actual results of the Revolution produced unforeseen difficulties for French policy.

3. THE NATIONAL SPIRIT AND THE REVOLUTION

In the north and centre of Italy hatred of the feudal régime was almost as strong as in France, and the clergy were detested. The philosophical spirit held sway over the enlightened classes. 'But', says a historian of Italy, 'if the wish for reform was felt by the great number, the idea of a revolution had occurred to no one; there were no individual ambitions; everyone expected time and the wisdom of the rulers to bring about the necessary and desirable reforms.'[16] However, France brought, complete and in one piece, both the revolution they did not want and the reforms which they did. The reforms, for which they were prepared, they joyfully re-

[15] *Mémoires*, IV, p. 269.
[16] Botta, *Histoire d'Italie*, bk. I. Paris, 1824.

ceived. As to the revolution, most of them gave it a passionate welcome, but they were acclaiming the liberation of Italy, not the domination of France.

It was in this light that they saw the Revolution, and in this way that they interpreted the *Declaration of the Rights of Man* and the establishment of the Republic. The philosophical doctrines which prefaced the Revolution met with so much favour in Italy only because they aroused and gave shape to ideas of national independence. The Italians, when they proclaimed the emancipation of the human race, were thinking first and foremost of the emancipation of Italy. Their literature was entirely classical, after the French fashion, but these Greek and Roman maxims of liberty, when translated into Italian, stirred in their hearts an ardent desire for Italian liberation. The subject and the setting of the tragedy seemed the same as in France, but the audience was very different, and in the literature that so pleasantly titillated French pride because it seemed to consecrate France's greatness the Italians found instead allusions to a lost glory and encouragement of their hopes for its renewal. The grand ideas which in Paris seemed destined to establish the worldwide domination of French thought appeared to the Italians the natural means of evoking, at least in Italy, a renaissance of Italian thought. Alfieri was an ardent and single-minded patriot. 'We are slaves,' he said, 'but slaves ever trembling with hope.' He wrote, as he himself said, 'in transports of fanatical liberalism'. He kept before him always the thought of Italy and the Italians. 'If the words nation and fatherland are not bereft of meaning,' said a Piedmontese, Count Napione, in 1791, 'if every civil society ought to have a character of its own with which every member is to be imbued, we must strive to stimulate it, to learn its language, to cultivate it and love it; this is the prime factor in the public welfare, the best and strongest bond of the body politic.'[17] There

[17] *Dell' uso e dei pregi della lingua italiana.* Turin, 1791. Bianchi, I, p. 452.

was, then, nothing cosmopolitan about the Italians, and the French Revolution made such easy progress among them because it took on the character of a national revolution. When people spoke to them of fatherland and republic, they took these to mean Italy and nothing more.

There the inevitable misunderstandings began. In summoning the Italians to freedom France intended to attach them to herself, but in fact they were alienated. The politicians of the Revolution imagined that through common principles and identical forms of government the links formed between the kings would become stronger ones between the peoples, and that France, having dominated the governments of Italy as their protector, would still more easily dominate the peoples as their liberator. The mistake was profound, and the future was to show how great was the danger. The same sentiment which urged the Italians to assist an invasion to set them free moved them in a very short time to detest their liberators. The rallying-cry of independence aroused them, in spite of everything, to distrust and hatred of any foreigner who tried to rule them.

France restored to the Italians their rights, gave them a fatherland, made them citizens. In becoming citizens they became sufficient unto themselves; consciousness of their rights awoke consciousness of their interests; and in recovering their fatherland they wanted to see it free, powerful, and glorious. All the passions that flared up in their hearts were Italian, and one of the most inveterate—which caught fire at the same time as the rest—was the hatred of France, which, as Bonaparte wrote in 1797, they had preserved 'through prejudice, through the habit of centuries and through their character'.[18] So there came about that strange evolution of ideas whereby France, far from simplifying her policy, made it more complicated. In Italy she no longer had to reckon with disunited states, rulers who were often weak, governments which were always unstable; she now found a

[18] Bonaparte to Talleyrand, 26 September 1797.

people who never ceased to aspire to independence and who took pride in their refusal to submit to foreign masters.

We shall see what part was played by the various governments that emerged from the Revolution in this transformation of the relations between France and Italy. What is important here is to fix the starting point of the development, and to see how the initial moves in the crisis led on to the conclusion drawn in 1814 by Massimo d'Azeglio and, with him, all Italian patriots. 'It is a hard thing to say,' he reports in his *Mémoires*, 'for no one feels more deeply than I do the debt we owe to the Napoleons, and no one appreciates better the value of each drop of French blood that has watered the soil of Italy and ransomed it, but I must be allowed to say, because it is the truth, that it was an immense and ineffable joy to see the French depart.'[19]

These same causes produced consequences in Germany which were even more extraordinary and even more baleful for France.

V.   *Germany*

I. THE HOLY ROMAN EMPIRE

It was Germany that furnished the pretext for the struggle which brought France into conflict with Europe in 1792; it was Germany that became the chief theatre of the war and the setting for the peace negotiations; her territories served in turn as battlefield and as booty for schemes of partition. At one time she was the most useful instrument of French power; later she became the most active of the forces that brought about France's decline and fall. Indeed, from Valmy to Waterloo, from the quarrel over the princely enclaves of

[19] *I mie Ricordi*, vol. I, ch. IX. Florence, 1866.

Alsace to the Treaty of Paris of November 1815 Germany was never absent from the scene of action; it was she who supplied the first impulsion and the last. In the general European turmoil no country suffered a more profound upheaval. Through all these remarkable vicissitudes, however, her own historical development proceeded according to her own traditions, and the Treaties of Vienna continued the work begun in the Treaties of Westphalia.

The Treaties of 1648 were still in 1789 the basis of German public law. In them can be found the raison d'être of the Holy Roman Empire, but also the causes of the dissolution that perpetually threatened it. In France and England the feudal system disappeared and gave place to a monarchy, mixed in England, absolute in France, but in each case ruling a unitary state. But in Germany, where national and political traditions were lacking, the constituent parts tended to form separate states. While in France the monarchy subjected and absorbed the great feudatories, in Germany these attacked and seized the Empire. The same era—the age of Louis XIV—that witnessed the fulfilment of the monarchy's aims in France saw the triumph of the chief princely families in Germany. In France the maxim that there must be no state within the state prevailed; in Germany the quasi-sovereignty of the states of the Empire was solemnly proclaimed. The alliances with foreign powers which were a matter of high treason in France became for the princes of the Empire the most essential of their prerogatives.

The tendency which drove the German princes to make themselves independent of the Empire led them also to increase their power and extend their territories. As political ties were loosened the map became simpler, for while the princes strove to free themselves from the imperial supremacy they sought to concentrate their own powers. Each was trying at the same time to secure the autonomy of his own state and to incorporate the lesser territories that were on his borders or shut up as enclaves within them. The confiscation, or—to use the official euphemism—the secularisation of ecclesiastical lands in the states of North Germany introduced into the political customs of the Holy Roman Empire a new and highly prolific procedure for the rounding-off of princely possessions and one capable of widespread application.

The Treaties of Westphalia gave recognition to these facts and erected them into rights. In the words of the French instructions to ambassadors to the Diet of the Empire, 'These treaties consolidated the liberty of the states and gave a definite force to the public administration of the Germanic Empire by balancing the power of the members against the authority of the head and by setting up fixed barriers to his ambition.'[1] This state of affairs was an admirable safeguard for Germany's neighbours,[2] but, truth to tell, it worked for the destruction of Germany herself. Voltaire's dictum has often been quoted: 'The Germanic body called itself the Holy Roman Empire, whereas really it was neither holy, nor Roman, nor an Empire.' Holy it had never had more than a claim to be; Roman it had become only in order to oppress Rome; an empire it had been intermittently in the Middle Ages, but it was so no longer in the epoch of the French Revolution. If you looked for this Empire it was nowhere to be found. Germany could show neither the institutions nor even the framework of a state.

The Empire extended in theory over 660,000 square kilometres and had from 28 to 30 million inhabitants. The map, especially in the centre, and in Swabia, the Upper Rhineland and Westphalia, was a veritable mosaic; towards the borders there were more or less compact masses, like larger patches in a flecked material. Frontiers were marked out in festoons of

[1] Instructions of the French envoy to the Germanic Diet, 1774, 1775.
[2] 'This part of Europe is a bulwark to France. It is as essential to the king to preserve it in its actual state as it is for him to preserve his own dominions. This is the reason why the guarantee of the Treaty of Westphalia has always been regarded as one of the finest jewels of the crown.' *Résumé de l'état actuel*, February 1787, by Gérard de Rayneval, *Affaires étrangères*.

fantastic shapes. In this medley of states everything seemed
strange and arbitrary. The feudal hierarchy appeared there
in full panoply. From the knight to the Emperor, every type
of seignory was represented; abbeys were found side by side
with republics. But in spite of this extraordinary fragmentation, Germany came little by little to be concentrated in some
of the more powerful sovereignties, which tended to encroach
on the others. These large states occupied about five-sevenths
of the Empire. The free cities and ecclesiastical principalities represented almost another seventh, and the small fragments formed the rest. In the first rank, and far above the
rest, was the house of Austria; this had ten and a half million subjects within the Empire, but in addition there were
nearly fourteen million Hungarians, Poles and Italians. Prussia came next with two and a half million German subjects,
and as many again of Silesians, Poles and Prussians outside
the Empire. Then came the dynasties of Bavaria and Saxony,
and those of Brunswick, Wurtemberg, Hesse, Mecklenburg,
Nassau and Baden; these last might have no more than 200,-
000 subjects, and were comparable with the ecclesiastical
territories, of which the largest, Mainz, numbered 350,000
subjects, while Trier, Cologne, Wurzburg and Bamberg varied from 200,000 to 350,000. The states on this level had
neither force nor influence; they only counted as makeweights in political combinations or divisions.

Germany was an empire without subjects, institutions or
sovereign. Such institutions as she had were only empty
forms. To judge cases reserved to the Emperor, 'imperial
cases', there was the Imperial Chamber at Wetzlar and the
Aulic Council at Vienna. These still sat, but rarely concluded any business. In 1772, when Goethe was attached
to the chancellery of Wetzlar, there were 20,000 cases
pending. To hold together the mass of territories there were
ten circles, whose diets were charged with providing for the
common defence and carrying out the laws of the Empire.
Except in the neighbourhood of France, where fear kept
them alive, these assemblies were unimportant, and the cir-

cles had no more than a geographical significance. To manage affairs common to all the states of Germany there was a Diet of the Empire. The one which was sitting in 1789 had been summoned to Ratisbon and had been prorogued perpetually since 1663. The Diet did not act, it conferred; it did not discuss, it heard lectures. It was a congress of notaries or public attorneys, for whom niceties of procedure were more important than reaching a conclusion. When it was seized of a question by the Emperor each delegate referred it to his government, which replied at its own convenience by a note which the delegate communicated to the Diet. It was composed of three colleges, equal in rights and voting separately. A majority of two colleges was required to pass a resolution or *conclusum* of the Diet. The votes were a matter of negotiation: in reality, the Diet did no more than register the decisions taken separately by the states represented in it. It must be remembered too that three foreign princes had their spokesmen there—the King of England in respect of Hanover, the King of Sweden for Pomerania, the King of Denmark for the duchies of the Elbe. 'A minister sent by a ruler to the assembly is like a farmyard mastiff baying the moon', said Frederick the Great.[3] So they stayed away. In 1788, of a hundred voters enrolled in the college of princes there were only fourteen at Ratisbon; only eight cities were represented out of fifty-one; the Diet was reduced to twenty-nine delegates.

The Emperor was no more than the pompous simulacrum of sovereignty. He commanded an army which was only mustered when the Diet of the Empire so decided, and only marched when the diets of the circles gave their consent. His normal budget amounted to 13,884 florins. His government consisted of a vice-chancellor and a few scribes. His functions were to introduce business to the Diet, and to ratify and promulgate its decisions. He was in fact the president of a confederation of quasi-sovereign states. He would have been

[3] *Mémoires*, Introduction, ch. I.

infinitely less important in Germany than was the President of the Republic in the United States had he not joined to the imperial status the dignity of the King of Bohemia and Hungary, which made him a more powerful ruler than all the rest of the German princes put together and enabled him to dominate them, not by law but by force.

What was important in Germany was not the Empire, which was decrepit, nor the institutions, which were obsolete, but the states of which the Empire was comprised and the political groups formed by the states. If these remained divided Germany was nothing; if they combined she became formidable. But they could only be united by a common peril and held together by an iron hand. Such a union of the Germans was a constant anxiety to their neighbours, and the basic object of the Treaties of Westphalia was to render it impossible.[4] Yet in fact they erected into a law of the Empire an antagonism as old as the Empire itself.

As far back as one can go, the north and south of the Empire seem always to have been divided and hostile. This opposition appears in every way. In the sixteenth century the north became Protestant, the south became Catholic; and from 1648 there were a *corps catholique*[5] and a *corps évangélique*[6] between which the Empire was officially divided. The house of Austria sought unity of rule through

[4] 'At the time of the conclusion of the Treaties of Westphalia, those who played the chief part in them regarded the privileges and rights which were secured for the princes and States of the Empire as essential to the stability and balance of Europe. Settling the rights of the court of Vienna, the Treaties prevented the Germanic body and this court, which could only act according to the common principles and interests of the princes, from ever constituting one and the same body politic, which would truly have been dangerous to all the powers of Europe.' Instructions of the duc de Richelieu, 1725. *Recueil*, t. i. *Autriche*, p. 208.

[5] The hereditary states of the house of Austria and Bohemia, Bavaria, part of Swabia and of Franconia, and the ecclesiastical Electorates.

[6] Brandenburg-Prussia, Saxony, Hanover, Brunswick, Hesse, Wurtemberg.

unity of religion; in opposition to it the Protestants in 1530 formed the Schmalkaldic League. Repulsed on this front, Austria tried to govern Germany by concentrating her own strength; in 1785 the same states formed the Confederation of Princes[7] to restrain her—in a new attempt to found that North German Confederation which was to become the master plan of Prussian statesmen and the main lever of Prussia in the grand design she had already formed to gain control of Germany. For the time being, as she was not yet in a position to absorb the other German states, she defended their liberties against Austria; it was a sure means of weakening that dynasty and insinuating herself into its place.

The secondary states did not like Prussia, her military government, her aggressive policy, her arrogant behaviour, or her strident claims; but they needed her against Austria, and made use of her, and when she tried to divide the Empire they supported her. There was nothing they feared more than that these two rivals, Prussia and Austria, should harmonise their ambitions and share Germany between them. It was because the constitution of the Empire guaranteed their existence and their autonomy that the small states were so strongly attached to it; but while they thought they were defending it, they were unwittingly doing as much as Austria and Prussia to destroy it.

The German princes had two ruling passions—the spirit of independence, and greed. Both sprang from egoism, which determined their whole conduct. This was the great betrayal of Germany, and by Germany of her allies. Each was for himself, and none was for Germany. Nor did Germany command the loyalty of the two great powers, Austria and Prussia. In their attacks on the Slavs they were seeking only to gather new forces to possess themselves of Germany; through the domination of Germany, thus taken in the rear, they aimed at the domination of Europe. The small states copied

[7] Treaty of Berlin of 23 July 1785 between Prussia, Saxony and Brunswick. See Ranke, *Die Deutschen Mächte und der Fürstenbund.*

them as far as their strength allowed: a Guelf became King of England, a Saxon King of Poland. They all coveted a royal crown, and sought outside the Empire the means to control the Empire—and if possible to dismember it. They considered, in fact, that the best way of containing Austria and Prussia was to follow their example, that is to grow stronger and expand.

There was therefore a tendency for territories to be concentrated in a few states of medium size which balanced each other, and by their total weight balanced that of the two great powers. The princes did not see that by simplifying the map of Germany they made its subjection easier. The task of unification, of which the Treaties of Westphalia represent only one stage, was thus pursued, and through the very operation of its principles destroyed the system of these famous treaties. Greed and ambition were universal, and the attendant dangers did not deter even the ecclesiastics. 'The Elector of Cologne', reports Frederick, 'has put on his head as many mitres as he can lay hands on.' The laymen, for their part, were always talking of secularisations. In 1778 it was said in the Rhineland that Prussia would let Austria take Bavaria, and that Austria, by way of recompense, would deliver up to Prussia the bishoprics of Münster, Hildesheim and Paderborn. The King of Prussia wanted Saxony, and the Duke of Brunswick Hanover. Mirabeau wrote in 1786: 'The only wish that the Duke clearly expressed to me was the separation of the Electorate of Hanover from the English monarchy, and the secularisation of certain states which could one day help to make an equivalent to Saxony.'[8] These rumours recurred periodically in the years before the Revolution. Frederick had summed up in a phrase the condition of things in Germany: 'The weak were slaves, the strong were free.' Germany was being devoured by her own greed.

The French Revolution aroused and excited the passions

[8] *Correspondance secrète*, letter of Brunswick, 22 October 1786.

of these princes but made no difference to their character. It threatened their existence, yet they saw in it only an opportunity to advance their schemes of emancipation and aggrandisement. When the crisis broke Austria and Prussia claimed that their aim was to defend Germany against the common enemy; this they did so well that the rest of Germany feared them more than it feared France. Moreover, the two powers were so jealous of each other and each was so intent on pursuing its own interests that in the end they left Germany to its own devices—that is, to suffer conquest and partition. Prussia first set the example of defection, and, having broken up the coalition, destroyed what was left of the Holy Roman Empire by separating the states of the north from those of the south, drawing a line of neutrality which was simply a new outline for a Confederation of the North. She accepted the principle of the dismemberment of Germany by agreeing to the cession of the left bank of the Rhine subject to the provision of compensation by the secularising of ecclesiastical territories on the right bank.[9] Austria held out longer but finally gave in on the same conditions.[10]

As for the small states, they did not wait for Austria's ratification of Prussia's policy before copying it themselves.[11] One after another they treated with the French Republic. In theory the Diet retained sole competence, and when they signed their armistice or peace agreements the German princes reserved the right of the Empire to consent. But when the leading members of the Empire had engaged themselves separately ratification by the Diet became nothing more than a matter of form, and all the reservation of the rights of the Empire in fact amounted to was a solemn denial of them.

[9] Treaties of Basle, 5 April 1795, and of Berlin, 5 August 1796.
[10] Treaty of Campo-Formio, 17 October 1797.
[11] Treaties and conventions of 28 August 1795 with Hesse-Cassel, 25 September 1795 with Wurtemberg, 25 July 1796 with Baden, 27 July 1796 with the Swabian Circle, 7 August 1796 with the Franconian Circle and Wurtemberg, 22 August 1796 with Baden, 7 September 1796 with Bavaria (armistice).

The German princes conducted the peace negotiations as they had conducted the war. Their mutual distrust had prevented them from defending themselves and their greed now led them to despoil one another. The war had entailed the defeat of the Empire; the peace brought about its dissolution.

Each state had in fact chosen its portion in advance; the French had only to put the distribution into effect. Under the violent pressure of the Republic and still more of Bonaparte, Germany underwent a crisis in which all the elements of opposition that smouldered inside her came to the surface. The Empire was completely overthrown; yet neither the Republic nor Bonaparte had begun this revolution; they found its causes at work in Germany and needed only to activate them to the utmost. That is why such a remarkable achievement was really so easy; it was only a matter of bargaining and statistics. For the Duke of Wurtemberg the cession to the Republic of the left bank of the Rhine had meant attaining the electoral dignity and the acquisition, in the form of abbeys and free cities, of double what he had lost. In 1805 this prince, warned of the arrival of the French, protested indignantly against the invasion of his lands. 'I shall repel this brigandage!' he exclaimed to the officer Napoleon sent to treat with him. The officer begged him not to be angry, and so successfully was the Duke appeased that at the end of the interview he whispered in the Frenchman's ear that 'his own possessions were much inconvenienced by having these others as neighbours; if he took them over and his electorate was erected into a kingdom everything might be arranged.'[12] Indeed everything was. The Duke, who at the time of the Revolution had 650,000 subjects, found himself, after Napoleon appeared on the scene, ruler over 1,350,000. In the meantime, it is true, the Holy Roman Empire had disappeared. When in 1806 Napoleon decided on its dissolution a word was sufficient; it had already long ceased to be.

[12] *Mémoires du général de Ségur*, vol. II, p. 355.

2. THE GOVERNMENTS

In the Empire as it was constituted the states were everything, the German nation was nothing. There was no fatherland and there were no parties, but only rival dynasties. During the wars of the seventeenth century whoever was not Austrian or Spanish was Swedish or French—or even English. Nevertheless, in spite of these divisions, there survived in men's minds a confused feeling for the whole. There were recollections of a past that was ill understood and aspirations towards a future that was ill defined; there was an instinct of nationalism that for the most part smouldered dully, yet was liable to burst forth from time to time.

Germany's neighbours were aware of this latent force and feared it. 'Who can say', wrote a contemporary of Richelieu, 'whether, if the Germany the Spaniards have divided wishes to reunite, and if the Germans tire of lending their hands and giving their blood to the enemy to enslave their country, all the trophies he has erected among them may not fall incontinently to pieces and the successes of ten years come to naught?'[13] Louis XIV had experience of this, to France's cost, and the eighteenth century began with those formidable wars in which, as Fléchier expressed it in his funeral oration on Turenne, 'The great and vast Germanic body, composed of so many peoples and different nations, had unfurled all its standards and marched upon our frontiers to terrify us by its numbers and overwhelm us with its force.'[14]

Though dispersed among so many rival sovereignties, the Germans retained and developed their natural character. 'This vast state', said Voltaire, 'was not strong externally, but it was strong within, because the nation has always been industrious and warlike.'[15] They were renowned for their discipline, which fitted them so well for military service. 'The

[13] Balzac, *Le Prince*, ch. XXXI.
[14] *Oraison funèbre de Turenne*.
[15] *Essai sur les moeurs*, ch. CLXXVIII.

dominant characteristic of the German nation', as a German wrote, 'is a strong passion for war, to which they sacrifice everything, even their liberty.'[16] Many became mercenaries; some their rulers sold into service, whole regiments at a time. They fought under every flag and on every battlefield. But some among them recalled that formerly Germans had shed their blood for Germany, had won glory, had made great conquests, had brought back rich spoils, had terrified their neighbours and caused the world to resound with the fame of their power. The wretched reputation which now remained to the Empire and the relic of honour which attached to the name of Germany were only a pale reflection of the glory of those remote times. At Frankfurt there survived a sort of historical museum of ancient Germany which from time to time was exhibited to the nation—at the coronation of the emperors. By such ceremonies the national tradition was kept alive.

In the eighteenth century it was revived. The words 'country' and 'patriot' appeared in diplomatic correspondence and in manifestoes. The sentiment must have existed since politicians appealed to it. Even those who were so busily dividing up Germany made a show of defending it and pretended to be the champions of its independence. In 1740, when the Austrian succession question arose, this was one of the arguments of Maria Theresa's enemies. A Venetian ambassador wrote: 'There can be heard the murmur of tumultuous voices saying that it is not fitting for the nation to be governed by a woman, and that it is in the common interest that a German prince be chosen.' Frederick, writing to the Emperor Charles VII, a Bavarian, boasted of being a 'good and loyal German patriot'.[17]

This patriotism declared itself principally in jealousy, mistrust and hatred of the French. 'Take care', said Frederick to Louis XV's envoy, M. de Valori; 'the only thing which puts your friend the Elector of Bavaria in the wrong in the eyes

[16] Bielfeld, vol. III, ch. VIII: *de l'Allemagne.*
[17] 8 October 1743. *Pol. Corr.*, vol. II, p. 440.

of all the German princes is his connection with you.' When Frederick invaded Silesia and wished to explain his venture to his confrères—or his co-states, as they were called—the German princes, it was to this sentiment that he appealed. 'In Hanover, Mainz and Ratisbon', he wrote to his minister, 'you must speak of the spirit of patriotism and my wish to preserve the Empire.'[18] Maria Theresa replied with the same weapons, and when in 1742 she tried to rouse the Germans against the French in Bohemia, she exclaimed, 'How long shall we allow the foreigner to trample the soil of our dear German country? Is not this the moment to free our country from the oppression of centuries?' The appeal was heard; the more energy and passion Maria Theresa showed against the French, the more she recovered the favour of the Germans. Frederick claimed to be defending the rights of the Empire when he allied with France to conquer Silesia; to get the Germans to recognise his conquest, he suddenly deserted the French and covered his defection with the same pretext—the interests of Germany.

This was the classic device of France's allies in Germany. 'They beggar my subjects by exactions which they have no right to claim from me', wrote the Duke of Wurtemberg in 1745. . . . M. le marquis d'Argenson has told you that the Swabians so hate the French that if there were a chance to massacre them all they would surely do it.' Frederick said to M. de Valori at the same time, 'You are right to be afraid of getting involved in Germany, my dear friends . . . be sure that the day after your troops cross the Rhine you will have the best part of Germany against you.'

As the century progressed these tendencies became clearer; the princes exploited them, and none more successfully than Frederick. In 1769, after the Seven Years War, in which France had so foolishly sacrificed her glory and her interests in the *idée fixe* of recovering Silesia for Maria Theresa, it was still on this basis of a 'patriotic German system' that the

18 Instruction to Podewils, *Pol. Corr.*, vol. I, p. 99.

Austrian and Prussian sought reconciliation and agreement to the detriment of France; having made use of her they were eager to humiliate her. They vied with each other in their ingenious ploy with the idea of 'patriotism'. The very word was a power in the land, and when used *à propos* it ensured a hearing throughout Germany.

How remarkable was the destiny of the reigning house of Prussia! The least of the German heads of state, the prince most alien in outlook and character to Teutonic traditions and German civilisation, he yet did most to reawaken the Germans to their national pride and a sense of independence. Though Prussia had many enemies, Rossbach made friends for her everywhere. It was forgotten that most of the fugitives in that famous rout were Germans; the fact that other Germans had put them to flight was enough to make the day renowned as a cardinal event in history. In addition to this there was the prestige throughout Europe of the philosopher king; flattery was lavished on him by the master spirits of the age and general homage was rendered by statesmen to the superiority of his rule. He raised Germany in the eyes of Europe and in her own. Goethe relates that the criticisms which in his youth he heard passed upon 'this unique man, so evidently superior to his contemporaries', made him feel the injustice of public opinion. 'I was for Prussia,' he says, 'or, to speak more precisely, for Frederick. What did Prussia mean to us?—It was the person of the sovereign that stirred all our hearts. I rejoiced with my father in his victories.' Some years after the Seven Years War he returned to this idea and pointed proudly to Frederick 'relying on his own strength and appearing as the arbiter of Europe and the world'.[19] This popularity reached even across the seas. A French agent wrote in 1766 of the Germans serving in America, 'They idolise the King of Prussia.'[20] This was the real foundation of Prussia's greatness: in spite of the deep disagreements which

[19] *Mémoires*, trans. Porchat, pp. 39, 254, 604.
[20] C. de Witt, *Jefferson*, p. 410.

estranged them from her in the internal affairs of the Empire, the Germans took pride in her victories over foreigners and became used to associating the idea of her power with their reborn sense of national pride.

'Patriotism' tended to become synonymous with support of Prussia in the jargon of the chancelleries. The Confederation of Princes gave substance to the aspirations it implied. Projects of federal reform were discussed, and means were sought of restoring its lost strength to the Empire by modifying its constitution. Germans of the older Germany like Hardenberg and Stein, to quote only the most illustrious, attached themselves to Prussia and devoted themselves passionately to realising such projects for the future. Frederick William II[21] tried to find in this policy a means of sustaining the crushing burden that devolved upon him. 'The King', wrote Mirabeau, 'has conceived the idea and the hope of becoming a great man by making himself German, purely German, and so defying the superiority of the French.' His apologists loudly praised him for it. One of them wrote in 1789, 'In so far as Germany was despised, and the trouble and disorder arising from her divisions were fomented by the policy of her neighbours, to that extent has she now become formidable under Prussian protection, and alliance with her been found desirable.'[22]

Whether enemies or friends of Prussia, all Germans declared themselves patriots, denounced the fragmentation of Germany as dangerous and demanded reforms. Towards 1789 this was the theme of the pamphlets which began to proliferate on the left bank of the Rhine as on the right. They not only looked to Joseph II, who also nourished his dream of the restoration of the great Empire, to realise their aim; they believed that Austria and Prussia must work for it together. Were they not of the same nation? Did they not

[21] Frederick II died on 17 August 1786. His nephew succeeded him under the name of Frederick William II.

[22] Trenck, *Examen de l'histoire secrète de la cour de Berlin.*

speak the same tongue, and should they not therefore share the government of Germany and of the world?[23]

These movements of opinion had their repercussions in Germany's relations with France. Bielfeld, the author of the *Institutions Politiques*, looking at the situation from the French point of view, declared that the plan of conquering the Rhine frontier seemed a 'dictate of wisdom',[24] but, considering the interests of Germany, he judged that 'the most important object of the policy of the Empire' must be to oppose the execution of this plan. 'If it be true', he said, 'that France seeks to extend her domination to the banks of the Rhine, the Germanic body must gather all its forces to prevent any further French advance in that direction, and to ensure that at least things remain as they now are.'[25] Meanwhile, he added, France was the guarantor of German liberties; without her these liberties would soon be no more than 'a matter of theory'. He concluded that the Germans must treat France with 'the utmost circumspection', must avoid meddling in her affairs, but, on the other hand, 'not suffer the court of Versailles to interfere in the internal affairs of Germany, still less to rob her of the smallest piece of her territory.' This was what the Duke of Brunswick indicated very clearly to Mirabeau in 1786: 'He frequently repeated to me that Protestant Germany and a good part of the rest would be indubitably on France's side if only she would fully reassure the Germanic body about her intentions.'

Meanwhile the Germanic body was not content with asking for guarantees and assurances; it put forward claims. These were not in fact new, but they were revived along with German patriotism and became popular as memories of Germany's former might were reawakened. The scholars and jurists of the Empire were busied with the same task as those

[23] *Réflexions*, 6 December 1786. Ranke, *Die deutschen Mächte*, vol. II, p. 299.

[24] Tome II, ch. IV, 20, and t. III, ch. III: *De la France*. See above, pp. 248-56.

[25] Tome III, ch. VIII: *De l'Allemagne*.

of the French king; their archives were as rich in rights, titles, interests and claims as those of Paris. It was, with a new look, the age-old litigation about the succession to Charlemagne, the eternal claim to the Kingdom of Austrasia. 'The German publicists', wrote Favier, 'have no more use for renunciations than the French jurists. You may say that in Germany claims are everlasting and imprescriptible.'[26] They never gave up demanding back what had been taken from them—and even what they had ceded themselves of their own free will in return for services rendered.

The very rulers who had been in such haste to give up to France the three bishoprics and Alsace, in order to obtain her guarantee of their independence from the house of Austria, showed themselves just as eager to support that house in its efforts to restrict and annul, if possible, the King's rights over these territories.[27] In 1709, when Louis XIV, vanquished by the European coalition, seemed to be on the point of capitulating, and when France, invaded, seemed at her last gasp, these were the most voracious in the rush for the spoils. 'Certain learned doctors', wrote Bielfeld, 'more notable for their knowledge than their judgement or penetration, pictured the Grand Turk and the crown of France as the two *hereditary enemies of the German name*. They inculcated this principle in their pupils, and as the prejudices of the schools are with difficulty dispelled, this dictum passed into a proverb, and the house of Austria has found it profitable to maintain the prejudice.'[28]

France was well aware of these tendencies, and was far from neglecting them in her policy. She had to take account of the 'patriotism' of the German princes, the more seriously because, far from tempering, it excited their traditional greed and furnished it with new pretexts. It was in fact to be expected that in negotiation they would now be found, not only intractable, but infinitely more demanding than hitherto

[26] *Doutes et questions sur le traité de 1706.*
[27] See above, book II, ch. II.
[28] *Institutions politiques*, t. III, ch. VIII.

in the matter of compensation. To obtain their consent to any further cession of territories to France they would have to be indemnified not only for the material but for the moral loss they would suffer; they would have to be paid not only for the territory they were giving up but for the discredit in the Empire which their pact with 'the hereditary enemy' would entail. The greater the apparent sacrifice, the higher the indemnity required. Their claims swelled with their patriotism, and to get them to give up a few patches of land on Germany's borders meant letting them extend their frontiers farther and farther in the heart of the Empire. For perspicacious diplomats these were considerations of much value. Louis XVI's advisers were well schooled in them, and found in them some of the most powerful motives for persisting in the system of moderation which they had adopted.

Towards 1789 this system had borne fruit: it could be said that the relations between France and Germany had never been so stable, so advantageous for the general peace and the interests of France as at this time. The Rhineland states, which alone could threaten France's enterprises, came under her influence, and in general showed deference to her advice. There was hardly a hostile ruler in this region other than the Elector of Cologne, and he was an archduke and brother of the French queen.[29] The King of France not only found allies and clients in the region—he raised regiments.[30] The cadet members of the better families, sometimes even the heirs-presumptive, counted it an honour to serve France, though it was not always wise to place much reliance on their loyalty. Most of them prided themselves, in this respect, on a great independence of spirit. The 'German patriotism' which allowed them to accept so much also bade them forget what they had received. So thought Prince Louis of Bavaria, for example, who was born in Strasburg, where

[29] Maximilian, born in 1756, Coadjutor in 1780, Elector of Cologne in 1784.

[30] Royal-Allemand, Royal-Deux-Ponts, Royal-Saarbrück, Royal-Bavière, Birkenfels.

his father commanded a French regiment. Louis XVI stood godfather to him, France saved his heritage for him in 1779 at the Peace of Teschen, and later the favour of Napoleon turned it into a kingdom. In 1806 he came to Alsace to greet the Empress Josephine and paid court to her most obsequiously—his sister was about to marry Prince Eugène de Beauharnais. But if the courtier abased himself in public the patriot protested in secret, and between two visits to his French protectors this German prince wrote in his diary: 'For me it would be the dearest prize of victory if this city where I was born could one day become German again!'[31]

France looked on the Confederation of Princes as a combination favourable to her policy; it was bound to be so as long as she kept to her rôle of guarantor of the Treaties of Westphalia. But if France tried to make conquests in Germany this confederation, formed almost under her auspices, would be transformed into a formidable alliance against her. This was one of the essential points in the schemes of federal reform which were under discussion in Germany in 1787 and 1788. Writing on this matter to Frederick William II of Prussia, the Duke of Saxe-Weimar led him to hope for the accession to their league of the Swabian circle, and added: 'This particular union, which would muster not inconsiderable forces (Swabia being able to furnish more than 30,000 combatants) could join them to those of the upper and lower Rhine, and all these together, reinforced by English, Hanoverian and Hessian cavalry and artillery, would compose a formidable force, well adapted for the defence of the Rhineland against France.'[32] The Margrave of Baden, who entered vigorously into this project, had no intention of being intimidated by his powerful neighbour; on the contrary he worked out a plan of defence based upon the same principles.

Such were the ideas of the German princes in the period

[31] Heigel, *Ludwig I, König von Baiern.* Leipzig, 1872.
[32] 17 February 1788. Ranke, *Die deutsche Mächte*, vol. II, p. 336.

when France worried them least and when they seemed most anxious to seek her alliance. Without understanding the motives of these princes it would not be possible to explain either the strange convolutions of their policy or the disappointments to which French policy was exposed by reckoning on their gratitude after speculating on their greed. As Forster* wrote in 1791, with cruel irony, 'Our policy is to deceive everybody, to treat with everybody, to keep our word to no one. It is in this way that some importance has for a long time been attributed to us.'[33] It was thus that Prussia had provided in the eighteenth century the precedents for the famous betrayals of the nineteenth. It was thus that, having stooped to France for a share in the great traffic in German lands, these princes, as soon as they judged her to be tottering, turned against her the power with which she had imprudently endowed them. Allied with France for the sake of conquest, they became her enemies to keep their gains. They wanted the profits of treason to be legitimised by patriotism.

But the patriotism they appealed to in 1813 was no longer the equivocal and venal patriotism on which they formerly prided themselves, and which they rated so highly only to exploit it to greater advantage. This was a sentiment much simpler and much stronger, patriotism true, sincere and violent like all primitive passions. This grand word, which under the ancien régime was current in Germany in only a distorted and debased form in the dubious vocabulary of chancelleries, now found a place in the language of the people, and sprang purified from its proper source, and, re-

---

* Georg Forster was born in Poland. His parents were German but of Scotch descent, and he spent much of his earlier life in England. In 1788 he was librarian to the University at Mainz. He gave a reasoned and moderate support to the Revolution. When the French occupied Mainz in 1793 Forster became a leader of the revolutionary club that was set up and advocated annexation to France. Sent as a representative to Paris he was rapidly disillusioned with the revolutionaries but continued to support the Revolution. He died in 1794.

[33] Forster, cited by Perthes, vol. I, p. 67.

covering its meaning, once more became the natural expression of the conscience of a great nation. It was now the German nation that took the field, a formidable force the existence of which the ancien régime hardly suspected; its intervention was to modify all the conditions in which French policy operated in Europe. Yet France, by a singular consequence of the Revolution, had in a sense aroused it against herself.

3. NATIONAL ASPIRATIONS

To consider appearances only Germany towards 1789 presented a similar spectacle to France. There were the same vague uneasiness and the same enthusiastic optimism, the same disgust with the present, the same confidence in the future, the same liking for universal ideas, the same concern for humanity, the same hopes for a radical and rational form of society, the same lack of legal rights with the same actual liberty of discussion in books and pamphlets, and finally the same opposition to established governments expressed in the same declamatory language.

But if the ideas are examined and the sentiments are analysed they are found to be quite different from those in France. There the nation was homogeneous and the government strongly centralised, and popular thinking, while it made use of abstract formulas, was fundamentally concrete; the French were becoming conscious of the notions and sensing the instincts accumulated through eight centuries of national life and monarchical discipline. When a Frenchman was told, 'The people is sovereign', his first thought was: the people—it is myself! And he saw himself on the throne of Louis XIV. The German could see in his country only individuals, split up by infinitely complicated internal divisions; he could see kings, dukes, counts, barons, knights, abbots, burghers, subjects, even serfs, but he could discover neither a people nor a sovereign; he could neither personify them nor form a total image of them; he could conceive of them only vaguely, and was unable to shape them in his mind or feel their presence within himself. All such notions remained for him in a state of abstraction.

The French believed passionately in themselves as a nation. But with the Germans even passions were speculative, and national feeling remained entirely theoretical and literary. There was no public spirit to form men's characters, no political customs or traditions to sustain them. The thought of the élite was vigorous and emancipated, but the mass of individuals remained passive, suppressed, almost servile.

'In Germany', said Mme de Staël, 'there are too many new ideas and too few common ones.'[34] It is precisely in common ideas that men find meeting-points where they can reach accord and find fellowship. In Germany there were only philosophical and literary schools, and they found their chief glory in their originality—that is to say their isolation. They were brought to this by the fragmentation of territories. There was no centre where ideas could be brought to bear or from which general impulses could radiate. Everything was diffuse. Ideas were universal but interests were still particularised, and men's thinking was straitened by their feelings. There were no traditions except those opposed to national unity. There were grand conceptions but only mean actions.

Germany held fast to her customs and took pride in them. 'Man is moulded by custom; custom is his nurse.' Several years after the Revolution this was to be said by Schiller, of all German poets the most enthusiastic, the most imbued with the ideas of Rousseau, the most eager to welcome new and generous ideas and noble illusions. 'A curse on those who would interfere with man's affection for the things of old, a precious heritage from his forefathers, consecrated in a sense by time itself! What is respected by the aged takes on a divine character in the eyes of the children.'[35] He believed that innovations must be in accord with custom, otherwise the

[34] *De l'Allemagne*, part 3, ch. XI.
[35] *Wallenstein*, act I, scene IV, 1799.

people would not accept them. This was the precise opposite of the spirit of revolution. And so it happened that the Germans stopped short on the road, scattered throughout the neighbourhood and calmly settled down in the adjacent fields, while the French, starting under the same impulsion and following at first the same route, pushed on to the end and into the abyss.

The Germans treasured their religious traditions. Those who were not believers nevertheless respected religion; for them it was an object of study, a subject for poetry, and always a source of moral edification. Voltairian scepticism only touched the surface of society and did not penetrate very deep. In the opinion of most Germans Frederick's glory was tarnished by it. In France irreligion preceded the Revolution, prepared the way for it and impressed on it an anti-Christian character; but in Germany rationalism turned pious. The Germans tried to harmonise their new ideas with their old beliefs. Protestantism lent itself to this process with remarkable flexibility; the North Germans had learnt in this great school the secret of wholesome change. The *Profession of Faith of a Savoyard Vicar*, which in France engendered only the paradox of the *Constitution Civile*, in Germany produced a kind of religious awakening. Compare Robespierre's 'Supreme Being' with the God of Schleiermacher,[36] the rhetoric of the one with the enthusiasm of the other, the sinister and ridiculous abortion of the cult of Prairial with the expansive evolution of German Protestantism, and you will have measured the distance between the two nations at the end of the eighteenth century, the ever-widening gulf that opened between them as they moved away from their common starting-point.

This disposition was so natural to the Germans that one finds it even among the Catholics. Joseph II wished to remain in the bosom of the Church; he protested against any suspicion of atheism or even of 'philosophical' ideas; and his

[36] Schleiermacher, born in 1768, published in 1799 his *Discours sur la religion, addressés aux gens instruits qui la dédaignent.*

conflict with Rome did not enhance his popularity. Nowhere in Germany can one find the elements of official irreligion.

Nor does one find the elements of democracy. The whole history of the French prepared them for democracy and led them to it; democracy was in their habits as national unity was in their character. In 1789 one decree was sufficient to introduce these principles into the laws, because in passing these laws they were simply conferring a definite title on ancient usages. In Germany society, as well as the nation and the state, was thrown out of gear by it; their political ways were based neither on aristocracy nor on democracy—there were only hierarchies.

Public spirit was entirely provincial, or even local. To a German Germany represented only the little state in which he lived immeasurably enlarged. Particularism seemed to him the very basis of the constitution. In France, where the nation was one, political parties recruited followers throughout the nation; in Germany, where the nation was broken up, there were no political groups that extended through the whole country. There were only separate states, with diverse interests and different policies. For the German the political party was the state to which he was subject, and political liberty was the independence of this state. Consequently he took pride in everything that magnified the ruling dynasty. Many no doubt would have liked to be better governed; very few had the idea of governing themselves—they well knew that they could not. They were too scattered and too lacking in every kind of necessary experience to lay siege to the state and take it over. The state was separated from them by dikes too deep to cross and walls too high to scale—it eluded their grasp. Besides, such endeavours were as foreign to their outlook as they were beyond their means. Enlightenment, reform, progress—all had come from the rulers. The state had provided for their needs, the ruler had fulfilled their wishes. They continued to place all their hopes in enlightened despotism, and if the despotism lacked enlightenment, they were wise enough, knowing they themselves could not supply the deficiency, to possess themselves in patience. If they turned away from their master it was only to put their trust in his successor, and their very discontent was a homage to sovereignty.

The *philosophes* who taught the new doctrines put no different interpretation upon them. They were most respectful towards the powers that be, not only through prudence and an accommodating temper, but because of their outlook and convictions. They wanted by reforming authority to strengthen, not to shake it. Levelling they found revolting, and anarchy filled them with horror. Consider the most revolutionary of the German thinkers, Kant. He led his disciples up to the giddy heights where his critique held sway so that they could better admire the scaffolding of balustrades, parapets and guard-rails he had so carefully erected to keep them from the abyss. Pure reason commands us to doubt everything, but practical reason bids us to respect everything. This superb dialectician who measures the extent of the infinite, disputes with God his raison d'être and questions the existence of the universe, proved himself in real life the most conciliatory of men, the most docile and submissive of subjects, the most moderate and accommodating of politicians. His conclusion in general is compromise and universal conciliation. His most radical propositions turn out to be maxims of common sense. He reconciled liberty with law and morals with policy. He does not confuse right with virtue, which everyone claims to have, nor with force, which anyone can exert. He is in favour of the separation of powers, and he admires—from a distance—representative government. Whatever ideal he pursues he marches towards it with measured steps and moderate pace, with no leaps or somersaults. He does not recognise any right of revolution. Obedience to authority is a *categorical imperative*. He does not even believe in the expedient of trusting government to philosophers. 'The profession of politics', he says, 'corrupts the free judgement of reason.' They can, however, be left in peace to speculate —there is no danger from them: 'This class of people is by its very nature incapable of forming groups and clubs, and consequently it cannot be suspected of propaganda.'

Such was the spirit of Germany at that time. 'Do not', wrote Lessing, 'throw away the dirty water before you can replace it with clean; do not destroy the temple, but build another beside it.' Goethe was to teach that one must cultivate one's garden, and as to reforms, needs should be consulted rather than desires, for needs are limited but desires are infinite. No revolution, but the peaceful evolution of natural forces; the whole art of government consists in promoting this development. He was understood in this sense by Justus Möser,* whom Goethe proclaimed an 'incomparable man,' and who from the beginning of the Revolution was to prove one of its most determined adversaries. Society founded on the family, the state founded on the commune, the spirit of tradition and the spirit of reform as complementary and mutually corrective—these were the principles of the great German statesmen, the Steins, Hardenbergs, and Humboldts; it was in this guise that the ideas of the French Revolution penetrated and fertilised German soil. In France, where the ground had been levelled, the torrent flowed over the land and flooded it; in Germany it was checked by dams, and formed lakes from which it issued tamed and pacified.

Such was the necessary outcome of the national character and tradition. When it came to translating political doctrines into action, it was character and tradition that determined the quality of the result. The Germans were not of the stuff of which revolutionaries and civic heroes are made. Mme de Staël was to say some years later, 'They are virtuous and full of integrity as private persons, heads of families, or administrators, but their pursuit of power, always, of course, conducted with charm and grace, is nevertheless painful to behold, especially when one loves them and believes them to

* Justus Möser, native and historian of Osnabrück, was a consistent critic of rationalism and the Enlightenment. He based an intensely conservative social philosophy on particularism, traditionalism and historic rights.

be, in the realm of speculative thought, the most enlightened defenders of human dignity. Assiduous in flattery and
anxious to submit to authority, they give harsh emphasis to
their words to hide the flexibility of their feelings, and make
use of philosophical ratiocination to explain the least philosophical thing imaginable—respect for force, and with it the
susceptibility to fear which changes this respect into admiration.'[37]

Nevertheless the Germans seemed to be moved by the
spirit of the age and moved profoundly. 'I can see', wrote
Mirabeau to his friend Mauvillon, 'that ideas are stirring in
your Germany, and I know that if the spark reaches com-
bustible materials there will be a real conflagration, not a
straw fire as with us. . . . The explosion will occur less
quickly than in a nation which is so dramatic and volatile,
and which inside a quarter of an hour can display both the
heroism of liberty and the idolatry of servitude.'[38] But this
agitation, the force of which Mirabeau foresaw without properly discerning its character, tended rather to estrange the
Germans from the French than to bring them together. The
great new drive of the eighteenth century was towards freedom. The French, already at an advanced stage in their history, and having, so to speak, attained a ripe age in their
social life, constituted a well-knit nation. They had a language and a literature and all the framework of a state; freedom for them meant freedom of thought, freedom of conscience, freedom of the person, freedom of property, and
above all political freedom through a revolution in the civil
laws of the nation and a revolution in the constitution of the
state. In Germany the nation's growth had been interrupted;
its people were dispersed, cut off from one another, with no
ties but vague memories; freedom for them meant the reawakening of national consciousness. Before asking whether
one should be free or what guarantees of liberty there should

[37] *De l'Allemagne*, part 3, ch. XI: *De l'influence de la nouvelle
philosophie sur le caractère allemand.*

[38] 3 December 1789. *Lettres à un ami d'Allemagne*, p. 489.

be, they had to exist as a nation, to be aware of living, meeting, talking, understanding one another.

The first thing was to think for themselves and to speak their own language, to disentangle and sort out the primary organs of national life. The first yoke to throw off was not that of the laws, even of the civil laws, but that of the pedagogues. And so the most decisive effect in Germany of the propagation of French ideas was to lead the Germans to free themselves from French influence in literature, philosophy and the arts. The whole history of German society at the end of the eighteenth century can be summed up in this proposition, which is only superficially a paradox—the more Germany came under the influence of French thought the more deeply she became separated from France.

Since for the Germans the Revolution consisted in becoming a nation, that is to say in living for themselves, all the passions which the French brought to the overthrow of the old social edifice were first turned by the Germans against the classical culture—the French culture. This was the foreign invasion that had first to be repelled. The Germans threw themselves fiercely into the assault on the positions the French had so long occupied. They began to speak and write in German. French remained the language of the aristocracy; after a few years it was only the language of the salons, of the reaction and the ancien régime. All who felt young, ardent, enthusiastic, all who found pride in patriotism, all who were exalted by grand ideas of liberty, humanity, virtue, in short all who corresponded to the party of the Revolution in France, all who had drunk of the same stream and felt the same stirring breezes, would henceforth speak German—and so escape the influence of France.

It was France however that opened the gates for them and showed them the way, incited them to break the old moulds, to tread conventions underfoot, and draw inspiration from Nature, source of all beauty, all virtue, and all justice. But to the German Nature meant the country where he was born, the language he had lisped as a baby, the race from

which he had sprung; it was himself, with all that was most
spontaneous in his impressions, his feelings, his passions. He
began to admire his native skies; the very rudeness of his
tongue, little refined as it was, charmed his ear; he renewed
his genius, desiccated by the arid platitudes of classical imitation, from the eternal springs of poetry—personal emotion
and popular song. These influences combined to develop
among the Germans an entirely different character from that
of the contemporary Frenchman. They knew this and they
gloried in it. Everyone worked to promote it—the most de-
terminedly anti-French, like Herder; the most enthusiastic
for French liberty, like Schiller; the most independent of
mind and most free from prejudice, like Goethe. A Lessing,
priding himself on his cosmopolitanism and regarding patriotism as a fetter on the soul, did more than anyone to reawaken
in his fellow-citizens the notion of the fatherland by his ardour in fighting foreign domination in literature and art.

'What German poetry lacked', said Goethe, 'was a basis,
and a national basis.'[39] What the German nation lacked was
a common basis of thought and poetry. Literature and the
nation arose together. However subordinate and equivocal
its political condition, Germany could, as 1789 drew near,
apply the famous Cartesian proposition and declare to Europe—somewhat disconcerted by this entry on the stage— 'I
speak, therefore I am!' It was in these troubled times that
the German genius achieved its most magnificent flights.[40]
To ignore the strength of this movement and think still in
terms of Voltaire and classical tragedy is to fail to understand
what followed or to explain the welcome given to the French
Revolution in Germany.

In this state of effervescence the first explosion of the Rev-

[39] *Mémoires*, part 2, bk. VII.

[40] Goethe produced *Goetz* in 1773, *Werther* and *Clavigo* in
1774; *Tasso, Egmont, Iphigenia* from 1786 to 1788; Schiller
Fiesco in 1785, *Kabale und Liebe* in 1785, *Don Carlos* in 1787;
Lessing published his *Dramaturgie* in 1767 and 1768, his *Emilia
Galotti* in 1772 and *Nathan* in 1779.

olution was bound to have deep repercussions. As soon as
they heard the generous appeal addressed by France to all
the nations the Germans rose with enthusiasm. The fine example she gave to men at the same time as she proclaimed
their rights, the exalting of the people, whom she declared
sovereign, and the patriotism which she acclaimed as the
highest of virtues, responded so well to the aspirations of
the Germans that they could not fail to be profoundly
moved. But the passion that aroused them was wholly German, and they translated into their own tongue, newly tempered and invigorated, the rousing words which the French
were casting to the four winds of Europe. It seemed to them
that the first of the rights of man was, for them, the right to
be German, and that patriotism par excellence was that which
consisted in loving their own country. They searched for
their fatherland, for their rights and titles; and as in recent
centuries these titles had been mislaid, and the rights misunderstood or obscured, they went back into the past, feeling
their way through the shadows, to pursue even into the
Middle Ages the phantom of Germany. As with the freeing
of thought and the return to Nature, so it was with the rights
of man and patriotism—the propagation of French ideas restored to the Germans the feeling for their language, the
spirit of their poetry, the cult of their history, respect for
themselves—in short, it brought them back in every way to
their traditions. The Revolution, which in France meant
breaking with the past and even erecting scorn for the past
into a principle, meant for the Germans renewing the ties
that had been broken for centuries and re-establishing the
cult of their ancestors.

The French demolished their bastilles and burned their
charters; the Germans restored their castles and built up their
archives. The Revolution, entirely classical in France, was
from the first romantic in Germany. This was because the
French maintained, in a different form, the most brilliant
tradition of their history—the intellectual conquest of the
world. Never had they displayed their national character

more splendidly than on the day when they undertook this astonishing crusade and launched into this prodigious *chanson de geste*. The Germans, on the other hand, in some sense lacking a fatherland for several centuries, had become like colonists in their own country, and were obliged, in order to rediscover themselves, to return to the past. The summons to a national revolution was not a call to clear away the débris of the Middle Ages; it involved them, above and before all else, in a break with the French seventeenth and eighteenth centuries.

Far from founding in Germany a cosmopolitan society, docile under French supremacy, the principles of the Revolution aroused in Germany a nation at first turbulent, then hostile, and finally, when it felt sufficiently emancipated and self-confident, rebellious. Realised in this way, the splendid French ideas were narrowed and deformed. But they could only spread in Germany by being quickened and so becoming German. They were in a way acclimatised, and, sown in this foreign soil, the seeds became remarkably fecund. But when after some years the French came to reap the harvest and gather in the fruits, they ran into brambles and thorn-bushes, into impenetrable thickets bristling with tangled branches; the field they had tilled was forbidden ground to them and they no longer recognised the trees they had planted.

4. THE GERMANS AND THE REVOLUTION

These peculiar consequences of the Revolution in Germany assumed different aspects according to the region. The Empire included populations very diverse in origins and traditions, further diversified because of their governments. The general conditions having been considered, it is necessary to look further to discover how the same cause could produce, in different regions, such opposite effects.

First one finds a region isolated from the rest of the Empire which during the course of the Revolution follows a special destiny—the country on the left bank of the Rhine. The territories were divided among heterogeneous sovereignties. Ignoring small lordships, there were the possessions of the Palatine branch of the house of Bavaria and of the Deux-Ponts branch, those which Prussia had acquired through the Jülich-Cleves successions, and then the ecclesiastical states of Speyer, Worms, Mainz, Trier, Cologne, Liége, with the imperial cities enclosed by them—Cologne, Aachen, Worms, Speyer. The populations that were divided among these principalities themselves present rather sharp contrasts.

In the lower Rhineland, around Bonn, Cologne, Jülich, Mörs, Cleves, where the land is flat, the peasant raised crops; he was industrious, thrifty, submissive, indifferent to politics. Towards the upper Rhine the picture changes. The country becomes picturesque; the vine was cultivated, and the inhabitants were of a gay, restless, lively and carefree disposition, more versatile and excitable and more likely to be aroused by political passions. The people of the lower Rhine accepted the Revolution, those of the upper acclaimed it. These regions had long been open to French influence. The governments looked to France for protection, the nobles for a career, the thinkers for guidance. A group had come into being, especially at Mainz, eager for liberty and drawn to new ideas, men like Forster and all the future leaders of the Rhenish Republic. They were recruited mainly from the professors, lawyers, journalists and booksellers; this was in fact the embryo of a third estate after the French fashion, and consequently the kernel of a French party.

These populations had few connections with the rest of Germany. The Revolution, which they were to adopt with enthusiasm, would separate them from it altogether. Their ideal would be to set up little autonomous republics like the Swiss cantons. But if they had to choose, they would prefer the domination of France, under which their ideas would prevail, to that of a German prince, who would stifle them.

Though hardly abreast of the new principles, the rural population was quite alive to their results. The condition of the peasantry in these territories was much like that of the French. They were proprietors, and had enough civil liberties to want more. The feudal system was sufficiently relaxed for them to conceive the idea of freeing themselves from it altogether. The French Revolution would be understood and welcomed as in France itself. Both ideas and interests would attract them to France, and it would be the easier to annex them because their links with Germany were weak and uncertain.

Most of them indeed had no historical traditions, no dynasty even which could take the place of a country. The only reigning family of ancient foundation was the Palatine house; but it was in its states that French influence was most pronounced and the attraction of France most keenly felt. Moreover, in the Palatinate government was worse than mediocre. That of Deux-Ponts was detestable and was detested. The inhabitants of Cleves scarcely knew the name of their Prussian sovereign; they had changed masters so often that it was all one to them whether they changed again. The feelings of most of the inhabitants of the left bank—those governed by the ecclesiastical princes—can be explained in a similar way.

The ecclesiastical princes were elective, brought in by varied political combinations from all parts of Germany. There was consequently no bond between them and their subjects, who would receive succeeding rulers as passively as they had received these. Bishops, commissioners, administrators, prefects—it mattered little to them; all were strangers, and they were used to seeing them arrive, pass and depart; drilled to obedience, they would continue to obey. They expected moreover to be 'secularised', that is, annexed to a lay state. They did not know the name of the master for whom they were destined; it might be the King of Prussia, whom they did not know, the Emperor, whom they had never seen, or the King of England, whose existence they may not even have suspected. The French master would be neither more familiar nor more foreign to them than the Prussian, Saxon, Austrian or Guelf. They would judge the government by its deeds; the authority that bettered their lot and treated them most favourably would have their sympathies.

They were not oppressed. The bishops half-heartedly exploited their lands, but did not really govern. The neutral part they played in politics freed them from the most pressing cares of a ruler—the defence of the state and consequently the good management of its finances and resources. Their only thought was to enjoy a quiet life in these royal and opulent prebends. 'Freed from all the duties, one might almost say from all the attributes, of an adult monarchy, they languished in a prolonged childhood.'[41] Those who in these last days attempted reforms, like Frederick Charles Joseph d'Erthal, at Mainz, called in reformers and tried to govern in an enlightened fashion, only increased the appetite for change and prepared the way for the Revolution.

As for the imperial cities, they were entirely senile and decrepit. Government was ineffective, the oligarchies discredited, the populace unruly, the bourgeoisie paralysed by its divisions. Neither the elements of independent existence nor those of resistance to conquest were present. They were altogether ripe for annexation, and what scattered elements of democracy there were could only facilitate French domination. France would, then, find it easy to establish herself on the left bank of the Rhine; it was not there that national passions would be aroused or that the impact of the French Revolution would bring such strange reactions. To find the scene of these surprising transformations one must proceed into German Germany, and cross to the right bank of the Rhine.

Several states on the left bank—the Bavarian Palatinate, Trier and especially Mainz—extended also to the right bank. There were other ecclesiastical states scattered more or less

[41] De Broglie, *Marie-Thérèse*, vol. I, ch. III.

everywhere, and a whole patchwork of counts, barons and knights in Westphalia, Franconia, Swabia. At first sight it seems that political conditions would be the same as on the other side of the river. The fragmentation of territories was even more marked. But if the ecclesiastical governments had a similar character, the populations were very different. No centre of agitation can be found here like that which formed around the professors of Mainz, nor any revolutionary elements like those represented by the restless peoples of the upper Rhineland. There was not even the apathy of the inhabitants of the lower Rhine; it was something more depressing—'the heavy slumber, the brutish repose' of which Heinrich Heine speaks.[42]

They were at the same time more fundamentally German, further away from France, less accessible to her influence and far less advanced in civilisation. The serfdom which had tended to disappear on the left bank survived on the right. The feudal system there remained oppressive: the peasant could not conceive the possibility of escape from it. Caring little for their masters or totally indifferent to them, these Germans would change them as easily as their compatriots on the other bank; but while just as submissive to conquest they would be much more resistant to assimilation; the French, even while setting them free, would still be foreigners and enemies to them. Given time, peace and good government, France could convert the people of the left bank into French citizens, but on the right bank she could only make Germans, the more hostile as they felt more free. To give them the idea of possible reform was only to suggest to them also the idea of working through and for Germany.

It was there, in the country of Nassau, that the famous German reformer Baron Frederick Charles Freiherr vom Stein was born—his country's greatest statesman, and one of the most noble and far-seeing geniuses who ever devoted himself to the management of men. He belonged to one of

[42] *De l'Allemagne*, part 3.

those rare families of barons of the Empire who preserved in their feudal ways their primary raison d'être, and legitimised their overlordship, like their medieval ancestors, by the services they rendered, progressively emancipating and raising to full human dignity those subjects whom their forefathers had once protected against misery, calamity and brigandage. Stein derived from the traditions of his family that instinct for the traditions of Germany which enabled him to guide his country in her hour of crisis. He was the principal agent of that grand metamorphosis whereby, out of a cosmopolitan revolution and the most remarkable partitions that any empire has ever suffered, there emerged a nation passionate for unity. He became in consequence the most formidable of France's enemies on the Continent, turning against her the weapons she had forged, and destroying her through the very benefits she had wrought. It was he who was to suggest to the German rulers the plan, so profound and yet so simple, of themselves accomplishing, to the advantage of their dynasties, what the Revolution had achieved against them and for the profit of France—the abolition of the feudal system; of robbing the Revolution of all motive by forestalling it with reforms better suited to the ways of the country; and of exalting the sentiments of their subjects by presenting themselves as the most ardent prophets of the patriotism which the French aroused by their propaganda only to crush it immediately by their conquests.

In regions where, as in France, the traditions of the Middle Ages were broken, the Revolution became radical—this was the case on the left bank of the Rhine. Where the old traditions survived or could be adapted to the new spirit, there was not revolution but reform.

The reforms were moreover congenial to the spirit and outlook of most of the governments. They saw how much the state might gain by identifying itself with what was really practical and politic in French principles. The populace who first asked their rulers to protect them from conquest next asked for the benefits which conquest would have brought with it, and finally asked that they be delivered from this conquest and the foreigners driven out. Germany was used to expecting and receiving everything from the rulers; she expected from them even freedom, and so the Revolution had the strange result of strengthening the attachment of the peoples to their dynasties. This was evident in Bavaria and Wurtemberg, in the states of Saxony, Brunswick and Hesse-Darmstadt. In the other countries of the right bank of the Rhine where the conquest operated directly and where France carved out either departments or vassal principalities, as in Westphalia, the peoples were led, through the very action of the French government, to long for freedom from French domination. Having seen its advantages, they wanted to preserve them under the rule of national princes.

The greed of the princes contributed just as much to this revolution as the patriotism of their peoples; it was activated no less by the scheming of French politicians than by the propaganda of the revolutionaries. By simplifying the map of Germany as she did from 1795 to 1803 France removed the material obstacles to a reunion of the German peoples. Through 'secularisations' and 'mediatisations' she seized from the ecclesiastical governments and the lesser nobility, who had isolated and held them in a kind of reciprocal exile, populations which, when poured into the lay states, instantly became merged in them. France gathered and concentrated the peoples of Germany, thus opening avenues to the national spirit which she fomented by her propaganda. In 1806 the Holy Roman Empire was abolished, but Germany was reborn. The bond between the states that was then destroyed had long been worn out, but the ties formed between the peoples were indestructible. Through the dissolution of the Empire, which was only the phantom of a state, the Germans were united, to become the most redoubtable of nations. It was the dispersion of these peoples that had rendered the destruction of the Empire so easy; by bringing them together, the way was prepared for its re-establishment.

VI. *Austria*

If the words 'the house of Austria' awakened in men's minds
in 1789 the idea of an empire on which the sun never set,
this was no more than a trick of memory, a historical phantasmagoria. The house of Austria held, it is true, the imperial
dignity, but it was no more than a dignity, and the fame
Austria derived from it was entirely due to her own power.
On the map the Austrian Empire appeared as a great but
strangely dislocated body, a colossus indeed, but a colossus
maimed and broken, its members scattered over the surface
of Europe, the bizarre fragments of a creature which had
neither skeleton, skull, nor entrails. It had not even a name.
It became customary in the chancelleries, first gradually and
then generally, to call this mass of possessions by the name
of the ruling house—Austria. In international law and in
pure theory the state remained nameless; it was described as
the hereditary states of the house of Austria. The sovereign
was entitled *King of Bohemia and Hungary*; if chosen by
the Electoral College he became Emperor; but the title died
with him, and his successor could only use it by virtue of a
new election.

These hereditary states of the house of Austria were in
fact merely an agglomeration of territories. To the south-east
was Hungary with its dependencies—Croatia, Slovenia, Transylvania, Bukovina; to the north, Galicia, recently taken from
Poland, and Bohemia with the fragment of Silesia that remained Austrian; next, connecting the Hungarian to the
Bohemian group, Moravia and the archduchy of Austria, and
to the south Styria, Carniola, Carinthia, and the Tyrol. The
Milanese was separated from these territories by the Valtelline

on one side and the lands of Venice on the other. There were also some towns and lordships scattered over Swabia, and finally, isolated from the rest and as it were stranded on the French frontier, the Netherlands (or Belgium) and the Grand Duchy of Luxemburg, themselves divided by the Bishopric of Liége. Altogether there were 140,000 square kilometres with about 24 million inhabitants. These were roughly of the same proportions as France; but whereas in France the nation was homogeneous and the state closely knit, in Austria everything was complicated and dispersed.

The empire was all extremities and no centre. To defend this enormous length of frontier required a considerable army, which absorbed most of the revenue in peace time and could not be concentrated in wartime. If it was directed against Germany, the Turks at once threatened the frontiers of Hungary, and the semi-barbarous peoples on the fringes of the empire, feeling the rein slacken, gave vent to their natural insubordination and turbulence. In 1778 war was imminent against Frederick over Bavaria, which the Austrians wanted to acquire. They only had Prussia to fight, and launched against her the whole resources of the monarchy, which tottered with the effort. 'All our forces, apart from the Netherlands regiments, will be mustered, and everything, so to speak, staked on one card', wrote Joseph II. Only with difficulty did they get together an army of 170,000 men, and then only half could be put into the field. 'You speak of war to the limit', said Maria Theresa. 'I do not see how it is possible; we shall be outnumbered by 30 to 40,000 men.' What would happen if Austria had to face a coalition, and the Turks joined in? 'Look then to our frontiers!'[1]

Still worse, money was lacking. In the great European crises Austria supplied men, her allies supplied money. During the Seven Years War she had 75 million livres from

[1] Arneth, *Correspondenz von Maria Theresia und Joseph II*, April-July 1778. In Galicia there only remained seven battalions of men unfit for service and 200 horses.

France. During the Revolutionary Wars England would pay. The consequence was that, failing a Louis XV—who was so blind as to follow Austria's lead—Austria could not make war at will. If she tried to undertake it with her own resources she would not be able to carry on for long. To concentrate the state's resources and escape from this need for alliance was the problem that constantly obsessed the minds of the Austrians. Joseph II wore himself out and nearly lost his empire in the attempt.

The essential element, the vital organ, was lacking. The building was fundamentally unsound, resting on shifting soil and adrift from its foundations. There was no Austrian nation and no means of making one. The Habsburgs could imitate neither the work of the Capetians in France nor that of the Hohenzollerns in Prussia. Either nation and state must be formed together as in France, or the nation must be formed by the state as in Prussia. Austria could adopt neither of these methods. With whole nations like the Hungarians, Czechs and Belgians, who had their own traditions and special interests, the Habsburgs had brought together in their inheritance fragments detached from a nation, like the Poles in Galicia, who made loyalty to their origins a point of honour. It was equally impossible to fuse these diverse populations into a homogeneous whole or to govern them together. Any attempt to subject them to the same laws and to centralise, after the French manner, produced resentment and rebellion. If on the other hand they were offered a measure of self-government and grouped into a federation, they were still too close to the days of their independence not to wish to regain it, and the liberty they were granted only served to detach them from the monarchy. Whatever was done, and however slightly one of the pieces of this curious erection was moved, there was a fear lest, in Montesquieu's vigorous phrase, all the pieces of the monarchy should come crashing down together.[2]

[2] *Esprit des lois*, liv. VIII, ch. IX.

When to this tangled structure is added the German Empire with its inextricably complicated wheels within wheels, one has some idea of the obstacles, to some extent constitutional, which continually hampered this apparently formidable power. Beyond its own boundaries the Austrian government seemed ubiquitous and ever-present; cosmopolitan by nature, it was like a foreign power in its own territories, and its internal affairs had to be conducted like the foreign affairs of a centralised state. It was not in strict parlance a state, for it had no institutions; it was not even a government, but an administrative diplomacy. Austria could only govern her provinces with an eye on Europe, and treat with Europe with an eye on her provinces. She had only one means of holding them together—that by which Europe itself was held together, the balancing of opposing forces. Michelet's description of Germany could be applied in fact to this empire—a little Europe within the great. There was an Austrian balance as there was a European, but as in the Austrian states there was a sovereign with armed force at his disposal the balance there became a fact, and took the place of a constitution.

The consequences were the same as in 'the European republic'. The Austrian monarchy had to adopt for itself the rules of conduct which, in their perpetual rivalry and constant opposition of interests, the powers of Europe observed in their dealings with each other. That is to say, the constitutional law of Austria was made up of contradictions. Because of its origins it should have been the power par excellence to preserve established law and custom and good political habits, for Austria was founded on nothing but contracts and laws of inheritance. In France the constitution could be overturned and the sovereignty of the nation substituted for that of the King without shaking the state to its foundations, but in the case of the Austrian monarchy nothing would be left. Apart from titles in legal documents there existed no justification for its claims, since it was not upheld by the peoples of its empire. Every alteration of the law on which its sovereignty rested compromised the existence of the state.

An appeal to the nations which composed it was equivalent to a declaration of bankruptcy. In France, the popular revolution was to make federalism a crime against the nation; in Austria any revolution, to be national and popular, must necessarily be federalist.

Besides, Austria was the most dynastic power in Europe; she remained nothing but a ruling family, and the laws of succession were in fact the fundamental laws of the state; consequently no court should have been more firmly attached to the defence and maintenance of dynastic law. But because of the strange structure of Austria she could never increase her power without weakening its foundations. To unite the scattered fragments of the monarchy, to defend it and rationalise its indented frontiers, territories had to be annexed. They were needed also to endow the younger sons of the royal family. And they were needed to avoid being robbed or reduced by greedy neighbours. If rival states annexed territory Austria had to do likewise; if not she would lose her relative superiority, and, what was worse, allow herself to be hemmed in. These motives induced her, if not always to commit usurpation directly and on her own account, at least to tolerate the usurpations of others so as to join in them—in short, to accept, with good or bad grace, the system of partitions, and to participate in them if not to provoke them.

So she came to negotiate the partition of Poland; to contemplate at the same time a partition of Turkey; to seize Bukovina from the Turks, her allies, in 1775, having taken Galicia from the Poles, her friends, in 1772; and, with the aim of annexing Bavaria in 1778, to offer Frederick as a bait Lusatia, which belonged to the Elector of Saxony.

Maria Theresa, however, was at that time still living, and never had a ruler had to suffer so much from the weakness of international law and the immorality of political behaviour in Europe. She showed herself deeply affected by this conflict of interests and principles and by the tragic yet subtle struggles which took place in her conscience—from which

principles always came out the losers—and finally by this
particular fall from grace, which concluded with the most
flagrant injustice a reign which had begun with the defence
of right. No one was so intent on virtue or manifested such
horror of sin. Yet she sinned, and quite deliberately, but
with so many sighs and scruples, so much anguish before
the deed and so much remorse afterwards! Remorse became
for her a kind of indulgence which took the place of con-
trition. She thus allowed herself, continually giving way, to
proceed by insensible degrees from equivocal suggestions to
iniquitous acts, and finally arrived at the strange conclusion
that the abundance of the gains covered the wickedness of
the proceedings. Her ingenious dialectic led her to find in
the deed of sin itself the 'satisfaction' which should have
come from atoning for it, and, twisting a famous passage of
Scripture from its sense in politics—as it had been too often
twisted from its meaning in ethics—cheerfully imagined that
much would be forgiven to him who had greatly usurped. In
her were combined a casuist and a marvellous actress. But
public opinion was not deceived, and accusations of duplicity,
suspicions of trickery, charges of insatiable greed, were
heaped upon the court of Vienna. The Empress complained,
groaned, protested, and confessed that really public opinion
was right. She beat her breast, poured out her plaints and
'jeremiads'—and continued on the same course. 'One wants',
she wrote on a day of sincere repentance, 'to act like a Prussian, and at the same time keep the appearance of honesty!'

At the end of the eighteenth century this was all that was
left of Austria's political morality, and never did prince so
completely personify the spirit of his house as this great empress. Her character was to reappear, without the great qualities of statesmanship of which Maria Theresa's genius was
comprised, in her grandson Francis. Joseph II, who was
reigning at the beginning of the Revolution, added to it a
touch of cynicism à la Frederick. But with less hypocrisy in
the manner and more violence in the execution he in fact
pursued, and carried to new lengths, the work of his prede-

cessors. Most of his enterprises had been begun in the lifetime of Maria Theresa and were carried out under the direction of the minister who prided himself on preserving all
the traditions of that classic reign, Prince Kaunitz.

2. POLITICAL DESIGNS

These enterprises, like those that followed, were no more
than the realisation of schemes long entertained at the court
of Vienna. They can be found formulated and defined with
remarkable foresight in a very curious work of the end of the
seventeenth century, the *Testament of Duke Charles of Lorraine*.[3] The first objective, according to this, is Germany and
the Empire. To gain control of it the first thing is, under
pretext of seeking conquest and glory, to exhaust the strength
of all the German princes, reducing them to the rôle of
provincial governors, as the house of Bourbon had so wisely
done in France. Germany having been thus enfeebled by its
own efforts, the house of Austria was to employ Swiss, Italians, and Hungarians, who detest the Germans, to dominate
the Empire, and 'reduce it by conquest to subjection to the
monarchy—an end which can always be achieved more
quickly and surely by naked force than by political manœuvre.' When Germany has been overcome in this way,
'rights of conquest must only be given up on condition that
the Germanic body will bestow an hereditary title on the
reigning family and give complete submission to its orders,
without any further representation of states at Ratisbon'.
Vienna was to be the head of the Empire, and 'from it will

[3] 'Political Testament of Charles, Duke of Lorraine and Bar,
deposited in the hands of the Emperor Leopold at Pressburg on
29 November 1687, in favour of the King of Hungary and his
successors in the Empire.' Leipzig, 1696. Extracts from a manuscript in *Affaires étrangères*: d'Haussonville, *Histoire de la réunion de la Lorraine à la France*, 1857, t. iii, p. 372 ff. On the
authenticity of this testament, see the study by du Hamel, *Revue
historique*, t. xlviii, p. 252; t. xlix, p. 1 ff.

issue only despotic and absolute decrees'. This would be the time to exert the formidable power of the reunited Germans abroad and to undertake conquests. Power must be firmly established in Sicily, Naples and the Milanese. The mainland territory of Venice should be seized, this being required to connect the new conquests to the heart of the Empire. The rulers of Italy having been brought under the yoke like those of Germany, and given the rôle of mere governors, then, to crown the achievement, 'the Pope must be reduced by the threat of force to lordship over the city of Rome alone, whether he likes it or not'. The Pope would not cease to protest, and if necessary hurl the Church's thunderbolts; but care would be taken 'to engage the services of learned doctors who will teach the people through sermon and text the futility and falsity of excommunications when the issue is that of the temporal power, which Jesus Christ had never intended the Church to have'.

The author of the Testament took long views, but did not look as far as Turkey, for the Turks at that time were too strong for anyone to start disposing of their property. But after the Treaty of Carlowitz in 1699, the house of Austria, having driven the Turks from its own domains, was planning to invade their territories. This was according to the advice Prince Eugene of Savoy gave to Charles VI.[4] Once such ideas entered the heads of the Austrians they were not forgotten; their corollary was the partition of Poland.

If the political traditions of the house of Austria are compared with those which Henry IV and Richelieu had bequeathed to the house of Bourbon it will be seen that there was an almost complete contradiction between the aims of the two states. That France should be brought to subordinate her own plans to those of Austria and to sacrifice her age-old interests to those of her rival seemed to the diplomats of Vienna too good to be true. Yet this was the good fortune

[4] See *Recueil des Instructions, Autriche*, t. I, p. 168. Instructions of the comte de Luc, 1715.

of Maria Theresa. No wonder her Chancellor, Kaunitz, rated as his masterpiece of policy this 'Austrian system', which all enlightened Frenchmen thought fatal to their country.[5] Antagonism broke out again as soon as France, under the direction of Louis XVI and Vergennes, recovered her independence, resumed the defence of her interests and sought to recover her proper place in Europe.

From that time Austria experienced nothing but setbacks, and in each of these she saw the hand of France. Joseph II could not resign himself to this situation. As soon as he was master he turned to Russia.[6] His ambitions agreed with those of Catherine, and they became allies in 1781. The aims of Austria in making this alliance determined her whole policy during the Revolution.

The central idea was always the mastery of Germany. From this it followed that Prussia remained an adversary and irreconcilable rival. If Austria wanted to expand in Germany, Prussia barred the way; if she wanted to expand in Turkey, Prussia threatened her rear; if she wanted to expand in Poland, Prussia demanded a partition. The annihilation, or at least the dismemberment, of Prussia was the essential condition for the success of Austria's plans. It was the thought always uppermost in her mind, and the factor by which everything was judged. Friendship between these two powers could only be hypocritical, troubled and transitory. At bottom, as Kaunitz summed it up, there could be no 'sincere association or common accord on interests which are and always will be opposed, until one of the two powers contrives to subordinate the other'.[7] As long as Prussia was not *extra statum nocendi*,* Austria would never, in Kaunitz's

[5] See in Arneth, vol. VIII, p. 6 the Memoir of 14 November 1764.

[6] Maria Theresa died on 29 November 1780. Joseph had been Holy Roman Emperor and co-regent of the Austrian monarchy from 1765.

[7] Ranke, *Die deutschen Mächte*, vol. II, p. 307. *Réflexions de Kaunitz*, December 1786.

* in a situation to do no mischief.

belief, have a free hand in the east.[8] 'I am on the look-out,' wrote Joseph to his brother Leopold in 1783, 'and at the first opportunity I shall try to swallow him before he knows what is happening.'[9]

Until he could recover Silesia from Prussia Joseph occupied himself with rounding off his territories in Germany. He returned to his favourite plan—the acquisition of Bavaria. Giving up the idea of conquest, he sought to exchange the Netherlands for it. This swap, as it was called, would relieve Austria of a distant possession, difficult to defend and always exposed to French attacks, and provide her with a thoroughly German country whereby she would reach into the heart of Germany and link her German states with her possessions in Italy. Though she failed in 1785 in face of the resistance of Prussia and the ill-will of France, Austria did not abandon this scheme; she pursued it through all the complications of her policy during the Revolution, and the resulting disquiet of the Germans had a considerable influence on her relations with France.

'I believe', wrote the French ambassador in Vienna in 1778, 'that if the Emperor gives rein to his ambitions in Italy, his first objective will be the possession of Venice. Anything he thinks easy he will also think just.'[10] Italy seemed ripe for his domination: an Austrian archduke reigned in Florence,[11] while another awaited the succession to Modena;[12] the Bourbon in Parma, married to an Austrian archduchess,[13] was thought to be under his wife's thumb, and the Bourbon

[8] Martens, *Traités de l'Autriche*, vol. II, pp. 135, 188. Extract from a despatch of 28 November 1788.

[9] Arneth, *Joseph II und Leopold*, 10 August 1783.

[10] Breteuil to Vergennes, July 1778. See Fournier, *Gentz und Cobenzl*.

[11] Leopold, brother of Joseph II, born in 1747, Emperor in 1790.

[12] Ferdinand, brother of Joseph II, born in 1754, husband of Maria-Beatrice of Este, heiress of Modena.

[13] Ferdinand, Duke of Parma, married in 1769 to Marie-Amélie, sister of Joseph II, born in 1746.

of Naples to be quite subservient to his Austrian queen.[14] The dismemberment of the Venetian republic would make the picture complete. Venice was one of the portions Joseph had reserved to himself in the partition plans he had prepared with Catherine II. 'The mainland possessions, with Venetian Istria and Dalmatia', he wrote, 'provide the only means of profiting by the export of the products of my states.' The Venetian lands would moreover link up with those that Joseph proposed to acquire at the expense of the Turks.[15] He was reckoning to demand from the latter a rectification of frontiers which would include Galicia and Bukovina, and also the cession of Wallachia up to the River Oltet, Vidin, Orsova, and Belgrade, with a zone of three leagues on the left bank of the Danube; from Belgrade a line was to be drawn 'as straight and short as possible, following the terrain towards the Adriatic, and including the Gulf of Drina'— which would give Austria Bosnia, Herzegovina and Monte-negro, with a slice of Serbia.[16]

As for Poland, it would seem that it was very much in the Austrians' interest to keep it as a buffer between themselves and Russia, and every consideration seemed to be in favour of protecting it from Prussia. Unfortunately the court of Vienna feared that if it was reformed the Republic of Poland might be dangerous, and thought it best to leave that country open to partition when need should arise. It was judged expedient to maintain in Poland a state of anarchy, so that there should always be the opportunity of lopping off further provinces.

All these plans estranged Austria from France, yet their successful execution required that France should remain

[14] Ferdinand, married in 1768 to Marie-Caroline, sister of Joseph II, born in 1752.

[15] See Arneth, *Joseph II und Catharina*: letter of Joseph II to Catherine, 13 November 1782. *Cf.* Arneth, *Joseph II und Leopold*: letters of Joseph, 24 November 1782; of Leopold, 16 December 1782.

[16] The Treaty of Berlin, 13 July 1878, assigned Bosnia and Herzegovina to Austria.

neutral. Austria needed particularly to keep her hold on
Russia, and she knew from experience that she would lose
it as soon as Russia felt herself to be indispensable. 'If she
found a way to make me break my links with France,' wrote
Joseph II, 'she would see that I was absolutely at her disposal, which would be very useful for her, but far from suit-
ing me; so it must not be.'[17] Thus he maintained the alliance
of 1756, but while submitting to it he detested it. At bottom
he envied and hated France. If bitter enemies of the 'Austrian
system' could be found at Versailles, implacable opponents
of the 'French system' abounded in Vienna.

The blind complaisance of France during the Seven Years
War had done little to soften these secular rancours. Austria
continued to think she had been sacrificed and was exasperated by the policy of Vergennes. Maria Theresa declared
herself strongly attached to the alliance; she loved France as
she loved Poland—because she had treated them so badly;
and her affection was the greater because of her scorn. Joseph
II and his brother Leopold felt the same contempt and with
it impatience. Their letters were full of recriminations against
France—'her deceitfulness, her wish to do them harm'; her
conduct was 'dreadful, contradictory, outrageous, and worthy
only of herself'. France only used 'the name of the alliance,
our relationship and friendship, to deceive us in an underhand way and to insult us with the more impunity'. Austria,
on the other hand, acted always with 'the utmost sincerity,
friendliness, trust and cordiality', which France had 'constantly abused in order to do as much harm as possible'.[18]
The brothers secretly harboured the intention of avenging
themselves on this ally who had previously been so weak as
to sacrifice her own interests for their benefit, and was now
committing the crime of defending them. 'If only', wrote

[17] To Leopold, 17 November 1782. See the letters of Catherine
to Joseph, Arneth, *Joseph II und Catharina*, pp. 198, 237, 247.

[18] Arneth, *Joseph II und Leopold*. See in particular: Joseph to
Leopold, 3 December 1784; Leopold to Joseph, 10 December
1784.

Joseph, 'we could have exchanged the Netherlands we should have been beyond reach of their claws, and perhaps one day we could make them feel sorry for it if they had a new war with the English.' 'But this is not the moment to show resentment. It must not be forgotten but kept well in mind, and we must act accordingly; but as long as we have need of her we must swallow our feelings and hide our true sentiments.'[19]

Thus disposed towards France, and contemplating an attack on the Turks to which France could oppose insurmountable obstacles, the Habsburgs were on the lookout for every sign of weakness that appeared in the French monarchy, and followed the progress of its internal troubles with a satisfaction they did not disguise. 'The French spirit of pride and liking for intrigue', wrote Joseph, 'can only be defeated by lack of means to carry out their ambitious plans. They can only come to grief through their own fault, and this they are in a fair way to do. If France has plenty of troubles on her hands and lacks money and resources, the King of Prussia alone will not dare to attempt anything and can be held in check by the two imperial courts. *We shall be able to do whatever we like*, and the Turks are lost.'[20] Here is the complete explanation of Austrian policy in respect of France during the early days of the Revolution.

In 1788 Joseph II judged the crisis at Versailles to be sufficiently serious for him to be able 'to do whatever he liked' in the east, and in concert with Catherine II he undertook the conquest of the Ottoman Empire. Thenceforth it was in his interests that France, though retaining the appearance of a state, should not recover her strength, vigour or activity. So the Revolution seemed to him singularly opportune. His policy and that of his brother Leopold, who succeeded him in 1790 and reigned till March 1792, may seem tortuous and complicated; it was in fact perfectly logical. Austria was following her tradition.

[19] To Leopold, 3 and 24 December 1784.
[20] To Leopold, 16 December 1782.

So long as the French Revolution paralysed the monarchy without destroying it, and did not threaten Europe with armed propaganda, Austria viewed it with indulgence; when it degenerated into anarchy, invaded the neighbouring states and appeared to be a menace to the Continent, Austria fought against it. But the *arrière-pensées* which had so retarded Austria's intervention trammelled it when it began. Austria had no wish to help in re-establishing a strong government in France; she intended that the restored monarchy should remain limited, weak and precarious. While seeking to restore the throne she meant to dismember the kingdom. At the very time when she appeared to be upholding the cause of the King of France she was busy reconquering the two provinces, doubly the patrimony of her dynasty, which she had been forced to cede to France and had never renounced— Alsace and Lorraine. Faithful to the tradition of centuries, she only saw in this great crisis an opportunity to pursue her plans of aggrandisement.

We shall see, and by reference to her past we shall understand, how Austria, deceived in her calculations and disconcerted by the French victories, speedily abandoned the policy of conservation to return to that of partitions; how she compensated herself for her losses at the expense of Poland, which had not attacked her, of Venice, which lay helpless at her feet, and of the German princes of the Church, whom she had a mandate to protect; how, losing the reputation for honesty she had gratuitously arrogated to herself—but which it was so much in her interest to deserve—she became the accomplice or the partner in insidious or violent enterprises which overturned all rights of possession deriving from the ancien régime in Europe; how, when she had tried to scheme against everyone and was schemed against by everyone, she became lost in the limitless plans she sought to pursue everywhere at once; how, having failed to beat France down she became her ally so as to await more safely the chance to betray her; how, to appease and placate the conqueror, she agreed to give up to the crowned head of the Revolution one of her archduchesses; how, defeated in every campaign from 1792 to 1809, at Jemappes, Lodi, Arcola, Marengo, Hohenlinden, Austerlitz, Wagram, she nevertheless managed, by dint of patience and suppleness, persistence and guile, to attain the position of arbiter in the greatest crisis modern Europe had known; how in the end she emerged more influential, more secure, and really more powerful than she had ever been, upsetting all the calculations of her enemies at the beginning of the nineteenth as she had done throughout the eighteenth century. It had been said that she was always one idea and one army behind. But she always had an idea and an army; this too was one of her traditions, and it was this one which allowed her to sustain the others.

3. RESOURCES

In 1740 it had seemed that the Austrian monarchy might collapse for lack of a head. In 1789 it was the head himself who put the monarchy in peril of dissolution. In his attempts to reform the state Joseph II had come up against the resistance both of the peoples and of the agents of the government. Trouble had broken out in several provinces; everywhere there were signs of restlessness. Joseph, deceived in all his hopes, was discouraged and confessed himself almost beaten. 'There is a complete lack of men,' he wrote one day to his brother, 'men of every sort, men to think out plans and to will their execution, and above all no one is inspired with zeal for the welfare of the country.'[21] This lamentation began with Maria Theresa and continued into the time of the great catastrophes of the monarchy, in the wars with France. The fact was that while the Empress had found a few capable ministers to deal with internal affairs, in general her subordinates were unequal to their task.

[21] To Leopold, 7 August 1782. Arneth, *Joseph II und Leopold von Toscana.*

In foreign affairs, the Empress conferred on important matters with her court and state Chancellor, Prince Kaunitz. Sixty-eight years of age in 1789, he had grown old with the century, and no one better represented the ancien régime in its decrepitude. Foppish in his person, conceited in his outlook and pretentious in his notions, he affected grand ideas and lofty principles. He excelled in deducing over-subtle sophisms from vacuous formulas, and would indulge in an occasional flight into the realms of pure reason. He combined, as is not unusual in diplomats, the pertness of a courtier with the pride of a pedant. Fundamentally cunning and sceptical—except of his own merits—well versed in all the political tricks, he was too self-sufficient, too narrow-minded, too frivolous, and really too worn out to understand or judge the new times. He could only think in syllogisms and deliver dissertations, a habit which declined with the years into mere drivel. The Revolution was a shock to his futile empiricism; but having known only the France of Louis XV, he thought he was dealing with a second Poland and acted accordingly.

This colossal mistake entailed disastrous consequences, and Kaunitz's successors were not the men to retrieve the situation.[22] Apart from Mercy, who died disoriented, deceived and discouraged in 1794, the court of Vienna not only had no one of genius to guide it in this crisis, but no one capable of clear vision, firm will, or consistent policy. Lacking counsellors, the house of Austria had to rely on its princes. When Joseph died, his rash and restless genius was in process of bringing all to ruin.[23] Joseph had no children; his brother Leopold, a man of subtle, steady and profound character, was capable of putting everything to rights. But Leopold passed from the scene at the moment when he seemed most needed,

[22] Kaunitz retired in 1792 and died in 1794.
[23] Joseph II died on 1 February 1790. Leopold of Tuscany succeeded him and died on 1 March 1792; his son and successor, Francis II, was then twenty-four.

leaving the succession to his son, who was young, inexperienced, without knowledge of affairs and almost without knowledge of himself. It required the ordeals of several years to bring out and develop the perseverance which was the chief quality of Francis II and his sole virtue as a statesman.

If perseverance was indeed enough to sustain the Austrian monarchy in face of the most formidable assaults, and if perseverance enabled it to await the change of fortune and the favouring circumstances from which the skill of Metternich was later to draw such great advantage, the monarchy must have possessed more consistency and endurance than it was commonly given credit for. What brought it into such jeopardy at the end of the ancien régime was precisely what saved it in the crisis of the Revolution. In intellectual development Austria was backward. Enlightenment was not admired; in fact it was feared. Up to 1764 men's minds were in the keeping of the Jesuits, and they were indifferently equipped for the task. They held sway in the schools, colleges and universities, and controlled the censorship. Teaching at every stage was puerile, formal, and slack; only the censorship was still rigidly maintained. An express command of the Empress was required to get *L'Esprit des lois* past the frontier. There was no scientific activity; philosophy was proscribed and literature stifled. The spirit of emancipation, passion and independence which animated Germany worried Maria Theresa and shocked her prudish mind. Besides, the land had been too carefully weeded by the Jesuits to lend itself to this disorderly kind of vegetation. In 1774 an attempt was made to found an academy in Vienna for the propagation of German literature, and it was even named after Lessing, but public opinion would have none of it. In those days of universal excitement Austria produced only musicians and it seemed interested in nothing but pleasure. This interest however was a lively one. The famous 'Commission of Chastity' set up by the Empress and the harsh examples she made at her court did not succeed in curbing the sensual frivolity that was displayed with such abandon in Vienna, transforming the capital into a veritable promised land of joyous intrigue and easy-going licence.

There was no corresponding intellectual licence, as in France, England and Germany. The Viennese brought no refinement to their diversions; they followed their fancies and made no pretence of putting the world to rights. They were amiable scatterbrains, and their profligacy had nothing deliberate about it. That is to say, it was all on the surface, entirely materialist. Their frivolity protected them from the contagion of philosophic doctrines more effectively than all the censorships in the world. Joseph II disturbed their peace with his reforms; they submitted to them only with a bad grace, and with a kind of fright. The French Revolution seemed to them an appalling event, and they strongly approved of their government's fighting against it. Most of them understood nothing about it but all detested it. Mirabeau, who had observed them when passing through in 1786, wrote of Joseph II: 'He is going against the nature of things, and so nothing succeeds with him.'[24] The same factors of resistance would, with stronger reason, put up insurmountable obstacles to the French Revolution. The force which elsewhere ensured its success—the popular will—was in the Austrian states opposed to it.

National feeling was entirely lacking in the patchwork monarchy, but in compensation for this there was no cause to fear a national revolution. Among these diverse peoples revolutionary propaganda only awakened the memory of their former independence, that is, of the traditions which set them against one another. Far from bringing them together, the idea of liberty divided them. For each of them this idea was involved with the aim of autonomy, but as none of them was strong enough to become free by its own efforts, as they were too widely separated by their origins and traditions to

[24] *Monarchie prussienne*, bk. VIII.

unite in a common effort, as none was in a position to defend
itself against the foreigners while all required protection,
even their mutual conflict rallied them to the imperial dynasty. The ruler had only to present himself to each country
as its national sovereign to win the hearts of the people. He
thus gained, in his task of keeping the whole together, from
the tendencies which drove each of the parts to separate
itself. An intelligent ruler—and Austria found one in Leopold
II—would associate himself with the liberal ideas that were
spreading among the nations of his empire in order thus to
strengthen his own power.

These peoples only thought of liberty in the forms consecrated by their history—they made much of their assemblies, liberties, charters. Provided they were granted these,
their traditions were revived, their institutions—which were
entirely aristocratic—were re-established, and far from the
ancien régime being abolished, it was renewed from its source
and in a sense regenerated. In these countries the spirit of
national independence and the spirit of political liberty naturally turned against the doctrines of the Revolution and
favoured any party whose interest it was to combat them.

That was why among the mass of the people, and among
the peasants in particular, these ideas of liberty met with
little response and aroused no enthusiasm. A system which
would strengthen the aristocracy and deliver government
largely into the hands of the nobles found no favour among
them; they much preferred the direct government of the
ruler. For the only reform in which they were interested—
the abolition or relaxation of the feudal system—they looked
to the state. They found themselves in the curious position
where the return of their country to political liberty would
leave them more remote than ever from civil liberty. So it was
that the civil reforms that were brought about by the government redounded to the profit of the state and the dynasty.

In place of a national spirit, which could not develop in
the lands of the monarchy, there was the dynastic spirit. 'All

the Austrian provinces are swarming with people', wrote Bielfeld. 'There they have an inexhaustible source of recruits.' These peoples were warlike and easily disciplined. For many of them war entailed no great change of habits. Trade was limited and industry little developed, so that war did not cause the profound disturbance in Austria that it did in England or France. The state was poor, the nobility rich; the nobles came to the help of the state in times of crisis because they knew that its fall would involve their own destruction. Austria was no more than an agglomeration of inherited lands; but because of her heterogeneous constitution she could suffer the loss of members with less damage than other states and effect additions with greater ease. All factors seemed to favour the monarchy. The dynasty was the sole bond between the peoples, but if it was broken in one place it could be renewed in another. The dynasty always survived, even if it had to shift its ground. Austria's life was like that of one of those primitive creatures that can be cut up without suffering harm and can reconstitute themselves from their own pieces, since they have no centre and no essential organ; their body in fact can never really be severed. The origins and names of the fragments of nations that composed this monarchy mattered little provided that the sum total and mass of the whole remained the same. Austria was the only power composed of mere statistics.

Being fated by circumstances to govern through and for the sake of external policy, and having, properly speaking, no internal policy, Austria had not to fear the crises which on occasion paralysed the governments of France and England, though of course she lacked the strength they drew from their national unity. No government was so quick to profit from the mistakes of others, so capable of waiting on events and taking advantage of an opportunity. Austria lived on Europe, through Europe and for Europe; a foolish policy could bring disaster, but a clever one could bring recovery. Her times of adversity under Thugut and Cobenzl were as much in the logic of her history as her great recovery under Metternich. Her periods of eclipse, her aberrations, her catastrophes, her recoveries, and that constant power of self-renewal which is the secret of her history—all these proceeded from the same cause.

VII. *Prussia*

I. THE NATION AND THE STATE

'Prussia is to-day the pivot on which both peace and war on the Continent turn', wrote Mirabeau in 1786.[1] In France in the last years of the ancien régime men's minds were full of Prussia, and her policy was eagerly discussed. All who aimed at conquest and glory paraded their alliance with her. Those with a taste for political speculation compared her to Macedon. Those publicists who were most ardent for reform extolled the Prussian monarchy and held it up as an example—'a great and superb machine of government which the finest practitioners of politics have spent centuries in perfecting'. Mirabeau closed his treatise on 'The Prussian Monarchy' with this aphorism: 'If Prussia should perish, the art of government would return to its infancy.'[2] Yet the fall of Prussia seemed to him to be near; he foretold it, and revealed the causes: 'Never has a kingdom more clearly shown signs of an early decline. The Prussian monarchy is so constituted that it could not survive any kind of calamity, not even that which is bound to befall in course of time—unskilful government.' This inherent contradiction was the basis of all contemporary judgements. Praise and criticism were equally jus-

[1] *Histoire secrète*, July 1786.
[2] Mirabeau, *Monarchie prussienne*, bk. VIII, 1788.

tified, and they were to be borne out, in turn, by the events of the revolutionary period.

This state, which to the *philosophes* represented the ideal of 'enlightened government', was to be the most determined adversary of a revolution made by the pupils of the *philosophes* and intended to spread 'enlightenment' throughout Europe. The enemy of the Revolution in its early days, Prussia became its complacent associate in its hour of victory. Then, having been the most sought after and the most lavishly paid ally of the Republic, the Prussian monarchy suddenly turned against the Empire, only to become its most illustrious victim. Having been raised up so quickly it fell with a greater crash. Yet, having suffered so complete a collapse, it was to rise again with even more astonishing *éclat*, and those who had so long been counted in Paris as natural and necessary allies would henceforth figure as the most implacable enemies of the new France. These vicissitudes in Prussia's history were closely linked with those of the French Revolution. It is therefore necessary to seek an explanation for them. This can be found in Prussia's past, and it will be seen that through all its curious changes this state was only working out the special characteristics which it bore from the very beginning.

It is impossible to imagine a state more different in character from Austria, which we have just been studying. Antagonism between these two states seemed to be part of the order of things. In Austria everything combined to produce a cosmopolitan monarchy, a government whose principal resource was diplomacy and whose existence was a series of reactions to outside events. In Prussia on the contrary all the social and political forces tended to bind a compact nation into a closely-knit state which, far from passively receiving impulses from outside, made an impact itself on everything around it. The house of Hohenzollern was, like the house of Habsburg, greedy, ambitious and restless; but, more sure in its conceptions and less divided in its aims, it pursued more clearly defined plans with greater method and tenacity. Prussia was as apt to concentrate her resources as Austria was to disperse them. This was because she found from the start what Austria always lacked—the constituent elements of a nation and a state.

The Prussian monarchy was formed in the sixteenth century by the union of the Mark of Brandenburg and Prussia. Between these two countries and completely separating them stretched Polish Prussia, but they readily lent themselves to government by a single head, for they had the same origins and had followed the same destiny. Both were German colonies in Slav countries. In the Mark it was a dynasty, the Ascanian, while in Prussia it was a military order, the Teutonic Knights, that carried out the conquest and founded the new system; but the same political necessities imposed similar methods. Both had to convert and subdue the Slavs, and then had to defend and exploit territories of a similar kind. The Order turned farmer and merchant, while the dynasty organized its army like a military order. In each case the same type of character emerged—warrior and colonist, man of action and mystic in one.

They worked on virgin soil. The conquered populations were practically uncivilised and had neither history nor traditions. Those who escaped extermination submitted to the conqueror; they merged with the German colonists, who imposed their own religion and customs. But the Germans themselves were changed by this environment, and from this crossing of stocks resulted a race apart, very different from both Slavs and Germans—more industrious, serious and tenacious than the former, more meticulous, enterprising and supple than the latter. They were superior to both as political material because in them clearer minds and a more docile spirit were put to the service of simpler passions. Above this solid and yet malleable population there was raised an aristocracy which owed its existence entirely to conquest. It was formed from the companions of the conquerors, who settled in the country as colonists or as rulers of the colonists. In Prussia the Teutonic Order was like an army in the field;

it included in itself all the ranks of a military nobility. In the Mark the noble emerged in the army and remained its natural leader. There were moreover no great fiefs—the Grand Masters and the Margraves took care to create none. Hard-working and thrifty, warlike by inclination as well as by necessity, this indigent nobility was scattered over a barren countryside. It never formed a united body, it had no tradition of independence, and it had need of the ruler to maintain and defend it. It was submissive and loyal, gave him its service, and had no thought of disputing his power, the benefit of which it was the first to feel. The ruler could count on this nobility instead of having, as elsewhere in Europe, to reckon with its opposition.

Thus by force of circumstances, in Prussia as in the Mark, everything was created by the state out of nothing; the state was all in all, the raison d'être and the mainspring of the whole country. In Prussia the Church was identified with the state, and submitted to it in the Mark because it needed its support. So complete was its submission, and so thorough was the confusion of religious and profane interests, that when the Margrave went over to the reformed religion and the Grand Master secularised his office, the clergy followed him, and the people followed the clergy, becoming Lutheran in just the same way as they had become Christian. Thus were the conquest and the assimilation completed, while by isolating themselves from the Catholic world these two colonies intensified and defined more firmly their original character. When in the course of events the Grand Master of the secularised Order, now Duke of Prussia, became also Margrave of Brandenburg, the fusion of the peoples and the governments took place spontaneously. All the elements of the Prussian nation were present, and all the elements of the Prussian state were ready to hand. It only remained to proclaim its unity: this was the work of the Hohenzollerns. Drawing inspiration from the traditions both of the Margraves and of the Teutonic Knights, rulers by divine right of an essentially secular state, mystic leaders of an entirely military nobility and a nation disciplined to arms, they proved to be skilful and conscientious administrators of the best-governed country—and the most amenable to government—in Europe.

Their history continued as it had begun. They had no frontiers; any neighbouring territory was there for the taking, but what was taken was not always easy to keep—hence the unavoidable emphasis on the military factor. Since they were greedy and vigorous their peril became their opportunity: the great plains on which they were established and which seemed open to every invader also opened the path of conquest to the Prussians themselves. Poland divided them into two parts—so they could never rest until they had expropriated the Poles. They became conquerors from necessity, and continued so through inclination and temperament. 'War', said Mirabeau, 'is the national industry of Prussia.' 'The physical constitution of the country', a French diplomat wrote later, 'makes ambition a kind of necessity for her. Any pretext is good enough; she is hindered by no scruples; expediency is her only law.'[3] From the available pretexts she excelled in choosing the most comprehensive, the most productive, the most brilliant. No dynasty had known better how to descry the main currents of events and how to exploit them, allowing itself, as men said, to be borne along by the spirit of the time. The Prussian sovereigns were born of a crusade, and grew in power through the Reformation. They first conquered for the sake of the Church and then secularised their countries for the sake of the state. Adroit in seizing on pretexts, they were no less diligent in profiting by their opportunities. In this respect they had a long-established reputation. 'All will go well', wrote an agent of Francis I, 'if we can satisfy the Margrave of Brandenburg. He and his brother, the Elector of Mainz, wallow deeper in avarice every day.' The King replied, 'I would that the Mar-

---

[3] Instructions of Talleyrand, for the Congress of Vienna, 1814, in the collection of Angeberg, *Le Congrès de Vienne*, vol. I. Paris, 1864.

quis Joachim were stuffed to repletion.'[4] It was done as he said; the bidding was opened, and the auction never closed.

The successive Prussian princes of the seventeenth and eighteenth centuries played complementary parts. Frederick combined all these in himself and surpassed all the others. He completed the work of his predecessors, and opened up paths to his successors for the future. A prince after the heart of the *philosophes*, he was at the same time the Prussian king par excellence. Inheriting from his ancestors the makings of a small state, he left to his descendants the framework of a great power. He took Silesia from Austria and Polish Prussia from Poland, and raised the number of his subjects from two and a half to five and a half millions. He both extended and concentrated his kingdom. Besides the agglomeration of territories in eastern Europe he possessed others in East Friesland, in Westphalia, and on the left bank of the Rhine; he could anticipate the inheritance of Ansbach and Bayreuth in central Germany. These were the foundation stones of new constructions, advanced posts for future conquests. But Frederick left the honour and the adventure of these conquests to his successors. 'You will share the Empire with the Emperor, like Octavius and Antony', his brother, Prince Henry, once said to him. Frederick no doubt thought that an imperial crown would not be out of place on the brow of a Hohenzollern, that Saxony would look very well on a map of his possessions, and that it would be expedient to join the lands in Westphalia, and even those of the Rhine, with Brandenburg, in the same way as Brandenburg had been joined to Old Prussia. But he replied, not without irony, 'It will not be for me, my dear brother, to bring to maturity the entente with the House of Austria!' And so he continued the struggle, and not finding himself within reach of sharing the Empire with Austria, he became the defender of the rights of the Empire against her. He was thus able to leave as his political testament the Confederation

[4] Guizot, *Histoire de France*, vol. III, p. 31.

of the Princes, the scheme which, when it was taken up in the following century by one of his nephews, was to raise Prussia to the peak of fortune which Frederick thought beyond hope of attainment by himself.

He indicated the goal, he planned the work, he showed the road, he marked the stages. Every path for Prussia's advance was opened or traced by his hands. He not only indicated the hereditary enemy who must be combated and expropriated, he identified the necessary ally and traditional associate. The advance of Russia was for him a prime preoccupation. 'This is a terrible power', he wrote to his brother Henry on 8 March 1769. 'Sprung from those Huns and Gepides who destroyed the empire of the East, they could well break into the empire of the West before long. I can see no remedy but to form, when opportunity offers, a league of the greatest rulers to stem this dangerous torrent.'[5] But it was the same with this league as with the division of the Empire between Octavian and Augustus—the time was never ripe. This was another task reserved for the third generation of his successors. Frederick's gaze hardly reached beyond another century; that was enough for him, and very few statesmen would have seen so far. The Russian threat in fact seemed to him dangerous only in those yet distant times where it became lost in the mists. As far as the eye could follow its course, Frederick calculated that instead of spending ruinous efforts in raising useless barriers, it would be more expedient to channel the waters and turn their force to the greater profit of the Prussian monarchy. He said in his *Mémoires*: 'There were two possible courses: either to stop Russia in her headlong career of conquest, or—which would be wiser—to try to profit from it.' This is what he had done with infinite skill at the time of the first partition of Poland, and this was the lesson he bequeathed to his successors.

Without the least liking for one another, and even vaguely recognising that it would be their destiny in future ages to

[5] Ed. Boutaric, vol. II, p. 335.

renew the legendary struggles of East and West, the Prussians and the Russians realised that for the present it was in their interests to make common cause. They both coveted Poland equally, and while Poland survived their greed was bound to lead them to join and share the spoils rather than fight each other to achieve exclusive domination. Moreover, the Russians thought only of the East, the Prussians of the West, the former thrusting into Turkey, the latter into Germany; their paths did not cross, their designs were not contradictory. Finally, they both had to face the same rival and enemy—Austria. Blind passions or mistaken calculations might for a time set them at odds with one another, but force of circumstances was bound to lead them as a rule to make common cause against common adversaries.

If Frederick's experience had needed confirmation, it could have been found in the vicissitudes of Prussia's fortunes during the wars of the French Revolution. Frederick died on 17 August 1786, at the moment when the great crisis occurred in France the sequel to which was to have such surprising consequences for his dynasty.

2. THE WORK OF FREDERICK

Frederick had come triumphantly through the two great tests of conquerors—he had kept what he had seized, and he had assimilated the conquered provinces with his hereditary states. He believed his work would last. He admitted that his death would mean a crisis for the Prussian state. 'But', he added, 'a monarchy is not so quickly destroyed, and mine is well established. Even if they wish to, they can hardly ruin it.' In this he deceived himself. He knew his own worth and did not exaggerate it; but he had great illusions about the value of his system of government. He personified Prussia; no sovereign could say with so much truth: '*L'état, c'est moi*'. This was the strength of the Prussian monarchy, but it was also its vice and its weakness. The state was the ruler, and the ruler was a great statesman. The defects of the work proceeded from the very qualities of the artist who had created it. Frederick's indefatigable activity, his imperious character and his military habits led him to organize everything, control everything, do everything himself. He raised all things to the dimensions of his own mind, which far surpassed the average of human capacity. He administered the state as a landowner manages his property. His whole system of government was reducible to this elementary principle—the exploitation of a great domain by an intelligent master.

'Frederick the Great', said a contemporary, who had served in a subordinate position in his cabinet, 'directed by himself all the activities of the state. His ministers asked in writing for his orders, and from his cabinet he decided with a stroke of the pen the most important matters just as he did the smallest details. His scorn for mankind, which he could not put from him, had given him a perfect detachment in his judgements, and never in his two-line instructions did he betray a motive. Two or three secretaries, people of no particular ability—mere machines—sufficed for this mode of work.'[6] He neither wanted nor asked for advice, nor entrusted anyone with his secrets. He would not even have tolerated underlings, in the manner of Louis XIV's later years. So he trained no pupils. Among servants accustomed to suffer his ascendancy in silence and to translate his infallible orders into the vernacular there were nevertheless men who were highly trained, distinguished, and abreast of the time—'enlightened ministers'—like Hertzberg, for example, or Zedlitz, Carmer, Struensee, Schulenburg, Finckenstein. But by reducing them to an inferior rôle Frederick had robbed them of the confidence of the public and confidence in themselves. In the dull mechanism of the chancelleries men's wills were destroyed and their characters suppressed. From the highest official to the lowest clerk, none was capable

[6] Lombard, *Matériaux pour servir à l'histoire des années 1805, 1806 et 1807.* Leipzig, 1808.

of anything but passive obedience. The bureaucracy which enveloped all elements of the state in its tangled net was an instrument, not an institution. In energetic and clever hands it could transmit vigour from the centre to the extremities, but by itself it was nothing and was worth nothing. It would with the same docility transmit contradictory orders and meaningless directives. Thus there was unity and purpose in government as long as Frederick ruled, but confusion and incoherence when he was replaced by a king of weak character, incapable of coherent planning. Frederick left behind him disciplined officials, but no counsellors or administrators. The country had not yet a tradition of government, and after Frederick it had nothing but a routine.

Frederick had no budget. He was his own controller of finance and kept his own accounts. It is well known with what parsimony he regulated his expenses, with what pittances he rewarded those who laboured for his glory. But imagine in his place a lavish prince surrounded by greedy favourites, and the system would be doomed to immediate collapse and ruin. There had been thrift, but no credit and no resources. Money lost could never be recouped. Only by prodigies of economy had Frederick been able to meet the cost of two long wars. In the poorest country in Europe, at a time when all states were overburdened, he had managed with a revenue of 17 millions to accumulate a treasure of 60 million crowns and maintain an army of 160,000 men.

The most skilfully devised and best constructed institution in the state was the army, but it was no more than a set of cogs in a machine. The motive power was the King's will. He required blind and automatic obedience. Initiative in an officer seemed to him as culpable as indiscipline in a soldier. He wanted service without the nobility by which it might be exalted, and he set no store by the military virtues. A third of his army was composed of foreigners, bought or kidnapped into service by his recruiting agents. The rest, the Prussians, were separate from the nation. Frederick approved of this, for war thus independently sustained did not disturb the life of the state; but if the war went badly the nation was incapable of self-defence. 'Prussia', Mirabeau wrote, 'has but one army and one treasure. If the Prussian army were destroyed it could no more be reconstituted than the treasure.' Without the soul that inspired it, that comprised its force, its intelligence and its life, this army must dissolve. All had learnt to obey, none to command. With Frederick no longer there, no one commanded and many ceased to obey. The soldiers were mere instruments; they had no country. The officers were cosmopolitan. Left to themselves, they spent their time arguing about *philosophie* and politics, for they belonged to their age, and the king did not forbid them to jest and debate. When they no longer had a master, or when their master was incapable of leading them, there seemed to be more merchants than captains among them. Certainly they fought with valour, but they were pedantic and irresolute, and combined presumption with indecision. This often denied them victory, and was in 1806 the chief cause of their defeat.

They had however retained their military outlook and habits. The army was admirably well-behaved in peace time and often played a great part on the field of battle. The diplomats, on the other hand, showed neither a grasp of ideas nor training in the ways of politics. Frederick's disciples copied only his defects; his imitators represented merely a caricature of the great man. Frederick's genius concealed his political methods from his contemporaries; his genius removed, only the methods remained, and they then appeared what indeed they were—odious. Frederick's moderation, and the political judgement which he possessed to such a high degree, compensated for the viciousness of his principles in the opinion of a public which would often excuse a crime but never pardon a mistake. He had achieved his ends, as he himself avowed, simply by dint of negotiation and intrigue. After him intrigue remained the only basis of Prussian policy. Frederick had appeased the cupidity of the Prussians by moderate satisfactions, but after his reign they broke out in all directions seeking greedily after all kinds of gains. There were temptations everywhere for Prussia. She thought nothing forbidden and nothing impossible, forgetting that Frederick had succeeded because he allowed himself to attempt only what was possible. He may have lacked scruples, but he had prudence. Those who took his place, infatuated by his strength and intoxicated by his success, employed conscienceless diplomacy in pursuit of unlimited ambition.

Even Frederick's greatest achievements had their hidden defects and carried within them the seeds of dissolution. The religious toleration of the Prussian kings was justly famous. It could be said, as Mirabeau said of war, but on a higher plane, that it was the national industry. Louis XIV's error in revoking the Edict of Nantes, the damage it had done to France, and the advantages Prussia had gained from it, were taught in Berlin as political maxims. The Jesuits profited from this in the eighteenth century as the Protestants had done in the seventeenth. The Huguenots proscribed by Louis XIV and welcomed in Prussia included engineers, officers, artists, men of learning. The Jesuits expelled by Louis XV provided her with pedagogues whose mechanical mode of instruction was quickly adapted to Prussian discipline; they gave Frederick powerful aid in assimilating the Catholic populations annexed from Silesia and Poland.

Religious liberty, which they alone in Europe enjoyed, was an inestimable benefit to the King of Prussia's subjects. But for the King it was simply an instrument of government, a means of attracting colonists and fusing together the diverse elements of the population. Frederick's tolerance sprang neither from respect for conscience nor from love of liberty; it was the result of scepticism and indifference to morality. 'The heterodox', wrote a French diplomat, 'hold that everyone should have freedom of belief, and that virtue without faith can bring salvation. Frederick II favoured them and never allowed them to be harassed. His principle was that only the wishes of the flock should determine the choice of a pastor. Many times he has deprived heterodox priests because

their parishioners wanted those who were attached to orthodoxy. But he did not care what doctrine was taught so long
as the flock were content. M. Schultz, minister at Gilsdorf
near Berlin, who was much loved by his parishioners, spent
ten years preaching materialism.'[7]

The higher Lutheran clergy were openly rationalist.
Preaching in the big towns reduced itself to moral exhorta-
tion, humanitarianism and sentiment. A senior councillor of
the consistory, Spalding by name, declared that the mysterious and the supernatural should be removed from religious teaching. The basis of their beliefs was English deism,
translated with commentary by the author of the *Dictionnaire
philosophique*. 'This is Voltaire in pastor's bands and gown',
wrote Forster. Many of them followed the master all the way,
and enlivened their sermons with jests. Frederick let them
have their say, as long as they praised the King and taught
obedience to his subjects. It was pure policy on his part; but
with his cold calculation went the impudent bragging of the
libertine and the cynicism of impiety.

This unworthy kind of tolerance produced disintegrating
effects. Because it did not proceed from respect for faith it
engendered scorn of it. As there was no tradition of social
morality other than the restraints of religion in this new society, corruption set in and began to erode it. The King's
scepticism spread to his subjects, who translated it into deeds.
It was the accepted fashion; everyone in Berlin took it up
and conducted himself accordingly. The leaven of licence
and sensuality which permeates all the literature of the age
fermented without hindrance in these unrefined souls. A
forced civilisation had overheated their imagination and
senses without mellowing their raw and primitive passions.
In Prussia there was none of the delicacy of taste, the habits
of elegance, the gaiety of spirit which in France provided a
corrective to the depravity of the age. She flaunted instead a
stupid profligacy. Civil servants, the upper class, women,

[7] The younger Custine, 1 April 1792.

nourished their minds on d'Holbach and La Mettrie,* taking their doctrines seriously and applying them to the letter. Moreover, in this recently built capital an altogether artificial society, an improvised amalgam of disparate elements, was as if predisposed to dissoluteness. Berlin swarmed with soldiers who had no families, and did not spend the whole day on parade. Men of letters, adventurers of the pen and the sword drawn by Frederick's reputation and reduced to living by intrigue and expedients; a poor, haughty and exclusive nobility on whom the royal discipline bore heavily, and who were bored; an enlightened and rich bourgeoisie, which nevertheless had an inferior status; between these groups, divided by etiquette or prejudice, a sort of 'demi-monde' grew up where they met, talked, and sought diversion at their ease. This was the home of 'French ideas,' the centre of affairs and intrigues—the Jewish society, the richest and the only elegant one in Berlin. With the marvellous suppleness of their race, they had assimilated the new civilisation, and avenged themselves for their exclusion from politics by gathering in their salons all that Berlin could offer in the way of men of intellect, as well as agreeable women and anyone desirous of liberty and free from prejudice.

This was the Berlin scene in the time of Frederick. 'One of the most beautiful cities in Europe', wrote Forster in 1779, 'but the Berliners! Sociability and a refined taste for enjoyment degenerate with them into sensuality and licence (I would almost say into a voracious appetite for evil), freedom of the spirit and love of enlightenment into unbridled effrontery and an unchecked debauchery of ideas. Women for the most part are morally ruined.' This was also the impression of an English diplomat, Sir James Harris, later Lord Malmesbury: 'Berlin is a city where, if one can translate *fortis* by honourable, one can say that there is neither *vir fortis nec femina casta.*'

Allowing for the fact that, except among the Jews, money

* Exponents of the materialist philosophy in France.

was scarce, and as temptations are all the stronger when there is less means of gratifying them, it is understandable that in many cases the profligacy of ideas and the corruption of morals opened the way to a new evil, assuredly the most dangerous and the most repulsive in the life of a nation—venality. Mirabeau in his *Secret History* delineated with ineffaceable strokes all the vices of 'this noble gaming house' of Berlin. In this respect his famous pamphlet is a ferocious picture but a true one. Cynicism seemed to be no more than the natural climate: 'Decay preceding maturity—I very much fear this may be the motto of Prussia. . . . What cannot money do in a house so poor?'

It needed Frederick's iron hand to set these complicated forces in motion, to control this unwieldy machine, to hold together these elements assembled by dint of contrivance and ever ready to fall apart. But it was a harsh and heavy hand. In the upper classes at least, the only ones which were thought to matter and of which people were conscious, there could be observed a kind of smouldering revolt against this implacable discipline. Besides, the Prussians entertained strange illusions about the future. Frederick had deceived his subjects as he had deceived himself about the durability of his work. They did not realise how far their power was personal to their king. Proud to the point of infatuation of the rôle he had made them fill, they imagined that they had a great destiny, and that the soul of Frederick would live on in them. They expected from a new reign the same glory abroad, the same security at home, the same relative prosperity, with at the same time a less harsh yoke and a less severe discipline, failing to understand that the harshness of the yoke and the severity of the discipline were the necessary conditions for Frederick's work to endure. The mercantile and protective system which had created industry, the tax system which had brought money flowing into the state's coffers, the economy which immobilised it in the treasury, all these hampered and annoyed everyone who wanted to work and do business, everyone who thought about the natural conditions of trade and industry. But these measures alone enabled the poorest government in Europe to be better armed than the richest states and to keep ahead of them. In brief, the people wanted the mainspring to be slackened and took no account of the fact that to slacken the mainspring was to destroy the state.

To reform Frederick's monarchy would have required as great a genius as to create it. This reform was nevertheless indispensable, for only Frederick was of the stature to hold up the composite structure he had raised; hence the threat of an almost inevitable catastrophe. 'Everything will continue all right, and almost by itself, as long as external affairs remain calm and unchanged', wrote Mirabeau after the King's death. 'But at the first shot of a cannon or the first sign of a storm the whole little fabric of mediocrity will collapse. All these servile ministers will shrink into insignificance! Everyone, from the frightened crew to the bewildered captain, will call for a pilot! But who will this pilot be?'

3. FREDERICK WILLIAM II

Frederick's nephew, who was called upon to succeed him, was not cut out for this great rôle. In all respects he presented a complete contrast to the prince whose heavy burden he inherited. Frederick had been frail in health and frugal in habits. His appearance had been striking only in the glance of 'his great eyes, which', in the words of Mirabeau, 'charmed or struck terror, at the pleasure of his heroic soul.' Frederick William II was 'a handsome man', sanguine and robust, a lover of violent exercise and gross pleasures. 'The stature and the strength of a Swiss guard', wrote the French minister d'Esterno, who did not much like him. 'An enormous machine of flesh', said an Austrian diplomat who saw him at Pillnitz in 1791. 'A true specimen of a king', was the verdict on the other hand of Metternich, who was presented to him in 1792 at Coblentz, at the time of the crusade of the Germans against France and the Revolution. 'His stature', he added, 'was gigantic, and he was corpulent in proportion. In any gathering he was a head above the surrounding crowd. His manners were noble and engaging.' He expressed himself with some effort, in little clipped phrases.[8] There was nothing about him to recall the masterly and implacable irony of Frederick. 'His look', said an apologist, 'did not denote a man of genius, but German candour shone upon his brow.'[9] A peculiar kind of candour, and a quality which it would be somewhat difficult to grant him if the word were taken in its proper and usual sense. It must indeed be interpreted as it was then understood in Germany, thanks to the translations of Rousseau—in the equivocal and refined sense which reconciled innocence with shamelessness, and virtue with every irregularity of impulse or imagination. Ecstatic and sensual, devout and licentious, stirred by violent appetites yet tormented by scruples of conscience, superstitious and debauched, a believer in spirits, and much given to intrigue, Frederick William had an inclination to morality and a sentiment for religion. He spoke of it with respect, fear and emotion. It was a natural tendency in him, but it was also an assumed attitude—the usual device of the heir-presumptive in regard to the reigning master, a means of winning admiration and gaining favourable opinions by force of contrast. Frederick's impiety had found only too many imitators among Frenchified Prussians, but it scandalised those Prussians who remained German; much inclined as they were to the debauchery of the age, they could not take to this raw and bitter beverage. Even in their cups they wanted something more unctuous and melancholic, something to nourish dreams on, the illusions of sentiment, the luxury of remorse, licence

---

[8] Metternich, *Mémoires*, vol. I, p. 14. Report of the Referendary Spielmann on the interview of Pillnitz. Vivenot, *Quellen*, vol. I, p. 208.

[9] Baron de Trenck, *Examen critique de l'histoire secrète de la cour de Berlin*.

baptised with tears. The clear sparkling wine of Voltaire did not suit them; they wanted Rousseau's subtle-tasting mead. Even in their diversions they were seeking some kind of German revenge for the French influence which had reigned despotically in Frederick's time. The new king shared in these trends and saw that he could profit from them. He made a point of speaking only German, of detesting France and the French, their frivolity, their principles and their literature, of combating their domination and condemning their morals.

He could easily be fooled by this 'German candour', and so could those around him. Not so Frederick. In his memoirs he paints his nephew as he was in 1756, at the age of twenty-one, at the time of his first marriage, to Elizabeth of Brunswick: 'The young husband, quite without morals, abandoned to debauchery, was daily unfaithful to his wife. The princess, who was in the full bloom of her beauty, was outraged by the small attention paid to her charms. She soon gave herself up to dissoluteness no whit less than that of her husband.'[10] They were divorced in 1769. Frederick William married a princess of Darmstadt. The second marriage was no happier than the first. The princess did not avenge herself on her husband, but she did not lack motive for doing so. The prince resumed his debauched habits. Besides plenty of passing fancies, he had a *maîtresse en titre*. This person, who always knew how to keep the favour if not the love of Frederick William, was a musician's daughter. She married the prince's *valet de chambre*, became Madame Rietz and was later made Countess of Lichtenau. By his first marriage Frederick William had had a daughter, the princess Frederica, who was brought up by the Queen—the wife whom Frederick the Great had put away, if not repudiated. The father, when visiting his daughter, was taken with one of her maids of honour. She was called Mademoiselle de Voss; she came of a good family, was cousin to one of the King's ministers, M. de Finckenstein, and had a brother who was president of

[10] *Mémoires*, ed. Boutaric, vol. II, p. 331.

a court. 'This beauty, who in my view is very ugly', wrote Mirabeau, 'is a mixture of prudery and cynicism, affectation and ingenuousness . . . she has a sort of natural wit and some education, but she has crazes rather than desires, and a *gaucherie* which she tries to retrieve by an appearance of naïvety. . . . For looks she has only the complexion common to people of that country, and I would describe it as more pallid than fair; a very fine bosom. Her unique combination of licentiousness with airs of innocent ignorance and the severity of a vestal, has, they say, seduced the prince.'

Frederick William was one of those complicated libertines who seek a sauce for their desires and also a relief for their scruples in a cunning resistance. Mademoiselle de Voss's little game lasted nearly two years. It had not reached its *dénouement* when the death of Frederick the Great suspended its course for several weeks. King on 17 August 1786, Frederick William seemed to forget everything except business. But from 8 September Mirabeau noticed that 'the fervour of the novice seemed to slacken. Mademoiselle de Voss', he added, 'was ready to yield.' The King, in order to see her more easily, had built a house for his daughter Frederica; Mademoiselle de Voss did the honours there. The year passed, however, before the vestal gave in. She loved the King; but family honour spoke louder than love. Moreover she set rigorous conditions on her surrender: a morganatic marriage, the written consent of the Queen, and the dismissal of the *maîtresse en titre*, Madame Rietz. On the last point the King was inflexible, but he gave way on the other two. The Queen gave her consent, subject to the reservation that there should be neither a real divorce nor a public separation—she was to keep her title of Queen and her position of legitimate wife. As to the rest, it seemed, she cared little. There was nothing to be done now but to perform the marriage, but under these conditions that would be a delicate and difficult business. It was indeed known that there were casuists as well as judges in Berlin, and that Lutheran pietists could in case of need show themselves as fertile in resource as the disciples of Sanchez.* The consistory deliberated, rummaged in the archives, examined precedents. One was discovered which seemed decisive.

In 1539 Philip of Hesse, who was not on good terms with his wife, a Saxon duchess, fell in love with a damsel from Saal. She wished above all things to be married. Philip, who used to read the Bible in the vulgar tongue, did not see why a German prince should be forbidden what was permitted to the patriarchs. The early Church moreover had shown itself conciliatory in this respect, and the Emperor Valentinian II had the benefit of its tolerance. This claim by a reformed prince threw the reformers into a cruel difficulty. Luther and Melanchthon, called upon to deliver their opinion, adjured him to restrain his passions, but concluded that nothing in the New Testament forbade, in this matter, what was authorised by the Old. Philip married Mademoiselle de Saal and became a bigamist, which caused a great scandal in the Reformed Church and outside it. Melanchthon developed feelings of remorse of which he nearly died; Luther formally retracted his opinion.

The Prussian consistory only took account of the historical fact. It invoked the letter and disregarded the spirit; it authorised the marriage, and, far from repenting of its lapse, was soon to repeat it, as will shortly appear. The marriage was celebrated in July 1787 in the royal chapel of Charlottenburg; Mademoiselle de Voss took the name of Countess of Ingenheim. Her good fortune was short-lived—she died in March 1789. There was general mourning in Berlin, reported M. d'Esterno. 'The Countess of Ingenheim is bitterly regretted by the people, the royal family, and even the Queen, much less because of the person of the said Countess than because of the improved status that her death will allow to the Lady Rietz, former *maîtresse d'habitude*, who is said to be very greedy and a great schemer.'

* Sorel probably means the Jesuit Thomas Sanchez (1550-1610).

The literature of the time made much of the royal sorrows, acclaimed the 'virtues' of this 'man of feeling', and against the arid scepticism of Voltaire and the shameful frivolity of the French the Prussians held up to admiration the tender passion with which Frederick William had yielded to 'the sweetest bidding of Nature'. 'The enemies of women', wrote the baron de Trenck, 'have been the scourge of mankind. The King of Prussia has a great and sensitive soul; in love he is capable of a tender affection; he knew the true worth of his mistress. Even supposing he gave her a million and these riches were distributed among the members of her family, they are citizens. He has not deprived an honest man of the spouse who has made him happy; he has not sacrificed Rome to Cleopatra.' He wished to be loved for himself alone. For twenty months he courted Mademoiselle de Voss, he married her, he was faithful to her, 'he has wept over her ashes. Every citizen enlightened enough to understand human weaknesses' must wish that if he should make another choice, it should light upon an object equally worthy of his heart. 'Let us then rejoice in a happiness which belongs to a simple peasant as it does to kings.' This farrago of hypocrisy, this licentious casuistry, was then quite the thing and much approved in Germany.

There was not long to wait for the distraction Trenck desired for the King in his desolation. In 1790, on the day of the anniversary of the Countess of Ingenheim's death, Mademoiselle Dönhof was presented at court, where they were much concerned to provide consolation for Frederick William. They had even, as was then said, 'put forward the claims' of a young lady named Viereck, a friend of Mademoiselle de Voss, whose place in the household of Princess Frederica she had taken. Unfortunately for the friends of Mademoiselle Viereck she was a brunette, and did not in the least resemble the deceased. Mademoiselle Dönhof on the contrary was, said the French minister, 'so perfectly blonde that she was pretty by artificial light, though in daylight she was as yellow as a lemon'. With the same charms as Mademoiselle de Voss she had the same spice of pietism and virtue. Marriage was therefore necessary. The King saw no difficulty in this. 'I am separated from the Queen', he wrote to Mademoiselle Dönhof, 'I am left a widower by Madame d'Ingenheim; I offer you my heart and my hand.' He hid nothing, declaring openly that he had reasons for repudiating the Queen, but that he preferred not to detail them, in order to maintain the dignity of the throne. There was nothing more for the consistory to discuss; the precedents had been set, and they followed them. The marriage took place on 10th April, 1790, and it was the court preacher Zöllner who blessed it, as he had blessed that of Mademoiselle de Voss. The Queen gave the bride clusters of diamonds. The Queen Dowager received her, and there was general celebration at court. At the same time she could no more obtain the dismissal of Madame Rietz than could Mademoiselle de Voss before her. This much-favoured lady, who had received 70,000 crowns to depart, remained, took an officer as her lover, and secured his promotion from the King.

Thus in 1790 the King of Prussia, widower of Mademoiselle de Voss, had three wives living—the Princess of Brunswick, who had been repudiated, the Princess of Darmstadt, who though divorced retained the status of queen, and Mademoiselle Dönhof, morganatic spouse. This third lady, a diplomat reported, would not be the last, for 'any whom the King now sets eyes on will also wish to be married'. Moreover the ruler was always ready. Polygamy seemed to him to be a prerogative of sovereignty. Following a court intrigue he arranged in 1792 a separation from Mademoiselle Dönhof, crowning by this underhand divorce his remarkable series of conjugal convolutions. He immediately offered his heart and his hand to a young lady named Bethmann, a banker's daughter, whom he had known at Frankfurt and whom he found much to his liking. This young person, in the words of Lord Malmesbury, 'was all sentiment and all fire';[11] but

---

[11] *Journal and Correspondence of Lord Malmesbury*, December 1793 and January 1794. Philippson, vol. II, p. 148.

she had principles and a sense of propriety; she developed scruples about the character of the marriage and doubts about the constancy of the husband. She refused, thus sparing the casuists of Berlin the embarrassment of deliberations even more scandalous than those that had gone before. I do not know whether these obliging theologians, reared in the school of Voltaire and Frederick, really took these simultaneous marriages seriously. Abroad they were matter for jest, and Catherine the Great, not herself inclined to be troubled with such formalities, was highly diverted by them. 'This great clod of a Gu'—this was the name she gave Frederick William in her letters to Grimm—'this great clod has just married a third wife; the fine fellow never has enough legitimate wives; he is a conscientious gallant if ever there was one.'[12]

Frederick William liked women, but he did not let them rule him. Yet he escaped the influence of mistresses only to fall under that of favourites, and his subjects were no better off. Badly brought up, kept away from affairs of state by his uncle, distrusting others because he was distrustful of himself, he knew nothing of the art of government but merely cherished vague projects of reform. He was cramped and constricted by the ministers left him by Frederick, inferior though they were. He feared to seem to be under their direction; besides, these ministers represented ideas and a system which he affected to condemn. 'The King will be led precisely because he fears to be', wrote Mirabeau. The fear of being governed by his ministers gave him over to lesser people. These soon dominated him though they abased themselves before him. They soothed his suspicious pride, flattered his passions, and exploited his weaknesses. Frederick William wished for the good of the state, and he had an obscure but fairly lively appreciation of the need to temper the excesses of Frederick's government. But his intentions went

[12] Letter to Grimm, 23 June 1790. Société d'histoire de Russie, *Correspondance de Catherine II avec Grimm.*

for nothing, and his vague desire for reform, more mystical than political, proceeded less from a conception of the interests of the state than from the influence of a secret doctrine with which he was imbued. In him the statesman was no more than an adept in magic, and he took mere charlatans as his ministers. At Potsdam Frederick's 'enlightened' ministers were replaced by clever conjurers. This was one of the most curious features of this troubled period.

Of these opportunist mystics the one whose influence was perhaps the most disastrous for the Prussian state, Wöllner, was a sheer intriguer. Son of a country pastor of the Mark, he was introduced into the family of General Itzenplitz; he first won over the mother and then married the daughter. Frederick, who was by no means indulgent to misalliances, shut him up in the Berlin prison. Wöllner's hatred for the philosopher king dates from this episode. He was at that time a rationalist and disciple of Wolf, and had become a Freemason. But already, in the high society of Germany, the wind was veering away from pure deism. Wöllner, who was a freethinker and always remained a complete sceptic, changed his convictions. Considering himself as well-fitted as another for the commerce of apparitions and the craft of mystery, he resolved to become an 'honest broker' between the powers of this world and of the next, basing his credit with the former on that which he claimed to have with the latter. He joined the Rosicrucians and soon became one of the white hopes of the Order.

He thus came to know the man who was to rival him in favour at the court of Berlin and one day to share with him the government of Prussia, the Saxon Bischoffswerder. Son of a member of the minor gentry, a soldier of fortune who had come like so many others to seek service in Prussia, Bischoffswerder had insinuated himself into the favour of the Prince Royal and had promptly taken his fancy. Unlike his future associate Wöllner he was genuinely superstitious, believed in his nostrums and appears to have been, at first at any rate, the dupe of his own phantasmagorias. While Wöll-

ner, simply greedy and grasping, wanted only to push his
way into high positions, Bischoffswerder sought the reality
rather than the appearance of power. And he was sincerely
devoted to Frederick William. Wöllner was the type of hack
employed in the censor's office or the secret cabinet. Bischoffswerder was a courtier and man of the world, of fine bearing, discreet demeanour, impressive glance, mysterious smile;
he was charming, and knew how to combine a dignified exterior with servile obsequiousness and how to conceal insatiable ambition behind a mask of modesty.

He presented Wöllner to the Prince-Royal, and it was
through their offices that Frederick William was received into
the Rosicrucians in 1781. From that time membership of the
Order became the best way of pleasing the heir-presumptive,
and later of gaining the favour of the King. That is how
Haugwitz, who was to play such a great rôle, began. They
formed a party, backing each other and helping each other
on, giving Frederick William consultations and, if necessary, orders through the mediation of spirits which appeared
and spoke at their command. Despite the mystery with
which they surrounded themselves, their secret was known to
all Berlin. Count d'Esterno shows us Bischoffswerder in
1790 'working the machine of ghosts and illuminati about
which people never cease to talk'. With him was another
Saxon, Lindenau, and Wöllner, who had 'the department of
spirits and religious affairs', and at need, wrote Biron, made
the Holy Spirit to speak and the shade of the great Frederick
to walk. A ventriloquist—'an illuminated domestic' was the
piquant description of a contemporary—played the part of the
great man and was five hundred crowns the better off for his
services.

Already a colonel and about to be promoted general,
Bischoffswerder had the rank of official favourite. 'In the
monarch's heart', wrote Custine in 1792, 'the favourite takes
precedence of the mistress. But it is above all in relation to
the ministry that he lords it in the most astonishing way. He
is the intermediary between the King and his ministers. It

is not, as you would perhaps think, that he alone works with them; it is the King who often works with the ministers and who reports to M. de Bischoffswerder, with whom he then makes the final decision. . . .' Mistresses and favourites, Rosicrucians and valets, theosophists and light ladies, they all lived indeed in great harmony and got on famously with one another. From the laboratory of the Rosicrucians to the boudoir of Madame Rietz was but one step, and these mystic personages passed shamelessly from one to the other. They contracted an intimate alliance with the *valet de chambre* and his wife, the *'maîtresse d'habitude'*, who throughout the King's matrimonial eccentricities contrived to maintain her credit by artifices similar to those which had so long sustained Mme de Pompadour at Versailles.

Around them milled a whole mass of minor intriguers, the 'clique' as they were called in Berlin, ready for any piece of backstairs work at the court, in the army, in politics, in diplomacy, above all in finance. Needy and grasping, they had a well-established reputation for venality throughout Europe. 'There is certainly a great difference', wrote M. d'Esterno, 'between the ministry and the people of the inner circles about the King of Prussia. The ministers are knowledgeable and practised in affairs, while the others are in every respect lower than anything you can possibly imagine. Their only interest is in money.' 'I can state as a fact', said Mirabeau, 'that with a thousand louis one could get complete information on all the secrets of the Berlin cabinet. . . . So the Emperor has a faithful record of all the moves made by the King from day to day, and would know of anything he projected, if ever he should project anything.' These were, as Custine averred in 1792, 'the means which all diplomats employed; all the ministers residing in Berlin made use of them, only with more success and more generally than elsewhere'. It is a fact that when in this same year it was desired to discredit the comte de Ségur, envoy of Louis XVI, in the King's opinion, it was enough to accuse him publicly of having wanted to buy the mistress and the favourites; everybody in Berlin and in Europe believed it—the King, the ministers, and the mistress and the favourites sooner than anyone.

Such was the strange band of adventurers who hastened to assault the monarchy and the treasure built up by Frederick the Great. Their plans of action, highly complex and highly effective, were well designed to gain a hold over a temperamental and sensual bigot. They would not however have risen to influence over policy, as distinct from antechamber influence, if they had not known how to pervert the highest as well as gratify the lowest of the King's inclinations. Mediocre and inferior as he was among rulers of the Hohenzollern line, Frederick William was not lacking in all kingly qualities. He was brave; he was good—or, rather, he was a man of 'sentiment'; he desired the public good; he had suffered, like the nation at large, under the pitiless régime of Frederick; he wished, like the rest of the nation, to reform the state by easing the yoke. He believed himself to be inspired from on high, '*illuminé*', and called by Heaven to restore morals and faith in a country which, he was told—and he believed it himself—was perishing through scepticism and the relaxation of morals. How did he reconcile these tendencies with his tastes, these aspirations with his appetites, these beliefs with his debauches? It was precisely here that he showed himself of weak character and a mystic; it was for this purpose that he joined theurgical sects instead of submitting to the Church; that he believed in visions rather than the Gospel, and listened to a ventriloquist counterfeiting the voice of Frederick instead of attending to the opinions of ministers who were disciples of that great king; so it was that he mistrusted wise, thoughtful and experienced men and gave himself over to domestics, charlatans and favourites.

4. REACTION

The results were not slow to appear, and they were disastrous. In home affairs Wöllner, who immediately gained a predominant influence and had a ministry allocated to himself, launched, of set purpose and with all the bitterness of personal revenge, a total reaction against Frederick's system. It was waged in the first place and with the greatest violence against freedom of thought. In 1788 two edicts were published, against freedom of conscience and freedom of the press. Deists and *philosophes* were forbidden to maintain publicly or teach their opinions. Heterodoxy was persecuted equally with impiety. There was a rigorous censorship of speech and books. 'The most meticulous inquisition is established', Custine reported; 'the police is the instrument of this theologian minister, who, thus holding all the strings in his hand, has presented the King with a complete engine of political repression.' The writings of the *philosophes* were submitted to inspection by orthodox pastors, writings on medicine to official doctors. No one wrote on politics. Science was stifled. The repression extended to the universities. To conceal its character and mislead those who were impatient of restraint it was given the colour of a national reaction—a German reaction against France. Here again there was a deliberate reversal of the policies of Frederick's reign.

The men who came to power with Frederick William were not only declared adversaries of France in politics, they were passionate enemies of the French mind and French ideas. They had submitted with resentment to French supremacy. In Frederick's time the French dominated the court, the academies, the theatre. The King would not have any person in society speak any language but French. Frenchmen came to Berlin to study government and the art of war. A publicist, politician or soldier who wanted to make his mark in the world felt obliged to visit Berlin. Officers in particular flocked there. Lauzun, the future General Biron, came there, and the two Custines foregathered with Mirabeau in 1786. These travellers were so numerous that the French minister complained. He was told of the arrival of another Mirabeau, the Mirabeau-Tonneau of the emigration, who was then travelling in Germany. 'We had enough of the first', he wrote. 'Permit me to observe on this occasion that most of the French who come here give a bad impression of the dignity and situation of the nation. Some of them, seized with a ridiculous enthusiasm, praise Prussia above everything else and decry the government and military standing of France. Others embrace the contrary opinion with so much warmth that they heap invective on the Prussians, so much indeed that people of less phlegmatic character would not endure it.' They did endure it, under orders, in Frederick's reign; afterwards they wanted their revenge, but Prussia gained nothing by it.

Whether the trouble came from the French or elsewhere, Wöllner's inquisition only made it worse. Frederick's indifference and tolerance had engendered scepticism and scorn for faith. The hypocritical intolerance, crude mysticism and pietism of Frederick William debased religion and alienated people from it. No law could be effective in face of actual behaviour, no censorship could prevail against example. While the cynicism of the great King vitiated his tolerance, the licentiousness of his successor paralysed his repression. Licence was not reduced, it was concealed. Piety, which was scoffed at under Frederick, seemed odious as soon as the government tried to impose it. By becoming bigoted Berlin society was only further corrupted. It even ceased to think. Frederick's philosophy might narrow men's minds, but at least it left them open to precise conceptions and clear reasoning. But the superstitious religiosity which was decreed to be the fashion after his time only led them astray. Authority was weakened, the crown's prestige collapsed, and the souls of men were degraded by the official Pharisaism.

Frederick's ministers had indeed been underlings, but they were trained, obedient and faithful. They were replaced by the creatures of favourites, who were incapable of building and could only destroy. The bureaucracy became slack; it lost its only qualities, which were blind respect and discipline, without acquiring independence. All the drawbacks of the previous régime were kept while its advantages—mechanical order and passive regularity—were lost. The finances were badly managed and fell into disorder. The disorganization which threatened the state extended even to the army. 'If ever that were neglected', said Frederick, 'it would be the end of the country.' They did worse than neglect it—they left it to its own devices. It became a sort of republic where all tried to get the most for themselves, busied themselves with intrigue, and pulled each other's reputations to pieces. In Frederick's time the army argued about politics; under Frederick William it took an active part in it. Unity disappeared, and the government disintegrated. The King was in the hands of a clique, yet he formed cabals against it. The favourites worked against the ministers, the malcontents worked against the favourites.

It was the survivors from Frederick's reign and the representatives of his tradition who formed this opposition. As the reaction against him was marked above all by hostility to the French, its opponents under the new king made a point of connecting themselves with France, seeking her alliance and propagating her ideas. This was the kernel of the French party which, much restrained and kept in the background in the early years of Frederick William, recovered favour in 1792, and in the following years exercised a considerable influence on Prussian policy.

Foremost in this party was the King's uncle, Frederick's brother Prince Henry, one of the heroes and most admired figures of the eighteenth century. 'Valiant warrior, skilful general, profound statesman, friend of justice, the sciences and the arts, protector of the weak, the succour of the unfortunate', said the comte de Ségur. He was the Maecenas of the French in Berlin. In fact he did them more harm than good, for he had the reputation of being a schemer and grumbler. 'His Gallomania has done us a bad turn', wrote Mirabeau. The great tribune, who had no reason to be pleased with Prince Henry, drew an unflattering portrait. 'He is false, and does not know how to hide it; though full of ideas, wit and talents, he is quite lacking in judgement. Petty devices, petty schemes, passions, views—everything is petty in the soul of that man, although there is something phenomenal about his mind.' 'He is a fussy old woman, and that's about all', was Catherine II's description of him.[13] He could never console himself for not playing the premier rôle, and so that he could claim the honour of having done so, this *philosophe* did not hesitate to boast of having woven the perfidious plot for the first partition of Poland.[14] He was one of the chief negotiators of the peace between France and Prussia in 1795, and always remained faithful to the idea of alliance between the two states. As a pledge of his sentiments, he made the Institute a present in the Year V of the manuscript of *Jacques le Fataliste*. The Director sent him in return arms of honour, with bound copies of the works of Diderot.[15]

Another of the 'French' prominent in Berlin and much in favour in Paris was the Duke of Brunswick, Mirabeau's Alcibiades. Among others who shared the ideas of Prince Henry and the Duke of Brunswick were included Struensee, minister of excise—'as favourable to the Revolution as a Prussian minister can be', said Custine—and Möllendorf, the most brilliant of Frederick's lieutenants, 'loyal, straightforward, sound, whose virtue would do honour to a land more productive of it than this one'.[16] Though well-known and popular at army headquarters, in the universities and above all among the Berlin bourgeoisie, on the eve of the Revolution these men were without influence at court. Brunswick only recovered credit there by sacrificing his principles. The others were only listened to when their apprehensions and criticisms had been justified by disaster.

5. DECLINE

As Mirabeau had foreseen, the decline began in diplomacy. Frederick had first astonished Europe by his audacity, and then surprised it by his moderation. In his latter days he be-

[13] Letter to Grimm, 8 April 1795.
[14] See Ségur, *Mémoires*, vol. I, pp. 145 ff.
[15] Procès-verbaux of the Directory, 2 and 7 vendémiaire an V.
[16] Mirabeau, *Histoire secrète*, letter of 2 December 1786.

came hermit-like and strongly conservative. While friendly with England and flirting with France, he remained the ally of Russia, and was feared by Austria. He had bound these two courts to Prussia in the only way in which, in the state of international law at the time, three powers mutually jealous and equally ambitious could be solidly united—complicity in crime. Frederick William could have enjoyed in peace the brilliant ease his predecessor had prepared for him. But he was avid for glory; he had at his disposal an army of a hundred and sixty thousand men and a well-furnished treasury. He thought the treasury was inexhaustible and the army invincible, and he wanted to be talked about. Far from restraining him, Hertzberg, his minister for foreign affairs, urged him on to great enterprises. Frederick William was very willing to listen to this kind of language from his counsellors. He began in 1787 with a great success. In Holland the patriot party had rebelled. France protected it, while England took the side of the Stadtholder. Frederick William saw a chance of humiliating France, and seized it. He sent an army to Holland which put the patriots to flight almost without firing a shot, and without France daring to resist it. The enterprise succeeded against all expectation. 'What Louis XIV, Turenne, Condé, Luxemburg, Louvois and 200,000 Frenchmen have not achieved in Holland,' wrote Mirabeau before this expedition, 'Prussia, watched by the Emperor, cannot possibly do in the same country when it is supported by France.' The Dutch submitted, and the Prussians thought themselves formidable. Their natural presumptuousness was increased tenfold. Taking no account of the motives which prevented France from intervening, nor of those which induced the majority of the Dutch not to resist, they attributed the success of their military promenade entirely to the terror engendered by the renown of their arms. Believing France to be stricken unto death, they ceased to take any account of her, and thought it the easiest thing in the world to re-establish a throne and smother a revolution.

The terrible miscalculation of their campaign of 1792 proceeded from the success of that of 1787.

But for the moment they were full of pride in their triumph. The treaties of the Triple Alliance which they concluded with England and Holland sealed their victory.[17] Prussia rose to the first rank, and Hertzberg thought he had control of Europe. We shall see in what complicated adventures he had involved Prussia by the time war broke out between France and Austria in 1792, after the Revolution. The tortuous combinations of Hertzberg brought Prussia nothing but failure; she thought that by throwing herself into the war against the French Revolution she would find the opportunity for a striking revenge and great gains. Frederick William joined the crusade of kings; he even commanded the vanguard. But though he abruptly changed his policy, he remained the same man, and brought to his new enterprise the same indecision and the same dreams of grandeur contending with the same greed for lucre. Total disinterestedness should have been the sole raison d'être and the sole condition of success in the war into which he threw himself. It upset all his forecasts and deceived all his hopes. Neither he nor his advisers measured up to the prodigious events they were called upon to face. The formidable resistance of France, the Machiavellianism of Russia, the disarray of the old Europe found them lost and bewildered. They vainly sought within themselves for some direction and support; they found there nothing but the love of gain and the habit of intrigue. By these their conduct was dictated. Thus tainted and vitiated from the beginning, their enterprises collapsed. The uncertainties of diplomacy hampered the movements of the army. The pursuit of the manifold objects of their greed resulted in contradictory measures. Seeking everywhere only for gain they saw it everywhere at once escape them. Hence the equivocation of their promises, the duplicity of their conduct,

[17] Treaties of 15 April 1788 with Holland, 13 June and 13 August 1788 with England.

the miscarriage of ill-conceived plans, and the changes of front, which have been justly described as betrayals.

And so they successively left Poland at the mercy of the Russians and shared her territory with them after promising to defend it; conspired against Austria and suddenly abandoned her after seeking her alliance and urging her to fight; gave the signal for the capitulation of the dynasties after preaching the crusade of the kings; joined in the dismemberment of Germany after taking up arms to protect it; became the first associates of the Revolution after being its first enemies; and coupled Prussian perfidy, shorn of Frederick's genius, with Austrian hypocrisy, shorn of Maria Theresa's virtues. Suspected by everybody, Frederick William brought about the isolation of Prussia in Europe, having already hastened the decline of the Prussian state within.

The ten years of peace which followed the treaty of 1795 only delayed the catastrophe; the causes which rendered it inevitable still continued to operate, and they were already present in 1792. 'In the army', says a German historian, 'caprice, presumption, egoism; no spirit of sacrifice, no devotion to King or country; in the administration intrigue, indolence, routine jealousy, little aptitude and less zeal; in the upper classes desire for enjoyment and dislike of effort; a dogmatising spirit which laid down the law and criticised everything without effort of will or of thought—such was the state of Prussia at the end of the eighteenth century. The firm discipline which had brought her to such a high rank had disappeared both in the government and among the people. There were doubtless still great vigour and resource within the nation, but they were useless under the government of a lot of conscienceless intriguers, wretched mediocrities and conceited debauchees.'[18] In face of a triumphant France Prussia found herself with an unstable government, a nation in disarray, a diplomacy in disrepute. Nothing re-

[18] Philippson, *Geschichte des Preussischen Staatswesens*, I, p. 468. Leipzig, 1880-2.

mained of the work of Frederick save his army. This was annihilated by Napoleon.

6. RECOVERY

After this catastrophe it seemed that the Prussian state was about to collapse and that the very name of Prussia would disappear from the map of Europe. Its decline had been obvious for a long time; Napoleon gave the final blow to a moribund state which had been irrevocably condemned by all the political doctors of the age. Nevertheless Prussia rose again, regenerated by her terrible ordeal. The men who conceived this great recovery and the factors they used to accomplish it were at hand even as the country approached its downfall, but they passed unnoticed. 'Prussia has only a façade to show Europe', said the abbé de Pradt. This façade, hastily built of heterogeneous materials, was already cracking in Frederick's time; it was easy to foresee its collapse. But what was not seen was that hidden in the ground were deep and solid foundations on which, when the rubble was cleared away, skilful architects could build a new edifice stronger than the first; all the materials for it had been patiently accumulated by the earlier kings.

The nation in Prussia, like the state, was artificial. As one historian has ingeniously expressed it, it was a mosaic cunningly put together.[19] But the mosaic was compact and solid; it formed a whole. Populations of diverse origins had been fused together by the institutions of government. In Prussia the state was both rational and national. Beneath the bureaucratic network, beneath the restless surface of the nation and the froth of the great cities, there was a mass of men in the provinces moved by the same aspirations, accustomed to live in close contact with one another and to love the same country, among whom had developed the kind of public spirit

[19] Lavisse, *Etudes; Formation de l'Etat prussien*. Inaugural lecture at the Sorbonne. *Revue politique*, Paris, 1881.

which in the time of Mirabeau had been, it was said, the
envy even of the English, and which in Germany was called
'the Prussian spur'. The corruption of the upper classes has
not been exaggerated, but this corruption was confined to
the capital.

The lesser nobility—the nerve-centre of the state—remained
untouched by it. They were poor and hardworking. It was of
them that Frederick was thinking when he wrote to the Duke
of Brunswick: 'You in your Lower Saxony and I in my sand-
pit, we have no need to fear that affluence will corrupt the
sentiments of our fellow-citizens.' Living in the midst of the
peasants and associated with local government, they were respected by the people, to whom they rendered services as
well as ruling them. The people were primitive and their
lives were rough; their education was poorly developed. The
veteran non-commissioned officers to whom Frederick had entrusted the direction of his schools had not taught their pupils
much in the way of systematic knowledge, but they had
taught them patriotism in action. The Prussians were habit-
uated to revere the King, to identify the fatherland with the
royal family and to combine discipline with duty.

It was not likely that this nation would disintegrate through
the breaking of the mould in which it had been shaped. The
army, recruited from foreigners, was destroyed, but there was
a people who could be called to arms, and a rural nobility
ready to form the cadres of a new army. The military bond
was strengthened by the feudal bond and the spirit of nationalism. The bureaucracy was decrepit and powerless, but
in the provinces could be found all the elements of an administration more alert, more vigorous, more personal, and
better fitted to the nation's needs. The state was dissolving,
but there survived in the people the forces on which states
are based. It was said that Prussia must perish because she
was artificial and of recent construction, but it was precisely
this that saved her.

She was formed from very disparate elements, from very
diverse countries of origin. The state had respected their us-

ages if not their autonomy. While absorbing them in itself, as the spirit of the age required, it had allowed to remain, or to speak more exactly had not had time entirely to destroy, the ancient customs of local administration in the provinces and especially in the communes. Memories, tastes, habits, traditions, survived; these were the elements of provincial society. In brief, administrative centralisation stopped at the surface— it had not penetrated to the nation in general. When the state was overturned and its elements had to be reassembled, it was not necessary to centralise further or push to extremes, under pretext of reforming it, the system that had made reform necessary. It was possible to go back and, renouncing an artificial organization which had been condemned by the fact of its collapse, to find in the natural development of the national elements of the monarchy the means of rebuilding the state. Hence the extreme difference between the political and social revolution in France in 1789 and the reform which was accomplished in Prussia after 1807. It was possible, as it would not have been in France, to reconcile changes as profound as those which Stein and his collaborators effected with respect for the past and the maintenance of outdated institutions—such changes as the successive abolition of the feudal system, equality of taxation, universal military service and open admission to employment.

The same motives explain why, in spite of the violent disturbances by which she was shaken, Prussia remained so refractory to the spirit of the French Revolution. This Revolution proceeded from principles and produced a centralised system of government which were precisely those against which Prussia was protesting, from which she had suffered and from which the reformers wanted to set her free.

The nation was not prepared for sedition: foreign conquest, far from provoking a revolution, produced on the contrary a sort of recrudescence and reawakening of royalist sentiment. Since the nation, the state and the King were identified, the defeat which revived the spirit of the nation revived at the same time its devotion to the state and attach-

ment to the dynasty. It was the French Revolution, armed
and personified in a conqueror, that had vanquished the Prussians. Their reform had as its motive and its aim a rising
against the military domination of France, but it was also a
revolt against the intellectual and political domination of
the French. And yet what was most noble in the ideas the
Prussian reformers applied to their country was the very essence of the ideas of the eighteenth century, and France had
been their home. Stein and his disciples appropriated these
ideas and applied them to the regeneration of the Prussian
state, as their predecessors of the sixteenth century had done
with Protestantism. In both cases their originality lay precisely
in the skill with which they reconciled monarchical traditions with great political and religious innovations. In becoming Lutheran, the Grand Master of the Teutonic Order
was thinking less of the welfare of his subjects than of founding a great dynasty; religious reform offered him the means,
so he adopted it. In adapting to Prussia's needs some of the
practical ideas of the French Revolution, the Prussian ministers of 1807 had no thought of creating an ideal state or
working for humanity—they thought only of reconstituting
the Prussian state. Social and political reform provided them
with the means, so they became reformers.

These men were born in Frederick's period; in their youth
they had witnessed the decline of the monarchy. The catastrophe enlightened them on the causes of the evil before they
themselves had experienced its effects. They belonged to a
generation which without having suffered the deleterious effects of the ways of thought of the eighteenth century was
nevertheless imbued with its spirit. They had acquired its
high intellectual and political culture, and to this their country's disaster forced them to add realism, a sense of proportion
and practicality. The ordeal hardened their characters. So in
the space of twenty years, from 1786 to 1806, there could
be seen evolving the causes which were to bring Prussia so
low and raise her again so high. Her astonishing decline could
be seen to result from her very prosperity and, yet more

astonishing, her regeneration to spring out of her decadence.

When Frederick died, his nephew, who succeeded him, was forty-two years old, and his great-nephew, who was to reign next, was sixteen. Frederick William II almost destroyed Prussia, Frederick William III restored it. If the former summed up in his own person the causes of her fall, the latter bore within him the elements of recovery. Mirabeau, who had a flair for understanding revolutions, and who in political matters had the presentiments of a genius, had discerned better than anyone what was solid and what was fragile in the work of Frederick. He had foretold its collapse, but at the same time instinctively felt that it would be rebuilt. 'Perhaps', he wrote after meeting the young prince who was to reign as Frederick William III, 'this young man has a great future before him, and when he becomes the pivot of some memorable revolution, men who view it from afar will not be surprised.'[20]

VIII.   *Russia, Sweden, Poland and Eastern Affairs*

I. TURKEY, SWEDEN AND POLAND

Turkey, Poland and Sweden occupied a place of considerable importance in the old French system. They were like so many counterweights attached to the extremities of Europe, allowing the centre to be detached from them. They provided the means for the diversion of interests from the central problems and the theatre to which they could be diverted. This rôle they continued to fill during the wars of the French Revolution, and the diversions they provided exercised a de-

[20] *Histoire secrète*, 30 December 1786.

cisive influence on the destinies of France. It was in the north and east of Europe that the crisis arose which from 1789 to 1795 incensed the great powers of Europe against each other, made plain their irreconcilable claims, caused their rivalries to break out, demonstrated the defects of their international system, distracted their attention from the affairs of France till the end of 1791, long retarded the formation of their coalition, paralysed it as soon as it was formed, and finally broke it up.

While a social and political revolution was taking place in the West, a territorial revolution was in progress in the East. There was no connection between these revolutions, which proceeded from absolutely different causes and produced quite dissimilar results, but they began at the same time and had a parallel development. The same powers were interested in both, and so the one reacted on the other. At the moment when France was under the most violent pressure, and Europe seemed about to stifle her, a great void suddenly appeared on the plains of Poland; the alignment of political forces was changed, and France, relieved, could breathe again. It was a sort of mechanical effect; the resulting reaction was equally efficacious, and France drew great advantages from it. This was a European counter-revolution of a sort; Sweden appeared only in episodes, Turkey supplied little more than pretexts, and even Poland, which succumbed to it, only provided opportunities for others. It was Russia that took the lead, and so this power, whose soldiers took no part in the struggle against France until 1799, was involved in the whole history of the French Revolution. Her intervention, though indirect, seemed decisive in some of the most grave crises. To conclude this study of Europe before 1789 we must traverse this vast battlefield of the East and North, and point out at least the main positions, the great folds of the terrain, and the watersheds.

The arrival of Russia on the political scene and her advance towards the centre of Europe were contemporary with the decline of the Turks and their retreat towards Asia. In the seventeenth century, to take only their external features, the two countries presented certain similarities. 'In Russia', said Voltaire, 'the government resembled that of the Turks in that the Streltsi, like the Janissaries, sometimes disposed of the throne and almost always disturbed the state as much as they strengthened it.'[1] But while in Turkey the continual palace revolutions, the uncertain tenure of power, and the decay of private and public morals under a despotism both feeble and tyrannical represented in some sense the natural character of Ottoman power and its whole development, the same phenomena in Russia only signalised the troubled ferment of a great nation seeking to establish itself and to emerge into the light of day.

There was no Turkish nation, only conquerors camped in the midst of hostile populations. The Turks did not form a state, but had only an army which was useful for nothing but conquest and tended to melt away as soon as it was brought to a halt. European civilisation was beyond their reach, for they could not undertake reform without breaking away from their traditions, that is to say without altering the essential sources of their power. Between themselves and the peoples they had enslaved religion opened an unbridgeable gulf. They knew no way to rule but by force, and their force was declining. In Russia, on the contrary, the peoples were united by the strongest of the primitive bonds by which nations are formed—religious belief. Their faith drew them towards the old European world and opened its civilisation to them. They were as amenable to outside influence as the Turks seemed recalcitrant. The Turks had based their empire on ruins, and the soil around their camp remained barren. The Russians spread over their vast plains, virgin soil which only awaited cultivation to become fruitful. Time, which in Turkey withered everything, with the Russians brought everything to life.

All things contributed to the growth of antagonism and

[1] *Histoire de la Russie*, ch. II.

hatred between these two peoples. The Russians had received their faith from Byzantium; this was their metropolis, and the Turks sullied it by their presence. The Turks oppressed the Russians' co-religionists, and every Russian looked upon the deliverance of his brethren as a religious duty. Popular passions agreed in this with the dictates of policy: it was towards the Black Sea, the Danube and Constantinople that the Russian rulers were naturally led to extend their sway; to liberate and to conquer became for them synonymous terms. The tsars had the rare fortune that their schemes of ambition were supported by the nation's instincts, so that they could turn against the Ottoman Empire a religious fanaticism like that which had hurled the Turks themselves against Europe and, not very long since, made their attacks so formidable.

These essential characteristics of Russian policy were nowhere so clearly marked as in relations with Turkey; but they could be seen elsewhere, and recognised wherever Russia's power advanced. From the beginning her claims were singular in being vast and simple at the same time. Never had a policy proceeded more directly and spontaneously from the very nature of things. Russia could only breathe, grow and prosper by opening the routes of civilisation and trade. The trade route was the Baltic, which was closed by the Swedes; the centre of civilisation was the old Europe, and Poland blocked all access to it. Hence arose Russia's primordial antagonism to the Swedes and the Poles as well as to the Turks. And history favoured the Russians in Sweden and Poland as in Turkey.

Sweden had played a large part in world affairs in the seventeenth century and the first years of the eighteenth, yet she made only a fleeting impression; she was prominent only sporadically. The first of her great warriors, Gustavus Adolphus, was no more than an illustrious auxiliary; the second, Charles XII, was a royal adventurer. He lost the Baltic provinces, gave over the empire of the North to Russia, and left Sweden exhausted, discouraged, and divided against herself. Her part was played out. The Swedes had suffered much from the caprices of their rulers; they tried to find safeguards in their ancient liberties, but these remained as empty forms inherited from the Middle Ages and only suitable to rough ways and simple passions. The Swedes infused them with the turbulent and *frondeur* spirit of the eighteenth century and all the habits of intrigue which had been introduced under the cover of despotism. This pretended return to liberty was nothing but a collapse into anarchy. The parties which were formed had no base in the country; they sought support from outside and sold themselves to foreigners. All their institutions were eaten with corruption, and the nation seemed to invite the intervention of neighbouring powers.*

Although they seemed no longer capable of governing themselves liberally, the Swedes were by no means an ungovernable people. They had a basic sense of discipline. Their differences were passionate, but they were not inveterate to the point of blinding them to their patriotic duty. They were aware of the peril involved in their divisions. They had not lost their liking for war, and brilliant enterprises could still divert them from factional strife. This explains the success of the coup d'état brought off by Gustavus III in 1772, which saved Sweden's independence. The *philosophes* applauded; Gustavus was their pupil, and loved the enlightenment; he 'overthrew the altars of fanaticism', and the sovereign power he had arrogated to himself he used for the reform of abuses.

But these purely pacific successes did not satisfy Gustavus.

* Sorel's description of Swedish politics in the eighteenth century is hardly fair. It is true that foreign influence and bribery exercised a considerable influence, as it did in all aristocracies and courts; but the Swedish parties were divided on grounds of policy. The Caps, who prevailed for a large part of the century, stood for a peaceful foreign policy, after the disastrous adventures of Charles XII, while the Hats—the name being taken from the more military type of headgear—increasingly pressed for a return to a forward policy. The *coup d'état* of Gustavus III in 1772, which restored monarchical power for a short period, was effected with the aid of French influence and money.

He was twenty-six; he was fearless, he loved glory, and he burned to astonish the world and fill with the renown of his exploits those famous Paris salons he had visited, which, from far and near, always fascinated him. He was always liable to *ennui* and restlessness, but along with signs of frivolous vanity there were also sudden bursts of chivalrous imagination. The other side of this volatile politician, this *philosophe* prince, this wooer of the world's opinion, was a knight-errant in quest of a crusade. In him the soul of Gustavus Adolphus sometimes seemed to stir, and he was as if obsessed by memories of greatness. But he lacked both resources and interests. Sweden's only interest was self-defence, and as to resources, she had to borrow them. She could only maintain her armaments by means of subsidies. Obliged to fight for foreign causes, she could only appear in important affairs in a subsidiary rôle. Expeditions, even if in the national interest, must be brief and successful. The King had always to fear party intrigue when he went to war, and his enemies too easily found allies among his own subjects. Nevertheless Sweden survived, and even seemed to be firmly established again; it was an improvement for her to be weak only when she was aggressive and to be in difficulties only when she was adventurous. Unhappily the same could not be said of Poland.

Poland was dispersed over the immense plains of Eastern Europe. The Polish state was a sort of fleshless body stretched out on the earth, covering a vast extent of land but not embracing it. Its boundaries were vague, its government precarious; it offered its enemies territories that were open to attack and a nation torn in fragments. What survived of her institutions tended to weaken the state and what remained of her national traditions tended to divide the nation. The Polish constitution combined defects of opposite kinds. It was an aristocracy, but 'the most imperfect of all', said Montesquieu;[2] the people lived in slavery to the nobility. It was a republic, but it was at once the most anarchical and least

2 *Esprit des lois*, liv. II. ch. III.

free; the object of the laws was independence for everyone, and the result was the oppression of all. A hundred thousand gentry held sovereign power over Poland; their ancestors had begun to rule in days beyond the reach of memory. A few great families, the richest and most powerful, lorded it over the rest. Beneath this nobility there were peasants still reduced to the condition of serfdom. There was no intermediate class, no bourgeoisie—for one could not so describe the German colonists, who were execrated and suppressed, or the Jews (taxable at pleasure as in France at the time of Philip the Fair) who were massed together in the towns, but formed no united body, and remained isolated from this republic of gentry like 'drops of oil in a swamp'.

The nation was thus reduced to an army of nobles, living as in a conquered country and indulging every kind of passion with impunity. They loved pleasure and fêtes, and to pay for them they ruined the peasantry, drying up their own sources of income by the oppressive burden they laid upon the land. The state belonged to them—they shared it out between them. The king was only a figure-head; he was elected by the nobility, and before the election they imposed on him, under the title of *pacta conventa*, an anticipatory abdication of power, only the insignia of which he was about to receive. When the king was proclaimed, the nobles kept him legally powerless by means of the Diet, without which he was impotent and in which he counted for nothing. The members of this assembly showed the same jealousy of each other as of the king. Power belonged to all; each could be master by paralysing its exercise. Unanimity was required for all resolutions—the *liberum veto* left the republic at the mercy of a madman's caprice or the schemes of a scoundrel.

Anarchy thus became the normal condition of the state. The only way of escaping it—a remedy worse than the disease—was civil war. To set up a state within the state, suspend the laws, impose the will of a faction by force—things which elsewhere would have been sedition and justly imputed treasonable—were for the Poles the exercise of a public right. It was called forming a *confederation*, and was the only check on anarchy that there was. The first principle of this government had insurrection as its indispensable corollary.

As for the obscure masses of the people, they seemed to be crushed by their yoke and brutalised by the sunless misery of their lives. 'Your peasants', wrote Mably to the Poles, 'are reduced to the most wretched servitude. Their lords have less idea of caring for them than for their horses.' The degrading indifference of their masters towards them made them indifferent to their masters' fate. The government was quite alien to them. They did not feel themselves to be citizens; the nation rejected them, and they did not recognise it. It mattered little to them that authority changed its name if it preserved the same character. If their lot was eased, they welcomed the change. They were only aroused from their torpor to give themselves up to blind fanaticism, and their fury was directed first against their lords. Arming them against the enemy always meant the risk of a peasant revolt.

Poland was simply an anachronism in eighteenth-century Europe. While she laid herself open to the intrigues and invasions of her neighbours, they on the other hand were concentrating their power. With all the resources of science and the formidable organization of modern states they set about besieging this citadel of the Middle Ages. To the artillery and engineers of the enemy Poland could oppose only outdated defences, dismantled ramparts, a troop of heroic but undisciplined knights-errant, while behind them, in the towns, there were conspiracies and factions, dismayed townsfolk, and a populace that was half-savage, famished, avid for pillage and massacre.

In 1772 Poland was dismembered by Prussia, Austria and Russia. Sweden learnt her lesson from this frightening example, and Poland in her turn seemed to be struck by the example of the Swedes. All Poles who genuinely loved their country knew it could be saved only by extensive reforms. They must abolish the *liberum veto*, which broke up the nation, the capitulations, the *pacta conventa*, which shackled authority, and the *confederations*, which rent the state. They must establish a system of taxation; fill the treasury instead of robbing it, and train regiments of the line and artillery to replace the brilliant but disorderly *pospolite*, who were to the Prussian and Russian forces what the French knights had been to the English archers at Crecy and Agincourt. And particularly they must arouse civic life and involve in the fate of the nation the enormous mass of inhabitants still excluded from it, and treat them as citizens who might one day be called to the defence of the city. Such were the ideas stirring in the minds of Polish patriots when that famous diet met at Warsaw in 1788 which seemed destined to regenerate the Republic, but which was on the contrary to complete its enslavement.

Among the Poles could be found—and this is why history cannot disregard their misfortune—a profound awareness of their evils, an ardent wish to remedy them, respect for their national origins, faith in the future, an exalted tradition of disinterested enthusiasm, a feeling for noble causes, readiness for sacrifice, and passionate love of country. These were their virtues, but unluckily for Poland everyone put these virtues at the service of party. Each party saw itself as the whole republic; to secure its own triumph none would scruple to call in foreigners to its aid, and all looked upon rival factions as enemies. Foreigners nourished and profited from these dissensions. It could be said that in Poland everybody had a party except the Republic, and that the Poles relied on everyone except themselves.

The state lacked a soul. The King, Stanislaus Poniatowski, had only one title to reign—he had been the lover of Catherine II. On the throne of his country he continued to be a time-server to his former mistress, and the obligations of the favourite always paralysed the patriotic aspirations of the king.* In the state of anarchy that prevailed in Poland even

* Stanislaus showed himself more worthy of his kingship when, in 1791, he put himself at the head of a great national movement for the reform of the Polish Constitution. This would not have

attempts at reform furnished the pretext for new divisions. Danger only served to disunite the Poles; each put the blame on his adversaries, and even patriotism became a motive for faction. We shall see how, in spite of the generous resolutions which the principles and example of France inspired in the Poles, the French Revolution still further increased discord between the parties by its propaganda. In so far as this penetrated among the people, it aroused the anger they naturally felt against their lords. Everything in Poland worked for the extension of anarchy, and everything contributed to the decline of the Republic. At the same time everything combined to increase the power of Russia.

2. RUSSIA AND CATHERINE II

Revolutionary propaganda could not touch Russia. It was not merely the remoteness, it was the actual character of the civilisation of that empire that rendered it inaccessible. Nothing in it was ripe for either political or civil liberty. The three essential elements of the French Revolution were lacking in Russia; a privileged but powerless nobility, an ambitious and strong middle class, and a proprietary peasantry. The Revolution of 1789 was above all a revolution in ownership, and it proceeded essentially from the principle of individual property. In Russia the peasants had not even a conception of this, and therefore the whole spirit of the Revolution escaped them. The noble alone was a landowner, but the Russian noble had nothing in common with those of the West. There was nothing feudal about the Russian nobility; it was a hierarchy, created entirely by the tsars, open to all state employees, and one rose in it according to one's grade in the service. It had been created to absorb and de-

---

amounted to much without a corresponding reform of the social structure, which the Polish nobles would never have contemplated; but in any case reform was the last thing that Russia would tolerate in Poland. The inevitable result was the Second and Third Partitions.

stroy—to swamp in a sort of 'noble plebs'—what was left of the ancient aristocracy of the country. This noble status dependent on function conferred no political rights on those who had it. The nobility did not compose a distinct body. In the towns, infinitely less numerous and populous than in France, there were merchants, artisans, and employees, but none of the elements of a middle class of the European type. There were only individuals prostrate before the majesty of the state and securely under its thumb, almost deaf to western ideas and hostile to their influence.

A group of 'patriots' was indeed formed in the years preceding 1789 who dreamed of 'enlightened government' and discussed and preached great humanitarian reforms. But they took no action, they were nowhere near attaining to power, and they had no place in government till the reign of Alexander I. Moreover they were far from being democrats, and prided themselves on remaining Russian in every respect. They only began to understand the Revolution and were only prepared to admire it after 18th Brumaire, as represented by the Civil Code, and in the despotic form of Bonaparte's Consulate. They were thus only inspired to reform the State for the purpose of strengthening it.

Most contemporaries saw in the events of 1789 to 1799 in France nothing but a series of inane or odious Saturnalia. Apart from her victories, which seemed inexplicable, France gave them the impression of another Poland—that is to say in their eyes the most wretched object in the world. This was the judgement of the 'enlightened' nobility, nourished on the manna of the *philosophes*. They were astonished from the very first. It must be remembered that the culture of these Russian gentlemen was entirely superficial, and that they recited French phrases rather than spoke the French language. At bottom they remained barbarous, changeable, and scornful of anything foreign that affected them only remotely and indirectly. 'With you', Joseph de Maistre told them, 'there is nothing constant but inconstancy.' The fashion and caprice which had favoured the *philosophes* were trans-

ferred to the émigrés, without any intermediate stage and
without any difficulty. What attracted them so strongly before the Revolution was the old French society, so free in
thought, so refined in civilisation, so noble in its sentiments
and aspirations. In 1793 it seemed to them that a Duc de
Richelieu represented this better than a Robespierre. The
revulsion of feeling was not really so strange as it seemed.
They had spoken French and paraded their *philosophie* to
distinguish themselves from others, through pride of caste and
in pursuit of elegance. As soon as *philosophie* became revolutionary and the Revolution became democratic—and France
became the people—they rolled *philosophie*, Revolution and
France into one, and arrogantly bestowed the same hatred
and condemnation on them all. As for the mass of the Russian nation, it remained perfectly indifferent. 'Peter I, to police this nation, worked on it like aquafortis on iron', said
Frederick.[3] The tsars had often met with difficulties in their
efforts to impose western civilisation on their subjects; so the
government found nothing was easier than to resist revolutionary propaganda.

There was only one bond that united men in Russia at
that time—religious faith—and only one idea that roused
men's spirits—the extension of the Empire, that is, the propagation of the national faith. A contemporary wrote: 'They
owe to their superstitious faith and to the concentration of
all power in a single hand their vainglorious and exclusive
character.'[4] Parallel to France they developed a power very
different in kind but not less formidable. Despite their modern armament the Russian troops were still barbarians. With
their immense quantity of baggage, their mass of camp-
followers, the devastation and contagion they left behind
them, they came on like the Asiatic hordes of old. But their
soldiers were excellent. Hardened to fatigue and inured to
suffering, their brutal enthusiasm and their fatalistic resigna-

[3] *Mémoires*, ch. I.
[4] Ségur, *Mémoires*, vol. III, p. 145.

tion made up for the inadequacies of their officers. A leader who could arouse the passions of these men, a Suvorov for example, eccentric and fanatical, could lead them to the end of the world. They did not enter the lists till 1799, but from the first onset the French found how redoubtable they were.

The tsars wanted only useful conquests and undertook only popular wars; they shaped in the interests of the state only plans that were sustained by national passions. Their policy, dictated by the nature of things, was obvious and simple, and that is why it was able to persist through incessant changes of power. The throne was unsteady in the extreme; violent usurpation and assassination seemed to be the only constant law of succession to the empire. The rulers brought with them a troop of favourites or accomplices, almost all of whom were foreigners or people of lowly origin. There were no institutions, no councils, nor even a court by which traditions could be maintained, and yet they were carried on without interruption. Peter the Great was succeeded by a Livonian peasant woman who could neither read nor write, assisted by a former pastrycook raised to be prince and regent.* Later it was the son of a Courland groom whom the caprice of an empress called to direct the state.† 'Four loose women', says a historian, 'two children, two madmen or maniacs—these were for a century the successors of Peter.'[5]

They all, however, actuated by the same instinct, thrust out in the same directions—to the Black Sea, the Baltic, central Europe. They all contemplated or attempted aggrandisement at the expense of the Turk, the Swede and the Pole.

---

* The Livonian peasant woman was Peter's widow, who became the Empress Catherine I, 1725-1727; the former pastrycook was his minister Menshikov, regent during the brief reign of Peter's grandson, Peter II, 1727-30.

† Presumably Ernst Johann Bühren, who had a predominant influence over the Empress Anna (1730-1740), though his highest official appointment was head of the imperial stables. His family, however, had been ennobled in Courland in the seventeenth century.

[5] Anatole Leroy-Beaulieu, vol. I, pp. 251-252.

When in 1762 a new barrack and palace revolution put the heritage of the Muscovites into the hands of a little German princess, all the routes were marked out and all the ways were open. Catherine II applied to the pursuit of these traditional plans the extraordinary vigour of her genius. Fortune, which had prepared such great destinies for Russia and presented her with such singular opportunities, afforded her at the same time the sovereign best fitted to make use of them.

Catherine of Anhalt was sixty years of age in 1789. More imposing than beautiful, she had energy in her features and fire in her glance, and in her physiognomy something noble, grave and restrained which contrasted with everything that was known of the incredible laxity of her morals. She gained the admiration of the *philosophes*, who found the principles of virtue in the instincts, but she would have been the scandal of the monarchy if its reputation had left any room for scandal. She had raised up her accomplices and lovers and she loaded them with honours and riches, made them ministers, generals, ambassadors, counts and princes. By 1789 Gregory Orlov had died in retirement, and Potemkin was a favourite only in respect of dignities and influence, but his influence was immense and his dignities prodigious; he was the second personage of Russia, he commanded her armies, and enjoyed a fortune estimated at 175 million livres. The other lovers, the *kyrielle* (roll-call) as they were described, were all ennobled and given places. There was always one lover *en titre*, but he changed fairly often, and while he remained current he did not fail to preserve his credit by using the artifices employed elsewhere by the '*maîtresses d'habitude*', Madame de Pompadour at Versailles and Madame Rietz at Berlin. The favourites themselves chose their understudies, and several presented their successors. The Empress, when she was tired of them or dissatisfied, dismissed them, married them off and gave them a dowry. At court they formed a faction which Rulhière wittily named 'the favourites' faction', and which was opposed to the more serious group which composed 'the ministers' party'. But, very different in this from the kings who were her rivals in licentiousness—more virile than a Louis XV, for example—and remaining always the sovereign in the midst of lovers like Louis XIV among his mistresses, this singular woman lived her life in two parts, one devoted to government, the other to love. She may have been liberal with her person, but she was jealous of her power. The weaknesses, jealousies and anxieties of a woman only troubled the Empress during the last period of her life, when she could not rid herself of an obsession with growing old, when she began to count the days left her for love and the enervating impatience of age upset the balance of her character.

In 1789 her genius was still in full flower, and never had the reign of a Russian sovereign achieved such greatness. And this was because there had never been a sovereign so completely Russian as this German princess. Having been called to succeed the tsars by the chances of politics, she meant to justify her good fortune and in some sort legitimate her usurpation. While Peter I gave himself so much trouble to become European, Catherine employed all her flexibility and all her resolution to become Russian. She only undertook reforms that were possible, so her reforms bore fruit. She left Russia transformed and prosperous. Her subjects, in any case inured to revolutions, only looked at the great results and willingly forgot the evil deeds in which they had originated. At St. Petersburg and Moscow they spoke of *the Empress*, as under Louis XIV, at Paris and Versailles, they spoke of *the King*.

In her correspondence with the leading lights of Paris Catherine appeared superior to her famous partners, Grimm, for example, and even Voltaire. But to know her only from her letters is to judge her by appearances and to do injustice to her genius. In particular it would mean totally misunderstanding her policy during the period of the French Revolution. It would make it impossible to explain how this 'Semira-

mis' of the eighteenth century could from the outset be such
a scornful and relentless enemy of a revolution which was,
at least to begin with, the realisation of the ideas of those
whom the Empress openly declared her masters and friends.
One is astounded to find her preaching the crusade of the
kings with an extraordinary vehemence of sarcasm, and raising against the Revolution the terrible war-cry of Voltaire
and the Encyclopaedists—the cry of *Ecrasez l'infâme!*—which
had not long since rallied the whole army of *philosophes* to
the attack on the Church. And it is surprising to find that,
upholding in Poland what she was combating in France, she
was as tenacious in maintaining anarchy in Warsaw as in
restoring absolute monarchy in Paris. We might be tempted
to conclude that she was not guided by principles, which is
true, and that she lacked consistency in her policy, which
would be a grave error.

The matter had nothing to do with principles; Catherine
was not in the least concerned with them. The Revolution
in France upset her calculations, so she detested it; anarchy
in Poland assisted her projects, so she fomented it. She ut-
tered fearful condemnations of the rebellious French, but
left the duty of acting upon them to the Germans. The disposition of her peoples and the remoteness of her states
screened her from propaganda, so she could afford to mis-
understand the character of the French Revolution. She
looked upon this great European crisis merely as a series of
opportunities for her policy. The cause of monarchy was for
her only a pretext for furthering her own enterprises. In this
respect she always judged correctly, and acted with a decision
and firmness that were truly extraordinary.

This princess must be taken for what she was—a German
by race and character who had become a great Russian ruler.
Of great genius, fine intelligence, unaffected in her private
life but dissembling in her policy, abandoned in her passions
but cautious in her public conduct, prudently nourishing immense ambitions, she possessed in an extreme degree the

master qualities of great statesmen, clear-cut policies and constancy of character. A freethinker and *philosophe* by inclination, she accepted orthodoxy for reasons of expediency, and was careful not to contradict the superstitions of her subjects. She dominated the Russians precisely because she viewed them with detachment. If she had been Russian she would have been lost in the confusion of vague ideas which stirred in Russian minds. But she was German, poised, clearsighted, methodical, less sentimental than Maria Theresa and more humane than Frederick. She had neither the private virtues of the former nor the fiendish spirit of the latter, but she shared with both an ability to see things as they are, a passion for certainty and rejection of the impossible.

In the chaos of Russia she distinguished and sorted out, as a matter of course, the real needs, the vigorous forces, the unformed aspirations, and reduced them all to proportion in her own mind, one of the best ordered and most consistent there have ever been. As she simply followed out her own thought, and as her thinking was always precise and firmly based, she was not at all bothered by the contradictions which foreigners found in her language and conduct. It was enough for her that there were no such contradictions in her policies. It was precisely her strength and her superior skill to make the most diverse elements combine in the accomplishment of a design. She spoke the language of the times, but she retained the simplicity of ideas, flexibility of mind, and intensity of passion of primitive natures. The ideas of the age passed over her like a gleam which sparkles on the surface of the waters without warming the depths. For intellectual diversion and political flirtation she had her *philosophe* courtiers, but for love she preferred to keep to her Russian grenadiers. 'You are a great statesman', she once wrote to Grimm. 'You survey all Europe in a couple of pages; but as the object of this is to tell me that I have only to do what my interests dictate, I am much obliged to you, and assure you I shall not fail to do so.'

3. WAR AND NEGOTIATIONS, 1787-8

She never did fail, and as the French Revolution was approaching she was turning over in her mind that vast design, known by the name of *the Greek project*, which was to serve as Russia's master plan for future action. It was not enough to have taken White Russia from the Poles and the Crimea from the Turks, to have watered the Russians' horses in the Danube and victoriously sailed their ships in the Mediterranean, the Adriatic and the Aegean, to have summoned the Greeks to a holy war and proclaimed herself protector of the Christian subjects of the Sultan. Catherine wanted to bring to its conclusion the traditional project of the tsars, realise the dream of the Russian people, drive the infidel from Europe and restore to the Orthodox faith its centre, cleansed of the heathen. To restore the Greek empire at Constantinople for the benefit of her grandson Constantine, whom she had destined for this from his birth, to form between this empire, which would extend to the Danube, and Russia, which would stop at the Dniester, an intermediate state which would have the name of Dacia—these were the plans the Tsarina had drawn up in 1782, and which she reckoned to carry out by means of her alliance with Austria. Joseph II was completely won over to it. He looked for great advantages from it, and the two allies, whose friendship grew closer each year, were only waiting for a favourable wind to embark on the conquest of this new golden fleece.

They awaited it until the autumn of 1787. The sky, so far threatening, then seemed to clear for them. They had no serious obstacle to fear except on the part of France, and France, having risen to such a height of power a few years previously, now entered a domestic crisis which seemed likely to keep her inactive for a long time. Vergennes had died in February 1787, and in October France was forced to give way in Holland to Prussia and England. This incident was a sign to the whole of Europe of difficulties the gravity of which no one until then had suspected. France's enemies rejoiced, and were quick to exaggerate the consequences. It seemed to them that France had fallen into decrepitude, and that Europe need no longer reckon with her.

These judgements, which were to have dire consequences for the ancient monarchies of the Continent, were pronounced at the end of 1787. Everything that occurred in France from that time till the end of 1793 seemed only to confirm these estimates in the minds of those who had formed them. The Prussian, Hertzberg, wrote: 'France has lost the alliance of Holland and the remnants of her prestige in Europe.'[6] Joseph II's verdict was, 'France has just fallen, and I doubt whether she can be raised up.'[7] 'This shows', he wrote to his brother Leopold, 'in how short a time so considerable a state, with great resources, position and possibilities, can lose credit, influence, vigour and power through the want of a capable leader and lack of order.'[8] Catherine wrote to Grimm in October 1787: 'One cannot say that Louis XVI is flattered. Everything has been done to persuade him to accept guidance and to convince him that he understands nothing of his task. At the same time he is diligent, good, has the right ideas, and wishes to do well. . . . If it is a case of going back in order to jump farther, well and good; but if they have retreated and are not going to jump, but are going to let the Ge and the Gu[9] get away with it as they will, well, then goodbye to the reputation acquired through two hundred years! And who will believe in people who have neither will, vigour, nor enterprise?'

This eclipse of France seemed most timely to the allies of Vienna and St. Petersburg, for it meant their time had come, and the opportunity they had been waiting for was presented to them. In fact it anticipated their preparations, if not their

[6] Hæusser, vol. I, p. 225.
[7] Flassan, vol. VI, p. 415.
[8] 21 October 1787, Arneth, *Joseph II und Leopold*.
[9] Ge: *George III*, Gu: *Frederick William II*.

desires. The Turks, feeling themselves threatened, had made the first move, and called on their adversaries to declare themselves. On 13th August 1787 the Russian minister at Constantinople, Bulgakov, was invited to a conference. The Turks required of him the restitution of the Crimea, and on his refusal shut him up in the castle of the Seven Towers, which by Turkish custom was a solemn form of declaration of war. The Russians were not ready. Joseph II thought he was, and though the Turks had committed no hostile act against him, he deemed it expedient to notify them 'by a brilliant stroke' of his intentions towards them. The brilliant stroke was a surprise attack on Belgrade; he had spies there and hoped 'to take it in one night'.[10] The assault was attempted on 3 December 1787, and it failed. Joseph then had to resort to open war, which he declared on 9 February 1788, but as the season forced a suspension of operations the diplomats made use of it to busy themselves; everywhere in Europe they were in quest of alliances and diversions.

Embarrassed as she was, the two conquerors were still preoccupied with France. Her actual neutrality did not suffice them; they wanted to involve her in their schemes and hold her if possible at their disposal. There was at St. Petersburg at that time a French minister who was full of grace, intelligence and patriotism, the comte de Ségur. The Russians made much of him—garlanded him with flowers, as people said. Their proposals, insinuating and specious, consisted of setting up, in opposition to the coalition of England, Prussia and Holland a *quadruple alliance* of Austria, Russia, France and Spain. A project for a treaty conceived on these lines was outlined in St. Petersburg. The French ministry received these overtures and listened to them but gave no answer, and when Ségur pressed them for a decision constantly evaded it.

The comte de Montmorin,[11] who had been in charge of

[10] Joseph to Leopold, 13 December 1787. Arneth, *op. cit.*

[11] The comte de Montmorin de Saint-Hérem, born in 1746, was a *menin* (appointed companion) of the Dauphin in 1771, minister of Louis XVI at Trèves in 1774, ambassador to Madrid

foreign affairs since the death of Vergennes, and directed them with a somewhat timorous prudence, thought France had an absolute need of peace to restore her finances and accomplish the reform of her government. Since she was unable to take part in war she must oppose it, and if she could not manage to prevent it, at least limit its extent and duration. To conclude an alliance with Austria and Russia would be to approve their designs, facilitate their execution and precipitate the issue instead of retarding it. This alliance would moreover put France into a posture of hostility to England and Prussia, which for the moment were not threatening her. Finally, France ought to rescue her old allies, Turkey, Poland and Sweden, from the greedy attentions of Austria and Russia; to join these two would be to associate herself with the system of partitions which she had only recently fought against with such good reason and condemned with so much emphasis. Montmorin decided for neutrality. But the moderating rôle which France had filled with so much dignity during the ministry of Vergennes demanded more resilience than she was capable of in 1788. Her neutrality was perforce turned into self-effacement. She was soon reduced to pressing on all the courts of Europe pacific advice which no one valued very highly and no one seemed inclined to listen to.

The expeditions of the Argonauts of the North had always had the effect of setting Europe alight. Venturesome politicians and warriors greedy for spoils were not only to be found at Vienna and St. Petersburg. The allies thought Prussia could be ignored, but Prussia meant to be taken into account, and, thinking she was certain of England and Holland, aimed at nothing less than regulating the bidding in the great auction that was about to open. Frederick William thought he was called on to dictate to Europe, and Count Hertzberg easily led him on with the promise of a brilliant

---

in 1775, and left diplomacy for the army in 1783. After having become *maréchal de camp* and Governor of Brittany, he was appointed to the Ministry of Foreign Affairs on 14 February 1787. See Masson, *Affaires étrangères*, p. 56 ff.

and profitable mediation. An uncomprehending, presumptuous and clumsy disciple of Frederick, Hertzberg seemed to have adopted as the principles of his policy the ironical sallies of his master on *Her Sacred Majesty Fortune*. 'The Prussian system', said Hertzberg, 'is to have none, but to be guided by events.'[12] Frederick relied on chance for nothing except opportunities, and as he was always ready to seize them, chance always appeared to favour him. Hertzberg laboriously worked out the most involved combinations, and by attention to the smallest details determined the part to be played by the unforeseen. But as this was in fact the principal rôle, and as the unforeseen by its nature is recalcitrant to formulas, chance, which was so constant and helpful to Frederick, proved wayward with Hertzberg, and seemed to delight in placing stumbling-blocks under his feet. The Russian envoy S. Rumiantzov, who was very hostile and disparaging, compared him to a Don Quixote nourishing his hollow dreams with the political romances of the news-sheets.

Hertzberg conceived a vague and far-fetched plan, like those of Alberoni. This was to ignite fires everywhere and stoke them up, so as to be handsomely rewarded by Europe for putting the fires out. There was indeed no lack of fuel, for Europe was full of inflammable materials. Joseph II had exasperated his subjects by his reforms; the Poles were chafing under the Russian yoke; Gustavus III was only waiting for trouble so that he might join in. No more than a sign was required for the Swedes to march; a promise of alliance would engage the Poles to hurl themselves against Russia; a few insinuations, and of course subsidies, would encourage the Turks. Catherine, attacked on three sides, would be hard put to it to defend herself. As for Austria, a double revolt, fomented in Hungary and Belgium, would oblige her to

[12] Report from Berlin, 6 July 1790—'One can easily believe that the comte de Hertzberg was telling the truth when he chanced to say that the system of the Prussian ministry was to have none and only to act according to circumstances.' 4 February 1791. *Affaires étrangères*.

recall the greater part of her forces. Thus divided, and beset at the same time by so many distractions, the two allies would be forced to capitulate to the armed mediation of Prussia, supported by Holland and England as possible reinforcements. Prussia would dictate peace, and would adjust it in such a way as to satisfy herself while contenting everybody else, except possibly the Swedes, who would have nothing but honour, and the Turk, who would foot the bill. Russia would obtain the Black Sea coast up to the Danube, that is to say Otchakov and Bessarabia; Austria would take Moldavia and Wallachia; in exchange, she would restore Galicia to the Poles, who would cede to Prussia, by way of recompense, Thorn and Danzig. This acquisition would complete those made in 1772, and ensure to the Prussians the trade of the lower Vistula. As for France, Hertzberg thought her in no state to intervene. However, to make more sure of her inaction, he gave Goltz, the Prussian minister in Paris, secret instructions to get into touch with the party of opposition to the crown, to nourish their illusions about a Prussian alliance, to stir them up against Austria, and, in short, to work secretly to undermine the French state and isolate it in Europe.

The plot was subtly hatched, but it entailed very great efforts to obtain mediocre results. So complicated a turning movement would require singular dexterity, great precision and favourable conjunctures. There was every chance of straying down a by-road, of being lost in the mist, of missing an opportunity, and ending up in one of those pitiful failures that come from a master-stroke missing its mark.

The opening of the war, however, seemed to bear out Hertzberg's calculations to the letter. The campaign of 1788 began wretchedly. The Russian army was unorganized, and it was decimated by epidemics even before it marched. Potemkin was so discouraged that he talked of evacuating the Crimea. To complete Russia's disgrace, the Sebastopol fleet was surprised by a storm and had to stay in port to repair the damage. The whole weight of the war thus fell on Austria. Joseph II, obsessed as always by Frederick's glory, wished to command in person, but as he was both jealous of command and incapable of its exercise, no one in fact commanded at all. All the disasters suffered by Austria in the wars of the Revolution were foreshadowed in this campaign. All the leaders who were destined to fight against France could now be seen in action, under the direction of Lascy—who had for a moment held Frederick's fate in his hands—Coburg, Clerfayt, Wartensleben, and even Mack, who fought his first campaign, formed his first plans, and emerged from the Turkish war with the reputation for genius which was to prove disastrous to Austria. These generals showed themselves on the Danube, as later on the Rhine, spineless and confused, ceaselessly debating what to do and more given to intrigue than to action. 'I find in our generals', wrote Joseph, 'neither determination, zeal nor energy. They are all in despair about the war. They would like to stay comfortably in their billets, and nobody will go farther than he is pushed. Everyone blames everyone else, and there is no cohesion among them. . . .'[13]

Joseph had managed to muster about 180,000 men. It was the biggest effort that the house of Austria had ever achieved. But these troops were dispersed over an immense length of frontiers. They were ravaged by epidemics; in June there were 12,000 sick, in July 20,000. Austria had hardly started the war, but already she found herself in danger. 'If with all this the King of Prussia and the English join in and force us to make war on them at the same time,' wrote Joseph, 'then the monarchy is lost, for we should have to reduce the number of troops engaged against the Porte simply to prevent the King of Prussia from occupying all Bohemia and Moravia and marching on Vienna.'[14]

Through the despatches intercepted by the Austrian police and expertly deciphered by the *cabinet noir*, Joseph was well apprised of all Hertzberg's manœuvres. He did not

[13] To Leopold, 13 May 1788.
[14] To Kaunitz, 26 August 1788. Beer, *Joseph II, Leopold II und Kaunitz.* Vienna, 1873.

think he had the strength to contend with two enemies at once. If he wished to contain Prussia, it was high time to bring back the army to face Germany. On 28th August and 14th September the Austrians suffered two reverses, of which the latter turned into a disaster.[15] 'We are forced to retreat,' wrote the Emperor, 'and to abandon the whole of the Banat to the enemy; it is impossible even to cover Transylvania, which will also be ravaged, and that without losing a battle, without even a shot being fired. These gentlemen have abandoned everything—chosen, prepared and advantageous positions . . . and we have not been able to attack the enemy. Nothing more dreadful, more unfortunate, more shameful, could have happened.'[16]

This proud enterprise of conquest ended in retreat, and Austria, having set out with a plan for the partition of Turkey, found herself instead invaded by the Turks and threatened on her own frontiers.

The situation of Russia was perhaps even worse, for the diversion which Joseph feared on the part of the Prussians Catherine actually suffered at the hands of the Swedes. Gustavus III declared war on 1st July; he demanded the restoration of Carelia and Finland to Sweden, and of the Crimea to the Turks. He made an agreement with the Turks on 12th July, and marched on St. Petersburg through Finland. Catherine then had, like her master and patron Frederick in the Seven Years War, her time of trial, and it was for her as for Frederick her real period of greatness. Hard-pressed in the south by the Turks and in the north by the Swedes, and with Poland in revolt on her flank, she faced trouble on every side. All her forces were in the south—37,000 under Rumiantzov, who was to invade Moldavia, 80,000 under Potemkin, who was to conquer Otchakov. They hesitated, but Catherine kept up their courage and showed them an example. She managed with great difficulty to muster 16,000

---

[15] The battles of Mehadia and Slatyna, in which the Austrians were attacked by the Grand Vizir, Jussuf-Pasha.
[16] To Leopold, 20 September 1788.

men to cover St. Petersburg. Her only means of defence against Sweden was the fleet, which numbered seventeen battleships and seven frigates. She kept 500 horses always ready to take her, in case of a surprise attack, to Moscow. On 17 July there was a naval battle at Hoogland which was indecisive.

The danger was great, but it was removed by political measures. Catherine had maintained her intelligence service in Sweden; a conspiracy broke out there, and disaffected troops from Finland took part in it. At the same time the Danes, whom Russia had persuaded to take her side, crossed the frontier from Norway and threatened Gothenburg. Gustavus III was obliged to return to his own country, and from that side the campaign of 1788 was at an end.

Meanwhile Potemkin decided to besiege Otchakov. The operations began at the end of June and dragged on into December. The Turks held fast; the Russians grew weary. Their troops lacked both fuel and bread; only a desperate stroke could right the situation. Potemkin ordered an assault; the place was taken on 17 December after a bloody struggle which was followed by horrible massacres.

This success renewed Joseph's courage. But his plans were changed—he now thought only of Prussia. Here was a problem that should be settled once and for all. 'As long as the power of Prussia is not curtailed,' wrote Kaunitz, 'all the intentions, plans and enterprises of the two imperial courts will be hampered and brought to nought.'[17] Catherine did not disagree, and on 21 December she informed the Emperor that she had no objection to his making peace with the Turks so that he should be free immediately to attack the Prussians. As to mediation, she wanted to have nothing to do with it. The English had addressed rather strange insinuations to her, and she had haughtily rejected them. 'It must be

[17] To comte L. Cobenzl, Austrian ambassador at Petersburg, 28 November 1788. Martens, *Traités de la Russie avec l'Autriche*, vol. II, p. 18.

admitted', she wrote to Grimm, 'that brother Ge[18] is an astounding statesman; what a charming proposal he has made for agreement on two points, namely that one remain master of India, and the other of the Levant and its trade, after signing a fine declaration of disarmament.'

This plan for the partition of the Oriental world was to be discussed more than once between London and St. Petersburg. For the English it was a delaying device, and in any case a *pis aller* which was always rather dubious. They were looking for more substantial safeguards, and as Prussia was disposed to furnish them, they undertook, by an instrument of 13 August 1788, to proceed in agreement with her in all affairs of the East and the North. The Prussians were busy encouraging the Turks, freeing Gustavus III from the Danish diversion, and stirring up the Belgians. Hertzberg reckoned that a revolution in the Low Countries would compel Joseph II to be more circumspect towards Prussia. As for Russia, it was a question of the Poles, and the Prussian minister did his best to rouse them to revolt.

The Diet, to which the Polish patriots were looking to regenerate the Republic, met at Warsaw on 6 October 1788. It hastened to form itself into a *confederation*, that is to say a revolutionary assembly, in order to substitute majority voting for the rule of unanimity, which made all reform impossible. The Prussian representative in Warsaw exhorted 'the good and enlightened citizens of Poland' to rely on his master to upset the perfidious calculations of Russia. He wrote: 'They can believe implicitly that His Majesty will afford them every support necessary to maintain the independence, liberty and security of Poland.'[19] The movement of troops, and 100,000 ducats judiciously distributed, confirmed these insidious suggestions. The Polish patriots were at one in their hatred of Russia; it sufficed that Prussia inflamed their passion for them to believe her sincere. The Prussians

[18] George III. Catherine to Grimm, 22 April 1788.
[19] Prussian note to the Diet, 13 October 1788. Ferrand, *op. cit.*, bk. VIII.

excelled at this game, which they had played for a long time
in Paris against Austria. It was a classic ruse, and the Russians were beginning already, with much finesse, to turn it
against the Prussians. As for the Poles, it did not appear to
them that they were compromising their position by listening
to the King of Prussia—he was considered 'virtuous', and he
was guaranteeing them everything while asking for nothing.
The Poles took cognisance of his declarations, and, strong in
the confidence he inspired, they decreed the raising of a force
of 10,000 men.

Catherine could not mistake their intentions, and she gave
them notice of hers: she would consider 'the least change
made in the constitution of 1775 to be a violation of the
treaties'.[20] They were thus enjoined to remain in a state of
anarchy, that is in subjection. The Diet replied by demanding the evacuation of the territory of the Republic by the
Russian troops that still occupied it. Prussia at that time had
as her representative in Warsaw one of the most insinuating
and crafty agents of Frederick's chancellery, the Italian Luc-
chesini. In a note of 19 December he announced to the Diet
that his master was ready to take all steps 'to ensure the independence of the Republic, though not wishing otherwise
to be involved in its domestic affairs, or to restrict the liberty
of its movements, which he would do his best to guarantee'.
On 8 December the Diet decided to enter into negotiations
with the King of Prussia with a view to a treaty or alliance,
and to send legations all over Europe to explain to the powers
the work of reform it was undertaking. It declared itself in
permanent session until the task had been brought to completion. It was sincerely hoped to accomplish this in 1789.
The Diet counted on the friendship of Austria; Prussia offered her protection; Russia had too much on her hands to
be redoubtable. And indeed in the last weeks of 1788 the
Russian troops began to withdraw. It was a purely military
movement—Catherine had need of these soldiers and so re-

[20] Russian note of 5 November 1788.

called them. She did not make and did not intend to make any concession to the Poles. But they thought that Prussia, having helped to remove the Russians, would be able to prevent their return. Poland blindly abandoned herself to gratitude. 'The fanatical partiality for the Prussians which prevails in Warsaw is such', wrote a French agent, 'that many Poles would not think the friendship of Prussia too dearly bought with the sacrifice of Thorn and Danzig.'[21]

4. THE EUROPEAN CRISIS OF 1789

The Poles were ripe for the execution of Hertzberg's designs, and he was very active in stirring up the Hungarians. The Prussian minister in Vienna, Jacobi, was in contact with the opposition and incited them to revolt. Already the Magyars were demanding the recall of the Hungarian regiments which Joseph II had moved into Bohemia to defend it against Prussia. In Galicia the Prussian emissaries were fomenting a national rising and encouraging the Poles to hope for a prompt reunion with their country. Other agents were promising assistance to the Belgians against Austria, and to the people of Liége against their bishop. The governments of the ancien régime had always behaved towards each other after this fashion, but never had these Machiavellian traditions been followed with such fervour as in Prussia by Count Hertzberg at the beginning of 1789. The French minister wrote: 'He wants Europe to be entirely occupied with him, and—if he can contrive it—with the King his master.'[22] His chief difficulties were with this prince. Frederick William loved glory, but he loved his pleasures more. While Hertzberg led him on through his ambition, the favourites held him back through his superstition. 'All these people', wrote M. d'Esterno, 'are most anxious that the King of Prussia should not escape them, as would necessarily happen if

[21] Report of the marquis de Noailles. Vienna, 15 July 1789.
[22] Report of the comte d'Esterno, 23 January 1789.

the monarch went off to command his armies. So these persons and the mistress are, without a doubt, in favour of keeping the peace, and England is even more so.'

Pitt was indeed, though for quite different reasons from the King of Prussia, reluctant to join in Hertzberg's plots. England was well embarked on a series of reforms for the achievement of which she needed peace. Never had the kingdom seemed more prosperous. The prime minister was all-powerful. 'His popularity is so great', said the French ambassador, 'that he could at this moment undertake anything he wished.'[23] It was precisely because he wanted to retain his popularity that he hesitated to go to war. He was reassured by the internal crisis in France, and far from seeking to open a struggle with her, he was aiming at a rapprochement. His agents in St. Petersburg worked against the projects for a quadruple alliance, and he proposed directly to the French ambassador an entente to restore peace in the East and North. France and England, he told M. de la Luzerne, had the same principle, which was to refrain from aggrandisement, and the same interest in maintaining Turkey and Sweden against the Russians. Pitt wished to act 'perfectly in concert' with the French government, and, to give good earnest of his intentions, he prevented Denmark from resuming hostilities against Sweden.

While England was trying to get France to declare herself against Russia and Austria, Russia asked her to pronounce against Prussia and England. The project of a quadruple alliance was again brought forward; it was to be an alliance like that of 1756, and Spain was to sign it at the same time as France. To win over the Spaniards Catherine sent one of her confidants, Prince Nassau-Siegen; the accession of Charles IV afforded a pretext for this journey. The Tsarina wanted Spain and France to abandon Sweden and Turkey and to take a high line with the King of Prussia.[24] The Russian Vice-Chancellor, Ostermann, pressed Ségur very

[23] Report of M. de la Luzerne, 9 June 1789.
[24] Report of M. de Ségur, 3 March 1789.

strongly. 'We should like to see you with us,' he said; 'but if you can do nothing for us, we must take other measures.' These measures would be a direct arrangement with the English. Ségur wrote to Montmorin: 'If our alliance is deferred, we shall rapidly see a collapse of our credit and influence here. We have a unique opportunity of gaining another ally against England.'[25]

This was the argument best calculated to convince Montmorin. He knew Europe and the political ways of the age too well not to suspect England of contributing by all possible means to the weakening of French power. This fear, by which the revolutionaries of 1793 were obsessed to the point of hallucination, was with the French ministry an instinctive and traditional dread.[26] As soon as any crisis arose in France, the hand and the gold of England were seen in it. The correspondence from London in 1789 was full of these accusations. 'This government is jealous of us and hates us', wrote Montmorin to La Luzerne on 8 February 1789; 'if we are friendly with them they will want to dominate us; if we resist their desires they will not scruple to betray us.' He was afraid of giving them the least provocation. Learning that Ireland was in a restless state, he quickly instructed the French ambassador: 'Above all we cannot and should not join in this in any way whatsoever. We give too many hostages to others through the troubles we have at home to want to incite them elsewhere.'[27] He was no less suspicious of the secret machinations of Prussia; but without entertaining any illusions about the friendship of that power he thought it was needed to keep a balance, and therefore had no wish to bring it down.

[25] Report of Ségur, 5 January 1789.

[26] 'I know beyond all doubt', wrote Bernis with reference to the troubles of 1756, 'that England is making every effort, both by intrigue and by bribery, to foment these first signs of division.' *Mémoires*, ed. Masson, 2nd part, ch. xxix; *des affaires du Parlement*.

[27] Montmorin to la Luzerne, 6 April 1789.

Besides, France was in no condition to take action. The opening of the States General was drawing near, and the circumstances were not favourable to an intervention of which Russia alone would reap the benefit. Montmorin therefore restricted himself to offering his good offices with the Turks. As to the alliance with Russia, he agreed with Spain that its conclusion should be postponed. France accepted it in principle, but did not admit that the treaty could apply to the current wars. She did not want to be involved in them at any price. Nevertheless she promised not to renew her alliance with Sweden, which would expire in 1790. The desertion of so old an ally was a sad blow to Louis XVI. And Russia demanded a still more painful concession—recognition of the partition of Poland. Montmorin had at one moment raised the question in Vienna and St. Petersburg of annulling this iniquitous act. The allies had replied by requiring that Louis XVI should explicitly sanction it. 'I will not conceal from you', Montmorin wrote to Ségur,[28] 'that it is with extreme repugnance that the King has undertaken to guarantee the boundaries of this kingdom (Poland) and that His Majesty has only set aside the principles which I have expounded since the commencement of the negotiation in order to convince the two imperial courts of the sincerity of his attitude and of the value he attaches to their alliance.' Was this sincerity reciprocated? Montmorin thought that the reservation stipulated by France on the subject of the war then in progress would be 'a touchstone which would make plain the true intentions of Russia', and would show whether her overtures were aimed at an equitable alliance or only at a treaty in which 'France would have the obligations and nothing else'.[29] If the attitude of the court of St. Petersburg is sincere and does not merely arise from the circumstances of the moment', he wrote,[30] 'it will adopt our proposals without the least difficulty; if on the contrary it disapproves

[28] 20 March 1789.
[29] Montmorin to Ségur, 19 March 1789.
[30] To the marquis de Noailles at Vienna, 4 June 1789.

of them, it will be evident that its anxiety to ally with us is only transitory; in this case we should congratulate ourselves warmly on having forced it to come into the open and itself to show us its real intentions.'

This showed more perspicacity than Catherine liked to find in her partners. She hid her mortification with banter. 'The reputation of the French court is completely lost through its inaction', she wrote to Grimm.[31] She took Louis XVI's scruples on the subject of Poland in very bad part, and launched into recrimination when Ségur spoke to her of putting off the practical operation of the alliance till after the war. Potemkin, who was strongly hostile to France, was constantly disparaging. Ségur, who had recently been so much sought after, now found himself deserted and almost isolated. 'I am only too conscious', he reported to Noailles, 'how difficult, alarming and painful my position has become.'[32] 'By our rapprochement with Russia we have embittered the league (England, Prussia, Holland), Poland, Sweden and Turkey. By not signing the alliance, we have given the two imperial courts a grievance. Thus we have got out of the alliance all the kicks and none of the halfpence. This is what our domestic troubles have brought us to. If England and Prussia are skilful, they can procure a peace advantageous to Russia, win her over, and completely overthrow our influence here, the pieces of which I am doing my best to pick up.'[33]

Such were the relations of France with Europe at the moment when the States General met. In considering these relations as a whole, we find France momentarily paralysed, but nevertheless envied for her resources and feared for her national strength, while other states watched her internal crisis with jealous anxiety; England alternately showing passive indifference and passionate interest in the affairs of the Continent, at one time surprising those who feared her too

[31] 19 March 1789.
[32] 14 April 1789.
[33] To the marquis de Noailles, 22 May 1789.

much by her lapses, at another time those who underrated her power by her sudden revivals; Prussia restless and acquisitive, with the most solid nucleus of an army in Europe to put at the service of an aggressive diplomacy; Russia thinking only of the East and Poland, and in every European crisis looking for opportunities of expansion; Austria with troubles everywhere and in no condition to act anywhere, always tempted by great enterprises but always hesitating to carry them out, hampered and almost stifled by the confused mass of her states, hindered at every turn by the rivalries and seditions of the diverse peoples she governed with so much difficulty; Poland in dissolution and her defences breached; Turkey in disarray and under attack—all these facts and relations were already old by the end of the eighteenth century and were to be reproduced time and again in the nineteenth. This remark alone is enough to demonstrate, even at the risk of stressing the obvious, how powerful and persistent was the action of the historical trends which I set myself the task of expounding in this book.

Conclusion

Before setting out on an exposition of the events which began in May 1789 I propose to summarise the facts we have just assembled and note in broad outline their connection and consequences, so providing the whole framework for this history.

The Revolution, which was imminent almost everywhere in Europe, broke out in France because the ancien régime there was more decrepit and at the same time more intolerable; because the government had made reforms necessary which it was incapable of bringing about; because authority was powerless to direct opinion yet lacked the strength to repress it; because financial bankruptcy was accompanied by the breakdown of government; because change seemed inevitable, and there was every opening for innovators; and finally because the doctrines of *philosophie* were more popular there than in any other country, had penetrated deeper into the nation and were better suited to its genius. It was this genius which impressed such a special character on the revolution in France, and this character, in its essential traits, was one that permeated the whole history of France.

The classical spirit, which guided the Revolution, and absolute government, which provided the immediate occasion for it, brought together its elements and determined its bounds, developed in France side by side. They followed from the same conception of man, society, the state, philosophy and art. The men who made the French Revolution were naturally influenced in their thinking by this spirit. They felt an urge to propagate their political principles and their system of government beyond their own frontiers. It was not so much the universal character of their ideas that led them on, but their own character. The same ideas were prevalent in London, Vienna, and Berlin; a national assembly meeting in any of those capitals would perhaps have put at the head of its laws, in imitation of the Americans, a declaration of the rights of man, but it would never have thought of carrying the gospel to humanity at large, still less of launching a crusade for the conversion and deliverance of the nations. In claiming to offer Europe, and then to impose on it, a rational model of democratic society, the French at the end of the eighteenth century were obeying the impulse which had made their ancestors the disseminators par excellence of modern civilisation. They renewed, in accordance with the spirit of the times, the work which their thinkers, jurists and artists had achieved for mankind in the Middle Ages, in the Renaissance, and in the seventeenth century. They did for the people what their fathers had done for the state, and thus continued to exercise that 'magistracy' over Europe for which history seemed to have destined them.

But just because they remained so consistent and so faithful to their traditions, their ideas continued to be 'wholly national and wholly passionate'. They appropriated the new doctrines but profoundly modified their sense and bearing. The terms they used were abstract, but their thought remained concrete and entirely French. The spirit of nationalism immediately changed the universal character of their principles. While these were only a subject of argument they remained in the realm of vague discussion and metaphysics, but when action was required, there was a return to reality —that is to the history of France. And so from the beginning an essential idea in the doctrine and practice of the Revolution was the idea of the fatherland.

Under the ancien régime the king was looked upon as the state itself. He represented to the French the living image of France, and love of country was identified with devotion to the king. When sovereignty was transferred to the people, the nation took the place of the king, and love of country was identified with respect for the laws. Meanwhile, as the law should be founded on justice, and justice on reason, whose reign the Revolution was to establish not only over one people but for all mankind, the idea of the fatherland became generalised as the idea of law. There was only one fatherland for the human race, and it could be found wherever reason held sway; patriotism was thus identified with attachment to the *Rights of Man*. The patriot was a citizen of the world. The great idea of the fatherland which the centuries had, so to speak, incarnated in every Frenchman was thus refined into abstractions and seemed to lose both its raison d'être and its reality.

While some Frenchmen, repudiating the whole past of their race, thus conceived of a fatherland without frontiers, country, nation, memories or memorials, others, starting from the opposite pole though moved by the same inspiration, substituted for this universal and intangible fatherland a kind of personal and nomadic fatherland which everyone carried about with him wherever he went. Led astray by the same spirit of logical abstraction which caused the revolutionaries to identify the idea of country with the idea of revolution, the émigrés identified it with the idea of monarchy. Conceiving for their part of a monarchy without a kingdom, a king without a state, a state without a nation, and a nation without a territory, they limned in their minds a chimerical France, a 'true France', which followed them everywhere, and which they set over against the real France, the France of nature and history, which they had been constrained to abandon.

A single cannon-shot was enough to demolish this baleful nonsense. The great mass of Frenchmen did not understand it and would have nothing to do with it. They saw in the Revolution something real and thoroughly practical, that is, the abolition of the feudal system, which was indeed the basis of it, and they saw in the armed emigration—and again they were right—an attempt to restore by force this execrated system. The Revolution took place to secure for Frenchmen the free enjoyment of the land of France; the foreign invasion took place to destroy the Revolution, dismember France and enslave the French. They naturally identified love of France with love of the Revolution, as they had formerly identified it with love of the king. The old patriotism reawakened in their hearts as simple, lively, strong and efficacious as it had been in the wars against the English or the great disasters at the end of Louis XIV's reign. There was no trace of abstraction in it. It was an instinct, a sentiment, a passion which every Frenchman had in his blood and which pulsated through him with every heartbeat. The fatherland remained for the French what it had always been for their fathers—the country in which they were born and where they wished to die, the home of all their affections, their memories, their hopes, the France they wanted to keep independent. These ideas constituted the whole force of the Revolution; they also produced its excesses, its aberrations and its ruin.

Dread of the emigration and of foreigners delivered France

into the hands of the terrorists. They usurped the Republic on the pretext of defending it, and the noblest of causes served as cover for the vilest of tyrannies. They did not stop at profaning liberty; they rendered it odious by associating it with the memory of their crimes. Of the great work attempted in 1789 the people retained only the civil reforms. As soon as success seemed assured they showed as much aversion to anarchy as they had done to invasion, and dread of the terrorists gave them over to the leaders of the army. They let the revolutionaries be proscribed as readily as they had let them rule. The Jacobins themselves had opened every avenue of the Republic to military despotism, and it was the more easily established because the Revolution, by turning national passions away from political liberty, had directed them towards conquest and glory.

The invasion had reduced the conception of the fatherland to its natural and primitive elements. Victory aroused in men's breasts, where they confusedly slept, all the ancient instincts of glory, crusade, triumph and adventure, love of the extraordinary and hunger for the impossible, the fund of chivalrous romance and the love of heroic exploits which every Frenchman carried within him, and which every age renewed in its own legends.

The French republicans believed themselves to be cosmopolitans, but this was only a manner of speaking. They felt, thought, acted, interpreted their universal ideas and abstract principles in the light of the traditions of a conquering monarchy which had laboured for eight hundred years to fashion France in its own image. They identified humanity with their country, and their national cause with the cause of all nations. Consequently, and quite naturally, they confused the propagation of the new doctrines with the extension of French power, the emancipation of mankind with the greatness of the Republic, the rule of reason with that of France, the liberation of peoples with the conquest of states, and the European revolution with the domination of Europe by the French Revolution. In reality they followed impulses which were as old as French history, and so exactly was this the case that the countries they tried first to deliver, then to conquer and annex, and which in fact they united and merged so easily with the body of the old France, were precisely those which the kings had for centuries claimed to inherit and methodically prepared to absorb. Humanity appropriated to itself the claims of the monarchy and asserted its rights. Furthermore, the French established dependent and subordinate republics which they kept in a sort of tutelage, applying, according to the precedent of feudal overlordships, the maxim of ancient republics that their citizens alone being free alone were fit to govern the surrounding peoples.

The Revolution degenerated first into armed propaganda, then into conquest; military government prevailed over civil; the Republic came to base its rule on its external power and to live by its armies. Finally, these armies invaded the Republic and took it over. The nation had long been familiar with such aberrations. Reviewing its history one is less astonished to find it, after an interval of so few years, rushing with equal passion down such diverse paths, showing such steadiness in defence and such rashness in conquest, endangering and losing the great rewards of the defence by excess in conquest. If one remembers the wars of 'magnificence' so vaunted in the fifteenth century, and recalls that it was just after the Hundred Years War that the French kings undertook the wars in Italy, one can better understand the career of Bonaparte. One can see how, acclaimed by the people for his achievements in vanquishing the foreigner, concluding peace, restoring order in the state, consolidating the civil revolution and ensuring the independence of the Republic behind magnificent new frontiers, he could beguile the French even while robbing them of their freedom, and lure them into the depths of Russia in an insensate pursuit of prestige and grandeur.

The French Revolution took Europe unawares, and being incapable of understanding it, Europe was powerless to combat it. The statesmen of the ancien régime were disconcerted not because the fact of revolution was novel or because they were surprised by the event—the French Revolution upset their calculations and threw their political ideas into confusion just because it did *not* surprise them. They only saw in it a crisis like many others which they knew of by tradition or experience. They judged it by false analogies and regulated their behaviour towards it by baseless conjectures. There had been many revolutions in Europe, especially in the seventeenth and eighteenth centuries, but none had taken on the universal character which the French Revolution assumed. Its character was inevitably misunderstood by Europe at the beginning of the Revolution, but Europe continued to deceive itself long after all illusions should have been dissipated by the actual outcome. The original misconception and the prolonged blindness to the facts were both due to the same cause—reliance on accepted ideas and precedents.

Europe first thought the French Revolution to be a purely internal crisis which would paralyse the French state, and accordingly sought ways of profiting from it, thus acting according to the precedents of Richelieu, Mazarin and Louis XIV towards England, and of contemporary governments towards Poland. It then witnessed the growth in France of a formidable society which, by its boundless affiliations, disseminated throughout Europe a doctrine subversive of all authority. As Europe had judged the Jesuits so it now judged the Jacobins, and reacted against them in the same way. A league was negotiated and formed to destroy the society at its heart and proscribe its emissaries and associates everywhere. But Europe could not get the better of France as easily as of the Holy See. In order to destroy Jacobinism, Europe would have to embark on a struggle with a powerful and warlike nation long disciplined to arms. The spirit of independence and revolutionary fanaticism multiplied the strength of France tenfold. To overcome her would entail a full-scale war and the formation of a coalition. At this point each state was to bring into play its own claims, ambitions, secret intentions, interests, and suspicions. A disunited Europe could not assemble cohesive forces, but at least an attempt was made to unite men's minds by recourse to principles. Those that were invoked were better known in the breach than the observance. To the rights of peoples were opposed the rights of rulers; but these were interpreted according to the traditions of centuries filled with jealousy, covetousness, conflict, disorder and usurpation. Europe spoke the language of law, but acted with the habits of intrigue and force. Even before they were engaged in battle the allies were disputing the fruits of victory. But victory eluded them. Then their concern was simply to indemnify themselves for their losses, so that the whole enterprise immediately turned into a crude pursuit of gain, which is to say that it reverted to the worst customs of the ancien régime.

It was then that Europe proposed peace to France, or rather was resigned to accepting it at her hands. France wished to complete the Revolution, reorganize the state, and ratify the results of her victories; but powerful as she was, she was not powerful enough by herself to lay down the law to Europe. She had only triumphed over the coalition by dividing it, and she still had to reckon with her enemies, beaten as they were. Not being able to destroy all the monarchies she had to come to terms with the monarchs. She had defeated her enemies, chased them back into their own territories, and carried out great conquests; but to keep these peacefully she needed treaties. Treaties meant negotiation, and negotiation involved going back to past customs. The ancien régime and the Revolution bargained not on principles, which are irreconcilable, but on frontiers, which are moveable. There was only one common ground on which the old Europe and republican France could meet and reach accord, and that was raison d'état. So it was this that determined their agreements. Geography remaining unchanged, and the ambitions of states being what they had always been, all the ancient political traditions reappeared spontaneously in these negotiations. These old traditions lent themselves all too easily to the plans of the revolutionaries, and custom offered only too many facilities for satisfying their desires. They knew that in this Europe which they had defeated and which was divided by its own rivalries force was everything, and he who had it was the master. Precedent showed them precarious agreements, unreliable engagements, wars being constantly renewed, states dismembered, dynasties made homeless and nations partitioned. They had been brought up, like all the politicians they dealt with, in the school of Frederick and Catherine, and they made the procedures of the ancien régime serve the purposes of the Revolution. They did not break with the traditions of this régime, they simply took them over. They did not innovate, they continued the same practices. Europe showed a most docile readiness to treat with them, and in these transactions it was not the old system that was in jeopardy, but the new.

Russia and Prussia had negotiated the second partition of Poland before France declared war on Austria. This partition was contemporary with the first coalition formed against France; indeed, it was the necessary condition of it. There was not even the sophisticated excuse for the secret plotters who cynically perpetrated this iniquitous and insolent spoliation of the weak by the strong that they were restoring for the benefit of the northern courts the balance which the conquests of France had destroyed. For France had not made any conquests by the spring of 1792, when the Russians invaded Poland and the Prussians decided to seize their share of the border regions. So far from being intended to compensate them for the extension of French power, the pact then concluded between the allies had as its secret corollary a plan for the subsequent dismemberment of France to their common advantage.

It was France, on the contrary, when she came to negotiate peace in 1795, that found herself faced with an enormous shift of power resulting from the partition of 1793 and the further one which, on 3 January 1795, completed the deplorable performance. It was France which, after the custom of the ancien régime and invoking its doctrine of balance, was thereby authorised to claim those additions to her territory required to maintain the degree of relative power and preponderance which she had formerly possessed in Europe. This she achieved, and without difficulty, since she actually held the territories which she wanted to keep. But as these territories were very extensive the other states in their turn demanded equivalent gains, and France was a party to the allocation of them.

The great treaties of the Republic and Empire were not simply ratifications of conquests, they were schemes of compensation and partition. They were in this respect entirely in keeping with the ways of the monarchies, though quite contrary to the spirit of the Revolution. By taking part in this traffic, which was the only way of retaining what she had conquered, France was departing from her fundamental principle, the sovereignty of the people. The populations which she allotted to various rulers remained subject to the ancien régime, and they were not consulted about the change of government they underwent. Yet such was the force of ideas, such were the decrepitude of the old European system and the expansive power of the new, that the principles of the Revolution, so to speak, penetrated Europe by this roundabout route and prevailed through the very effect of the transactions which appeared to sacrifice them. This upheaval in Europe, effected according to the custom of the ancien régime, necessarily led to the destruction of that régime.

In the countries which France joined to her own territory or shaped to her own pattern she proclaimed her principles, destroyed the feudal system and introduced her laws. When the inevitable disorders of war and the first excesses of conquest were over, this revolution was enormously beneficial to the peoples concerned. This is why the conquests of the Revolution must not be confused with the conquests of the ancien régime. They differed from it in this essential feature —that, despite the abuse of the principles of the Revolution and deviations from its original ideas, the work of France was done for the benefit of the nations. The nations had been, though for a long time without their knowing it, the whole raison d'être, the vital force—as one might say, the sap —of history. The French Revolution summoned them to self-consciousness and brought them into action, and France evoked this response from them even when she did not bring it about herself.

By destroying the petty states and uniting under the same government people whose origins and ways were similar, France diminished the number of frontiers that divided the nations of Europe. At the same time she propagated the ideas best fitted to bring them together. When anarchy had disappeared and the Republic had been pacified and organised, France taught the princes of Europe by her example that the reforms which were most precious to the people redounded directly to the profit of the state; that the chief act of the Revolution, the one which had made it so popular and powerful—the suppression of the feudal system—far from weakening the government, favoured the concentration of power and facilitated its exercise; that consequently nothing was easier or more expedient for rulers than to become the emancipators of their subjects and thus to suppress the causes of revolution; that since the age of nationalism was bound to come, the rôle of kings must henceforth be to gather their peoples around them; that they could in future govern them only by representing them; and that the future was to those best able to discern the great currents of history and to exploit their force. It was thus that the French Revolution produced a remarkable simplification of the map of Europe, and instead of propagating universal anarchy and a general revolt of peoples against kings, it did much on the contrary to make states more powerful and attach nations more closely to their rulers.

New destinies were opening for Europe, and she was prepared for them. The doctrines of the eighteenth century, which in France had given rise to the Revolution, in Europe had produced the rule of the *philosophes*. Europe by 1789 was tending to enlightened despotism; France returned to it with Bonaparte's Consulate. It was in this shape that the Revolution seemed to become defined and fixed in France; it was in this form that Europe understood and copied it. The princes, taking over the French reforms, and the people, gratefully receiving them at their hands, were only following the tendencies of the whole of the eighteenth century.

France did more than conquer Europe—she converted it. French civilisation prepared the way for the victories of her armies and outlived them. It had opened the avenues by which the armies of France marched upon Europe, but by their withdrawal they opened even wider and more far-reaching ways to the Revolution. Victorious even in their defeat, the French won over to their ideas the very nations which had rebelled against their domination. When they were no longer shifting the old frontiers by their policies they transformed the old laws by their principles. The most hostile of the princes and those most eager to throw back the Revolution into France and crush it there by a single blow returned from their crusade to see it, so to speak, germinating in the soil of their own lands, so long tilled by the French armies and watered with their blood. The French Revolution only ceased to be a cause of conflict between France and Europe to engender on the Continent a political and social revolution which in less than half a century changed the face of the European world.

Yet by these very successes the Revolution was abated and French power reached its limit.

In France the whole force of the Revolution proceeded from its national character; among foreign peoples it took on the same character and derived from it the same force. The same sentiment which had inspired the French to conquer tended to rouse up, wherever they propagated their principles, nations eager for independence and therefore impatient of a foreign yoke—even that of their liberators. These nations were as jealous of their prerogatives, as thirsty for glory, as much concerned for their interests, honour and prestige as France had been.

None of these peoples, when the *Rights of Man* and national sovereignty were preached to them, thought of man in the abstract, man without body or soul, or of some ideal nation without territory or inhabitants. They did not pursue the elusive phantom of a metaphysical liberty into the mists of abstraction. Each people, in imitation of the French people who had launched these great ideas upon the world, conceived of them with notions built up in their own minds, and embodied them in images accumulated in their memories for many generations. They nourished these conceptions with their blood, and in giving them life infused them with all the passions of their race.

Through the conflict of claims and historic interests, of the actual necessities of life and of national character, these passions had been opposed to one another for centuries. But what had been a veiled hostility pursued under cover of dynastic rivalries now came into the open, became, so to speak, personal to each citizen and therefore more formidable than it had ever been. So it was that a revolution which had appealed to all mankind, and would admit into its ideal city only citizens of the world, substituted for the relatively cosmopolitan Europe of the eighteenth century the ardently national and deeply divided Europe of the nineteenth. France was to suffer from this alike in her interests and in her glory. Round her arose rival nations, which first disputed her supremacy and then entered into formidable competition with her. Language being one of the chief signs of nationality, the influence and prestige of the French language declined in Europe, and the rivalry of national tongues signalised the opposition of nations.

But this revolution of Europe was in fact the reverse of the French Revolution. It lacked precisely what had constituted the originality of France in this adventure, had remained the motive-force of her greatness and at the same time the excuse for her aberrations—the enthusiasm, the generous impulse and the belief that she was working for mankind. Her imitators thought only of themselves; however legitimate their desire for independence, whatever devotion individuals may have put at the service of national passions, these passions contained something of jealousy and bitterness, a basis of rancour and a ferment of envy which clouded and debased them; the gleam of altruism was lacking. Doubtless this gleam had appeared in France only in the dawn of a day to be filled with shadows, storms and tempests, but brief and transitory though it was it left behind a reflection which enlivened the whole history of this epoch and ensured that it should always remain one of the most marvellous episodes in the history of mankind. It is the honour and consolation of France to remember that even when they hurled themselves upon her, hated her, disowned her, the peoples of Europe were in spite of themselves subject to her ascendancy, and took from her hands the weapons they used to fight her. At the very moment when they were turning against her the ideas of national independence which she had spread throughout the world they were still following the generous impulses of her genius.

Moreover, these bitter disappointments and cruel misunderstandings, this aggressive reaction which turned the revolution against France, these things were not inherently necessary. Nothing in the broad current on which French thought was carried boded this disordered reflux of the waters. Nothing in the great declarations of 1789 was incompatible with the peace of the world. Nothing made it impossible to conceive of a powerful, prosperous and free France amid a Europe peacefully invited to follow her example. France before 1789 was the most populous, the richest, the most fully developed state on the Continent; she was to become the most free, and was to consecrate through the example of most beneficent reforms the noble mastery she exercised over Europe. Her prestige could not but increase. This was what Mirabeau expected when he wrote in

1790 those lines that sum up the finest hopes of his contemporaries:

'The influence, sooner or later irresistible, of a great nation of 24 million people, who speak the same language and have reduced the art of living together to the simple notions of equity and liberty—ideas which, endowed with an irresistible attraction for the human heart, find missionaries and proselytes in every country of the world—the influence of such a nation will without doubt win over all Europe to truth, moderation and justice, though not all at once, not in one day or in a single instant.'[1]

These ideas, by themselves and of their own force, were bound to conquer the world, and this belief excluded all thought of war. On this essential point, the principles of the Revolution were in accord with the experience of the most wise and discerning statesmen. This was understood by the men of 1789 when they laid it down as one of the fundamental laws of the state that France would not attack any people who did not attack her, and renounced thenceforth all wars of conquest. The Revolution of 1789 was quite reconcilable with the policy of Henry IV and Richelieu, but not with that of Louis XIV and Louvois. It was the strange destiny of the French Revolution to turn against France as soon as the French themselves betrayed its principle and converted it into an instrument of conquest and domination.

[1] Speech of 25 August 1790. *Moniteur*, vol. V, p. 480.

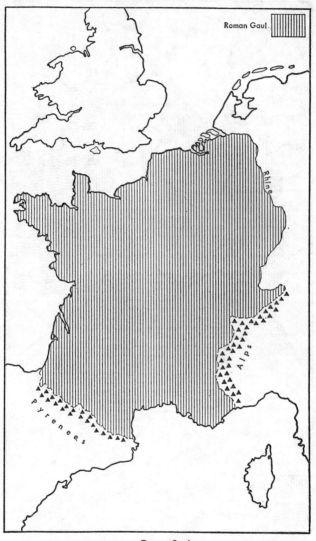

Roman Gaul

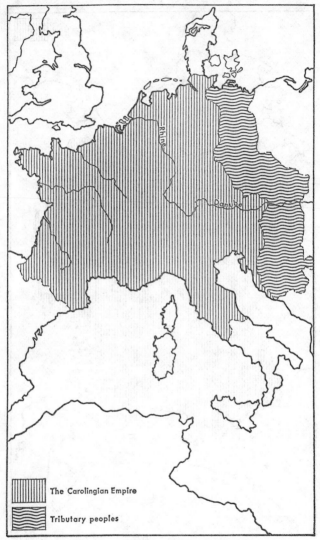

The Carolingian Empire

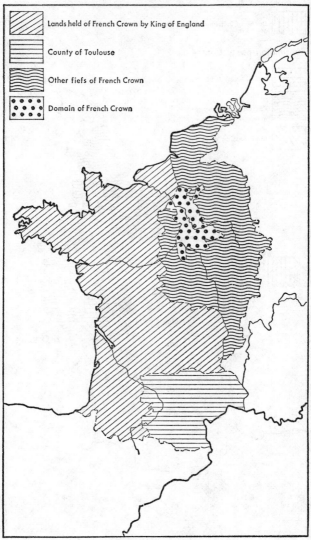

Lands held of French Crown by King of England

County of Toulouse

Other fiefs of French Crown

Domain of French Crown

France in the Twelfth Century

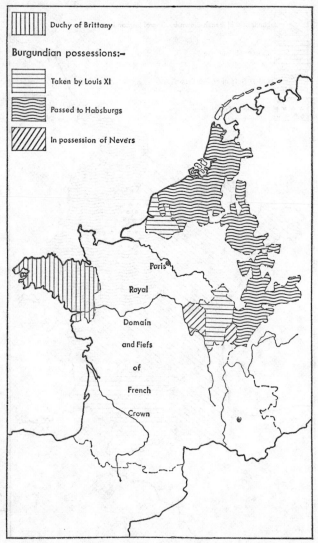

Duchy of Brittany

Burgundian possessions:—

Taken by Louis XI

Passed to Habsburgs

In possession of Nevers

Paris

Royal

Domain

and Fiefs

of

French

Crown

France and Burgundy in the second half of the Fifteenth Century

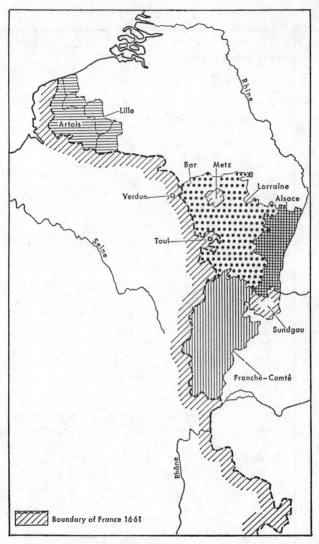

Lille

Artois

Bar   Metz

Verdun   Lorraine
Alsace

Toul

Sundgau

Seine

Rhine

Franchè-Camté

Rhône

Boundary of France 1661

The Eastern Frontier of France in the Seventeenth
and Eighteenth Centuries

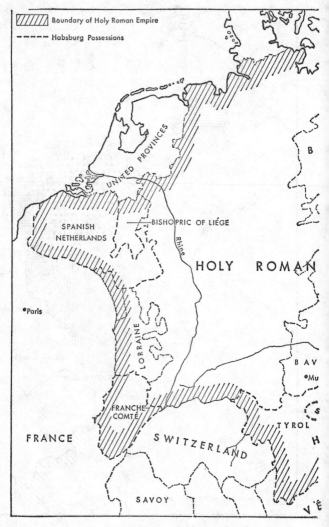

Central Europe after the Treaty of Westphalia, 1648

PRUSSIA

POLAND   Warsaw ●

ANDENBURG
● Berlin

SAXONY   SILESIA

EMPIRE

BOHEMIA

MORAVIA

A U S T R I A
Danube
●Vienna

 B STYRIA
LZBURG

CARINTHIA

NICE

CARNIOLA

HUNGARY

OTTOMAN
EMPIRE

POSSESSIONS

Europe in the Eighteenth Century

BALTIC SEA

Riga

PR·USSIA

Danzig

SILESIA

1772

1795

1793

Warsaw

AUSTRIA

1795

Cracow

Lvov
1772

HUNGARY

RUSSIA

1772

1795

Minsk

1793

Kiev

OTTOMAN

EMPIRE

BLACK SEA

	Lands annexed by Russia
	Lands annexed by Austria
	Lands annexed by Prussia

The Partitions of Poland

Index